A COMPANION
TO
ROMAN RELIGION

BLACKWELL COMPANIONS TO THE ANCIENT WORLD

This series provides sophisticated and authoritative overviews of periods of ancient history, genres of classical literature, and the most important themes in ancient culture. Each volume comprises between twenty-five and forty concise essays written by individual scholars within their area of specialization. The essays are written in a clear, provocative, and lively manner, designed for an international audience of scholars, students, and general readers.

ANCIENT HISTORY

Published

A Companion to the Roman Army
Edited by Paul Erdkamp

A Companion to the Roman Republic
Edited by Nathan Rosenstein and Robert Morstein-Marx

A Companion to the Roman Empire
Edited by David S. Potter

A Companion to the Classical Greek World
Edited by Konrad H. Kinzl

A Companion to the Ancient Near East
Edited by Daniel C. Snell

A Companion to the Hellenistic World
Edited by Andrew Erskine

A Companion to Late Antiquity
Edited by Philip Rousseau

A Companion to Ancient History
Edited by Andrew Erskine

A Companion to Archaic Greece
Edited by Kurt A. Raaflaub and Hans van Wees

A Companion to Julius Caesar
Edited by Miriam Griffin

A Companion to Byzantium
Edited by Liz James

A Companion to Ancient Egypt
Edited by Alan B. Lloyd

A Companion to Ancient Macedonia
Edited by Joseph Roisman and Ian Worthington

A Companion to the Punic Wars
Edited by Dexter Hoyos

In preparation

A Companion to Sparta
Edited by Anton Powell

LITERATURE AND CULTURE

Published

A Companion to Classical Receptions
Edited by Lorna Hardwick and Christopher Stray

A Companion to Greek and Roman Historiography
Edited by John Marincola

A Companion to Catullus
Edited by Marilyn B. Skinner

A Companion to Roman Religion
Edited by Jörg Rüpke

A Companion to Greek Religion
Edited by Daniel Ogden

A Companion to the Classical Tradition
Edited by Craig W. Kallendorf

A Companion to Roman Rhetoric
Edited by William Dominik and Jon Hall

A Companion to Greek Rhetoric
Edited by Ian Worthington

A Companion to Ancient Epic
Edited by John Miles Foley

A Companion to Greek Tragedy
Edited by Justina Gregory

A Companion to Latin Literature
Edited by Stephen Harrison

A Companion to Greek and Roman Political Thought
Edited by Ryan K. Balot

A Companion to Ovid
Edited by Peter E. Knox

A Companion to the Ancient Greek Language
Edited by Egbert Bakker

A Companion to Hellenistic Literature
Edited by Martine Cuypers and James J. Clauss

A Companion to Vergil's *Aeneid* and its Tradition
Edited by Joseph Farrell and Michael C. J. Putnam

A Companion to Horace
Edited by Gregson Davis

A Companion to Families in the Greek and Roman Worlds
Edited by Beryl Rawson

A Companion to Greek Mythology
Edited by Ken Dowden and Niall Livingstone

A Companion to the Latin Language
Edited by James Clackson

In preparation

A Companion to Sophocles
Edited by Kirk Ormand

A Companion to Aeschylus
Edited by Peter Burian

A Companion to Greek Art
Edited by Tyler Jo Smith and Dimitris Plantzos

A Companion to Tacitus
Edited by Victoria Pagán

A Companion to the Archaeology of the Ancient Near East
Edited by Daniel Potts

A COMPANION
TO
ROMAN RELIGION

Edited by

Jörg Rüpke

WILEY-BLACKWELL

A John Wiley & Sons, Ltd., Publication

This paperback edition first published 2011
© 2011 Blackwell Publishing Ltd

Edition history: Blackwell Publishing Ltd (hardback, 2007)

Blackwell Publishing was acquired by John Wiley & Sons in February 2007. Blackwell's publishing program has been merged with Wiley's global Scientific, Technical, and Medical business to form Wiley-Blackwell.

Registered Office
John Wiley & Sons Ltd, The Atrium, Southern Gate, Chichester, West Sussex, PO19 8SQ, United Kingdom

Editorial Offices
350 Main Street, Malden, MA 02148-5020, USA
9600 Garsington Road, Oxford, OX4 2DQ, UK
The Atrium, Southern Gate, Chichester, West Sussex, PO19 8SQ, UK

For details of our global editorial offices, for customer services, and for information about how to apply for permission to reuse the copyright material in this book please see our website at www.wiley.com/wiley-blackwell.

The right of Jörg Rüpke to be identified as the author of the editorial material in this work has been asserted in accordance with the UK Copyright, Designs and Patents Act 1988.

Library of Congress Cataloging-in-Publication Data

A companion to Roman religion / edited by Jörg Rüpke.
    p. cm. — (Blackwell companions to the ancient world)
  Includes bibliographical references and index.
  ISBN 978-1-4051-2943-5 (hardcover : alk. paper)
  ISBN 978-1-4443-3924-6 (paperback : alk. paper) 1. Rome—Religion.
I. Rüpke, Jörg.

BL803.C66 2007
292.07—dc22

                         2006025010

A catalogue record for this book is available from the British Library.

Set in 10/12pt Galliard by Graphicraft Limited, Hong Kong
Printed in Malaysia by Ho Printing (M) Sdn Bhd

1 2011

Irene
filiae carissimae

Contents

List of Figures   x

List of Maps   xiii

Notes on Contributors   xiv

Acknowledgments   xix

Abbreviations   xxi

Maps   xxviii

1   Roman Religion – Religions of Rome   1
Jörg Rüpke

2   Approaching Roman Religion: The Case for
Wissenschaftsgeschichte   10
C. Robert Phillips, III

Part I   Changes   29

3   The Religion of Archaic Rome   31
Christopher Smith

4   Pre-Roman Italy, Before and Under the Romans   43
Olivier de Cazanove

5   Urban Religion in the Middle and Late Republic   58
Eric Orlin

6   Continuity and Change: Religion in the Augustan Semi-Century   71
Karl Galinsky

7   Religions and the Integration of Cities in the Empire in the
    Second Century AD: The Creation of a Common Religious
    Language   83
    William Van Andringa

8   Old Religions Transformed: Religions and Religious Policy
    from Decius to Constantine   96
    Hartmut Leppin

9   Religious *Koine* and Religious Dissent in the Fourth Century   109
    Michele Renee Salzman

Part II   Media   127

10 The History of Roman Religion in Roman Historiography
    and Epic   129
    Denis Feeney

11 Religion and Roman Coins   143
    Jonathan Williams

12 Reliefs, Public and Private   164
    Katja Moede

13 Inscriptions as Sources of Knowledge for Religions and
    Cults in the Roman World of Imperial Times   176
    Rudolf Haensch

14 Religion in the House   188
    Annemarie Kaufmann-Heinimann

Part III   Symbols and Practices   203

15 Roman Cult Sites: A Pragmatic Approach   205
    Ulrike Egelhaaf-Gaiser

16 Complex Rituals: Games and Processions in Republican
    Rome   222
    Frank Bernstein

17 Performing the Sacred: Prayers and Hymns   235
    Frances Hickson Hahn

18 Music and Dance: Forms of Representation in Pictorial and
    Written Sources   249
    Friederike Fless and Katja Moede

19 Sacrifices for Gods and Ancestors   263
    John Scheid

Part IV Actors and Actions 273

20 Religious Actors in Daily Life: Practices and Related Beliefs 275
   Nicole Belayche

21 Republican *Nobiles*: Controlling the *Res Publica* 292
   Veit Rosenberger

22 Emperors: Caring for the Empire and Their Successors 304
   Peter Herz

23 Urban Elites in the Roman East: Enhancing Regional
   Positions and Social Superiority 317
   Athanasios Rizakis

24 Living on Religion: Professionals and Personnel 331
   Marietta Horster

Part V Different Religious Identities 343

25 Roman Diaspora Judaism 345
   Jack N. Lightstone

26 Creating One's Own Religion: Intellectual Choices 378
   Attilio Mastrocinque

27 Institutionalized Religious Options: Mithraism 392
   Richard Gordon

28 The Romanness of Roman Christianity 406
   Stefan Heid

Part VI Roman Religion Outside and Seen from Outside 427

29 Exporting Roman Religion 429
   Clifford Ando

30 Religion in the Roman East 446
   Ted Kaizer

31 Roman Religion in the Vision of Tertullian 457
   Cecilia Ames

Bibliography 472

General Index 511

Index of Personal Names 526

Index of Places 537

Figures

4.1   Ancient Italy.   48

11.1   Roman silver didrachm, c. 275 BC, showing a wreathed head of Apollo and horse.   143

11.2   Roman silver *denarius*, c. 212 BC, with Roma and Dioscuri.   144

11.3   Etruscan cast bronze coin, third century BC, with priestly accoutrements.   145

11.4   Roman gold stater, c. 220 BC, showing oath-taking scene.   145

11.5   Seleucid silver tetradrachm, 129–125 BC, depicting the altar of Sandan.   145

11.6   Roman silver *denarius*, c. 135 BC, showing the Columna Minucia.   146

11.7   Roman silver *denarius*, 42 BC, showing Octavian on horseback holding a *lituus*.   147

11.8   Roman gold *aureus*, AD 69–79, depicting the temple of Vesta.   148

11.9   Ephesian bronze coin, AD 138–61, showing the temple of Artemis.   149

11.10   Silver shekel, AD 132–5, depicting the destroyed Jerusalem Temple.   149

11.11   Bronze coin of Heliopolis, AD 193–211, with an aerial view of the temple.   149

11.12   Bronze coin of Ephesus, AD 218–22, showing the city's four neocoric temples.   150

11.13   Gold *aureus* of Augustus, c. 16 BC, showing the *clipeus virtutis* and sacred laurel trees.   151

11.14   Gold coin made for Sulla, c. 84 BC, with his priestly symbols.   151

11.15   Silver *denarius*, 44 BC, showing the bust of Julius Caesar with priestly symbols.   151

11.16   Ancient British silver coin of Verica, early first century AD, showing a naked figure holding a *lituus*.   152

11.17 Bronze coin of Carthago Nova, Spain, mid-first century BC, with Roman priestly symbols. 152

11.18 Silver didrachm from Syrian Antioch, AD 41–54, showing the young Nero and Roman priestly emblems. 152

11.19 Bronze coin of Ephesus, AD 218–22, showing athletic prize-crowns. 153

11.20 Roman silver *denarius*, c. 97 BC, showing King Numa sacrificing. 153

11.21 Gold *aureus* of Augustus, 17 BC, showing the emperor sacrificing. 154

11.22 Brass *sestertius* of Caligula, AD 37–41, showing the emperor pouring a libation like a god and sacrificing. 154

11.23 *Denarius* of Augustus, 16 BC, showing Apollo Actius pouring a libation. 154

11.24 *Denarius* of Julius Caesar, 44 BC, with sacrificial implements combined with symbols of prosperity. 155

11.25 Base-metal coin of Constantine I, AD 321, showing a globe resting on an altar. 155

11.26 *Denarius* of Vitellius, AD 69, with temple and image of Jupiter Capitolinus. 156

11.27 Gold *aureus* of Elagabalus, AD 218–22, showing the stone image of the god Sol Elagabal being drawn in a chariot. 156

11.28 *Denarius* of Commodus, AD 187, with an image of Pietas sacrificing. 157

11.29 Bronze coin from Alexandria, AD 81–96, with the figure of *Elpis Sebaste*. 157

11.30 Copper *as* of Domitian, AD 84, showing the figure of Moneta Augusta. 157

11.31 Gold *solidus* of Constantine I, AD 317, mounted for wearing as a personal ornament or amulet. 158

11.32 Base-silver coin of Diocletian, c. AD 301, depicting Sacra Moneta. 158

11.33 Base-metal coin of Constantine I, AD 327, celebrating the foundation of Constantinople. 159

11.34 Gold *solidus* of Constantine I, c. AD 325, showing him "at prayer." 160

11.35 Bronze coin commemorating the death of Constantine I, AD 337. 160

11.36 Bronze coin of Magnentius, AD 350–3, with prominent *chi-rho* symbol. 160

11.37 Base-silver coin of Vetranio, AD 350, showing him holding the *labarum*. 161

11.38 Base-silver coin of Constantine I, AD 318, one of the last issues to depict the image of Sol. 161

11.39 Gold *solidus* of the empress Eudocia, c. AD 423–4, showing an angel with the True Cross. 161

11.40 Base-metal coin, AD 326, showing Fausta, wife of Constantine I, and an image of the goddess Salus. 162

11.41	Base-metal coin, c. AD 388, showing Victory dragging a bound captive.	162
11.42	Base-metal coin, c. AD 430, with a simple cross motif.	162
11.43	Gold *solidus*, AD 704–11, with the image of Christ on the obverse and the emperor Justinian II with his son Tiberius displaced onto the reverse.	162
12.1	Altar of the *magistri* of the *vicus Aescleti* (Rome, AD 2/3).	166
12.2	Sacrifice on the occasion of the twentieth anniversary of Hadrian's reign (Rome, AD 137).	169
12.3	Testing a sacrificial animal (Rome).	172
12.4	*Suovetaurilia* sacrifice on the *Anaglypha Traiani* (Rome).	174
13.1	The Roman calendar before the reform of C. Iulius Caesar.	179
14.1a	Wall painting of Apollo and Daphne, Pompeii.	190
14.1b	Wall painting of Perseus and Andromeda, Pompeii.	191
14.2	Center of a silver dish, third century, found at Chaourse.	194
14.3	Lamp from the early Roman military camp of Haltern.	196
14.4	Mercury with money-bag and staff on a money-box from Italy, c. AD 200.	198
14.5	*Lararium*, Pompeii.	200
15.1	Temple precinct of Apollo on the Palatine.	216
15.2	Sacred precinct of Fortuna Augusta, Pompeii.	219
18.1	Marble relief of a triumphal arch, AD 176.	250
18.2	Marble relief of a triumphal arch, AD 176. Rome, attic of Constantine's arch.	251
18.3	Fragment of a marble frieze from the temple of Apollo Sosianus, c. 20 BC.	251
19.1	Initial libation at a portable altar.	265
20.1	Votive epigraph from imperial Phrygia.	282
20.2	Charm on a tablet found in Berytus.	290
24.1	Fragment of a frieze of the Trajanic period.	333
28.1	Reconstruction of the *memoria* of Peter at the Vatican, second half of the second century.	411
28.2	Constantinian church buildings outside the gates of Rome.	420
28.3	Reconstruction of the presbyterium of the Constantinian Lateran Basilica.	421
28.4	Stational churches of Rome, sixth century.	425

Maps

The Roman empire.   xxviii

The center of Rome, late republic.   xxx

Contributors

Cecilia Ames studied at the National University of Cordoba, Argentina, and at Eberhard-Karls-Universität Tübingen. Since 1994 she has been professor of ancient history and of myth and religion in Greece and Rome at the National University of Cordoba. Invited as a researcher to Tübingen and Erfurt universities and to the Kommission für Epigraphik und Alte Geschichte/German Archaeological Institute at Munich, she is also a research member of CONICET (Consejo Nacional de Investigaciones Cientificas y Tecnicas, Argentina) and director of the "Discursive Practices in Greco-Roman Times" research project.

Clifford Ando is professor of classics and of the college at the University of Chicago. He studied at Princeton and Michigan and was formerly professor of classics, history, and law at the University of Southern California.

Nicole Belayche studied at the University of Paris IV–Sorbonne and the École pratique des hautes études (Paris). She was maître de conférences of Roman history at the universities of Orléans and Paris IV–Sorbonne 1989–99, then professor of Roman history at the University of Rennes. Since 2002, she has been directeur d'études at the École pratique des hautes études, sciences religieuses (Paris). She coordinates the following research programs within the Centre Gustave Glotz (UMR 8585): "Les communautés religieuses dans les mondes grec et romain," "Les identités religieuses dans les mondes grec et romain," and "Cohabitations et contacts religieux dans les mondes grec et romain."

Frank Bernstein studied at the universities of Düsseldorf, Oxford (Brasenose College), and Duisburg. From 2002 he was Hochschuldozent of ancient history at the University of Mainz, then replacement teaching chair and full professor at the University of Bielefeld. Since 2007 he has been chair of ancient history at the University of Frankfurt/Main. He is working on Greek and Roman political and religious history.

Olivier de Cazanove studied at the Sorbonne, at the Ecole normale supérieure (Paris), and at the French School at Rome. Formerly director of the Jean Bérard Centre in

Naples, then maître de conférences of ancient history at the University of Paris I, and professor of archaeology at the University of Burgundy at Dijon. He is currently professor of Roman archaeology at the University of Paris 1. He directed excavations in South Italy and works on the "Inventory of Sacred Places in Ancient Italy" program, promoted by the French National Center for Scientific Research, Italian universities and archaeological *soprintendenze*.

Ulrike Egelhaaf-Gaiser studied at the universities of Munich and Tübingen. She was a research assistant at the University of Tübingen 1994–5, then a research associate at the Berlin-Brandenburgische Akademie der Wissenschaften (Inscriptiones Graecae) and a research assistant at the University of Giessen. Since 2006 she has been a research associate at the Collaborative Research Centre (SFB 434) working on "Memory Cultures" at the University of Giessen. She is currently replacement teaching chair of Latin at the University of Hamburg, and will be professor of Latin philology at the University of Göttingen from 2008.

Denis Feeney studied at Auckland University and Oxford University. He has held teaching positions at Edinburgh, Wisconsin, Bristol, and New College, Oxford, and is Giger Professor of Latin and chairman of the Department of Classics at Princeton University. In spring semester 2004 he was Sather Professor at the University of California, Berkeley.

Friederike Fless is professor of classical archaeology at the Institute for Classical Archaeology, Freie Universität Berlin. She studied at the University of Trier, the Julius-Maximilians-Universität, Würzburg, and the Johannes Gutenberg-Universität, Mainz. Her current research focuses on Attic red figure vases as a part of Greek culture in the necropolis of Pantikapaion, toreutics and jewelry in the North Pontic region, and sepulchral representation in the Bosphoran kingdom.

Karl Galinsky studied at Princeton University. He is the Floyd Cailloux Centennial Professor of Classics and University Distinguished Teaching Professor at the University of Texas at Austin. He has directed several projects, including faculty seminars on Roman religion, for the National Endowment of the Humanities and received many awards both for his teaching and for his research, including grants from the Guggenheim and von Humboldt Foundations and from the Max-Planck Society.

Richard Gordon studied at Jesus College, Cambridge. He was a research fellow at Downing College 1969–70; then a lecturer and senior lecturer in ancient civilization at the University of East Anglia, Norwich. He was a visiting fellow at Darwin College 1979–80, and since 1987 has been a private scholar resident in Germany. He was made honorary professor in the history of ancient religions at the University of Erfurt in 2007.

Rudolf Haensch studied at the universities of Cologne and Bonn. He became a member of the Institute of Advanced Study, Princeton, in 2001, then replacement teaching professor of ancient history at Hamburg and Cologne, then visiting professor at the Ecole des hautes études en sciences sociales (Paris). Since 2004 he has been second director of the "Kommission für Alte Geschichte und Epigraphik des Deutschen Archäologischen Instituts" (Munich).

Stefan Heid has been professor of the history of liturgy and of hagiography at the Pontifical Institute for Christian Archeology at Rome since 2001.

Peter Herz studied at the universities of Mainz and Oxford. He was professor of ancient history at the University of Mainz 1986–94, then chair of ancient history at the University of Regensburg. In 1990 he became a member of the Institute for Advanced Study, Princeton.

Frances Hickson Hahn studied at the University of North Carolina in Chapel Hill. She was assistant professor of classics at the University of California, Santa Barbara, 1987–93, then became associate professor of classics.

Marietta Horster studied at the University at Cologne, where she was a researcher in ancient history 1990–4. She was assistant professor in ancient history at the University of Rostock 1995–2001, researcher at the Prosopographia Imperii Romani 2003–6, replacement teaching chair at the Universitites of Bamberg, Humboldt University Berlin, Hamburg, and Heidelberg 2006–9, and has been chair of ancient history at the University of Mainz since 2010.

Ted Kaizer studied at the University of Leiden and Brasenose College, Oxford. He was an associate lecturer at the Open University 2001–2, then British Academy Postdoctoral Fellow at Corpus Christi College, Oxford. Since 2005 he has been a lecturer in Roman culture and history (senior lecturer since 2008) at the University of Durham.

Annemarie Kaufmann-Heinimann studied at the universities of Basel and Bonn. She is a fellow of the Society of Antiquaries of London, and a research associate of the Archäologisches Seminar of the University of Basel. She works as a freelance archaeologist, and her main fields of research are Roman bronzes and religion, and Roman silver.

Hartmut Leppin studied at the universities of Marburg, Heidelberg, and Pavia. He was replacement teaching chair of ancient history at the University of Greifswald 1995–6, then Feodor-Lynen Fellow at the University of Nottingham, and Heisenberg Fellow at the University of Göttingen. Since 2001 he has been chair of ancient history at the University of Frankfurt/Main. He is a member of the editorial board of the *Historische Zeitschrift* and editor of *Millennium Studies* and the *Millennium Yearbook*.

Jack N. Lightstone studied at Carleton University and Brown University. He is currently president and vice-chancellor, as well as professor of history, at Brock University. He previously served as professor of religion and provost and vice-rector, academic, at Concordia University. He has been a visiting research fellow at the Hebrew University in Jerusalem and at the University of Miami, and vice-president and subsequently president of the Canadian Society of Biblical Studies.

Attilio Mastrocinque studied at the University of Venice. He was a fellow of the Istituto Italiano per gli Studi Storici (Naples) 1975–6 and of the Consiglio Nazionale delle Ricerche 1978–81, then a researcher in ancient history at the University of Venice.

He was professor of Greek history at the University of Trento 1987–95 and at the University of Verona 1995–2002. Since 2002 he has been chair of Roman history at the University of Verona. He is also Alexander von Humboldt-Stiftung research fellow at the universities of Cologne, Aachen, and Freiburg im Breisgau, and in 1993 he was invited professor at the Ecole normale supérieure (Paris).

Katja Moede is a researcher at the Institute for Classical Archaeology, Freie Universität Berlin.

Eric Orlin studied at Yale University, the American School of Classical Studies at Athens, and the University of California, Berkeley. He was an instructor in ancient history at California State University, Fresno, 1995–6, then assistant professor of history and classical studies at Bard College, and since 2000 he has been associate professor of classics at the University of Puget Sound. He was a participant at the NEH Seminar on "Roman Religion in its Cultural Context," American Academy in Rome, 2002.

C. Robert Phillips, III studied at Yale, Oxford, and Brown universities. He went to Lehigh University in 1975, where he became professor of classics (1987) and professor of classics and ancient history (1990); he chaired the Department of Classics 1982–8. In his free time he practices Chopin's *Etudes*.

Athanasios Rizakis studied at the universities of Thessalonika, Paris, and Lyon. He was a lecturer in Greek language and civilization at the University Lyon III-Jean Moulin 1974–8, then assistant and maître assistant associé at the University of St-Etienne. He became a research fellow and, in 1984, director of research at the National Hellenic Research Foundation, where he is head of the "Roman Greece" program and of many other European or bilateral research projects. He was an invited member at the Institute of Advanced Study, Princeton (1994), and visiting professor at the universities of Creta (1980–1), Lyon II (1987–8), and Cyprus (1996–7). Since 1998 he has been professor of ancient Greek history at the University of Nancy II (France).

Veit Rosenberger studied at the universities of Heidelberg, Augsburg, Cologne, and Oxford. He was an assistant at the University of Augsburg 1992–2003 and exchange professor at Emory University (Atlanta) 2000–1, and has been professor of ancient history at the University of Erfurt since 2004.

Jörg Rüpke studied at the universities of Bonn, Lancaster, and Tübingen. He was replacement teaching chair of Latin at the University of Constance 1994–5, then professor of classical philology at the University of Potsdam. Since 1999 he has been chair of comparative religion at the University of Erfurt, and since 2008 fellow of the Max Weber Centre and co-director of the International research group "Religious individualization in historical perspective" of the German Science Foundation. He was visiting professor at the Université Paris I-Sorbonne Panthéon in 2003, at the Collège de France and at Aarhus University in 2010, and T. B. H. L. Webster lecturer at Stanford University in 2005. In 2008 he received the Gay-Lussac Humboldt Prize.

Michele Renee Salzman studied at Bryn Mawr College. She was assistant professor of classical studies at Columbia University 1980–2, then assistant to associate professor at Boston University. Since 1995, she has been associate to full professor of history at the University of California at Riverside. She has been chair of the Department of History and professor-in-charge of the Intercollegiate Center for Classical Studies, Rome. She is senior editor of the Cambridge History of Ancient Mediterranean Religions.

John Scheid's PhD thesis was supervised by Robert Schilling and Hans Georg Pflaum. He was a member of the Ecole française de Rome 1974–7, then assistant professor of ancient history at the Université de Lille III, and afterwards professor and directeur d'études at the Ecole pratique des hautes études, sciences religieuses. Since 2001 he has been a member of the Collège de France.

Christopher Smith studied at Oxford University, and was appointed to St Andrews University in 1992. He is currently Director of the British School at Rome. In 2001 he gave the Stanford Lectures at Trinity College Dublin.

William Van Andringa studied at the universities of Toulouse and Oxford. He was a member of the French School at Rome 2002–3 and maître de conférences in Roman history and archaeology at the university of Picardie Jules-Verne. Since 2007, he is professor of Roman history (history of ancient religions) at the university of Charles-de-Gaulle Lille 3. Having supervised the excavations of the necropolis of Porta Nocera at Pompeii (2003–7), he is now Director of the archaeological journal *Gallia* and responsible for the research programme of the Temple of Fortuna Augusta at Pompeii.

Jonathan Williams studied classics at the University of Oxford. He was a lecturer in ancient history at St Anne's College, Oxford, 1992–3, then curator of Iron Age and Roman coins at the British Museum. Since 2005 he has been policy adviser on international affairs for the British Museum. He is now Keeper of the Department of Prehistory and Europe at the British Museum.

Acknowledgments

Very few pages of this book were written by me. My first thanks go to my colleagues, who agreed to collaborate in this project, and made the bricks of this building. Their contributions combined the attempt to give an overview of the field, to introduce methodological problems of research into historical religions, and to give an individual face to each chapter. More reliably than in many projects before this, deadlines were held, limits kept to, questions quickly answered, and suggestions taken up or (for the benefit of the reader) rejected. The result attests to the various traditions of research in Italy and Greece, in Northern and Southern America, in Britain and France, in Germany and Switzerland. At the same time it attests to the coherence of an international scientific community that is willing and able to read and react to contributions in each other's languages. I am grateful to those who provided English texts, to those who translated texts, and to those (mostly anonymous) who helped in improving these texts.

It was Al Bertrand who contacted me on July 30, 2003, about embarking on this project and who accompanied the Companion through all its stages, in particular the early phase of defining the project. Ben Thatcher, Sophie Gibson, Kitty Bocking, and Angela Cohen accompanied it at important steps along the way; Fiona Sewell as copy-editor was extremely helpful, sensible to intentions and mistakes, and last but not least efficient.

From the staff at the Department of Religious Studies at the University of Erfurt, Diana Püschel, Mihaela Holban, Blossom Stefaniw (for translations), Astrid Willenbacher (for the bibliography), and Elisabeth Begemann (who compiled the index) must be gratefully mentioned.

As our daughter started to read my last book, I felt I should dedicate this one to her, thus finally providing my excuse for missing a number of sunny afternoons and cozy evenings.

The cafeteria of the Ashmolean Museum in Oxford, Paris and Rome, Córdoba and Los Angeles, the Villa Vigoni on the Lago di Como, Munich and Erfurt offered places to discuss the book as a whole or individual chapters. I hope that it will find its way back to these places and many others. The fact that a paperback edition could appear is an indication that this wish is being granted.

Erfurt, September 2010

Abbreviations

Journals and Works by Modern Authors

AE	*Année épigraphique.*
AJAH	*American Journal of Ancient History.*
AJP	*American Journal of Philology.*
ANRW	Temporini, Hildegard, and Haase, Wolfgang (eds.), *Aufstieg und Niedergang der römischen Welt.* Berlin 1972–.
BEFAR	Bibliothèque des écoles françaises d'Athénes et de Rome. Paris.
BHG	Socii Bollandiani (eds.), *Bibliotheca hagiographica graeca.* 3 vols. Brüssels 1909². Halkin, F. (ed.), 1957³.
BHL	Socii Bollandiani (eds.), *Bibliotheca hagiographica latina antiquae et medii aetatis.* 2 vols. Brussels 1898–1901. Suppl. editio altera, 1911.
BMC	Mattingly, Harold et al. (eds.), *Coins from the Roman Empire in the British Museum.* London 1923–.
CCL	*Corpus christianorum, series Latina.*
CFA	Scheid, John, *Commentarii fratrum Arvalium qui supersunt: les copies épigraphiques des protocoles annuels de la confrérie arvale (21 av.–304 ap. J.-C.).* Collection Roma antica 4. Rome 1998.
CIJud	Frey, Jean-Baptiste, *Corpus inscriptionum Judaicarum.* 2 vols. Rome 1936–52 [repr. New York 1975].
CIL	*Corpus inscriptionum Latinarum.* Berlin 1863–.

CIMRM	Vermaseren, Maarten J., *Corpus inscriptionum et monumentorum religionis Mithriacae*. The Hague 1956–60.
CP	*Classical Philology*.
CQ	*Classical Quarterly*.
CR	*Classical Review*.
CSEL	*Corpus scriptorum ecclesiasticorum latinorum*.
CstipiVot	*Corpus delle stipi votive in Italia*. Rome.
CW	*Classical World*.
EJ²	Ehrenberg, Victor, and Jones, Arnold H. M., *Documents Illustrating the Reigns of Augustus and Tiberius*. 2nd edn. Oxford 1955.
EPRO	Etudes préliminaires aux religions orientales dans l'empire romain.
FIRA²	*Fragmenta iuris Romani antejustiniani*.
FIRBruns	Bruns, C. G., Mommsen, T., and Gradenwitz, O. (eds.), *Fontes Iuris Romani Antiqui*. 3 vols. Tübingen 1909–12.
FPL	*Fragmenta poetarum Latinarum*.
FRH	Peter, H. W. G. (ed.), *Historicorum Romanorum fragmenta*. Leipzig 1883. Repr. 1993.
GL	*Grammatici Latini*, ed. Keil.
GRF	*Grammaticorum Romanorum fragmenta*.
HABES	Heidelberger althistorische Beiträge und epigraphische Studien.
HLL	Herzog, Reinhart, and Schmidt, Peter Lebrecht (eds.), *Handbuch der lateinischen Literatur*. Munich 1989–.
HSCPh	*Harvard Studies in Classical Philology*.
HTR	*Harvard Theological Review*.
ICUR NS	*Inscriptiones christianae urbis Romae. Nova series*.
IG	*Inscriptiones Graecae*. Berlin.
IGLS	*Inscriptions grecques et latines de la Syrie*. Paris.
IGRR	Cagnat, René, *Inscriptiones Graecae ad res Romanas pertinentes*. Paris 1906–27.
IGUR	Moretti, Luigi, *Inscriptiones Graecae urbis Romae*. Rome 1968–90.
ILCV	*Inscriptiones latinae christianae veteres*.

ILLRP	Degrassi, Attilio, *Inscriptiones Latinae liberae rei publicae.* Florence 1957–63.
ILS	Dessau, Hermann (ed.), *Inscriptiones Latinae selectae.* Berlin 1892–1916.
JdI	*Jahrbuch des Deutschen Archäologischen Instituts.* Berlin.
JRA	*Journal of Roman Archaeology.*
JRS	*Journal of Roman Studies.*
LIMC	*Lexicon Iconographicum Mythologiae Classicae.*
MEFRA	*Mélanges de l'École française de Rome, Antiquité.* Ecole française de Rome. Paris.
NGSL	Lupu, Eran, *Greek Sacred Law: A Collection of New Documents.* Leiden 2005.
NP	Cancik, Hubert, et al. (eds.), *Der Neue Pauly.* Stuttgart 1996– 2002 (English trans. Leiden 2004–).
ODB	*Oxford Dictionary of Byzantium.*
OGIS	*Orientis Graeci inscriptiones selectae.*
Orph. fragm.	Kern, O. (ed.), *Orphicorum fragmenta.* Berlin 1922. Repr. 1963.
P&P	*Past and Present.*
PawB	Potsdamer altertumswissenschaftliche Beiträge. Stuttgart 1999–.
PCPS	*Proceedings of the Cambridge Philological Society.*
P. Dura	Welles, C. Bradford, Fink, Robert O., and Gilliam, J. Frank, *The Parchments and Papyri: The Excavations at Dura-Europos. Final Report 5.1.* New Haven, CT, 1959.
PG	Migne, *Patrologia graeca.*
PGM	Preisendanz, K., and Henrichs, A. (eds.), *Papyri Graecae Magicae.* Repr. Stuttgart 1973–4.
PGMtr	Betz, Hans D. (ed.), *The Greek Magical Papyri in Translation.* Chicago 1986 [2nd edn. 1992].
PL	Migne, *Patrologia latina.*
PLRE	Jones, Arnold H. M. et al., *The Prosopography of the Later Roman Empire 1: A.D. 260–395.* Cambridge 1971.
RDGE	Sherk, Robert K., *Roman Documents from the Greek East.* Baltimore 1969.

RE	Wissowa, Georg (ed.), *Paulys Realenzyklopädie der Classischen Altertumswissenschaften: Neue Bearbeitung.* Stuttgart, 1893–1980.
REA	*Revue des études anciennes.*
RG-RW	Religions in the Graeco-Roman World. Leiden.
RGVV	Religionsgeschichtliche Versuche und Vorarbeiten.
RIB	Collingwood, Robin G., and Wright, R. P., *The Roman Inscriptions of Britain. I, 1: Inscriptions on Stone.* Oxford 1965.
RIC	*Roman Imperial Coinage.* 10 vols. London 1923–94.
RICIS	Bricault, Laurent, *Recueil des inscriptions concernant les cultes isiaques.* Mémoires de l'Académie des Inscriptions et Belles-Lettres 31. Paris 2005.
RPAA	*Rendiconti della Pontificia Accademia Romana di Archeologia.* Vatican City.
RPC	Burnett, Andrew M., and Amandry, Michel (gen. eds.), *Roman Provincial Coinage.* London 1993–.
RRC	Crawford, Michael H., *Roman Republican Coinage.* 2 vols. Cambridge 1974.
SC	*Sources chrétiennes.*
Schanz/Hosius	Schanz, M., and Hosius, C., *Geschichte der römischen Literatur bis zum Gesetzgebungswerk des Kaisers Justinian.* 3 vols. Munich 1927.
SEG	*Supplementum epigraphicum Graecum.* Leiden 1923–.
SGG	Mastrocinque, A. (ed.), *Sylloge gemmarum Gnosticarum, I.* Rome 2003.
SIRIS	Vidman, L. (ed.), *Sylloge inscriptionum religionis Isiacae et Sarapiacae.* RGVV 28. Berlin 1969.
Syll.[3]	Dittenberger, W. (ed.), *Sylloge inscriptionum Graecarum.* 4 vols. 3rd edn. Leipzig 1915–24. Repr. Hildesheim 1984.
TAM	*Tituli Asiae Minoris.*
TAPhA	*Transactions of the American Philological Association.*
ThesCRA	*Thesaurus cultus et rituum antiquorum.* 5 vols. Los Angeles 2004–6.
WUNT	Wissenschaftliche Untersuchungen zum Neuen Testament.
YCS	*Yale Classical Studies.*

| ZPE | *Zeitschrift für Papyrologie und Epigraphik.* |

Works by Ancient Authors

Amm.	Ammianus Marcellinus, *Historiae.*
App. *Civ.*	Appian, *Bellum civile.*
Apul.	Apuleius.
Apol.	*Apologia.*
Met.	*Metamorphoses.*
Arnob.	Arnobius, *Adversus nationes.*
Aug.	Augustinus.
Civ.	*De civitate Dei.*
Conf.	*Confessiones.*
Aur. Vict.	Aurelius Victor.
Cass. Dio	Cassius Dio.
Cat. *Agr.*	Cato, *De agricultura.*
CI	*Codex Iustiniani.*
Cic.	Cicero.
Div.	*De divinatione.*
Har. resp.	*De haruspicum responsu.*
Leg.	*De legibus.*
Leg. agr.	*De lege agraria.*
Nat.	*De natura deorum.*
Const Imp. Or. ad sanct.	Constantinus I imperator, *Oratio ad sanctorum coetum.*
CTh	*Codex Theodosianus.*
Dion. H.	Dionysius of Halicarnassus, *Roman Antiquities.*
Epist.	*Letters.*
Eus.	Eusebius.
HE	*Historia ecclesiastica.*
Theoph. syr.	*De theophania* (Syrian fragments).

V. Const.	*Vita Constantini.*
Fest.	Sextus Pompeius Festus, *De verborum significatione.*
Hdt.	Herodotus, *Historiae.*
HE	*Church History.*
Hist. Aug.	Historia Augusta.
Hor.	Horace.
Jos.	Flavius Josephus.
Lact. *DMP*	Lactantius, *De mortibus persecutorum.*
Lib.	Libanius.
Libanius, *Laud. Const.*	Libanius, *Laudatio Constantini et Constantis.*
Livy, *Per.*	Livy, *Periochae.*
Macr. *Sat.*	Macrobius, *Saturnalia.*
Mart.	Martial, *Epigrams.*
Min. Fel.	Minucius Felix.
Or.	*Orationes.*
Ov.	Ovid.
Am.	*Amores.*
Fast.	*Libri fastorum.*
Pont.	*Epistulae ex Ponto.*
Rem.	*Remedia amoris.*
Trist.	*Tristia.*
Paul. *Fest.*	Paulus Diaconus, *Ex Festo.*
Plin. *Nat.*	Pliny the Elder, *Natural History.*
Plut.	Plutarch.
Sall.	Sallust.
Seneca, *Epist.*	Seneca minor, *Epistulae morales ad Lucilium.*
Sozomenus, *HE*	Sozomenus, *Historia ecclesiastica.*
Suet.	Suetonius.
Tac.	Tacitus.
Ann.	*Annals.*

Hist.	*Histories.*
Tert.	Tertullian.
Apol.	*Apologeticum.*
Nat.	*Ad nationes.*
Spect.	*De spectaculis.*
Val. Max.	Valerius Maximus.
Varro	
Ling.	*De lingua latina.*
Rust.	*Rerum rusticarum de agri cultura.*
Vell.	Velleius Paterculus, *Historia Romana.*
Virg. *Aen.*	Virgil, *Aeneid.*
Vitr.	Vitruvius, *De architectura.*

Dates

In dating, BC/BCE and AD/CE are used.

Maps

The Roman empire.

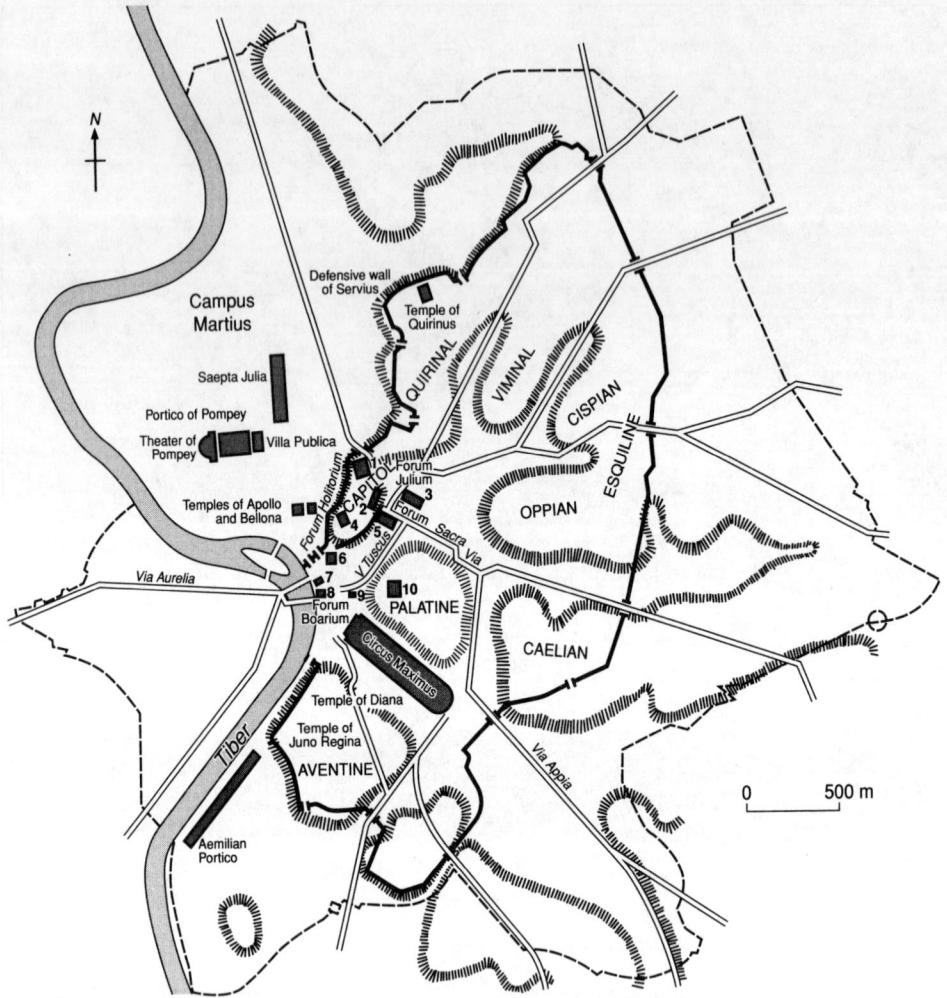

1 Temple of Juno Moneta   2 Tabularium   3 Basilica Aemilia   4 Temple of Jupiter Capitolinus   5 Basilica Iulia   6 Temples of Fortuna and of Mater Matuta   7 Temple of Portunus   8 Temple of Hercules Olivarius   9 Ara maxima   10 Temple of Cybele or Magna Mater

The center of Rome, late republic.

CHAPTER ONE

Roman Religion – Religions of Rome

Jörg Rüpke

Roman Religion

Why dedicate a book of over five hundred pages to a religion as stone-dead as that of one of thousands of ancient Mediterranean cities?

For the choice of the city, it is easy to find arguments. Rome was one of the most successful cities ever to build an empire, which comprised millions of square kilometers and lasted close to a millennium. It was and is a cultural and religious center, even if the culture was frequently Greek and the religion is known nowadays as Catholic Christianity. Finally, Rome remains a tourist center, a symbol of a past that has succeeded in keeping its presence in school books and university courses. And yet, what has this all to do with Roman religion?

"Roman religion" as used here is an abbreviation for "religious signs, practices, and traditions in the city of Rome." This is a local perspective. Stress is not given to internal differences between different groups or traditions. Instead, the accent is placed on their common history (part I) and range of media (part II), shared or transferred practices (part III), and the social and institutional context (part IV).

Many religious signs were exchangeable. The fourth-century author of a series of biographies on earlier emperors (the so-called *Historia Augusta*) had no difficulties in imagining an emperor from the early third century venerating Christ among the numerous statuettes in his private rooms. Gestures, sacrificial terminology, the structure of hymns were equally shared among widely varying groups. Nevertheless some stable systems, sets of beliefs, and practices existed and were cared for by specialists or transported and replicated by traveling individuals. They were present in Rome, effective and affective, but a set of beliefs, a group, or even an organization had a history of its own beyond Rome, too. Here, the local perspective is taken to ask how they were modified in Rome or the Roman period (part V).

"Rome," the name of the city, finally, is merely a cipher for the Roman empire. In the long process of its expansion and working, the religious practices of the center were exported, in particular the cult of the living or dead emperors and the cult of the dominating institutions, the "goddess Rome" (*dea Roma*) or the "*Genius of the senate*" (*Genius senatus*). This was part of the representation of Roman power to its subjects (see chapter 22), but at the same time it offered space for the activities of non-Roman local elites to get in touch with the provincial and central authorities and to distinguish themselves from their fellow-citizens (chapter 23). As communication between center and periphery – and other attractive centers in a periphery that was marginal in administrative terms only – these activities touched upon the religious practices in the city of Rome, too. "Roman religion" cannot be isolated from the empire, at least for the imperial period, if we take for granted the character of earlier Rome as a Hellenistic city on the margins of Hellenic culture (Hubert Cancik, p.c.). Again, that perspective holds true in both directions. The history of Mediterranean religions in the epoch of the Roman empire must acknowledge the fact that Persian Mithraism, Hellenistic Judaism, and Palestinian Christianity were Roman religions, too. It is the final section of this book that explicitly takes this wider geographical stance (part VI).

An Ancient Religion

Roman religion did not grow out of nothing. Italy, above all in its coastal regions, was already party to a long-distance cultural exchange in the Mediterranean basin in a prehistoric phase. The groups that were to grow into the urbanization of the Roman hills did not need to invent religion. Religious signs and practices were present from the ancient Near East, via Phoenician culture, at least indirectly via Carthage, and via Greece and the Etruscans. Speaking an Indo-European language, these groups shared a religious "knowledge" in the form of names or rudimentary institutions in the area of cultural practices that we call religion. Even if historians of Roman religion do not any longer privilege the distant common heritage of Celts, Romans, Greeks, Persians, and Indians over the intensive cultural exchange of historical times and the immense diffusion of practices from the non-Indo-European Near Eastern cultures, some constellations might find an explanation in those distant areas by comparing cultures more isolated from each other in later times.

Cultural exchange – as said above – was not restricted to the founding phases. It is hard to overestimate the diffusion of religious practices within and from the Latins, Umbrians, and Etruscans. In detail, the range is not clear at all. There are definite similarities, a shared culture (or, to use a Greek term, *koine*), in votive and burial practices. To say the same for the architecture of sanctuaries is neither contradicted by the evidence nor massively supported. We can suppose that many characteristics of the gods, the fascination of statuary and anthropomorphic representation, were shared. The very few longer non-Latin texts demonstrate surprising similarities in calendrical practices (the Etruscan *tegula Capuana* from the fifth century BC) or in priestly organization and ritual detail (the Umbrian *tabulae Iguvinae* from the second to first centuries BC). Unfortunately, non-Latin Italian languages ceased to be spoken (and especially to be written) in the first century BC and the first century AD as a consequence of Roman domination. Latin antiquarian writers adduce many instances of the borrowing of middle Italian practices and symbols in order to explain contemporary Roman institutions.

The continuous presence of self-conscious Greek writers is not the only reason to pay an ever-growing attention to Greek influences and their (frequently deeply modifying) reception. From the beginning of the great "colonization" – that is, especially from the eighth century – onward, Greeks were present in Italy and served as translators of the achievement of the earlier civilizations of Egypt and the "fertile crescent" of Anatolia, Syria, Mesopotamia, Palestine. Anthropomorphic images, temple building, and the alphabet came by this route. Influences were extensive and continuous. Despite the early presence of the alphabet it was not before the third century BC that Rome started to adopt Greek techniques of literary production on a larger scale. Many of the rivalries of Italian townships of the second century BC – frequently resulting in large-scale temple building – were fought out in terms of Greek cultural products. Competing with Roman elites meant being more Greek. Much of what provincials thought to be Roman and adopted in the process of Romanization during the following centuries stemmed from Greece.

The "Greece," however, of this intensive phase of cultural exchange – intensified by Roman warfare and plunder in Greek territories – was Hellenistic Greece, a cultural space that faced large territories. In the aftermath of the expansion by Alexander the Great (d. 323 BC) and on the basis of the earlier establishment of Greek ports and trading centers on Mediterranean coastlands, this Hellenistic culture had developed techniques of delocalization, of universalizing ancient Greek traditions. It offered grids of history, a mythic geography that could integrate places and societies like Rome and the Romans. Greeks thought Romans to be Trojans long before Romans discovered the usefulness of being Trojans in talking with Greeks.

Religion for a City and an Empire

Roman religion was the religion of one of hundreds of Mediterranean cities. It was a Hellenized city and religion. Yet it found many a special solution, for reasons of its geographic location, local traditions, immigrants. The most important contingent factor, certainly, was its military success. At least from the fourth century BC onward, Rome organized an aggressive and efficient military apparatus, managing hegemony and expansion first within Italy, then within the Mediterranean basin, finally as far as Scotland, the northern German lowland plain, the southern Carpathians, the coast of the Black Sea, Armenia, Arabia, and the northern edge of the Sahara. Preliminary to that was the orchestrated growth of the Roman nobility through the immigration of Italian elites.

These processes had consequences for the shape of religion at Rome. There is a strong emphasis on control, of both centralization and presence (see chapters 21 and 16). Public rituals were led by magistrates, priestly positions filled by members of the political elite, mass participation directed into temporary and then more and more permanent architectural structures in the center of Rome. At the same time, religion remained independent in a peculiar sense: gods could be asked to move, but not ordered to do so; priesthoods could be presented with candidates, but co-opted them in their own right; the transfer of public property to imported gods was the subject of political decisions, but their rituals were not. Being not directly subjected to political decision, religion offered a powerful source for legitimizing political decisions; it remained what Georg Simmel called a "third authority."

The dominant Roman model for religion was not expansionist; it was rather absorbing. Numerous "gods" – that class of signs the centrality of which within a set of social interaction makes us term these practices a "religion" – in the forms of statues, statuettes, images, or mere names, were imported, and – what is more – stories about these gods, practices to venerate them, molds to multiply them, knowledge about how to build temples for them, even religious specialists, priests, accompanied them or were invented on the spot.

For the ancient metropolis, a city growing to the size of several hundred thousand inhabitants, maybe close to a million by the time of the early empire, the usual models to describe the religions of Mediterranean cities do not hold. Surely, publicly financed cult – *sacra publica*, to use the ancient technical term – held an important share. The large buildings of public temples did provide an important religious infrastructure. So did the publicly financed rituals. Yet the celebrations of many popular rituals were decentralized. This holds true for the merrymaking of the Saturnalia (not a public holiday in the technical sense!) lasting for several days, and for the cult of the dead ancestors and the visits to the tombs during the Parentalia. We do not know how many people fetched purgatory materials from the Vestal Virgins for the decentralized rituals of the Parilia, the opening of the "pastoral year." Many "public" rituals might have remained a matter of priestly performance without a large following. The life-cycle rituals – naming, leaving childhood, marrying, funeral – might utilize public institutions, but were neither spatially nor temporally coordinated. In times of personal crises, people often addressed deities and visited places of cult that were not prominent or were even outside of public ritual. Indeed, the growing importance of the centralized rituals of the public games – to be witnessed especially from the second half of the third century BC onward – were meant to compensate for these deficits of "public religion." Hence the "civic cults" (or "polis religion") does not form a sociologically useful category.

Neither does "pantheon." The idea of "pantheon" as a concept for the history of religion derives from the analysis of ancient Near Eastern and especially Greek mythological text. These seem to imply the existence of a limited group of deities (around ten to twenty) that seem to be instituted in order to cover the most important needs of the polity. Internal coherence is produced by genealogical bonds or institutions by analogy to political ones: a council of the gods, for instance. For Greece, the omnipresence of the Homeric poems gives plausibility to the idea that local deities were thought to act within or supplement the circle of the around twelve most important gods, even if these were not present in the form of statues or individually owned temples. For Rome and Italy this plausibility is lacking. The aforementioned centralizing rituals might further the idea of such a "pantheon" – technically, by the way, a term to denote the exceptional case of a temple owned by "all the gods." In contrast to the frequently used term *di immortales*, designating the gods as an unstructured ensemble, the circus processions would present a definite number of gods. Yet we do not know whether the order of the gods was fixed or subject to situational and individual decisions. Even if tradition – that is, precedent – had its share, there was no codified body of mythological tales that would constitute an order of gods or even an inner circle of divine figures. The multitude of gods venerated in the city of Rome was always increased by individual decisions – those of generous members of the nobility and victorious generals investing parts of their booty, as well as those of immigrants with a foreign ethnic background. Likewise the decrease in number was due to individual neglect of cultic performances or lack of interest in maintaining and repairing sanctuaries.

These findings corroborate the earlier characterization of Roman religion. Of course, Roman religion was an "embedded religion" (see the introduction to chapter 25 for further methodological considerations). That is, religious practices formed part of the cultural practices of nearly every realm of daily life. Banqueting usually followed sacrifice (chapter 19) and building a house or starting a journey implied small sacrifices and prayers, as did meetings of the senate, parades, or warfare. Religion, hence, was not confined to temples and festivals; it permeated, to repeat this point, all areas of society. Yet politics – to concentrate on the most interesting realm in this respect – was not identical with religion. Many stories, the huge number of non-public rituals, individual "superstitions" (doing or believing more than is necessary), the complicated procedures for installing priests: all this demonstrates the independence of the gods and the possibility of distinguishing between religion and politics, between *res sacrae* and *res publicae*, in everyday life. It was religion thus conceptualized, thus set apart, that could be used as a seemingly independent source of legitimization for political action. This set the guidelines for liberty and control and explains the harsh reaction to every move that seemed to create an alternative, a counter-public, by means of religion. To define these borders of religion – one might say, from without – the technique of law was employed, developing a body of regulations that finally appeared as an important part of the law collections of late antiquity (see chapter 29) and were of the utmost importance for the history of religion in Europe.

If the Romans did not export their religion, they certainly exported their concept of religion. Of course, the outcome varied from area to area. The impact of particular Roman religious signs (names and images of deities, for example) and practices (rituals, festivals) was small in the Hellenized territories of the Hellenistic east, even if Mishnaic Judaism can hardly be imagined without the impact of Roman law and administration. Yet for parts of northern Africa and the more northern European provinces of the empire, the diffusion of stone temples and plastic images, of writing and permanently individualized gifts to the gods, the permanent visibility of votives, and the self-representation of the elite by means of religious dedications – these traits (by no means exclusively Roman practices) fundamentally changed the shape of religion and its place in provincial societies, shaping Christianity no less than paganism. Roman religion became an inseparable strain of the history of religion in the Mediterranean world and what much later came to be termed "Europe."

Religion

In terms of the history of religion the afore-mentioned process is no "history of reception" or *Wirkungsgeschichte*. For reasons of disciplinary traditions and political history, the end of the fourth and the beginning of the fifth century offer an easy borderline for this book. Publicly financed polytheistic religion was ended, and non-Christians (with Jews as a special, frequently not privileged exception) were discriminated against for the filling of public offices. Yet cultic practices continued for centuries, Christians being perhaps not willing or able to stop them or to destroy the architectural infrastructure on which they were the performers. As transmitted by texts, ancient – that is, Greek and Roman – religion, together with the polytheistic practices in Judah and Israel described in much less detail in the Bible, offered the typological alternative to Judaism and Christianity and formed an important pattern on which to describe and classify the practices of "heathens" in the colonial expansion of Europeans. Thus, "religion" could be coined as a general term encompassing Christianity and its illegitimate equivalents: Asian, American, African, and Australian idolatries.

The latter process, to be dated to early modern times, implied that our perspective on religion is informed by Christianity, a religion that developed from antiquity onward, and furthered by centuries of theological faculties within European and (in this perspective) lately non-European universities, a complex and well-ordered theory to reflect on its beliefs and practices: theology. Yet the ancient history of religion is no field to be analyzed within the framework of the standard topics, the *loci communes*, of Christian dogma, even if many of them found their counterpart (and origin) in ancient philosophy. By the late nineteenth and early twentieth centuries, the independent discipline of "comparative religion" or "history of religion" tried to supplant this scheme with series of topics like gods, beliefs, temples, rituals, priests. These are helpful as appealing to common sense, but ahistorical if applied as a system.

What is described as "Roman religion" in this book is of an astonishing variety. Various are the phenomena, from Mithraic caves to hilltop Capitolia, from the offering of paid services by divinatory specialists (*harioli*) to colleges of freedmen whose members met on a monthly basis. Various are the social functions, from the *pater familias* who led the sacrifice to his own *Genius*, and thus underlined his position as head of the family, to neo-Pythagorean convictions that informed the preparation of one's own burial and offered the prospect of a post-mortal existence.

For the purpose of a historical analysis, "religion" is conceptualized by the authors of this book as human actions and communication. These were performed on the presupposition that gods existed who were part of one's own social or political group, existed in the same space and time. They were to be treated by analogy to human partners and superiors. That offered space for wishful projections and experiments. What was helpful as regards human superiors should be useful in dealing with the gods, too. What was assumed to function among the gods should offer a model for human behavior, for consuls and kings.

Without doubt, "gods" were important symbols, either in direct representation or by their assumed existence behind the attempts to communicate with them ritually. Methodologically, however, it is important neither to engage in a debate about their existence nor to expect to find them or their traces empirically. Thus, the lack of a chapter on "gods" is intentional. Analyzed as "signs," the "gods" have neither an essence nor biographies. To represent the immortal god in social space, one has to produce new or use established signs, and these signs vary according to the media used. Narratives are an important medium, for example in historiography or epic (chapter 10); images could appear on coins (chapter 11), on reliefs (chapter 12), or independently as sculptured statues (chapter 15); and conventions of representation, of the use, and of the audience vary from genre to genre. Rituals (part III), too, are an important – perhaps the most important – means of not only communicating with the gods but demonstratively, publicly performing this communication, of defining the respective god by the strategy and content of the communicative approach (animal or vegetable sacrifice, female or male name, choice of time and place). Rituals stage-manage the gods' existence and one's own piety at the same time. Thus, it seems important to concentrate on the human actors in the center of the book (part IV): on ordinary individuals, on members of the changing elites, on those, finally, who made a living out of religion.

If the renunciation of a chapter on the gods prompts an explanation, the lack of a systematic treatment of "cults" should prompt another. "Cult" as applied to ancient religions is a very convenient term, as it takes ancient polytheism to pieces that are gratifyingly similar to the large religious traditions like Christianity: defined by one god, be it Venus or Mithras, supposed to be connected to a specifiable group of persons, be it loosely or densely organized, characterized by common interests or social traits, be it women or members of the military, Syrians or freedmen. Without doubt, voluntary religious associations existed, but they were not necessarily exclusive, they did not necessarily concentrate on one god, and certainly, the sum of their activities did not comprise all or even most of ancient religious practices. According to socio-historical research, there was hardly a significant difference between the followers of the god Silvanus, a forest-god by name, sometimes venerated by colleges, and the god Mithras of Persian origin, whose exotic features were thematized in the cult of small and strictly hierarchical groups. Neither the sum of individual choices, ever changing or keeping within the limits of familiar or professional traditions, nor the identity of the name of a god from one place to another justifies speaking of "a cult" in the aforementioned sense. Thus, part V deliberately illustrates the wide spectrum of religious groups or options and does not attempt to map ancient polytheism as the sum of different "cults."

FURTHER READING

Any further reading should start with ancient *sources*, many of the literary texts being accessible in the bilingual editions of the Loeb library. There are no "scientific" accounts of Roman religion from antiquity, but some extensive descriptions exist in different literary genera. The most fully preserved account of Roman ritual is given in Ovid's commentary on the Roman calendar (*Libri fastorum* VI), written in late Augustan times and trying to integrate traditional Roman worship, the cult of the emperors, and the natural cycle of time. His near contemporary, the Greek Dionysius of Halicarnassus, dedicated a long section in his *Roman Antiquities* to religion (2.63–74, trans. E. Cary). Varro's *Antiquities of Divine Things* survived in fragments only (a shorter self-quotation might be found in his *On Latin Language* 6); the polemical usage of it by the Christians Tertullian, in his *To the Nations*, and Augustine, in his *City of God* (books 4–7), give the best idea of its contents and later reception. From the first half of the third century, Minucius Felix's dialogue *Octavius* offers another polemical and informed view on early (rather than middle) imperial Roman religion (trans. and comm. G. W. Clarke, New York 1974). The most important documentary texts are the acts of the Secular Games (new ed. and comm. for the Augustan games: Schnegg-Köhler 2002) and the protocols of the Arval Brethren (ed., comm., and French trans. Scheid 1998b).

Religion is central for a number of institutions discussed by the Greek politician and philosopher Plutarch in his *Roman Questions*; his account of *Isis and Osiris* (trans. and comm. J. Gwyn Griffiths, Cambridge 1970) is not only an ethnographic piece, but a contemporary perspective on a cult flourishing widely in the Greek and Roman world. Tacitus' *Germania* shows how a Roman viewed foreign cultures (and religion) at the turn of the first to the second century AD (trans. and comm. J. B. Rives, Oxford 1999).

For the religion of the imperial period the most interesting texts stem from genera of fictional literature: book 11 of Apuleius' *Metamorphoses* on the cult of Isis (comm. J. Gwyn Griffiths, Leiden 1975), Philostratus' *Life of Apollonius of Tyana*, Lucian's *Alexandros* and *The Syrian Goddess*, and Aristeides' autobiographical *Hieroi Logoi*. One should not forget the Christian New Testament, in particular the Acts of the Apostles, and the early acts of martyrs, which narrate the confrontations of Christians with the Roman administration in provincial centers. Finally, the emperor Julian's *Letters* attest the project of an anti-Christian revival and Neoplatonic modification of traditional cults.

Cicero, prolific author, rhetor, politician, and philosopher from the late republic, deals frequently with religion, yet his *On the Nature of the Gods* (comm. Andrew R. Dyck, Cambridge 2003–) is more revealing for the history of Hellenistic philosophy than for Roman practice. The same does not hold for the subsequent *On Divination* (comm. A. E. Pease, Cambridge, MA, 1920–3, repr. Darmstadt 1963). The speeches *On His House* and *On the Reply of the Haruspices* do give interesting insights into the fabric of religious institutions. Other important sources are less easily accessible. Livy's Roman history remains basic to the history of republican religion. Religious information, however, is widely scattered. The lexicon of Festus, abridging the Augustan Verrius Flaccus' alphabetic account of his linguistic and religio-historic research, has not been translated so far. Beard et al. (1998) offer good commentary on a selection of sources for the late republican and early imperial period; Valantasis (2000) does so for late antiquity.

Literary as well as archaeological sources are extensively documented in the *Thesaurus cultus et rituum antiquorum* (*ThesCRA*) (Los Angeles, 2004–6). For reliefs Ryberg (1955) remains essential, frequently supplemented by Fless (1995). Schraudolph (1993) and Dräger (1994) publish numerous Roman altars; sarcophagi are shown and interpreted by G. Koch

(1993) and by Zanker and Ewald (2004). Muth (1998) offers a glimpse into private mytho-logical mosaics.

Recent monographic accounts of Roman religion are given by Beard et al. (1998) and Rüpke (2001 [2007]); shorter introductions are offered by North (2000) and Scheid (2003). The manual of Wissowa (1912, repr. 1971) remains indispensable (for a recent assessment of Wissowa's achievements see *Archiv für Religionsgeschichte 5*, 2003). For monographic accounts of the religious history of individual provinces see now the series Religion der römischen Provinzen (Belayche 2001; Spickermann 2003, 2007; Kunz 2006; further volumes are forthcoming).

The best guide to recent research is given by survey articles every three to four years organized by epochs and provinces (Belayche et al. 2000, 2003, forthcoming).

For the concept of religion see J. Z. Smith (1978, 1990, 1998) and Gladigow (2005).

Many chapters of this book offer frequent references, usually to the most important type of "reading," the reading of the ancient evidence. This is mostly available in annotated and trans-lated form, as far as standard literary texts are concerned; often conveniently put together into multi-volume *corpora*, as far as inscriptions are concerned; often widely scattered, analyzed without image or photographically represented without analysis, as far as archaeological evid-ence is concerned. Here, the attempt is made to provide the interested reader with direct references, even if these refer to rather specialist publications.

CHAPTER TWO

Approaching Roman Religion: The Case for *Wissenschaftsgeschichte*

C. Robert Phillips, III

A comprehensive history of the study of Roman religion does not exist, and this despite the upsurge of contemporary interest in *Wissenschaftsgeschichte* for other areas of classical studies. It is true that there have been overviews of the *Wissenschaftsgeschichte* of Roman religion (Latte 1960: 9–17; Wissowa 1912: 10–17), surveys of recent scholarship (e.g. Rose 1960) and the occasional discussion of interpretive developments (Michels 1954/5; Wide 1912: 268–71), and studies devoted either wholly or in part to re-evaluating the work of past scholars (Bendlin 2000; Scheid 1987). Then there are varia, a plethora of widely scattered observations, such as Latte's view of animism (Weinstock 1961: 206) or Wissowa's Janus-like dismissal and utilization of Frazer (Wissowa 1912: 248 n. 3, 104 n. 3). Finally there are archival materials. Some have been published, such as the correspondence between Usener and Wilamowitz (Dietrich and Hiller 1994). Many have not seen the light of day, such as letters from, to, and about Stefan Weinstock (Phillips 2004); there we learn, for example, that Eduard Fraenkel's negative report on Weinstock's "Triumphus" manuscript led to its rejection by Oxford University Press (Phillips 2004: 1043–4). The reasons, definitely not bruited about at the time, remain unknown and we are forced to conclude from Fraenkel's published works that while the great Latinist knew much about Roman religion, he did not know as much about it as he thought. But *totum pro partibus*, none of these items provides either a synoptic whole or, *per se*, the materials for constructing one. Writ large, there exists no history of the study of Roman religion which attends to its socio-intellectual context, nothing along the lines of what has been done, say, for Roman history (Christ 1982). Consequently, I begin with the axiomatic as I briefly identify reasons why this is so; the elaboration of those reasons and their significance will ensue along with cross-references to these axioms.

A   The methods of classical studies

1   All areas of classical studies have traditionally originated in the study of the ancient languages in the empirico-positivist context "the facts speak for themselves." This entailed (a) belles-lettres outlooks which privileged ancient literary texts over other evidence and (b) widespread skepticism and sometimes hostility to interpretive guidelines and comparative information from disciplines such as anthropology, religion studies, sociology.

2   Since mastering Greek and Latin requires an enormous amount of scholarly training, all thought there was no time to think philosophically about scholarship or to consider interpretive guidelines from other disciplines, especially since such thinking was considered *parerga* (A1). Thus rejection of theory and comparative material arose from empirico-positivist concerns (A1) and from lack of attention to those theories and material.

3   It followed from the empirico-positivist concerns (A1) that scholarship by its nature should be scientific (*wissenschaftlich*) and thus follow the model of the natural and physical sciences, a point which the nineteenth-century philological handbooks were wont to stress. This led to a kind of cognitive dissonance, in that scholars expressed fidelity to the scientific method while in practice they often utilized aesthetic and hermeneutic methods. Further, as a result of this expressed allegiance to the sciences all felt that older views of classical antiquity existed only to be refuted, that the latest was best. Exceptions could of course be made for those whose empirico-positivist results seemed eternally veridical. Thus *Wissenschaftsgeschichte* became, in the opinion of many classicists, a history of erroneous past views, and as such it was deemed marginal to the pursuit of "scientific" classical scholarship.

4   Lack of training in other areas (A2) meant that criticism of "theory" in the study of ancient religion ignored a crucial point. Much of the theory, and almost all of the excesses, arose in the study of Greek religion; theory and comparative material seemed to "work" for that religion. Any theory employed for Roman religion usually postdated its use for Greek religion.

B   The conceptualizations of classical studies

1   Greek civilization was long considered the archetype of Mediterranean antiquity; thus Roman civilization became derivative. Worse, the Romans were measured against the Greeks, and, for example, their failure to have mythologies of the Greek kind was considered not merely a religious and cultural difference but, rather, symptomatic of the Romans' total reliance on Greek cultural norms imperfectly assimilated (Bendlin 1995; Phillips 1991a). Hence the assumption arose that knowing Greek religion meant knowing Roman religion; excellent scholars of Greek religion could and did pronounce on Roman religion from a position of considerable unfamiliarity with that latter religion (Phillips 2000a).

2   Classical studies long belonged to members of the white, male, Judeo-Christian, and European socio-economic elite; thus that elite's socio-cultural prejudices came into play. Cults of the lower ancient socio-economic orders became

"primitive" while cults of the higher ancient socio-economic orders became normative.

3 Training in classical studies consequently inculcated those biases (B1, B2). They seemed not bias but patent truth since they arose "scientifically" (A3).

C Consequences of methods and conceptualizations (A, B)

1 Neglect of patent evidence that nineteenth-century British scholars considered the three alleged fields of classical studies, anthropology, and religion studies aspects of but one field. Likewise, utilizing Darwin meant that scholars considered themselves to be "scientific." Thus empirico-positivism in classical studies (A1) possessed competing visions.

2 Neglect of patent evidence that the circumstances of C1 differed radically in nineteenth-century Germany. Only a minority felt the three fields (C1) kindred; the immense power of the professors and their "schools" rendered such a view moot.

3 Neglect of the resultant intellectual competition as a result of the conceptual differences (C1, C2), a competition marked by scarcely concealed jingoism. Scholarly criticism, although couched in empirico-positivist terms, decidedly betokened conceptual differences.

4 Unfortunate excesses in the study of Greek religion (A4), which led non-specialists to dismiss any scholarship other than empirico-positivist. Those dismissals are not persuasive since their authors did not proffer detailed critiques of the theoretical excesses but rather took refuge in vague, sometimes emotional, generalities such as "forcing the facts into the theories." This is perhaps a function of the empirico-positivism of classical studies (A4, B3).

5 Contemporary intellectual bifurcation. Too often classicists who would never utilize the concept "primitive" in other cultural connections continue to use it to characterize aspects of Roman religion.

6 Field bifurcation. Theory continues in religious studies and continues to be refined. But scholars in that field left Roman religion to classical studies and do not demonstrate the same interest in the Roman evidence as did their predecessors; likewise, the formerly close links between classicists specializing in Roman religion and scholars in religious studies have virtually vanished today.

Thus, while deplorable, it is understandable why there is no *Wissenschaftsgeschichte* of Roman religion. It seems highly specialized to do *Wissenschaftsgeschichte*, but for Roman religion one must attend not only to the *Wissenschaftsgeschichte* of classical studies, but also to the *Wissenschaftsgeschichte* of anthropology, sociology, the history of universities, religious studies; thus the study becomes a specialty inside a specialty. Further, there arises the issue of perspective. It is certainly fruitful to focus on the various conceptual models in the study of Roman religion, and this enables the detailed consideration of important details and gradations of interpretation. But it is equally fruitful to shift the focus to how those models came into being, how they were influenced by contemporary large intellectual and, often, historical concerns. It is this latter perspective which the following pages would trace.

Finally, there exists an issue of contemporary influence, the *Rezeptionsgeschichte* of scholarship on Roman religion in other areas of classical studies, especially the literary. Of course it requires time for specialist views to percolate through a wider venue. But the situation is not so good for Roman religion. For example, most specialists nowadays reject the idea that Roman religion constituted "cult acts without belief," yet there currently exists only sporadic evidence that non-specialists in classical studies generally have appropriated that point.

Classical Antiquity through the Renaissance

Here the distinction between evidence for Roman religion and evidence for *Wissenschaftsgeschichte* blurs. Thus the earliest literary reference to Roman religion will be the appearance of Camena in Livius Andronicus' version of Homer's *Odyssey*. A position on Roman religion is implied; still, although the word is specialist, its literary context is not. Put differently, Andronicus knew about the relation between Camena and the Muses, but we cannot hope to recover it with certainty. Likewise what did the elder Cato know about Ares in connection with Mars (*Agr.* 141)? Indeed, Cicero's famous statement on the aridity of the chronicles of the *Annales Maximi* (*Leg.* 1.6), combined with the enormous numbers of later commentaries on the pontifical *acta*, suggests that this earliest example of extensive writing about Roman religion constituted facts useful for the activities of the pontifical compilers. Scholarly interpretation and refutation lay in the future. Consider as parallel how Roman private law handled delicts; they begin with particular instances in the Twelve Tables (e.g. *Digesta* 9.2.4.1), are expanded and replaced by the early third century BC *Lex Aquilia* (*Digesta* 9.2.1), but only appear as a focus of scholarly interest from the later republic onward, when the need arose to harmonize the actions granted by the urban praetor.

Scholarly interest in Roman religion, as for many topics, appears in the late second century BC. Since even the most substantial remains of that activity, Varro's works, survive in fragments, judgment on the *Wissenschaftsgeschichte* must be conservative. Nevertheless, certain general tendencies appear from now until the early third century AD. First there is an empirico-positivist position on earlier views; an earlier savant's views of a knotty cultic question exists either to be praised or to be censured, but never to be discussed beyond demonstrating contradictory evidence or logic. Second, with the exceptions of Varro and possibly Nigidius Figulus (both first century BC) there exists no attempt to create a comprehensive view of Roman religion, surely for the obvious reason that such a view is impossible in a diffuse polytheistic system. Third, we may never be sure who knew what or who constituted a specialist in Roman religion in classical antiquity. Aulus Gellius (2.10) outlines a scholarly debate on the *fauissae* of the Capitoline temple involving three figures not usually identified as specialists; compare Verrius Flaccus (Paulus Festus 78.10–13 L) of the Augustan period, showing a lexicographer attending to this combined religious and topographical issue. Compare, too, Lucius Cincius (first century BC), absent in Gellius (*supra*), surely knowledgeable on the *fauissae* (*GRF* 11), who definitely authored treatises on lexicography, topography, and politics as well as Roman religion. Fourth, the range of ancient scholarly debate on an issue remains unknowable, thus the *fauissae* and the various fragments on the Novensides (*GRF* Cincius 22, Cornificius 8, Stilo 22). Fifth and consequently, much specialist religious information lurked in works whose titles did not promise it; consider the late example of the important opinion lurking in Dionysius of Halicarnassus' *Roman Antiquities* (2.19–20, late first century BC). Sixth, the works were "armchair"; their authors seem to have relied on personal libraries, memories, and personal interactions with other writers. Consider a mid-second century example: Fronto on Anagnia's cults (*Epist. ad Aurelium* 4.4 = 60–1 van den Hout[2]), sole literary evidence of same, arose from spontaneous detour rather than scholarly determination, although the town lay close to Rome. Seventh, no known Roman author, Varro included, devoted himself largely to the study of Roman religion as did, say, St. Augustine for Christianity.

There is also the issue of religious knowledge, and discussion thereof, in legal texts literary and epigraphic, sometimes anonymous, sometimes not. Consider the case of "magic." *Malum carmen* ("noisome metrical charm") seems to have appeared in the XII Tables (Rives 2002), to judge from the host of explicit and implicit quotations, and it continued to remain a live issue (Seneca, *Naturales quaestiones* 4.7.2). But on what terms? Did theorizing about the relation between magic and religion exist in any form (Phillips 1991b)? The famous decision of the senate *de Bacchanalibus* (186 BC: *ILLRP*[2] 511) betokens knowledge of and thought about the cult: the rites are secret (10), but it is recognized that the goddess may require some to participate (2). What about the much-discussed "Nazareth Decree" (*FIRA*[2] 1.69)? Does it reflect knowledge of the alleged resurrection of Jesus (Matthew 28.12–13) or does it rather reflect an ongoing Roman concern for legal issues in exhumation and reburial (Pliny, *Epist.* 10.68f.)? We cannot say; the emperor issuing the decree remains anonymous, while the pontiffs as referenced in Pliny gave rulings advisory rather than binding (Wissowa 1912: 402, 513). The *Lex Lucerina* (*FIRA*[2] 3.71b), through its prohibition on manuring, involves the complexities of what makes a grove sacred (Bodel 1986: 24–9), which we know from other evidence could include such arcana as the legal status of its soil (*ILS* 4915). But given the nature of a polytheistic religious system founded on local religious knowledge it seems unlikely that the precise regulations were universally known, let alone observed; regulations in later legal compilations represent juristic ideals rather than actual local practice (Buckland 1963: 183–4). Finally, the Arval *acta* of AD 224 mention three *Sondergötter* (Summanus, Adolenda, and Coinquenda; Scheid 105v verso) – did the Arvales possess detailed and archival knowledge of those divinities or, rather, were they merely following *mos maiorum*? In all of these cases the circumstances appear not much different from the other examples we have considered. It is impossible to determine whether the evidence betokens substantial and specialist study or whether a combination of legal and religious traditions was simply reused and sometimes modified without significant scholarly thought.

Finally, looming large over all considerations of the Romans' scholarship on and possession of religious information are the pontifical books. They may have been physically *reconditi* (hidden), but a certain fraction of information clearly got out.

The problem lies with determining details in the obvious absence of the books themselves and the annoying presence of widely differing and wildly contradictory testimonia (G. Rohde 1936). Specialist attempts to cut the theological Gordian knot have produced solutions at once complementary and contradictory (Linderski 1985; North 1998; Rüpke 2003). We can, however, assert certain things which bear directly on *Wissenschaftsgeschichte*. First, the pontiffs were neither professional scholars nor professional priests; thus whatever the books really contained, scholarly treatises they did not. Second, factual information from the books did come into the hands of scholars. Third, knowledge of the books' contents was limited by considerations of book production and literacy as well as the agreed-upon although not yet demonstrated difficulties of moving the information via a pre-industrial transportation system. At the one extreme, then, even if the books teemed with treatises and archival religious information, the circulation of that information would be limited by physical factors. At the other extreme, there is no reason to think they teemed with such information at all, in which case it made little difference whether or not they could be circulated. In short, they resemble nothing more than a grandiose, possibly grandiloquent, version of the records which local temples kept throughout Italy and the empire (MacMullen 1981: 11–12). This is not to minimize the importance of such records; they could offer substantial libraries of religious information, a notable example of which appears with the Serapeum of Alexandria and its religious education activities in the late fourth century AD (Watts 2006: 145–6, 189–90). But Alexandria was of relatively easy access, while the libraries of small temples in lonely venues would be far less accessible and, hence, their records' influence would be rather less. Indeed, the very existence of such libraries provides a further important reason for the Christians' promiscuous destruction of temples in the later Roman empire. Thus on practical grounds the pontifical books loom large, but on empirical grounds they loom larger than they should, and this for scholarship of both ancient and modern times.

Further confounding factors begin with the third century AD. The "military anarchy" between the death of Caracalla and the accession of Diocletian occasioned an almost total dearth of contemporary scholarship apart from Dexippus, and a sharp decline in epigraphic evidence. Cornelius Labeo, plausibly but not provably third-century (*HLL* 4.78), appears along with Censorinus (*infra*) as the only author with provable interests in Roman religion. Labeo wrote on, among other topics, the Roman calendar as well as the *disciplina Etrusca*, and possibly the Di Penates (Macr. *Sat.* 3.4.6), although this is disputed (Mastandrea 1979: 113–19); his writings were notable enough to earn the censure of Arnobius (2.15) and Augustine (*Civ.* 2.11, 9.19) while John Lydus, Servius, and Macrobius also utilized him; interestingly, Arnobius seems to have known Varro only from handbooks while Augustine may well have had access, at the least, to very substantial excerpts. Here we must not speculate freely. Varro's works remained very popular in late antiquity, Servius frequently cites them by title, and thus Arnobius represents the exception while Augustine the rule. Contrariwise, the works of Nigidius Figulus passed out of general interest after the second century AD, making it far more likely that later quotations attributed to him come from handbooks. We can cautiously assert that there was an overall tendency toward that which Isidore of Seville exemplifies, the promiscuous use of handbooks and lack of acquaintance with those handbooks' sources. To return and recapitulate, Labeo points to substantial scholarly interest in Roman religion, an interest which his contemporary Censorinus may have shared through demonstrable use of Suetonius' lost *De anno Romanorum* (*On the Year of the Romans*), but they remain the sole exemplars of such interest in his era, and this accords with the period's general tendencies and contrasts with earlier eras. In general, the patristic authors as they prosecute their polemical agenda present occasional bits of information as mere snippets of indifferent probative value hastily culled from larger works; Tertullian may constitute a significant exception (see chapter 31 in this volume).

Despite the third-century issues, it is clear from works of the next two centuries that interest in and resources for Roman religion had not perished. Unfortunately, it becomes impossible to generalize. For example, the fifth-century polytheist Martianus Capella shows some knowledge of Etruscan arcana, although the quality of that knowledge remains debatable since he clearly used earlier scholars' work without attribution (Weinstock 1946). Certainly he relies heavily on some combination of Nigidius Figulus and Varro; likewise, he probably had access to the late republic's Latin translations of the Etruscan sacred books. Nevertheless we cannot know if he knew his sources complete. *Pars pro toto*, consider the case of the aforementioned Lucius Cincius. His 31 fragments preserved in *GRF* (pp. 372–81) come from Arnobius (1 fragment), Charisius (1), Festus (22), Aulus Gellius (1), John Lydus (2; three further quotations are absent from *GRF*), Macrobius (3), Servius (1). Perhaps the most obvious inference becomes that there existed substantial knowledge of Cincius in the second century AD, but this inference totters when we recall that Festus (second century AD) epitomized Verrius Flaccus. Thus we should rather assert that Flaccus, a contemporary of Cincius, had substantial, possibly total, access to his work and that later authors did not but rather borrowed from Flaccus and Festus. Indirect references slightly expand this; Gellius (16.4) quotes from him promiscuously, Livy uncharacteristically praises him as a source (7.3.7), Varro used him (Macr. 1.12–13), one late direct quotation may be expanded by a paraphrase (Servius, *Georgica* 1.10). But we cannot be doctrinaire; the grammarian Charisius could have quoted from a now-lost anthology, but it is not impossible that he used his own antiquarian copy, and possibly other grammarians did as well (Marius Victorinus *GL* 6.23.19–20; Consentius *GL* 5.349.11). Writ large, how much Varro could, and did, Augustine know? Again, the *Carmen contra Paganos* clearly has scholarly knowledge of Roman polytheism, but from where (Phillips 1988)? Of course, "handbooks" constitute one possibility. "Libraries" constitute a better one, since through the fourth century AD polytheists remained a significant group with means and motive and opportunity to preserve antiquarian religious treatises – after all, *pace* Ammianus Marcellinus (28.4.14, 14.6.18) not all senators hated learning like poison and kept their libraries closed like tombs. Productions like Symmachus' Third *Relatio* or much of Ausonius betoken substantial research resources. And we should not overestimate Augustine's ken; he mined Varro but did not expand his researches, both for theology and, interestingly, for music (*De musica*). Christianity had conceptually liquidated Greco-Roman divinities to the status of demons or delusions, in part by citing nuggets of polytheist information.

Matters soon change. Symmachus (c. AD 340–402) had no *epigonoi* and his socio-economic-theological class was vanishing. Thus, in the fifth century, Macrobius and Servius conserved information from much earlier authors, but no one produced a significant new work on Roman polytheism. This lack of scholarly activity, combined with the movement of Rome to Constantinople, killed further scholarship in the west. But consider Constantinople as famous repository for classical texts, and the activities there of John Lydus (sixth century). He may have seen a relatively complete Cincius, because the majority of the Latin authors proffering religion references to Cincius parallel each other, while most of Lydus' citations of Cincius are not otherwise cited. Any hope of scholarly continuity on Roman religion was stillborn, however, as a shrinking minority knew Latin, and in some cases were forbidden to use it (John Lydus, *De magistratibus* 3.68).

Changing east–west dynamics meant changing scholarly interests. Christians no longer viewed "paganism" as a major threat and no longer conned texts for polemical material. Instead, Christian scholarship turned to the various "heresies" within Christendom and the encroachments of Islam. Certainly, "pagan" texts could be useful antiquarian relics, patriotic reminders of *Romanitas*, and justification for contemporary politics (Charlemagne) and the educational system (trivium, quadrivium). But those uses required no scholarship, merely anthologies, and thus came mistakes, often obscenely egregious as in the eighth-century Merovingian claim that Venus was male (Levison 1946: 302–14). More promiscuously, the glossaries which begin by the fifth century AD only rarely conserve truly antiquarian knowledge and even less often show significant comprehension of the texts they gloss (Lindsay and Thomson 1921: v–xii). Likewise scholarly compendia, for example Paul the Deacon's abridgment of Festus (eighth century). Where there was once fertile debate, as on *fauissae* (Paul. *Fest.* 78.10–13 L and *supra*), there was now an account potted to unintelligibility. Traditionally arcane theological and legal points become almost illogical twaddle (*euerriator*: 68.8–13 L); significant toponyms shrink to their barest meaning (*Crustumina*: 48.12 L). Moreover, given the almost total lack of Greek works, knowledge of Roman religion was conflated with knowledge of Greek religion via the preservation of various "myth" handbooks from classical antiquity (Rossum-Steenbeek 1998: 119–56), those handbooks conflating Greek and Roman; the popularity of Ovid made matters all the worse. Rome continued as "then," only occasionally "now," as in the verse of Hildebertus Cenomannensis (c. 1056–1133): *Par tibi, Roma, nihil cum sis prope tota ruina / quam magni fueris integra, fracta doces* (A. Scott 1969: no. 36.1–2), "nothing is like you, Rome, even if you lie almost totally in ruins, / broken you teach how great you were whole." The Renaissance marked an expanded interest in classical antiquity, especially after Greek texts reappeared widely. Interest devolved on the traditional mythologies, especially those useful for fine art and literature, or on the necessary processes of finding and restoring the widely scattered texts (often in a deplorable state of preservation). Hence it is understandable that humanists such as Poggio and their *epigonoi* (e.g. Valla, Politian) spent more time simply recovering the texts and gleaning their most obvious meanings; plumbing the meanings lay later, for the Scaligers of Europe. In short, none seems to have possessed an urgent need for the detailed exegesis of Roman religion.

Early Modern Europe through the Eighteenth Century

The detailed study of Roman religion reappeared, but in its earlier patristics guise as polemical cudgel wielded against theological opponents, and this continued even during the Renaissance conflation and utilization of Greek and Roman religion and their mythologies. For rationalists, particularly of the Enlightenment, the ancients' religion demonstrated savagery combined with stupidity, apparently an excellent justification for anti-clericalism. The Christian view of late antiquity reappeared: Greco-Roman religion trafficked in false gods, the Foul Fiend's invention. Finally, the deists, partially co-extensive with the rationalists, saw the ancients' religion as organized religion of the Judeo-Christian ilk. Their misconstruction justified their problems with contemporary organized religion. In all these cases, precise understanding of Roman religion went by the board in favor of honing the attractive intellectual weapon provided by "ancient wisdom."

Martin Luther looms large with the critique of ritualism, both in his Theses and elsewhere, that Christianity meant an inner state, from which it followed that absent the appropriate inner state, external ritual has no effect. Thus Roman Catholic rituals, relying on ritual efficacy (*ex opere operato*), became meaningless. Luther's followers elaborated, the more so since the Roman church unrepentantly reaffirmed the principle at the Council of Trent in 1543–65 (7.8). Geography helped; the city of Rome constituted the seat of not only Roman Catholicism, but also the "pagan" past, from which it seemed patent then that Roman Catholicism had inherited its allegedly godless attitude to ritual from the "pagans."

But the way was clear for a further development, which reached an apex in the early eighteenth century (J. Smith 1990) and actually led to an interest in Roman religion *per se*. Conyers Middleton produced in 1729 a treatise which went off at least like a firecracker if not a bombshell: *A Letter from Rome, Shewing an Exact Conformity between Popery and Paganism; Or, The Religion of the Present Romans derived from that of their Heathen Ancestors.* Here Middleton built on the combination of Luther and geography to demonstrate an exact equation between Roman Catholic and "pagan" rituals. First, he marshaled substantial quotations from Greco-Roman sources to prove the equation once again. Second, he expanded the logic through demonstration that ancient "pagans" trumped Roman Catholics because the former had rejected allegedly odious aspects of their rituals while the latter had remained perversely mired in their allegedly odious rituals. Put differently, Roman Catholics were "bad pagans." For example, Numa and the religion traditionally ascribed to him appears frequently, notably in his chapter 4 (Middleton's emphasis): "As to that celebrated act of Popish idolatry, *the adoration of the host*, I must confess that I cannot find the least resemblance of it in any part of the Pagan worship . . . ," which he supported with Cicero *Nat.* 3.41 (*sed ecquem tam amentem esse putas, qui illud, quo vescatur, Deum credat esse*). Here lies the reappearance of scholarship on Roman religion, albeit for polemical purposes.

Deists and rationalists alike in the Enlightenment used Greco-Roman texts both traditionally and originally. For some, the alleged "primitive" observances provided further evidence that all religion was depraved. For others, the "primitive" obser-vances were signs of primeval virtue, from which contemporary religions, especially Christianity, had departed to their detriment. But a new kind of evidence was flooding in from the European explorers and the nascent colonial empires of their sponsors. The explorers, and missionaries who often accompanied them, found non-European peoples whose religions offered apparent parallels to what the Greco-Roman texts seemed to say about religion. If the ancient texts had previously provided a mighty cudgel for earlier savants, this new evidence inserted metal spikes into the weapon which should, on their view, make the truth of their conceptions irresistible. Thus the very beginnings of what might be styled a comparative anthropology of Greco-Roman religion were pressed into the service of the Enlightenment's theological agenda.

A development in the British colonial empire expanded the terms of the debate once again. Although substantial quantities of Indian religious texts had existed in the west since the early eighteenth century, full texts and knowledge of Sanskrit did not achieve intellectual significance until the British conquest of India and the con-sequent academic activities of Sir William Jones and his followers (Schwab 1984). Jones amassed ancient Sanskrit texts and translated them, but also he published *On the Gods of Greece, Italy, and India* (1799), in which he noted frequent similarities, principally in what he styled "mythologies," between those three religions, and others besides. This provided not only yet more ammunition for the Enlightenment's *philosophes*, but also an unwitting charter for the "scientific" scholarship of the next century and beyond.

Nineteenth Century and Early Twentieth Century I: Colonialism, Darwin, Universities

The Sanskrit evidence enormously influenced the direction of studies of Greco-Roman religion. Friedrich Schlegel's *Über die Sprache und Weisheit der Indier: Ein Beitrag zur Begründung der Alterthumskunde* (1808) combated earlier romanticized views and sought to provide a scholarly explanation for the kinds of correspondences Jones had observed. Its emphasis on comparative grammar influenced scholars such as the classicist Bopp and the Brothers Grimm; it furthered the Enlightenment's driving emphasis on logic and comparative material to unravel riddling cultural *Streitfragen*. Friedrich Max Müller, who as a student attended Bopp's Berlin lectures, himself an Indologist by training and academic appointment, yoked logic and comparativism to produce his famous and notorious assertion of myth as a "disease of language." K. O. Müller's *Prolegomena zu einer wissenschaftlichen Mythologie* (1825) narrowed the focus to Greco-Roman religion; he conceived myth as Hellenic myth, apparently plausible in light of the Sanskrit connections. This Müller influenced classical studies and Roman religion far more; as long as Greek and Roman mythologies were con-sidered identical there had been no problem, but now it appeared that since the Romans possessed no mythologies as Müller had defined them, they had no mythologies at all. Thus the title of Ludwig Preller's *Römische Mythologie* (1881–3, 3rd edn. H. Jordan)

constitutes no coincidence, as it sought an ecumenical solution in contrast to J. A.
Hartung's *Die Religion der Römer* (1836), but to no avail. German scholarship proceeded, from what it appropriated as Müller's axiomatic demonstration, to enshrine
the view that either the Romans had no mythology, or had totally lost a very early
mythology; these scholars did not consider that perhaps the Romans had no mythology of the Greek variety (Phillips 1991a). In this the specialists in Roman religion
unwittingly supported the more general "common knowledge" view of classical studies
that "real" classical civilization was Hellenic (*supra* C1).

Classicists agreed on the value of the Sanskrit evidence but soon they began to
disagree on the use of other comparative evidence, a disagreement centered on Britain
and Germany. The former, with an enormous colonial empire, possessed a huge and
rapidly increasing stock of comparative ethnography, the immediate basis, along with
Darwin's theories, on which apparently to explain notorious conundrums ancient and
modern of human societies and their institutions. It cannot be overemphasized that
academics in mid-nineteenth-century Britain conceived anthropology and religious
studies and classical studies as but parts of one overarching discipline. The organizational change did not begin until 1883–4, with Tylor's appointment as reader
in anthropology. Nevertheless, despite the place of anthropology as a sub-faculty
of natural sciences, Tylor regularly lectured on topics such as "Anthropological
Elucidations of Greek and Latin Authors" (1888); his "Anthropology in Ancient
History" (1904) was cross-listed (often the case with his lectures) with the ancient
history sub-faculty of litterae humaniores, and note that the very next year (1905)
Cyril Bailey offered his lecture series on Roman religion. Such juxtapositions, and
there were countless others of this ilk, speak volumes. As for publications, Tylor cited
classical sources aptly and promiscuously; the classicists Farnell and Fowler quoted
Tylor; and R. R. Marrett imbibed R. H. Codrington's *The Melanesians* (1891), anthologized the observations about *mana* in his notebooks, and prefixed a stage of
pre-animism to Tylor's theory of animism, as he strove in *The Threshold of Religion*
(1909) to provide a comparative-ethnographic solution to the vexed issue of *numen*
in early Roman religion. Whatever the value of the comparative material (it is still
disputed), the work on *numen* had little *Nachleben*; Weinstock's empirico-positivist
position still remains one with which, unfortunately, most today would agree
(Weinstock 1949). There was a conceptual gap which would not be bridged; the
author of the book Weinstock was reviewing, H. J. Rose, had just earlier written
that Tylor's animism was "still popular today because it contains a large measure of
truth" (Rose 1943: 362, Rose 1935).

Germany's relatively tiny colonial empire provided scant ethnographic data in comparison to Britain's. While nationalistic and evolutionary issues blocked attention
to the British material, German Romanticism's idealization of the people, especially
evident in *Des Knaben Wunderhorn* of Arnim and Brentano (1806), led scholars
to utilize German folklore in many areas of classical studies, including Roman religion. The British had a long tradition of folklore studies, often tinged with nation-
alism, but their folklorists largely remained antiquarians with scant influence on
the Oxonians' work on Roman religion. Wilhelm Mannhardt's *Antike Wald- und
Feldkulte* (1875–7) remains famous (Kippenberg 2002: 81–7); Ernst Samter utilized

Tyrolean poetry to demonstrate that the Romans conceived ghosts as inhabiting the floor, on the basis of an enigmatic passage of the Elder Pliny (*Nat.* 28.27; Samter 1901: 108–14); Hermann Usener's *Götternamen* (3rd edn. 1896) took comparative linguistics and ethnography to new heights in attempting to make sense of those enigmatic Roman divinities (Phillips 2001), an approach which Wagenvoort much later significantly expanded (1947). Retrospectively, though, German classicists' use of ethnographic material seems short-lived for two interrelated reasons. The conceptual hostility of senior academics such as Wilamowitz (*supra* C2) was itself a function of the dominant post-Kantian idealist tradition with its double epistemology, in which human historical development was inevitably separated from the natural sciences and their views of evolution. Perhaps the clearest example appears with Wilamowitz's qualms about the "Frankfurt School," although the works of some of those (Kerényi, Otto) did not make the best possible case for their position (Schlesier 1994: 215–18). Not all were hostile, of course; Ludwig Deubner, himself a pupil of Usener, welcomed the comparative material of Samter's *Geburt, Hochzeit und Tod* (1911) even though demurring from some of the conclusions (Deubner 1920: 419–21). Finally, of course, there was outright scholarly jingoism. Two quotations suffice: from the United Kingdom: "It is absolutely impossible in these days to dispense with the works of a long series of anthropologists, many of them fortunately British . . . ," and from Germany on Wissowa: "Ethnologische Gesichtspunkte werden von ihm sorgfältig vermieden . . ." (Fowler 1911: 19; Wide 1912: 270). Of course there exist exceptions, and thus in 1911 Hermann Diels proposed Frazer for membership in the Prussian Academy in a letter which shows considerable appreciation for comparative ethnography (Calder and Ehlers 1991); that Diels was a regular correspondent with the generally despised (in Germany) Usener (Calder and Ehlers 1991: 141 n. 5) should caution us against overly interpreting public pronouncements, valuable though they be.

Darwin and his theories further differentiated studies of Roman religion in the two countries. Although Darwin treated only biological speciation, not using the word "evolution" in his first edition, others soon expanded his views to societal evolution, arguing that since biological speciation was "scientifically" proven, so must be societal evolution (Burrow 1966). The way seemed clear, finally and "scientifically," to answer the crucial questions, as Oxford scholars combined comparative ethnography, evolution, and classical studies. German scientists nationalistically rejected evolution in favor of their own rather different theorizing, further dooming larger vistas for those German scholars who had dared to utilize ethnographic material (Burrow 1967).

Finally, there is the striking difference of academic venue between Germany and Britain. Much of the Prussian plan for German unification devolved on universities, part of Humboldt's grandiose humanistic scheme. Humboldt's enormous influence, though, could not counteract German classicists' long-standing affection for Kantian empiricism, which provided philosophical support for their rejection of the British comparative evolutionary anthropology; thus German classical scholarship focused on what is often called "Big Scholarship," the editing of and commenting on classical texts, literary and otherwise; the compilation of enormous reference works; the relentless flow of *Einzelerklärungen*, "explanations of individual problems" (Grafton 1983). Larger perspectives were either neo-Humboldtian (Wilamowitz 1931–2; Henrichs 1985) or sporadic attempts to utilize comparative material (E. Rohde 1898; Samter 1901), and these latter predictably (*supra*) encountered nearly total hostility. Thus it scarcely seems coincidental that Wilamowitz in his Latin autobiography placed Usener among those (*inter philologos*) *quibus nihil debeo* (Calder 1981: 48), although Usener received vindication of a kind when Ernst Cassirer utilized his work in *Philosophie der symbolischen Formen* (1925). British universities, by contrast, remained sleepy places until the reforms of Oxbridge in the second half of the century. The reforms had an intellectual base, but it is scarcely coincidental that they took place at the time of alarm at the rise of the mighty Prussian intellectual and industrial-military machine; hence the "endowment of research" at Oxbridge to counteract the Prussians. The British could not meet them on the grounds of "Big Scholarship" directly, but with their comparative evolutionary perspectives they felt they could go where the Prussians refused to tread. Hence it should not surprise that the British found Usener's magnum opus congenial (Fowler 1911: 161–4; Rose 1913; but cf. Farnell 1907) while the scholars in the USA, largely following the German model of scholarship, did not (Gildersleeve 1896). The effects of all of these developments on the study of Roman religion were enormous.

Nineteenth Century and Early Twentieth Century II: Developments in Germany and Britain

It is not surprising, that given the differences on colonialism and comparative material, Darwin, and the role of universities, the study of Greco-Roman religion would differ greatly in Britain and Germany. Oxford had rapidly become the training-ground for future colonial administrators. These future administrators imbibed the intellectual ferment of classics and anthropology in Oxford's "Greats" curriculum, popularly considered to be the curriculum of choice for future civil servants, despite the introduction at Cambridge of the Special Board of Indian Civil Service Studies (Symonds 1986; Vasunia 2005). After taking degrees, the new colonial administrators often reported to their erstwhile mentors, reports inevitably colored by the mentors' theories. Thus Frazer (until recently unpublished; see now Ackerman 2005: 96–7) to Tylor, December 4, 1896, of a projected history of Uganda by a Mr. Pilkington, "a Cambridge man who took good honors in classics and works as the linguist of the mission in Uganda." The British were not unappreciative of the German efforts, but they felt that they could go them one better by way of the comparative ethnographic material, use of which was just as "scientific" (Darwin was, after all, "scientific") as the Germans' "Big Scholarship." Thus Fowler on Wissowa: "I cannot but think it a pity that this eminent scholar should so absolutely decline to learn anything from the despised comparative anthropologists" (Fowler 1902: 119). Despite cooperation between classics and anthropology, the study of Roman religion remained highly specialized. For example, Fowler never lectured on Roman religion; nor did Arthur Darby Nock during his brief tenure at Cambridge; Bailey did so only infrequently; and despite Weinstock's long tenure at Oxford and regular lectures on Roman religion, the questions on Roman religion posed in the Oxford "Greats" examinations in the 1960s were virtually identical to those posed in the previous century. Compare "What do we gather from Tacitus respecting the worship of the numen of Augustus?" (1876) with "What conditions determined the decision to deify Augustus in September, A.D. 14?" (1964). The sorts of questions posed in the Oxbridge exams did not rely so much on specialists' research as on the traditional views. That is, although specialist Oxford dons might write on Roman religion in light of the latest evidence and theorizing, their influence on the examinations was nil. This should not surprise when we consider, for example, that Stefan Weinstock did no tutorial work, and of the three research students who began work with him, only one (John North) completed his DPhil with him.

Many of the British anthropologist-classicists were religious skeptics. On their view, "magic" and animism were almost co-extensive, the starting point for evolution to science by way of religion. The less skeptical saw an evolution to religion by way of science, but all agreed that "magic," often equated with animism, lay at the evolutionary base and thus constituted something different from religion. Although "magic" and its synonyms had appeared in the ancient texts, in virtually all cases it constituted a term of convenience with which to blacken one's theological opponents. Now it was not only opposed to religion, but in light of the ethnographic material a "primitive" mode of thought of "savage" peoples, and for "peoples" read "those who were not Christian and not European" (Phillips 1986: 2711–32, Phillips 1991b). Despite those divisions, they shared a common language, and thus J. G. Frazer's commentary on Ovid's *Fasti* (1929: 426) remarks of 2.520 (*primitias Cereri farra resecta dabant*) "to eat of them was to partake of the body of a god, in other words, it was a sacrifice or communion." Hence the origin of today's unfortunate common parlance that Roman religion was of primitive origins which not even later developments could eradicate. Hence too the unfortunate common use of Christian-centric words such as "pagan orthodoxy" in studies of Roman religion.

As for Germany, the measured compliments of, for example, Warde Fowler (*supra*) were not returned; comparative material and anthropology had acquired a bad smell for German classicists. Since Niebuhr, German classicists had an important role in providing an intellectual and historical charter for the rise of Prussia; many German ancient historians concerned themselves with the constitutional basis of government along with law and imperialism. The rest, including Roman religion, deemed peripheral to the study, was consigned to *Privataltertümer*. One might say Roman religion lost in both countries. It lost in Britain as a primitive religion of "magic" and animism. It lost in Germany as irrelevant to historical studies except insofar as *Reichsreligion* could be fractioned from it. It also lost because the unfortunate circumstance of World War I resulted in the deaths of a number of young scholars whose scholarly inclinations lay with the incorporation of the best of British and German scholarship on Roman religion. Nevertheless, the fact remained that there were issues and evidence in Roman religion, and so hardy classicists in both countries kept the study alive in the face of such dispiriting and disparaging classicist ideologies in both countries (A4, B3, C).

The Twentieth Century until 1960

By the 1920s the previous fascination with evolution as a means of explaining religions had largely run its course. Indeed, there arose a strong counter-reaction in all the disciplines, including classical studies, a reaction which was largely occasioned by the evident excesses of evolutionist theorizing; inside classical studies the ire devolved especially upon the so-called Cambridge ritualists. But the counter-reaction was curious.

> Students of religion sought other approaches to understanding religion that ranged from positivistic philological and historical studies of religious texts and communities to phenomenological and hermeneutical "studies" of particular aspects or elements of religious belief, ritual practice, and behavior, and of religions and religion in general, that produced what might well be called "virtuoso scholarship," dependent more upon the idiosyncratic ideas of the individual scholar than on the nature of the subject matter and general rules of inquiry. (Wiebe 2004: 234–5)

But notice that only "positivistic . . . studies" and "virtuoso scholarship" apply to what happened in classical studies generally and the study of Roman religion specifically. Classicists remained, and continue to remain, albeit with scattered significant exceptions in recent years, innocent of and often hostile to concepts such as the phenomenological and hermeneutical. From the teeming scholarship I select three items.

First is H. J. Rose's summary of scholarship for 1910–60 (Rose 1960). The "idiosyncratic" appears with the various works of George Dumézil and Franz Altheim (cf. Rose 1934); there are sympathetic observations on the evolutionists Frazer and Tylor. Far the most part of the scholarship Rose identifies falls squarely into the category of "positivistic" studies, which he overtly considers the prime desideratum. Second is Agnes Michels's justly celebrated survey of recent trends; unlike the other two authors, and most specialists in Roman religion then, she takes on its own merits each theory and approach of the "happy chaos" (Michels 1954/5: 27). Her view has much in common with the very recent words of Wiebe. Third is Stefan Weinstock's review of Kurt Latte's *Römische Religionsgeschichte* (Weinstock 1961). To his credit, Weinstock here and elsewhere does not reject animism out of hand, *contra* Latte (Weinstock 1961: 206; 1960: 116–18). To his discredit, he takes Roman religion as a religion without belief. The bulk of his review, however, devolves on the positivistic corrections and additions of scholarship and evidence. But herein lies a fundamental problem of the field, a problem unresolved. If three notable specialists can disagree on the scholarship appropriate for Roman religion, where does that leave the field and its place inside classical studies?

Recent Developments

Some continued earlier tendencies; thus Stefan Weinstock without apology followed Mommsen (Weinstock 1961: 206; Phillips 2004), while Arthur Darby Nock continued the positivism but with less of Mommsen's influence (Z. Stewart 1972). Likewise again, Robert Palmer made the very best possible case for an empirico-positivist approach as he extracted seemingly every plausible meaning from a panoply of recalcitrant evidence; his superb results should give pause to those who consider that theoretical approaches constitute the only way to further advances in the study of Roman religion (Palmer 1974). Gerhard Radke continued the earlier emphasis on etymologies and origins in his *Die Götter Altitaliens* ([1965] 1979) and rather speculatively in *Zur Entwicklung der Gottesvorstellung und der Gottesverehrung in Rom* (1987); we should remember that Weinstock considered it high praise that in his view Latte knew linguistics even better than Wissowa (Weinstock 1961: 207). The idiosyncratic continued with Dumézil's *La religion romaine archaïque* (1966, 2nd edn 1974), which pushed comparative linguistics almost to the limit. Finally there are the revisionists. Louise Adams Holland wedded empirico-positivism to a respectful yet skeptical use of the earlier British anthropologists, consequently demonstrating that the earlier theorizing should not be rashly dismissed (Holland 1961), while we have seen Weinstock's use of Samter amidst his self-identification with the Mommsen tradition. More frequently, though, the same scholar who dismisses theories and comparativism will not be above using them almost on the sly, as it were; thus Kurt Latte dismissed Samter's use of animism while approving of the concept of sympathetic magic (Latte 1960: 94 n. 1, 69).

Recent years have also seen the expansion of an unfortunate tendency in literary studies into studies of Roman religion. There has long existed a legion of literary studies of, say, "myth in Propertius" or "ritual in Ovid" either standing alone or as parts of a larger work. Too often those studies show scant familiarity with Roman religion beyond misconceptions prevalent among the literary scholars, sometimes buttressed by handbook forays to cull that which seems to support the misconceptions. Specialists in Roman religion have previously and profitably shunned such *cacata carta*. But since Ovidians have turned to his *Fasti*, the situation becomes critical. Their lack of attention to Roman religion now inevitably leads to the misrepresentation of a substantial poem on Roman religion and hence all Roman religion. Symptomatic: a recent commentary on part of the *Fasti*, a commentary deficient on Roman religion, received a positive review by a respected Latinist in a respected journal, despite the review's thunderous silence on any issue of Roman religion.

Writ large, as I have put it in a review (Phillips 1996: 285) of an excellent small survey of Greek religion, equally applicable here by changing "myth" to "Roman religion":

> because all classicists possess that necessary linguistic training, it follows that everyone thinks he or she knows what myth is and is competent to pronounce on it . . . Put differently, there exists as common knowledge in classical studies an enormous amount of interpretational twaddle promulgated by those without any knowledge of Greco-Roman religion beyond what they read in the ancient texts.

Of course, literary studies have a fundamental contribution to make to Roman religion, and specialists in Roman religion have long, through inattention to literary qualities, produced distorted views. But it can be no help when literary specialists continue almost perversely to ignore any and all scholarship on Roman religion. Literary scholars do not have to specialize in Roman religion, but they do need to learn about it; Denis Feeney (1998) has shown it can be done with superior results.

Scholarship from specialists in Roman religion has an eclectic quality. That is good, in that various theoretical guidelines can be appropriated on a basis of intellectual integrity. That is not so good, I think, because now we are less sure than ever what Roman religion "is," and this despite, say, an excellent, sympathetic and accurate two-volume survey (Beard et al. 1998). Likewise, there has been a recent meticulous historical analysis of the early republic to cast important light on early Roman religion and the calendar (Rüpke 1995a). But what are the implications for a general view of Roman religion? Similarly, articles by all the aforementioned scholars and others such as Bendlin, Scheid, and myself (Bendlin 2000; Phillips 1991a; Scheid 1987) offer illuminations of specific issues, but what of the whole? If previous generations of scholarship on Roman religion have been marked by a tendency to fit evidence to theory, it may be that a counter-reaction, theory only when appropriate to a small-scale issue, is inevitable. But one cannot help but think that something is lost. It is true that we no longer characterize Roman religion as one of cult acts without belief, mired in primitive animistic practices. It is true too that we possess enormous quantities of *Einzelerklärungen*, whether of specific evidence or specific cults and rituals. But sometimes it can seem all trees and no forest; we miss the grand sweep with which the scholars of earlier generations traversed the evidence. This grand sweep arose not just from concern with specific models, but in counterpoint, sometimes harmonious and sometimes dissonant, with the intellectual and sociopolitical climate of the times. Put differently, we have lost the majestic Bruckner symphony and now hearken to often atonal Albumblätter. Perhaps it is time for specialists in Roman religion to renew contact with their erstwhile colleagues in religious studies and anthropology – those fields are rife with promising approaches such as the cognitive. The large-scale urgently needs to return to the study of Roman religion.

FURTHER READING

Given the assertion of my opening sentence, the suggestions here aim for a brief orientation to a selection of the sorts of materials available; the "overviews" mentioned in the second sentence will remain basic, to which add the *Year's Work in Classical Studies* 1906–45/7 (vols. 1–34), especially Fowler's notices "Roman religion and mythology," which appeared 1906–17. One usually has to mine more general works. Calder (1981/2) introduces the value of archival material, while Calder and Kramer (1992) with Calder and Smith (2000) provide a rich starting point for quarrying bibliography. Of the many histories of classical scholarship, the most immediately useful here are L. D. Reynolds and Wilson (1991), Schlesier (1994), and Wilamowitz (1921), with Hummel (2000) for the larger context. Necrologies are often very valuable; although widely scattered, *Gnomon* and *Proceedings of the British Academy* provide a point of departure. No one should miss Briggs and Calder (1990), where 50 generous entries include masterly articles on Frazer, Harrison, Müller, Norden, Erwin Rohde, and Usener. Many of the themes and concepts raised throughout this chapter appear in Phillips (1986).

One should always remember the cross-disciplinary aspects of *Wissenschaftsgeschichte*; thus for definitions of religion compare Fowler (1908) and Michels (1976) on the classical side with McCutcheon (1995) and J. Smith (1998). Comparative religion looms large over the entire subject, reliably introduced, albeit with a regrettable slighting of classical studies, in Sharpe (1975).

Classical antiquity through the Renaissance: For classical antiquity, one must quarry from the relevant volumes of *NP*, *RE* (with electronic index), Schanz/Hosius, and *HLL*; L. Reynolds and Wilson (1991), with the bibliographies in its chapter notes, will provide orientation. One should be prepared to deal with obscure and fragmentary works, and Rawson (1985) provides a reliable point of departure; for example, all will know of Varro's *Antiquitates rerum divinarum* and the voluminous scholarship on it, but his less familiar works have much to offer (Cardauns 1960; Mastandrea 1979), even though the good modern editions just referenced remain the exception rather than the rule. Temple destruction has received frequent scholarly attention; Sauer (2003) provides a sound introduction; I shall soon be publishing at length on the connections between temple destruction, geographical accessibility, and religious knowledge. Tracing the Byzantine *Nachleben* constitutes a task both toilsome and obscure even for classical studies; see *ODB* on the various topics and Maas (1992) for John Lydus. For the medieval and Renaissance periods, L. Reynolds and Wilson (1991) provides the best short entry; the important but wretchedly difficult issue of the medieval glosses can best be approached via the voluminous papers of Wallace Lindsay, many of which are conveniently reproduced in Lapidge (1996).

Early modern Europe through the eighteenth century: For this teeming period, I mention three works which bear directly on issues raised *supra*: J. Smith (1990) for post-Reformation appropriation of Greco-Roman religion; the tremendously exciting and superbly documented Gay (1966–9) for the Enlightenment; Schwab (1984) for the Sanskrit connections. Important texts on "mythology" from the period are anthologized in B. Feldman and Richardson (1972), but the documentation and commentary are not entirely free from errata; comparative religion texts from the United Kingdom are anthologized with a valuable introductory study in Pailin (1984).

Nineteenth century through 1960: The question of myth and ritual hangs heavily over the period. For a valuable collection of primary texts together with even more valuable introductions by the editor, himself a classicist by training, see Segal (1998); an exciting *au courant* study of the theories appears in Bell (1997), while Ackerman (1987) produced a model biography of Frazer now accompanied by (Ackerman 2005), a model selection of Frazer's correspondence. The perspectives I have presented in these sections do not, obviously, appear with the same emphases in other authors' works, and much relies on archival material. Nevertheless, in addition to the documentation given, some general works will provide guideposts. For the UK, Rothblatt (1968) covers Cambridge; Engel (1983) covers the academic side of Oxford; Brock and Curthoys (1997, 2000) exhaustively cover Oxford in the nineteenth century; Symonds (1986) demonstrates Oxford's dominance in the administration of the British empire generally, with Vasunia (2005) on the case of India; while Stray (1998), a work whose perspectives regularly parallel my own, puts British classical studies in societal perspective. For the study of Greco-Roman religion the experience of the British in India is crucial, and these salient aspects appear in Bayly (1996) and Cohn (1996). For Germany, McClelland (1980) provides an overview, Grafton (1983) details the formative period of the early nineteenth century, while Gildenhard and Ruehl (2003) offer essays on developments in the later nineteenth century.

On the social sciences in the UK, see Stocking (1987, 1996a); for Darwinism, see Sharpe (1975: 47–71) and Burrow (1966). For British folklorists, see Dorson (1968); for German folklorists, see Stocking (1996b).

Recent developments: Dumézil remains a live issue, on which see Littleton (1982). Discussion of some very contemporary tendencies appears in Phillips (2000b). Finally, my forthcoming book on Roman religious knowledge will present extended analyses of Oxbridge lectures and archival material along with detailed analysis of the connections between classical studies and anthropology and empires both in Germany and in the UK.

ACKNOWLEDGMENT

Thanks to Andreas Bendlin for suggesting improvements in the material from antiquity and early modern Europe. The staff of the Bodleian Library, University of Oxford, regularly surpassed even its legendary reputation for helpfulness during my many research visits; two archivists, Simon Bailey (keeper of the archives, University of Oxford) and Martin Maw (archivist, Oxford University Press) generously and *in situ* taught me the basics of archival research and supplied material I would never have found unaided. It is no exaggeration to claim that *Wissenschaftsgeschichte* cannot be done without constant reference to the many perceptive works of William M. Calder III, and my exchanges with him over several decades have been a wise and constant inspiration; although he will be reading this chapter in print for the first time, I hope he will consider it a not inapposite thank-offering.

PART I

Changes

CHAPTER THREE

The Religion of Archaic Rome

Christopher Smith

The obscurity surrounding early Roman religion is profound. Writing about ancient religious experience is difficult in itself, but especially in the case of early Rome, in the absence of any substantial written record, and with a scattered and incomplete archaeological record, it is bound to be a task fraught with uncertainty and doubt. There is no doubt, however, that the subject has been, and continues to be, attractive to scholars. Rome has been considered to be a society whose religion is so static and whose customs so conservative that one might have hoped to find the traces of the earliest forms of Roman religion in present practice, and Rome has also been regarded by some as peculiarly bound to its religion, so that some facts of unusual value ought to be concealed within the origins of its practices (e.g. Fowler 1911; Ogilvie 1969).

Neither of these views would command much support today; Roman religion is regarded as dynamic, and scholars tend to eschew grand claims about the Roman identity (Beard et al. 1998). Nevertheless, we have to make some sense of the evidence that survives, and this is particularly the case because the history of early Rome has received so much attention of late that it is now appropriate to reconsider the religious aspects, in light of the kinds of arguments that are currently mounted in support of a degree of optimism in relation to the possibility of recovering some kind of narrative, or at least some degree of understanding of the structural underpinning of archaic Roman history (Cornell 1995; Forsythe 2005).

We should briefly reflect on the history of scholarship in this area. Roman religious practice was of interest to antiquarian scholarship in the Renaissance and Enlightenment, but largely in matters of detail (see chapter 2). The point at which historians started to take the early myths of Rome more seriously was when these began to be scrutinized for their historical accuracy and deconstructed according to modern, skeptical, and analytical methods; the pioneer in this area was Niebuhr, who, early in the nineteenth century, began to analyze in detail the foundation stories and early myths (Niebuhr 1828–32).

From this point on, Roman mythology and religious practice began to be considered as a historical resource. Let us take an example which has been well studied recently: the story of Romulus and Remus, the twin brothers who founded Rome. Niebuhr excavated from this account a story about two cities, Rome and Remuria, the latter defeated by the former (this is universally discounted now). Schwegler thought that the twins were derived by ancient thinkers from the very early twin Lares Praestites, the protective deities of the city. Mommsen, who wrote a great account of the constitutional history of Rome, found in the story of the twins an explanation of the shared power of the consulship. More recent accounts have emphasized broad folktale motifs, but there is still the possibility that there is a political interpretation which can explain the myth (Wiseman 1995a).

All this depends on how we read the available sources. At this stage it is at least worth stating that a gulf has opened up between different traditions in the study of Roman religion. Anglo-American scholarship has tended to be skeptical about everything to do with early Rome, whereas French and Italian scholarship has sought to uncover the deepest and earliest religious history of Rome through the study of etymology and ritual, without placing much faith or interest in the validity of the historical accounts of the period (compare for instance Forsythe 2005 with Carandini 1997). As more scholars in the Anglo-American tradition adopt various strategies legitimately to recover a historical understanding of early Rome, a degree of rapprochement with the long European tradition becomes appropriate.

At the same time, we should not overlook the importance of the recovery of Roman religious activity through archaeology. In the context of Rome and its hinterland, Latium, and the fascinating yet mysterious civilization of the Etruscans across the Tiber, some elements of the material correlates of religious action have been long known, either as standing ruined temples, or as scattered finds. For the earlier phases, however, only careful excavation could reveal issues of context and sequence. Equally, for archaeologists of the late Bronze and early Iron Age across Europe, the scope and definition of what might be called religious, or more usually ritual, material, was developing. Archaeologists of this period usually have no texts on which to base their arguments, and therefore rely upon theories of human activity, and chief amongst those is the identification of recurrent and repeated activity which is invested with meaning. One recent and important definition (Bell 1992: 74) speaks of "ritualized" action, defined as the way in which certain ritual actions strategically distinguish themselves in relation to other actions, and this same account emphasizes issues such as power relations, knowledge, and knowledge as power, and the relationship between ritual and the human body, all of which are significant features in archaeological accounts. So archaeology brings to this period in particular a degree of theoretical sophistication, and we shall see how this has begun to draw out interesting and challenging interpretations of Latin religious behavior. At the same time we should acknowledge that as the historians of religion focused on behavior that was identifiable from literary texts, and as archaeologists sought behavior which they could identify as ritualized, the two approaches did not necessarily converge. To give a single example, the ritual of the Parentalia, which was intended to appease the spirits of the dead, is archaeologically invisible, but the ritualized activity relating to burial is the commonest and most significant aspect of the archaeological record for Latium, the area surrounding Rome, between 1000 and 500 BC, with Osteria dell'Osa being the most extensive necropolis yet excavated (Bietti-Sestieri 1992).

This introduction has outlined two problems. First, different traditions of scholarship have led to radically different interpretations of the early religion of Rome; second, the gulf between the approaches driven by literary texts and those inspired by archaeology and archaeological theory is wide. To bring these together is a substantial and perhaps impossible task; I will simply outline the major elements of available evidence, before indicating a particular way in which archaic Roman religion can be located in wider discourses of political structure and narrative.

Ancient Sources

Early Rome might be thought to suffer from a lack of written evidence. No narrative history exists, even in fragments, from a period earlier than the second century BC, and our earliest continuous surviving narrative of Rome comes from a political treatise, the *Republic*, by Cicero in the middle of the first century BC, some five hundred and more years after the events it describes. Moreover, it is not at all clear that there was anything before the third century BC, either in Latin or in Greek. The first history of Rome by a Roman, Fabius Pictor, was written at the end of that century, and the stray comments in the fourth-century BC Greek historian Theopompus about the dining habits of the Etruscans do not clearly betoken a wider and more substantial treatment of central Italy. It is tempting to believe that substantial accounts were written by the Greeks in Campania (the region to the south of Latium), but it is merely an optimistic guess. Even if such accounts did exist one would not necessarily find them of substantial use for writing the religious history of Rome, just as one would struggle to write an account of Greek or even Athenian religion relying solely upon its historians.

The gap between the composition of histories of Rome and the events which they claim to describe is long, and the development of specialized accounts, which we loosely describe as antiquarian, comes even later. The key name here is Varro, who was writing toward the end of the first century BC, but whose works are sadly mostly lost. Inevitably, one must ask whether the historical or antiquarian authors had any reliable information from which to create their accounts, and whether and how any such information could have survived from the earliest periods of Roman history.

In addition, we must acknowledge that a persistent interest in making their past justify or condemn their present made Roman historians and antiquarians of the late republican and early imperial periods both indefatigable researchers, and unreliable ones. The desire to discover the past, and to present it in a highly wrought fashion, was given added impetus by the claimed connection of the Julii (the family to which Julius Caesar and Augustus Caesar belonged) with Aeneas and therefore with the earliest history of Rome. Virgil's epic poem, the *Aeneid*, and Livy's history reflect this obsessive interest in and reinvention of the past, and they were in turn commented upon right into late antiquity. The distortions of the late republic and the

Augustan period, and the multiplication of those distortions over time, are hard to push aside, yet each was a coherent and in its own way fascinating reconstruction of early Rome (Fox 1996).

At this stage we should first give some indication of our own chronological definitions, and within those some idea of what claims the ancients made. Rome had two founding myths. One told how Aeneas escaped from Troy and came by a difficult path to the shores of Italy, where his son founded the city of Alba Longa a few miles from Rome. The other told how the twins Romulus and Remus, after a miraculous escape from an early death, came to found the city of Rome, and how one of them, Romulus, killed his brother and ruled Rome alone. These two myths could be made compatible by making Romulus and Remus distant descendants of Aeneas. Aeneas' mythical adventures belonged to the very distant past, but this was located to what we call the twelfth century BC by ancient scholars. Rome itself was founded, again according to ancient scholars, in what we call 753 BC, and for Romans, this was the date from which their history ran forward; year one, in other words. There were seven kings, who ruled Rome to 509 BC, when the last king, Tarquinius Superbus, was expelled, and the Roman republic began, characterized by two annually elected officials called consuls. On the whole, we tend to think of the Rome of the kings as archaic Rome, making some allowance for the fact that there is archaeological evidence for a settlement at Rome back at least as far as the tenth century BC. The first century of the republic, or the early republic, ends with two watershed moments: the capture and destruction by Rome of Veii, its great Etruscan neighbor, in 396 BC, and the capture and destruction of Rome by the Gauls in 390 BC (Cornell 1995 gives valuable guidance on all the above).

Archaeology

For the earliest periods the evidence is predominantly archaeological, and here we are in a stronger position. Not only is the material evidence more rewarding than the literary evidence because of its bulk and contemporaneity, we also know more about aspects of the material culture of this period than we do about subsequent periods because of the intensity of excavation, and the nature of the preservation of material (C. Smith 1996a for a survey). One important element of the archaeological evidence which is also borne out by the literary sources, and has a significant impact on archaic religion, is the intimate relationship between Rome and its hinterland Latium. The community of language (Latin), the overwhelming similarity of archaeological material, and indeed the contemporaneity of urban development – most towns build temples, monumental houses, and walls at roughly the same time – suggest that one may supplement the archaeological record at Rome, where massive subsequent building in antiquity and of course until the present day has obscured the earlier regions of the city, with information gathered from the surrounding region.

In brief, the more or less uniform material of the tenth and ninth centuries BC, largely found in burials, is supplemented in the eighth century by imports either of

material, or of ideas, originating in the east and carried to Italy as part of the movement of peoples which was stimulated by the Phoenicians and carried on by the diaspora of Greeks in the colonization period. By the later eighth and seventh centuries,
this had led to rising levels of luxury in the material record, particularly in burials
which have been called "princely" (*tombe principesche*) and are some of the most
famous features of Latin archaeology; the great tombs of Praeneste just outside Rome
being prime examples. This period is also characterized by the beginning of practices of votive deposition which are visible to archaeology. As we move into the later
seventh and sixth centuries, we find fewer burials and more evidence of public and
private building throughout Latium, and this includes the emergence of substantial
temples across the region. One way of beginning to understand this change is to
see a shift away from expenditure on elaborate funerals, which are singular events,
into monumental display (but cf. chapter 5). There is no lack of competition
between the wealthy aristocrats, but this is channeled increasingly into activities which
emphasize communal goods, and make permanent marks on the landscape of Latin
settlements. By the beginning of the fifth century, this shift is complete, but the
subsequent period is extremely problematic archaeologically, with significant gaps
which may reflect the rather unsettled period of the fifth and fourth centuries.
Nevertheless, unless fire or other disaster intervened, the sixth-century building achievements remained. As one example, it would appear that the temple of Jupiter
Optimus Maximus Capitolinus at Rome, which was destroyed in Sulla's march on
Rome in 83 BC, was essentially the same as the one built late in the sixth century
(L. Richardson 1992: 221–4).

It is notable and perhaps significant that there is a similarity of material between
burials and votive deposits, and in the case of a particular type, the miniature statuette of a human with a hand outstretched in the act of offering, it is likely that this
object represents cult activity. We also find models of cakes which may represent
food offerings, and from the eighth century onward we find remains of animals which
had presumably been sacrificed and eaten, and the accoutrements of wine drinking,
a custom imported from the east (Bouma 1996). In the seventh century, we see that
identical architectural frieze decorations are found in temples and in domestic settings
(C. Bruun 1993). By the classical period, we can demonstrate that there is huge
overlap between the individuals who hold political office and those who hold priestly
office. In the fifth century at Rome, efforts were made to confine both kinds of office
to a hereditary aristocracy, the patricians – efforts which were ultimately unsuccessful
(Szemler 1972; Raaflaub 1986). It is likely that in the early period, we see predominantly
elite behavior in the material record, and what this behavior seems to show is that
the close association of political power with religious authority is of long standing.
It is not simply a lack of available options that brings this continuity from sacred to
secular, but rather an absence of that division. Archaic Rome and Latium was a world
full of religion, if not of gods.

It is also important to stress that individual sites demonstrate continuity of
religious practice over very long periods. There are a number of major temple
complexes which are preceded by a sequence of votive deposits. One example is San
Omobono at Rome, about which we shall have more to say below, and where the

religious connection is preserved through a Christian church to the present day. Another excellent example is at Satricum, where it would appear that religious activity may have begun around 800 BC around a natural spring, and then developed with successive votive deposits and a sequence of religious buildings, culminating in a major and impressive temple, which included the dedication stone with the now famous inscription to a Publius Valerius by his *suodales*. The temple is dedicated to Mater Matuta, who is the partner of Fortuna in the S. Omobono site, and is surrounded by buildings which may be dining halls rather than private dwellings (C. Smith 1999). Certainly the existence of communal dining spaces in relation to cultic space is paralleled in the Greek world, and the *curiae* of Rome, early divisions of the Roman people, dined together and worshiped together (Palmer 1970; C. Smith 2006). Once again, though, we are reminded that the continuity of cult, as well as similarities across Latium, make Rome's religion as complex and highly developed across time and space as was its social and political development.

Festivals and Gods

The centrality of the festival is obvious, and work at Satricum on distinguishing the different layers of votive deposits may demonstrate recurrent visitation and worship (Bouma 1996; C. Smith 1999). Whilst the funeral cannot be predicted, and however public and ostentatious it may be, it is also fundamentally about a private event, and whilst at least some depositions in votive deposits may be private acts, Roman and Latin festivals give a strong structure to the year and to the nature of religious practice. Much of Latium was shaped by the activities of the now extinct volcanoes that form the mountains around Alba Longa, and which were, and still are on a fine day, visible from Rome. Standing on the Capitol, and looking down the Via Sacra, one's eye is drawn to the distant shape of the mountains, and this was precisely the line which was used to divide the sky and watch for omens, especially birds. Such augural lore is probably of great antiquity but developed by precedent and elaboration. In the classical period, there were still festivals at Alba Longa in which the Roman and Latin elite participated together, and nearby at Bovillae, the clan of the Julii, around 100 BC, dedicated to the god Vediovis (who may have represented their and Alba Longa's founder, Iulus). Cult, festival, and religious symbolism therefore clung to Alba Longa for centuries after it had ceased to be a significant population center (Alföldi 1965; the key passage is Pliny *Nat.* 3.69–70).

This was only one of several festivals where Romans and others from Latium gathered. Perhaps the most famous archaeological setting is at Lavinium, allegedly the burial place of Aeneas, where a complex of altars, all in a line, has been found; though we cannot date with precision the procession of magistrates from Rome to Lavinium (it is sometimes placed in the fourth century), the three altars of the sixth century and the archaic dedications suggest it was a major cult center (Torelli 1984; see Beard et al. 1998: 2.12–14). We also know of a temple to Diana at Aricia where the Latins worshiped, and Servius Tullius built a temple to Diana, perhaps as a claim that Rome was now the center of such communal activity (Livy 1.45; Beard et al. 1998: 2.15–17). A similar action may be represented by the construction of a temple to Castor and Pollux at Rome early in the fifth century. Castor and Pollux had been worshiped at Lavinium (we have a dedication naming them; Beard et al. 1998: 2.21), but they were also said to have announced at Rome the victory over the Latins at the battle of Lake Regillus (Cic. *Tusculanae* 1.28; Dion. H. 6.13; Val. Max. 1.8.1c; Plut. *Coriolanus* 3.4). The temple may be a visible sign of Roman claims, not dissimilar from the act of *evocatio*, by which the deity of a defeated town was "evoked" into victorious Rome (see e.g. Livy 5.21 in relation to Juno at Veii). Whilst much of this activity represents the centralization of some Latin festivals at Rome, or at least the construction of rival variants, this takes place against the background of more federal and dispersed religious authority.

There was a theory current in antiquity that the earliest Roman deities were not anthropomorphic. Varro is quoted by the later St. Augustine for this view, and also for the account of the many deities of natural events or phenomena who were worshiped at Rome (Aug. *Civ.* 4.31 with Beard et al. 1998: 2.2–3; Aug. *Civ.* 4.16–24). A good example is Robigo, the goddess of grain mildew, who was appeased by an elaborate ceremony involving the sacrifice of young dogs (C. Smith 1996b). At the same time, the Romans developed a pantheon not dissimilar to the Greek one, and whilst it is indubitably the case that the Romans imported substantial amounts of myth, and made their gods both look Greek and in some instances sound Greek (Apollo is a good example), there must also have been a process of syncretism. The words for god and goddess are from the earliest strata of Latin, and one does not need to follow Dumézil's more elaborate theories to recognize the deep antiquity of the worship of Jupiter and Juno, for instance. This is important, because it is clear that there are important deities who were worshiped across Latium, and who represented core values of the community, and Juno is one. The cult of Juno Sospita in particular seems to have been connected with the defense and reproduction of the citizen body.

Equally there are striking examples of the import of eastern myths and deities who then operate across central Italy. Unsurprisingly, it is at port sites that this phenomenon is most marked. Study of the port sites of Pyrgi, Gravisca in Etruria, and S. Omobono in the Forum Boarium at Rome has revealed a dense complex of associations in the sixth century (Coarelli 1988). Hercules has substantial similarities to the Phoenician deity Melqart, and there are traces of his cult in coastal Etruria. These incarnations are connected with the Etruscan deity Uni, who characteristically has spheres of interest in sex and reproduction. The sanctuary at S. Omobono, near the Ara Maxima which was said to have been dedicated by Hercules, was a center for the worship of Fortuna, also a deity of fertility and fortune. At S. Omobono, a statue has been found of Hercules and Athena (or Minerva in Latin). It is interesting that this divine pair is the one referred to by Pisistratos during one of his attempts to gain tyranny at Athens (Hdt. 1.60); Servius Tullius, a Roman king who is described by Roman historians in much the same way as one of the good tyrants of Greece, prior to the bad tyrant Tarquinius Superbus, is said to have founded the cult of Fortuna, and his traditional sixth-century dates cohere roughly with the sixth-century finds at S. Omobono. Much of this depends on somewhat speculative connections, and it is not demonstrable and perhaps not plausible that the actions of a Greek tyrant were precisely imitated by a Roman king, who added a touch of the Phoenician world. The deduction one can make, though, is that in the Roman world, and indeed across central Italy, patterns of behavior had developed by later in the sixth century that are sophisticated and demand to be read intelligently, and with some knowledge of a narrative mythical framework. There is no doubt that in the fourth century and after, Roman religion developed, imported new deities, elaborated its ritual calendar, and to some extent reinvented or maybe invented archaic rituals; but this was not wholly new or unprecedented, and middle republican innovation is predicated upon the groundwork laid in the archaic period.

Most of what has been discussed above relates to public cult. There is every reason to suppose that private and domestic cult developed at least alongside the cults of the state. One interesting area which is still to be fully explored is the relationship between the state and the domestic Lares and Penates. Every *domus* or house had its own such deities, and the Lares were often envisaged as twins. In their form as the Lares Praestites they were guardians of Rome. The Penates, on the other hand, were identified with sacred objects rescued from Troy by Aeneas, and in some accounts located and worshiped at Lavinium. It is tempting to attribute great antiquity to such stories and deities (see e.g. Carandini 1997), but it is worth emphasizing that these stories can also be connected with much later story-telling, of Greek-influenced tales of nymphs and fauns, and indeed the whole Trojan cycle. The difficulties inherent in securing these particular stories do not remove the likely antiquity of private domestic religion.

It is important briefly to acknowledge here that one difficulty in the study of archaic Roman religion is that one may reasonably guess that Etruscan religion has a large part to play in its development, since throughout the sixth century Rome shows substantial Etruscan material in its archaeological record, and the literary sources claim a period of Etruscan domination through the kings Tarquinius Priscus and Superbus. The absence of substantial reliable source evidence for the Etruscans and in particular their religion is a serious obstacle here. It may well be that Etruscan influence can be overstated – recently, an attempt has been made to limit it to the external trappings (dress, cultic implements, the odd word) but not the substance of festivals, rites, or political institutions (Cornell 1995: 151–72). Undoubtedly Rome shared with its neighbors a whole package of practices and customs, and that may well include a degree of cultural eclecticism, which led all the people of central Italy, and the elite most particularly, to pick and choose appropriate behaviors that underpinned their own ambitions. The most important role of the Etruscans, and the Campanians to the south, may have been in mediating the tremendous impact of Greek, Phoenician, and other eastern ways of thinking. The success of this may be symbolized by a fragment of an Attic black figure cup, representing Hephaestus, found in the cult site in the Forum which the Romans called the Volcanal, proving that by the early sixth century at least the Romans had identified their own deity with a Greek one (Cornell 1995: 163 for illustration).

The Roman Calendar and Roman Priesthood

We have already stated that no literary accounts have survived from this early period, but there is one kind of evidence which may indeed preserve detailed and vital information that predates the republic, and that is the Roman calendar. The calendar is preserved in a number of ways. There are inscribed or painted versions, for instance a first-century BC version from Antium, and one from the beginning of the first century AD from Praeneste, with learned commentary believed to come from Verrius Flaccus. Ovid's *Fasti*, a substantial poem giving highly sophisticated accounts of the festivals, is also a vital source, but the advantage of the calendars is that they pick out a set of festivals, identified by the use of capital letters, none of which can be demonstrated to be of republican date, and which exclude a number we know to be republican (e.g. the festival of Apollo, whose worship at Rome did not begin until the fifth century). This evidence has been pushed too far. The calendar was said to have been fixed by the second king of Rome, Numa, but that is no more valuable as a statement than that Rome was founded by Romulus, and it has recently been argued that the function of the creation of the calendar was more political than religious (Rüpke 1995a). Without a written calendar, power lies deep in the hands of the religious elite of Rome; indeed the sources tell us that the ritual cycle was originally simply announced by the priests, so the fixing of the calendar deprives them of a specific task. However, there seems little reason to doubt that the calendar preserves a degree of accurate information about a sequence of festivals which are of great antiquity, and it is tempting therefore to look at the way that the year is shaped around agricultural festivals, and to see how narratives can be constructed around their juxtapositions and coincidences (Scheid 2003: 41–59 identifies as instances two great cycles of agrarian and civic festivals). It should be noted, however, that many of these associations are observed by modern scholars, rather than commented upon in antiquity.

We have indicated that priestly and political offices were closely related, and that a cycle of public *feriae* existed, but it remains to say more about the role and development of these offices in the regal period. There was no single order of priests, but rather a mixture of different ways of organizing the public religion of Rome, and characteristically the Romans allowed these different ways to co-exist whilst their relative importance shifted (Scheid 2003: 129–46). It is usually believed that the earliest priests were the *flamines*. The *flamen Dialis*, the priest of Jupiter, labored under a remarkable number of prohibitions and duties, and only the Vestal Virgins were as constrained. The major *flamines* of Jupiter, Mars, and Quirinus had to be patricians. Twelve so-called minor *flamines* each dealt with the worship of a single deity.

At some stage the *pontifices* become more significant. Also originally patrician, with a chief priest or *pontifex maximus*, their role in law and in advising on the performance of public and private ritual placed them increasingly at the center of Roman life. Another figure in this picture is the *rex sacrorum*, sometimes called the *rex sacrificulus*, whose role is obscure. However, there may be a way of discerning a glimmer of what was happening in the later sixth century. The clue is the complex

of buildings in the Forum including the Regia (which contains two small shrines to
Ops and Consiva, very old agricultural deities), the *domus publica*, and the house of
the Vestals. We have yet to be certain of how the story should be told, but one version would argue that the *rex sacrorum* carried on the priestly roles of the king, at
first in the Regia and next to the Vestals who may well have been very closely tied
to the kings. At some point, the *pontifex maximus* displaces the *rex sacrorum* and
takes over the *domus publica* and responsibility for the Vestals. It is notable that the
rex sacrorum retains the duty of announcing the fixed *feriae* (the ones we noted as
written in capital letters in the calendar). At least some of these changes represent
the restructuring attendant on the removal of the king and the creation of the republic; the Regia receives a major overhaul at the end of the sixth century, but retains
that final form for centuries thereafter. What the new republican situation seems to
have achieved is a diffusion of religious power, a situation which thus makes any
individual's position stand out less from those of others, and which introduces various balances. The *flamines, rex sacrorum*, and *augures*, who advised on the auspices,
thus shared a complex pattern of religious rites and prerogatives, whilst the magistrates preserved the right to take the auspices. The king may have controlled Roman
religion, but he was supported and perhaps to a degree constrained by others who
had religious responsibility; over time the diffusion of responsibility represents a
continuation of a process (Cornell 1995: 239–41; Beard et al. 1998: 1.54–61).

Earlier we expressed radical doubts about our ability to tell a coherent story of
Roman religion, and those doubts must not be forgotten. Reconstructions like
the ones we have discussed depend on complex associations of bits and pieces of
topography, ritual, archaeology, and narrative, all from different periods, and none
intended to tell that particular story. However, it should be clear that the problem
of early Rome is not the complete absence of evidence but the difficulty of fitting a
mass of disparate evidence together coherently, when there is clearly much still missing. One can take a position of radical skepticism, and more often than not what
this means is that the archaic period is written off as unknowable and all innovation
and change is attributed to a later period. This is, it seems to me, unnecessary, for
if there are assumptions and guesses which need to be made for the archaic period
they may at least proceed from an attempt to understand what the sources tell us,
and may derive some corroboration from the archaeological record.

Religion and the City

The study of archaic Roman religion is dominated by the figure of Dumézil. His
many studies and the great synthesis translated as *Archaic Roman Religion* (Dumézil
1970) are remarkable works of scholarship, but hardly trusted any more. Dumézil
started from a belief that one could extract a core Indo-European tripartite structure (warrior, farmer, priest) from a careful re-reading of the sources. In some ways,
his approach owed something to a belief first that the sources had to be decoded (a
good structuralist belief, but also derived from the distance between the sources and
the events they describe), as well as to earlier accounts of Roman religion which had

identified a primitive core in a form of animism, itself based heavily on Varro's unhelpful claim that early Roman religion was not anthropomorphic. Wagenvoort, for instance, in a book translated by H. J. Rose, had no difficulties comparing Roman beliefs with Melanesian accounts of *mana* (Wagenvoort 1947).

Nor was Dumézil alone in his approach. A number of French and Italian scholars have similarly gathered hints and allusions from all over ancient literature, and used analogies from other societies, to reveal hidden stories and unknown versions of key events, or found in the historical accounts rituals which had been rationalized (see e.g. Gagé 1950, 1976; Hubaux 1958; Mastrocinque 1988; Carandini 1997). The more sober German handbooks, and skeptical Anglo-American scholarship, largely eschew this adventurous approach. Is there any way that these traditions can come together?

The archaeological discoveries of the past thirty years or so indicate with increasing clarity both the sophistication of Latin culture between the eighth and sixth centuries, and the importance of that period in the development of an urban society across the region. It is very important always to remember that, significant as Rome was, it was not unique in developing public space, public buildings, and the other indices of what we tend to call urbanism (C. Smith 2005). This process is accompanied universally by the development of votive deposits and subsequently temples, and by the establishment of some kind of ritual order, which we see most clearly at Rome through the calendar and the priestly offices which can be dated to the regal period.

The significance of this should not be underestimated, and it is intimately bound up with the development of religion. Although early Roman festivals do preserve in various ways some of the concerns of an early agricultural society, and after all, agriculture was crucially important to all contemporary societies, the development of the community brings other associations and other meanings to every ritual act. The act of processing around Roman territory in the ceremony of the Robigalia – purifying the fields – takes on new meanings as Roman territory expands, and becomes a statement about boundaries as well as about mildew (C. Smith 1996b). The calendar's evolving complexity both preserves the great agrarian cycle, built around the solstices, and adds a more civic layer, including, quite possibly, some ritualized memory of the flight of the king, the Regifugium, which perhaps marked an end of a civic year, which began again in the Liberalia on March 17, when young men assumed the toga (Scheid 2003: 50–1; Wiseman 2004: 64, 68).

In order fully to understand archaic Roman religion, one needs all the methodological tools at our disposal. As archaeology increasingly gives shape and substance to our picture of ancient society, we still need the careful analysis of the written sources to enrich and secure our accounts. Much detailed analysis was predicated on a view of the texts as concealing truths even from the ancients, which needed to be excavated by the diligent scholar. This was of a piece with a view of early Rome as deeply primitive; but archaic Rome was nothing like Melanesia, and whilst anthropological methods and analogies are invaluable to the ancient historian, they should not mislead one into a false image of the Roman past. Philological and analytical skills need now to address the kinds of patterns of thought and behavior which existed in the regal period and were productive of the remarkable edifice which is the republic and its historiography.

Here again, the development of the city and the impact on religion are vitally important. The relationship between the king and the priests, between different orders of priests, and the significance of the citizen community as object of the gods' protection and active partner in securing the gods' favor, are all parts of the story we must tell to explain Rome's political development. It is absolutely core to the understanding of the rise of the plebeian movement which sought to break patrician monopolies of power that the language in which they frame their own self-image is profoundly religious; the alternative triad of Ceres, Liber, and Libera, with connections to Greek cult (Spaeth 1996), the development of the plebeian games, the sacrosanctity of the plebeian tribunes all arise at the very beginning of the republic and evolve from the world of regal Rome. The study of archaic Roman religion is now more open and more exciting than ever before.

FURTHER READING

The standard introduction is Beard et al. (1998: 1.1–72), but see also Scheid (2003) for an excellent overview, and on Etruscan religion, see Jannot (1998) and de Grummond and Simon (2006). On all issues relating to the history of early Rome, Cornell (1995) is indispensable; see also Grandazzi (1997) and C. Smith (2006). For the historiography of early Rome and its myths see Fox (1996) and Jason Davies (2004: 1–142).

For the archaeology of early Rome and Latium, see C. Smith (1996a, 2005), Bietti-Sestieri (1992), and Carandini (2000). For individual sites, see as follows: the Forum Boarium, Coarelli (1988); Lavinium, Torelli (1984); Osteria dell'Osa, Bietti-Sestieri (1992); Satricum, C. Smith (1999) with full references. For votive deposits see Bouma (1996). There is a challenging and problematic account of early Rome in Carandini (1997), on which see Wiseman (2001).

Dumézil (1970) is a remarkable work, but there are also challenging and valuable contributions in Dumézil (1968–73, 1975). For a devastating critique see Wiseman (1995a: 25–30). On Roman mythology see Preller (1883) and, more recently, a controversial but fascinating attempt to establish the political and dramatic context of Roman myth-making in Wiseman (2004). For the Roman calendar see Michels (1967), Scullard (1981), Rüpke (1995a, 2006c), and Beard et al. (1998: 2.60–77). For Roman priesthoods, Wissowa (1912) and Latte (1960) are again vital, but see more recently Vanggaard (1988) on the flaminate, and on the *auspicia* and the roles of the augurs Linderski (1986). There is no reliable English treatment of the pontificate.

For the development of the city of Rome and the consequences for Roman religion and history, see Raaflaub (1986); Momigliano returned repeatedly to this subject and his thoughts are collected in his *Contributi* (Momigliano 1955–92).

CHAPTER FOUR

Pre-Roman Italy, Before and Under the Romans

Olivier de Cazanove

Sentinum and the Impossible Religious Unity of the Italian Peninsula

Pre-Roman Italy, broadly understood, cannot be said to have been unified in any meaningful sense, not least in the field of religious representations and practices. One episode is emblematic of this situation: all the people of Italy actually formed an alliance together on only one occasion, to counteract the imminent rise of Rome. Nevertheless, the event reveals their habitual disunity, their lack of common foundations, including common religious rites. In 295 BC in Sentinum, in Umbria, the Samnites, Gauls, Etruscans, and Umbrians met to face the Roman armies. This battle represents to some extent the climax of the Roman conquest of Italy. Its perceived importance at the time is confirmed by the fact that it became the theater of completely exceptional divine signs and rites. First a double sign (*omen*): a hind pursued by a wolf appears between the two armies (Livy 10.27). The hind moves toward the Gallic lines, the wolf toward the Roman lines. The latter open in front of it, while the Gauls kill the hind. By killing the animal dedicated to Diana, as a Roman soldier called out, they called down judgment upon themselves in the form of forced retreat and the destruction of their army. In contrast, the wolf of Mars left the confrontation victorious and unscathed, reminding the Romans that they were, they and their founder (Romulus), worthy descendants of Mars.

The lesson to be learnt from this episode is that the Romans have a well-defined legendary identity, well known also to their enemies. Two centuries later (in 82 BC), Pontius Telesinus, the chief of the Samnites, the last Italic to raise arms against the Romans, would compare Rome, which he wanted to demolish, with a den of wolves which had ravished the freedom of Italy. On the contrary, the hind cannot function as a representative symbol for the allies as a whole, although attempts have been made to see the hind as a symbol of Celtism in Italy. Even if this were true, it would be still only be the identifying animal of the Gauls, not of the Samnites. The opposition between the animal of Mars and the animal of Diana perhaps better recalls the old antagonism between Romans and Latins.

The account of the battle of Sentinum brings up a few things about the various people who faced the Romans, but nothing about their religion. The *omen*, in spite of all appearances, is entirely Roman. Also Roman are the rites Livy describes: one of the consuls dedicates a temple and the spoils from the enemies to the victorious Jupiter, the other carries out the frightening rite of *deuotio*. He devotes himself and the enemies to the earth and the Manes. We don't learn anything, on the other hand, about possible prayers or ceremonies in the camp of the allies before the beginning of combat. Is this simply because that does not interest the Romans, only concerned with their own religion? Perhaps, but Livy describes in detail some chapters further (10.38) a "sacrifice according to the old religion of Samnites" (*sacrum . . . ex uetusta Samnitium religione*), which takes place two years later, in 293, within the camp of Aquilonia. A certain interest of an antiquarian or ethnological nature, with respect to the customs, rites, armaments, etc. of the former enemies of Rome thus cannot be excluded. This interest is not without distortions: Livy places the ceremony in Aquilonia, not in an Italic sanctuary as one might think, but in a camp planned in the Roman manner (de Cazanove in Ribichini forthcoming). We don't have any similar information for Sentinum, but it is rather doubtful that the other tribes of the Samnites, Gauls, Etruscans, and Umbrians could have conceived rites to be celebrated together. For this reason, and also in order to preserve a certain unity of presentation, the pages which follow will be almost exclusively dedicated not generally to pre-Roman Italy, whose ethnic mixture is too varied to be treated as a whole, but specifically to the Italic populations, in the precise, dialectal meaning of the term: the peoples who left us the Umbrian, Oscan, and south-Picenian "Sabellic texts" (Rix 2002).

The battle of Sentinum may be seen as a sign of "the unfinished identity of Italy" among other such signs, to paraphrase the title of an important study (Giardina 1994). The author refers to the political identity of Roman Italy, but one can extend the matter to the religious identity of pre-Roman and Roman Italy. Or rather: one can speak about Italy as a whole, on the religious level as well as on all others, only in comparison with Rome; first as a common enemy, then as a power exercising its hegemony upon all, within the framework of unequal treaties, and finally, starting with the Social War, as common *ciuitas* of all the Italians, which involved an in-depth reshaping of local religious life, as we shall see below.

Shared Sanctuaries or Exclusion of the Other?

The absence of a common religious identity does not necessarily imply absence of contact between ethnic groups in the same sanctuaries. The frequenting by foreigners of particular holy places is epigraphically documented. However, the best testimony that we have on a multi-ethnic sanctuary in Italy comes from a literary source. According to Dionysius of Halicarnassus (3.32.1), the sacred grove of Feronia in the territory of Capena was the site of the most famous fair in Italy. During the feast days, one made deals both with the gods (vows taken and fulfilled, sacrifices) and with other merchants. Dionysius adds that the place of cult was jointly venerated by Latins and Sabines. He doesn't mention either the Etruscans or the Faliscans, but these were surely present: Livy (26.12) writes for his part "of the Capenates and of the other neighboring people . . . who had filled the sanctuary with gold and silver." Its treasures were plundered by the troops of Hannibal in 211 BC. Feronia, goddess of wild nature and also of the transformation of the uncultivated into cultivated – she had a role to play in the emancipation of the slaves – was mainly venerated in the Sabine and Sabellic area, but she was also introduced in Rome, and even in the *conciliabulum* of Pisaurum, a later colony of Roman citizens.

In addition to the sanctuaries with multi-ethnic worshipers, like that of *lucus Feroniae*, there are also places of cult managed together by two towns of the same ethnic group, like that of Hercules in Campania, about which an exceptional epigraphic document, the *cippus abellanus* from the second century BC, informs us that it was the common property of Abella and Nola (Franchi De Bellis 1988); or the sacred grove of Juno Sospita in Lanuvium, whose administration the Romans demanded to share with the Lavinates after the Latin war (Livy 8.14). But all these shared places of cult seem to have remained an exception. Each community (city, people, or ethnic league) had a religion of its own, which concerned in principle only its members, while non-members of the community could be excluded. In Rome, in certain sacrifices, the lictor shouted: "out of here (*exesto*) the foreigner (*hostis*), the chained prisoner, the woman, the young girl! It was forbidden for any such individuals to be present" (Paul. *Fest.* 72 L). At Gubbio, in Umbria, before a ceremony taking place at the boundary stones, one solemnly banished "the people of Tadinum, the tribe of Tadinum, the nations of Etruria and of the river Na(ha)r, the *iapuzkum nomen*" (Rix 2002: 48). A little earlier in the ritual, the execration prayers against the same people are addressed first collectively to three divinities, Cerfius Martius, Prestota Cerfia of Cerfus Martius, Tursa Cerfia of Cerfus Martius, then to each of the two goddesses in the transparent names Praestota, "the-one-who-protects," and Tursa, "the-one-who-terrifies." The ban concerns with one exception the adjacent populations of Umbria: the Etruscans in the west, beyond Tiber, the Sabines in the east, on the other side of Na(ha)r (these rivers would still be the limits of the Augustan region VI: Umbria). The *iapuzkum nomen* is probably located on the Adriatic coast, that is, in the direction of Picenum. The exception is Tadinum (today Gualdo Tadino). This is an Umbrian city, like Iguvium–Gubbio. But precisely this Umbrian city is treated in the prayers of execration in a different way than the other peoples. One excludes the *tuta tarinate*, the *trifu tarinate*, the "community" and the "tribe" of Tadinum, while speaking about *turskum numem*, the "Etruscan nation."

The Italic Religious Cultures:
Similarities and Differences

In Italic religious cultures we can observe exclusion of the other, but at the same time a considerable similarity. The similarity between the *exesto* of the Roman lictor and the ban of execration in Gubbio is one of the numerous rapprochements one can identify between Roman religion and Italic religions. One can likewise point out numerous similarities between the religions of the different Italic peoples. These are in fact homologous religious cultures, but they do not coincide exactly. In order to study them, it is necessary to pay as much attention to the contrasts as to the similarities.

Let us go back to the problem of the religious identities and their representations. There was indeed, as we have suggested, a lack of a positive and coherent image of the whole of Italy in the face of Rome. But, on the other hand, the symbol of the Italics in revolt at the time of the Social War (91–89 BC) is well known: the bull crushes the Roman she-wolf on the coins of the insurgents with the legend *víteliú*. There is a complex network of implicit references here (Briquel 1996): first the etymology, distorted but current, which made out of Italy "land of the calves" (Italia/*Ouphitouliôa* < calf/*vitlu* Umbr.); then the reference to the civilizing epic of Hercules, who brings back the oxen of Geryon through the peninsula; finally the allusion to the legendary Samnite origins. On another *denarius* of the Social War (Rutter 2001: 409) the bull appears reclining, next to a standing warrior with spear. Lengthways on the lance runs the legend *safinim* (Samnium). The scene must actually illustrate the foundation account of the Samnite nation. The young Sabines were expelled from their community in execution of a vow. They emigrate under the guidance of a bull, which lies down to indicate the place where they must settle. They gratefully sacrifice to Mars the animal which guided them.

This type of migration is an essential element of the "sacred spring" (*uer sacrum*). The sacred spring is presented by a little corpus of sources (de Cazanove 2000a) as a *mos*, a typical Italic custom (Paul. *Fest.* 519–20 L). This large-scale gift consists in dedicating to the divinity, under the pressure of exceptional circumstances, all the living beings which will be born in the year: the animals will be sacrificed, the devoted men expelled once they have reached adulthood. The *uer sacrum* is placed under the patronage of the god Mars and almost exclusively concerns the ethnos *safinim* and its ramifications. It aims to explain that the different native populations from the center of the peninsula come from a single origin: the common Sabine trunk. The *Aborigines* settle down in the core of Sabine land, at *Cutiliae*. The *sacrani* (the "dedicated ones"), coming from Reate, settle down on the Roman *septimontium*. Some Sabines emigrate to Samnium, others to Picenum under the guidance of a woodpecker, others still to the Hernician country, to the Paelignian country, to Hirpinia led by a wolf; the Lucanians come from the Samnites and the Brutti from the Lucanians. We won't discuss here the degree to which these migratory movements are realistic or consistent (all the possible solutions, or almost all, have been considered: ethnic awakening without displacement, movements of mercenaries, infiltrations of armed gangs: Tagliamonte 1996: 17–21). The majority of authors refuse to consider the *uer sacrum* as historic (Dench 1995: 183) and only admit that it "perhaps never had another existence, but retrospective and legendary" (Heurgon 1957: 51). So it wouldn't be – but this is already much – more than a number of myths of origin following a common pattern. I am not sure for my part that the *uer sacrum* is entirely to be ascribed to legend and that it never had a ritual reality. In any case, it should be admitted that this myth is still productive in historical time, since the conquest of Messana by the Mamertine mercenaries of Agathocles toward 285 BC is presented as a sacred spring. The *uer sacrum* is to be found even in Rome: after the catastrophe of Trasimene, at the beginning of the Second Punic War (in 217), one is promised, but it is carried out only approximately twenty years later (in 195–194). One offers then – to Jupiter, not to Mars – only the newborn animals from March–April 194: a singularly restrictive interpretation of the expression "sacred spring," while the Italic *uer sacrum* concerned all *animalia* of the year! Moreover, only the cattle are concerned: it is not a question of expulsion of young people. The Roman sacred spring illustrates perfectly the complex interplay of the similarities and differences between neighboring religions. In the hour of the utmost danger of the invasion of Italy, after the consultation of the Sibylline Books, Rome reaches for a tradition, an Italic *mos*. But the complete rite is reinvented from Rome's own perspective (Scheid 1998c: 418–19).

Meaningful cultural gaps can also be observed on a quite different level: the votive practices of private persons in sanctuaries, public or not (fig. 4.1). The increase of Italic epigraphic documentation has made it possible to observe that all the Oscan speakers, from *Vestini* to Lucanians, fulfill their vows using the same formula: *brateis datas*, "for given favor" (Rix 2000). There are 14 occurrences of this formula so far identified, and the list is of course expected to grow longer. The most recently published one was a limestone base of a statue from the second century BC bearing a dedication to Hercules (Poccetti 2001): it was found in the large sanctuary of Mefitis in Rossano di Vaglio (Lucania), but a little apart from the paved court which constitutes the core of the place of cult. We already know other instances of the same formula at Rossano. It is considerably different from the Latin formula *donom dat lubens merito*, "he gave his offering willingly and deservedly," which appears in the first half of the third century (Panciera 1990: 910). The Latin formula insists on the fact that the carrying out of the vow is owed, since the one who has made it sees it as fulfilled. The Oscan formula stresses the "favor" granted by the divinity, as in this Paelignian inscription, which is still known to us by handwritten copies: "Ovia Pacia, to Minerva, for the favor granted, because she gave the favor which she asked for her and her children" (Rix 2002: 4). One can see how, starting from stereotyped forms, one can draw the geographical and intellectual contour-lines between religious cultures, within which the conceptions of the relationship with the divinity do not coincide exactly.

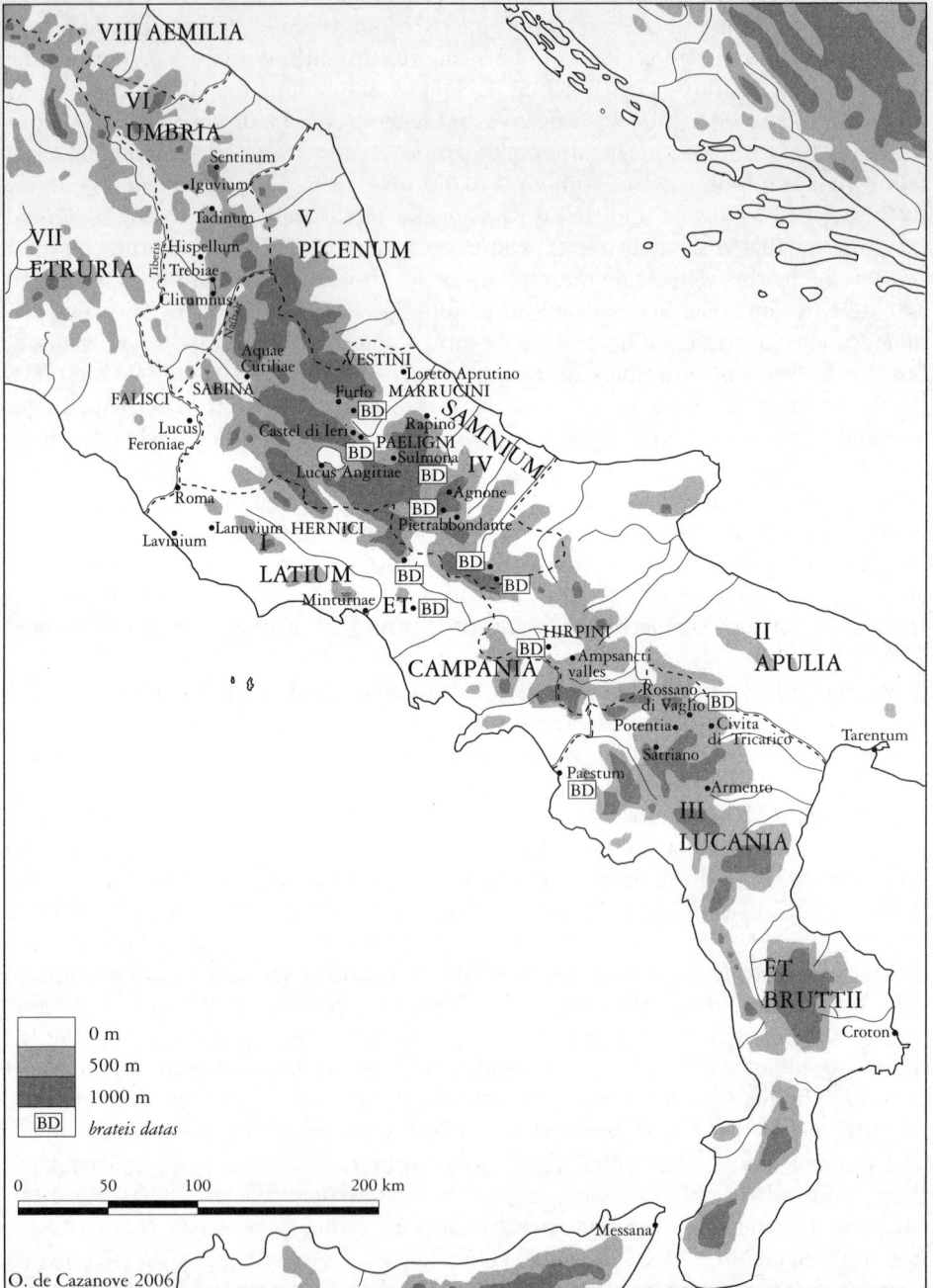

Figure 4.1 Ancient Italy (cult places, frontiers of Augustan regions, distribution of the votive formula *brateis datas*).

The Great Public Rituals: Possibility and Limits of Comparison

In order to clear up Roman realities, or some other Italic ritual documents, one often calls upon the famous Iguvine Tables, already quoted. As we will see, these comparisons, useful in detail, can be carried on only up to a certain point. One generally regards the bronze Tables of Gubbio as the most complete document on an Italic religion (*an* Italic religion, it is necessary to stress here once again, and not the Italic religions in general). The seven bronze tables found at Iguvium (Gubbio, Umbria) in the fifteenth century, all written in Umbrian, are noted in an alphabet derived from the Etruscan for the oldest, in a Latin alphabet for the most recent ones. They are to be dated between the end of the third century BC and the Social War (Sisani 2001: 237–45). They have been made the object of innumerable attempts at exegesis (among others Devoto 1940, 1977; Poultney 1959; Prosdoscimi 1989). They are in fact ritual protocols, of a high degree of accuracy, relating to the public ceremonies carried out on behalf of the city (*ocre fisia*) and of the community (*tuta ikuvina*). On tables I and VI is described the complex rite (*persklo*) (Prosdoscimi 1985) which takes place around the three gates of the city, after the preliminary consulting of *auspicia*. Two groups of three victims are sacrificed at each gate: at the Trebulan gate, three oxen to Jupiter Grabovius and three pregnant sows to Trebus Jovius (in front of and behind the gate respectively); at the Tesenacan gate, three oxen to Mars Grabovius and three suckling pigs to Fisus Sacus; at the Veian gate, three oxen to Vofionus Grabovius, three ewe-lambs to Tefer Jovius.

The "*Grabovius* triad" was many times compared with the "archaic" or "pre-Capitoline" triad of Rome (Dumézil 1974: 161–2). In Rome, Jupiter, Mars, and Quirinus are invoked together on certain solemn occasions and are represented by three priests, the *flamen Dialis*, the *flamen Martialis*, the *flamen Quirinalis*. For Dumézil, these two structures are exactly parallel and are to be explained as originating from an inherited model, which he calls "trifunctionality" (sovereign and priestly function, warrior function, productive and social function). The sovereign god (Jupiter) and the god of war (Mars) are the same in Gubbio and in Rome, but apparently the last term of the equation is not so. In fact – and on this point Dumézil has enjoyed general agreement – Quirinus and Vofionus can be regarded as equivalents (Benveniste 1969). According to the generally accepted etymologies, Quirinus comes from **co-uiri-no*, "(the god) of the community of the *viri* (men)," and Vofionus from **leudhyo-no*, "(the god) of the people."

The relationship between the two triadic arrangements Jupiter–Mars–Quirinus and Jupiter Grabovius–Mars Grabovius–Vofionus Grabovius is beyond doubt, regardless of whether one interprets the overlap as fossilized common heritage or, on the contrary, opportunistic update of the potential of the neighboring religions. I favor the view that the reference to the three Grabovius gods is in Gubbio only one part of a complex ritual and should not therefore be arbitrarily isolated even when doing so serves to underline theoretical parallelism with the Roman situation. There is parallelism, certainly, but it relates to only one segment of the ceremony. There are indeed three gods inside every gate, who correspond symmetrically to the Grabovius gods. These three gods belong to the circle of Jupiter. It is explicitly the case with two of them (Trebus Jovius and Tefer Jovius), and it is implicitly the case with the third (Fisus Sancius, perhaps to be related to Semo Sancus Dius Fidius, god of the oath). However, the ceremony described on the Iguvine Tables I and VI does not stop after the sacrifices at the gates: it continues in two sacred groves: at the grove of Jupiter, one sacrifices two ewes and three calves to Mars Hodius; in the "core-tian" grove three calves to Hondus Cerfius. Then only, the formula concludes "the city will be purified" (*ukar pihaz fust*). But if there is a ritual flaw, it is necessary to start all over again from the beginning, that is, from the consulting of *auspicia* and the sacrifice at the Trebulan gate. This statement points out that the entire ritual series (*persklo*) is seen as a whole and the final sacrifices in the grove must not be separated out.

Limited comparisons are likely to be found not only between Gubbio and Rome, but also between the bronze tablets and the great Roman ritual protocols. There are also other Italic religious inscriptions of public relevance: the "bronze of Rapino," datable toward 250 BC, carries a "law for the Marrucine community" (*totai maroucai lixs*) (Rix 2002: 77). After a preliminary invocation (*aisos pacris*: "gods, be favorable!"), it seems to be a question of how to divide sacrificial meat (*asignas*, an interpretation to be preferred to the one which supposes that it regulates sacred prostitution: Zavaroni 2004). The ceremony relates to "Jupiter Father of the Jovian citadel Tarincris" (*ioues patres ocres tarincris iouias agine*). The "citadel" in question is generally identified with the fortified site on the height of Civita Danzica. Grotta del Colle, where the bronze of Rapino comes from, opened on a neighboring slope. It is one of the increasing number of places of cult in pre-Roman Italy on which there is now an archaeological publication (Guidobaldi 2002).

The Names of Gods

The very form of the theonyms on the Tables of Gubbio itself cannot fail to surprise (Prosdoscimi 1989: 484–7). They are not composed of only one term, but of two, three, even four:

- substantive + epithet: "Hondus Jovius," "Torsa Jovia," "Pomonus Popdicus";
- substantive + possessive phrase + epithet: "Vesona of Pomonus Popdicus";
- substantive + epithet + possessive phrase + epithet: "Prestota Cerfia of Cerfus Martius," "Torsa Cerfia of Cerfus Martius."

As I mentioned before, Prestota is "the one-who-protects" and Torsa "the one-who-terrifies." These purely functional divinities have their equivalents in Rome. They were invoked in the prayers according to the Roman rite, as recorded in the sacer-dotal books (quoted by Gellius 13.23.2): "*Lua* of Saturn, *Salacia* of Neptune, *Hora* of Quirinus, *Virites* of Quirinus, *Maia* of Vulcan, *Heries* of Juno, *Moles* of Mars, *Nerio* of Mars" (i.e. "the efforts of Mars," "the boldness of Mars"). An action power of the divinity is to some extent extracted from it here (Scheid 1999a). It will be noted that in Gubbio, Torsa, "the one-who-terrifies," is alternatively Cerfian and Jovian. In the same way, Hunte is Cerfian in the coretian sacred grove, where three calves are sacrificed to him. But on table IIa, it is a Jovian Hunte, to whom the sacrifice of a dog is offered.

In Gubbio, one thus meets "Jovian," "Martian," and "Cerfian" divinities, with possible permutations, as we have shown. In the Oscan area, there are "Jovian," "Cererian," and "Mefitanian" divinities. We find these last only in the Lucanian sanctuary of Mefitis in Rossano di Vaglio (Lejeune 1990). One can thus consider that "Mefitanian Venus" and "Mefitanian Mars" are hosts of Mefitis, in the place of worship of which she is titular. Their epiclesis indicates a certain ratio of dependence. In the same way, several of the divinities from the sanctuary of Ceres close to Agnone, about which further discussion follows, are described as "Cererian" for obvious reasons (Rix 2002: 82 Sa 1). One finds in the same place of cult of Mefitis in Rossano a "Jovian sovereign," but she is associated with Jupiter on a monument, found in an angle of the paved court of the sanctuary, of which the platform carrying two profiled bases or altars has survived. The double monument constitutes a small cult ensemble inserted in the large one, belonging to Jupiter and his *paredra*.

The Rossano sanctuary, attended between the fourth century BC and the first century AD, has been excavated since 1969, and today is one of the best-known Italic places of cult epigraphically and archaeologically: of the 58 inscriptions found, 10 are dedications to Mefitis, sometimes with an epiclesis: *Utiana, Aravina, Kaporoinna*. A certain number of other divinities are also attested, as we noticed: Jupiter, the "Jovian sovereign," Venus, Mars, Hercules . . . The sanctuary does not include a temple (or it has not been found, which is less probable). A wall of the *temenos*, endowed with a monumental entry framed by fountains, and, on the three other sides, a portico and elongated halls surround a rectangular paved surface crossed longitudinally by the altar (Adamesteanu and Dilthey 1992). The abundance of the available data should not, however, seduce us into treating Rossano as a pattern for the rest of Italy. The diversity of the sanctuaries of pre-Roman Italy does not allow it.

The Sanctuaries of Pre-Roman Italy

The archaeological study of the pre-Roman places of cult must avoid two pitfalls. The first consists in looking too intensely for a specificity, a clearly definable "Italicity" of the Italic places of cult. But it would also be dangerous, on the other hand, to see the perspective from a too distant point of view by overlooking differences between the sanctuaries of the peninsula, which are Etruscan, Roman, Samnite, Lucanian, Greek, etc. It is necessary to be attentive to cultural and regional particularity.

The places of cult in the open air, without any actual cult edifice, were certainly very numerous, but one should not make them into a prototype of the indigenous sanctuary. After all, one of the main extra-urban sanctuaries of Lavinium, "metropolis of Latins," until its abandonment at the beginning of second century BC, never consisted of more than a line of 13 altars, in addition to the neighboring *heroon* and an archaic building, demolished in the fifth century. The same applies to many sacred groves (*luci*). At the border with Latium, in the Sabine land, the lake of *aquae Cutiliae* was a cult place, sacred to Victory, surrounded by a palisade and inaccessible "except that at certain times each year those whose sacred office it is go to the little island in the lake and perform the sacrifices required by custom" (Dion. H. 1.15). This island was supposed to be a floating one and thus was never built on. In these cases, if the place was left in its natural state, it is above all because it represents a "geological wonder." In a more general way, the Greek and Latin literary sources are very often interested in the old sanctuaries of Italy only insofar as they belong to the category of the *thaumasta*, of the *mirabilia*, of natural curiosities to be reported to the scholar and the tourist. These sources are interested in landscape rather than in the cult, in the works of nature more than in human ones. Ovid (*Am.* 3.13) described in picturesque terms the feast of Juno Curitis and her sacred grove within the land of the Faliscans, without mentioning the temple of Celle, which was built in the sixth century BC. Strabo and Plutarch insist on the celebrity of the sacred grove of Marica at the mouth of the Liris, on the border between Latium and Campania. It is only incidentally that Plutarch mentions the existence of a temple – where a votive picture representing the escape of Marius from *Minturnae* was deposited. This temple, which goes back to the end of the archaic period and was replaced by a new building in the imperial period, was excavated between the two world wars. In the valleys of *Ampsanctus* in Hirpinia, Virgil locates a "mouth of the underworld" (Virg. *Aen.* 7.563–71) because the water, charged with carbon dioxide, is fatal. Only Pliny the Elder (*Nat.* 2.208) reports the existence of a temple of the goddess Mefitis. None of the places of cult which I have just quoted is, contrary to what one might think at first sight, a sanctuary in open air – at least not entirely, and not in the last phase of their architectural evolution.

In other cases, when we are faced with missing or too limited excavations, it is quite difficult, using only the literary sources, to reconstruct the appearance of the sanctuary and to come to a conclusion about the presence or not of a cult building inside. We know only by one famous inscription from the second century BC, found in 1848 in Capracotta near Agnone, in Samnium, the *húrz* of Ceres. What does *húrz* stand for? The translations suggested differ slightly: "garden" (cf Lat. *hortus*), "sacred grove," "enclosure," and simply "sanctuary" (Del Tutto Palma 1996). All that we do know about this place of cult is that it included an "altar with fire" and (temporary?) altars for 15 divinities or groups of divinities, among them Ceres, while six others are described as "Cererian." Moreover, outside the *húrz*, one sacrificed at the time of the *fiussasiai* (the feast of *Floralia*?) to four other divinities, of which three are again known as "Cererian."

Let us return to the place of cult of Mefitis in the *Ampsancti ualles*. It is composed of two parts. The small valley is the actual domain of the goddess, where one only enters to sacrifice: the animal victims are killed simply by putting them in contact with water. The hill, delimited by a portico, is the part of the sanctuary which allows for human access: it is a space which people to some extent share with the goddess, since there she had her temple, perhaps on the site of the current church of S. Felicità. If this reconstruction of the place of cult is right, it had truly vast proportions: 700 meters as the crow flies and 100 meters of slope separate the sulfurous lake from the top of the hill of S. Felicità (de Cazanove and Scheid 2003: 145–79). This cannot, however, be considered an isolated case. In central Sicily, the sanctuary of *Palikoi* presents very similar geomorphological characteristics: over the slopes of Roccichella, a recently discovered architectural complex composed of a *hestiatorion* and perhaps a temple towers over the plain where the sulfurous lake of Naftia lies. A third example of the vast dimensions of certain Italic sanctuaries, which juxtapose a natural site and a monumental sector, is provided by the grove of the Marsian goddess Angitia. It dominated the banks of Lake Fucino, drained in 1875 by Prince Torlonia, so that the site of the sanctuary lost much of its expressiveness. Recent excavations have brought to light three temples from the third to first centuries BC (Campanelli, in Ribichini forthcoming), along a way parallel to the ancient bank, which leads to the church of S. delle Maria Grazie (*Sancta Maria de Luco* is mentioned from the tenth century). An enclosure in polygonal masonry, dated to the fourth century BC, also runs parallel to the bank for approximately 600 m, then climbs the heights by forming a prominence in the south, in order to shelter the church. Once more, we find an Italic sanctuary of astoundingly vast proportions.

The erection of proper temples in the Italic sanctuaries is a rather late phenomenon, more or less contemporary with the Roman conquest of Italy. Exemplary from this point of view is the evolution of the Samnite sanctuary of Pietrabbondante (Coarelli and La Regina 1984: 230–56). It appears to have been related from the beginning to the rites of victory and the exhibition of enemy weapons. The majority of these weapons date from the Samnite Wars (343–290 BC). Almost nothing is known about the structure of the sanctuary at that time: perhaps there was a simple square enclosure. We must wait until the second half of the third century before we can observe an Ionic temple, with a short existence before its destruction during the Second Punic War.

The rebuilding of the sanctuary began around 180–170 BC with the erection of temple A. It is in fact in the second century that the majority of the monumental temples of Samnium were built. The great Samnite families, grown rich after the Roman conquest, played a decisive part in this. In Pietrabbondante, there are especially the *Staii*, the ones who supervise as *meddices tutici* the works. Are these "public magistrates" of a community or of an ethnic league? An incomplete inscription mentions a *safinim sak[araklum*, apparently a "Samnite temple," which could have related to the whole ethnos. In the years 100–90 a vast temple-theater complex, whose pattern comes from Latium and Campania, was built. The tripartite temple B is characteristically Tuscan. The cult ceased to exist after the Social War.

The Italian Cults in Roman Italy: Ruptures and Continuities

The development of the sanctuaries of Italy after the Roman conquest is more diverse than has previously been thought. For a long time it was believed that there had been a clear turning point: an almost general shipwreck of the pre-Roman cultures, including their cults; abuse of power, even acts of sacrilege by the Roman generals in the sanctuaries of the allies; then, after the Social War, and especially from the beginnings of the principate, the introduction in the new *municipia* and colonies of an enlarged, renewed pantheon: the Roman gods and *diui* (divinized emperors) appear, next to a few large local sanctuaries, which would have been allowed to remain, even favored because of their power of attraction. An exemplary case for this new religious framework is the *lucus Feroniae*, noted above. The ancient sacred grove was the site for the foundation of a colony in the second half of the first century BC, the *colonia Iulia Felix Lucoferonensium*. We know little about the topography of the old sanctuary: the archaeological data are primarily reduced to a deposit of anatomical statuettes, ex-votos, and inscriptions. On the other hand, on the axis of the forum, opposite to a prostyle temple, an exedra was built, which included a beautiful series of statues of members of the imperial house (*domus diuina*) (Sgubini Moretti 1982/4). In addition, hardly 800 meters from there, the luxurious villa of *Volusii Saturnini* (first century BC to first century AD) was built. On the whole, through the eyes of the modern visitor at least, the panorama of the small urban center, the statues of *diui*, a great senatorial domain, are much more visible than the old sanctuary of Feronia. But isn't this an effect of the remaining archaeological data, which we must remind ourselves is only partial and influenced by previous excavations?

It was precisely the increase in recent field investigations that led to a questioning of the idea of a drastic rupture. This gloomy vision was already partly shared by contemporaries, as can be illustrated by the disillusioned reflections of Strabo (6.1.2): "The Leucani . . . and the Brettii, and the Samnites themselves . . . have so utterly deteriorated that it is difficult even to distinguish their several settlements; and the reason is that no common organization longer endures in any one of the separate tribes; and their characteristic differences in language, armor, dress and the like, have completely disappeared." Strabo also adds that the effort to push the ethnological investigation further is not worth it, since the Italics from his time on, for example Leucani or Campanians, "are Campanians only by name and Romans in fact; they have become Romans." In modern historiography, it is the famous work of A. J. Toynbee, *Hannibal's Legacy* (1965), which strongly stressed the concept of Italian "desert" (*solitudo*) starting from the second century BC: an annihilation of Italian identities in all respects, which would have affected more especially the south and the inner zones, and would have been the combined effect of the Roman conquest of the peninsula, the Second Punic War, and the subsequent confiscations.

Toynbee's great book has been the object of several recent reappraisals. It is especially, as I said, the decisive contributions of archaeology and epigraphy which have made it possible to make progress by increasingly more regional investigations. In Lucania, it is true that the majority of the small places of cult around the Greek cities and the indigenous settlements of the interior disappear during the Hellenistic period, but not necessarily (as has generally been thought) around 273–272 BC (as deduced from the Latin colony of Paestum, the conquest of Taranto: emblematic dates of the "end" of Magna Graecia). Some of them continue to be attended in the second century BC (Serra Lustrante d'Armento, Civita di Tricarico: de Cazanove

2005), and even until the time of the empire. In the Sabellic territories, the vitality of the rural districts is characterized by the building of sometimes monumental temples. They were built *ex pagi decreto* or *ex pagi sententia*, "on the decree of the *pagus*," by the north Oscan populations, Vestini and Paeligni (Letta 1992). Among other examples, one can note the splendid tripartite temple on a profiled podium from Castel di Ieri. The inscription in mosaic mentioning the construction *ex pagi decreto* dates from the middle of the first century BC (Buonocore 1996). It was found by the entry of the *cella*, where the fragments of a marble cult statue of Minerva with the aegis were also recovered. The famous law of dedication of the Jupiter Liber temple in the *vicus* (village) of Furfo (*CIL* 9.3513) dates from 58 BC. Also within the territory of *Vestini*, a particularly clear case of continuity of cultural frequenting can be mentioned: the sanctuary, recently and attentively excavated, of Feronia in Loreto Aprutino. The small temple with *alae* but without a podium, which can be reconstructed as distyle in antis, was built in the second century BC, perhaps on a former place of cult. Restored during the Augustan period and endowed with a bronze cult statue, it provides material datable to the first half of the third century AD.

Otherwise, the cult continued, but at the cost of change. The sanctuary of Mefitis in Rossano, Lucania, about which I have already spoken, continued to exist even after the disappearance in the third century BC of the neighboring settlement in Serra di Vaglio. The importance of the sanctuary is indicated by the number of official dedications (in the Oscan language) which were found there. A senator, a censor, and several quaestors are mentioned, without it being clear to what these magistratures refer (are they federal? municipal? purely indigenous or under Romanization in progress?). Beginning in approximately 100 BC (i.e. undoubtedly with the Social War), the inscriptions are in Latin. The sanctuary is restored for the last time by Acerronius, in the second half of the first century BC or during the time of Tiberius. In the imperial time, the cult is transferred to the neighboring *municipium* of *Potentia*. The magistrates of Potenza, the *quattuorviri*, continue to make dedications to Mefitis, who maintains the epiclesis Utiana that she already had in Rossano (*CIL* 10.131–3).

The cult of Mefitis Utiana, like a certain number of local cults of the peninsula, thus had to be categorized as *municipalia sacra* (municipal cults), defined by Festus (146 L): "One calls municipal cults those owned originally, before the granting of Roman citizenship; the pontiffs desired that people continue to observe them and to practice them in the way they had been accustomed to from ancient times (*eo more quo adsuessent antiquitus*)." These cults, which people had deliberately chosen to fossilize in the forms considered original, were undoubtedly those which were regarded as most representative for the religious identity of the various communities and Italic ethnic groups. Unfortunately, we do not have the list of them, but one could be tempted to include the sanctuaries that Virgil mentions in Book VII of the *Aeneid*, when he enumerates the people of Italy going into combat in a spirit which is that of the Augustan restoration of traditional values: the fields of Juno of Gabii, the Soracte, the sacred grove of Capena (= the *lucus Feroniae*), the *nemus Angitiae*, the sacred grove of Egeria (= the *nemus Aricinum*), Jupiter Anxur, and the sacred grove of Feronia.

Still higher in dignity than the *municipia* are the colonies. It is perhaps for this reason (Scheid 1997, forthcoming b) that the Umbrian sanctuary of the sources of Clitumne, which stand before the *municipium* of Trevi, was given by Augustus to the colony of Hispellum.

What became of the local cults which did not enjoy this attention? If they did not simply disappear, they did not have more than a private status and could be found on rural property. It is apparently the case of the temple of Ceres, "old and narrow," located on the property of Pliny the Younger, in the upper valley of the Tiber or close to Como; it was restored by his own initiative, *inter alia* by replacing the old wooden cult statue (Pliny, *Epist.* 9.39). Scheid proposes "to regard Ceres as the guardian divinity of a *pagus*" (1997: 244). In fact, this private temple was further attended, on the day of its annual feast (undoubtedly the anniversary day of the dedication), by a great number of people, coming from the whole region.

This annual feast is on the Ides of September, that is, on the day of the *epulum Iouis* (Scheid 1997: 244). The reference to the religious calendar of Rome was chosen here, although it was a private and regional temple. Another probable example of the overlapping of a local cult and a Roman feast is provided by a graffito from the temple of Hercules Curinus, close to Sulmona, by the Paelignians. Somebody comes to fulfill the vows and to consult the oracle "on the feast of August" (Buonocore, in Mattiocco 1989). One should recall the feast of the Great Altar of Hercules in Rome, on August 12, as another graffito reports on the practice of the tithe, well attested by the *Ara Maxima*.

I subtitled this last section, dedicated to the Italian cults in Roman Italy, not "rupture *or* continuity," but "ruptures *and* continuities." The two phenomena unfold in different proportions according to the cultural areas examined and to the perspective one adopts. The status of the temple of Hera Lacinia in south Italy, described as "the most famous temple of this area," didn't hinder the plundering of its marble tiles by the censor Q. Fulvius Flaccus in 173 BC. However, it is significant that the injury is redressed: the only abuses of the power of the Roman magistrates which the senate remedies between the Second Punic War and the Social War relate precisely to sanctuaries of Magna Graecia, the temple of Persephone in Locres, and the *Lacinion* close to Crotona (de Cazanove 2005).

The conclusion of the episode could be used to substantiate contradictory verdicts: the returned tiles remain gathered in a pile in the *area* of the temple, because a specialized craftsman, able to replace them on the roof, cannot be found: a sign of chronic technological involution, that seems to indicate abandonment. And yet, nearly three centuries later, the sanctuary is still active: one freedman dedicates an altar to Hera Lacinia for the health of Marciana, the sister of Trajan (*CIL* 10.106). As stated by the senate in 173 BC, "the immortal gods are the same everywhere," *iidem ubique di immortales* (Livy 42.3.9).

FURTHER READING

A comprehensive treatment of the cults of pre-Roman Italy is lacking. There are some short syntheses on Italian religions, such as Prosdoscimi (1989), Bianchi (1978), and de Cazanove (1993). For Etruscan religion see Colonna (1985) and Briquel and Gaultier (1997). For the relationship with Roman cults see Dumézil (1974) and Beard et al. (1998). For the historical development of the conflictual Italian–Roman relationship (religion included) see especially Cornell (1995) and Hinard (2000).

Some large inscriptions have been regarded as the main access to Italian cults. Epigraphical sources are collected by Rix (2002), who replaced the early *Handbuch* of E. Vetter, brought up to date by Poccetti (1979); M. Crawford (forthcoming) promises a vision of the inscriptions in their material quality. The *tabulae Iguvinae* have been edited since Renaissance times; see more recently Devoto (1940, 1977), Poultney (1959), Prosdoscimi (1984, 1985, 1989), and Sisani (2001). The tablet of Agnonia has been studied by a recent conference (Del Tutto Palma 1996). A commented edition of the *iuvilas* of Capua has been offered by Franchi De Bellis (1981); of the *cippus* of Abella by Franchi de Bellis (1988); of the dedication in the sanctuary of Mefitis at Rossano di Vaglio by Lejeune (1990), to be supplemented by Poccetti (2001); of the inscriptions of Pietrabbondante by La Regina (1966). The legends and monetary types are fundamental for our understanding of the political, cultural, and religious identity of the pre-Roman communities, too (Rutter 2001). Recently, interest in the sanctuaries has grown (de Cazanove and Scheid 2003; Ribichini forthcoming). The series *Fana Templa Delubra* (in preparation) intends a systematic treatment of all the relevant sources. For the moment, a multitude of most informative regional studies exists (*Luoghi* 1996).

CHAPTER FIVE

Urban Religion in the Middle and Late Republic

Eric Orlin

Religion and the *Res Publica*

Roman religion in the middle and late republic, a period stretching from the beginning of the Punic Wars in the early third century to the death of Julius Caesar and the ascension of the first emperor Augustus in the late first century BCE, concerned itself with the city of Rome. This statement may seem to be a truism, but it actually expresses the two fundamental features of Roman religion: that the Roman religious system concerned itself primarily with the health of the Roman community, and that it was a religion of place. The primary purpose of the public religious system was to protect and enhance the community of the Romans; the modern notion of a separation of church and state would have been unthinkable to the Romans. The welfare of the city and its inhabitants was ensured by a series of rituals by which the Romans attempted to secure the goodwill of the gods, and the primary role of the religious authorities in Rome was to ensure that these rituals were performed in the proper way, at their proper time, and in their proper place. The second point follows from the first: Roman rituals were performed in specific places around the city of Rome in order to protect the city. Some of these places had been considered sacred from time immemorial, while others had gained their status over the years, but each location had its specific ritual that needed to be performed on that spot, and at a specified time of the year. Religion permeated almost every element of both space and time for the inhabitants of Rome, leading the Romans to believe themselves the most religious of all people and to ascribe their military success to their superior cultivation of the gods (Cic. *Har. resp.* 19).

To ensure the favor of the gods, the Romans relied on the correct performance of ritual (*orthopraxis*). Questions of belief or morality were not central to the religious system, though this statement should not be misinterpreted as meaning that the Romans did not believe in their gods or that they did not concern themselves with morality. The Romans did have a well-developed sense of what constituted appropriate behavior, but they did not believe that moral standards emanated from divine pronouncements; for reasons we shall explore below, divine revelation in the form of specific commands played a very limited role in Roman religion. In regard to belief, such questions are exceedingly difficult to answer at all times, even more so for an ancient society that has left us limited records. The evidence available from Rome dates mostly from the middle of the first century BCE, which makes it virtually impossible to know what Romans of an earlier period may have believed. This evidence suggests that late republican Rome may have been largely similar to modern societies; some members of the community, such as Cicero, can be found expressing some skepticism, but there is no reason to think that the overall level of belief was any greater or lesser than today. Romans performed religious actions on a regular basis in different contexts – in public as citizens, in their houses as members of their family, and perhaps on their own – but for the Romans these formed a continuum of religious activity. While the following remarks concentrate on the public religious system, that focus is not intended to privilege that sphere as more important, but acknowledges it as the most visible manifestation of religion in Rome, in terms of both the surviving evidence and its impact on the city as a whole.

Religious Authority

Undoubtedly the most salient feature of Roman republican religion lies in the fact that religious authority and religious institutions were tightly interwoven with political authority and the political institutions of the *res publica*. The political system during the republic operated on the principles of collegiality and cooperation, as the system succeeded by balancing the needs of numerous different actors. On the one hand Polybius noted that the *populus* retained the final authority to enact laws or decide whether or not to go to war, but he also noted that the aristocracy in the senate maintained control over Roman policy through its management of finances and foreign affairs (Polybius 6.13–14). Within the ruling elite, a balance needed to be maintained between the desires of individuals to take initiative and to win glory for themselves, and the desire of the ruling elite to share collective power and thus to prevent any one individual from gaining a position of dominance. Political authority was thus diffused throughout the ruling elite, as two consuls jointly held the highest executive authority for a single year, which allowed scope for individual accomplishment while not allowing any one individual to obtain an excess of power. The senate as an institution played a pivotal role in this balancing act; comprised exclusively of members of the aristocracy, it set priorities and articulated policies in the crucial areas of foreign relations and financial affairs that the popular assemblies ultimately approved. As the collective authority of the ruling elite, it also could check the ambitions of individual members of the aristocracy. The ability to manage these balances – between mass and elite authority, and between individual and collective authority – served as an important element in the success of the Romans, and the inability to maintain these balances in the late republic led directly to the demise of the republican political system.

These same balances appear in the religious system: during the middle republic, the ruling elite balanced the scope for individual initiative with the need for collective control while maintaining the decisive authority over Roman religion, and again the senate served as the focal point for these balances. Just as political authority was diffused, so religious authority was diffused throughout a number of different religious colleges: the pontiffs, the augurs, the *decemviri*, or 10 men, in charge of the prophetic Sibylline Books. The existence of these colleges served an essential role in maintaining the balance of the system in several ways. Since the Romans believed that the gods did not reveal their will directly, but through signs and portents that these men as a body needed to interpret, no one man could claim a special authority to interpret the will of the gods and place himself above the system. A further sign of the link between religion and politics can be seen in the membership of these colleges, for these men were drawn exclusively from the same elite who dominated political life at Rome (Cicero, *De domo sua* 1.1). There was no separate priestly class in which religious authority was vested, but the same men who made decisions regarding the relationships of the Roman community with other human communities also made the decisions regarding its relationship with the divine community. When a vacancy occurred in one of the colleges, the remaining members chose a replacement (a process known as co-option), which kept these positions within a narrow circle; one important criterion, that of avoiding the selection of a personal enemy of an existing member, aimed at ensuring the harmonious operation of each group (Cicero, *Ad familiares* 3.10). Furthermore, one of the key principles governing these colleges held that no person should be a member of more than one college, again guaranteeing the diffusion of power in just the same way that political authority was diffused.

Numerous examples throughout the republic demonstrate that the senate retained the final authority to enact decisions relating to religious matters, just as it served as the highest consultative body on political matters. The handling of prodigies offers perhaps the clearest example. The Romans considered unusual phenomena – meteor showers, lightning strikes, congenital deformities – as indications that the *pax deorum* (peace with the gods) had been ruptured and that they needed to take action to repair that relationship and restore themselves to the favor of the gods. The reporting of an unusual phenomenon, however, did not in itself constitute a prodigy; the senate needed to meet and confirm that the report did in fact indicate a rupture in the Romans' relationship with the gods. Only after making this decision might they refer the problem to one of the priestly colleges; the pontiffs or the *decemviri* did not act unless they were specifically called upon by the senate. The college would then recommend a course of action to expiate the prodigy and report its decision back to the senate, but it was the senate that made the final decision to order that the recommendation be carried out. This procedure illustrates the close cooperation between the senate and the priestly colleges, and of course the fact that the members of the colleges were themselves senators minimized any possibility of conflict between religious and political authority. It also demonstrates that it was the senate that played the decisive role regarding religious matters that affected the Roman people.

A similar procedure may be seen on matters of religious law: a religious college might render an opinion, but the senate ultimately issued the order resolving the case. The most complete record of a religious hearing in Rome bears out this conclusion. When Cicero sought to have his house restored to him after his return from exile, on the grounds that the shrine erected there during his absence had not been properly consecrated, the debate was held before the pontifical college (Cicero, *De domo sua*). Even when the pontiffs ultimately rendered a decision in Cicero's favor, Cicero still needed the vote of the senate to restore the property to him (Cicero, *Ad Atticum* 4.2). As in the case of prodigies, the senate almost always accepted the recommendation of the priestly college, revealing again that essential element of the Roman political, and hence religious, administrative system: the cooperation between the senate and individual office-holders. The place of the senate in the religious structure of Rome may be symbolized by the locations where the senate met: such meetings always took place in a *templum*, a religiously consecrated space (though not necessarily a temple in the modern sense of the word). This fact symbolizes the relationship between the senate and religion; in a very real sense the senate was the caretaker of the Romans' relationship with the divine, just as it was the caretaker of their relationship with other humans.

Effects of Expansion

From the fourth through the second centuries BCE, Rome developed from a small city on the banks of the river Tiber to an empire that dominated the Mediterranean basin. By 270 the Romans controlled all of peninsular Italy, and over the next hundred years, they expanded their influence overseas to include Sicily, north Africa, Spain, Greece, and Asia Minor; some areas, such as Sicily, they governed directly as provinces, while others they oversaw from Rome and intervened when necessary. This expansion wrought changes in every fabric of Roman society. At the most basic level, and most obvious to the inhabitants of Rome, the population and size of the city expanded, and the amount of wealth, both in the form of war booty and in the form of trade, increased even more dramatically. The growth of Roman hegemony and the increasing disparity in wealth between the elite and the *populus* brought difficulties to the political system, threatening the internal balances that kept Roman society functioning smoothly. The influx of foreigners, and foreign cultural elements, posed further challenges for the Romans. Roman society had always been open to foreign influences; Roman foundation myths, including the arrival of Aeneas as a refugee from Troy (Virg. *Aen.*) and the establishment by Romulus of an asylum on the Capitoline (Livy 1.8), reveal the Romans' understanding that their city had not begun as a closed or exclusive circle. Rome's domination of the Greek-speaking eastern part of the Mediterranean, as well as north Africa and Spain, and the large numbers of citizens serving overseas on military campaigns brought the city into much more direct contact with these other cultures. Because of the close relationship between religion and politics at Rome, the impact of these developments was felt in the religious sphere as well as the political.

Perhaps most obvious to the inhabitants of Rome, the expansion of hegemony brought with it an expansion in the Roman pantheon, as new temples to new gods were erected throughout the city. Greek cults had found a place in Rome since the fifth century BCE, and the Romans on at least one occasion had made use of a ceremony known as *evocatio*, whereby they promised a home in Rome to the protective deity of a military enemy if that deity abandoned the enemy in favor of Rome (Livy 5.21). But these cults had either come from other towns in Italy or been mediated through them. The increased contact with the Greek world beginning in the late third century BCE led to both an increased number and an increased pace in the adoption of foreign cults. The Romans had taken possession of Sicily at the end of the First Punic War in 241, and in 217, at the outset of the Second Punic War, they brought Venus from Mount Eryx in Sicily and installed her in a temple on the Capitoline hill, not far from the religious heart of the city (Livy 23.31). Simultaneous with that war, the First Macedonian War brought direct Roman involvement in the Greek east, and in 205 the Romans brought the aniconic black stone representing the Magna Mater from Asia Minor and installed it in the temple of Victory; in 191 they built a temple for the goddess on the Palatine hill, traditionally the oldest part of the city (Livy 29.10–11, 36.36). These locations, and the fact that both these goddesses were brought following a consultation of the Sibylline Books and hence a vote of the full senate, reveal that these goddesses had broad support from the ruling elite. Nor did the introduction of foreign cults cease after the Second Punic War; a second temple was built for Venus Erycina in 181, and M. Fulvius Nobilior erected a temple to Hercules of the Muses in the following decade. The expansion in the divine community that the Romans cultivated paralleled the expansion in the human communities over whom the Romans held power.

These cult introductions and temple constructions present many features characteristic of Roman religion that deserve emphasis. The notion of expanding the pantheon in response to the expansion of territory is not a necessary one or typical of the ancient world. The Babylonians brought the worship of their own god Marduk into conquered lands rather than adopting foreign worship; even the Athenians, who did introduce new gods into Athens, did so on a much more limited basis than Rome and never, as best we can tell, from a defeated enemy. The Romans, however, displayed an unusual willingness to extend citizenship to others, so here again Roman religion mirrors Roman politics. The expansion of the pantheon, and especially the incorporation of foreign divinities, reveals that same willingness to extend the Roman community beyond the mere walls of the city of Rome. At the same time as the Romans signaled this openness, they also demonstrated their superiority; while the Romans did not deprive the local communities of their cults, they indicated their power over these communities by taking on responsibility for the proper cultivation of the gods' favor in Rome. The procedures by which these cults came to Rome also exemplified the principles of Roman religion. The great bulk of the new temples resulted from a vow made by a general in the field, a response to a crisis, and thus provided scope for an individual to parade both his piety to the gods and his *virtus* ("manliness") to the Roman people. In order for these temples to become part of the Roman religious system, however, the senate had to give its assent, which it regularly did, underlining both the ultimate senatorial control over Roman religion and the habitual cooperation between the senate and individual actors. On many levels, the addition of foreign cults to Rome exemplifies the main features of the Roman religious system.

In addition to new cults, expansion brought changes in the ritual practice of existing cults in Rome. Festivals since the early republic had included *ludi* (games), mostly horse races (*ludi circenses*), though by the fourth century plays (*ludi scaenici*) had also formed part of the program (see chapter 16). In the late third century, the same era which saw an increase in the pace of the introduction of foreign cults, the direction of these festivals turned more toward the stage than the race track, due in part to the influence of the culturally Greek areas of southern Italy. The sheer number of *ludi* proliferated as well: the plebeian games were founded, and annual games were added in honor of Apollo, the Magna Mater, and the goddess Flora, all within a fifty-year span, marking a dramatic shift toward this type of religious activity and a striking increase in the number of days devoted to this ritual. The Romans even created a new college, known as the *epulones*, to supervise the rituals of the games (Livy 33.42). Contact with the Greek world led to other changes as well. The cult of Ceres underwent a significant transformation, adding Greek rites, apparently along the lines of the Eleusinian mystery cult, to those of the original Italic cult that had been founded in the early fifth century; Cicero (*Pro Balbo* 55) informs us that priestesses were invited from the culturally Greek towns in southern Italy especially to officiate at these rites. The temples built in the second century reflect Greek influence as well, often employing Greek artists and adopting Greek techniques and styles, including the beginnings of the use of marble in temple construction. The closer Roman contacts with the Greek world in the late third century left their marks all over Roman religious practice.

A Response to Expansion:
Defining "Roman" Religion

These ritual and cult introductions brought a variety of new practices into Rome, but in doing so, they posed a problem: what was "Roman" about Roman religion? One can observe the Roman elite working out an answer to this question over the course of the second century BCE by placing limitations and restrictions on a variety of rituals. The case of the Magna Mater mentioned above provides a good example. The senate placed a series of restrictions on the practice of this cult in Rome, banning native-born Romans from serving as priests of the cult or walking in procession, and limiting the activity of the *galli*, the Phrygian eunuch priests, to the specific days of the goddess's festival (Dion. H. 2.19). At the same time, the senate organized *ludi*, a Roman form of worship, for the Magna Mater and provided for a Roman magistrate to preside at sacrifices held according to the Roman custom, and members of the aristocracy formed *sodalitates* (brotherhoods) to organize dinner parties in honor of the goddess. While welcoming the goddess to Rome and allowing for her traditional forms of worship, the Romans created another set of rituals to be practiced in her honor; these parallel sets allowed the Romans to see "Roman" practices and "foreign" practices set side by side, even as the cult itself was made part of the "Roman" system of worship.

Similar issues appear in the most famous religious incident of the Roman republic, the measures taken against followers of the Bacchic cult in 186 BCE. In that year, rumors of criminal activity and sexual debauchery among the followers of Bacchus led the consuls to seek out the perpetrators; eventually over four thousand people throughout Italy were executed (Livy 39.8–19). Many features of this episode remain obscure, because Livy, our sole literary source, has included many details unlikely to be true in an effort to portray the repression as a reaction against the sudden infiltration of too many Greek elements into Roman worship. His presentation is enough to alert us that questions of the "Romanness" of religious practice were still live issues in Livy's day, nearly two hundred years later. But it is unlikely that the senatorial reaction of 186 was motivated by anti-Greek sentiment; the cult had had worshipers in Italy for many years prior to 186 and Greek elements continued to find a home in Rome even after this date. More to the point, Bacchus continued to be worshiped after 186; we are fortunate enough to possess a copy of the senate's decree relating to this incident, and that decree makes no effort to ban the worship of Bacchus entirely, only to specify the conditions of worship (see Beard et al. 1998: 2.290–1 for a translation of the decree). Many hypotheses have been advanced concerning both the worship of Bacchus and the senatorial reaction, ranging from the ways in which this cult may have represented a social, economic, and/or political challenge to the Roman state to the senate's fear of allowing members of a religious group to swear allegiance to each other, or its desire to extend its control of religion over all of Italy. What is most striking about the decree may be the similarities to the treatment of the Magna Mater, ranging from the people who may and may not serve as priests to the places and manner in which the cult rituals may be performed. Rather than the repression of a conspiracy, the Bacchic incident may reveal the concern with ensuring a "Roman" form of worship for a Greek cult.

Similar concerns with Romanness can be seen in religious practice as well as in the response to individual foreign traditions. In the third century the Romans began to refer to the practice of sacrificing with a bare head as being *Graeco ritu* ("according to the Greek rite") (Scheid 1996). In Roman practice, the *pontifex maximus* sacrificed while pulling the hem of his toga up over his head; Roman emperors in general, and Augustus in particular, would come to portray themselves in this fashion. The curious feature of this terminology is that the "Greek rite" was not used for all Greek cults; Aesculapius, for instance, imported directly from Epidaurus in 293 BCE, did not fall into this category. Nor was the Greek rite used only for Greek cults, for it was applied to the ancient cult of Saturn. Several elements may be seen at play here, including the desire of the Romans both to emphasize the presence of Greek elements within their religious system and to draw a clear distinction between Greek and Roman styles of worship. As the Romans came to dominate the culturally separate Greek world, their religious system responded to the needs of the community and reflected the Roman desire to incorporate aspects of foreign cultures that they found desirable while still maintaining a clear sense of their own Roman identity.

Competition in the Late Republic

The late republic, which conventionally begins with the tribunate of Tiberius Gracchus in 133 BCE, witnessed the gradual disintegration of the balances that had kept the republican form of government operating smoothly. The increasing riches coming into Roman society led to increasing disparities among the Romans in wealth and also heightened the competition for power. The system for mediating between the desires of individuals and that of the aristocracy as a social collective began to break down, while the *populus*, often encouraged by members of the elite who saw popular support as a means to power, demanded a more direct role in decision-making. Reforms in army recruitment allowed the commanders to wield their armies as political weapons, and the late republic is well known for the series of military dynasts who dominated the political stage: Marius, Sulla, Pompey the Great, Julius Caesar. Historians often present this period as one of decline, from a harmonious and selfless republic to petty bickering and selfish civil war that ultimately culminated in the demise of republican rule in favor of an autocratic system.

This narrative of decline attached to the politics of the late Roman republic has often been transferred to Roman religion, but recent studies have emphasized the fallacy of this approach. The notion that Roman religion was in decline stems largely from the notion that religion was manipulated by a disbelieving elite in order to advance political aims during the late republic. In fact the central place often occupied by religion in the struggles of the last century of the republic is the surest sign of its vitality; the link between religion and politics suggests that we should expect to find religion involved in political wrangling. But we should expect to see changes in Roman religion that correspond to the changes in Roman society: as the political struggles began to transform Rome, the religious system needed to adapt to the new circumstances. These innovations carried further processes that had been underway in Roman society, and helped mark the next stage in the evolution of Roman civilization.

Some developments in the late republic reflected the changed structure of the political system, as the processes set in motion by Tiberius Gracchus resulted in the *populus* obtaining a larger role in the decision-making process. Whereas in the middle republic, new members of the priestly colleges were chosen by the remaining members of the college, that is, the political elite, in 104 BCE a law handed selection of priests for the major colleges to the tribal assembly. Although other priests continued to be appointed and the priestly colleges drew up the list of candidates to be submitted for the election, this law marked a significant shift of decision-making authority from the aristocracy to the people, as can be gauged by the subsequent continuing legislative battle. Sulla felt this transfer significant enough that his legislative program, as part of its short-lived attempt to limit the authority of the *populus*, repealed the provision, while the tribune Labienus sponsored legislation in 63 to restore the selection to the people. As a result of this reform, election to the priestly colleges became a matter of heightened political importance: the surprise election of Julius Caesar as *pontifex maximus* in 63, amidst widespread allegations of bribery, signaled his emergence as a major player in Roman politics. The selection of members of the priestly colleges signified the changed conditions of the late republic: where once it revealed the control of the elite over Roman society, in the late republic it signaled the increased power of the people. And although we have no signs that election brought divisions into the priestly colleges, the new procedure no longer revealed fundamental cooperation among the aristocrats, but intense competition between them for public honor.

Religion thus became another site of contestation among the political elite as the restraints on the competition for status and power were less and less enforced. Even such straightforward matters as the necessity of the pontiffs to add intercalary days in order to make the Roman calendar conform to a solar year became a matter of intense political concern, for the addition of days at a particular point in the year could affect the outcome of elections or trials by delaying or interrupting proceedings. Cicero's triumph over Verres in 70 BCE was all the more remarkable since the orator needed to overcome the obstacle of religious holidays that threatened to interrupt his prosecution and deprive him of needed witnesses. The device of *obnuntiatio*, whereby an official with religious authority declared a halt to public business because he claimed that he had observed signs that the gods were unfavorable to the conduct of public business, became a regular feature of political life. One of Cicero's letters details what seems to many readers a comical game of cat and mouse, as one magistrate tracked another through the forum in order to make the necessary public proclamation that the omens were unfavorable (*Ad Att.* 4.3). Sometimes practical means served better than legal ones to overcome this religious objection: Caesar effectively restricted his co-consul Bibulus to his home as a means of preventing him from announcing unfavorable omens, though Bibulus claimed to be watching the heavens anyway, creating at least some grounds to argue that Caesar's legislation had not been legitimately approved (Suet. *Caesar* 20). That politicians attempted to make use of religion to advance or halt a political agenda does not imply that they did not believe in their religious system, but rather confirms its importance. Roman politicians did not ignore religious objections, but argued that their own actions were more religiously correct than their opponents'. The necessity of making an argument on religious grounds implies strongly that religion was still taken seriously by the Roman elite and testifies to the continued vitality of the religious system. As the political aims of individuals came to challenge the interests of the community in the later years of the republic, it became increasingly important to claim that the gods favored particular individuals rather than the *res publica* in general.

The construction and reconstruction of temples in late republican Rome provides one way to see this modification in the nature of Roman religion. A number of temples built or rebuilt in the late republic were known colloquially by the name of their founder. For example, the temple that Marius built to Honos et Virtus following his dramatic victory over the Cimbri and Teutones in 102 was known as the *aedes*

Mariana, while the god to whom Pompey built a temple was called Hercules Pompeianus. Nor was this phenomenon limited to just the "great men" of late republican Rome; the temple of Diana Planciana was called after the consul of 55 BCE, Cn. Plancius. Prior to the late republic, only non-religious buildings, such as the *basilica Aemilia* or *columna Minucia*, were known by the names of their builders. As noted above, temples had long served as a means for Roman generals to advertise their prowess and their piety, and it had been sufficient in the middle republic for the general's name to appear in the dedicatory inscription. In the late republic, as the balance between the collective needs of the aristocracy and the desires of individuals shifted decisively in favor of the latter, a direct connection between the temple and the individual became more important.

This connection might even take the shape of a direct relationship between the individual and the gods. This feature is particularly associated with Julius Caesar, as we shall see in the next section, but it is important to note that Caesar's generation was not the first to claim this special connection. As early as the second century, Scipio Africanus was reported to have cultivated a close personal connection with the gods, visiting the temple of Capitoline Jupiter every day and doing nothing to refute stories that "he was a man of divine stock" (Livy 26.19). In the middle republic, Scipio's exceptional individualism was checked by the collective body of the senate, but in the late republic the attempt by individuals to claim a special divine favor for themselves became a regular feature that the senate was unable to prevent. Marius carried a Syrian prophetess around with him – a woman whose prophecies had even been rejected by the senate – and after his great victory over the Cimbri and Teutones, the people proclaimed that they would make offerings to the gods and to Marius at the same time (Plutarch, *Marius* 27.9). It is worth noting that the decision to include Marius was apparently made by "the masses" and not by the senate, a further sign of the increased role of the *populus* in religious decision-making. Sulla took the surname *Felix*, by which he indicated the good fortune with which the gods had blessed him, but the Greek translation of this term reveals the goddess from whom he claimed special favors: *Epaphroditus*, beloved by Aphrodite, or Venus (Plutarch, *Sulla* 19.9). If the hegemony of the Romans was to be ascribed to the favor of the gods bestowed on them, then one logical explanation for the dominance of individual men was the favor of the gods bestowed upon those men.

The Religious Programs of Pompey the Great and Julius Caesar

Over the last forty years of the republic, Venus became a focal point of the contest between the leading Roman politicians, as both Pompey the Great and Julius Caesar followed the example of Sulla and sought to establish their claims to her special favor. By the late republic, the legend of Rome's foundation by the offspring of Aeneas had become well established, which may account for the prominence of Venus at this time, for as the mother of Aeneas she was therefore the mother of the entire Roman race. Venus also had strong military connections in some guises, and the

Romans had already availed themselves of this aspect of the goddess when they invited
Venus Erycina to Rome in the midst of the Second Punic War. There is, then, nothing unusual about the prominence of Venus or the significance of her presence at
this time; the innovation of the late republic again lies in the attempt to divert the
divine connection from the community to the individual. In their competition for
predominance, both Pompey and Caesar took further steps down the path that had
already been marked out, and in so doing paved the way for the religious developments that occurred under Augustus.

Pompey's attempts to claim the patronage of Venus date back to the beginnings
of his career under Sulla; even as a young man he may have competed for the favor
of Venus with the dictator. Pompey's connection to the goddess is revealed most
clearly in the temple he built to Venus Victrix in 55 BCE as part of a vast complex
in the Campus Martius. The project is most famous for the stone theater that was
attached to it, which was the first permanent stone theater to be constructed in Rome.
Christian sources would complain that Pompey evaded the objections to a stone
theater by claiming that the seats in the theater were merely steps for the temple, just
as the steps of the temple of the Magna Mater provided seating for the audience at
the Megalesian games in her honor (Tertullian, *Spect.* 10). Such extreme skepticism
is misplaced; since the second century the Romans had included temples as part of
larger complexes, and the theater was not the only element of Pompey's building
program. The complex also included a massive garden laid out in the Hellenistic
Greek style, complete with numerous statues including representations of the 14 nations
conquered by Pompey. Even more than other temples built by late republican military dynasts, this complex clearly placed primary focus on Pompey himself as a man
who had achieved a significant number of "firsts": first to build a stone temple in
Rome, first to conquer the specified territories. Since such complexes were often connected with ruler cult in the Hellenistic east, Pompey may even have been the first
to aim at divine honors in Rome. The temple to Venus Victrix is a far cry from the
displays of devotion to the gods and *res publica* represented by most mid-republican
temples.

Caesar, as he did so often in confronting Pompey, chose not to give ground, but
competed with Pompey directly to see who favored, and was favored by, Venus the
most. In this contest, Caesar was able to claim an immediate advantage; the Julian
clan traced its ancestry to Iulus, the son of Aeneas and hence the grandson of Venus.
Many other families in the late republic claimed heroic lineages to build support,
but Caesar could go one step further and claim divine lineage, and this aspect became
an important part of his public image. Even Pompey recognized this problem; an
anecdote tells how on the night before the climactic battle of Pharsalus with Caesar,
he dreamed of spoils decorating the temple of Venus Victrix, but was afraid that the
dream favored Caesar rather than himself (Plutarch, *Pompey* 68). When it came time
to give the watchwords for the night, Pompey gave Hercules Invictus while Caesar
stayed with Venus Victrix (Appian, *Civil Wars* 2.76). Though these stories may have
originated as a way of explaining Pompey's defeat, they indicate that competition
for the favor of Venus was seen by Romans as essential to the contest between Pompey
and Caesar.

At the battle of Pharsalus, Caesar also vowed a temple, in best republican fashion, to Venus Victrix, almost as if he were summoning Pompey's protectress to his side in the manner of an *evocatio*. Several years earlier Caesar had begun preparations to build an additional forum adjacent to the traditional one in Rome; when the complex was dedicated three years after the battle of Pharsalus, it contained a temple to the goddess Venus Genetrix, apparently in fulfillment of the vow. The new epithet for the goddess is significant, for it clearly marked her as the ancestor of the Julian clan and of the Roman people, and not merely as the bringer of victory. In raising a private family connection to the level of a public cult and in claiming descent from a divinity in order to enhance his personal stature, Caesar laid the groundwork for further innovations. Though he followed in the footsteps of Pompey and the other late republican leaders of Rome, Caesar sought to create a divine aura around himself more clearly than any of them. Apparently even before his assassination in 44 BCE, Caesar was given a special priest, or *flamen*, of the type that were attached to the most ancient cults of Rome, the right to have his statue carried among the gods in processions, and other honors that assimilated him closely to the gods (Suet. *Caesar* 76; Dio 44.4–6.). Though the degree to which he desired to be considered a god himself during his lifetime remains a matter of controversy, these honors made it easier after his death for the senate to pass a formal decree of deification, enshrining Caesar in the Roman pantheon (Suet. *Caesar* 88; Dio 47.18).

A discussion of the cult of the emperors must be reserved for subsequent chapters (see chapter 22), but here it is worth noting that again there are good republican precedents for what at first glance may seem the most significant religious innovation of the imperial period. As early as 196 BCE Titus Flamininus, the "liberator" of Greece, had received divine honors in Greece for his actions in restoring freedom to the Greeks (Plutarch, *Flamininus* 16). Over the subsequent century two relatively obscure proconsuls, Manius Aquilius and Mucius Scaevola, would be honored with a special sacrifice, complete with a special priest, and a festival respectively. But these honors were offered by Greek cities of the east; Pompey and Caesar brought these types of honors to Rome itself, and so made a lasting impact on the religion of the city as well as the empire. When Caesar was deified in Rome after his death, it set an important precedent, and Octavian was able to capitalize on this development both politically, in his struggles with Mark Antony, and religiously, in his subsequent religious program. Roman religion had consistently developed hand in hand with political events, and the Roman revolution was to prove no different.

FURTHER READING

The fundamental study of Roman religion in the middle and late republic is Wissowa (1912), though it is badly outdated; Beard et al. (1998) has now become the indispensable tool for all aspects of Roman religion, both specific incidents and broad theoretical issues. On priesthood and the role of the Roman senate, see Beard (1990) and Rüpke (2005a); Szemler (1971) established the essential identity between priests and magistrates. MacBain (1982) is fundamental to the study of prodigies, but now see also Rosenberger (1998) and Rasmussen (2003);

on augury see Linderski (1986). There is not yet any overall treatment of the Roman reaction to foreign cults, though Montanari (1988) touches on several important issues. Gustaffson (2000) is the most recent treatment of the vexed question of *evocatio*, while Ziolkowski (1992) and Orlin (1997) focus on the temples built in Rome during the republic. The work of Degrassi (1963) on the stone calendars marked with festivals is invaluable. On *ludi*, see Bernstein (1998) and his contribution in this volume (chapter 16). The bibliography on the cult of the Magna Mater is vast; Vermaseren (1977) is a good starting point in English, while Beard (1994) discusses how the paraded foreign aspects contributed to a sense of Roman identity. The bibliography on the Bacchanalia is even larger: Pailler (1988) is now essential, but see also Gallini (1970) and Gruen (1990: 34–78). On the late republic, Weinstock (1971) is required reading not only for Caesar's religious behavior, but also for the antecedents; see also Taylor (1931). Schilling (1954) offers a history of Venus in Rome, to be supplemented with Sauron (1994). The narrative presented in this chapter might be considered part of a "new orthodoxy" on Roman religion; for a critique of that approach, see Bendlin (2000).

CHAPTER SIX

Continuity and Change: Religion in the Augustan Semi-Century

Karl Galinsky

It is clear from the preceding chapters that religion was an integral part of the fabric and the workings of the Roman state. As can be expected, therefore, it continued in that role in Augustus' reign (31 BC–AD 14) and became even more multi-faceted, befitting the character of the age. As such, it is a paradigm, in many ways, of the special characteristics of that vital period and must be approached from the same perspectives as other Augustan phenomena. That means, first and foremost, that the dichotomies which are often applied to them do not work. To give one prominent example: Augustus' *res publica* was not republican *or* monarchic; rather, it was both. Similarly, in Augustan culture in general, we are looking at *both* tradition *and* innovation and at *both* continuity *and* change. In the area of religion in particular, the posited dichotomies would not hold up anyway because change was part of the tradition of Roman religion (North 1976). In fact, operative terminology from the religious sphere is helpful for understanding the much-debated meaning of Augustus' "restored" republic (*res publica restituta*). Romans would see the term "restitution" used routinely in inscriptions on restored temples; such restorations occurred all the time because of frequent fires and the like. We know from archaeology that such rebuilding hardly ever involved an exact replica of the old structure. Instead, a new and changed, even if not radically changed, edifice would be erected on the old foundation – precisely the image Augustus uses in one of his best-known quotations, namely that he "left the city, which he found made of bricks, as one of marble" (Suet. *Augustus* 28). The phrase follows his statement that he built his "new state" on a secure foundation (*fundamenta*) – architecture is both reality and metaphor.

Both the metaphor and the reality – another famous claim by Augustus was that he rebuilt 82 temples in the city of Rome besides constructing several others (*Res Gestae* 19–21) – fittingly apply to the development of religion in the Augustan reign.

Like the god Janus, it looked in two directions at once: back to existing traditions and forward to the future; we can see in retrospect that the foundations for many religious developments and practices in the empire were laid in the Augustan age.

Some Fundamental Aspects of Continuity and Change

"Continuity and change" or "tradition and innovation" are perspectives that apply to just about all manifestations of Augustan religion, as was rightly seen by J. Liebeschuetz (1979: esp. 55–100). Before we take up particular topics, however, it is important to call attention to two underlying and connected developments.

During most of the republic, religion had been solidly in the hands of magistrates or priests who, for the most part, came from the aristocracy and staunchly resisted any attempt to diminish their power by admitting others to the club. It is telling that the admission of plebeians to the highest political office, the consulship, occurred a full 67 years before plebeians were granted access to the pontifical and augural colleges (*Lex Ogulnia*, 300 BC). That meant anything but parity: to the end of the republic, membership in these colleges remained a closely guarded aristocratic prerogative, and broader participation remained minimal. Characteristic of the Augustan age, the change that comes about at the end of the republic and solidifies under Augustus is not political, but cultural. Most of the members of the priestly colleges in Augustus' time continued to be aristocrats, but the real power and control over religion and the calendar now flowed from professional experts, such as the polymath Varro, because they had the power of knowledge. The phenomenon, which pervades all areas of Augustan culture, has been fittingly called "the Roman cultural revolution" (Habinek and Schiesaro 1997; Wallace-Hadrill 2005) in contrast to the narrowly political view of the Augustan transformation that forms the basis of Sir Ronald Syme's classic *The Roman Revolution* (1939).

One key area was control over the calendar. More is involved than a mere reckoning of time: "Calendars belong to the most important instruments of a society's temporal organization" (Rüpke 1995a: 593). In Rome, the calendar determined the flow of public life and, through the annual *fasti*, marked identity by singling out individuals for the offices they held and their activities. There was a great deal of latitude for those who knew how to handle such matters or, at any rate, handled them. They were, of course, members of the nobility and they often proceeded at will. The calendar reform of Caesar marks the arrival of expert professionals. They bring their knowledge to regularizing a haphazard system, and they are employed and appropriated by the new leader of the state. The process continues under Augustus with the additional dimension that, like control over the calendar, *fasti* are not a privilege any more that is limited to the aristocracy, but spring up all over for local festivals, magistrates, and functionaries, including freedmen and slaves. In Andrew Wallace-Hadrill's succinct formulation: "In slipping from the nobility, Roman time becomes the property of all Romans" (2005: 61). Far from being isolated, this occurrence is part of a broader phenomenon: one of the defining aspects of the

Augustan reign is precisely the opening up of formerly restricted opportunities to a much larger segment of the populace (with the obvious exception of governance at the top). Paradoxical as it may seem, a shift to autocratic government is accompanied by an authentic involvement of much wider strata of the population. Everyone, and not just the city of Rome and the consuls, gets to publish their *fasti* now, whether monthly calendars or annual list of functionaries, or in combination. We find them in towns like Praeneste, for the officials (*vicomagistri*) of the 265 neighborhoods in Rome who were freedmen (see the section on increased participation, below), the slaves of the Tiberian imperial villa at Antium, and many more. Augustan religion is a perfect reflection of both trends: on the one hand, greater concentration on the ruler – when Augustus rebuilt temples, for instance, many of their anniversary dates were changed so as to coincide with important dates for him, such as September 23, his birthday – and, on the other, much wider participation by far more people in the life of the state via religion.

Such participation extended to all strata that had traditionally been left out, such as freedmen, slaves, and provincials, and I will follow up with some specifics below. But the principal shift is clear: the aristocracy lost its formerly exclusive control in the area of religion just as it did in other important areas like law, language, public speaking, and military science. When it came to knowledge of religious practices and their origins, you now could turn to Varro's compendium on *Human* [i.e. Roman] *and Divine Antiquities*, which, not by coincidence, was dedicated to the *pontifex maximus* Julius Caesar. It is such developments, and not just the loss of the old order's political power, that are behind the laments about the "decline" and "decay" of the republic. Religion continued to serve as a cohesive force in the state. The reason for this function, however, altered because of the changes I have outlined. In his famous characterization of Roman religion, Polybius, the Greek Alexis de Tocqueville of the second century BC, praised it because the aristocracy used "awe of the gods" to instill fear into the populace and thereby keep it unified (*Historiae* 6.86). In diametrical contrast, the role of public religion in achieving cohesion and unity under Augustus was the result of greater inclusiveness and opportunity for participation. This was all the more important as the Augustan panorama extended not just to Rome and Italy but to the entire Mediterranean.

A final aspect is that the changes that took place in Augustus' reign were not sudden – not for nothing, his motto was "make haste slowly" – but took place over time. That time includes, as John Scheid (2005a) has recently pointed out, the Octavianic period of Augustus, that is, the years from 44 to 27 BC. From the beginning, Octavian/Augustus pursued the establishment of divine honors for the ruler (his slain adoptive father Julius Caesar, for the time being) and the restoration of some ancient traditions. I want to turn to this second aspect first.

Restoration

Augustan culture was highly visual. Augustus marshaled the media of art and architecture like no Roman before him (Zanker 1987 [1988]). We can begin with what would have been most obvious to Augustus contemporaries, the rebuilding of Rome. It is a paradigm of Augustan-style restoration, as defined earlier: the city was not simply rebuilt in its prior form, but the urban plan was clarified and reorganized, with new buildings being deliberately so arranged as to form coherent ensembles with the older structures and with one another, thereby serving as focal points (Favro 1996, 2005).

Temples and other sacred building figured prominently in this endeavor. As mentioned before, Augustus himself lists many of the restored and new buildings in the extensive summary of his achievements, the *Res Gestae*. The quantity alone was impressive: "In my sixth consulship" [28 BC], he states, "I restored 82 temples of the gods in the city on the authority of the senate, neglecting none that required restoration at the time" (20.4). We can assume that the rebuilding took longer, even if these temples were not massive stone buildings but mostly smaller shrines made of less durable materials, such as wood and terracotta. And we should note that Augustus, quite typically, shows himself as deferential to the senate, which had the traditional say over the building of temples (see chapter 5). More importantly, what did it all mean? It is not that the populace forthwith became more "religious" or "pious" – we always have to be careful not to transpose later notions of religion back into Roman times. The rebuilding, first and foremost, was a matter of signifying the return to stability. Roman religion was not a religion of salvation, but it was intimately connected with the civil order of the state. No question, as always in times of distress – and the preceding decades of internecine war were horrendous – people would wonder whether the gods had turned away from Rome or were punishing the city for its misdeeds; such sentiments are readily found in Roman authors, including the poet Horace. The basic phenomenon, however, is very simple: religion, in the end, is an alternative and response to chaos, and chaos had ruled, reaching new extremes in the civil war between Antony and Octavian. The gods were there to protect the community, to safeguard its values, and to help instill proper civic behavior. When their shrines fell apart it was a sign of the fraying of this fabric. Their restoration signified the return of divinely ordered civic stability.

Part of that stability was that, like so many of its other functions, the aristocracy's competition in temple building came to an end. Munatius Plancus, who was a former partisan of Antony's but introduced the motion to name Octavian "Augustus," still had the privilege of being in charge of the restoration of one of Rome's oldest temples, that of Saturn in the Forum. That temple is a fine example of the nexus between religion and the state, as it also housed the state treasury. New temples, however, were built exclusively by the emperor or members of his family. They were true, eye-catching cynosures as they were sheathed in gleaming, white Luni marble (the same Carrara marble Michelangelo used later). First among them was the temple of Apollo on the Palatine, dedicated in 28 BC. It was closely integrated with Augustus' house and thus prepared the way for that house to become in part a shrine to Vesta after Augustus assumed the office of *pontifex maximus* in 12 BC and did not, of course, move to the pontiff's residence in the Forum. Another standout was the temple of Mars in the new Forum of Augustus, which was dedicated in 2 BC and commemorated the revenge taken both on Caesar's murderers and on the Parthians in the east for the defeat they had inflicted on Rome's armies; Augustus celebrated a bloodless "victory" over them in 20 BC and they returned the Roman army's standards. With the exception of Apollo's role in the Secular Games of 17 BC, this did not lead to increased cultic activities for either god (more on Augustus' association with Apollo below). Rather, the splendid architectural celebration of these deities, which was enhanced by grand pictorial and sculptural programs, invoked their many associations, such as Mars' connections with the beginnings of Rome (he was the father of Romulus and Remus) and Apollo's with both victory and peaceful cultural pursuits. The gods' renewed patronage of Rome was now literally set in stone.

So was another aspect of Roman religion that reached new heights under Augustus. From the beginning, Roman religion had been one of appropriations, resulting in an ever developing mix of Italic, Etruscan, Greek, and other traditions; the practice of "evoking" gods (*evocatio*), described in the previous chapter, from conquered territories signified both conquest and integration into the Roman system. The temple of Mars is a paradigm of the expression of these characteristics in architecture. In the Italic tradition, it was built on a massive platform; at the same time, the elaboration of some of the column bases was carefully modeled on precedents from the Acropolis in Athens, and the exuberance of colored marble in the interior recalled the orient. All in all, this showcase temple, which was built in the most lavish of three main architectural orders, the Corinthian one, was a far cry from the "standard" temple recommended for Mars by the architect Vitruvius (Vitr.1.2.5), who dedicated his work to Augustus.

There was also an appropriation of a different kind. As I have already mentioned, the anniversary dates of several rebuilt temples were changed to dates important for Augustus; the temple of Apollo in the Circus Flaminius is good example (from June 13 to September 23). Other temples would receive an even more obvious Augustan coloration. The temple of Concord in the Roman Forum, for instance, was reconfigured as the temple of Augustan Concord, *Concordia Augusta*, and dedicated on the thirty-seventh anniversary of Augustus' assumption of that name (January 16, AD 10). Indeed "Augustus," which was chosen for its many associations (including *augur*) and therefore can be translated only imperfectly as "The Revered One," set the first citizen (*princeps*) apart from his contemporaries because it hinted at his being part of more than the human sphere.

Much has been made in this connection of Augustus' association with Apollo. Its beginning was not altogether auspicious: at a time when Rome was racked by famine, the young Octavian and 11 of his friends threw a lavish party dressed as the 12 Olympian gods, with Octavian being Apollo; the event earned him a great deal of bad publicity (Suet. *Augustus* 70). "Apollo" actually was the watchword of Brutus and Cassius at Philippi (42 BC); like so much else, Octavian appropriated it. Later, the god's new temple on the Palatine, dedicated in 28 BC, became a landmark. We have already noted its integration with Augustus' house, but its insertion on the Palatine into the context of two pre-existing temples of Victory is just as important. It was the goddess Victory, Victoria Augusta, who became the signal deity of Augustus. Her image was ubiquitous because warfare was unceasing; the *pax Augusta*, as Augustus himself put it succinctly, was "a peace born of victories" (*Res Gestae* 13). In particular, we should not overemphasize, let alone narrow down, the role of Apollo because of Octavian's struggle against Antony. The schema of Apollo versus Dionysus goes back to Nietzsche, who saw in it the key to Greek civilization, but it is another dichotomy that works with only limited success in the Augustan context. Antony styled himself as the "New Dionysus" in the east, but there is no evidence that this riled the inhabitants of Rome and Italy: the cult of Dionysus, identified with Bacchus and Liber, kept enjoying great popularity. Dionysus is a frequent theme in both Augustan poetry, including Virgil's and Horace's comparisons of him to Augustus, and Augustan art; the floral and vegetal decoration of the famous Altar of Augustan Peace (*Ara Pacis Augustae*), for one, is permeated with Dionysiac motifs. Certainly, however, one impact of Augustus' religious building activity was the enhancement of his own "Augustan" aura: he was clearly destined to join the gods at the proper time, even if Horace begged him not to "return to heaven till late" (*Odes* 1.2.45).

Similar perspectives emerge from the Augustan restoration of the priesthoods. They were, as we have noted, prestigious offices and highly coveted by the nobility. Augustus was intent on keeping them that way and revitalizing them at the same time. Because of the disarray of the late republic and the civil wars some of the positions had not been filled, a prominent example being that of the priest of Jupiter (*flamen Dialis*), which had stood vacant for some 76 years. In this case, we have the explicit testimony of Tacitus (*Ann.* 4.16) that "Augustus brought certain things up to date for present practice out of that horrid antiquity," and the example stands for many. Restoration was not a mindless recovery of archaic rites but was adaptive. Another good illustration is Augustus' transformation of the "Brotherhood of the Cultivated Fields" (Arvales) from a group that had rather insignificant functions to a high-profile college of 12, of which he was a member. It bears out Suetonius' summary statement that "he increased the priesthoods in numbers and dignity, and also in privileges" (*Augustus* 31); the Vestal Virgins received several of the latter, including special seats in the theater and lands in the vicinity of Rome. At the same time, there was another distinction that set Augustus apart from ordinary mortals: he was the first Roman to belong to all the major priestly groups. In the *Res Gestae* (7.3), he in fact prides himself on that, quite in contrast to his insistent refusal, in the previous paragraphs (5–6), to accept any offices and powers that were "inconsistent with the custom of our ancestors." Religion was a priority for many reasons. Therefore, and analogous to his role as temple builder, Augustus now was in charge of selecting the priesthoods' new members, and thereby replacing previous contentious mechanisms such as co-optation.

The restoration also involved religious festivals. When Suetonius enumerates them (*Augustus* 31), he typically uses the word *restituit*, which, as we saw at the beginning, implied change as well as continuity. The most outstanding and best-documented example is the Secular Games (*ludi saeculares*) that Augustus celebrated with the Roman populace for three days and nights in 17 BC. The title comes from the Latin word *saeculum*, which could connote periods from one generation to a hundred years. The only previous celebrations of the festival that are attested securely, if not unproblematically, took place in 249 BC, at the height of the First Punic War, and in 146 BC, coinciding with the final stage of the wars against Carthage and Greece. The underlying idea clearly was that of a historical marker and of an extended *lustrum* or periodic occasion for purification; the regular Roman *lustrum*, which also marked the election of the censors, was every five years. Accordingly, the ritual centered on the gods of the Underworld, Dis (Pluto) and Proserpina, who had to be propitiated in various ways.

The changes that Augustus made were significant. Characteristically, they began with the choice of an expert, Ateius Capito, to design the new format and, just as characteristically, they aimed at widespread participation, as torches, sulfur, and asphalt were distributed to the entire free population of Rome. As for the ritual itself, its expiatory and retrospective function was complemented with a forward-looking orientation: the festival marked both an end and a beginning. The war with the Parthians had been settled, internal stability had returned, and the newly passed legislation on family and moral life, along with the ongoing rebuilding of Rome, pointed to a promising future; this latter aspect is the central theme of the hymn Horace wrote for the occasion (*Carmen Saeculare*). Accordingly, the Underworld gods disappeared from the ritual altogether and were replaced with more beneficent deities: the Fates (Moirai), goddesses of Childbirth (Eilithyai), and the Earth Mother (Terra Mater). The sacrifices to them were still made at night, as they had been for Dis and Proserpina. But, in line with the festival's new dimension, there now were sacrifices on each day, too: to Iuppiter Optimus Maximus, to Iuno Regina (both on the Capitoline), and to Apollo at his new site on the Palatine. As can be seen from the names of some of the deities, another characteristic of the festival, and of its ritual, is that it combined both Latin and Greek elements and thus typified a major strand of Augustan religion and culture.

Ever respectful of traditional customs, Augustus waited patiently for Lepidus, his former fellow triumvir, to die before assuming the office of *pontifex maximus* himself in 12 BC. Not that he was lacking earlier opportunities, as he does not fail to point out in the *Res Gestae*. And he makes some other points as well (10.2):

> I declined to be made *pontifex maximus* in the place of my colleague who was still alive, when the people offered me this priesthood which my father had held. Some years later, after the death of the man who had taken the opportunity of civil disturbance to seize it for himself, I received this priesthood, and such a multitude of citizens poured in from the whole of Italy to my election as has never been recorded at Rome before that time.

It was the wish of the people, and not a small clique, that he become *pontifex maximus* (a title, incidentally, taken over by the popes and abbreviated as P. M. in their inscriptions). Julius Caesar had held that office and, as his heir, Augustus implies that he was entitled. Indeed, all Roman emperors after Augustus automatically were made *pontifex maximus* upon their accession. Lepidus, who is not even named, is cast as a usurper, but Augustus abided by the legalities and did not push him out.

It made for an interesting situation. Lepidus was not an activist but lived in virtual exile on the Bay of Naples. Augustus studiously avoided all situations that would require the direct involvement of the *pontifex maximus*. The *ludi saeculares*, for instance, could be carried out without any role for Lepidus, but the *flamen Dialis* could not be appointed by anyone except the *pontifex maximus*, and Augustus promptly made that appointment in 11 BC. In the meantime, he engaged in a lot of adroit maneuvering and obviously exerted considerable influence and power over religious affairs. Cynics might argue, therefore, that the office really was not needed, just as the mechanisms of the traditional *res publica* were not needed because Augustus ultimately was in charge anyway. This argument, however, misapprehends both Augustan realities and mentalities. The maintenance of the *res publica* and the office of *pontifex maximus* was not simply window dressing. Augustus clearly craved that office, but held himself in check. Once he could legally occupy it with the enthusiastic consent of the governed – citizens could not mail in their ballots but had to come to Rome for elections – he promptly engaged in a burst of activity. One of them was the expansion of cultic activities to freedmen and even slaves.

Increased Participation for the Non-Elite

Population estimates of Augustan Rome vary, but the consensus is that it was upward of a million inhabitants. Many, if not most, of these were not Roman citizens but freedmen and slaves. Roman household slaves could generally expect to be freed before the end of their lives and, often, much sooner. They would attain the status of freedmen, while their descendants would become Roman citizens. We should note, therefore, that there was a constant influx into the Roman gene stream and that Rome was a vast, multi-ethnic and multi-cultural cosmopolis. Participation in the political process was restricted to Roman citizens. It made sense, therefore, to involve the large number of non-citizens in the life of civic society by other means, and for Augustus that other means was religion.

The best-documented example is his reform of the cult of the Lares at the crossroads. Fittingly enough, it demonstrates the intersection of political social, civic, and religious aspects. The overriding goal was constructively to integrate especially the lower-class dwellers in each neighborhood into the fabric of civic responsibility and the Augustan state. Typically, the way this was done was again not by imposition from above, but by mutual endeavor that built on existing practices and refocused them.

Neighborhoods (*vici*), and organizations related to them, had existed in Rome for centuries. They often were the locus for providing services like food and water just as they were a locus for political organization at the grassroots level. Cults and ceremonies pulled the neighborhood together and were centered on the shrines or altars of the Lares, who were protective deities, at the major crossroads (*compita*). Like everything else, the *vici* and their cults had their ups and downs in the last century of the republic before Augustus systematized the existing socio-religious institution in 7 BC, having laid the groundwork, probably starting in 12 BC, with the orderly division of the city into 14 regions and 265 neighborhoods. It was an important step: it marked the first time the city was actually known and is another example of the Augustan revolution that was based on power resulting from the control of knowledge.

Each individual *vicus* was led by four freedman magistrates (*vicomagistri*), whose administrative task was to assist with the food and water supply, fire fighting, and policing the streets. This constituted the beginning of an effective imperial bureaucracy and could easily have been their only dimension. The fact that it was not illustrates once more the close nexus between religion and the state. For the monuments on which we encounter the *vicomagistri* are those of the compital cult, which was reorganized at the same time. The old festivals were maintained, but two new holidays were added; on purpose, they did not coincide with a significant Augustan date but fell on days that already had a connection with the Lares' cult in the city. Augustus' role was not intrusive, but the freedmen eagerly seized on the opportunity and made the most of the recognition they were given in the new order. The altars often show them sacrificing with their attendants, the slave *vicoministri*. The images on the other sides of the altars commonly include the Lares, two animated, youthful figures who hold laurel branches or pour libations, and imperial emblems such as the oaken wreath, a symbol of saving the citizens. Some show Augustus and members of his family or a *Genius*, the representation of male life force, but while it is true that the Lares now were styled "Lares of Augustus" hardly any of the altars display the *Genius* of Augustus. There was no mandate from above to do so, and the sculptural decoration of the altars is a good reflection of the dynamic that shaped the cult. Each altar is different; certain key motifs recur, often in competition with other altars. There is tremendous pride in self-representation coupled with a display of loyalty to the new order that made this possible. In other words, there is no standardization, and that was another reason for the cult's vitality.

At the same time, the cult brought Augustus into each neighborhood in both stone and actuality. We know that he visited many of them and gifts were exchanged. The cult fostered cohesion, and Augustus, a single patron instead of the former many, provided another unifying dimension. The impact of the cult went beyond the city's boundaries: it showed the denizens of the Roman empire how a multi-ethnic constituency could come together and that all social classes now could become participants in a shared enterprise. We will see similar trends in the practice of the imperial cult in the provinces (see next section).

Another successful institution whose membership was composed of wealthy freedmen was the *Augustales*. These were members of newly created collegial associations in Italy and the western provinces in particular whose function was to take care of the cult of Augustus. Not being citizens, they could not aspire to membership of the governing classes in their towns, but their participation was sorely needed to help out with financing community projects, including buildings. Hence religion functioned once more as a means to give them status and recognition. As in the case of the *vicomagistri* in Rome, the *Augustales* were not priests and their functions were far broader than cultic. Another typical aspect is that the institution did not operate on Augustus' directives. Instead, the Augustan system simply provided opportunities that were overdue. The response was overwhelming and often resulted in a competition between towns in terms of buildings and benefactions, just as there was competition between the *vici* in Rome; this far more broadly based competition replaced the temple-building competition of the Roman nobility (see chapter 5) and is another example of the nobility's loss of exclusive control. By the mechanism of cult an important social order, freedmen, was given a conspicuous and active role in the Augustan order, which thereby was strengthened. It is mutual processes like these that provided the stability of the *pax Augusta*, and religion was a major arena.

The Divinity of Augustus and the Imperial Cult

When the senate bestowed the title "Augustus" on Octavian in January, 27 BC, it marked the temporary culmination of developments that had been underway from the start of his career. Being a mere 18 years old at the time of Caesar's death and having no political or military résumé, Octavian literally had to hitch his star to Julius Caesar's: a comet appeared in the summer of 44 BC and Octavian saw to its interpretation as the soul of Caesar ascending to divinity. The star was subsequently affixed to all representations of Caesar, including coins. Caesar now was a *divus*, which made his adoptive son *divi filius*, son of the divine, and the letters DF became part of his name wherever it appeared, in inscriptions and on the coinage in particular. Later that year, Octavian openly announced that he "aspired to the honors of his father" (Cic. *Ad Att.* 16.15.13), though certainly not by having his life cut short. But the construction of his divine aura was deliberate and steady, and marked by a variety of milestones. To list only the most important: grant of the sacrosanctity of tribunes; libations decreed by the senate to his *Genius* before private banquets; membership in all major priestly colleges; Italy and the west swearing a sacred oath of allegiance in his battle against Antony; dedication of the temple of Divus Julius in the Roman Forum; insertion of his name into the oldest Roman prayer hymn (cf. *Res Gestae* 10.1); omens, starting at his birth, and stories of Apollo being his real father (Suet. *Augustus* 94). The appellation "Augustus" ratified and enhanced his placement into a sacred context because, as Dio (53.16.8) notes, it designated him as someone "more than human, for all the most honored and sacred things are called *augusta*." The trend then accelerated; the poets, for instance, likened Augustus to a god or called him a god outright (Ovid did so, especially from exile: *Trist.* 2.54, 3.1.34, 4.4.20; *Pont.* 1.2.97). In the arts, he continued to be linked with Caesar's apotheosis, as, for example, on the so-called Belvedere Altar that is today in the Vatican, and while the interior part of the newly built Pantheon included a statue of the Divine Julius Caesar, Augustus was placed in the entrance hall. Outside of Rome he began to be worshiped directly as a god. The distinction between *divus* and *deus* was no more than a semantic nicety as both appellatives were used in inscriptions.

Before we briefly survey the phenomenon, a few basic points need to be made. Emperor worship had nothing to do with belief in a personal deity who could guide one to eternal salvation. To be sure, a grateful populace in Italy and around the Mediterranean could easily regard Augustus as a savior from decades of turmoil, and for them he was *praesens deus*, a god who was present rather than dwelling in a far-away heavenly abode. He was a deity related to order, law, and right, very much like the deity of what Robert Bellah (1967) has called "the American civil religion," a concept that goes back to Jefferson, Washington, and others and bears no relation to sectarian agendas. And, as for the United States, the Roman emperor's task was to find *e pluribus unum*, that is, to identify some issues, values, institutions, and emblems that would give his vast and diverse constituency some sense of unity. We are back to the theme of Roman religion serving as a means for cohesiveness, and the cult of Augustus became its imperial variant. The empire now was the Roman, and improved, version of Alexander's *oikoumene*; it is fitting that the term "ecumenical" today is operative mostly in the area of religion.

In the east, the imperial cult was the natural successor to the cults of the Hellenistic rulers. At the provincial level, permission was required from Rome, and Augustus authorized a joint cult of the Divine Julius and the goddess Roma for Roman citizens at Ephesus and Nicaea, and of himself and the goddess Roma for non-citizens in Pergamum and Nicomedia. Far more numerous were the municipal cults in his honor which did not need formal authorization. The reasons for them ran the usual gamut: gratitude for tax relief, peace, and liberty; show of loyalty especially on the part of those cities that had sided with Antony; and demonstration of local pride. This last element in particular again led to competition with other cities, not just in the same province, but throughout the Augustan *oikoumene*; the city of Mytilene on the island of Lesbos, for instance, in 27 BC sent ambassadors as far as Spain to advertise the exceptional honors it had voted to Augustus. In the individual cities, much of the impetus came from the Romanophile local aristocracies that were the agent of "Romanization" throughout the empire. It implied anything but standardization, but was a constant work in progress, and the cult of the emperor was part of that. Besides the basic distinction, inherited from the previous ruler cult, of making sacrifices not *to* Augustus, but *for* him to the gods, there were nuances like granting him honors "like a god" – in Greek there was no real equivalent to *divus*, nor was Augustus called a god (*theos*) outright in the provincial cults. In most of the municipal cults he was, but when he shared a temple with another deity or more, care was taken not to represent him as the gods' equal. These are only a few examples of the many variations that kept the cult vital rather than routine.

As in so many other ways, things were different in the western provinces. There was no indigenous tradition there and hence the two provincial cults, centered at Lugdunum (Lyon) and Cologne, were established almost twenty years after their eastern counterparts, and through the action of the Roman government at that. Loyalty and security in these areas were the main issues. Municipal cults did not wait that long and flourished especially in Spain. Even in many of these we find a strong military ethos, which is yet more obvious in the establishment of altars to Augustus by Roman commanders from the northwest corner of Spain to the Elbe. But there were other variations, such as a cult for the *numen* of Augustus at Narbo, which was supervised by a body of three knights and three freedmen, and at Forum Clodii in northern Italy where the inscription relating to the cult makes it plain that worship of the emperor's divinity (*numen*) was the same as worshiping him directly as a god.

It has often been noted that one of the legacies of Augustus was a much more unified empire. Religion and his cult played a major part because they allowed for many outlets, variations, and autonomous responses that nonetheless had a central focus instead of being centrifugal.

FURTHER READING

As for the study of the religion in the republic, Wissowa (1912) is still the basic handbook for much relevant source material relating to the Augustan period in Rome and Italy. The scope of Beard et al. (1998) is much more interpretive and takes into account the great amount of new material since Wissowa; volume 2 offers an excellent collection of sources, all translated into English, from texts, inscriptions, art, and architecture. J. Liebeschuetz (1979: 55–100) is fundamental; so is Rüpke's study (1995a) of the role of the calendars. For the larger perspective on the Augustan "cultural revolution" of which religion is a part see Wallace-Hadrill (2005); similarly, for the social changes in the Mediterranean world, Purcell (2005). The wider historical and cultural context is delineated by Galinsky (1996) and, with emphasis on art and architecture, Zanker (1987 [1988]); Kienast (1999) is a useful digest of the scholarship on all aspects of the Augustan period, including religion. Favro (1996, cf. 2005) offers a detailed discussion of Augustus' reorganization and rebuilding of Rome; compare, with a focus on temples, Stamper (2005: 105–29). A good recent take on the Secular Games is Feeney (1998: 28–38). On the compital cult see now Lott (2004), and for the *Augustales*, Ostrow (1990) and Abramenko (1993). Scheid (2005a) is essential for a definition of Augustus' religious policy. For the cult of Augustus, Price (1984), Fishwick (1987, 1992), and Gradel (2002) are basic while Ando (2000) provides the larger panorama. The *Res Gestae* of Augustus is quoted from the 1967 edition of Brunt and Moore, which also has an excellent commentary.

CHAPTER SEVEN

Religions and the Integration of Cities in the Empire in the Second Century AD: The Creation of a Common Religious Language

William Van Andringa

An inscription discovered in 1973 in the city wall of Lugo (Léon), capital of a *conventus* of northwest Galicia, reveals much about the religious situation in the empire in the Severan era: "To the divine powers of the Augusti, Juno Regina, Venus Victrix, Africa Caelestis, Frugifer, Augusta Emerita and the Lares of the Callaeciae, Saturninus, freedman of Augustus" (*Inscripciones romanas de Galicia 2, Provincia de Lugo*, 23; *AE* 1985, 494; 1990, 939). As Le Roux demonstrated, the status of Saturninus as well as the divinities invoked are enough to explain that the patronage of the gods mentioned is linked to the administrative career of an imperial freedman connected to Africa and called on to serve in Lusitania and Galicia, the hierarchy being a religious one (*AE* 1980, 595 bis) rather than reflecting the career itself. At the beginning of the text, the imperial *numina* appear as the normal and inevitable religious representations of the reigning power: here, the successive Augusti, protectors of the freedman, and Juno Regina, the divine evocation of Julia Domna as well as Venus Victrix, bring to mind the emperor, guarantor of the imperial system. For their part, Africa Caelestis, Frugifer, and the Lares of the Callaeciae demonstrate the continuing existence, several centuries after the conquest of Africa, of divinities of provincial origin, some of which, among them Caelestis, the goddess of Carthage, even had temples in Rome. The name of the city Augusta Emerita in this list may seem unusual, but it was normal religious custom at the time to associate cities or groups of people with the gods and imperial power within the sphere of the divine.

The first thing we learn from this valuable text, therefore, is that, in this period, the large number of provincial and Roman deities allowed for various divine combinations. Imperial cults, Roman gods, and local gods all guaranteed a fine network of protection that could be adapted to any situation and accrued religious insurance, as Robin Lane Fox rightly said (1986). Saturninus' devotion evokes another characteristic typical of the religion of the imperial era: the religious language of rites performed at the altar not only helped to fight against or to prevent life's daily worries, but also played a decisive role in one's perception of the world. Sacrificing to or for the emperor was a means of recognizing that peace and the preservation of one's city were directly linked to the sovereign's ability to accomplish his difficult task as head of the empire. It was also a recognition of the established order, guaranteed by an institutionalized hierarchy of gods: Iuppiter Optimus Maximus, even though not mentioned in the Lugo text, assisted by the emperor, who possessed powers beyond that of ordinary men, made it possible for the Roman world and its gods to exist. Everyone was conscious of this during the time of the *pax Romana*. Thus, in a way, the ceremony organized by Saturninus was a means of placing his administrative activities and life under the tight and benevolent yoke of divine patronage, composed of poliad or local deities (the great goddess of Carthage and the Lares of the *conventus* of Braga and Lugo) encountered during his travels and the gods who represented Roman order. All in all, city cults, cults representing the state and Roman power as established in the world, though permutated in a thousand ways in reflection of the myriad communities that formed the structure of the empire, dominated the religious landscape of the empire in the second century AD.

Taking this into consideration, it is difficult to accept the classification adopted since Jules Toutain, in which Roman gods are distinguished from local gods and "oriental" gods. If this last concept has now been challenged (Belayche 2000; Bonnet et al. 2006), the distinction between Roman and indigenous cults, which is difficult to characterize, fails to take note of the integration of the cities and provincial populations in the empire as a whole. As the imperial government rested on an amalgam of autonomous cities, the starting point is the creation of religious constructs defined by each city in relation to its specific history and the political dialogue it had established with Rome. With time and under the effect of the *pax Romana*, the spread of divine powers of universal character (Iuppiter Optimus Maximus, Magna Mater, the deified emperor or his *numen*, etc.) and the call on the city gods to safeguard the emperor and the empire contributed to the appearance of a common religious language. A common religious language and a variety of pantheons specific to each community – this is how one can define religion in the Roman empire beginning in the second century AD.

Provincial Particulars and Integration: The Diversity of the Pantheons

It is never easy to board a moving train. Under Trajan, the imperial system had been in existence for over a century and – by a process of integration – was adapted to historical, political, and cultural contexts which varied extremely from one end of the empire to the other. The cities of Greece and Asia Minor had retained their civic pantheons into the imperial era. When, under Trajan, Dio of Prusa (*Speeches* 39.8) praises the gods of his city, Nicaea, he mentions the old, ancestral gods, whose main role, so he tells us, is to ensure concord within the community: "I therefore pray to Dionysus, first ancestor of this city, Hercules, founder of this town, Zeus Polieus, Athena, Aphrodite Philia, Homonoia, Nemesis and the other gods." In the same way, Athena and Artemis remained, unchanged, the great patron goddesses of Athens and Ephesus. Indeed, the Greek and Roman gods were part of the same family and the same religious culture, as the texts sometimes state: a letter addressed by Trajan Decius to the Carian city of Aphrodisias specifies that the close links tying Aphrodisias to Rome find their justification in their shared religious tradition (J. Reynolds 1982). Was not Aphrodite/Venus, from whom the city took its name, also the mother of Aeneas, founder of Rome?

It is true that the foundation of colonies under Caesar and Augustus had sometimes led to significant changes: for example, the goddess of Calydon, Artemis Laphria, whose temple stood on the city's acropolis, was moved to the other side of the Strait of Corinth to the colony of Patras. However, these interventions were only occasional and related to the organization of the provincial system at the very beginning of the empire – they were certainly no longer undertaken in the second century AD. On the other hand, the public spaces and main sanctuaries of the Greek cities were progressively encroached on, if not taken over, by cults and images representing the emperor and the imperial family, as seen in the case of the 136 statues of Hadrian erected in the sanctuary of Zeus at the Olympieion of Athens (Alcock 1993). It is obvious that, in these regions, Rome's sway over local religion was very different from that it had in the west, taking the form of cults that connected imperial power with the traditional civic cults through subtle combinations (Price 1984). In a religion characterized by a multiplicity of gods and divine representations (Petronius 17.5; Seneca, *Naturales quaestiones* 2.5), it was only logical that the integration of religious forms relating to imperial power also took the form, as is normal for polytheistic religions, of multiple images and religious manifestations.

The same can be said for Egypt, which had also preserved its ancestral sanctuaries and religious organization (Frankfurter 1998a; Willems and Clarysse 2000). Under the empire, sacred animals continued to be mummified and buried according to the funeral rites of the old kings. Titus was even present at the enthronement of a new Apis bull in AD 70 (Suet. *Titus* 5). Suetonius reports that he wore a royal diadem for the occasion in accordance with the traditional rites of the Egyptian religion, though it caused great consternation among the Romans. Despite the undeniable persistence of traditional rites, Kaper and others (e.g. Frankfurter 1998a) have brought to light changes which indicate that the Egyptian gods, like the other gods integrated in the empire, were in step with their times, in which Rome dominated: for example, one notes the importance which Serapis came to have alongside Isis in Egypt – an association well known in the rest of the empire, notably in Greece and Italy, but less so in Egypt itself, where tradition normally associated Osiris with Isis. In the same way, the success in Egypt of the cults of Bes and Harpocrates, the son of Isis, seems to echo that of these gods in numerous other imperial provinces. It must also not be forgotten that, in Egypt as elsewhere, religious life was pervaded by feasts organized in honor of the emperor. In one example, from Apollinopolis Heptakomia, the accession of Hadrian to the imperial throne resulted in sacrifices and processions coupled with a play, of which part of the text survives (*Papyrus Gissensis* 3). In it, Phoebus announced to the *demos* of Apollinopolis the new sovereign's accession to the empire!

One must admit that, in the western provinces, religious integration took other forms. In Asia Minor, Greece, or the Greek cities of Egypt, the gods already wore togas and were conversant with civic life; in the west, the gods changed and adapted in response to the changes imposed by the spread of the civic system (Van Andringa 2002). There were exceptions: in Italy or in provinces long since conquered, such as Baetica, where people had been Roman for some time, the cults, despite a variety which reflected the history of each community, were all Roman. Consider what we find as revealed by the chance discovery of inscriptions of various periods: Hercules, Iuppiter Optimus Maximus, and Pietas Augusta at *Tucci*; Diana, Venus, Libertas Augusta, Mars Augustus, and the Lares Augustorum at *Singili Barba*; Apollo and Aesculapius Augustus – the two healing deities – in the company of *Fons divina* and the *Genius municipi* at *Nescania*; Iuppiter Optimus Maximus and Victoria Augusta at Cortijo del Tajo; Bonus Eventus, Mars, and Pietas at *Astigi*. The impression given is no different in one of the cities of the Levant, again in Hispania: Aesculapius Augustus, Isis Pelagia, Mars Augustus, Mercurius Augustus, the Lares Augusti, and Diana Maxima, the patron goddess of the city mentioned by Pliny (*Nat.* 16.216), rule over Saguntum. The contrast with other regions of Hispania only recently conquered and pacified is striking, as in the case of the northwest, integrated into the empire under Augustus, which had pantheons composed mainly of indigenous gods (Tranoy 1981): at Lugo, it is true that inscriptions of the second and third centuries mention Iuppiter Optimus Maximus, but most of the texts refer to Lahus Paraliomegus, Poemana, Rea, Rego, and Veroca (or Verora) in the city and, in the country, to Bandua Boleccus, Cohvetena, or rather peculiar Lares, because these, unlike those in Rome, guarded not the crossroads (*Lares Compitales*), but roads (*Lares Viales*).

These colorful pantheons are the result of communal processes triggered by the organization of the indigenous peoples into cities. In several regions, from north Africa to Britannia and the frontier regions along the Rhine–Danube axis, municipalization was the catalyst for the progressive recomposing of the religious systems already in place. With the autonomy of the cities defined and framed by Rome, it is easy to understand that the changes in question, encouraged by the cities themselves, hinged on the religious expressions of Roman power, the inevitable point of reference. Integration was inseparable from control of the provinces, as noted by Price.

In fact, from the first century on, the town centers of the new *civitates* developed around tripartite forums which included a temple dedicated to Augustus or the imperial family, very frequently with a time-lag between the planning of the urban network, which set aside a location for the forum, and the actual construction of the monument by local benefactors. These urban innovations paralleled an archi-tectural reconsideration of the rural sanctuaries, often more ancient, as can be seen in the particular architecture of the Romano-Celtic temples specific to the provinces of the northwest. This plan, frequently encountered at archaeological sites and pre-senting a portico surrounding a *cella*, does not correspond to any known Celtic model and appears, indeed, to have been created during this period (Derks 1998; Van Andringa 2002).

The changes noted in the rites performed are similar; notwithstanding the occa-sional local peculiarity, Roman forms of animal sacrifice gradually took over. Martin Henig, in an evocative passage, has reconstructed the ceremony performed at a temple in the province of Britannia (Henig 1984): a procession penetrates into the sanctuary, bringing the animals for sacrifice, invariably the three main domestic species (oxen, sheep, pigs); the doors of the temple are open, revealing the silhouette of the cult statue, carved from local limestone; the Latin used in the prayer is a bit odd and the divinity has a local epithet, but one uses the *patera* and *oinochoe* for the *praefatio*, filled with wine from Gaul or Spain. Inside the sanctuary, vows are uttered, others fulfilled in the form of sacrifice and offerings. Such a scene is, of course, fictional – we do not possess any description of a ceremony – but the architectural settings, as well as the acts described, are duly attested by the archaeological docu-mentation. Moreover, it must be noted that, as regards the very forms of the cults, the image presented is not that far off the one given by Pliny the Younger in rela-tion to the sanctuary of Ceres on his property (*Epist.* 9.39).

This rearrangement of religious space took place in parallel to the transformation of the gods themselves via the *interpretatio romana*. This process of naturalizing indigenous divinities which had taken on Roman names has its origins in similarities noted between the physiognomy or sphere of action of the gods in question. As demonstrated by the translations of Caesar and Tacitus of certain Gallic or Germanic divinities which they describe, the choices regarding divine similarities could be entirely personal (Caesar, *Bellum Gallicum* 6.17; Tac. *Germania* 43). Nevertheless, epigraphic records of the Treveri or the Riedones (Gallia Belgica and Lugdunensis) demonstrate that the process in question became official once it had been used for the city's public cults (Scheid 1991; Van Andringa 2002). Thus, the Treveri's ancient tribal divinity became Lenus Mars, his cult inserted into the city's calendar. The attribution of a flaminate and the construction, during the first century AD, of a large temple 500 meters outside the city crowned the cult's transformation.

At Rennes, inscriptions from the reign of Hadrian show that there was a temple dedicated to Mars Mullo either in the city or just outside it (*AE* 1969/70, 405a–c). It seems likely that the naturalization of the ancient local divinity (his name appears in the patronage of three out of four *pagi*) took place during the first century AD, perhaps in relation to the city's obtaining the *ius Latinum*. The composite name, in which the indigenous epithet Mullo is connected with the Roman theonym, should not deceive us: this was no hybrid deity, half Roman and half Gallic – religious lan-guage, on the contrary, is very precise – but Lenus Mars or Mars Mullo were muni-cipal deities whose powers were specific to the regions in question. The process that took place was decisive, especially once an indigenous divinity adopted a Roman name.

There was no fusion or syncretism or simple dressing up – these gods changed both names and identities.

Of course, many divinities retained their local names, either because there was no Roman equivalent – one thinks notably of the god bearing stag antlers, named Cernunnos, found on a bas-relief from Paris, whose image is well known from the Celtic provinces – or because the god in question had a topical and local dimension. In the city of the Convenae, one finds at least 60 gods with indigenous names, a diversity which, in the end, reflected the fragmentary nature of the lands and communities. One encounters a similar situation in the comparably mountainous regions of Galicia, which teemed with indigenous divinities very frequently flanked by Jupiter the omnipotent, father of the gods. Sometimes, the aura of these gods stretched well beyond the frontiers of the city, as seen in the example from the Germanic provinces of the goddess Sunuxal, studied by Spickermann (2001: 36). She possessed an important temple at Kornelimünster, yet her cult is also attested at Bonn, Cologne, and other locations. Such a widespread presence is most certainly explained by the goddess's well-known powers, honored by Roman citizens throughout the second and third centuries AD. Of course, one must not forget that similar processes took place in the Greek east – one thinks in particular of the indigenous gods specific to the rural zones of inner Asia Minor.

In such a context – that of specific pantheons of the imperial era adapted to the history of each of the thousands of cities which comprised the empire – it is obvious that the classification formerly suggested by Toutain, which distinguished indigenous gods from the Roman and "oriental" gods, loses its probative character. The very rigidity of such categories fails to take account of the inner evolution of cities and people, ultimately masking the harmony that these gods, together, were meant to represent for each community at any given time. Rather than focusing on "indigenous" or "Roman" gods, the point was to worship familiar gods and cults whose power was guaranteed by municipal investiture, gods who also established a connection with Rome and were adapted to their times, the situation of individuals and their place in society. This explains the naturalization of gods in numerous cities, which simultaneously allowed them to integrate and keep in step with their times. This also explains the continuity – never denied – of sanctuaries as powerful and wealthy as the Serapeum of Alexandria, the sacred wood of Apollo at Daphne (Antioch), or again the temple of Aesculapius at Pergamum.

Religious Autonomy and Empire: Rapprochement with Rome

The great variety of situations was in large part due to the system of cultic organization overseen by the autonomous city. Each city has its religion, Cicero said, and we have our own (Cic. *Pro Flacco* 69). The notion still held true for the imperial era, notwithstanding the progressive rapprochement of the empire's communities with Rome. Thus, so-called Roman tolerance was in fact simply due to an autonomy defined and controlled by Rome. Indeed, the Romans were no more tolerant than anyone else, but a city, like any other autonomous community, by definition determined its own cults and religious calendar. This was particularly true of peregrine cities, where cultic sites were not managed according to Roman sacred law (Pliny, *Epist.* 10.50). The notion of religious autonomy was equally valid for the colonies, even if, as the altar regulations at Narbonne or Salona testify, the foundation and management of cultic sites followed Roman rules. If, indeed, we believe one of the rare surviving municipal laws (M. Crawford 1996: no. 25), from Urso in Baetica, the document issued at the foundation of a colony only foresaw, in principle, the establishment of a cult of the Capitoline triad: the adoption of the great gods of the Roman state as patron gods of all Roman communities followed on logically (Beard et al. 1998). As regards all other cults, the authorities had free choice, guided as much by the basic criteria of ancient tradition as by the community's specific needs.

It is no surprise, therefore, to see that, in the provinces of Africa, most of the Capitolia were constructed in the second and the beginning of the third centuries AD, the period when most of the cities were promoted to the status of *municipium* or colony. At Sabratha, the successive procurement of the status of *municipium* and then colony was further sanctioned by the construction of an imposing Capitolium in the monumental center that already contained a temple to Liber Pater and Serapis. At Cuicul (Djemila), it seems that the Capitolium was built at the time of the colony's foundation, under Nerva or Trajan. Nevertheless, the link between legal promotion and the implantation of a cult was not automatic. Thus, at Thugga, the Capitolium was consecrated under Marcus Aurelius by both the *pagus* (rural district) and the *civitas*, even though the city was still attached to the colony of Carthage. However, this was probably undertaken in response to the cult of the Capitoline triad, long established in the colony of Carthage, at a time when Thugga was about to obtain the status of an autonomous city.

On the other hand, it is obvious that *municipia* and colonies, once promoted, operated publicly like Roman communities. That was when cults which further ratified the institutional rapprochement with Rome established themselves in the city, as it can be seen by the statues erected in the forum of Cuicul. The 20 effigies identified from the second century AD are all representations of the emperor or civic concord: the colony lived in step with Roman power. One also wonders if these institutional transformations were not sometimes at the root of the abandonment of certain practices that were no longer adapted to the new communal reality. Thus, archae-ologists have noted that Sabratha's tophet ceased to be active toward the end of the first century AD. At Vertault in Gaul, the sacrifice of horses and dogs attested at a suburban cultic site appears to cease around the middle of the first century AD, perhaps in connection with the development of the nearby city that is known to have obtained the status of *vicus*.

The provincial cities' ongoing and ever more frequent promotion undeniably played an important role in the Romanization of cults. In the beginning, the generalization of the *ius Latinum* – in Gaul and Hispania, this phenomenon took place during the first century AD – made it possible to frame religious changes within municipal struc-tures. Rapprochement with Rome and its cults was later reinforced by numerous pro-motional policies throughout the second century AD, notably under the Antonines and Severans. It is in the very specific context of municipalization that the cult of Iuppiter Optimus Maximus spread through the western world. As god of public oaths, he was the appropriate guarantor of the cities that had become local republics. At Chaves (Aqua Flavia) in Hispania Citerior, he was even known as Jupiter of the Municipium (*Iuppiter municipalis*, *AE* 1992, 992). This civic Jupiter provided also the ideal means for any one community that wanted to express its political rapprochement with Rome.

It is in this same context of political rapprochement with Rome that the so-called "oriental" cults established themselves, as these were the Roman forms of the cults. The spread of the cult of Magna Mater throughout the west from AD 160 onward testifies to this phenomenon. Yet the instigation for this came rather from Rome, which instituted the rite of the *taurobolium* for the security of the empire. The *taurobolium* of Lyon, dated December 9, 160, actually commemorates the investiture of a local priest by the quindecemviral college of Rome (*CIL* 13.1751). Therefore, this was no response to the attraction of a new, "oriental" cult, but a partaking in a common interest, that of the safeguarding of the empire, through the installation of a cult defined in Rome itself. The growing success of the cult of Mithras at this time had nothing to do with any public impulse in Rome or the cities, but rather fell within the framework of a broadening of religious options typical of polytheism. The installation of a *mithraeum* in the enclosure of the Altbachtal sanctuary at Trier or in the shade of the enclosure wall of the great temple of the *vicus* of Nuits-Saint-Georges also demonstrates this. In both cases, the cult openly implanted itself in the religious district of the civic group, city or *vicus*, without entering into competition with the traditional religion, which continued to be largely dominated by the great communal cults.

This was not only a question of collective behavior, as individuals could also promote these deities. A man from the provinces, once he gained Roman citizenship, embraced a new homeland – Rome – and was expected, in principle, to respect its gods. In AD 137 in Salona (Dalmatia), Iuppiter Optimus Maximus was invoked in the public square to ensure the safety of the magistrates, the members of the municipal council, the citizens of the colony, and also women and children (*CIL* 3.1933). Among the Consoranni of the province of Aquitaine, Valerius Iustus consecrated two altars in two different locations, one to Iuppiter Capitolinus, the other to Fortuna Augusta. Obviously, religious language founded on the cults of Jupiter and the emperor was enough to forge a common identity, even if the local dimension, again and necessarily, was not forgotten. In the same region, among the neighboring Convenae, a great landowner worshiped the topical gods installed on his land in a sanctuary in which Iuppiter Optimus Maximus was present: L. Pompeius Paulinianus thus made a gift of an altar to Idiatte in the sanctuary of Saint-Pé-d'Ardet for the health of his family, while another member of that family – unless the same person is concerned – consecrated a monument to Artahe, the local goddess (*CIL* 13.65, 70). Being a citizen did not mean renouncing the ancestral gods; on the contrary, piety demanded that cults be perpetuated. Thus, we see the man from Bordeaux who went to consult the Sybil of Tibur, who, though far from his homeland, had no other gods but his local goddess, Onuava (*CIL* 13.581):

I wander, never ceasing to pass through the whole world, but I am first and foremost a faithful worshiper of Onuava. I am at the ends of the earth, but the distance cannot tempt me to make my vows to another goddess. Love of the truth brought me to Tibur, but Onuava's favorable powers came with me. Thus, divine mother, far from my home-land, exiled in Italy, I address my vows and prayers to you no less.

We learn from this evolution that, as a result of the political integration of the various populations, the place of provincial communities became less and less distinct from that of truly Roman groups in the provinces – military units and the associations of Roman citizens settled in foreign lands. The calendar of the Palmyrene cohort of Dura-Europos, dated to AD 225–7, presents us with a long litany of Roman cults and imperial birthdays celebrated in the camp's enclosure (Fink et al. 1940). One expects no less of an institution of the Roman state, but it has been noted that the sanctuaries found around camps still welcomed numerous divinities, including those from the military units' own regions or whose local char-acter helped to ensure the safety of their quarters. The fort of Maryport, occupied by the Hispanian cohort along Hadrian's Wall, has produced 21 altars consecrated to Iuppiter Optimus Maximus (*RIB* 813–35), something that must be seen as bear-ing witness to official ceremonies celebrated in honor of the Roman state's great god. The other gods known in the military circles of the province of Britannia could also reflect the ethnic origins of the recruited soldiers (the goddess Syria or Astarte, Viradecthis, deity of a Romano-Celtic *pagus*). Nonetheless, one most frequently encounters local gods, such as Conventina, or those adapted to military activity, such as Epona, goddess of horsemen, as well as Iuppiter Dolichenus, Mars, Hercules, Disciplina, or Victoria, other gods directly associated with the military profession. A cohort recruited in Emesa in Syria and stationed along the Danube beginning in AD 160 brought along its own national gods as well as certain Roman gods, including Jupiter.

For the associations of Roman citizens settled throughout the empire, origin and the community to which they belonged became one and the same: the national gods were Roman (Van Andringa 2003). This can be seen in the impressive series of altars erected throughout the second century AD along the summit of Pfaffenburg, near Carnuntum, in the sanctuary of Iuppiter Optimus Maximus. These monuments commemorate ceremonies celebrated by the Roman citizens living in Carnuntum in honor of the father of the gods for the health of the reigning emperor or emperors (Piso 2003). In a Dacian sanctuary at Turda, expatriate Romans established a cult to Jupiter and Terra Mater. We have the date for the celebration of the cult of Iuppiter Optimus Maximus by the Roman citizens settled in a *vicus* of Histria on the Black Sea: December 13, the same date as that of the feast celebrated in Rome in honor of the Capitoline god. Since the very beginning of the imperial era, the status of Roman citizen also demanded the performance of the cult of the deified emperor (Cass. Dio 51.20.6–7). However, religious activities were not limited to cults which focused on politics or identity: expatriate groups, as well as the other communities, created their own religious systems, systems which took into account the activity exercised just as much as the local context. It could not happen otherwise in the paganism of the ancient world, which is why one sees *cives romani* honoring Mercury in Gaul and Frugifer in a temple of Alma in Africa.

The Roman gods took an even more important place in the background noise of the polytheistic religious diversity so well adapted, ultimately, to the imperial structure, something which affirmed the provincial communities' political rapprochement with Rome. If there were numerous combinations possible from city to city, the importance taken by Jupiter Capitolinus and the divine honors granted to the emperor and the imperial family are undeniable. At the same time, this phenomenon cannot be dismissed as banal allegiance, as these cults were the manifestation of a sincere impetus on the part of the people in question, quite simply because integration was taken for granted and meant that those in the provinces shared Rome's destiny. The safeguarding of the city was inseparably tied to that of the empire. This was the very justification used officially for Caracalla's edict of 212, which extended Roman citizenship to all free men of the empire: "I believe that I can serve the glory of the immortal gods (the Greek gods and the gods of Rome) by making all those who are part of my people participate in the cult of the gods with me. This is why I grant Roman citizenship to all the *peregrini* of the earth." Rome had become the common homeland of all (*Digesta* 50.1.33).

The Gods of the Cities and the Gods of Rome: A Shared Destiny

Let us admit right away that, even in the first half of the third century AD, it is difficult to see any sort of failure in the system so far described or even signs of this failure's approach: the immortal gods invoked by Caracalla reign supreme over the empire and still favor imperial endeavors. In the totality of the *oikoumene*, the fragmentation of divine patronage made it possible for communities and individuals to be harbored within a fine network of protection. Moreover – as it should have – piety played first and foremost an essential role in putting people's minds at rest. "I prayed to the gods on your behalf every day," we find in letters from Egypt. People continued to turn to local gods known, of course, to be powerful and capable of ensuring day-to-day stability, whether for a birth, illness, or good harvest, as can be seen from the thousands of ex-votos found in public and private sanctuaries throughout the Roman world.

Among the many examples are the numerous votive dedications found in Phrygia addressed to Zeus Alsenos, Zeus Patarenos, or Zeus Thallos (Drew-Bear et al. 1999). Sometimes, eyes are represented on these steles in such a way as to draw the god's attention, or hands are depicted palms up in the normal attitude of piety. We should note that these steles come, for the most part, from illegal excavations, which means that we lack crucial information concerning the sanctuaries themselves and the cults celebrated in them. Parallel to these testimonies from the eastern empire, one can cite for the western empire, in random order, the numerous ex-votos found at the source of the Seine, domain of the goddess Sequana, or those in the mountain sanctuaries of the Convenae. At Thibilis in Africa in the third century, every year the magistrates of the city made the 17-kilometer voyage to the cave of the god Bacax in order to leave a dedication on the wall. The numerous gods installed in the sanctuaries of the mountain Rosia Montana in Dacia near Alburnus Maior dealt in the same way with the daily worries of the people who lived in this mining district. From the numerous lead tablets found in the temples of the province of Britannia, we learn that the main concern was the theft of personal property – a tunic, a purse, etc. However, limiting the religious phenomenon to this type of activity would obscure the second essential function of religion in the Roman world.

The gods, owing to their patronage of all types of things, places, activities, or human groups, played an essential role in the communal definition of societies and power relations as established within the city and between cities. That is already the gist of the speech by Dio of Prusa quoted above, given near the end of the first century AD for the gods of Nicaea. Essentially, it was just as important to ensure one's own preservation, or that of one's household, through repeated vows to the local gods as it was to participate in ceremonies or sacrifices whose goal was to preserve civic concord. One understands, then, how the ever-increasing integration of provincial communities in the empire came to be translated into an active participation in cults that established a link with the imperial power. The accounts of the Capitolium of Arsinoe for the period of January to June 215 reveal that the ceremonies celebrated focused primarily on imperial birthdays and victories. Of course, one knows that, from the beginning of the imperial era, attachment to the empire was symbolized in the provinces by the consecration of altars to Rome and Augustus as well as celebration of annual vows for the emperor (Tac. *Agricola* 21; Pliny *Epist.* 10.35–6, 101–2). However, after the passing of a few generations, the meaning of these cults had evolved in step with the Romanization of the people and institutions. In the second century and well into the third century, the increasing number of altars erected for the health of the emperor demonstrates that the annual official ritual of January 3, during which vows were made for the health of the emperor, was extended through frequent and standardized acts of piety that involved the greater part of the population. A profound conviction that the destiny of the empire, which linked Rome with the provincial cities and depended on the ability of the emperor to take on his enormous task, took its place beside official acts of piety. Was the emperor not known as savior of the world, the *sôter tou kosmou*, in the cities of the eastern empire and as the *conservator orbis* in the west?

The future and preservation of the city depended directly on the peace that the sovereign imposed on the earth – this is what the numerous dedications and sacrifices made to the gods for the health of the emperor indicate. At Heliopolis in the province of Syria, Moralee counted 13 dedications to Jupiter Heliopolitanus for the health of the emperor from the time of Hadrian to that of Gordian III (Moralee 2004). Each time, individuals acting on their own behalf signed the documents, such as the plumber (*plumbarius*) who had a group of statues erected for the health of the emperor that included Sol, Luna, and Victoria, Sol and Luna revealing the extent of the world over which peace was guaranteed by the imperial victories. During the same period, at Dura-Europos on the eastern limits of the empire, international gods such as Adonis, Zeus, and Artemis were invoked just as frequently as the local Aphlad and Azzanathkona, again for the health of the emperor. At Gerasa, at least 50 dedications for the health of the emperor can be found from the second century AD, some of which, in a revealing way, link the emperors' health with the concord of the people. Also beginning in the second century, African populations started to invoke the gods for the health of the emperor (Smadja 1986). The safety of the world and the preservation of the city: these were the major questions which preoccupied provincial communities at a time when political integration had joined the destiny of Rome with that of the provincial populations.

All communities were involved, as can be seen from the altars erected on Mount Pfaffenberg throughout the second century and at the beginning of the third century by the Roman citizens settled in Carnuntum. In Germania, most of the public and private dedications made to the gods from the middle of the second century AD onward contain the abbreviation *in h(onorem) d(omus) d(ivinae)*. The Divine House and the gods – thus piety located individuals within the established world. Again during the same period, the stage of the theater of Belginum-Wederath, *vicus* of the Treveri, was inaugurated with a joint invocation of the *domus divina*, the god Cretus and the *Genius* of the *pagus*: imperial power, the local god, and the *Genius* of the district – the inaugural sacrifice drew the precise institutional limits of the community at a specific moment in its history. The formulae were many and varied, as witnessed by the use of different phrases linked to local customs in the provinces of Gaul: among the Bituriges Cubi, imperial power was invoked in the form of the divine power (*numen*) of Augustus; the Aedui preferred to invoke Augustus in religious dedications. Such invocations appeared on most of the edifices paid for by the civic elites: arches, temples to the gods, theaters, fountains – all the monuments which defined *urbanitas* were built thanks to the prosperity of the elite and the city itself (the two were indistinguishable in ancient societies), a prosperity made possible by the emperor.

The result of provincial integration strictly defined in relation to the Roman power in Rome, the piety of this era universally demanded that people worship the gods for the emperor's sake. The populations of the empire knew that peace and happiness depended as much on divine benevolence as on the emperor's immense powers. This conception of world order resulted in the appearance and spread of peculiar monuments. In Egypt, statuettes represented the gods Horus, Bes, or Anubis in Roman military attire, following the example of cuirassed imperial statues. In the frontier provinces of Germania and eastern Gaul, columns crowned with a horseman trampling an anguipede, symbol of the triumph of civilization over barbarism, appeared throughout the region (550 are known) in cities as well as in rural domains between, essentially, AD 170 and 240. At a time when the Roman empire was encountering its first problems along the borders, such monuments clearly spelled out the communities' desire to encourage imperial victories and the health of the empire with which they were connected.

Conclusion

The network of divine patronage and deified imperial power, the city and the empire: the forms of religion which gradually fell into place as communities became municipalized and Roman citizenship spread reflected the permanent need to live with the times, when autonomous cities were completely integrated into the empire. The people of the provinces progressively emerged from submission to become conquerors, sharing this with the local gods. Of course, the great homeland, Rome, did not substitute itself for the local one as Roman citizenship became more widespread; however, the fact of gradually belonging to both homelands clearly led individuals as well as communities to share in Rome's destiny. This is how the cults of the cities came to be directly associated with cults which served to support the sovereign in his task of governing. The religious language constructed around this was not merely one of convenience; on the contrary, it enabled a collective and regular definition of the framework in which one lived, putting men in phase with the times – that of a pacified and civilized Empire. This established order, which depended as much on divine benevolence as on imperial victories, would be increasingly challenged by the troubles of the third century and the end of the *pax Romana*. As imperial power was gradually challenged by its inability to guarantee the security of the empire, the institutionalized piety that required that sacrifices be made to the gods on behalf of the emperor inevitably lost touch with reality.

FURTHER READING

The numerous recent works concerning the integration of the provinces in the empire (e.g. Le Roux 1998; Sartre 1997) have rendered the classifications adopted by Toutain (1907–20) obsolete, and allow an analysis of the cults of the empire in the second century from the point of view of municipalization and the relations established between the autonomous cities and the central Roman power (Scheid 1991; Beard et al. 1998; Van Andringa 2002). In this religious language, which made it possible to transcribe institutionalized forms of power within and without the city, the divine honor given to the emperor and to the imperial family played an essential and unifying role (Fishwick 1987–2004; Price 1984; Moralee 2004). Numerous regional studies also attest the variety of religious situations encountered in the cities in the second century (Alcock 1993; Belayche 2001; Derks 1998; Frankfurter 1998a; Henig 1984; Le Roux 1995; Spickermann 2003; Tranoy 1981; Van Andringa 2000, 2002; Willems and Clarysse 2000; etc.).

(trans. Tamar Nelson)

CHAPTER EIGHT

Old Religions Transformed: Religions and Religious Policy from Decius to Constantine

Hartmut Leppin

The epoch from the death of Alexander Severus (235) until the acclamation of Diocletian (284) has often been deemed as being a time of imperial crisis. In recent times, however, the concept of a general third-century crisis has been differentiated and modified (Strobel 1993; Witschel 1999). But one should not go too far: there were a lot of symptoms of crisis and the corresponding feeling was widely spread among the population. One of the most visible was the fact that most emperors only remained on the throne for a few years, if not months, often being deposed (and killed) by usurpers or in action. Even some inner regions of the empire experienced barbarian incursions. In many provinces prosperity declined, and the economy became less stable.

Contemporaries were predisposed to decode any crisis in religious terms. The mercy of the gods (or God) had to be regained somehow. Some people strove to practice the old cults with more care; others sought a more personal contact with the gods; many went both ways. These developments obviously had an immediate impact on the history of Christianity and paganism in the third century.

The religious history of those years seems to be marked by a clear and simple development: the Christian religion, which had been oppressed and persecuted in the beginning, namely by Decius, Valerian, and Diocletian, triumphs over paganism; Constantine's conversion brings about the adoption of Christianity as the religion of the Roman empire. If we follow this line, we fall victim to the Christian interpretation of history with its antagonistic concept of "true" and "false" religions. But history is more complex.

Paganism is a Judeo-Christian notion, which subsumes a lot of religious manifestations and ideas under one name: the monotheistic philosophy of some intellectuals as well as the *polis* religion, magic rituals as well as the veneration of Isis – and this list could be continued at length (Leppin 2004). Even Christianity was by no means homogeneous; there had always been intense competition between divergent doctrines and conflicting leaders; the practices and doctrines could be contradictory, even within a single town, although there was relatively intense communication between the different Christian groups.

To make things even more complex, there also were a number of common concepts between "paganism" and "Christianity," which were deeply rooted in the *Zeitgeist*. Both groups accepted the importance of miracles as signs of godly intervention; both admired holy men; many people believed in the existence of the soul after death. Monotheism itself was by no means limited to Jews or Christians, even though the exclusive, personal god had special importance for Christians. Common to all groups was the idea that the emperor bore responsibility for the well-being of his empire, which could only be guaranteed by the support of the gods. This idea was particularly powerful for an epoch in which many people felt they were living through difficult times.

An Empire of Religious Variety

Traditional religious practices met two main challenges in the third century: the challenge of Christianity and of other new, universalistic religions on the one hand and the challenge of political instability on the other. Nevertheless, the religious traditions of paganism remained vigorous: public religion lived on although there were without doubt restrictions, engendered by the political and economic difficulties; the cults of the cities were celebrated as well as the festivals, to which people flocked even from far away. The great number of private dedications to Roman and local gods all over the empire show that the traditional religious bonds were still strong (Alföldy 1989b: 72ff.).

Among the gods revered by the Romans there was a variety of divinities which have been categorized as oriental by contemporaries and modern scholars, such as Mithras or Isis and Serapis. This can be misleading. Truly, those gods had their origin in oriental regions, and some of their cults had been regarded as mere superstitions in former times; but many had won recognition progressively, since the borders between legitimate religion and superstition were always negotiable; new cults could always hope for acceptance. They should therefore not be seen as rivals to the traditional religion of the cities, but as an integral part of the religious landscape of Rome, which could always be enriched by new cults.

There were new developments, which set the old traditions in a new context. In the middle of the third century Plotinus taught his philosophy, regarded as the beginning of Neoplatonism. His philosophical teachings were far from the academic skepticism of former centuries. These texts revealed ways of knowing and achieving union with the "One," thus being monotheistic in their core and interpreting Plato in religious terms. Plotinus also had a special, in part ascetic way of life, which he shared with his pupils. Many educated pagans turned to those ideas. Plotinus' teaching was continued and changed by the next heads of his school, Porphyry and Iamblichus. Both opened Neoplatonism to the multifarious forms of contemporary paganism, which were regarded as appropriate for those uninitiated in Neoplatonic ideas. However, they were revolted by certain practices, as for example Porphyry was by animal sacrifices.

Neoplatonists became intellectual champions of paganism; hence Porphyry wrote a treatise against the Christians, which shows a good knowledge of their ideas. Iamblichus legitimized rituals and theurgical practices of all kind, so as to integrate multifarious expressions of religion which had been tagged as pagan by Christian polemicists and which had only in part been regarded as legitimate by the traditional elites. Numerous holy men with a Neoplatonic background rivaled Christian saints by teaching and by doing wonders.

With all its internal differences Christianity was much less inclusive and multifarious than paganism (see chapter 28). The "Old" and the consolidating New Testament served as a common text fundamental in the eyes of all Christians, and there were a growing number of tenets considered as essential by a majority, but which could not be enforced in all communities. Moreover, the local churches were marked by a strong hierarchy with a bishop as the local leader. Many were connected to each other by intense communication; synods became ever more important as instruments for the creation of a dogmatic and organizational consensus among believers from different towns. This could not prevent heresies, but the clashes were less explosive than later, because the contending groups were not able to rely on public authorities to resolve their problems.

In spite of internal quarrels and external pressure Christianity became ever stronger. Valerian's (253–60) second edict gives an impression of Christian influence even within the traditional elite, because it presupposed senators and *equites* among the Christians. In the forty years of peace after his demise the Christians grew in number; large churches were erected. A general stabilization of what was to become "the church" of the empire is clearly discernible.

As distinct from pagan literature, Christian literature flourished during that time; a general intensification of theological reflection took place. Hippolytus (first half of the third century) drew up a refutation of all heresies, which he denounced as being based on pagan traditions. Theological thinkers such as Clement of Alexandria (c. 200), Origen (c. 185–253), who was tortured under Decius, and Lucian of Antioch (martyred 312) undertook to speak about Christianity in a language based on Greek philosophy. This philosophy was mainly Neoplatonist in character. Therefore pagans and Christians came closer to each other on the intellectual level. Not surprisingly, Christian thinkers were able to impress pagans; Origen, for instance, was invited to several talks by members of the elite and even wrote a letter to Philip the Arab (244–9; Eus. *HE* 6.19.15; 21.3–4; 36.3).

In the wake of Tertullian (c. 200), Latin became ever more important as a language of theology, in particular thanks to the contributions of Cyprian (martyred 258). But philosophical terminology was used to a lesser degree than in Greek authors.

The anti-Christian stance of some emperors triggered a problem within Christianity, which perhaps was even more menacing than the imperial measures in themselves. The Christian communities became divided between the confessors, who had withstood the pressure of the government and had not perpetrated a sacrifice, and those who had given way to force, the so-called *lapsi* (fallen). Many of them, willing to do penance, yearned for forgiveness. Others were not even convinced that they had done anything wrong by making what were minor concessions in their eyes.

Yet many of the confessors scorned all those who had "fallen" as traitors, who should not be received back into church. Disputes must have broken out in many towns. The conflicts in Carthage (Cyprianus, *Epist.* 44–55, esp. 55) and Rome (Eus. *HE* 6.42–45) are very well documented. In Carthage, bishop Cyprian seems to have managed to reintegrate the *lapsi* after long conflicts, on condition that they did penance for their sins (cf. his *De lapsis*). In Rome though, a minority group, led by Novatian, completely separated from the other Christians and had him consecrated bishop; this schism lasted many decades. The conflicts over the readmission of the *lapsi* should not be seen in political or tactical terms only. They rather had a deep theological impact, concerning the question of the role of penance, which was central to Christian ethics and justified the return of the *lapsi*. Therefore those arguments intensified the theological debates.

Another significant conflict centered on Paul of Samosata. The bishop of Antioch (since 260) was deposed in 268 by a synod for dogmatic reasons – his doctrine on the human nature of Christ was rejected – and for his lifestyle, which reminded his brethren of the habits of the administrative elite. This resolution was made known to Rome, Alexandria, and other sees. All the same Paul remained in office until Aurelian's victory over Palmyra in 272, when he was forced to leave the "building of the church" (Eus. *HE* 7.29–30). Political conflicts, local rivalry, and theological debates converged in this quarrel. Interestingly, the pagan emperor was accepted as an arbitrator in an argument which concerned Christians only: Aurelian had been asked to decide the dispute over the ecclesiastical buildings.

The measures of Diocletian against Christians caused similar arguments to those raised by earlier persecutions: disputes about the treatments of those who had given in to the authorities. In Africa these tensions escalated when, about 312, Caecilian was consecrated bishop of Carthage. One of his three consecrators was charged with having been a so-called *traditor*, that is, of having handed over Christian books to the authorities. His enemies deposed Caecilian, making bishop first a certain Maiorian and, after his untimely death, Donatus, from whom his adherents received the name of Donatists.

Another dispute divided the eastern part of the empire: in Alexandria, the priest Arius came into conflict with his bishop, Alexander, about dogmatic issues, but perhaps also about the priest's right to preach. As it seems, Arius contended that there was a moment at the beginning of the world when Christ did not exist, whereas Alexander denied this. Many bishops of the east, such as Eusebius of Nicomedia, were dragged into the affair, perhaps not completely against their wills, because the disagreement with his priest promised to weaken the powerful bishop of Alexandria. This conflict was deepened by another dispute, the so-called Melitian schism, which again had been caused by disputes over the treatment of traitors during the

Diocletianic persecution. The Melitians sided with Arius, thus strengthening his moral authority.

To sum up, Christianity had become stronger during the third century, the number of adherents growing significantly. They were well educated and well organized, but exactly those factors caused heavy disputes because they forced the Christians to develop clearer criteria for the adherence to their churches. Rifts occurred, schisms which weakened the Christian communities to a certain degree, but did not lead to a complete disintegration of Christianity.

There was still space for a new religion: Manicheism. Its Persian founder Mani (216–c. 276), being influenced by Christian-Gnostic and Persian (Zoroastrian) traditions alike, perhaps also by Buddhism, had developed a religious system to which the idea of a conflict between good and bad was central. This dualism and the rigorous norms applied to the way of life to be led by believers contributed to the appeal which the new religion had for many people. Although Mani at first had demonstrated his loyalty toward the Persian king, he was persecuted in Persia and finally killed. Nevertheless, his ideas survived, spreading at home and across the Roman empire. For traditional Romans this new religion was barely distinguishable from Christianity, whereas Christians struggled to show their difference from this cult.

Imperial Intervention I: Reshaping Paganism

More than every other inhabitant of the Roman empire, the emperor was obliged to ensure the peace of the gods, and all of them strove to show their endeavors. Philip the Arab (244–9) celebrated the thousandth birthday of Rome on April 21, 248, with splendid games, commemorating the long tradition of Rome (only to lose his reign and life a year later). On the other hand, his benevolence toward Christianity – reminiscent of some Severan emperors or empresses – was so striking as to give to some later Christian authors the certainly false impression that he was a Christian himself.

The reign of Decius (249–51), who had come to the throne as a usurper, resulted in a break with tolerance. He energetically tried to renew Roman traditions. Obviously, his main concern was to make clear that only the traditional gods could grant the well-being of the empire and to show his piety by a *supplicatio*, a special kind of religious sacrifice to be made in difficult times.

The relevant edict is not preserved, but its outlines can be reconstructed on the basis of a variety of sources (namely Eus. *HE* 6.41.9–13; Cyprianus, *Epist.* 5–43): Decius apparently commanded every inhabitant of the Roman empire to sacrifice, to taste the sacrificial meal, and to swear that they had always sacrificed. The most unusual element was that special commissions, consisting of local magistrates, supervised the sacrifices and made written confirmation of every perpetrator, in so-called *libelli*. Several of them have been found on Egyptian papyri (for example *Papyrus Oxyrhynchos* 4.658). Those refusing could be fined, apparently not by the commissions, but by higher magistrates such as proconsuls. Even if there is no doubt that Decius was a traditionalist, his edict *de facto* meant a deep change in Roman traditions. The public religion of Rome had been collective and local; now Decius issued a decree that was universal and individual (Rives 1999).

Seen from a Christian perspective Decius' order was a clear provocation, although the Christians, as far as we can see, were nowhere mentioned explicitly. Yet they had been attaching importance to the act, as for a long time many of them had declined to make an offering to the emperor and had thus suffered martyrdom. Now they were expected, even forced to make the offering.

A substantial number of Christians rejected the sacrifice and suffered cruel punishments; some even died as martyrs. The letters of Cyprian, which are addressed to confessors, give a vivid impression of their afflictions (for example *Epist.* 6, 10, 20); Eusebius (*HE* 6.39–42) tells edifying stories about them. On the other hand, no small number, even some bishops, succumbed to the pressure or tried to elude the authorities by bribery or deceit. For obvious reasons, such cases are documented to a lesser degree.

There is no doubt that Christians bore the brunt of Decius' edict – but did Decius focus his attention merely on the Christians? This is doubtful, as it would have meant an immense waste of energy. All those Romans who were not Christians would have had to make their offerings only to isolate this group, which cannot have been too numerous. Thus, what the Christians regarded as a persecution was apparently only a side effect of a wide-ranging campaign to enforce loyalty to the emperor and to renew the old religion.

After two years Decius suffered what Christians saw as a just punishment: in 251, he was slain in a battle against the Goths. His first successors did (possibly could) not take up the idea of religious purification. Only Valerian (253–60) pursued the idea again, in 257, by explicitly attacking Christians (Eus. *HE* 7.10–11; Cyprianus, *Epist.* 76–81). His first edict aimed at the clerics, who had to make sacrifices; in addition, whoever performed service in churches or cemeteries was to be punished by death (Eus. *HE* 7.11; *Acta proconsularia Cypriani* 1, 4). The second edict was directed against Christians in general. Those who persevered in their habits – there were even senators and *equites* among them – were to lose their property together with their dignity and, in the end, their lives, if they did not renounce their belief. Women of high standing were deprived of their property; imperial officials and imperial freedmen had to be sent to the mines (Cyprianus, *Epist.* 80).

These edicts were obviously focused on the Christian elite, on the elimination of clerics and of Christians from leading families. In fact, many Christians died. Among these was Cyprian, bishop of Carthage, whose letters give a lively impression of the plight of the persecuted Christians, and Sixtus II, bishop of Rome. In contrast, Denys of Alexandria, having been exiled, survived.

In 260 Valerian suffered a heavy defeat against the Persians and was taken prisoner himself. In Christian eyes this evidently resulted from God's vengeance. The Christians were confirmed in their belief that even a bad emperor was not able to destroy their religion.

When Gallienus, Valerian's son, became sole emperor in 260, he revoked his father's anti-Christian edicts (Eus. *HE* 7.13). This did not imply that he neglected paganism. Gallienus himself was in contact with Plotinus (Porphyry, *Vita Plotini* 12). He seems to have taken a special interest in Greek rituals and games. Possibly, he was initiated into the Eleusinian mysteries, but he did not therefore discount Roman traditions; it was only a slight shift of balance.

Politically the crisis deepened under his reign as so-called *Sonderreiche* (independent empires) emerged in Gaul and in Syria (Palmyra). But in the years after Gallienus' death in 267, a series of strong and efficient emperors managed to stabilize the Roman empire and to make good the losses to a high degree.

Foremost among them was Aurelian. Much more than his predecessors he laid emphasis on the fact that a god had invested him as emperor. After his victory over Palmyra in the summer of 273 he established the cult of *Sol invictus* (Invincible Sun) in Rome. The god received his own magnificent temple, the *templum Solis*, and the priesthoods were restructured in order to give the priestly college of Sol a special rank. Moreover, a special *agon Solis* (games for Sol) was introduced, to be held every four years. This cult has an air of monotheism, insofar as there was a central god, but it did not exclude the veneration of other gods. It was new, but remained within the framework of traditional religious practice and could happily co-exist with the older cults.

It is a matter of debate whether Aurelian planned measures against Christians in his last days. Even if he drew up orders for persecutions (Eus. *HE* 7.30.20–1; Lact. *DMP* 6), they were never issued. Several accounts of martyrdoms refer to his reign, but they may represent local incidents. There was no heavy oppression of Christianity in his times.

After several short-lived, but mostly effective emperors, Diocletian, proclaimed in 284, was the first to reign for a longer period. He created a new political system, the tetrarchy, by installing four rulers, two *Augusti* (at first Diocletian and Maximianus) and two *Caesares*, the latter subordinated to the *Augusti* and their prospective successors. In doing so, he made usurpations unattractive, because potential usurpers could be integrated or had to reckon with four legitimate rivals.

The legitimacy of the dynasty was propagated in religious terms. The emperors were regarded as holders of an office which was given to them by the providence of the gods (*providentia deorum*). But they themselves also had divine qualities and virtues by birth. Their closeness to the gods was expressed by epithets: in 286, Diocletian received the surname of *Iovius* and Maximianus that of *Herculius*, connecting them with Jupiter and his son respectively; in 293, those titles were also bestowed on the *Caesares*. Even if they were not called gods officially, the tetrarchs and their gods (not their natural family) formed a *domus divina*, a divine family, the emperors being considered as sons of the gods (Kolb 2004). This systematic concept was a clear innovation, but remained integrated in a range of measures intended to demonstrate respect toward the temples and traditional customs.

Part of the policy of religious restoration was the elimination of cults which could offend the traditional gods, first of all Manicheism. Probably in 297, by an edict answering to a request of the proconsul of, as it seems, Africa (but which possibly had an impact on the whole empire), Diocletian ordered the leaders of Manicheism to be burnt alive together with their books (*Collatio legum* 15.3). These were unusually hard measures, which, however, did not destroy Manicheism.

Perhaps about 300, after a traditional sacrifice had failed, Diocletian, being told that this was due to the presence of Christians, ordered first the members of the palace, soon all of his soldiers and officials to make sacrifices (Lact. *DMP* 10; *Divinae institutiones* 4.27.4–5; Eus. *V. Const.* 2.50–1). Whoever refused to do so was dismissed. Four years later the Diocletianic persecution began, which was to become the longest and most thorough persecution of Christians. The details of its history are partially ambiguous: the accounts of our main sources, Lactantius, whose *De mortibus persecutorum* narrates the gruesome fates of the persecutors, punished by God, and Eusebius, who devotes the eighth book of his *Church History* as a whole to the persecution and its martyrs, differ insofar as only Eusebius distinguishes several edicts. Here a harmonizing interpretation is adopted (following Corcoran 1996: 179 ff. in the main outlines), an approach which is arguably controversial (see e.g. Schwarte 1994), particularly as the edicts released for the various parts of the empire may have shown discrepancies.

It seems to be clear that several edicts threatened Christianity with ever harder oppression. The first edict, legitimized by an oracle of Apollo and promulgated at Nicomedia on February 24, 303, ordered the destruction of church buildings and Christian texts, forbade services to be held, degraded officials who were Christians, re-enslaved imperial freedmen who were Christians, and reduced the legal rights of all Christians. But physical or capital punishments were not imposed on them (Lact. *DMP* 13; Eus. *HE* 8.2.3–4).

When not much later fires broke out in the palace, arson by Christians was suspected. Several adherents were executed because they were regarded as being guilty (Lact. *DMP* 14.2; Eus. *HE* 8.6.6). A second edict menaced clerics with imprisonment (Eus. *HE* 8.2.5); a third, offering a kind of amnesty, ordered them to make sacrifices, promising freedom to those who did (Eus. *HE* 8.2.5, 8.6.10). Even in 304, a final edict, seemingly going back to Decius, enjoined universal sacrifice (Eus. *Martyribus Palaestinae* 3.1; Lact. *DMP* 15.4). With this edict, Diocletian took up Decius' measure, but the times had changed, so as to make it a plainly anti-Christian decree.

The edicts did not fulfill their aims; they were not enforced in every part of the empire with equal vigor. Constantius, *Caesar* and then *Augustus* of the west, ignored them; other rulers or governors did not put them into effect wholeheartedly. Even in those parts of the empire where the rulers tried to apply the edicts rigorously, Christians proved to be locally powerful, although as during former persecutions a considerable number of Christians accommodated themselves to the authorities. When Diocletian retired in 305, his successor Galerius became the main champion of anti-Christian politics. On his deathbed, however, Galerius, acknowledging his defeat, revoked the politics of persecution in 311. In a new edict he allowed the Christians to assemble and asked them to pray for the emperor (Lact. *DMP* 34; Eus. *HE* 8.17.3–10). This meant an official recognition of their importance in the religious world of the Roman empire, although one of the tetrarchs, Maximinus Daia, still oppressed Christians in his part of the empire up to 313.

Imperial Intervention II: Reshaping Christianity

Constantine (the Great) was the eldest son of the tetrarch Constantius. Excluded from legitimate succession by the tetrarchic system, he seized the throne after his father's death in 306. After long debates he was accepted as a *Caesar* within the tetrarchy, but he did not comply with its regulations. Instead, he went further, extending his power. His main opponent in the west was Maxentius, another tetrarch's son who had usurped power on his part. Constantine defeated him decisively near Rome in 312.

Constantine's personal religious convictions have often been discussed, which is a fruitless effort. There is no serious way to discern what he "really" thought, because all the sources we have are reflecting his representation or his image. Possibly he had known Christianity since his youth, but he cannot have been a confessed Christian from the beginning. It is plain from a panegyric, an oration in praise of the emperor (*Panegyrici latini* 6[7] 21.3–7), that he had special reverence for Apollo. His coins show that for a certain time he made public his special relationship with Sol, who was closely connected to Apollo.

Nevertheless, the year 312 was soon regarded as a decisive date in the development of Constantine's religious policy: Constantine's Christian supporters claimed that, inspired by a sign from God, he had made his soldiers place the *chi-rho*, the symbol of Christ, on their shields, before he defeated Maxentius; the accounts by Lact. *DMP* 44 and Eus. *V. Const.* 1.26–32, 37, which is much later, again differ in several details. Thus, his victory was ascribed to the Christian God. Henceforth Constantine showed his support for Christianity in many regards. Even so, it is difficult to say that he had become a Christian in 312. First of all, his main interest in the Christian God seems to have been in his power to grant victory, which is a fundamentally pagan concept and not specifically Christian. Moreover, the emperor's politics were by no means unambiguous.

Several measures facilitated Christian life. Constantine and Licinius, who reigned in the east, convened in Milan and agreed to release the so-called Edict of Milan in 313. This granted all inhabitants of the Roman empire, specifically the Christians, the right to worship the gods they preferred, and restored the property which had been lost during the persecution to Christians as individuals and to the churches. (Two letters by Licinius, which published this agreement if not in a completely identical form, have been preserved; Lact. *DMP* 48; Eus. *HE* 10.5.1–14.) By contrast to the Edict of Galerius, the whole text displayed sympathy to Christianity.

In the years that followed Constantine backed Christianity in many regards, at the same time beginning to use Christianity as a political instrument, namely against his rival Licinius, who was soon depicted as a new persecutor. After his final victory over Licinius in 324, Constantine was to reign as sole emperor for 13 years. The situation at the frontiers was not precarious, except for the menace of a Persian invasion in his last years, thus giving Constantine the time to pursue his political goals within the empire.

The emperor sustained his support for the new religion, issuing several edicts which must have been sympathetic to Christians, such as the ban on disfiguring human faces, "which are formed after the celestial beauty" (*CTh* 9.40.2 [315]), or the interdiction on inscribing convicted persons as gladiators (*CTh* 15.12.1 [325]); crucifixion as a penalty was abolished (Aurelius Victor, *De Caesaribus* 41.4), but several other cruel forms of punishment were preserved. Celibacy, which had been sanctioned by Augustan marriage laws, was freed from disadvantages (*CTh* 8.16 [320]). Besides, respect for the Christian Sunday was enforced (*CI* 3.12.2; *CTh* 2.8.1 [both 321]). Immunity from fiscal burdens was given to clerics (*CTh* 16.2.2 [319]). But, shortly afterwards, Constantine made clear that people who, being relatives of decurions, were obliged to take over the financial burdens of the city councils must not become clerics (*CTh* 16.2.3 [320]; cf. 16.2.6 [326]). Churches were allowed to accept bequests (*CTh* 16.2.4 [321]); the bishops obtained the right to act as judges, when they were appealed to (the *episcopalis audientia*; *CTh* 1.27.1 [318]). Many Christian buildings were erected by the emperor (or his mother Helena) in Rome, Constantinople, and the Holy Land, as the whole of Palestine began to be transformed into a Christian landscape. In his last days Constantine intervened with the Persian king (Eus. *V. Const.* 4.9–13), allegedly in order to protect the Christians in the neighboring empire, perhaps also to find a suitable pretext for a military attack on Persia.

However, as has been said repeatedly, Christianity had never been a uniform religion. The success of Christianity within the Roman empire corresponded to intensified conflicts among Christians, which had a new quality because they were expressed with an obstinacy unknown before and could win the support of an emperor. Soon after his victory over Maxentius, Constantine was confronted with the Donatist dispute, which ultimately resulted from the Diocletianic persecution (for the sources see Maier 1987). Constantine initially gave his support to Caecilian, Donatus' counterpart. But after an intervention of the Donatists he agreed to assign the decision to the bishops. For the first time in history a synod tried to counsel the emperor in religious matters. In the end, four synods had to be convened, in part with the emperor present. All of them recognized Caecilian as the legitimate bishop of Carthage. This created turmoil, most notably in the rural regions of Africa. Constantine's efforts to suppress this were in vain, and the emperor resigned about 321, leaving, as he told the Catholic bishops and laics of Africa, the vengeance to God (Maier 1987, no. 30). The conflict continued over the next centuries.

After his victory over Licinius, Constantine turned his attention to the Arian conflict. He tried to mediate between the groups with a letter to Arius and Alexander, which played down the theological contrasts (Eus. *V. Const.* 2.64–72), yet without success. Shortly afterward he convened a general synod in Nicaea, which was to be regarded as the first ecumenical synod. The ancient accounts of this synod (most important Eus. *V. Const.* 3.10–16) have been idealized in order to prove the holy character of the assembly, which was to release a new creed that formed the basis for Catholic and Orthodox doctrines up to today.

Yet the members of the synod were not able to find a solution by themselves. Constantine intervened by proposing to introduce the word *homooúsios* (of the same substance) into the creed in order to describe the relationship between God the father and God the son. This formula was an apt one to disguise the differences between

Alexander and most of his opponents, but had the disadvantage of not being a biblical term. Nevertheless, the council fathers accepted the word, even Eusebius of Caesarea, who had to change his position and was forced to explain this to his parishioners at length (Theodoretus, *Historia ecclesiastica* 1.12). In the end, only two opponents remained, and they were exiled, as was Arius. Other decrees of the Council of Nicaea concerned the date of Easter and canonical questions.

The council did not find general acceptance at first, and many other councils, partly of regional and partly of more general importance, followed; before long Arius was rehabilitated. In several towns adherents of Alexander and Arius (or rather of Eusebius of Nicomedia) fought against each other. Soon, Athanasius, who had succeeded Alexander in 328, rose to the center of the conflict. Charges against him were discussed in various councils and brought before the emperor. Formally, they did not regard dogmatic questions, charging him with murder and other criminal offenses. After long debate Athanasius was exiled to Trier; the rows went on. Constantine's attempts to unify Christianity had failed. Possibly an anti-heretical law which forbade the assemblies of certain heretic groups, such as Novatians and Montanists, which were rejected by Athanasians and Arians alike was an attempt to bring those groups together by drawing attention to common enemies (Eus. *V. Const.* 3.64).

Although Constantine was willing to lend his support to Christianity, he did not fight against paganism directly, with the possible exception of a short period after his victory over Licinius. At that time he seems to have published a general ban on sacrifices (Euse. *V. Const.* 2.45.1, historicity in dispute), which was soon abolished (Eus. *V. Const.* 2.56). Nevertheless, paganism was affected by several measures, which were not necessarily anti-pagan in their intent. Temple possessions were confiscated, allegedly to embellish Constantinople (Lib. *Or.* 30.37). Certain apparently immoral practices were forbidden, as for example temple prostitution – but customs of this kind had also been criticized by pagans. Even the interdiction on *haruspicina* in private houses (*CTh* 9.16.1–2) is not necessarily to be interpreted as a specifically Christian measure, because private divination had always posed a serious threat to Roman emperors. Public *haruspicina* were expressly allowed and even requested when public buildings were struck by lightning (*CTh* 16.10.1). A special case is the destruction of a pagan temple in Mamre, which was also a holy place for Christians (Eus. *V. Const.* 3.52–3).

Apart from this, traditional practices were not obstructed by the authorities. The emperor remained *pontifex maximus* and the cult of the emperor persisted; pagan symbols continued to be used in official representation. A famous inscription from Hispellum documents an imperial letter which even allows the building of a new temple for the emperor and his family, on condition that no superstitious acts (probably a hint at sacrifices) be performed (*CIL* 11.5256 = *ILS* 705).

It was still a time of co-existence. Officially, the emperor praised tolerance in itself, but he must also have been driven by political reasons. Paganism and Christianity were strong and the emperor needed support from both spheres, not least because many members of the administrative elite still harbored pagan sympathies.

In his last days, Constantine was baptized, demonstrating his adherence to the Christian god. This may show personal conviction, but it is unclear whether he had theologically nuanced ideas about this religion. If it is true that he wanted to be buried among the cenotaphs of the 12 apostles, so aspiring to be like Jesus Christ (Eus. *V. Const.* 4.60.1–4), he revealed a deep misunderstanding of Christianity at least in a theological sense. His Christian belief seems to have been inspired by pagan ideas.

Constantine aimed at religious unity within the empire and to be able to use Christianity for his personal purposes. His reign definitely furthered Christianity. For the first time, the religion was supported by an emperor; its public presence was enforced, and those Christians who were close to the emperor could make use of political instruments to enforce their religious ideas, most often in intra-Christian disputes. Being the religion of the emperor, Christianity, as expressed by the majority, changed its character.

But Christianity did not become the state religion of the empire: Paganism was not generally forbidden or suppressed. However, paganism had to change in character, because one element which was constituent for pagan religious practices had been lost: civic religion. The public sphere was religiously neutralized. Local magistrates were deprived of cultic functions, which had been essential to their office. After many changes in paganism resulting from the emperors' influence, it now had to change without their support.

Conclusion

Religious history from Decius to Constantine is characterized by many conflicts between paganism and Christianity, but also by periods of peaceful co-existence. Neither paganism nor Christianity was homogeneous, although the universalistic religion of the Christians possessed more binding elements. Both changed considerably during this period. The attempts to preserve paganism under changing circumstances resulted in a change of paganism, because the universalistic principles of Christianity were transferred to its realm. Christianity on the other hand had to change by its growth and by the mere fact that a religion which had been persecuted or at best tolerated now became the one favored by the emperor.

Paganism was reshaped several times in different ways by various emperors, all united by their eagerness to preserve it; in the end, an emperor who apparently had no clear ideas about the theological issues of Christianity lent his decisive support to this religion. Imperial interventions were forceful, but no emperor got through with what he wanted, not even Constantine, who was unable to suppress the quarrels between Christians.

Constantine had sided with a powerful religion: even if it is under debate how many Roman citizens around the year 300 were Christians, the spread of Christianity during the third century is impressive. It can be understood as the result of several causes, among them the extraordinary commitment of its believers, the intensity of charitable work, the large-scale and efficient organization of the church, the willingness to reintegrate *lapsi*, and the obvious failure of its most rigid enemies, which confirmed the Christian belief in being the people of God. In a time of suffering, Christianity seemed to give the best answers and to set the most impressive examples in the eyes of many contemporaries.

Constantine felt he was supported by the power which gave the Christians their strength, and made use of it for his political aims. Although the Christianization of the Roman empire cannot be put down to a single person, Constantine's decision made the process of Christianization completely irreversible. Thus, Christianity had been victorious against persecutors in the end. However, the official recognition of Christianity conjured up another enemy of this religion, which had previously only lurked in the background: dogmatic disputes and internal quarrels, which were to weigh heavily on Christians for centuries, in particular when they were linked to political conflicts.

FURTHER READING

A brilliant historical overview is given by Potter (2004). For the religious developments see Lane Fox (1988); on the concept of paganism, Leppin (2004); on the cult of the Sun, Berrens (2004). Strobel (1993) doubts whether the third century was actually perceived as an epoch of crisis by contemporaries. Witschel (1999) draws attention to the regional differences within the Roman empire. See also the contributions in Swain and Edwards (2004) (on the problem of monotheism especially Edwards 2004) and Alföldy (1989a). For a history of Christianity, see Chadwick (2001) and Piétri (2004). On Manicheism, see S. Lieu (1994). On Philip the Arab, see Körner (2002) and Rives (1999); for an alternative interpretation, Selinger (2004); for the following periods de Blois (1976), Alaric Watson (1999: esp. 183f.), Corcoran (1996), Kolb (2004), Bleckmann (2003), and Drake (2000). On the persecution of Christians, see Schwarte (1994). Local studies like Bratož (2004) give a clearer picture of the real extent of the Diocletianic persecution. For Donatism, see Maier (1987).

CHAPTER NINE

Religious *Koine* and Religious Dissent in the Fourth Century

Michele Renee Salzman

In a justly famous passage, the historian Ammianus Marcellinus described the visit to Rome of Constantine's heir, the emperor Constantius II, in 357 CE (Amm. 16.10). Constantius had come to Rome to celebrate his *vicennalia* and the return of peace after the defeat of the usurper Magnentius. After entering the city, the emperor admired its monuments and stood in awe, as Ammianus observes, also of its religious shrines – the sanctuary of Tarpeian Jove, the Pantheon, and the Temple of Urbs Roma (Amm. 16.10.14). This respect for Rome's pagan monuments is much in keeping with what we hear about Constantius II from the late fourth-century Roman senator Symmachus: Constantius "with no anger on his face, viewed the holy shrines, read the names of the gods inscribed on the pediments; he inquired about the origins of the temples, expressed admiration for their founders and preserved these as part of the rites of the empire, even though he followed a different religion himself" (Symmachus, *Relatio* 3.7). In addition, Constantius filled the pagan priesthoods with men of noble rank and spent monies on the pagan ceremonies and games (ibid.). This pious Christian emperor found much that was of value in the religious traditions attached to the state cults at Rome, and so he maintained them.

The willingness of Christian emperors to find common ground with pagans in their religious and civic traditions is a result of the political reality of the mid-fourth century; large numbers of pagans and Christians were living together still in the empire. To persecute pagans outright would not work, as Diocletian's failed persecution of Christians had shown. But at a deeper level, Constantius' support for pagan cults is tacit acknowledgment of a truth that tends to escape modern historians, namely that Christians and pagans did, indeed, share certain beliefs, attitudes, and practices. As Robert Markus noted: "There just is not a different culture to distinguish Christians from their pagan peers" (1990: 12). Markus went on to claim that "only religion distinguished the Christian from the pagan" (1990: 12). What I will argue here, however, is that even in religion, in terms of practices, attitudes, and beliefs, there was much that pagans and Christians shared. Moreover, recognition of a religious *koine* into the late fourth century should not be surprising; religion in antiquity had always been intimately integrated into Roman culture and society, and deeply embedded in the state and its institutions.

Yet the willingness of Christian emperors to find common ground with pagans did not survive the fourth century. Although some practices and attitudes inherited from pagan religion continued without any question into the fourth century or later, many came under attack; over the course of the fourth century, bishops and monks widened their definitions of "pagan" practices and attitudes and then preached against them as sinful or sacrilegious. By the end of the fourth century, late Roman Christian authorities and emperors had undermined and reshaped the religious *koine* that pagans and Christians had shared in public and private; religious practices and beliefs once considered acceptable were increasingly prohibited by imperial legislation and canon law. Even the notion that a shared religious outlook was desirable came under attack. The tolerance for religious difference that had once comprised part of the shared religious outlook of many early fourth-century pagans and Christians disappeared under the increasingly hostile assaults made by clerics, monks, and emperors. In the 380s and 390s, as we shall see, the laws issued by the Christian emperor Theodosius mark the official end of tolerance for religious differences; by the early fifth century, the validity of alternative religious traditions – be they pagan, Christian, or Jewish – was denied by emperors and clerics in search of a unified and more uniform Christianity.

The growing willingness on the part of late Roman Christian emperors and bishops to prohibit practices and beliefs labeled as "pagan," and the desire to silence religious dissent of any kind and especially within the Christian community, are signs that the empire was indeed moving closer to orthodoxy. The growth of intolerance is, I would argue, one of the most negative legacies of the fourth century, but one that survived, with destructive consequences, into the Middle Ages and beyond. Admittedly, certain elements of the early fourth-century religious *koine* continued into the new Christian empire of the late fourth and early fifth centuries, but these elements were increasingly subjected to reinterpretation along "acceptable" Christian lines, so as to be stripped of any "pagan" meaning. By the end of the fourth century, the new religious *koine* was imperial Christianity, and it was a Christianity that was unwilling to brook religious dissent, both within and without the church. This chapter will explore these changes in Roman religion and society over the course of the fourth century.

Religious *Koine* in Public Cult and Ritual: Shared Religious Traditions in Roman Religion in the First Half of the Fourth Century CE

As Constantius' visit to Rome showed, Romans of all religious affiliations – Christians, pagans, and Jews – inhabited the same city and encountered each other in its civic and public religious spaces. They also, as we shall see, shared private religious space and ritual in Rome as in the Mediterranean world at large.

The official calendar for the city of Rome in the year 354 CE is perhaps the best source for the public religious *koine*. This calendar attests to the continuing prominence of the pagan state cults and ceremonies; it included holidays and festivals in honor of the pagan gods and goddesses, as well as those to celebrate the ruling imperial house and the cult of the deified emperors (Salzman 1990: 16–19; 116–92). Because the holidays and ceremonies recorded in the public calendar were for the benefit of the people as a whole, they were funded by state monies (Festus 284 L; Macr. *Sat.* 1.16.4–8). So too did public monies support the public games or *Ludi* held in conjunction with these holidays and festivals, be they circus games, gladiatorial combats, beast hunts, or theatrical performances in honor of the gods or the emperors (living and deified). At the games in particular, but so too at imperial cult, civic, and traditional pagan holidays, pagans and Christians rubbed shoulders with one another in a shared religious space and time.

The religious *koine* reflected in the public calendar of Rome had, however, come under attack from Christian clergy even before Constantine's well-known conversion near the Milvian Bridge in Rome in 312 CE; the third-century Christian father Tertullian decried these venues and what happened there: "We have, I think, faithfully carried out our plan of showing in how many different ways the sin of idolatry clings to the shows, in respect of their origins, their titles, their equipments, their places of celebration, their arts; and we may hold it as a thing beyond all doubt, that for us they are utterly unsuitable" (Tert. *Spect.* 13.1). Christian clergy focused their attacks on blood sacrifice performed in front of the temple of the divinity by the priests of the pagan cults in conjunction with religious holidays and/or public games. So Tertullian specifically noted these practices: "I shall break with my Maker by going to the Capitol or the temple of Serapis to sacrifice or adore, as I shall also do by going as a spectator to the circus and theater" (Tert. *Spect.* 8.3). For Tertullian, the *sacra* that "preceded, intervened in, and followed" the games (Tert. *Spect.* 8.3) were idolatry, and so Christians should not attend either the games or the pagan ceremonies.

Constantine's open support for Christianity and his public unwillingness to sacrifice (Curran 2000: 178) may well have altered that element of pagan ritual in certain public settings; there is no evidence for animal sacrifice in conjunction with the *Pompa Circi* in the fourth century, for example, and scholars dispute whether or not Constantine actually legislated against blood sacrifice, as Eusebius of Caesarea claimed he did in 324 in the east (Eus. *V. Const.* 2.45; Bradbury 1994: 120–39; Salzman 1987: 172–88). Even if Constantine did legislate against blood sacrifice as a "deterrent designed principally to clear public spaces of that aspect of pagan cult considered most unacceptable in the eyes of Christians" (Bradbury 1994: 138), he nonetheless continued state support for the ceremonies, rituals, and games of the pagan religious holidays and civic festivals noted in public calendars.

Constantine's support for the state cults was potentially problematic, since not just the public holidays but also the spectacles attached to them had retained their essentially pagan religious meanings in the eyes of many fourth-century Romans. This

was the case for certain pagans for whom not just the holidays but even the spectacles and games in the Circus Maximus in Rome, along with their ritual *Pompa
Circi*, as well as the statuary and physical adornments, "lent religious sustenance"
(Curran 2000: 259). Certainly, the amount of religious feeling experienced by the
participants at the public *ludi* and civic festivals varied; some attendees, pagan and
Christian alike, felt nothing akin to "religion" as they filed past the traditional gods
of the Roman pantheon, intent on observing the games and spectacles. For some,
the religious element was overshadowed by simple excitement or civic pride. Yet this
religious element was noticeable to Christian clergy; the sermons of late Roman
Christian bishops indicate that the games and civic festivals, and not just the religious ceremonies and rituals, still held pagan meanings and hence Christians should
avoid them (see, for example, Jon Chrysostom *Contra ludos et theatra* [PG 56,
253–60]; Salvian *De gubernatione Dei* 6.129–30 [*PL* 53, cols. 120–1]; and for
Augustine, Markus 1990: 107–23). I emphasize this fact since it indicates that to
a significant number of Christian authorities and laypeople, as well as pagans, the
holidays and festivals of the public calendar, as well as the games and spectacles, formed
part of what we can call the public religious *koine*.

Not surprisingly, and in no small part because of the pagan public cults' broad
appeal, Christian emperors through the mid-fourth century tended to follow the religious policy established by Constantine; by and large, they focused on and restricted
or prohibited the most offensive element of these cults, namely animal sacrifice, but
continued to support and fund the pagan holidays, ceremonies, and games associated with the Roman state cults until the last decade of the fourth century; games
and circuses continued even later than this date (see "Emperors on Religious *Koine*
and Religious Dissent," below).

One key reason for the ongoing imperial support for the public religious *koine*
was the continued attraction of the imperial cult; the reformed cult of the Second
Flavians flourished in Rome, in north Africa, and throughout the provinces through
the fourth century. Here, too, Constantine had set a precedent; in his reply to a
request from the town of Hispellum in Umbria (*CIL* 11.5265) for an imperial cult
center, he established a *flamen* (priest) and games (*ludi* and *circenses*), but he stipulated that *superstitio* be absent from this cult. What he meant by *superstitio* at the
time is a matter of some debate (Salzman 1987: 172–88; Grodzynski 1974: 36–60),
but even if he had intended to prohibit blood sacrifice, Constantine and his successors continued their support for the traditional Roman ceremonies and games. It
remained an honor to serve as a *flamen* in the imperial cult throughout the fourth
century, and we find Christian *flamines* even into the fifth century in Gaul (Diehl,
ILCV 391) and into the Vandal period in Africa (Chastagnol and Duval 1974: 87–118),
although by the late sixth century, we cannot be certain if the *flamines* are honoring the Roman emperor or the Vandal king. Nonetheless, only after 386 CE were
restrictions placed on Christians so that they were no longer allowed to attain the position of chief civil priest (*archierosyna*) (*CTh* 12.1.112). The provincial assemblies,
whose delegates were called *sacerdotes provinciae*, continued as well; their principal
religious role was to arrange games at a temple dedicated to Rome and the emperor
(Cecconi 1994: 83–106).

Religious *Koine* in Private Cult and Ritual: Shared Religious Traditions in Roman Religion in the First Half of the Fourth Century CE

The religious *koine* reflected in the public calendar of Rome was very much alive in the middle of the fourth century in public ceremonies and rituals which, in origin and meaning, still had strong religious implications. But in private cult too, there is ample evidence for shared traditions – this religious *koine* – surviving among pagans and Christians. Here, I will stress two elements of private religiosity that reveal this shared outlook. First, there is ample evidence that especially among educated pagans, but also even in the lower orders, a religiosity that approached monotheism was very much alive; and second, religious practices and burial places for the dead were shared by pagans and Christians alike. In both of these areas concerning private religiosity, we see the persistence of shared attitudes among fourth-century Romans of the Mediterranean world, pagan and Christian. And, as in the case of public cult, we find Christian clergy and emperors attempting to redefine these private shared religious attitudes as sinful.

Pagans approaching monotheism

Monotheism was "perfectly compatible with belief in the existence of a plurality of divine beings" in the view of certain Greek philosophers (Athanassiadi and Frede 1999: 8). Platonic teaching had proposed a strict hierarchy subordinated to the supreme God. "These lower gods were executors or manifestations of the divine will rather than independent principles of reality. Whether they are called gods, demons, angels, or *numina*, these immortal beings are emanations of the One, and their degree of reality depends on their proximity to the apex of the theological pyramid" (Athanassiadi and Frede 1999: 8). The principle of polyonymy, articulated, for example, by the Neoplatonist Maximus of Tyre (39.5; cf. 2.5), stated that: "the gods have one nature but many names." This was a wide-spread belief that extended notions of monotheism beyond those who were philosophically oriented to the upper classes more generally. Such a system was made more understandable by the drawing of parallels with the human order; the lesser gods were like provincial governors who were subject to the emperor (Celsus *CC* 8.35; Aelius Aristides 43.18ff).

Among the educated upper classes of the fourth century especially, there are indications that some pagans seem to have been approaching monotheism. So, around 390 CE, the grammarian Maximus of Madaura argued in a letter to Augustine that pagans and Christians agreed about the nature of the one God, but that only their systems of veneration differed (Maximus *apud* Augustine, *Epist.* 16.1 [*CSEL* 34.1.37, 34.1.38–9]). Another pagan, Longinianus, in another letter to Augustine similarly describes his pagan journey toward the "one, universal, incomprehensible, ineffable and untiring Creator" (Longinianus *apud* Augustine, *Epist.* 234.2 [*CSEL* 57.520]). Perhaps one of the fullest expressions of pagan monotheism survives in a fifth-century text; Macrobius' *Saturnalia* portrays one of the leading pagans of the late fourth century, Praetextatus, as arguing that "the supreme god, of whom all the others are aspects, is the Sun" (Liebeschuetz 1999: 186). The solar monotheism attributed to Praetextatus has a long history in Greco-Roman thought. Here it is enough to remark that the worship of Sol was one of the key cults in the fourth century; Constantine (prior to his conversion) and his father were alleged by some to be Solar monotheists (*Panegyrici Latini* 6 (7) 14.3; Drake 2000: 189–90). The emperor Julian (361–3 CE), too, was especially devoted to the Sun and viewed him as the supreme god, approaching the sort of pagan monotheism expressed by Macrobius (Julian, *Hymn to Helios, Oration 11*, ed. C. Lacombrade, *Works of Julian*; and Athanassiadi and Frede 1999: 19). Although the historical Praetextatus was known as a prominent polytheist (*PLRE* 1.723 s.v. Vettius Agorius Praetextatus), the solar monotheism ascribed to him in the *Saturnalia* is in accord with well-attested strands of fourth-century religiosity, and not at odds with Praetextatus having been a practicing polytheist.

Interestingly, it has been argued that monotheistic trends spread beyond the educated pagan elites and philosophical schools to the lower orders of society. The cult of *Theos Hypsistos*, although attested mostly in the eastern Roman empire, had also spread to the west; its worshipers, according to Mitchell, included the members of all classes – peasants simply praying for good harvests alongside men and women of all classes asking for health and fertility (Mitchell 1999: 106). Mitchell and others have argued that this cult was essentially monotheistic, for in it "pagans worship a single, remote, and abstract deity in preference to the anthropomorphic figures of conventional paganism" (Mitchell 1999: 92). This cult continued into the fourth century in the east (Epiphanius, *Panarion* 80.1–2; Gregory of Nazianzus, *Oratio* 18.5 [PG 35.990]) and thrived in the western empire as well, if we accept that the inscriptions noting *metuentes* or god-fearers from Rome, from north Italy at Pola, and from Numidia can be tied to this cult (Mitchell 1999: 118). Hence, a monotheistic approach to private religious belief should also be seen as part of the religious *koine* of private cult among certain pagans, educated and not, as well as among Christians in the fourth-century empire.

Shared burial spaces and rituals

As early as the second century CE, pagans and Christians throughout the Mediterranean world had turned from cremation to inhumation of the dead. And as they shared similar burial practices, they also shared sacred burial spaces and religious rituals for the dead. These similarities in the care for the dead are, I would argue *contra* Rebillard (2003b: 47–55), elements of a shared religiosity, or what I have called the religious *koine* of the fourth century.

Despite modern sensibilities to the contrary, there was no legal reason why pagans and Christians could not share the same private or non-church *collegia* burial grounds. Under Roman law, the tomb was considered a sacred space (*res religiosa*) (De Visscher 1963: 43–63); the tomb monument itself became sacred after the body was placed in it (*Digesta* 11.7.2.5). Because of the sacred nature of the tombs, the pagan *pontifices* oversaw the construction and use of the tombs, even after the advent of Christian emperors; a law of Constantius dated to 349 CE indicates that this continued to be the case (*CTh* 9.17.2). Hence, private burial grounds were sacred spaces under Roman law for pagans and Christians alike, and there was no legal reason why members of the same family, but of different religious orientations, could not be buried together in private or non-church *collegia* burials. Only in church cemeteries, from the third century on, could clerics prevent pagans from being buried next to Christians, but from the fourth century there is no evidence to indicate that the church interfered with private or non-church *collegia* burials (Johnson 1997: 42–3). And indeed, throughout the fourth century there is ample evidence that pagans and Christians continued to share private and non-church *collegia* tombs across the empire, even if some localities did at times regulate this practice (Johnson 1997: 37–59). Perhaps the most striking instance of such shared space from the fourth century is the Catacomb of Vibia located on the Via Appia outside of Rome. The style of the paintings, the epigraphy, and certain words indicate that the catacomb was at the height of its use from c. 350 to 400 CE (Ferrua 1971: 58–61). The paintings and inscriptions indicate pagan worshipers of *Dei Solis Invicti Mithrae* were buried here; so too were a good number of Christians (Ferrua 1971: 44, 33, 56–62). The religious *koine* represented by such shared burial space remained protected by Roman law throughout the fourth century.

In addition to sharing tombs, Christians and pagans also shared certain rituals for the dead. The *Apostolic Constitutions*, a late fourth-century compilation of various sources, provides information about Christian burial practices; it supplies a prayer for the deceased and stipulates that the third, ninth, and thirtieth days after the death should be commemorated (*Constitutio Apostolica* 8.42: for the edition and dating, see *Les constitutions apostoliques*, SC 320, 329, 336, ed. M. Metzger, 1985–7; Johnson 1997: 43). This practice is closely related to pagan usage which stipulated that a funeral feast and sacred rites, known as the *novemdialis*, be held on the ninth day after death (Johnson 1997: 43). Similarly, pagans and Christians shared the custom of offering food and wine to the dead. We hear about Augustine's mother, Monica, who was about to make such an offering of cake, bread, and wine to honor the memorials of the sainted dead in a suburban cemetery outside Milan when bishop Ambrose prevented her "both for fear that to some they might be occasions for drunkenness and also because they bore so close a resemblance to the superstitious rites (*parentalia*) which pagans held in honor of their dead" (Aug. *Conf.* 6.2). Augustine follows Ambrose (Aug. *Epist.* 29) in viewing this custom of *refrigerium* as a disguised version of the annual pagan feast of the dead, the *Virgo Vestalis Parentat* (or Parentalia) on February 13, when mourners visited the tombs of their dead relatives and gave gifts of cake and wine. These private rites culminated in two public holidays for the dead: the Feralia on February 21, which included sacrifices and offerings to the Manes, the ancestral spirits of the dead; and the *Cara Cognatio* (= Caristia) on February 22, when families gathered for a meal and to offer food and incense to the family gods (Lares) to maintain good relations with the dead (Ov. *Fast.* 2.631ff). Such annual honors were publicly recorded in the official state calendars, and Christians performed these as well, as evidenced by attempts to halt such practices as late as the 567 CE Canons of the Council of Tours (Council of Tours, Canon 23 [22], ed. C. de Clercq, *CCL* 148A).

Of course, Christian clerics and laypeople interpreted these rituals for the dead in markedly different ways. Most obviously, Christian inscriptions tended to note the date of death and celebrated the anniversaries of the deceased as "a new life" (Fontaine 1989: 1. 152). Pagans, however, tended to note the day of birth and the lifespan of their deceased on their tombstones, and the public rites of the Caristia and Feralia were intended to keep good relations with the dead, from a distance. Indeed, pagans saw the bodies of the dead as polluting; hence burial outside of the city was necessary to maintain the purity of the living. The Christian veneration of the bodies of the martyrs, especially as it developed in the fourth century, was repugnant to many pagans (Brown 1981: 4–6).

These differing attitudes toward the dead changed the religious *koine*; "by the end of the fourth century, above-ground Christian burial sites associated with churches or with mortuary chapels began to appear within the city walls" (Jon Davies 1999: 193). Such differences in burial practices were accompanied at the end of the fourth century by a lively debate among clerics concerning the funerary customs of their congregations. A number of late Roman clerics, like Ambrose in the 380s, delivered homilies criticizing their congregations' funerary customs, especially the drunkenness and riotous behavior that accompanied the funerary banquets at the graves of the dead, either at the family tombs or in the *memoriae* of the martyrs (Marrou 1978: 225–37; Brown 1981: 26–30; Gaudentius *Sermones et tractatus* 4.14). Augustine proposed a Christian understanding of funerary meals; not only should there be no drunkenness or scandalous behavior, but Christians should invite some of the poor to the tombs of their dead or reserve some food for them, thus making the funerary meals into a form of almsgiving (Aug. *Epist.* 22.6). Nonetheless, the shared burial practices and rituals – funerary banquets on the ninth day after death, food offerings, and shared tombs – provide ample evidence that a religious *koine* persisted in private rituals for the dead among pagans and Christians in the first half of the fourth century, with some elements clearly continuing into the latter half of the century and beyond.

Constantine's Legacy, 337–61 CE: Imperial Policy on Religious *Koine* and Religious Dissent under Constans and Constantius II

When Constantine died in 337, the pagan state cults and the institutions supporting them remained essentially unchanged, even if this emperor had indicated through his laws, actions, and orations that he would place certain restrictions on the rituals attendant on the public and imperial cults. As noted above, Constantine had himself refused to sacrifice publicly, and if Eusebius is to be believed, he had also restricted blood sacrifice, although this is much disputed. According to Eusebius, Constantine had also closed certain pagan cult sites where practices objectionable to Christians occurred (ritual prostitution at two temples of Aphrodite is noted by Eus. *V. Const.* 3.55). Christians were excused from attending pagan rituals that they found offensive, such as lustral sacrifices (*CTh* 16.2.5). Yet these pagan rituals were continued with state monies and Christians attended them, along with the games and circuses offered at state expense.

Constantine's tolerant policy on paganism was adopted by his heirs, Constans and Constantius II, who, however, increased restrictions on the public cults. A code of 342 CE, directed to the prefect of Rome by these two *Augusti*, specifies certain sanctions imposed for the first time on Rome: "all superstitions must be completely eradicated"; but this code also stipulates that pagan religious sites and rituals be upheld: "Temples outside the city walls shall remain untouched since certain plays or spectacles of the circus or contests derive their origin from some of these temples" (*CTh* 16.10.2). This code justifies the maintenance of such buildings because of the "regular performance of long-established amusements for the Roman people." In an attempt to neutralize the paganism of these rituals, the code redefines them as amusements (*voluptates*). Hence, this code supports much of what I have discussed as part of the public religious *koine*; the games, circuses, holidays, and temples are protected and continued, even as the emperors attempt to desacralize the activities associated with them. Hence, I would argue, *contra* Markus (Markus 1990: 1–17), that imperial propaganda attempted to widen the range of the secular by making the games and circuses into mere "amusements." This effort at desacralization, as I will show, continued under imperial guidance throughout the fourth century.

Once Constantius had gained sole control of the empire by the mid-350s, he broadened the definition of the public religious *koine* that was no longer acceptable. A code (*CTh* 16.10.6) dated to 356 CE prohibited sacrifice and the veneration of pagan images upon pain of death; another code (*CTh* 16.10.4), dated 356–61 CE, also closed the pagan temples. The language of the codes, widely promulgated, expressed in more vehement fashion the reasons for these prohibitions. Nonetheless, Constantius did not put an end to public cult or to the celebrations that formed part of the public calendar of the city of Rome or of its empire. Indeed, independent literary and archaeological evidence attests to the policy of toleration for paganism and for continued public sacrifice at Rome: Libanius, in *Oratio* 30.33–4, dated to 386 CE, observed that "They [the officials] have not yet dared rob Rome of its sacrifices." The toleration of sacrifice and the ongoing funding for public cult at Rome can also be observed in other cities of the empire; much depended, I would contend, on local magistrates and local politics. In Athens, for instance, Praetextatus, as proconsul, convinced Valentinian I to allow the celebration of sacrifices at night (Zosimus, *Historia Nova* 4.3.2–3). Christian administrators could take a more restrictive position vis-à-vis public cult worship, but similarly, pagan administrators could take more tolerant ones (Salzman 1987: 172–88). In essence, then, the key components of the public religious *koine* were still in place in the middle of the fourth century.

Constantius' attempts to redefine the public games and ceremonies as entertainment not religion is important. If this approach succeeded, it would deny any shared religiosity to pagans and Christians. This approach, however, did have a positive political aim; by desacralizing the games and ceremonies attendant on the public cults, Constantius was attempting to find a way for pagans and Christians to continue participating in these activities, united behind one emperor.

Unity was the justification, too, for Constantius' attempts to put an end to religious dissent. In this regard, Constantius, like Constantine, appears mostly concerned with religious dissent within the Christian communities of the empire. Constantius' energies were largely focused on resolving a controversy that had arisen under his father's rule; the presbyter Arius had been excommunicated for denying Christ was fully divine. "Arius was understood to teach that, just as a human son is later in time than his father and obedient to him, so also the Son of God is posterior to and subordinate to the Father" (Chadwick 1998: 564–5). Arius and his supporters attacked the idea that the Son could be said to be "identical in essence" with the Father, which was the compromise creed that Constantine had had passed by some 220 bishops at the Council of Nicaea in 325 CE. Constantius, too, sought compromise, but his interventions could not put an end to the ongoing theological and political controversies roused by these disputes about the creedal definition of the relationship of the Holy Trinity.

There are many instances of Constantius taking on his role as arbiter of religious dissent among Christians (see especially T. Barnes 1993: 165–75), but perhaps one example will show the difficulties of such a position. Constantius summoned Athanasius, bishop of Alexandria, to Milan, and accused him of undertaking "practices repugnant to the purpose of the religion over which he presided" (Amm. 15.7.8). To win support for removing this dissenting bishop, Constantius directed Liberius, then pope in Rome, to condemn Athanasius as well. Liberius would not play along, and so the emperor had the bishop removed in the middle of the night (Amm. 15.7.10). Such heavy-handed intervention was not always Constantius' style, but it was evident that this emperor would use force if necessary to put an end to religious dissent within the Christian community, as he tried to establish a new religious *koine* more to his liking.

Emperors on Religious *Koine* and Religious Dissent, 361–423 CE: Julian and the Dynasties of Valentinian and Theodosius

The emergence of Julian as Constantius' Caesar was an unexpected event in many ways; similarly, his eventual accession in 361 CE was the result in no small part of good fortune, since Constantius died before civil war could decide the issue of succession. With Julian's accession, the empire had, for the first time since Constantine, a pagan emperor. Yet Julian's religious policy was not like Constantius'; he did not aim to allow for much common ground between pagans and Christians. On the contrary, Julian's efforts were largely divisive and served to fuel the rising tide of intolerance.

Once Julian became Augustus (361–3 CE), he openly embraced paganism and emphasized the pagan religious element in public life. He restored the temples, and both encouraged and performed numerous animal sacrifices (Amm. 22.5.2; Lib. *Or.* 18.126). He also tried to reform pagan organizations; so, for example, pagan priests were to be more like Christian priests in terms of their spiritual authority and charitable works (Lib. *Or.* 18.236; 84.429c Bidez, Julian, *Epist.* 84, 89). Julian publicized his brand of paganism by an aggressive ideological campaign; he wrote speeches and published them. He wrote letters and urged others, like the notable pagan Neoplatonist Sallustius, to promulgate paganism, as Sallustius did in his book *On the Gods and the World*. Julian was convinced of the value of animal sacrifice, but his theology has also been described as approaching a Solar monotheism, especially in his *Hymn to Sol*, as noted earlier. In this regard only, Julian could be seen as encouraging the religious *koine*.

It is an irony that did not escape even supporters like Ammianus Marcellinus that Julian was an emperor who would only allow limited dissent on religious matters. He was, we know, happy to bring back Christians exiled by Constantius for heresy in the hope (or so says Ammianus Marcellinus) of fueling religious tensions within the Christian community (Julian, *Epist.* 110.398d, 114.436a–b; Amm. 22.5.3–5). But Julian could not brook those pagans and Christians who, at Antioch, disapproved of his own brand of religiosity; his bitter satire, *The Misopogon*, reflects an emperor who, had he lived, would have no doubt taken revenge on religious dissenters in this city. Indeed, Julian was clever in attacking those who disagreed with his brand of paganism; his most famous ruling in this area may well be his edict of June 362 that stipulated that only those who were morally upright and who could sincerely practice what they preached could teach classical literature (Julian, *Epist.* 61, Bidez; Lib. *Or.* 18.157). Christian professors of rhetoric had to step down; dissenting Christians had no opportunity for self-defense. It is an important sign of the general willingness to maintain some shared cultural and religious options that Julian was criticized even by his supporter Ammianus for this law which deepened the divide between pagans and Christians (32.10.6); even the pagan Libanius omits this law from his praises for the emperor's deeds as patron of learning (*Or.* 18.157ff.).

Many Christians interpreted Julian's early death in a military fiasco in Persia as proof of the just anger of God against this apostate (cf. Gregory of Nazianzus, *Oratio* 4 and 5). To signal the new imperial rule, Julian's immediate successors – Jovian (363–4 CE), Valentinian I (364–75 CE), and Valens (364–78 CE) – adopted a more tolerant attitude toward the pagan–Christian religious *koine* even as they continued to restrict religious dissent in Christian communities. So, for example, funding approved by the emperors Valentinian, Valens, and Gratian led to the restoration of the temple of Isis at the Port of Ostia between 375 and 378 CE (*SIRIS* 562 = *AE* [1961], no. 152). Although sacrifice was restricted, the ceremonies and rituals of public state cult continued with public monies.

However, tolerance of the ongoing pagan–Christian public accommodation in society did not translate into acceptance of religious dissent within the Christian community. Valentinian was an orthodox Nicene Christian who passed laws hostile to certain sects deemed heretical and attacked fraudulent clerics (*CTh* 16.2.20, 370 CE; against Manichees, *CTh* 17.5.3, 372 CE). Valens also intervened in church matters, but in support of Arians. He upheld the canons of Ariminum (Rimini) and Seleucia from the last years of Constantius' reign which had supported non-Nicene formulations of faith.

Under the last years of the reign of the emperor Gratian (367–83 CE) and the early years of "the most Christian of emperors," Theodosius I (379–95 CE) with Valentinian II (373–92 CE), official imperial policy concerning the public religious *koine* and religious dissent changed dramatically; in the 380s pagan state cult and its supporting institutions came under attack as emperors and Christian authorities set about institutionalizing Christianity in the east as in the west. In an important edict of 380 CE addressed to the people of Constantinople, the emperors Theodosius, Gratian, and Valentinian II prescribed the Orthodox Catholic faith: "It is Our will that all the peoples who are ruled by the administration of our Clemency shall practice that religion which the divine Peter the Apostle transmitted to the Romans. It is evident that this is the religion that is followed by the pontiff Damasus and by Peter, bishop of Alexandria" (*CTh* 16.2). This law further defined correct Christian belief: "We shall believe in the single Deity of the Father, the Son and the Holy Spirit, under the concept of equal majesty and of the Holy Trinity." The imperial view of Christianity was the only acceptable one now. This edict labeled those who dissented – evidently aiming only at Christians – as "demented and insane," and guilty of "the infamy of heretical dogmas"; as to Catholic dissenters, "their meeting places shall not receive the name of churches, and they shall be smitten first by divine vengeance and secondly by the retribution of Our own initiative" (*CTh* 16.2.1).

Even if the edict of 380 was not easily enforced, and even if it was only issued in the eastern empire, the implications of this view of the religious *koine* and of religious dissent for Christians and pagans across the empire were ominous. Indeed, less than two years later, in 382, the boy emperor in the west, Gratian, inspired by Theodosius' activities in the east and with the support of his bishop, Ambrose, confiscated revenues earmarked for maintaining public sacrifices and ceremonies, diverted to the imperial treasury property willed by senators and Vestals for the upkeep of pagan ritual, and put an end to the exemption of pagan religious officials from compulsory public duties (*CTh* 16.10.20, 415 CE, refers to Gratian's edict). He also ordered the removal of the Altar of Victory from the Roman senate house (Symmachus, *Relatio* 3; Ambrose, *Epist.* 17–18). Soon after, he renounced for the first time ever the title of *pontifex maximus* of the pagan cults (Cameron 1968: 96–9).

Gratian's undermining of public state cult was extended by the emperor Theodosius in 392 CE to include the prohibition of all pagan rites and ceremonies, private as well as public (*CTh* 16.10.12). Prohibition not only of animal sacrifice but of the offering of incense and candles and the hanging of garlands would have also affected even private practices, such as the funerary rituals for the dead. Hence, not only what I have deemed the public religious *koine* but its private elements fell under attack with this 392 law of Theodosius'.

These changes in ritual accompanied changes in the legal status of the public holidays associated with them; in 389 CE a code stipulated a limited list of holidays that had legal standing (i.e. the courts were closed). Sunday and the holy days of Easter were to be so recognized, along with Harvest Holidays, Vintage Holidays, the New Year, the *Natales* of Rome and Constantinople, and the birthday and accession day of the emperor (*CTh* 2.18.19). In 395 CE, under the sons of Theodosius, Arcadius and Honorius, the pagan holidays were explicitly removed from the calendar and abolished (*CTh* 2.8.22).

Such legal action did not take effect immediately, nor did it mean that laypeople, pagan and Christian, did not continue to celebrate certain rituals and ceremonies attached to the traditional pagan public holidays. Popular holidays like, for example, the Lupercalia and the Saturnalia continued to be widely celebrated long after they were no longer officially recognized as public religious holidays by the state (Salzman 1990: 239–46). Moreover, the laws undermining the legal standing of the pagan holidays did not affect at all the legal status of the games and circuses; most of these had never been, legally speaking, "holidays" on which court actions had to be halted. Hence, they could be continued as public "entertainments," a view already articulated by laws as early as 342 CE.

The logic of the imperial position on games and circuses is expressed succinctly in a code issued by Theodosius' sons, the emperors Arcadius and Honorius, in 399 CE:

> Just as we have already abolished profane rites by a salutary law, so do we not allow the festal assemblies of citizens and the common pleasure of all to be abolished. Hence we decree that, according to ancient custom, amusements [*voluptates*] shall be furnished to the people, but without any sacrifice or any accursed superstition, and they shall be allowed to attend the festal banquets whenever public vows so demand. (*CTh* 16.10.17)

Laws did restrict the *ludi* insofar as their celebration was not allowed on Christian holidays, like Sunday and Easter, now given official status as public holidays (*CTh* 15.5.5, 425 CE; 2.8.23, 399 CE; 2.8.24, 400–5 CE).

But much did continue as before. Gladiatorial combat (unsuccessfully forbidden by Constantine as early as 325 CE) continued at Rome probably until 438 CE, well after the emperor Honorius closed the gladiatorial schools in 399 CE. Wild beast fighting and hunting persisted much longer, at least until 523 CE. Chariot racing survived in Rome even later; the last recorded races in the Circus Maximus were held under Totila in 549 CE (Salzman 1990: 237).

Although the *ludi* and *circenses* continued into the Christian empire of the late fourth and fifth centuries, scholars have debated how much of the pagan elements of the earlier religious *koine* persisted. I have argued that the religious dimension of these games varied, depending on the attitudes, background, and beliefs of the participants. To the diminishing number of pagans who attended these games, there may still well have been religious meaning, even if the age-old rituals, like animal sacrifice, were gone. However, official imperial propaganda, expressed so clearly by the *Theodosian Code*, tried to put an end to the religious meaning of the games, as they also did, by the 390s, to the religious meaning of private rituals for the dead and the household Lares. In their efforts to undermine a religious *koine* for pagans and Christians, as in their attempts to legislate a uniform Christianity with no room for dissenting views, emperors were encouraged, supported, and at times manipulated by Christian authorities; most important in urban contexts were the bishops.

Bishops on Religious *Koine* and Religious Dissent, 350–423 CE

In the cities of the fourth-century empire, it was the bishop who claimed that he had the authority – spiritual, ascetic, and pragmatic (Rapp 2005: 16–22) – to deal with the twin issues discussed in this chapter, notably the possibility of a shared religious *koine* with pagans and tolerance for religious dissent within and without the Christian community. The growing importance of the church as an institution in the cities across the empire lent weight to the authority of the bishops. By the end of the fourth century, some bishops claimed priority even over and above the emperor as the ultimate arbiter about what was and what was not acceptable Christianity.

We can begin by looking at what I have defined as the public religious *koine* manifested by public cult festivals and practices, especially blood sacrifice. By the last decades of the fourth century, the bishops uniformly opposed state support for these activities. Perhaps the clearest and best-attested example of their position is the rejoinder of the bishop of Milan, Ambrose, to the pagan senator Symmachus' request for the return of the Altar of Victory; in matters of religion, this bishop stated, the bishop, not the emperor, has the right to decide (Ambrosius, *Epist.* 17.13). Ambrose claimed that it was not tolerable for pagans to sacrifice in the presence of Christian senators (Ambrosius, *Epist.* 18.31). Symmachus had crafted an eloquent plea for tolerance for the pre-existing religious *koine*: "It is reasonable to regard as identical that which all worship. We look on the same stars; we share the same heaven; the same world enfolds us. What difference does it make by what system of knowledge each man sees the truth? Man cannot come to so profound a mystery by one road alone" (Symmachus, *Relatio* 3.10). In response, Ambrose proclaimed the superiority of Christians, who "have found through the real wisdom and truth of God" the path that pagans could only vaguely hint at (Ambrosius *Epist.* 18.31). Any notion of shared religiosity or tolerance for religious difference or dissent was denied.

Not only the pagan religious ceremonies but also the civic festivals, games, and circuses were now deemed unacceptable even as "entertainments" by many a late fourth-century bishop. Perhaps the best-known expression of this opposition was articulated by John Chrysostom, bishop of Constantinople, in his homily *Contra ludos et theatra* (PG 56, 263–70). In opposing the games and the theater, Chrysostom was joined by other bishops and monks who, by the end of the fourth century, had become, like Augustine, increasingly intolerant of Christians who participated in civic banquets or went to the shows. In sermons delivered in Carthage and Bulla Regia from 399 on, Augustine "lament[s] over Christians who fill the theaters on the festivals of Babylon; over the fortunes squandered by the rich on the shows while Christ's poor go hungry; and is constantly exhorting Christians to turn from the enjoyment of the great civic occasions (*munera*) to the enjoyment of spiritual delights" (Markus 1990: 117–18, citing, among other texts Aug. *Sermo* 51.1, 32.20; *Enarratio in Psalmos* 61.10, 102.28, 80.23). In opposing the spectacles, bishops took a somewhat different position from that of the emperors whose laws had attempted to desacralize and hence continue the games and circuses. In this regard, the emperors, not the bishops, had greater success, as the games continued for centuries in Rome and in Constantinople.

In terms of private cult, too, late Roman bishops claimed the authority to define what was and what was not acceptable. Indeed, notions about the correct way to honor the dead and the growing emphasis placed on the veneration of martyrs made private rituals concerning the dead of community import as the empire became increasingly Christian (Brown 1981: 1–49). As already noted, it was with his authority as bishop that Ambrose prohibited Christians from offerings for the dead and the martyrs (Aug. *Conf.* 6.2). He, like other late fourth-century bishops, sought to teach his flock about the correct rituals for the deceased and emphasized how very different these were from pagan practice. Augustine discussed these at length in his tract *De cura gerenda pro mortuis.* Clearly, private rites for the dead practiced by Christian laypeople did not conform in all respects to the views of the bishops, nor, in the late fourth century, was there uniformity in Christian practice in this area. Nonetheless, within each city, it was the bishop who, like Ambrose, claimed the authority to decide this matter.

It is consistent with their claim to authority that the bishops also asserted themselves in dealing with religious dissent, especially in matters pertaining to the Christian community. Ambrose presented a paradigmatic example of episcopal behavior when he asserted his authority in dealing with the empress Justina, widow of Valentinian I. Gratian had granted those Christians not of the Nicene persuasion a basilica in Milan for their worship. The basilica was handed back to the pro-Nicene bishop Ambrose. But in 386 CE, "the Empress Justina had enacted freedom of assembly for upholders of the creed of Ariminum, leading to a confrontation with Ambrose, who mobilized his people to resist her" (Chadwick 1998: 581–2). Ambrose succeeded in reclaiming this basilica, although the non-Nicene position remained a viable one in Italian cities for at least another century.

Ambrose's intolerance for dissenting Christianities was typical of the rising tide of orthodoxy that accompanied the growth of an imperial Christianity in the late fourth century. In dealing with Justina, Ambrose was successful without the use of force, but violence did erupt at times. The struggle for the episcopacy of Rome in 366/7 CE included substantive as well as political differences between the supporters of Damasus and Ursinus; it erupted into a violent conflict that left the religious dissenters from both sides, some 137 of them, dead after a battle in the basilica of Sicinus in Rome (Amm. 27.3.11–13). And after Theodosius' laws of 391 and 392 CE, bishops could more effectively lead the charge against groups now labeled as heretics or schismatics. So, in north Africa, Augustine preached and acted against the schismatic Donatists at the end of the fourth century, as well as against pagans and heretics (Chadwick 1998: 583–6).

Thus, in private and in public, in episcopal courts if need be, bishops denied the validity of Christians sharing in many of Rome's civic and public traditions. They attacked what they defined as pagan elements of the public and private religious *koine* even as they repressed dissenting religionists; in this latter movement, they focused first on Christians, but pagans and Jews were also, logically, dissenters from the truth who, too, could be confronted and converted.

A New Religious *Koine*

By the late fourth/early fifth century, the wide spread of Christianity with imperial and episcopal support had effectively altered the traditional religious *koine* of the empire. One way to assess this transformation is to look at what happened to the public cultic celebrations that had formed the essence of the early and mid-fourth-century religious *koine* reflected by the Calendar of 354 from Rome. The games and circuses which did indeed continue were justified as custom or entertainment. Pagan holidays were illicit, and so many disappeared. Others, although illicit, retained their rituals and customs, but acquired new Christian meanings; so, for example, the carrying of pictures of Isis on board her sacred ship, part of the popular festival to Isis celebrated in March (*Isidis navigium*) and associated with public vows on behalf of the emperor's well-being by the fourth century, continued in the early fifth century in the Christian festival of the *Carnevale*, held in conjunction with Easter; at this festival, the ship or a representation of it was carried by assembled celebrants, its meanings now linked with Christ's resurrection (Alföldi 1937: 46ff.). And the rites of the Caristia to honor the ancestral spirits of the dead were likely continued under the guise of the Christian festival of St. Peter's chair on February 22 (Salzman 1990: 47).

Other pagan holidays were still popularly celebrated but desacralized. A good example of one of these is the celebration of the pagan holiday of Lupercalia. From earliest Roman times, this holiday had been a purificatory rite which, with the lashing of women with whips, promoted fertility. By the third century CE, the holiday had been reinterpreted into a rite of the punishment and public penance of women; purification was interpreted as spiritual, not only sexual, but still within a pagan context. The ritual of female flagellation fell under attack at the end of the fifth century when, in 494, the pope labeled these rites as "*diabolica figmenta.*" A Christian senator opposed the pope, arguing that the Lupercalia was merely an *imago* of the former pagan festival and its continuance was important for the well-being (*salus*) of the Roman community. Individual flagellation was necessary for individual purification for sin. Moreover, this senator argued, this ritual was a long-standing Roman tradition (Gelasius I, *Lettre*, p. 162, ed. G. Pomarès [*SC* 65]). In this instance, the pope won; he successfully labeled this ritual as paganism and used it to undermine the influence of Rome's senatorial aristocracy (Markus 1990: 131–5). But the holiday could have had another trajectory; although the Lupercalia died out in Rome, it continued to be celebrated in Constantinople until the tenth century as a Christian holiday (Wiseman 1995b: 17).

As arbiter of religious matters, it was the bishops who, by and large, determined which festivals and practices were acceptable or not. Much would depend on the local initiative of the bishop, and even his attitude could change over time. Hence, when confronted with festivals in north Africa which he deemed pagan, Augustine took it as his duty to repress them only in his later years as bishop, after 399 CE (Aug. *Epist.* 29.9; *Enarratio in Psalmos* 88.14 = CCL 88, 1294; and *De catechizandis rudibus* 25.48 = CCL 46, 172). Similarly, as bishop, Augustine took it upon himself to determine which dissenting opinions were or were not acceptable within the Christian community. Religion in the ancient world had always been a local affair, and at the end of the fourth century, it was the bishop who took the lead concerning such matters in local contexts.

The growing authority of the bishop over local and urban religious matters was also the direct result of the gradual abandonment of the western empire in the fifth century by the eastern emperors. As the bishop became, increasingly, the sole advocate for the city in the face of attack, the possibilities for religious dissent were increasingly limited. What had once been accepted as civic and traditional, like the festival of the Lupercalia, was denied validity by late fifth-century Christian bishops who desired to secure their authority in the western empire. In the east, too, the need to unify the *populus* behind the bishop and the emperor undercut any positive views of a religious *koine* that was anything other than imperial Christianity, even as such unity simultaneously destroyed traditional tolerance for religious dissent. One could say the Middle Ages had begun.

FURTHER READING

For a deeper understanding of the role of individual fourth-century emperors in shaping religious *koine* and religious dissent, a reader should look at the works devoted to individual emperors. For Constantine, see especially Drake (2000). For the impact of the emperors Julian through Theodosius II on fourth-century religiosity, a good introduction is to be found in Fowden (1998). The essays in Athanassiadi and Frede (1999) shed much light on this particular component of the religious *koine*. For further reading on funerary rituals and tomb monuments of pagans and Christians, see Jon Davies (1999), and for more on the church's attitudes in particular, see Rebillard (2003a). On religious *koine* in the fourth century as reflected in pagan festivals and Christian attitudes to these, see Markus (1990) and Salzman (1990). On the role of the bishop, see Rapp (2005).

PART II

Media

CHAPTER TEN

The History of Roman Religion in Roman Historiography and Epic

Denis Feeney

It is now impossible for us to know how – or even whether – the Romans represented divine action and religious practice in narrative or song before they began their project of adapting Greek literary forms into a literature of their own in the second half of the third century BC. More and more contemporary scholars wish to believe the once discredited Roman traditions about ballads of the men of old supposedly sung in the pre-literary period. If such songs were sung (and that remains a big "if"), it is imaginable that they portrayed the help of the gods and the pious rituals of the Roman people and its generals. Again, if the Romans told stories about their past on occasions such as festivals, funerals, triumphs, and anniversaries of victories or the dedication of temples, then it is likewise imaginable that these stories included human ritual or divine manifestations. None of this can now be securely known. What can be known is that the new literary forms of historiography and epic which came into being in the late third century BC included religion as a vital component from the beginning. Already in the fragmentary remains of our very first texts, it is clear that the histories and epics of the Roman people are a venue for exploring the relationship between gods and men, and this crucial preoccupation continued to be central to both literary traditions for as long as they endured.

While sharing this common concern, each tradition had its own distinctive techniques and priorities, which were to a large degree the inheritance of the developed Greek literary forms which provided their starting point. The student who is reading these texts with an interest in their religious dimension must always be conscious of the fact that they are specific kinds of literature, which are interacting with other religious discourses in their own distinctive ways. These texts have much to teach us about the possibilities of Roman religion, but we can never simply "read off" information about Roman religion from them without allowing for the particular kinds of narratives that they are. For many years the histories and epics of the Romans were commonly regarded as only "literary," with no relation to the "real" religion of the society. That phase of scholarship is thankfully passing, and the deep importance of the religious dimension of these texts is now generally acknowledged; the challenge now is to try to recover that religious dimension without making it conform to the norms of other kinds of religious discourse – without, in other words, blurring over the specific and distinctive literary characteristics of the work in question.

The Divine Sanction of the First Roman Epics

The earliest epics in the Latin language to be preserved and transmitted were written by men who were not native speakers of the language. A Greek from Tarentum called Andronikos became a Roman citizen with the name of Lucius Livius Andronicus; sometime in the second half of the third century BC he translated Homer's *Odyssey* into Saturnians, a non-Greek meter of uncertain origin and nature. Toward the end of the century a Campanian named Gnaeus Naevius wrote the *Bellum Punicum*, an epic, likewise in Saturnians, about the first war between Rome and Carthage (264–241 BC). Some thirty years later, some time around 180 BC, a man from the Messapian area on the heel of Italy, Quintus Ennius, took the decisive step of using Homeric hexameters for the first time in his composition of the *Annales*, a huge poem which described the history of Rome all the way from the fall of Troy down to his own day. The understanding these outsiders display of the Romans' language, culture, and religion is phenomenally deep, yet they all knew Greek before they knew Latin, and their poems are a fascinating amalgam of Greek and Roman in every aspect, not least that of religion.

The fundamental divine scenes of Homer reproduce themselves in all of these poems, with divine councils and interventions, gods speaking to humans, and so forth. The poems show the gods and goddesses of the Homeric tradition in action, yet in a Latin and a Roman guise. As characters, they have Latin names (Jupiter for Zeus, Juno for Hera, and so on), and the work of creating parallelisms between the Greek and Roman gods is clearly one that had been going on in cult for centuries before Livius and Naevius. Although many of the Greek aspects of the gods overlap with Roman ones, the poets knew that their narratives had to accommodate Roman gods to new roles. The familiar Roman healing god Apollo appears in Naevius as the god of Delphi (*Pythius*, frag. 24.2 Blänsdorf 1995), discharging a role that had only just become important for the Roman state, which consulted the Delphic oracle during the war against Hannibal. The Roman Mercury shared many of his mercantile affinities with the Greek Hermes, but in Rome he was not a god associated with escorting the dead, as he was in Greece. When he appeared in this role in Livius' *Odyssey* it will certainly have been a new piece of casting, and Roman readers will have had to cross mental boundaries to accommodate their Mercury to this new persona.

By far the most significant rewriting of Greek and Roman categories may be seen in the case of the supreme god, Jupiter Optimus Maximus, "Best and Greatest."

Naevius and Ennius are careful to blend together Greek, Homeric epithets with these special cult titles of the god. In Naevius Jupiter is addressed as "highest" of the gods, just like Zeus in Homer, and also as "Best," *optumum* (frag. 15); in Ennius he is addressed not only as "our father, son of Saturn," to correspond to the Homeric "our father, son of Cronus," but also as "Greatest," *maxime* (frag. 444 Skutsch 1985). These deft transcultural interstitchings are just one token of the way in which Jupiter becomes in these poems not only the supreme god of the Roman state but also the counterpart of the Greek Zeus, not just in his cultic dimension but with all the mass of interpretation which had accrued to his personality over centuries of Homeric scholarship. In this Greek tradition of exegesis Zeus is the god who stands above all gods and humans, guaranteeing a cosmic order and embodying a providential wisdom. In accordance with this kind of view, in the Greek world Zeus was not a partisan of any one city or state, but stood above them all, as for example at Olympia, where his temple was the focus for the whole Hellenic world in its celebration of the Olympic games. To identify this supranational and potentially cosmic figure with the supreme god of the Roman republic was a strategy of enormous symbolic power, beyond the capacity of any Greek state: the supreme god of the universe now has a partisan affinity with the new empire, and the destiny of the world is now the destiny of Rome. The Greek god has taken on Roman attributes and the Roman god has taken on Greek ones; from a Roman point of view, neither Zeus nor Jupiter will ever look quite the same again.

Zeus is intimately associated in Greek epic with an ability to foresee and foretell the future, and in Roman epic these capacities are also present, in even more potent form. Prophecies in extant Greek epic do not extend more than one human generation into the future, yet already in Naevius we see Jupiter prophesying the future greatness of the Roman people in the immediate aftermath of the Trojan war, looking hundreds of years ahead as he consoles Venus during a storm which threatens her son, Aeneas (frag. 14). In general, the epics of Naevius and Ennius show a determination to anchor the history of the Roman people in a divine plan and a deep mythic past, as if to show that their rise to hegemony was inevitably destined (Barchiesi 1962: 224–68). Naevius narrated the voyage of the Trojans to Italy in the first third of his poem, presenting the Roman triumph over the Carthaginians as part of a divine plan that had been in place for centuries. Ennius began his epic with the fall of Troy, although he narrated continuously from there to the contemporary present, to show the new Troy rising triumphantly from the ashes as the Romans achieved victory over the old enemy, the Greeks: the culmination of his original 15-book plan was the foundation of the temple of Hercules Musarum, built to house the statues of the Muses looted from Ambracia, home of the ancestral enemy Pyrrhus, and dedicated possibly in 184 BC, one thousand years after the sack of Troy (Gratwick 1982: 65).

These perspectives resonated with a Roman readership accustomed to thinking of their success in war as depending on their strenuous maintenance of good relations with the gods, yet the panoramas of the epics are not just a mirror of what everyone was thinking at the time anyway. Rather, they are a unique vision of Roman destiny, capitalizing on Greek epic strategies and Greek literary and philosophical scholarship in addition to Roman practices of commemoration. The new Roman epic, with its distinctive religious vision, has its own contribution to make to the way the Romans were reconceiving their role on the world stage in these days of unparalleled expansion. And we should never forget that the Roman epic led the way in exploring these questions: Naevius was the first person to write a history of Rome in an integrated narrative with literary aspirations (Barchiesi 1962: 242–3), and Ennius was the first person to write a history of Rome in Latin in an annalistic format (Rüpke 1995b: 200–1).

The first epics were also full of descriptions of religious practice of all kinds. In the first part of his *Bellum Punicum*, Naevius engagingly presents Aeneas' father Anchises behaving like a Roman priest – in fact, like three kinds of Roman priest. Greek epics contained many descriptions of prophets and seers in action, yet Anchises predicts the future on the basis of sacred books he received from his former lover, Venus (frag. 4): in this way he behaves not like a Greek seer but like one of the *decemviri*, who consulted the Sibylline Books in the temple of Jupiter. Anchises also knows how to "watch for his bird in the right area of the sky" like a Roman *augur* (*avem conspexit in templo Anchisa*, frag. 25.1), and how to lay the banquet for the gods like a *pontifex* (frag. 25.2) – it is just possible that Naevius knew of the new priestly college of the *tresuiri epulones*, established in 196 BC to take over the duties of providing sacrificial banquets (Rüpke 2005a: 1625–7). Ennius likewise describes many cult actions, and the institution of many Roman religious practices and institutions, especially with Numa's monarchy at the beginning of Book 2. One of the finest surviving fragments is the unforgettable scene in Book 1 where Romulus and Remus take the auspices to see which one of them will found the city of Rome (frag. 1.xlvii Skutsch 1985). Here the language of Roman augury is carefully staged at the crucial inaugural moment of Rome, with all its religious and political future ready to be bodied forth. The Roman nobility's sense of their place in a succession of religiously sanctioned predecessors underpins the entire poem, and their religious piety was scrupulously commemorated throughout (Gildenhard 2003: 95–7).

In Ennius' poem such self-consciously "Roman" moments are jostling with other discourses – not just the Homeric one, but philosophical and religious schemes with which Ennius will have been familiar from his upbringing in the orbit of Greek culture in southern Italy: Pythagoreanism, Euhemerism, and the natural philosophical rationalizing of the Sicilian Epicharmus, to name only the most prominent (Jocelyn 1972: 1010–11). The temptation, for students of Roman religion even more than for students of Roman literature, is to seize on the ritualistic moments in the poem and identify them as what really counts as religiously significant, so that the other religious discourses can be demoted or discarded. This would be a mistake, however, and not only because it is poor literary criticism. Such a procedure is also poor intellectual and cultural history. It would make it impossible to see how the poems of Naevius and Ennius are welding together disparate traditions in order to create novel visions of the destiny of Rome in a world undergoing bewilderingly rapid change.

The omnivorous reach of Roman epic's religious power reflects the society's involvement with the religious and cultural systems of many neighboring and distant states: the Romans are now heir to Greek concerns in the east, in ways that make their mythical Trojan status newly powerful; they are turning themselves into the heirs of Greek culture in more general terms, with an ambitious program of competition in the field of what we now call "literature"; their rivalry with Carthage enforces a new vision of their imperial destiny in competition with that of Carthage, framed in epic as a struggle between two divine systems centering on Carthage's Juno and Rome's Jupiter. The new Roman epic has many religious and philosophical discourses to deploy in pursuit of these ambitious goals, and the new genre cannot be reduced to a template which maps on to any identifiable correlative in the rest of the society.

The Religious Order of Virgil's *Aeneid*

While capitalizing on the determinative patterns of the epics of Naevius and Ennius, Virgil's *Aeneid* takes their concerns with fated dominion much further. By the lifetime of Virgil (70–19 BC) the Roman empire had grown to engulf the entire Mediterranean, and had fallen under the sway of a single man, the emperor Augustus (63 BC–AD 14). Through his adoptive father, Julius Caesar, Augustus was able to claim descent from Iulus, the son of Aeneas: by a gigantic historical fluke, the careful prophetic programs of Naevius and Ennius, guaranteeing rule to the descendants of Aeneas in general, have now acquired a new end-point, for the whole of Roman history now appears to be heading toward its culmination not just in the collective dominion of the Roman people but in the personal rule of Aeneas' direct familial descendant.

The ambition of the *Aeneid* also includes the project of showing how Rome has taken over the role of guarantor of civilized order from Greece, as the new heir to the cultural patrimony of the older and more distinguished culture. Ennius was already feeling his way toward this theme, but Virgil strongly foregrounds the *translatio imperii*, the process by which the Romans have taken over from the Greeks as the latest in the series of empires. Rome's religion has in the process become a global religion, with Rome's gods taking on a definitive role as the gods of an empire, not just a city. Virgil's Jupiter is now unquestionably the supreme cosmocrat of Greek philosophy and Homeric scholarship as well as Jupiter Optimus Maximus; Apollo is now the favorite god of Augustus as well as the god of prophecy, music, and healing; Juno is now starting to outlive her old persona as the inveterate enemy of Troy and Rome, as she used to be in her partisan roles as the Homeric Hera, the Carthaginian Tanit, and the Italian Juno/Uni of the resistance to Roman expansion in Italy.

As part of this larger objective of outlining a new imperial reach to Roman religion, it is striking how Virgil's interest in evoking Roman ritual is less strong than Naevius' and Ennius'. In taking over Homer into the center of Roman self-awareness in his new poem, Virgil interestingly downplays the distinctively Roman elements of his characters' prayers, for example, in contrast to Ennius, whose prayers had been more closely modeled on pontifical ritual (Hickson 1993: 27–31, 141–4): the "half-Greeks" at the beginning of the tradition seem more intent on adapting the form of Homer to accommodate the novel language of the culture they had learnt to know in their childhood or teens. Once again we see that the undeniable cultural power

of this deeply engaged poetry does not straightforwardly derive from the directness
of its ties to other forms of religious discourse, even those which modern scholars
might envisage as more "real" or "practical."

It is very hard to know what kind of impact the early epics of Naevius and Ennius
might have had on the Romans' thinking about their religion or their empire's place
in the Mediterranean scheme of things. In the case of the *Aeneid*, however, it is
plain that the poem rapidly became indispensably part of the way educated Romans
conceived of their mythic past and religious present. Within 10 years of the poet's
death in 19 BC, Augustus' Ara Pacis (dedicated January 10, 9 BC) shows an iconic
scene of sacrifice taken from *Aeneid* 7, with Aeneas sacrificing in the Roman garb
as if to ground the sacrificial actions to be performed there by his descendant in
contemporary time. Some years later, the Forum of Augustus (dedicated in 2 BC)
exhibits a statue group of Aeneas and his father and son, fleeing from Troy to their
new destiny in the west. The myths of the *Aeneid* have become central to the emperor's
self-representation. The power of this form of art derives not so much from its
successful tracking of existing patterns of thought or behavior as from its creation
of systems of meaning with their own distinctive – though not autonomous – power.
The myth of Troy and the narrative of a divine sanction grounded in more than a
millennium of history are not frameworks of Roman religious practice outside the
Aeneid or its epic ancestors, but the poems have their own unique ways of working
with the Roman state's techniques for guaranteeing the gods' support in all of its
operations. What the state attempted to guarantee through scrupulous observation
of inherited religious custom, the epics declared to be guaranteed through the involvement of personalized divine agencies whose relationships involved the Roman people
in a deep and wide mythical system.

Order Denied: Lucan and Statius

In many ways, the most striking proof of the *Aeneid*'s power to encapsulate vital
elements of Roman religious thought is to be found in the massive efforts made by
the Neronian poet Lucan (AD 39–65) to demolish the religious sanction which the
Aeneid had given to the new Roman order. In the *De bello civili*, his narrative of
the civil war between Caesar and Pompey in 49–48 BC, Lucan is determined to show
that Virgil was wrong to think that a beneficent world order emerged from the destruction of the republic. As part of this goal, Lucan systematically undermines the *Aeneid*'s
representations of both Roman history and religion. He shows the organs of religion in a state of collapse, with the state's rites failing to shore up the republic. He
also deliberately writes the gods out of the narrative, making it impossible for the
reader to find in his poem the kind of divine oversight that the *Aeneid* embodies in
the figure of Jupiter, above all. The gods do not act as characters in the poem, and
are unavailable as a point of reference for the reader trying to make sense of the
catastrophes described in the narrative. When Lucan refers to the gods' perspective
on the action of the poem, it is with irony and disgust. Early in the first book
he tells us that the gods may have backed the winning side but Cato backed the
losing side (1.128); here the gods' perspective on the direction of Roman history is

emphatically the inferior one, while the human character Cato has the "right" view. The gods back Caesar because he is going to become one of them, as the new deity "Divus Julius"; Lucan exposes the ruler cult as a sham rather than a vindication, and exposes the new imperial religion as a process of corporate raiding by the ruling family rather than an evolution of old forms into new meanings.

The fall of the republic and the emergence of the principate are unmitigated catastrophes for Lucan, and he represents Virgil as complicit in papering over the disaster with his creation of divine sanction for the new order. Lucan's refusal to endorse the new religious dispensation is shocking enough in itself, but he goes even further, entertaining the possibility that the gods simply do not care about what is happening to the Roman state. In the climactic moment of the battle of Pharsalus, as Pompey is defeated by Caesar, Lucan accuses the gods of total unconcern and irrelevance: the world is whirled along by blind chance and the fate of the empire means nothing within any cosmic framework (7.445–55).

Even though the gods do not act as characters, then, the religious dimension of the poem is still extremely important and powerful. Its nihilism is intimately bound up with its passionate disavowal of the expected patterns of Roman epic, especially of the *Aeneid*'s attempts to use the inherited religious forms of epic to validate the new regime. Both Virgil and Lucan understand how profoundly the sanction of the empire is bound up with its religion, even if one of them is trying to support the nexus and the other to undo it.

Lucan's vision of the relations between gods and humans had a deep influence on Statius (c. AD 50–c. 95), whose *Thebaid* narrates the legendary story of the Seven against Thebes. The story may be set in the time before Troy, without the clear reference to Roman history which its predecessors had, but the contemporary resonances of Statius' religious vision are nonetheless very strong. In Statius' poem, the gods certainly participate actively and involve themselves in human affairs through epiphany and prophecy, and in this respect his poem differs very much from Lucan's. As the *Thebaid* continues, however, the gods withdraw more and more from the human action, leaving the field to furies from the Underworld and to allegorical figures without the gods' cultic associations: by the end of the poem, even these replacement figures have gone, and the last book of the epic is one in which the only agents are human beings. The supreme god, Jupiter, appears early in the poem as a vindictive and authoritarian figure, and then he removes himself from the action and washes his hands of the humans. The sum effect is a very disturbing one, with a religious vision of humans attempting to carry on their lives within inherited forms which no longer have the meaning they once had. By Statius' time the dynamics of the Roman epic tradition have become so strong that they have become available for a vision of human experience which is related only obliquely to the experience of empire.

The Religion of the First Roman Histories

If we return now to the late third century BC, when the first epics in Latin were being written in response to the dramatic transformation of Rome into an international empire, we also find a new historiography emerging, composed by Roman senators who were attempting to explain and justify the rise of Rome. For the first two generations, these new histories were written in Greek, and not until the *Origines* of Cato in the middle of the second century BC do we find a Roman writing the history of his city in Latin prose. Part of these first Roman historians' motivation for writing in Greek may well have been their wish to reach a wide audience not only in Rome but elsewhere in Italy and in Magna Graecia, where knowledge of Latin was rare. Still, they probably had little choice in the matter: writing a full-blown history in Latin may strike us as a natural thing to be able to do, but in the late third century BC it is far more likely that anyone wishing to write a history of Rome was more or less obliged to use not just the only system of historiography available but also the language in which that historiography was couched, namely, Greek (Dillery 2002).

The first histories, then, were not only written in the Greek language; in certain basic and inescapable ways, they were written in conformity with the norms of historiography current in Greece at the time, norms which had for the most part been laid down over two centuries earlier by Herodotus, the founder of the genre. Herodotus had shown a great interest in matters of religion, and his history contains many reports of ritual, prophecy, miraculous events, and divine actions. As part of his new genre, however, Herodotus established a vital departure from the techniques of Homeric epic, for he never allows the gods to be part of the action of his narrative, and he never stakes his own authority on the veracity of the reports he transcribes of divine prophecy or intervention.

The first works of Roman historiography have been lost, so that it is impossible to know for certain how closely they followed the mainstream of Greek historiography in this regard. But on the basis of the surviving fragments and testimonia, there is no reason to believe that the first Roman historians did depart from the ground rules of their tradition so as to represent the gods in characterful action in the manner of Homer – certainly the surviving histories of Livy, Sallust, and Tacitus never do so. Here, then, we see immediately a major difference between the histories of Rome and the epics we have been discussing so far. While epic can have gods in the action as characters in addition to the human actors, history cannot.

The Roman historians had a powerful interest in the religion of the state and in questions of the relation between the state and its gods, but their interest had to find different expression from that of epic. They described prodigies and ritual actions, and had explicit discussion of the meaning of portents, yet the basic ground rules were different from those of Homer and his epic successors. Both in Greece and in Rome, an inspired poet might claim access to divine knowledge which he could represent through reporting divine prophecy or describing particular deities in action; but other authors did not use such language, and referred to "the gods" as a generalized collective, without claiming privileged insight into their actions or motivations. In many ways the Roman historian is in the same position as any senior figure in Roman life, making decisions about which signs to interpret and how to interpret them; in addition, as we shall see, the historian is crafting a narrative in which the manifestations of religion are an element of narrative art along with all the others. Religious events in Roman histories are therefore part of a complex series of creative and interpretive acts: magistrates and senate invested time in composing new rituals; interpreting the divine signs was a long-standing art with its own complex and sophisticated hermeneutics; debating the interpretation of signs was a long-standing feature of Roman public life; and incorporating such exegesis in a narrative introduces another layer of interpretive problems for the reader to decipher.

The first Roman historian, Fabius Pictor, writing sometime around 210 BC, was not working in a vacuum. Plutarch tells us that Fabius' source for the Romulus and Remus story was a Greek historian called Diocles of Peparethus (*Life of Romulus*, 3.1), and the great historian of western Greece and Sicily, Timaeus of Tauromenium, had incorporated a good deal of material about Rome's mythical past in his *Histories* of c. 280 BC. We know that Timaeus had a keen interest in the Trojan origins of the Romans. He explained the Roman ritual of the Equus October, in which they killed a horse on the Campus Martius, by referring to the Trojan horse and a resulting inherited hostility to horses (Polybius 12.4b-c1); more cogently, he said that he had heard from people at Lavinium that their holy objects included iron and bronze heralds' wands and a Trojan earthenware vessel (Dion. H. 1.67.4). As we now know from a painted inscription on a wall in Tauromenium, discovered in 1969, Fabius Pictor certainly referred to the arrival in Italy of Aeneas and his son Ascanius, to the birth "much later" of Romulus and Remus, and to the foundation of Rome by Romulus, who became the first king (Chassignet 1996: frag. 1). Whether or not Timaeus was trying to dignify the Romans' pedigree by incorporating their origins into the mainstream of Greek mythology, it seems reasonably certain that Fabius meant to achieve this end, and he was very probably, in addition, aiming at the same objective as Naevius, of showing how the gods had been watching over the Roman enterprise from the beginning.

How Fabius' narrative about Rome's mythic origins worked in practice is unknowable, since all we have remaining is later authors' summaries and references. He told the story of the rape of the mother of Romulus and Remus by the god Mars, for example, but we cannot tell whether this was part of his narrative like any other part, recounted as part of tradition, or given as the maiden's report. In the properly historical portion of his narrative he recounted prodigies and significant dreams, and gave accounts of the origins of temples (Frier 1979: 266). Once again, the actual technique is irrecoverable for the most part, but the overall strategy may be reasonably surmised – the meticulous acting out of the piety of the Roman people, scrupulous in their maintenance of relations with the divine, correcting religious error and appeasing divine anger when necessary, and guaranteeing the success of their enterprises from the time of Aeneas down to the war against Hannibal, their worst threat since Achilles and Odysseus (Frier 1979: 283–4; cf. Linderski 1993 on these themes in Livy). Other early Roman historians, now fragmentary, show a similar array of religious material, reporting prodigies and so forth (Frier 1979: 271); to assess how their narratives really worked is no longer possible, and we have to wait for Livy to have a body of real evidence.

Religion in Livy: Creating and Preserving a System

With Livy's history of Rome from Aeneas to his own day, we finally meet a substantially surviving text (even if we have lost 107 of the original 142 books), in which we may analyze religious discourses in the historian's own words without having to rely on the testimony of other authors. In the case of Livy, together with his successor Tacitus, modern discussion of the issues has tended to revolve, even more than in the case of the epic poets, around the question of skepticism and belief. Scholars have regularly read Livy and Tacitus in order to find out what they really thought about religion, and especially whether they really believed in the apparatus of omens, prodigies, and expiation which takes up so much of their description of religious matters. Quite apart from the theoretical objections which many literary critics would level at the project of making an author's personal beliefs the focus of reading a narrative, we need to remind ourselves that framing the question in terms of belief and skepticism misses the point that "these men were writing for a society that was not, for the most part, concerned with *whether* the gods existed but rather with how they would impact on the human world, how they should be understood to act and, more importantly, the effects and means of placation – and the consequences of failing to do so" (Jason Davies 2004: 2). The Roman state had a system for dealing with such matters, and any history of the Roman state will inevitably have to engage with that system.

In other words, the proper focus of inquiry is not whether Livy or Tacitus really believed in this or that, but rather how representation of religion actually works in the historians' narratives. It is the great merit of two major recent studies of religion in Livy (Levene 1993) and in Livy, Tacitus, and Ammianus (Jason Davies 2004) that we have been brought back to the task of reading these histories as sophisticated examples of a subtle genre of narrative in which various religious discourses have a distinctive part to play. As a result of this realignment of priorities, the theme of religious meaning is now available for wider interpretation: what kind of picture of Roman religion and of the Roman past emerges if we take the historians' representations of religion seriously as part of a narrative with powerful didactic intent?

As we have already seen, history's way of engaging with manifestations of the divine is not going to be the same as epic's, for historians do not claim inspiration, and the intervention of the gods "is represented from the point of view of the City's interest rather than any individual's, and by deduction rather than explicit identification. These are matters of literary genre, not personal belief, or philosophical speculation" (Jason Davies 2004: 141). Accordingly, throughout Livy's narrative, reports are made of prodigious events (talking cows, monstrous births of animals or humans), and then it is up to the responsible authorities in Rome to decide what to make of them. It is also up to the reader to decide what to make of them, for Livy involves the reader directly in the act of interpreting, and hardly ever analyzes these phenomena on his own account or gives his own explicit view on their meaning. This strategy is in accordance with the generally self-effacing narrative technique of ancient historiography, where larger thematic meaning is conveyed through narrative as in a novel, rather than through explicit editorializing as in modern histories.

Departures from this technique of not endorsing or vouching for divine motivation are extremely rare, just as they are in Herodotus. A striking example comes in Book 29, where the sacrilege of Pleminius and his Roman garrison at Locri draws Livy's angry contempt, and the tempo of the narrative escalates to the level of the tragic. Here Livy describes their despoiling of Proserpina's temple, whose treasure had never before been stripped, except by Pyrrhus; just as Pyrrhus' ships were wrecked, and only the treasure survived, so now the Romans were punished for their sacrilege when the pilfering of the money caused a madness amongst them (29.8.9–11). Even this extreme example has an element of authorial self-erasure, as Livy introduces the story of Pyrrhus' despoliation of the temple, leading into the miraculous survival of the money, by saying that the treasures "were said" (*dicebantur*) to have been looted by him. Livy's usual technique is to hold back from vouching for the authority of such anecdotes on the same footing as the rest of his narrative. In Book 2, for example, the consul Valerius is unable to push an attack on the Aequi because of a violent storm; when he withdraws, the sky clears so completely "there was a religious scruple against attacking for a second time a camp that was defended as if by some divine power" (*adeo tranquilla serenitas reddita ut uelut numine aliquo defensa castra oppugnare iterum religio fuerit*, 2.62.2). Here the "as if" (*uelut*) is not a sign that Livy is "skeptical" about the interpretation that a divine power was actually defending the Aequi; rather, it is his way of maintaining his authorial persona by refraining from vouching for this as a fact.

In general, the repeated prodigy notices and references to divine manifestations help to structure large-scale patterns of narrative, creating dynamic tension through their evocative foreshadowing technique, and inviting the reader to work at discovering the shapes into which the overall narrative may be falling. The rhythm in the narrative of the war against Hannibal (Books 21–30) is particularly distinctive, with its recurrent oscillations of religious dereliction followed by failure in the field, in turn followed by expiation, all underpinned by the fundamental assurance of eventual victory (Levene 1993: 77). One of the great strengths of the work of Levene is that it brings out how Livy's techniques can vary from one part of his work to another, in accordance with the varying demands of his ever-changing larger canvas. In particular, when Livy's focus turns from the war against Hannibal to the overwhelming scale of Roman expansion into Greece and Spain (Books 31–40) he finds it difficult to integrate his disparate narrative in the taut way he had managed so far. In this decade he downplays the religious dimension very much, and this is best seen as part of a larger artistic decision about how to structure the newly complex interrelations between Rome and Greece in particular: when the climactic Third Macedonian War arrives in Books 41–5 he returns to an integrated narrative with a newly organic interweaving of religious material, as if to highlight the new common destiny of times and places (Levene 1993: 124–5). This is not a matter of saying that Livy saw the gods' hand at work in the events portrayed in Books 41–5 and not in the events of Books 31–40; rather, his customary artistic use of religious

material in Books 31–40 would have been at odds with the narrative effect he wished
to achieve in that particular section of his work.

Levene's findings are the most economical illustration of the fact that it is never
possible to pick the religious items out from the overall effect of the narrative and
regard them as discrete pieces of data. In a way, this is just good formalist literary
criticism, but Livy's accounts of religious matters are impossible to detach from his
narrative in a deeper sense as well. In a famous passage in Book 43 he comments
that thanks to *neglegentia* prodigies are currently no longer announced or recorded
in the annals, but that his own spirit becomes antique as he writes of former times,
so that he will include in his narrative what the learned men of the past thought
worthy of note (43.13.1–2). This passage is a vivid illustration of how far the religious element of Livy's history is inextricable from its representation. For Livy's
history is itself a monument: "Like the city it describes and constitutes the *Ab Urbe
Condita* is a growing physical object through which the writer and the reader move
together" (Kraus 1994: 270). As he progresses through his monstrous project, the
religion of the Roman past comes to seem inextricable from Livy's narration of
it, just as in general his text becomes more and more co-extensive with what it
describes. Livy is *both* reflecting *and* constructing a meaning-making system. His
society's use of that system, however, is passing away as he writes, and his history is
attempting to anchor and restore that meaning-making system, along with the set
of republican values which, according to him, made it and were made by it: "for
Livy AUC history *is* his own work, the *Ab Urbe Condita*, and in reconstructing Roman
history he is in a moral sense reconstructing contemporary Rome" (Moles 1993:
154; cf. Liebeschuetz 1979: 59–60). The religious elements of Livy's narrative are
not reducible to being a transcription of Roman religion in action; they are part of
an evocation of a world, targeted at a contemporary audience who will lose their
contact with that world if Livy fails in his mission.

Religion in Tacitus: The System Subverted

The contemporary *neglegentia* lamented by Livy, by which prodigies were increasingly no longer publicly announced, was part of a general movement in the late
republic which saw the manifestations of divine concern shift from the corporate
focus of the ancien régime to a new interest in signs and omens associated with the
charismatic individual (North 1990: 69–71; Levene 1993: 4; Linderski 1993: 63–4).
By the time we reach the works of Tacitus, this movement has reached its culmination: the senate, formerly the communal center for adjudicating the meaning of
prodigies, has become a venue for elaborating the imperial cult, and the emperor is
now the person around whom portents and their interpretation cluster, along with
everything else. The republican system of religion is in disrepair, just as all other
aspects of the republican system are in disrepair, and Tacitus' narrative of religious
matters adapts in parallel. He uses the same techniques of dissonance here as in his
treatment of the principate in general: the inherited republican forms of behavior and
narrative are still present but have lost their real meaning, becoming a background

rhythm against which the new, discordant realities play out their disturbing effects (on the general technique see Ginsburg 1981).

Tacitus' *Histories* and *Annals* are accordingly full of portentous signs which derive much of their narrative effect from their conformity to and divergence from the kind of manifestations we know from Livy. Warning signs cluster around the doomed figures of Galba (*Hist.* 1.18) or Otho (1.86), while the rise of Vespasian turns out in retrospect to have been foreseen by astrologers, soothsayers, and priests in Italy, Cyprus, Judea, and Alexandria (*Hist.* 2.4; 2.78; 4.8; Liebeschuetz 1979: 192–6). Again, in the *Annals*, hyperbolically portentous signs refer to the house of the emperor, ominously pointing to impending conspiracy (15.47). Or else, as if in sympathetic derangement after the murder of Nero's mother, "frequent and unavailing" portents occur, most melodramatically in the form of a woman giving birth to a snake: as if to point up the failure of the system to generate sense in the way it should, Tacitus then remarks that all these "occurred without any concern of the gods, to such an extent that for many years afterward Nero continued his command and his crimes" (14.12: trans. Woodman 2004). The meaning of the signs is obvious – glaringly so – yet no one can do anything and the evident derangement of the world continues.

Such episodes are not to be read as evidence of personal skepticism about the interaction of the divine realm with the human, or indeed of personal belief. They are part of a general technique which Tacitus uses to create an unrelieved sensation of high-pitched strain, with a continual dissonance between form and reality: the overall effect of his treatment of religious phenomena is to create a fearful and oppressive atmosphere which does not allow for the rituals of expiation and relief which punctuate the narrative of Livy. Once, Tacitus gives us a possible example of a restorative breathing-space in the form of ritual, when he provides a detailed description of how the Romans began the rebuilding of the burnt and desecrated temple of Jupiter Optimus Maximus on June 21, AD 70 (*Hist.* 4.53). It is a stately passage, more meticulous in its evocation of the scene than anything of the kind in Livy, and unique in surviving Roman literature for the detail of its presentation of cult action (Jason Davies 2004: 209). According to Davies, "the refounding of the Capitoline is no less than the textual and religious reconstruction of Rome's proper relations with the gods," signaling "a reversal of the trend that had continued almost unabated and with increasing momentum since early in the reign of Tiberius" (Jason Davies 2004: 209). This is certainly one possible reading, though it is also possible to pay attention to the fact that the real ritual and laboring work of clearing the site began later in the year, when Vespasian arrived in the city: what we have here is "some preliminary ceremonial," involving "some preliminary disposal" of the *lapis Terminus* "before the restoration proper could be undertaken by the emperor on his return" (Chilver 1985: 65–6). Here too, in other words, we may be seeing mere displacement activity, an enactment of republican form which does no more than anticipate the real religious work which will take place when the person who really matters arrives.

Contemporary readers of Tacitus will no doubt have been able to read this scene on the Capitol in either an ironic or an ameliorative mode. It is characteristic of Roman historiography that they should not be nudged too overtly by the author, but should be left to draw their own conclusions about what the scene means as part of the larger work. The scene has something to say about ritual, and about the society which generates the ritual, but readers both ancient and modern must work at teasing out these meanings within the context of the meaning-making system which is the literary work as a whole.

FURTHER READING

The role of religion and the gods is discussed for each of the Roman epics in Feeney (1991), with bibliography on each; Feeney (1998) is a more theoretical discussion of the issues of the interaction between literature and religion. Liebeschuetz (1979) discusses Livy, Virgil, Lucan, and Tacitus. On Naevius, the large and difficult book (in Italian) by Barchiesi (1962) has great treasures. On Virgil, see Thornton (1976), Hardie (1986), and Braund (1997); on the impact of Virgil's poem on contemporary myth-making and religious representations, see Hölscher (1993) and Scheid (1993). For Statius' Jupiter, see Schubert (1984).

There is less discussion of the issues in Roman historiography than in Greek: on Herodotus, for example, see now Harrison (2000) and Mikalson (2003). Levene (1993) opened up the question of religion in Livy, and Jason Davies (2004) vigorously carries on the debate, continuing it to Tacitus and Ammianus. On Livy, see also Kajanto (1957), Linderski (1993), Feldherr (1998: 64–78), and Forsythe (1999: 87–98). Syme (1958: 521–7) is still worth reading on Tacitus' religion, even if the focus is the personal views of the historian.

CHAPTER ELEVEN

Religion and Roman Coins

Jonathan Williams

Ever since its first appearance in western Asia Minor in the seventh century BC, ancient coinage was intimately bound up with religion. The earliest known coin hoard from classical antiquity was found concealed in a pot buried in the foundations of the mid sixth-century BC temple of Artemis at Ephesus. Divinities and their attributes regularly adorned the coin issues of the Greek cities – Athena and her owl in Athens, Helios (the Sun-god) at Rhodes, Arethusa at Syracuse – and those of the Hellenistic kings, beginning with Alexander the Great, whose mythical ancestors Zeus and Hercules dominated on his silver coins, Athena and Nike (Victory) on the gold. Even before Alexander, some Persian provincial governors and other rulers in Asia Minor had suggestively usurped the place of divine portraits, supplanting them on the obverse with their own likenesses.

Designs on Greek coins typically remained unchanged for decades or even centuries, varying only in style or detail over time. The earliest Roman coin types in the late fourth and early third centuries BC drew heavily on the Greek repertoire, commonly depicting gods such as Mars, Hercules, or Apollo, and religious symbols – tripod, eagle on thunderbolt, caduceus (the herald's staff) – familiar from the Greek coinages of Italy and elsewhere (fig. 11.1). Apart from early diversions into unwieldy cast ingots of bronze, both oblong and circular (the so-called *aes signatum* and *aes*

Figure 11.1 Roman silver didrachm, c. 275 BC, showing a wreathed head of Apollo and horse in a typically Greek style. 19 mm (diameter measured along a horizontal axis on the obverse).

Figure 11.2 Roman silver *denarius*, c. 212 BC, with Roma and Dioscuri. 19 mm.

grave), Roman coinage down to the late second century BC did not differ fundamentally from its Greek civic counterparts with regard to form or designs, aside from
the occasional intrusion of specifically Roman figures such as Janus. The long period
of unchanging designs in the second century after the introduction of the *denarius*
in around 212 BC saw a fairly fixed range of types in use for both silver and bronze
denominations, dominated again by profile busts of different gods on the obverse –
Roma, Saturn, Hercules, etc. Action scenes dominated on the reverse of the *denarii*,
galloping Dioscuri and a range of divine charioteers becoming standard (fig. 11.2).

In the 130s BC something happened in Roman coin design that would change its
character for the next four centuries or more, and make Roman coins stand apart
from all that had gone before in the Greek world. Types began to change annually
as successive monetary magistrates, the *tresviri monetales* (the board of three in charge
of the mint) began to exercise what can only have been personal choice over what
types were to appear on the Roman coinage, often drawing on themes from their
family's history. This is a familiar story which has been most commonly understood
as a function of changes in Roman political life – the introduction of secret ballot-
ing at elections leading to the rise of a new form of self-promotion on the part of
rising stars among the political classes. More recently it has been reinterpreted as
an aspect of a wider trend toward the monumentalization of various aspects of
Roman public life, seen also in the late second-century BC expansion in historical
and antiquarian writing, in reaction to a changing social and political environment
(Meadows and Williams 2001). One of the main characteristics of the new-style coin
types was the enlargement of the range of religious imagery available for use far beyond
what had previously been normal in Greek traditions. No longer restricted to portraits of gods in profile or full length, the coinage came to depict, often in considerable detail, the material culture of Roman religious practice, from sacrificial vessels
to temples and monuments. Such motifs had occurred on Greek coinages, but much
less frequently (for a useful overview, see Anson 1911–16: parts iv–v). Italic bronze
coins from Etruria dated to the third century BC showing sacrificial implements on
one side and a male head wearing what looks like a priestly hat, or *apex*, on the
other perhaps betray the local antecedents of the new religious imagery (fig. 11.3).
An exceptional issue of Roman gold dated to about 220 BC, showing two figures
taking an oath by touching their swords onto a pig in the Roman fashion, points in
the same direction (fig. 11.4). There were parallel developments on some Hellenistic
city coinages around the same time. Specific cult statues begin to appear as civic types
in western Asia Minor from the 170s onward (Carradice 1995: 79). Similarly, Seleucid

Figure 11.3 Etruscan cast bronze coin, third century BC (*Historia Nummorum Italia* 68), with priestly accoutrements. 38 mm.

Figure 11.4 Roman gold stater, c. 220 BC, showing oath-taking scene. 19 mm.

Figure 11.5 Seleucid silver tetradrachm, Demetrius II (second reign), 129–125 BC, depicting the altar of Sandan. 31 mm.

silver coins in the late second century BC made at Tarsus illustrated the altar of a local deity, Sandan, in a new monumental style (fig. 11.5). The focus on the building perhaps emphasizes the connectedness between the king and the place and institution of the god's cult, rather than the abstraction of the divine person as patron or ancestor. It certainly prefigures any number of designs on provincial coins of the Roman east featuring the temple or cult object of the city in question, as we shall see below.

One of the earliest of the new monumental types foreshadows many of the typical features of the religious imagery on later Roman coinage. A *denarius* of about 135 BC in the name of C. Minucius Augurinus shows a column identifiable as the Columna Minucia, a monument mentioned in scattered literary sources (fig. 11.6). It has an Aeolic capital, from which hang bells. There are two crouching lions at

Figure 11.6   Roman silver *denarius*, c. 135 BC, showing the Columna Minucia. 19 mm.

the base, above which sprout corn-ears. Two figures stand one on either side and
the column is surmounted by a third who holds a staff. The standing figure on the
right holds a *lituus*, distinguishing him as M. Minucius Faesus, one of the first
plebeian members of the college of augurs. The other is probably identifiable as
either P. or M. Minucius, consuls in 492 and 491 BC respectively, from the loaves of
bread which he seems to be holding and the fact that his foot rests upon a *modius*
(grain-container), recalling grain distributions which took place in those years.
Scattered literary references argue that the figure on the top is probably L. Minucius,
who also distributed grain when consul in 439 BC.

It is worthwhile dwelling on this complex design, which is among the first of its
kind in the Roman coin series. What are its characteristics? It is meticulous and specific
as to the monument and the various attributes of the three figures, combining architectural observation, historical detail, and appropriate symbolism, in an imaginary
scene suggestive of familial piety, which profiles the great public achievements of
C. Minucius' ancestors and celebrates the monument dedicated to one of them by
a grateful state.

The design encapsulates many of the ways in which religion and religious symbolism are deployed on later Roman coins. Religious buildings and monuments of
various kinds are important – temples, altars, statues, cult objects, columns – and
they are individuated by the inclusion of telling details, which, however, does not
necessarily mean that they constitute an architecturally accurate elevation of the structure. The material trappings of Roman religion also make frequent appearances – as
here the *lituus* – whether as attributes or as motifs in their own right. Scenes of
sacrifice are common – as the left-hand figure on this coin, who appears to be
making an offering of his loaves at the column and looking upward in an attitude
of devotion toward the figure atop the monument. Finally, another kind of symbol
represented on this type completes the range of motifs with religious significance on
coins, exemplified here by the corn-ears either side of the column. Factually, they
refer to the grain distributions made by the moneyer's ancestors in the past. But
they also stand for the state of divinely sanctioned plenty and material prosperity
which accrues to the Roman people as a benefit of their communal piety, of which
the Minucii are here figured as outstanding traditional exemplars.

What kinds of effects were being sought, what sorts of responses were intended
to be evoked by the expansion of religious material on the Roman coinage? What, for
example, was the significance of the *lituus* as a motif or as an attribute? What kinds
of associations and resonances did it have for the informed viewer? On one level, it
might simply indicate that the person depicted was a member of the politically

Figure 11.7 Roman silver *denarius*, 42 BC, showing Octavian on horseback holding a *lituus*. 19 mm.

influential college of augurs, as in the case of M. Minucius Faesus on the coin discussed above, or that of the young Octavian whose equestrian statue appears with *lituus* in hand on a coin of 42 BC soon after he himself had joined the college the year before (his coin legends from that year already list the augurate among his titles) (fig. 11.7). But beyond its function as a badge of office, the *lituus* as symbol also connoted a host of specifically *religious* associations with the expert role of the augurs in interpreting the divine will and regulating sacred law in public life, the pious observation of which was one of the reasons which Romans gave for their rise to power. It also recalled a host of famous individuals and events connected with augury, not least Romulus, whose famous auspicy, the sighting of 12 vultures, marked the extraordinary divine favor which accompanied the foundation of the city of Rome. The story circulated that it had been repeated on the occasion of Octavian's first consulship in 43 BC – six vultures appearing to him when he was elected and six more when he took office, indicating that he would be another founder of Rome (Beard et al. 1998: 1.182). Whether Octavian's *lituus* on this coin suggests that the story was already in existence in 42 BC or not, it certainly refers to the same richly evocative nexus of religious tales and ideas surrounding the history and science of Roman augury that gave rise to the narrative.

The *lituus*, then, was a symbol with emotional power as well as providing factual information about the curriculum vitae of the individual with whom it was associated on the coin, a symbol capable of summoning up in Roman viewers strong feelings about their community's unique relationship with their gods, and about the augurs who played a large part in mediating that relationship. What the increasingly frequent appearance of religious symbols on the coins from the 130s BC onward also reveals is that the power of these images was not merely an Augustan innovation on the coins or elsewhere for that matter, but something which had its roots and antecedents in the late republican period. Let us now turn to each of the groups of scenes and symbols mentioned above and look at them in greater depth.

Temples and Monuments

The appearance of religious and other buildings and monuments on Roman coins in the late second century BC marked a considerable departure from the Greek tradition, one which remained characteristic of the Roman coinage throughout, and influenced the iconography of the city coinages of the eastern empire.

Figure 11.8 Roman gold *aureus* of Vespasian (AD 69–79), depicting the temple of Vesta. 19 mm.

Despite the fact that architectural designs are among the most illustrated and discussed for the information they provide on the lost monuments and cultic practices of antiquity, the significance of the phenomenon itself has been little discussed. Andrew Burnett has argued that the importance of the so-called *architectura numismatica* has been overdone, pointing out that of the 818 types on the imperial coinage of the reign of Vespasian (AD 69–79), only 34 are architectural (Burnett 1999: 156) (fig. 11.8). But by treating the subject under the heading of public building and architecture rather than religion, a more meaningful perspective from which to consider these types has perhaps been missed. For the obvious point about buildings on Roman coins, imperial and provincial, is that they are mostly temples or altars. Despite the occasional appearance of more obviously secular structures such as Nero's Market, Trajan's Forum, or the Colosseum, buildings mostly appear on Roman coins not *qua* public architecture, but as religious monuments.

They are, in a sense, the numismatic correlates to the section on buildings in the *Res Gestae* ("The Achievements"), Augustus' inscriptional autobiography (chapters 19–21). The majority of them are temples, and they appear as signs of the emperor's extraordinary piety and generosity, not primarily as indications of his devotion to public works. Not that these are omitted or unconnected – in the same passage Augustus also mentions his restoration of the Theater of Pompey and the Via Flaminia, just as the coins celebrate his restoration of the roads. The appendix to the inscription also mentions his immense expenses on wider acts of euergetism in Rome and elsewhere – theatrical displays, shows, moneys donated to cities damaged by earthquakes, and gifts to individuals. But the temples take pride of place, not merely because he built more of them than any other class of building, but because their construction was of particular significance for the restoration and maintenance of the Roman community's cultic and religious life, which was an immensely important theme.

Images of temples on Roman coins bespeak the emperor's exemplary devoutness, especially when he is their author or restorer. In the same ways as other kinds of religious symbols we will go on to look at, temples served as potent emblems of communal religious identity, which was also an important element in the civic and ethnic identities of ancient communities. This relationship is perfectly encapsulated in the slogan "Great is Diana of the Ephesians," which the people of Ephesus took up in response to the preaching of the apostle Paul, whose activities, they believed, threatened both their goddess *and* their city (Acts 19.23–41).

Figure 11.9 Ephesian bronze coin from the reign of Antoninus Pius (AD 138–61), showing the temple of Artemis with cult statue. 34 mm.

Figure 11.10 Silver shekel of the Second Jewish Revolt (AD 132–5), depicting the destroyed Jerusalem Temple. 27 mm.

Figure 11.11 Bronze coin of Heliopolis (modern Baalbek in Lebanon) from the reign of Septimius Severus (AD 193–211), with an aerial view of the temple. 25 mm.

Taking their cue from the Romans, many other communities of the Roman empire, both cities and neighboring kingdoms, adopted images of buildings as badges of communal identity appropriate for adorning their coins. Well-known examples include the Ephesians, whose famous temple of Artemis makes regular appearances (fig. 11.9), the Jews, whose destroyed temple reappears on the coins of the Second Revolt in the 130s AD (fig. 11.10), and the Heliopolitans, whose great temple of Jupiter appears on coins from the reign of Septimius Severus (fig. 11.11). The coins suggest that, for these communities, the symbolized idea, as well as the experience of the physical reality, of their great temples, or, in the case of the Jews, their painful experience of its absence, was central to the public articulation of their identities.

Figure 11.12   Bronze coin of Ephesus from the reign of Elagabalus (AD 218–22), showing the city's four neocoric temples. 34 mm.

   A further aspect to the spread of temple types on early provincial coins, as Burnett points out, was that many of the temples represented were associated with the imperial cult. It is well known that this was one of the main vectors of Roman identity in the east. The coins therefore reflect the Romanization of the religious culture of many eastern cities, to which, in the second and third centuries AD, was lent a competitive aspect in the development of the neocorate, as cities vied with one another for the honor of being granted the right to a provincial temple to the emperor, with which came the title *neokoroi*, meaning "temple-guardians" (Price 1984: 64). Particularly ambitious cities sought the honor several times over: the Smyrnaeans and Pergamenes eventually became "three times *neokoroi*," advertising the fact, and their three temples, on the coins, while the Ephesians achieved the rank of four (fig. 11.12).

Religious Realia and Scenes of Sacrifice

The preceding Greek repertoire of coin motifs had focused on divine attributes as religious symbols appropriate for coins – thunderbolts, caducei, cornucopias (horns overflowing with fruit), bunches of grapes, and so on. The accoutrements of religion are relatively rare on pre-Roman Greek coins, apart from tripods, which occur very frequently, though in most cases they probably stand for Apollo. Nor is sacrifice a major theme, though, as mentioned above, altars do make occasional appearances and other symbols such as *bucrania* (bulls' skulls) clearly allude to it. On Roman coinage, by contrast, the material culture and the actual business of religious practice was depicted very frequently. The coins betray a real fascination with objects associated with the great priestly colleges, and with liquid and animal sacrifice, a sign of the importance of orthopraxy – the proper performance of ritual – for Roman religion. The full range is well illustrated in a frieze of Augustan date probably from the Porticus Octaviae, where symbols of both priesthood and sacrifice appear side by side, flanked by a pair of *bucrania*, and clearly representing a familiar and coherent set (Zanker 1987 [1988]: 126–7, fig. 102a). The frieze also reminds us that what we see on the coins, as so often, participates in a wider set of iconographical contexts.

Figure 11.13 Gold *aureus* of Augustus, c. 16 BC, showing the *clipeus virtutis* and sacred laurel trees. 20 mm.

The high point of this style is, not unexpectedly, reached in the Augustan period, when these symbols combine with those specifically associated with Augustus himself, and especially with the honors accorded to him in 27 BC – the olive bushes, the *clipeus virtutis* ("shield of virtue"), the *corona civica* ("civic crown") – to constitute a new repertoire consisting of traditional Roman religious symbols now repurposed so as to refer to a single individual whose very name, Augustus, adverted to the mysteries of augury (fig. 11.13). This set the pattern for successive later emperors, whose coins regularly refer to the symbols of the four great priestly colleges, representing the emperor's continuing leading role in Roman public religion. But the background to this Augustan phenomenon lies in the earlier deployment of symbols of this kind on the coins of the late republic: first as descriptive attributes of an ancestral or historical figure, and later as insignia proper to a living individual named or depicted on the coin. Not surprisingly perhaps, the first instance of this phenomenon is provided by Sulla, whose coins refer to his membership of two of the major priesthoods, the augurs and the *pontifices* (fig. 11.14). All of the major players on the late republican scene for whom coins were struck with their names and images – Pompey (posthumously), Caesar, Brutus, Octavian, Lepidus, Mark Antony – and some of the second-order figures – Antony's brother Caius, Q. Cornificius, Lentulus Spinther, Cn. Domitius Calvinus – use priestly symbols among their types (fig. 11.15). The relevant designations also occur in the developing styles

Figure 11.14 Gold coin made for Sulla, c. 84 BC, with his priestly symbols. 19 mm.

Figure 11.15 Silver *denarius*, 44 BC, showing the bust of Julius Caesar with priestly symbols. 18 mm.

of personal titulature that accompany the images – AVGVR, PONT, and so on – anticipating later imperial styles where the title of *pontifex maximus* appears continually, conventionally abbreviated to P M.

As in the case of the temples, so the variable adoption in the provinces and beyond of the Roman habit of depicting sacrificial scenes and implements on coins is of particular interest, as it may assist in charting the spread not necessarily of Roman cultic practice itself, but of the symbolic attraction of its things. On the coins of Verica, a king in pre-Roman southern Britain in the early first century AD, there appear a number of motifs from the Roman religious repertoire including an altar, a temple with a cult statue, and a figure seemingly holding a *lituus* (Creighton 2000: 80–125; J. Williams 2005; fig. 11.16). There is little archaeological evidence for the adoption of the material culture or architecture of Roman religion in Britain before the conquest. But its symbols had already begun to exert a considerable fascination on the minds of some Iron Age Britons. On the provincial coins of early imperial Spain, various combinations of *apex, lituus, simpulum, patera*, jug, knife, and axe appear at a number of cities (fig. 11.17). This has been plausibly interpreted as an indication of a desire among the provincial cities of Spain to assimilate the things and symbols of Romanness (Burnett 2005: 178). In the east, by contrast, such symbols are to be found only at Antioch in the first century AD (*RPC* 1.4171, 4178), where a range of other unusually western-style features are also present, including the use of Latin legends on the city's bronze coinage down to the reign of Nerva (AD 96–8; fig. 11.18).

Figure 11.16 Ancient British silver coin of Verica, early first century AD, showing a naked figure holding a *lituus*. 11 mm.

Figure 11.17 Bronze coin of Carthago Nova, Spain, mid-first century BC, with Roman priestly symbols. 20 mm.

Figure 11.18 Silver didrachm from Syrian Antioch in the reign of Claudius (AD 41–54), showing the young Nero and Roman priestly emblems. 18 mm.

Figure 11.19 Bronze coin of Ephesus, reign of Elagabalus (AD 218–22), showing athletic prize-crowns. 34 mm.

Roman sacrificial implements and priestly symbols continue to make occasional but regular appearances on Roman imperial coins down to the late third century AD. By contrast, after the final demise of the western provincial coinages in the reign of Claudius, they seem all but absent from the provincial coinages in the east. Unlike the depiction of temples, this particular aspect of Roman religious iconography clearly did not resonate there. What we see instead is the depiction of objects relating to the festivals and games that sprang up in the eastern provinces: agonistic tables, crowns, and wreaths (Klose 2005; fig. 11.19). In parallel with their quest for neocoric titles, the cities competed with one another to secure imperial permissions to celebrate prestigious festivals. Ninety-four different cities are known to have issued coins with agonistic types. The roots of this provincial style lay in the Roman sensitivity to depictions of cultic realia. Its subsequent development in the realm of festivals and games in the Greek east is a function of the manner in which the cities related to the emperor, and to one another.

Since the introduction of varying types in the late second century BC, scenes of sacrifice and offering played an increasingly significant part on the Roman coinage. They make a slow start in the republic with a scattering of mythological scenes (fig. 11.20). Interestingly, and in contrast to the use of priestly symbols, none of the late republican figures mentioned above is shown in the act of sacrifice. Sacrificial scenes are also rare on the coins of Augustus (fig. 11.21), though he often appears in a sacrificial context on other visual media. Thereafter, emperors are regularly shown sacrificing throughout the imperial series, one of the earliest, from the reign of Caligula, being also one of the most complex (fig. 11.22).

Apart from emperors, there is another category of persons regularly shown in the act of pouring sacrificial libations, namely divinities. From the depictions of Apollo

Figure 11.20 Roman silver *denarius* of c. 97 BC, made by L. Pomponius Molo, showing King Numa sacrificing. 19 mm.

Figure 11.21   Gold *aureus* of Augustus, 17 BC, showing the emperor sacrificing. 21 mm.

Figure 11.22   Brass *sestertius* of Caligula (AD 37–41), showing the emperor pouring a libation like a god on the obverse and sacrificing on the reverse. 35 mm.

Figure 11.23   *Denarius* of Augustus, 16 BC, showing Apollo Actius pouring a libation on the reverse. 19 mm.

Actius under Augustus through to the recurrent types of Concordia, Salus, Pietas, Vesta, and *Genius*, among others, down to the early fourth century AD, they form an important group of types with parallels on other media (fig. 11.23). We will return to them later.

Symbolic Motifs

As well as depicting the actual places and things of cult religion, Roman coinage illustrated a range of more allusive symbols with a general religious content. These usually referred to a presumed state of good fortune, peace, plenty, order, and prosperity, all of which were believed to flow as much from divine favor elicited by Roman piety as from the secular success of Roman arms. This category includes symbols such as the caduceus, cornucopia, rudder, and corn-ears, all of which appear both as symbols in their own right, often combined with one another, and as attributes of various appropriate divinities. In contrast to the very specific reference of the

Figure 11.24 *Denarius* of Julius Caesar, 44 BC, with sacrificial implements combined with symbols of prosperity. 19 mm.

Figure 11.25 Base-metal coin of Constantine I, AD 321, showing a globe resting on an altar. 19 mm.

cultic imagery discussed above, this group of images is general in its meaning. They all refer in a non-specific fashion to a desired condition of material abundance and serene tranquility for the empire and its inhabitants. These two sets of motifs could be combined as, for instance, on a *denarius* issue of 44 BC showing Caesar on the obverse and, on the reverse, a caduceus crossed with *fasces*, with a globe, clasped hands and a sacrificial axe in the corners (fig. 11.24); or again four centuries later in the 320s AD on an issue with the reverse legend BEATA TRANQVILLITAS ("blissful tranquility") with the type of a globe resting on an altar (fig. 11.25). The implicit meaning of both designs is that there is an intimate connection between sacrifice, as represented by the axe and the altar on these types, and the longed-for state of universal harmony signified by the caduceus, the clasped hands, and the globes; and that the liberal performance of the former is a prerequisite for achieving the latter. A similar meaning must lie behind the puzzling scenes of sacrificing gods mentioned above, which make the same point by paradoxically ascribing the human act of sacrifice to its divine benefactors, who are in fact its recipients.

Gods, Personifications, and the Emperor

From the republic through to late antiquity, Roman coins continually depict the major divinities of the Roman state. Together, gods and personifications made up 84 percent of *denarius* reverse types on coins in circulation between AD 69 and 235 (Noreña 2001: 155). However, there is little evidence of system in the selection of which individual gods to depict, and the occurrence or absence of different divine figures at different times may at first sight seem fairly arbitrary, as may the relationship of the aspects or titles of the gods shown to those that were prominent in Roman public cult. Take, for instance, the figure of Jupiter, whose Capitoline manifestation as

Figure 11.26 *Denarius* of Vitellius, AD 69, with temple and image of Jupiter Capitolinus. 19 mm.

Figure 11.27 Gold *aureus* of Elagabalus (AD 218–22), showing the stone image of the god Sol Elagabal being drawn in a chariot. 20 mm.

Optimus Maximus ("Best and Greatest") is all but missing from the coinage apart from a brief flurry of references in the civil wars of AD 68–9 (fig. 11.26). Jupiter is far more often surnamed Conservator with the frequent addition Augusti ("Savior of the Emperor"), Custos ("Guardian"), or Victor. The most significant factor in guiding the choice and description of divinities on coins, in the imperial period at least, seems to have been the relationship of the god in question to the emperor or the empire. Hence, presumably, the absence of the figure of Jupiter from Augustus' coinage, and the presence of Mars Ultor ("the Avenger") and Apollo Actius ("of Actium"), both of whom had a close relationship to the emperor, being regarded as patrons of his early military victories at Philippi and Actium; or the dominance of Minerva on the coinage of Domitian, a goddess to whom we know he was particularly devoted, and the brief prominence of types and legends referring to Sol Elagabalus on the coins of his devotee, the emperor Elagabalus (fig. 11.27).

Personifications fall broadly into two categories: those that refer to the emperors' virtues – Aequitas ("Fairness"), Clementia ("Mercy"), Liberalitas ("Generosity"), Pietas ("Religiosity") and so on – and those that refer to desired qualities or attributes of the empire as a whole – Salus ("Safety"), Spes ("Hope"), Securitas ("Security"), Felicitas ("Prosperity"), Hilaritas ("Joyousness"), etc. Some of these received public cult, others seem to have had no life apart from their imagery on coins and elsewhere. The imperial virtues as a group first become popular in the reign of Nerva and continue so for the next two centuries or so. Noreña has shown that, as a medium for conveying the emperor's qualities, they are far more frequent than scenes involving him and the imperial family (Noreña 2001: 154). In other words, the coins will tend to show a figure of Pietas rather than the emperor sacrificing (fig. 11.28). As with the depiction of religious apparatus, the preference for depicting the imperial virtues is a particularly Roman style that is mostly absent from the provincial coinages, except

Figure 11.28 *Denarius* of Commodus, AD 187, with an image of Pietas sacrificing on the reverse. 19 mm.

Figure 11.29 Bronze coin from Alexandria of the reign of Domitian (AD 81–96), with the figure of *Elpis Sebaste*, modeled on the Roman type *Spes Augusta* ("the imperial hope"). 24 mm.

Figure 11.30 Copper *as* of Domitian, AD 84, showing the figure of Moneta Augusta. 28 mm.

for the coinage of Egypt made at Alexandria, which in this, as in other, respects tends to follow the pattern of the mint of Rome (Bland 1996; fig. 11.29).

The emperor came to be regarded as the effective author of the Roman public coinage and the regulator of its system of production at the imperial mint at Rome. Both the institution itself and its output were represented on the coinage as *Moneta Augusta* ("the mint of the emperor"), a recurring reverse legend that first appears in the reign of Domitian in AD 84, accompanied by a standing female figure holding a balance for equity and a cornucopia for plenty (fig. 11.30). The emperor was a figure, or an idea, capable of provoking a strong religious response in a variety of ways. So indeed could his image. In the early principate, the appearance of his revered profile on the coins provoked an uncertain response from some users of these otherwise mundane objects. In the heightened atmosphere of denunciation and accusation under Tiberius, taking a ring or a coin bearing the emperor's head into a latrine or brothel could be regarded as a capital crime (Suet. *Tiberius* 58.3). Suetonius clearly regarded this as a monstrous absurdity, and we hear of nothing similar from later

Figure 11.31 Gold *solidus* of Constantine I, AD 317, mounted for wearing as a personal ornament or amulet. 20 mm.

reigns, at least until late antiquity (see below). It is unclear whether this should be understood as a specifically religious reaction. There is no precedent for it with regard to images of gods on coins. It seems to belong to a new, and short-lived, category of offense particular to the emperor and his image.

The habit of mounting coins in rings or other items of jewelry, usually showing the obverse imperial portrait, shows how, when taken out of the routine world of daily exchange and highlighted in a special context, coins could act as objects of personal veneration, and as portable icons of the imperial person (Bruhn 1993; Johns 1996: 58) (fig. 11.31). This is distinct from their frequent role as offerings at temples or sacred springs, a subject that cannot be considered in detail here, but which ought to be borne in mind when thinking about the associations between Roman coinage and religion (Sauer 2005: 110–16).

The connection between the sacred person of the emperor and his coin had become significantly closer by the late third century AD. Under Diocletian, coin legends referred to the *sacra moneta Augustorum et Caesarum nostrorum*, the "sacred mint [or money] of our emperors and Caesars" (fig. 11.32). Imperial rescripts of AD 381 and 385 exclude the counterfeiter from receiving pardon at Easter, along with murderers, adulterers, prisoners, magicians, and others guilty of the most horrendous crimes, describing him as one who has "copied the sacred visage and assailed the divine countenance and, schooled in sacrilege, has minted the venerable images": *CTh* 9.38.6; cf. 9.38.8). Hard though it is to make sense of any of this within a Christian context except as theologically inexact and hyperbolic language, behind the florid eloquence is a real sense of the new sacredness of the imperial image on coins, and of its utter inviolability.

Figure 11.32 Base-silver coin of Diocletian, c. AD 301, depicting Sacra Moneta. 27 mm.

Christianity and the Roman Coinage

Over the fourth century AD, there are only intermittent indications of the increasing Christianization of the Roman order on the empire's coinage, now unified after the demise of the provincial coinages and the establishment in the late third century of a network of imperial mints all producing coins with standard types. The designs remained substantially public or imperial, in the sense that they proclaim the empire's perpetual victory over its enemies and its internal coherence, rather than drawing explicitly on the new religion to which the emperors now subscribed. In the fourth century, the *chi-rho* symbol, representing the Greek monogram of Christ, appears as a subsidiary motif on a number of different coin issues – either as a mint mark in the field, or as an element in the design of the imperial banner, the *labarum*, which various emperors are shown brandishing in triumphant mode. An unusually clear example of the style is the remarkable design used on coins minted in AD 327 at Constantinople to celebrate its foundation, showing a *labarum* adorned with three pellets to represent medallions of Constantine and two of his sons, Constantius II and Constantine II. The whole is surmounted by the monogram of Christ and the shaft is plunged into a writhing snake, usually interpreted as referring to Licinius, Constantine's vanquished rival (fig. 11.33). Eusebius (*Life of Constantine* 3.3) describes a similar scene painted on a tablet mounted on the portico of Constantine's palace, presumably in Constantinople. Much of the symbolism of the coin is clearly Christian. Even so, as the legend SPES PVBLIC ("the people's hope"), makes clear, this is a type in celebration of the triumph of the Roman people marching under a Christian flag and led into battle by a Christian emperor, rather than of the triumph of the religion itself, much less that of the church. This is equally true of the remarkable silver medallions of about AD 315 which show the emperor in a helmet decorated with the Christogram (P. Bruun 1997).

No doubt many Christians read all this Christian imagery in a straightforwardly partisan manner. Eusebius, for instance, describes the coins of Constantine showing his head looking upward as depicting him in the act of prayer, ignoring the long, pre-Christian tradition of royal busts with eyes raised heavenward in imitation of Alexander the Great (*Life of Constantine* 4.15; fig. 11.34). Nevertheless, compromises continued to be struck between the new religion and Roman religious traditions. So, on coins struck posthumously for Constantine, he is shown in the traditional Roman manner ascending into heaven on a chariot as a divinized emperor, with the hand of God reaching down to greet him, and is titled *Divus*

Figure 11.33　Base-metal coin of Constantine I, AD 327, celebrating the foundation of Constantinople. 15 mm.

Figure 11.34 Gold *solidus* of Constantine I, c. AD 325, showing him "at prayer." 21 mm.

Figure 11.35 Bronze coin commemorating the death of Constantine I (AD 337). He is welcomed into heaven by the hand of the Christian God on the reverse, but called "Divine Constantine" on the obverse. 15 mm.

Figure 11.36 Bronze coin of the usurper-emperor Magnentius (AD 350–3), with prominent *chi-rho* symbol. 26 mm.

Constantinus (Divine Constantine) in the legend (fig. 11.35). Christianity did not fully convert the coinage until the fifth century AD.

The exception to the rule in the fourth century are the coins of the western usurpers Magnentius and Decentius in AD 350–3, who use the *chi-rho* symbol as their principal type on their base-metal coins, flanked by an *alpha* and an *omega*, referring to Christ's description of himself in the Book of Revelation as the "Alpha and the Omega, the beginning and the end" (Revelation 22.13) (fig. 11.36). This design is accompanied by the legend SALVS DD NN AVG ET CAES ("The salvation of our masters Augustus and Caesar"), presumably referring to Christ himself in this instance. Their contemporary, Vetranio, who was briefly elevated to the purple in Illyricum in 350, also proclaimed his Christianity on base-metal coins which cite the famous vision of Constantine at the Milvian Bridge in AD 312 with the legend HOC SIGNO VICTOR ERIS ("With this standard you will be victorious"), around a type of the emperor being crowned by Victory and holding the *labarum* emblazoned with the *chi-rho* symbol (fig. 11.37). All three usurpers were proclaiming their Christianity, as well as advertising their loyalty to the dynasty of Constantine, with which the *chi-rho* motif as a public emblem was intimately associated (Dearn 2003).

Figure 11.37 Base-silver coin of the usurper-emperor Vetranio (AD 350), showing him holding the *labarum*, a standard decorated with the Christian *chi-rho* symbol. 19 mm.

Figure 11.38 Base-silver coin of Constantine I, AD 318, one of the last issues to depict the image of Sol, the pagan Sun-god. 19 mm.

Figure 11.39 Gold *solidus* of the empress Eudocia, wife of Theodosius II, c. AD 423–4, showing an angel with the True Cross. 22 mm.

There is also negative evidence for a change in what was regarded as appropriate on Roman coins in the new religious atmosphere. Designs may not have undergone a thorough-going Christianization, but they were substantially de-paganized. After 318, then, no more images of Sol the Unconquered Companion of the Emperor (fig. 11.38), or of the *Genius* of the Roman People on the base-metal coinage made in Constantine's realm in the western empire, a change that spread empire-wide after Licinius' defeat in 324. Some less offensive figures persisted, especially Victory, who remained common throughout the fourth century and would eventually turn into an angel bearing the True Cross under Theodosius II in the fifth (fig. 11.39). The personifications of Roma and Constantinopolis also retain a foothold. But others peter out in the fourth century: a type from the 320s with the legend SALVS REI PVBLICAE ("the salvation of the state") still shows a figure of the goddess Salus holding two small children to her bosom (fig. 11.40). In the late 380s the same legend is illustrated by Victory dragging a bound captive accompanied by a *chi-rho* symbol in the field (fig. 11.41). At Rome in the mid-fifth century, the type is simply that of a cross (fig. 11.42). This sequence provides an illuminating commentary on changing notions of what made the Roman state secure. The increasing lack of a full range

Figure 11.40 Base-metal coin, AD 326, showing Fausta, wife of Constantine I, and an image of the goddess Salus. 20 mm.

Figure 11.41 Base-metal coin, c. AD 388, showing Victory dragging a bound captive. 14 mm.

Figure 11.42 Base-metal coin, c. AD 430, with a simple cross motif. 14 mm.

of divinities and virtuous personifications to provide figural types also resulted in a far greater concentration in the fourth century on the emperors shown in various poses, mostly military and triumphant, than was the case in earlier centuries.

It is one of the paradoxes of Roman history that veneration for the image of the emperor was in some senses at its most intense in the fourth century AD after the emperors themselves had disavowed emperor worship. This was certainly the moment when the image of the emperor came to dominate both sides of the coinage more pervasively than at any other time, whether before or subsequently when, in the fifth century, a range of more explicitly Christian symbols began to take over on the reverse. Much later, in the early eighth century, Christian iconography moved onto the obverse, when, under Justinian II (reigned 685–95 and 704–11), the image of Christ displaced the emperor onto the reverse (fig. 11.43), a fashion which became standard after the restoration of the icons in 843.

Figure 11.43 Gold *solidus*, AD 704–11, with the image of Christ on the obverse and the emperor Justinian II with his son Tiberius displaced onto the reverse. 19 mm.

Sacra Moneta?

For most of their circulating lives, Roman coins were not treated as religious objects, despite the fact that they were often decorated with images of gods, emperors, and other symbols of Roman religion and cult. Indeed, coins were typically described in legal contexts as public things, not sacred. What made them into legitimate currency was that they were marked with "the public type of the Roman people" (*forma publica populi Romani*). This formula meant not just that the coins had been made in the public mint. It also implies that the designs chosen to represent the public type were part of what made the coins public currency, and identified them as Roman. From the *lituus* of the late republic to the cross of late antiquity, religion continued to supply most of the key motifs that constituted the public type. The prominence of religious coin designs persisted, despite significant changes in religion itself, surviving even the change from paganism to Christianity, manifesting the abiding significance of religion in the articulation of the Roman civic identity. Coins were one of the most deliberate symbols in antiquity of public identity (Millar 1993a: 230); to which, the coins reveal, religion was utterly fundamental.

FURTHER READING

The best introduction to Roman coinage in English is Burnett (1987). For a good introduction to the interpretation of coins in a wider context, see Howgego (1995). The quickest way to get a sense of the range and frequency of religious symbols on coins is to start with the catalogues. Roman republican coinage is discussed and fully illustrated in Crawford's seminal *Roman Republican Coinage* (*RRC*) (1974). For the imperial period, the key works, both started by Harold Mattingly in 1923, are the catalogue of the British Museum collection (*BMC*), *Coins from the Roman Empire in the British Museum* (6 vols., London, 1923–), which goes up to AD 238, and the series *Roman Imperial Coinage* (*RIC*) (10 vols., London, 1923–94), which covers everything down to AD 491 but is less comprehensively illustrated. For the hugely informative, mostly base-metal coinages produced by cities in the Roman provinces, see the ongoing series *Roman Provincial Coinage* (*RPC*) (Andrew M. Burnett et al. eds., London 1993–) which is also fully illustrated.

CHAPTER TWELVE

Reliefs, Public and Private

Katja Moede

Rituals and cultic events are among the predominant themes of Roman art, which amply reflects religious contents and their symbolism (Ryberg 1955; Fless 1995; Siebert 1999; Moede 2004). Various ways to treat the pictorial subject occur. It is either symbolized by both sacrificial implements and animals, or the actual ritual itself is portrayed as processions or sacrifices (Ryberg 1955; Ronke 1987; Fless 1995). Yet the question arises how many of those rituals performed in reality and attested by our sources are actually represented in art. In order to give an answer at the end of this chapter I shall first demonstrate the scope of public and private representations of rituals. Monuments or groups of monuments will be confronted with the respective ritual as reconstructed from written sources. From a thorough comparison of ritual sequences as they were performed to their actual representation, it will emerge which elements are significant in an iconographic sense and have been judged characteristics of a ritual for the purpose of representation.

At the Altar: The Peculiar Religious Reality of the Images

At the beginning of the principate there was a notable increase of representations with a religious content. Yet historical reliefs in general multiplied with the advent of the empire and its change of political conditions. Moreover it was Augustus who resuscitated a plethora of priesthoods, cults, and rituals at Rome and for the Roman empire, who took an unambiguous stance regarding the importance of religion and its part in running a state, and who did his utmost to translate this into action. Nonetheless those elements used by imperial art to represent rituals are already extant on republican monuments with religious topics. The performer of the sacrifice and his attending acolytes, who bring the required *instrumenta sacra* (implements of cult) or offerings to the altar, are visible on the terracotta gable from Via S. Gregorio at

Rome (Ryberg 1955: 130; Fless 1995: cat. 1 pl. 40 fig. 2; Ferrea 2002), on the Munich/Paris Census Monument (the so-called Domitius Ahenobarbus Ara: Ryberg 1955: 27 pl. 8 fig. 17 a–c; Kähler 1966: 14 figs. 4–10; Stilp 2001), on the Ara Borghese (Ryberg 1955: 23 pl. 7 fig. 15 a–b; Schäfer 1989: 383 cat. B 19 pl. 90 fig. 4), or on the circular base from Cività Castellana (Kuttner 1995: figs. 28–30). Yet unlike many scenes of sacrifice from the empire, these show the gods as present, ready at the altar to accept their offerings. The direct dependency of ritual and deity is made palpable by the image. The republican monuments' dedicators, unknown today, must have found it important to put themselves next to the deity and, con-comitantly, his or her divine assistance. One may call it the most balanced option to achieve this by making both sides face each other at the altar. As the mortal performs the sacrifice it is clear enough who is asking for assistance and who is granting it.

Part of the pictorial tradition's nucleus is the simple libation performed at an altar or tripod, a sacrifice in itself or the preliminary rite required for the more costly animal sacrifice. Thus the depiction of a libation is borrowed for that of a preliminary sacrifice. Adding acolytes and animals expands the altar scene to hint at an animal sacrifice. Since handing the offered substance to the deity is the main action and even the purpose of most Roman rituals, representations that adopt this very sequence are frequent. Altars to the Lares of the *compita* (crossroads) use the simple altar scene for many monuments (Hölscher 1988; Schraudolph 1993; Fless 1995; Hänlein-Schäfer 1996). These images do not combine any sumptuous ritual sequences with sundry attendants but are limited to showing the ritual's crucial action. Among their elements are the *togatus* (man in a toga) emptying his *patera* (bowl) with his head covered (*capite velato*) over the altar or tripod and a *victimarius* leading a sacrificial animal toward him. There may be acolytes assisting the performer by holding the *acerra* (incense box) or bringing the jug and *patera*. Usually a flute-player is behind or beside the altar. The *compita* altars were set in the *vici* (districts) newly organized by Augustus, who imposed the restructuring of Rome into 14 regions and 265 *vici* in 7 BC, thereby renewing cult associations, which had partly ceased to exist. Every *vicus* was from now on led by a college of four *vicomagistri*, who were elected from the inhabitants of their district and began their one-year tenure of office on August 1. Their duties included the cults of the Lares and the *Genius Augusti* as well as the upkeep of the shrines. Four *vicoministri* assisted. While in office the *vicomagistri* were entitled to wear the *toga praetexta* and to be accom-panied by two lictors.

The representation of the regular post-reform rituals at the compital shrines which is considered the most exact is the front scene of the *vicus Aescleti* altar (fig. 12.1). It was consecrated during the cult's ninth year (AD 2–3) by the four *magistri* of that *vicus*. They are shown in common sacrifice, two *togati* facing one each side of the altar *capite velato* and offering a libation over the *mensa* (table) with their right hands. Behind the altar the flute-player *en face* accompanies the (seemingly) common rite while two acolytes lead in the sacrificial pig for the Lares and the bull for the *Genius* from the left. A lictor with his *fasces* in the left part of the scene denotes the official rank of the *magistri*, just as the *toga praetexta* did as part of the original painting

Figure 12.1 Altar of the *magistri* of the *vicus Aescleti* (Rome, AD 2/3) (photo: Rome, Musei Capitolini. Archivio Fotografico dei Musei Capitolini).

of the relief. Both insignia combined, otherwise restricted to higher offices, were accessible to freedmen in Rome only through the office of *vicomagister*.

This sacrificial scene's importance is aptly summarized by I. Scott Ryberg (1955: 59): "The historical value of the relief is, however, much greater than its artistic value, for it constitutes the earliest evidence, literary, epigraphical, or archaeological, of the offering of a bull to the *Genius Augusti*." Moreover the *vicus Aescleti* scene has been repeatedly seen as the most comprehensive image of those rites the *vicomagistri* performed at the *compita*. The *magistri* in office are gathered in the presence of the inhabitants of their *vicus*. The four are grasping the *patera* for the preliminary sacrifice at the altar while the procession leading the animals, a pig and a bull, arrives. Animal sacrifices like this had been performed in the same way for thousands of times. If a single person is in charge the action will follow a clearly prescribed choreography with well-defined roles. If a four-person *collegium* is to share in that function, however, considerable difficulties arise. No single official would bear the definite responsibility to the deity should they collectively consummate the sacrifice. According to the juridical Roman understanding of religion one party to the "contract" would not be clearly defined, this deficiency invalidating the contract. But if they performed the symbolic sacrifice taking turns, using the same animal, this would be tantamount to a multiple sacrifice of one animal, which, again, the sacrificial rules prohibit. Yet it is not only the theoretical reflections presented above that preclude the explicit meaning of that picture. Nobody would doubt the absurdity of such an interpretation were it transferred to the Vatican Lares altar at the Sala delle Muse (Ryberg 1955: 85 pl. 16 fig. 29a). Here there are two *togati* on each lateral face, performing a libation *capite velato* while each pair is again accompanied by a flute-player. If we followed the impression of these scenes they would prove that the college split to perform the simple libation, two per altar offering fruit, wine, and incense. At the same time this would imply for the *vicus Aescleti* Lares altar that only one member of the college sufficed to sacrifice a bull. For the first time there emerges the contradiction of pictorial and written tradition I mentioned at the beginning.

Consequently the *vicus Aescleti* representation of a sacrifice is not to be considered a comprehensive rendition of those rituals performed at the *compita* but must be read in the same symbolic sense as this altar's side and back faces. The lateral faces show the Lares on a plinth, the same kind as for statuettes used in the compital cult. Each one's attribute is a great laurel branch, which, of course, refers to the laurel trees in front of the house of Augustus (Alföldi 1973). The list of honors to the *princeps* is completed by the *corona civica* on the back face. Several symbols of a similar kind are combined in the front-face scene. Just as the *toga praetexta* of the *vicomagistri* does, the lictor marks the official status granted to those persons for performing their duties, as discussed above. The servants (*servi publici*) assisting the college during their religious performances place the compital cult on the same level as other cultic activities of state interest and therefore denote its rank. The animals refer to the objects of veneration, since the ascriptions of the pig to Lares and of the bull to the *Genius* are unambiguous. Likewise the seemingly common sacrifice does not only represent "consensus (*concordia*) under the auspices of an imperial religion of loyalty" (Hölscher 1988: 319 cat. 217), but shows the *vicomagistri* performing their foremost duty. The only link between reality and the scene as depicted is the figures' appearance at the most important action; every single one of them is in theory allowed to perform by cultic prescriptions. In the self-same way the sacrificial animals denote that sacrifice which might – ideally – be performed at the *compita*, but do not exclude the possibility of regular libations without sacrificing an animal.

This is also how the lateral faces of the Vatican Lares altar are to be interpreted. Although the *magistri* are distributed on both faces, all of them are shown at the same ritual act, their most important task during their one-year term of office and their privilege, raising them above the other participants in the cult for that period. As the sacrificial scene is to mark their area of responsibility, it must not be read as a narrative report on the ritual in question; it does not have to respect any ritual prescriptions. This is why the *collegium* may appear together around one altar or be divided into pairs. Our examples show very clearly how the pictorial rendition of ancient rituals persistently follows its own laws and demands and how poorly they qualify as a mere illustration of written sources.

Rituals and their Special Iconography

After all, it is quite clear that the simple libation performed at an altar or tripod is one of the basic elements of religious scenes. It can be increased and specified as much as you like, yet at the same time it is the unambiguous and rather general formula for ritual action. This scene could be used to represent all religious rituals containing the sacrifice at the altar as central element. Through other elements the altar scene could be expanded and transferred into animal sacrifice. By this combination of non-synchronous ritual sequences the generalized images became the characteristic representations of Roman rituals. The peculiarities of visual art made it necessary to amalgamate non-synchronous moments of a coherent sequence into one unified scene. The contemporary beholder was able to relate the elements to the familiar ritual of his reality. Unlike modern viewers, he was not tempted to view these images as documentation of the actual event of the ritual, because he very well knew the sequences of the ritual.

Usually the animal stands beside the altar and is escorted by *victimarii*. Rarely, images combine the altar scene with the killing of the sacrifice (fig. 12.2 below). Roman historical reliefs show only the killing of bulls. Sheep and pigs do not have to die on these monuments. To reproduce the *immolatio boum* the Romans use a defined iconographic scheme (Brendel 1930): the bull's head is pressed down by one *victimarius* while another swings back the axe or hammer. The first representation of this scene is preserved on one part of the Boscoreale cup of Tiberius (Ryberg 1955: 114 pl. 50 fig. 77 c–d). It is on the opposite side of the cup from the triumphal procession and shows Tiberius during the sacrifice in front of the temple of Jupiter on the Capitolium (Hölscher 1980). Only for this sacrifice before a military campaign is it allowed to act inside Rome in military clothes.

The key information for explaining these scenes is readily offered by the so-called *Feldherrensarkophage* (for example, the sarcophagus of Mantua: Fless 1995: cat. 38 I pl. 39 fig. 1). The bull-killing sequence is also shown on these sarcophagi in a military ambience, but not in relation to the triumph. Here it is one of three illustrations of the life of the general between the subjugation of the barbarians and the get-together with his wife. Additionally the general of these sarcophagi is acting in military clothes in front of the Capitoline temple on his departure. This sacrifice alone is the guarantee for his victory or his success in the Roman provinces.

The bull-killing scene is not limited to the objects mentioned so far. Big historical monuments deal with our iconographic scheme, too. One of the most famous

Figure 12.2 Sacrifice on the occasion of the twentieth anniversary of Hadrian's reign (Rome, AD 137, today in Florence) (photo: Alinari Archives, Florence).

reliefs is in Florence today and shows the *Vicennalia* of Hadrian in AD 137, but was found in Rome in 1569, where it was part of the famous Villa Medici collection (fig. 12.2). Altar and emperor are not preserved, but the rest of an altar at the left part of the relief leaves no doubt that this example of Roman art also presents both the bull-killing scene and the *praefatio*. But a new scene is also preserved: two naked boys are holding a shield. Behind the shield are two standing (and often restored) figures. These two male figures are the *Genius populi romani* and the *Genius senatus*, both in the typical iconography of such personifications. The architecture in the left part of the picture is badly preserved and today offers no help for the understanding of the relief. But the shield is important, and a starting point for the examination of the monument in Florence. On coins, the *vota* that are promised during the sacrifice were inscribed on such shields. The latter stand on the reverse of the coin alone or, as in our relief, accompanied by the *Genius populi romani* and the *Genius senatus*. Quite often Victoria also stands beside the shield and demonstrates the future success of the Romans (Hölscher 1967). But in Roman coinage there is another way to characterize the success of the Romans. Here the bull-killing sacrifice is shown in front of the temple to Jupiter and the inscription *vota publica* describes the reason for sacrificing the bull in this pictorial scheme. The same scheme is used on coins for the sacrifice after a five- or ten-year period of reign by a Roman emperor. A medallion of Antoninus Pius from AD 158/9 also uses the bull-killing scene, and the inscription identifies the occasion: *votis susceptis decennalibus tertium*. That means that the vows for the last *decennium* are offered and those for the next ten years are defined (Gnecchi 1912; Fless 1995: pl. 3).

All these various representations so far have made clear how closely the bull-killing scene is linked with sacrifices before war, the inauguration of periods of reign, or the assumption of office by consuls or censors. The sacrifice at the Capitolium is a big honor and allows the general or censor to take the position of the emperor for this special moment. For this reason the private altar vowed for the censor C. Manlius in Caere (Ryberg 1955: 84 fig. 39 a–c) has special interests for us. The inscription leaves no doubt that C. Manlius held the Roman post of censor and that the altar was consecrated in honor of him by his *clientes*. The reliefs of the altar also present scenes of the life of Manlius. The front shows the bull-killing scene, and it is quite clear that he has chosen this to remember the assumption of his censorship and thereby the only moment in his life when he has acted in the same position as the Roman emperor during the inauguration of his periods of reign. This use of official Roman cult iconography on private monuments shows how well known the link between these special sacrifices and the bull-killing scene was for the ancient observer.

Big Events, Lavish Processions

All the images we have seen so far are concentrated very closely on the events around the altar. Roman imagery is full of representations showing religious processions, too, and the long and lavish processions of some Roman religious rituals distinguish them from one another. Sometimes all the participants, the priests, acolytes, and sacrificial animals, walk through the city; the Roman triumph will be treated later. Conspicuously for both the ancient participant and the modern viewer of the monuments are the rituals with the sacrifice of three different animals (ram, boar, and bull). For this sacrifice two names (*solitaurilia* and *suovetaurilia*: Scholz 1973) and a lot of occasions are preserved in ancient written sources. During the rituals the procession played an exceptional role, because it did not only go from a point A to a point B like the triumph. Instead it orbited the object (a group of persons, a city) three times for lustration. This sequence is suited to defining an integrated topographical or sociological situation. Any space is clearly connected with a group of persons. This community was constituted by the procession and everybody resting outside is clearly marked as a non-member. A place which was lustrated during this Roman ritual is marked as a Roman place, too. At the same time the ritual produces an atmosphere of transparency because the hierarchical structure of a community becomes visible. The person who is acting in a special role during the ritual also has a big responsibility for the society (Baudy 1998: 105–6).

But to which deity is this ritual addressed? If there are a lot of monuments and sources that show Mars at an altar (e.g. the Altar of Domitius Ahenobarbus), he is not only a deity for lustration. A deity could be the addressee in other specific situations, too. A frieze from Beaujeu in the Museum of Lyon (Ryberg 1955: 115

fig. 60 a–e) shows the inauguration of an altar for the goddess Ceres (Veyne 1959). The goddess herself is shown in the frieze between the ritual processions of sacrificial animals. However, is the presented ritual really an inauguration or its anniversary? A similar problem is offered by the case of the Ara Pacis in Rome (Ryberg 1955: 38 figs. 22–4). From the archaeological point of view it is not possible to decide whether the big frieze from the outside of the altar really shows the inauguration. This ambiguity may in fact be the solution to the problem: it is possible that the ancient Roman pictures are multi-functional. If both rituals – the one of the inauguration and the one on a fixed day once a year – are identical, the monument can record both, if there are no specific links to one or the other.

The most famous representations of *suovetaurilia* in Roman art are present on the column of Traian (Ryberg 1955: 109ff., 121ff. figs. 55–8; Fless 1995: pls. 3.1, 6.1, 22.1, 44.1). Three religious scenes (scenes 8, 53, 103) out of eight (the others are 80, 83–5, 86, 91, 98–9; Settis et al. 1988) show the common sacrifice of ram, boar, and bull. The composition of all three is identical. In the center the emperor in a toga and *capite velato* stands in front of the altar inside a camp. From the bird's-eye view the procession during the walk around the camp is also visible. The ritual shown, *lustratio exercitus*, is the perfect pictorial formula to demonstrate the unity of the Roman military. For these reasons this scene is shown before every big military action (Baumer et al. 1991). Beside the perfect arms and the secure camp the protection of the deities was the most important thing that made military actions successful.

The most lavish procession in the Roman world is that of the triumph. The military triumph is not only an important historical incident; it is also part of a religious ritual to Iuppiter Capitolinus. If the state of preservation is not too bad, it is easy to identify the scenes of Roman triumph. One of the famous monuments from the early imperial period is the rest of the frieze of the temple of Apollo Sosianus in Rome (fig. 18.3 in chapter 18 below). Behind a group of *ferculum*-bearers (stretcher-bearers) the highly decorated animals walk in step. Nothing remains of other sequences of the ritual, like the libation or the killing of the animals. All official monuments of Roman triumph have this fact in common; only the procession is presented and there is no necessity for other scenes. All the actors of the ritual are shown in an optimal position during the procession. For the emperor, the triumphal chariot is the perfect place to show his role, position, and success. Before the campaign he had offered to the gods and let everybody know his promises in case of success. The procession is the perfect form to demonstrate his keeping of the vows. The participant in the real procession in Rome and the observer of the monument can see that all the bulls the emperor promised are ready for sacrifice. Thus anybody can testify to correct dealings with the deities. Of all the triumphal ritual only the procession is able to show unmistakably how important the emperor is and how impressive his success during his reign.

Not all sequences of religious rituals are shown in the archaeological monuments, and every time there are specific motives for their representation. Certainly, there were exceptions, like the relief showing the examination of entrails that is today in Paris (Ryberg 1955: 128–31 fig. 69 a–b). Of all the Roman priesthoods and their rituals, only a few are represented in archaeological monuments. And if some of them are shown as members of processions (as on the big friezes of the Ara Pacis) they do not perform their specific cults. They only represent and symbolize the large number of the Roman priesthoods and their cooperation in a moment – mostly a big event under the rule of the emperor – important for the Roman community.

Realities of Religious Life Beyond the Evidence of Public Monuments

Frequently private monuments take up elements of the official imagery. Beyond these common traits, however, images from the private sphere can shed light on aspects of Roman religious life otherwise unknown in the iconographic record. Occasionally, there is room for the depiction of the whole *familia* (Fröhlich 1991: pl. 28 figs. 1–2) carrying out the sacrifice; even the communal meal following the sacrifice (Fröhlich 1991: pl. 48 fig. 1) can be shown. A small-scale statuary group in the Vatican Museum (fig. 12.3) is a rather extreme instance of such glimpses into a religious reality that differs widely from the one presented by official monuments. As has been clearly demonstrated by H. R. Goette (1986) this figure is not at all a

Figure 12.3   Testing a sacrificial animal (Rome, Musei Vaticani) (photo: Vatican Museums).

cow being milked, but rather depicts the testing of a sacrificial victim. Though heavily restored, the original parts of the group belong to a male animal and a kneeling priest examining its reproductive organs.

A number of cults had strict rules concerning the victims' sexual status as cow, male bovine (*bos mas*), or bull (*taurus*). *Bos mas* in this context indicates a fully procreative bull, and not – as has been held in the past – an ox. Consequently, it is argued by Goette, this quality, too, had to be checked before proceeding to the sacrifice proper, an operation called *probatio victimae* (Plin. *Nat.* 8.183; Cic. *Leg. agr.* 2.93). The group therefore focuses on a ritual sequence unparalleled among official monuments; this sequence constitutes a necessary and unquestionable element of any sacrifice, but one of such little importance as to be totally neglected by public imagery. It neither allows an identification of the deity receiving the sacrifice, nor involves any action by the decisive participants in the ritual. Just like adorning the victim, leading it to the altar, and killing it, the *probatio victimae* is rather a task to be carried out by second-rank religious staff. Since its depiction is unsuitable to emphasize any superior responsibilities for the ritual as a whole, the reasons for choosing such a sequence must be of a private nature. The person carrying out the *probatio* was a *pontifex minor*, who probably covered this task for the whole span of his priesthood. This particular sequence may have been chosen as representatively stressing his office, rather as the emperor chose to have himself depicted as performing the libation in front of the altar.

A similar statue in the Badia di Grottaferrata (Goette 1986: fig. 5) museum shows that such a decision was not necessarily exceptional. In this case, too, the subject matter is likely to have been chosen for entirely private motives. The actual function of the statue is unknown, but we can assume it served as a votive in some sanctuary or as a representative accessory to a tomb. It remains an impressive testimony to the much broader imagery of religious ritual within Roman private monuments. Furthermore, it serves as a reminder of the limitations of archaeological finds in illustrating written sources. The choice of the ritual sequences to be represented, the stress on particular performers within the ritual, and the slight distortions of the proceeding aimed at creating a clear-cut message all add up to creating a perspective on Roman religion specific to images. The images in themselves are a rich source for religious practice and contemporary views of this practice, but they cannot be read as continuous and coherent protocols of ritual illustrating the everyday (or the extraordinary) proceedings of Roman religion.

Sacrificial Victims: Showing, Not Acting

Besides the great number of narrative scenes, a large series of public and private monuments restricts itself to merely showing cult instruments and/or sacrificial victims. The animals' rich adornment usually leaves little doubt as to their destination of immolation, probably the most prominent example being the two depictions of *suovetaurilia* on the back of the Anaglypha Traiani (fig. 12.4). Again, parallels from Beneventum and Rome show the Anaglypha to be no exception in the record

Figure 12.4 *Suovetaurilia* sacrifice on the *Anaglypha Traiani* (Rome) (photo: Alinari Archives, Florence).

of public relief monuments. In private dedications the subject matter appears frequently, often constituting their only relief decoration. These depictions do without an altar, or persons carrying out or helping in the sacrifice; ritual is reduced to the sacrificial gift itself, without any sequences or performers clarifying which aspects of the proceedings are considered as significant. Obviously, representing the victim alone must imply the gift being handed over to the deity within the framework of a correctly performed ritual. Thus, even in their radical reduction, the images stress the regular and, above all, appropriate character of the deity's veneration. The adorned animal functions as a symbol for this veneration's continuity; since it is through the monument itself that the dedicator declares his constant readiness to sacrifice. Moreover, these representations presuppose a univocal relationship between deity and victim: as has already become clear, the choice of animals to be used in sacrifice is far from arbitrary, but subject to rules narrowly defining correct cult. It is only this strict interdependency between deity and victim that allows for sacrificial imagery being reduced to the depiction of the mere animal. As in the case of the simple altar scene, it is hard to establish the actual frequency with which the ritual alluded to is to be repeated. In any case, a high rate of repetition seems necessary to make the visual reduction of the ritual possible.

Furthermore, to only depict animals on state reliefs and private dedications underlines to what extent getting in touch with the deity is conceived to be accomplished by ritual and the gift offered in its course. Although an altar is a dedication occasioned entirely by specific individual experiences, the dedicator neither asserts his ideas about the deity in question, nor hints at his reasons or expectations. There is no personal encounter between dedicator and deity to be visualized; the only emphasis lies on the raw matter playing the central part in this act of communication. On the grounds of this gift, the dedicator feels entitled to confront the deity with his prayer and to hope for its fulfillment. The image, in short, indicates the price for divine protection.

FURTHER READING

Ryberg (1955) remains a thesaurus of material. Recent monographs that include fully documented catalogues and images address several subjects: cultic personnel and musicians (Fless 1995); priestly symbols (Siebert 1999); self-representations of magistrates and priests (Ronke 1987); and rituals (Moede 2004).

CHAPTER THIRTEEN

Inscriptions as Sources of Knowledge for Religions and Cults in the Roman World of Imperial Times

Rudolf Haensch

On the one hand, one can say that without inscriptions, we would know nothing about the more than eighty *matres* and *matronae* (e.g. Eck 2004: 495) and the ritual of the Arvales (Scheid 1998b). On the other hand, one can point to the few aspects of ancient cults of which we are informed by means of inscriptions: they provide us with a large number of names, certain indications where these gods were venerated and by whom. But if we take a closer look even these facts reveal their problems. We often do not know whether a Roman name was simply given to an originally indigenous god. It is almost every time open to doubt how typical these persons were who venerated the gods in question. Even if we know thousands of persons who dedicated altars, we know that they were a small minority of an elevated social status in comparison not only with the whole population of the Roman empire, but also with the adherents of a certain god. The fact that the inscriptions normally tell us nothing about rituals and myths is even more problematic.

But before discussing the advantages and problems of inscriptions as sources for religions in the Roman empire, a few preliminary remarks are necessary. Discussion about the importance of inscriptions for religion and cults in the Roman empire requires that all inscriptions referring to religion and cults during the late republican and imperial periods have to be taken into consideration, not only those referring to cults which originated in Rome. In the Roman empire of imperial times – the period from which most of our inscriptions date – there were numerous contacts between the cults on the local level, on the regional level, and of empire-wide importance, resulting in numerous processes of exchange of various degrees. We have to deal not only with Latin but also with Greek inscriptions (other languages were seldom used for inscriptions referring to religion and cults until the late empire – the case of Egypt is a special one). Accordingly, we have to discuss not only the gods of the Greek and Roman pantheons, but also the Near Eastern ones and the huge mass of regional and local ones. If we define our subject in such a way (cf. Cancik and Rüpke 1997, 2003) there are almost no comparable introductions. Certainly, all introductions to Greek or Latin epigraphy normally have a chapter about "dedicatory inscriptions" (e.g. Guarducci 1967–77: II 121ff., III 1ff.; Schmidt 2004: 44ff.). But they take a linguistic phenomenon and not the historical reality as the starting point for their remarks. Only recently some very short attempts in a new direction have been made (Rives 2001: 126ff.; cf. Corbier 1998: 97ff.; see also Rüpke 2005a: 1501–16). Given this traditional proceeding, it goes without saying that a different approach in this field cannot pretend to give a complete and exhaustive overview for the time being.

Secondly, we have to deal with various kinds of epigraphical evidence. On the one hand, some inscriptions preserved texts which originally were written on other materials, as for example on wooden tablets (Eck 1998), papyrus, or parchment. These texts – as for example sacred laws (*ILS* 4906–16), the *commentarii* of the fratres Arvales, the decisions of Roman priests (*ILS* 4175, 8380) or of authorities concerning religious matters (Haensch 2006), municipal decrees referring to religious matters (*ILS* 112, 154), calendars, ritual texts (*ILS* 112, 4907), inventories (*ILS* 4423, 4921), lists of participants in a cult – were originally not conceived as inscriptions. Therefore, the texts are often long and of a more literary nature than the great majority of inscriptions.

The most important group of those inscriptions were the so-called dedications, that is, the tens of thousands of inscriptions on dedicated monumental objects such as temples, altars, statues, vases, etc., or referring to these things. The first examples date as far back as early republican times (see for example *ILS* 2988 = *CIL* 1^2.1439; cf. pp. 840, 987 and *AE* 1979, 136 = *CIL* 1^2.2832a with Beard et al. 1998: 17f. and now Hartmann 2005: 138ff., 200f., 213, 260f.). In ancient times, there were probably even more graffiti and other painted inscriptions of a religious nature (see for example Pliny, *Epist.* 8.8.7; Beard et al. 1998: 316ff.; Geraci 1971; Scheid 2005b: 219), which got lost without doubt more easily than the monumental stone inscriptions. The same is true for inscriptions on wood (Scheid 2005b) and on metal objects, which were often melted down (e.g. *CIL* 1^2.383 = *ILS* 6132 from Firmum Picenum; *RIB* 218 from Britain; *ILS* 1010 from Germania Superior; *CIL* 5.6881 from the St. Bernhard). The number of tomb inscriptions is even higher than that of the dedications. We find reflections of religious convictions in their texts, but in a very indirect way only, and often of such a kind that we cannot decide if we are confronted only with a formula or with the result of a conscious conviction.

Calendars

During the high empire, the number of inscriptions that hand down Latin texts referring to religious matters, originally not intended for publication as monumental inscriptions, is quite small, even if they are important ones as for example the *lex de flamonio Narbonensis* (*ILS* 6964). Their number is much more restricted than the so-called *leges sacrae* of Greek *poleis*, dating mostly from the fourth to the first century BC (from imperial times, for example, *NGSL* 5, 10).

Thus, during the high empire the most important group of inscriptions conserving Latin texts originally not conceived as inscriptions is probably that of the calendars. We can focus our discussion on the calendar used in Rome and in the cities under direct Roman influence, especially the Roman colonies, because until late antiquity there was never a unique calendar for the whole empire and not much influence of the Roman calendars on others, as for example the Greek ones. During republican times, calendars must have been published for centuries on perishable material, especially wooden tablets (see Eck 1998; more confident than Rüpke 1995a: 187f.). Publishing them in a more permanent way became apparently a fashion during the last decades of the republic and – above all – the reigns of Augustus and Tiberius. Apparently private and public walls were decorated for large parts (up to 4 square meters) with wall paintings or marble slabs containing calendars. The *Fasti Antiates maiores* date from republican times (the sixties of the first century BC?), from the times of Augustus and Tiberius date 39 examples, and from later times only a handful (Rüpke 1995a: 39ff., chart 1). But this fashion – a so-called epigraphic habit (Chaniotis 2005: 75 with n. 1) – was limited to Rome and Italy. The most remote example comes from Tauromenium in Sicily, a city which was during imperial times a Roman *colonia* (Plin. *Nat.* 3.88), not a Greek city. There are no examples even from such Romanized provinces as Baetica or Narbonensis. Without doubt, this epigraphic habit has to be connected with the so-called "Augustan epigraphy" (Alföldy 1991) and the reforms of the calendars by Caesar and Augustus. But we cannot determine the precise motives which induced so many individuals, *collegia*, and cities of Italy to monumentalize the calendar used in Rome (with the exception of the *Fasti Praenestini*, there are almost no adaptations to local dates or special social groups).

Thus, we are quite well informed about the fundamental characteristics of the Roman calendar during the early empire, but not during other periods and in other places of the Roman world. These calendars have to be reconstructed by using other evidence – literary sources, mentions of individual data in inscriptions, and especially *P. Dura* 54 (see Herz 1975). Within the limits pointed out, these Latin calendars are a very important source not only for the dates of major rituals of the Roman cults, but also for the causes and contents of these rituals. The typical layout and the information resulting from it can best be explained by the scheme shown in fig. 13.1.

In a certain way connected with these calendars are the inscribed regulations of individuals about endowments to celebrate particular days of a year, often their birthdays but also certain feasts of gods, and especially important dates in the context of the imperial cult (for example *ILS* 3546; see now Wörrle forthcoming). Generally, the imperial feasts adopted by the Roman calendar had probably the most important influence on other calendars in the empire. The most prominent example is the decision of the provincial council of Asia to fix the birthday of Augustus as New Year's day in the calendars of its members, that is, of all the cities of the province of Asia (*RDGE* 65).

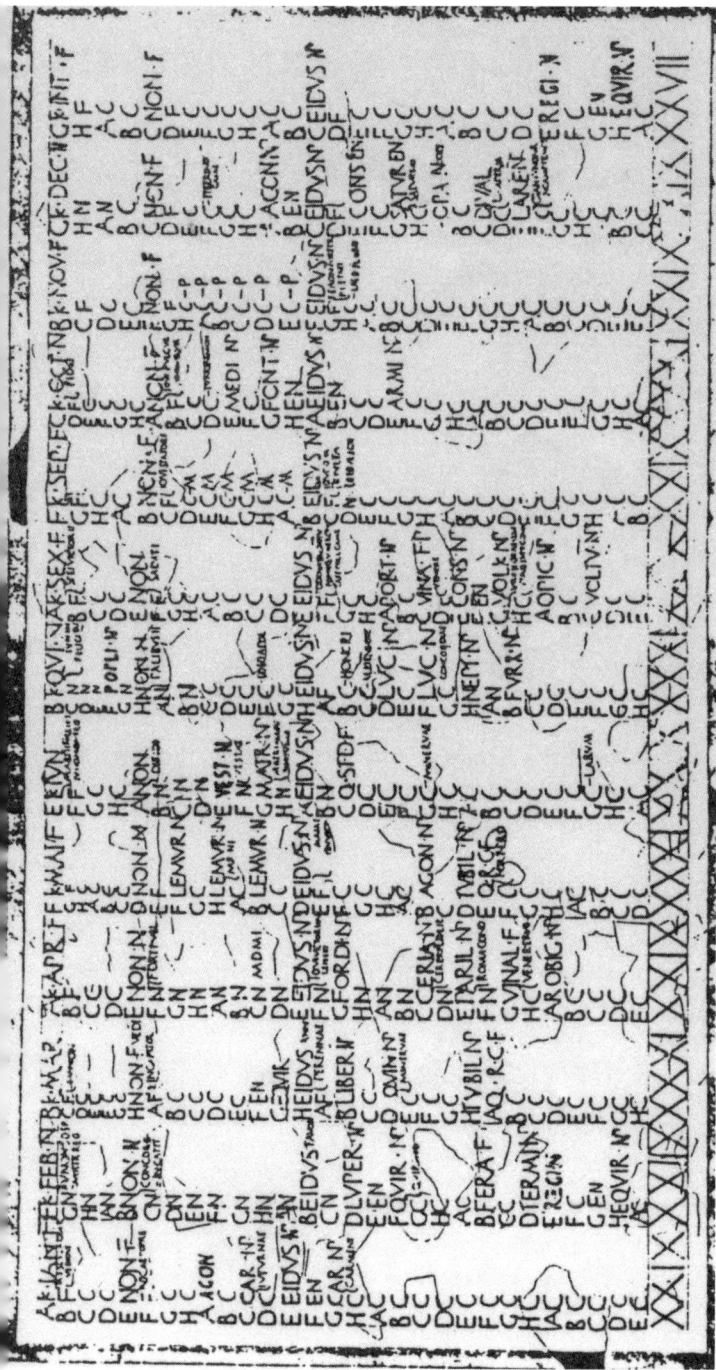

Figure 13.1 The Roman calendar before the reform of C. Iulius Caesar, as shown by the intercalatory month on the right (Fasti Antiates maiores, reconstruction Rüpke 1995a: 40). The letters A to H on the left of every monthly column serve to follow the Roman week of eight days; K(alendae), Non(ae), and Eidus ("Ides") structure every month and form the starting points for counting days (January 2 = ante diem IV Nonas Ianuarias). The letters F, C, and N indicate the juridical quality of the days (*dies fasti/comitiales/nefasti*); NP indicates religious holidays, *feriae*. For these days festival names are given in abbreviated form: AGO(nium, January 9); CAR(mentalia, 13th); LUPER(calia, February 15); QUIR(inalia, 17th); FERA(lia, 21st); TERMI(nalia, 23rd); REGI(fugium, 24th); EQUIR(ria, 27th, March 14); LIBER(alia, 17th); QUIN(quatrus, 19th); TUBIL(ustrium, 23rd); Q(uando) R(ex) C(omitiavit) F(as, 24th); FORD(icidia, April 15); CERIA(lia, 19th); PARIL(ia, 21st); VINAL(ia, 23rd); ROBIG(alia, 25th); LEMUR(ia, May 9, 11, 13); AGON(ium, 21st); TUBIL(ustrium, 23rd); Q(uando) R(ex) C(omitiavit) F(as, 24th); VEST(alia, June 9); MATR(alia, 11th); Q(uando) ST(ercus) D(elatum) F(as, 15th); POPLI(fugium, July 5); LUC(aria, 19th, 21st); NEPT(unalia, 23rd); FURR(inalia, 25th); PORT(unalia, August 17); VINA(lia, 19th); CONS(ualia, 21st); VOLK(analia, 23rd); OPIC(onsivia, 25th); VOLT(urnalia, 27th); MEDI(trinalia, October 11); FONT(inalia, 13th); ARMI(lustrium, 19th); AGON(ium, December 11); CONS(ualia, 15th); SATUR(nalia, 17th); OPAL(ia, 19th); DIVAL(ia, 21st); LARE(ntalia, 23rd).

Dedicatory Inscriptions

The most numerous sources for religions in the Roman world are the so-called dedicatory or votive inscriptions, that is, inscriptions on dedicated monumental objects such as temples, altars, statues, vases, etc. or referring to these things. They were already a frequent phenomenon in the Greek world. They informed the reader to which god or goddess the object in question had been consecrated and by whom. Generally these texts are brief and highly formalized. Standard elements are: the name of the god (normally in the dative, sometimes in the genitive), the name of the donor (normally in the nominative and during imperial times regularly in the second position – differently in earlier Greek inscriptions: Naumann 1933: 70, 72), and an often abbreviated dedicatory formula, such as *d(ono) d(edit)* or *v(otum) s(olvit) l(aetus) l(ibens) m(erito)* – in Greek *anéthēken* (is the wider use of *aphierōsen* and *kathierōsen* in Greek inscriptions of imperial times the consequence of a Roman influence?). These elements were only left out in cases where the context made them really superfluous – as for example if a *pater familias* dedicated an object in the *lararium*, the shrine of the Lares, of his house. There was apparently no equivalent to the practice of some Jews and Christians in late antiquity who explicitly renounced giving their names because these were known to the Jewish and Christian God and only this was important. Even if only the initials of a donor were engraved, as was sometimes the case in inscriptions of the high empire (*ILS* 3225), his contemporaries could probably identify the donor all the same.

These three standard elements tell us the things about which we are best informed: the names of the donors and the names of the gods. Both are important tools to determine certain aspects of religious life in the Roman world, and both are problematic ones. The Roman nomenclature with its three elements – the *praenomen*, the *nomen gentile*, and the *cognomen* – is a complicated and distinctive one compared to the nomenclatures used in other societies. Therefore, Roman names can be a good indicator in order to ascertain the identity of a person mentioned in two or more sources and to determine the geographical and – in some cases – social origin of a person. But there were only about two handfuls of first names. What is even worse is the fact that all people who obtained their Roman citizenship from a Roman emperor and all persons descending from such people or liberated by them took the *nomen gentile* of the emperor in question. Because of this, certain *nomina gentilia* also lost their value as a distinctive element of a name, and we are left with only the *cognomen* as a distinctive element. If the donors were given by their parents a very common *cognomen* or if the Roman army did it, as was common in the east, there are no possibilities of determining the donors' ethnic origin.

Donors quite often – but not always (Eck 1989: 39) – give not only their names, but also indications of their social status. They point to their senatorial or equestrian offices or to their rank in the Roman army or in the *familia Caesaris*, that is, the slaves and freedmen of the emperor. Thus, we are in general relatively well informed about the social structure of these adherents of a certain god, who venerated him by dedicating objects with inscriptions. In some cases we even get information about the donors' status not only at the moment of the dedication but also at the time when the vow was undertaken – as for example the *libertus* who fulfilled a vow made as a slave (*ILS* 3491), or the senior clerk in the staff of a Roman procurator (*cornicularius procuratoris*) who had made his vow as a recruit in the moment of being sent to a war on the Crimea (*quot* (!) *tiro proficiscens in bello Bosporano*; *AE* 1991, 1378). But it has to be emphasized that these people are only a part of those who venerated a god and we cannot even approximately determine the percentage. Only two things are certain: it was only a (very?) small percentage, and it was not a representative sample, because dedicatory inscriptions required money and an interest in this Greco-Roman form of cultural act. Even people who could read and write did not all belong to this group. Votive inscriptions are unevenly distributed throughout the Roman world geographically and especially chronologically (e.g. Derks 1998: 83). We can observe larger groups of adherents of a certain cult only in those cases where a whole religious community paid for something (*ILS* 3082, 3609, 3840, 5466, 5470).

Were all these hints of posts and honors motivated by the efforts of self-representation? That this was not the only motive at least in some cases has been shown by Eck (1989: 32ff.). He pointed out that Roman governors and other dignitaries mentioned their priesthoods only in two contexts – if a whole *cursus* was given, and in religious contexts (that is, if they dedicated a temple or erected an altar). Apparently, these senators did not consider their priesthood just as an honorary post, but acknowledged at least to a certain degree religious elements in these functions.

Two problems arise with regard to the names of the gods. In a provincial context – and 90 percent of the Roman empire was provinces – we can almost never exclude the possibility that behind a god of a Greek or Roman pantheon an indigenous god lurks who had been assimilated by the process of the so-called *interpretatio Romana* (or *Graeca*) to a Roman or Greek one with some similar characteristics (for a comprehensive discussion of the problems connected with the *interpretatio Romana* see Derks 1998: 94–118). But it is also impossible to exclude the possibility that the Roman deity was accepted by the local people, imitating the beliefs of Roman dignitaries such as the governors.

It is a clear-cut case of a local god if his name is derived from a local language, as for example the Dea Nehalennia (*ILS* 4748ff.), Bindus (*ILS* 4878), the Dii Magifae (*ILS* 4493), Bacax (*CIL* 8. 18828), or the Deus Turmasgada (*ILS* 4073–4). It is also possible to identify a local god where there was a standard equivalence – as for example in the case of Mercurius and the Celtic god Teutates – or where the equivalent chosen is a strange one – as for example in the case of a Roman veteran from the Hawran who venerated *[the]ô Lykoúrgo̦* (*IGRR* 3. 1294, cf. Stoll 2001: 467). These local gods, like all *dei patrii*, were without doubt for the majority of the population of the empire much more important than the gods of the Greek or Roman pantheon (and the gods of the *mysteria*). However, in all these cases, we know almost nothing about the rituals during which these inscriptions were erected. And even if the so-called *interpretatio Romana* took the form of an expressive paralleling by using the indigenous name as an epiclesis, as for example when our examples combine Bindus with Neptunus or Turmasgada with Iuppiter, or, as *AE* 1969/70, 405, does, connect the Celtic gods Atepomarus and Mullo with Mercurius and Mars, we know only that a part of the ideas of these gods recalled another. Only if we get further information – by bilingual parallel or divergent formulae (Scheid 2005b), by the archaeological context (characteristics of the sanctuaries; representations on the dedicated monument – very rare in the west: Spickermann 2003: 17f.) – do we get insights into the specific characteristics of these gods and eventually of their cults.

The Romans often presumed a divine presence but were not interested in determining its precise character, as the dedications to the *genii loci*, to *sive deus sive dea* (*ILS* 4015–17), and to such abstractions as *disciplina* or *pax* (*ILS* 3809–10, 3789) show. It was probably only in the later third century – under the impression of the crisis of these decades and its repercussions on religious beliefs – that a larger number of individuals used the epigraphical medium to explain explicitly the typical characteristics of a certain god (*ILS* 2996, 2998–9, 3170, 3257).

Thirdly, there are the formulae. Generally modern research puts them lightheartedly aside. Most researchers think apparently that the dedicators never took an interest in the formulae and that they were only added by the stonemason, who thought them to be part of a "normal" dedicatory inscription of a certain type. However, Scheid (2005b) has shown, by comparison between the Palmyrene and Greek or Latin parts of trilingual inscriptions from different places in the Mediterranean world, that the adherents of certain cults approached their gods in different ways in these parts of the inscriptions. In Latin (or Greek) the inscriptions recorded conditional vows typical of the Greek and Roman religions – the devout man had made a vow and thanked the god if he had gotten what he wanted. Such a contract, which placed an obligation on the god, was not possible in the context of the Palmyrene concepts of divinity. Thus, we find no equivalent to *votum solverunt* or *euchē* in the Palmyrene texts.

The examples used by Scheid are typical in another way, too. The inscriptions he discusses can show that the devout had different religious viewpoints according to the languages used. But Scheid cannot prove that all Palmyrenes who addressed their gods by means of a Latin or Greek inscription had the same complex way of thinking. We are almost never able to demonstrate how typical a certain behavior was.

We meet the same problem in the context of the rare cases in which dedicators informed us of their motives. For instance, it is quite surprising that somewhere in the Alps (near Seben), a slave of the emperor would thank *Mars Augustus conservator corporis sui* by dedicating a statue *ex iussu numinis ipsius* (*ILS* 3160, cf. 3704). The combination of the emperor, Mars, and the characteristics of a healing god seems astonishing, but apparently this slave had had a very impressive revelation of the god addressed by him. From the surroundings of Capua came a dedication to Silvanus (*ILS* 3523) by a *vil(icus) Dian[ae] (Tifatinae?)* and of eight *candidati* (to his post?). The constellation points to a ritual, routine act, but at the end of the inscription we find *ex viso*.

Rarely do we know what was dedicated (apart from the inscribed monument). In many cases the erection of the monument was part not only of a ritual, but also of a complex donation. But only seldom are the objects donated mentioned, because they could be seen at the time when the monument was dedicated and they became part of the inventory of the sanctuary, or were represented by the building inscription of the temple (or parts of it). Inscriptions like the altar (*ILS* 3039) dedicated to *Iuppiter paganicus* by a public slave of the *municipium Asisinatium* are more of an exception than the rule. He mentioned that he not only dedicated the altar, but also *aedem cum porticibus a solo sua pec(unia) fecit item mensam* (other examples: *ILS* 5453–4, 5457–9, 5461). These problems are aggravated by a certain tendency in the first collections of inscriptions to conserve only the text of an inscription and not to refer to the (archaeological) characteristics of the stone itself (see for example *ILS* 3876–7; in the case of only one of these dedicated objects was the object given explicitly named). The worth of the object donated is also mentioned rarely, whether by indicating the sum spent (*ILS* 5460) or the weight of the metal used (*ILS* 3192).

It was apparently a new phenomenon of imperial times – to be more precise, probably of the decades between c. 160 and 230 (see Derks 1998: 90) – that the adherents of a certain cult dedicated to the god venerated altars and other inscribed monumental objects of stone in huge numbers. As a consequence we can observe in certain sanctuaries hundreds of similar inscribed dedications. This phenomenon is known at least in all regions of the western provinces of the empire. In the sanctuaries of the *Matronae* at Pesch and Morken-Harff in the Rhineland respectively more than two hundred dedications to these gods were found (e.g. Eck 2004: 497). In northern Spain at Monte de Facho almost one hundred very similar *stelae*, dedicated to a *Deus Lar Berobreus* (otherwise unknown), were found (Schattner and Suárez Otero 2004) and at Thignica in Africa Proconsularis about three hundred votive *stelae* (*CIL* 8.14912–15199). Of course, even in these cases not all adherents of a certain god dedicated such an inscribed monument, and probably not even a major part of them did so. But the sheer number of such monuments and the manner in which these rural sanctuaries were dominated by inscribed monuments are very impressive – with regard to the interest in scripts and inscribed monuments in these rural contexts and with regard to the degree to which these monuments were part of the rituals of veneration.

In the cases where *arae* were dedicated, we find apparently a new understanding of the concept of the altar. Until then the adherents of a certain god or goddess had used the altar erected at the time of the founding of the sanctuary to burn incense or immolate the parts of the sacrificed animal destined for the god (e.g. *ILS* 112, 4907). But now at least many of the dedicators did not use an altar erected by another person but preferred their personal one (1,034 from 1,773 "dedicatory inscriptions" from Germania Superior are *arae* or fragments of such monuments: Spickermann 2003: 14, 17; for the Greek inscriptions see Naumann 1933: 70). As a result, the sanctuary was filled up with *arae* to such an extent that new ones blocked the way to the older ones. We can observe this phenomenon especially well in the so-called *Benefiziarierstationen*, as for example Osterburken, Sirmium, and above all Obernburg (Schallmayer et al. 1990: 145–75; Mirkovic 1994; Steidl 2005). In these cases, apparently a major percentage of these soldiers (certainly more than 10 percent, sometimes even up to 50 percent) felt themselves obliged not only to bring offerings to the Roman gods and – normally – to the not very well known, but important *Genius loci* at the customary dates, but also to erect their own altar.

This phenomenon is not restricted to stations of *beneficiarii*. We know it also from commanders of auxiliary units (Maryport: *RIB* 810, 812, 814, 816, 818–20, 824–9, 832–4, 846–7, 850), *primipili legionis* (Mogontiacum: *CIL* 13.6694, 6749, 6752, 6762), or *tribuni legionis* (Aquincum: *AE* 1990, 814–15, 817–19). Even a number of *praetores urbani* of the third and early fourth centuries wanted to honor Hercules with a separate *ara* (*ILS* 3402–9; cf. Scheid forthcoming b).

As a parallel and perhaps even connected phenomenon, we find during the same second century an ever growing number of altars and other monuments, dedicated especially by soldiers, that are addressed not to one god only but to a number of different deities, concluding sometimes even with the formula *et diis deabusque omnibus* (e.g. Cadotte 2002–3; for the earlier practice, see *ILS* 3208). This phenomenon was surely connected with the imperial cult, too. It was especially this cult which was often combined with other cults, whether the members of a ruling dynasty were equated with particular gods, whether deities were addressed *pro salute* of the reigning emperor, or whether certain dedications were made *i(n) h(onorem) d(omus) d(ivinae)*, as became a widespread practice in the northern provinces from Severan times on (Raepsaet-Charlier 1993; Schmidt 2004: 47).

Only a small number of all the dedicatory inscriptions are precisely dated – by way of naming the *consules ordinarii* of the year, or by referring to a provincial era or to local magistrates. Even the most widely known way of dating – by citing the consuls – became a more general practice only in the last quarter of the second and the first quarter of the third centuries. Not much more can inscriptions be dated in an indirect way – for example by prosopographical means or by our knowledge of the history of the units of the Roman army and their location. Dating by the form of the letters is only possible if the inscriptions come from a place where many well-dated inscriptions of the same kind were found. Even then we get only dates of such an approximate kind that we cannot base historical conclusions on them. This renders a difficult problem even more problematic. Dedicatory inscriptions are often used to determine the spread of a certain cult in space and time. For many cults not mentioned in the literary sources, inscriptions are our most important source of knowledge. But we should not forget that inscriptions can only provide *termini ante quem* for the introduction of a certain cult at a certain place. And the inscriptions known to us are normally only a small part of all those erected in ancient times. Finally, a cult could have been practiced at a certain place for centuries before the first inscription was erected. Thus, it will always be the absolute exception if our inscriptional evidence of a cult dates really from the time of its introduction to the place in question (for a comparable problem see Eck 1995: 349ff.). This problem is even more aggravated by the fact that precisely datable inscriptions are wanting. Thus, it is almost impossible to determine the precise routes and dates of the spread of a certain cult through the empire.

Another problem which has to be confronted by studies evaluating dedicatory inscriptions in bulk to get answers to questions of a more general nature is the fact that most inscriptions were not found *in situ*, that is, in the place where they were erected in ancient times. For excavations to reveal a higher number of inscriptions in their original place is the exception and not the rule (see e.g. Derks 1998: 83; Spickermann 2003: 14ff.). Normally we find dedicatory inscriptions (as all other inscriptions) in a secondary or even tertiary context – as part of a town wall, built into medieval churches, etc. Thus, it is often impossible to combine archaeological and epigraphical data. But in many ancient sanctuaries not only one god was venerated but also *theoí sýnnaoi* (e.g. *ILS* 3536). Therefore it is sometimes difficult to determine the principal god of a sanctuary known only by an archaeological excavation. If neither the central inscription of the temple itself was found nor a greater number of dedications to a certain god, but only one or two altars, there is no certainty that the god addressed was the principal one (see for example the so-called temple of Aesculapius at Augusta Treverorum: Haensch 1997: 76; Scheid 1998d).

Finally, two points should be made. Despite the fact that probably more inscriptions were lost through the ages than we will ever get knowledge of, cases are not so rare where two or three dedicatory inscriptions were put up by one and the same person. As for the *beneficiarii*, we find among the soldiers responsible for about six hundred and fifty dedications more than thirty who erected two or more *arae* (Nelis-Clément 2000: 31). We cannot determine whether this phenomenon was typical of other people to the same degree because we cannot identify in their case groups of persons and – consequently – individuals in the same precise manner. But there are a number of examples – e.g. *CIL* 1².4849 (Tusculum); *ILLRP*² 64, 237 (Veii); *ILS* 3424 (Rome), 3561, 3767 (Verona), 3747a/b (Pola, in a *fullonica*), 3886, 4253 (Aquincum), 3268a/b; and *CIL* 3.1096 (Apulum) – which seem to suggest that our epigraphical tradition was influenced at least to some extent by a quite small number of people who were especially impregnated with the epigraphical habit. But on the other hand, one should not underestimate the number of people who were sufficiently literate to be interested in such written forms of ritual acts. The people who frequented the sanctuaries of Pesch and Morken-Harff, Monte de Focho, and Thignica were apparently simple peasants living in a rural country and being only marginally influenced by "city life." What is more, the same can be observed in the case of the users of the *tabellae defixionum* (see the next point) and the authors of the "Beichtinschriften" (Petzl 1994). Apparently, much depended on the local situation influenced by many factors which we will never know.

Curse Tablets (*tabellae defixionum*)

One of the most important sources for ancient magic is the so-called curse tablets. These are inscribed pieces of lead, usually in the form of small, thin sheets, rolled up into scrolls or folded into small packets (but in Roman times not pierced by a nail), intended to influence, by supernatural means, the actions or welfare of persons or animals against their will (Jordan 1985: 151; cf. Jordan 2001: 5). They were left in water, in chthonic sanctuaries, and in tombs. In consequence of careful excavations and the widespread use of metal detectors, the number of detected tablets is increasing, sometimes in an exponential way. Until 1965, for instance, only seven examples were known from Britain. At present we have almost two hundred and fifty (Tomlin 2002: 165; for a general corpus see Audollent 1904; cf. Gager 1992; for the early examples from Spain, see Stylow 2005: 255, 261; for Germany, see Brodersen and Kropp 2004). The increase in the case of Britain is exceptional, but the number of Greek documents also grew by 100 between 1985 and 2001 (Gager 2001: 5).

As R. S. O. Tomlin and others have underlined, there are principally two different types. On the one hand, there are spells intended to eliminate a rival by invoking a demon and forcing it to act by writing its real name or by reciting words of power (e.g. *ILS* 3001, 8749). On the other hand, we have what should better be called "judicial prayers" (the majority of the British ones are of this type). The author of such a prayer, who often gave his name, voiced his grievance (usually theft) to a god, treating him or her like a Roman official larger than life. The writer is asking for justice (Tomlin 2002: 167f.).

Those tablets found in Great Britain are particularly well researched. Two hundred of these almost two hundred and fifty tablets come from two sites: one was originally urban and sophisticated – the great classical temple dedicated to Sulis Minerva at the Roman spa of Bath. The other one was a rural shrine of a Celtic god at Uley, twenty kilometers from the nearest town. It is important that apparently even in Bath, according to the names and the objects stolen, the petitioners did not come from a socio-economic elite. But it seems that they all wrote their own texts (probably after consulting "experts" concerning the formulae necessary).

Tomb Inscriptions

Even if each burial was a sacral act and even if each tomb inscription marked a *locus religiosus*, the number of inscriptions which give us insight into ritual and religious aspects of these acts is quite restricted. The reason is that most tomb inscriptions are brief and extremely formalized, too. After the introductory phrase *D(is) M(anibus)*, which we find quite regularly during imperial times, the name (and the functions) of the deceased are mentioned (in the dative or genitive), in the later second and third century often supplemented by a laudatory epithet such as *dulcissimus* or *incomparabilis*. Then follows the name of the person or of the persons who arranged the burial, with some indications concerning their relationship to the deceased. The inscription normally closes with a formula referring to the erection of the tomb – *f(aciendum) c(uravit)* or *ex t(estamento) f(ieri) i(ussit)* – or with one concerning the burial – *h(ic) s(itus) e(st)* – or last, but not least, with good wishes – *s(it) t(ibi) t(erra) l(evis)*. We find these texts on a number of different and often regionally specific forms of monuments: *stelae*, square stone slabs, put on edge, often with a crowning gable and sometimes with an image of the deceased; altars, which can only by their texts and the archaeological context be distinguished from *arae* dedicated to gods and goddesses; ash-cists, typical of Rome and its surroundings; sarcophagi, which were used in the western provinces with very few exceptions only from the late second century on; etc.

Of course, we get some general indications from these texts and monuments concerning burial rituals and the current religious concepts of death – for example, the ash-cists typical of the Roman *columbaria* are a manifest proof of the Roman practice of cremation (Tac. *Ann.* 16.6.2). But the problems arrive if one tries to get more specific information. To begin with a question already mentioned: were the formulae used consciously or only applied as a standard element of such a tomb inscription? The practice of abbreviating them seems to point to the second answer. But the other one is suggested when we find, in Greek inscriptions made by people who had come into deeper contact with Roman concepts (for example, through service in the Roman army), a translation of *Dis Manibus* (*theoîs katachthoníois*, *IGRR* 3.917 [a soldier, citizen of Athens], 1007). At Lugdunum (Lyon) and its surroundings, tomb inscriptions were often dedicated "under the trowel" (*sub ascia dedicare*). What constituted this ritual and where did it come from? Generally, only metrical inscriptions speak sometimes about the ideas of the people in question concerning death and burial. But they often pronounce nothing but very general phrases – "nobody is immortal"; specific religious ideas are rarely proclaimed (*IGUR* 432). Even then, we are sometimes confronted with such abbreviated allusions that we do not understand them (Merkelbach and Stauber 2002: 20/28/02).

To sum up, inscriptions are the only means by which to reconstruct the religious beliefs of all those people who are not represented in our literary sources; that is, not only the lower social classes in the centers of the ancient world, but also almost the whole populations of the provinces of the Roman empire. But even then we are informed only of the beliefs of certain parts of these populations – those interested in a very particular form of expressing their religious ideas. It depended on very specific local conditions how these parts were constituted. But this is not the only fundamental problem in dealing with inscriptions as sources for religious knowledge. Inscriptions are normally brief and formalized. Thus, we get insight into only some aspects of the cults mentioned in them.

FURTHER READING

There is no comprehensive introduction to the epigraphy of Roman religion.

CHAPTER FOURTEEN

Religion in the House

Annemarie Kaufmann-Heinimann

Religion, amazingly to the modern eye, was present everywhere in the Roman house. For some media – namely sculpture – we can fall back upon information given by ancient writers like Pliny the Elder or Cicero, whereas there is hardly any commentary by a contemporary author which might help us to understand the underlying meaning of the myths painted on the walls of Pompeian houses or displayed on mosaic floors of the later empire.

Our best source of archaeological information for getting an insight into a multitude of media, all present together, is the house interiors in the cities buried by the eruption of Vesuvius in AD 79. There a large quantity of the original furnishings has been preserved. If for instance we look at the small House of the Ara Massima in Pompeii (VI 16.15–17) (Stemmer 1992), owned by people of the lower middle class, the mass of religious and mythological motifs is baffling: Narcissus and the couples of Bacchus and Ariadne, Luna and Endymion, Mars and Venus represented in the wall paintings of the dwelling rooms, the Lares and the *Genius* painted on the *lararium* wall, Eros depicted on the handles of two bronze vessels, a sphinx used as a table foot. Evidence from other houses, such as lampstands, fountains, decorated couches, and garden sculpture, adds to the picture – not to mention small items like jewelry, often decorated with religious subjects. What was the meaning of all this? Were the Pompeians particularly pious people? Were any cult activities going on in their houses?

The phenomenon of religious subjects in a domestic context is, of course, not restricted to the cities near Vesuvius. There is evidence for it in all parts of the Roman empire and down to the late Roman period, for instance the mythological mosaics adorning sumptuous villas in north Africa (Dunbabin 1978), or the great dish decorated with Dionysiac scenes which forms part of the late Roman silver treasure from Mildenhall (Painter 1977). By studying some specific examples of interior decoration, therefore, we can try to discover what they meant to Roman imperial society. First, however, it is important to know where this style of life had its roots.

The Hellenized House in Italy

As a result of Rome's conquest of the Mediterranean world during the second century BC, Roman aristocrats came into close contact with the Hellenistic way of life. The Hellenistic palaces, equipped with porticos, libraries, picture galleries, and marvelous interior decoration, set new standards. Equally important, however, were the surroundings of the houses: the architecture was harmonized with the adjacent garden, and the view into a carefully chosen landscape added much to the new way of living. In order to blur the distinction between inside and outside, and to intensify the effect of grandeur, stage-like architectural prospects and idyllic scenery were painted on the walls. Certain parts of the house were given Greek names (*gymnasium, palaestra*, etc.), thus testifying to the inhabitants' education (D'Arms 1970: 1–72; Zanker 1998: 135–42).

Understandably enough, this new type of housing was in sharp contrast with the republican ideals of austerity stressed by writers such as Varro (*Rust.* 1.13.6, 3.2.3–4) from the first century BC or Pliny the Elder (*Nat.* 35.118) in the first century AD. This might have been a reason why in Italy the Greek model was first copied in the countryside, not in towns. Cicero gives us a vivid picture not only of his many purchases of statues and paintings to be installed in his villas at Tusculum and elsewhere, but also of the social life marked by *otium*, that is, intellectual activities and discussions with friends about art, philosophy, and literature (Neudecker 1988: 8–18).

One of the favorite regions for establishing large villas was the coast of Campania. The small town of Pompeii was in this area, with a population of around 10,000 inhabitants by AD 79 (Wallace-Hadrill 1994: 98–103), and there the conditions for observing this process of adoption and transformation are particularly favorable.

Wall Painting

There have been many attempts to track down the meaning of Pompeian wall painting and to decipher its underlying message. A very comprehensive and at the same time extreme view was put forward by Karl Schefold. He pleaded for a coherent religious interpretation of all the paintings (e.g. Schefold 1962, 1998: 361–77). To summarize and simplify his ideas: the decoration of a single house followed one coherent concept, illustrated by mythological and divine figures, be it a conflict between a hero and an evil-doer, or a more abstract concept like music or education. The main divine concept is represented by the Egyptian goddess Isis, who is present as well in the many landscape paintings often adorned with Egyptian motifs. Landscapes in general are thought to be sacred, and still-lifes represent offerings. Schefold's rigid, all-embracing system, however, despite many valuable observations and analyses, has not met with much scholarly acceptance (see Ling 1991: 136–7).

In recent years, Paul Zanker – amongst many others – has reconsidered the question of myths in domestic context, thus summing up one aspect of his many contributions to Pompeian problems (Zanker 1999). He stresses three points. First, images

Figure 14.1a Wall painting of Apollo and Daphne, House of the Ephebe (I 7.10–12, 19), Pompeii. The nymph Daphne does not try to escape her pursuer Apollo, as she does in mythological tradition, but rather flirts with him while unveiling herself (photo: © 2003 photo Scala, Florence/Fotografica Foglia. Courtesy of the Ministero Beni e Att. Culturali).

of myths were not tied to one specific interpretation but could be interpreted in different ways according to the personal experiences and situations of their viewers. Secondly, they gave their viewers the welcome occasion to display their knowledge of mythology and to prove themselves to be educated people. Thirdly, despite the wide range of subjects, the stress very often seems to lie not on the action of the tale which is represented, but on a general illustration of harmony and love, expressed usually through two protagonists. Thus, in the House of the Ephebe (I 7.10–12, 19), Daphne does not try to escape her pursuer Apollo but unveils herself in front of him (fig. 14.1a); in the House of the Colored Capitals (VII 4.31, 51) the mirror image of the Medusa's head does not disturb the tender meeting of Perseus and Andromeda (fig. 14.1b). Especially revealing is the fact that in some paintings the features of the gods are contemporary portraits, or they at least have contemporary hairstyles (e.g. the House of M. Lucretius Fronto [V 4.11]: Venus and Mars in the *tablinum*; a medallion with a child's bust as Mercury in a *cubiculum*). This reminds us of a scene at the beginning of Trimalchio's feast (Petronius 29.4) where Encolpius and Ascyltos are looking at the painting in the entrance hall depicting their host Trimalchio, who carries Mercury's staff and is guided by Minerva.

If we try to sum up what wall paintings might tell us about religion, there is certainly not a simple, one-track relation between the two. The paintings may have been ordered to demonstrate the culture of the owner, in other words for the

Figure 14.1b Wall painting of Perseus and Andromeda, House of the Colored Capitals (VII 4.31, 51), Pompeii (now in the National Museum Naples). The loving couple seem not to be disturbed by the menacing Medusa's head above them (photographed from Wilhelm Zahn, *Die schönsten Ornamente und merkwurdigsten Gemalde aus Pompeji, Herkulanum und Stabia*, Berlin, 1829. The Bodleian Library, University of Oxford, Mason EE51d, III Taf. 24).

simple purpose of having a picture gallery. This would explain why very often there is no system, and different topics are combined. On the other hand, the painted world of the gods and heroes illustrates models of (mostly) good experiences in life, and at the same time expresses the wish of the inhabitants of the house to share in these Dionysiac and erotic pleasures. There is hardly any connection to the people's daily world and to their religious activities, except for the paintings and statuettes of the household shrines, which seem to belong to a quite different sphere.

Mosaics

If in the first century AD the main medium for illustrating mythological subjects was, apart from sculpture, wall painting, in the later Roman empire this preference shifted to floor mosaics. In this period, the body of evidence comes mostly from sumptuous villas of the second to fourth century in Spain, north Africa, and the eastern provinces. As far as the subjects are concerned, there are no fundamental differences from wall painting. Here too, it is not possible to prove a common iconographic program for all the mosaics in one house. Dining rooms tend to be decorated with Dionysiac scenes, with scenes of the marine *thiasos*, or with *xenia* (small presents for the guests). Of growing importance are topics taken from the experience of the villa's owners, such as hunting and amphitheater scenes. When mythological subjects are represented, specific scenes out of a story are chosen, namely those representing important values in society like *virtus*, or illustrating *otium*. A preference for the erotic aspects of mythology is undeniable, although this is most probably not the primary and almost exclusive idea behind it, as a recent theory of Susanne Muth's would like to suggest (Muth 1998).

Sculpture

Sculpture is also a medium for religion in the house. Here we have better evidence from ancient writers than in the case of wall painting or mosaics. Polybius (second century BC) tells us about the first Greek works of art being transported to Rome after the conquest of Syracuse in 211 BC, "using such as came from private houses to embellish their own homes" (9.10.13). Cicero's letters to Pomponius Atticus and his speeches against his enemy Verres inform us in great detail about his own purchases of statues as well as about Verres' collections of stolen art. They not only testify to the very high appreciation of Greek statues (and Roman copies) but specify as well where within the house or garden the statues were set up.

If we go through the lists of statues Cicero ordered from his friend Atticus in Greece for decorating the various parts of his Tuscan villa, we realize that his main concern was not the subjects of the statues but that they should be suited for his so-called *gymnasium*, built following Greek traditions (Neudecker 1988: 12–14). Thus in the end he got some herms (amongst them Minerva and Hercules), some unspecified statues of Megarian marble, and a few terracotta reliefs. Obviously, religious concern was not the decisive factor for his choice. In his house in Rome, however, there was a statuette of Minerva, whom he regarded as his personal protector and whom he took with him when fleeing from home into exile in 58 BC.

Despite the difference of almost a century we might perhaps compare the arrangement in Cicero's Tuscan villa with the sculptures in the peristyle of the House of the Golden Cupids (VI 16.7, 39) in Pompeii (Seiler 1992). Here too, the guiding principle seems to be the allusion to Greek models. Herms, suspended marble tondi (*oscilla*), and masks, all covering Bacchic subjects, were meant to evoke the atmosphere of a Greek sanctuary's sacred landscape. On the other hand, the religious character of a Hellenistic votive relief with Venus and Amor, fixed in the peristyle wall, cannot be denied, even if its owner might have purchased it mainly for the sake of having a Greek original piece of art.

Interestingly, the display of sculpture in the domestic realm remained in fashion for many centuries down to late antiquity, as is demonstrated by the richly equipped villas of southwestern Gaul (Stirling 2005).

Collections of small bronzes were another kind of sculpture present in the home. The most desirable were the very expensive so-called Corinthia. Here it is particularly difficult to draw a line between statuettes bought and valued as pieces of art and others used in the domestic rituals. One of the most famous bronzes in Novius Vindex's big private collection was certainly the Herakles Epitrapezios ("Hercules at [or on] the table") which the poet Martial admired when invited to his patron's house (Mart. 9.43–4) (Bartman 1992: 147–86). It is obvious that less importance was attached to the subject itself than to the artist (in this case allegedly Lysippus) and the piece's pedigree. Still, there is a close connection between the motif – Hercules drinking at the symposium – and the function of the statuette as a table adornment. This same function is attested for *lararium* statuettes as well (cf. Petronius 60.8–9).

Silverware

Petronius' "Feast of Trimalchio" provides evidence not only of mythological wall paintings and *lararium* statuettes but also of decorated silverware used at the banquet (Petronius 52.1–3). The possession of richly decorated silver vessels was compulsory for well-to-do people, and it was equally important for the host and his guests to comment upon the mythological subjects represented on the silver. The ignorant freedman Trimalchio boasts of his enormous drinking cups (*scyphi*), but mistakes Medea for Cassandra when trying to explain one particular scene, and he is just as unlucky with other topics. The fact that in the first century AD such decorated *scyphi* were the focal point of interest is confirmed by the two big silver hoards found in the Vesuvian area, one discovered in the cellar of the House of the Menander (I 10.4) at Pompeii, the other on the premises of a *villa rustica* at Boscoreale (Painter 2001; Baratte 1986). They both consist of silverware for drinking and eating (*argentum potorium/escarium*), but relief decoration is to be found almost exclusively on the drinking cups. The topics represented on them and on other Campanian silver cover a range comparable with the one chosen for wall paintings: the worlds of Bacchus and Venus prevail, whereas within the realm of other religious and mythological scenes no preference for specific subjects can be made out (Künzl 1979: 220–1).

Under the exceptional conditions of the Vesuvian cities, silver services have been found more or less in the places where they had been in use, that is, in amply equipped private households. However, there are other cases where several successive phases of use can be distinguished. In this respect the Campanian plate within the temple hoard discovered at Berthouville (Eure, France) is of special interest. Five drinking cups and two jugs, mostly decorated with mythological scenes, had certainly been used in the context of private banquets somewhere in Campania before a certain Q. Domitius Tutus decided to donate them to the sanctuary of Mercurius Canetonnensis in northern Gaul (Babelon 1916; Baratte and Painter 1989: 79–97). It is clear, therefore, that religious subjects do not in any way prove religious use; they can just as well decorate secular silver plate, as is the case with the treasures from Pompeii and Boscoreale.

The same phenomenon proves true with later silver of the second and third centuries AD, in a period when the figured decoration on plate had shifted from

Figure 14.2 Center of a silver dish belonging to a third-century treasure found at Chaourse near Montcornet (Aisne, France): Mercury accompanied by a ram and a cock. The treasure, which consisted of a rich silver service and some coins, seems to have belonged to some private persons for their personal use, so the scene depicted does not allude to any cult activities (photo: Monnaies, médailles et antiques, Bibliothèque nationale de France RC-C-08692).

drinking to serving silverware. Imagery is now to be found on the medallions and/or the rims of large open dishes. In one particular case, Mercury has been chosen as a topic for the medallions of three dishes, each being part of a Gallo-Roman silver hoard (fig. 14.2). The god is accompanied by his favorite animals and represented, on two of the dishes, in the middle of a rural sanctuary. One dish was dedicated to the same sanctuary of Mercury at Berthouville mentioned above and was most probably made for this very purpose, which from an iconographic point seems quite suitable. The second one, however, belongs to a hoard of private table silver discovered at Chaourse (Aisne, France) which does not have any connection either with

Mercury or with cult activities in general, whereas for the third dish, found at Vaise near Lyon together with other dishes, coins and jewelry, secular use is quite likely, too (Baratte 1999: 37–41). Again, we are confronted with a wider range of connotations of religious images than we might expect.

Ceramics

Tableware

If we again take Pompeii as a model case, it is clear that, while several families had at their disposal a certain amount of silver plate, the possession of large silver services with decorated plate was restricted to very few persons (Painter 2001: 1–3). The situation is slightly different with ceramics: if we leave aside the coarse ware like cooking pots and amphorae, quite a large part of the fine ware, the so-called *terra sigillata* (Samian ware), is plain or simply covered with decorative motifs such as ornaments, scrolls, flowers, animals, etc., and a small amount only had figured relief decoration. But the dates and places of manufacture show, of course, that there are huge differences in quality within the relief-decorated ware.

The finest and most precious vessels, manufactured for instance at Arezzo in the Augustan period, betray the contemporary tendency to classicize, and they are, in terms of quality and choice of subjects, very close to contemporary silverware (for the motifs see Porten Palange 2004). In several cases it has been possible to prove that silversmiths and potters used the same models for illustrating mythological scenes (Roth-Rubi 1997; Porten Palange 2004). There is no doubt that the relief-decorated Italic drinking cups, as well as silver plate, wall paintings, and mosaics, gave ample reason for discussing and showing off with mythological knowledge to those invited to a symposium.

In the late Augustan period pottery production partly shifted to southern Gaul, and the enormous output there resulted in a more standardized production without much sophistication behind it. Nevertheless, drinking and mixing bowls decorated with animals, scrolls, ornaments, and small divine or human figures were highly fashionable in Italy, too (for the motifs see Stanfield and Simpson 1990). This interest may account for the wooden box filled with 90 bowls and 37 lamps, all fresh from the factory, found in the *tablinum* of house VIII 5.9 in Pompeii, which had most probably been ordered by a local tradesman. It is quite obvious that on this level the relief decoration has a purely decorative function, although some religious motifs are inserted (e.g. on no. 50: Minerva and Cupid, each in separate fields and surrounded by animals and scrolls: Atkinson 1914: pl. IX, 50).

Lamps

Mold-made lamps with decorated disks are closely related to relief-decorated pottery, as both artifact groups were made in the same workshops. In fact, in several cases it can clearly be demonstrated that punches from lamp disks were used for pottery molds. Of particular interest in this respect is a mold from the early Roman

Figure 14.3 Lamp from the early Roman military camp of Haltern (Nordrhein-Westfalen, Germany) (Haltern, Römisch-Germanisches Museum): Minerva voting in favor of Orestes, with a Fury present to the left. The type of the Fury, repeated and lined up in a row, has been reused in a mold for relief-decorated bowls where the original meaning cannot be made out (photo: Haltern, Römisch Germanisches Museum).

camp of Haltern with a procession-like frieze of women (fig. 14.3). It only makes sense when compared to the original scene they were taken from: it is an Erinye (Fury) from the scene of Minerva voting in favor of Orestes (von Schnurbein 1974; Kühlborn 1988: 594–5, no. 435). There are many other motifs which testify to this phenomenon (e.g. Klumbach 1961); nevertheless, they do also give evidence of the rich repertoire which was at the potter's disposal.

This is even more astonishing when one takes into account the restricted space available on the disks of the lamps. At first sight there is an overwhelming abundance of decorative topics which do not seem to have been selected to match the lamp's purpose. At Pergamum, for instance, of the 11 lamps with relief disks found in the house of Attalos Paterklianos, which was renovated around AD 200, six had been placed in a shrine for Cybele(?); but none of the reliefs makes allusion either to the goddess or to cult activities (Heimerl 2001: 85, 218). On the other hand, it is certainly not surprising that gladiator and sex scenes are preferred topics in military camps (e.g. Leibundgut 1977: 190–1). One would not, however, have expected them to be much more frequent on lamps found in the Idaean cult cave in Crete than representations of Zeus (Sapouna 1998: 120–2, 158–9). Such inconsistencies appear to be part of the ancient reality, even if we cannot find any convincing explanation. It is quite likely that any personally cherished object could be used as an offering.

On the other hand, a lamp disk with an isolated figure of a god might indeed have reminded the ancient viewer of all the statues he was familiar with in daily life, be it in temples, in household shrines, or on coins (P. Stewart 2003: 201–7). For the early empire we have to take into account Augustus' deliberate use of mass media like lamps for promoting his political and religious ideas (Alföldi 1973; Leibundgut 1977: 193–6; Zanker 1987: 88–90, 264–79). This is the case, in the first place, with lamps representing the Lares Augusti or Victoria with an inscribed shield, but cornucopias, capricorns, and laurel fall into the same category.

Money-boxes

Proof, however, that a deliberate choice of religious subjects was made, when thought suitable, is demonstrated by one specific category of objects for daily use: terracotta money-boxes. Apart from a specimen of the later first century AD with Victoria and inscribed New Year's wishes – obviously used as a *strena* (New Year's gift) – the bulk of the evidence is to be dated to around AD 200 and resembles in shape the mold-made lamps or, more often, a kind of beehive (Graeven 1901: 178–87; D. Robinson 1924; Fabbricotti 1967/8: 117, figs. 856–81, pl. LXIII; Reeder Williams 1984: no. 96). On the front there is decoration in relief: in most cases either Mercury or Fortuna standing within an *aedicula*, thus resembling a cult image. According to the inscriptions the money-boxes were made by lamp-makers, who had a wide repertoire of subjects at their disposal (Bailey 1980: 90). However, for the decoration of money-boxes they explicitly chose the two gods most responsible for wealth and welfare, a function most welcome in connection with the saving of money (fig. 14.4).

Artistic Evidence for the Domestic Cult

We have been moving around within a Roman house, have looked at the painted walls and the mosaic floors, have been admiring the garden sculpture and the art collection of the *dominus*, and have been drinking out of silver cups teaching us mythology, while some dim light was shed by relief-decorated lamps; but so far we have left aside one kind of straightforward evidence for domestic religion, namely the household gods and their shrines. For a first impression we can again go back to Petronius. When Encolpius and Ascyltos entered Trimalchio's house, they "saw a large cupboard containing silver Lares and a marble image of Venus" (Petronius 29.8). Later on, after a few courses, the statuettes of the Lares – certainly the ones mentioned before – were put on the table and a bowl of wine was carried round, followed by the blessing *dii propitii* ("May the gods be gracious unto us!") (Petronius 60.8–9). While this last scene probably does not correspond to daily practice – other authors speak of the daily sacrifice to be performed near the fireplace

Figure 14.4 Mercury with money-bag and staff on a money-box from Italy (c. AD 200). Out of a large range of subjects, the potter, who stamped his product on the back of the box, chose a topic to match the object's function, Mercury being responsible for luck and material welfare (photo: the Johns Hopkins University Archaeology Collection).

(Fröhlich 1991: 22–7) – the archaeological evidence confirms the existence of household shrines and gives an insight into various other aspects of religious activity in the house, especially in the case of the cities buried by Vesuvius (Boyce 1937; Orr 1978; Fröhlich 1991).

The media closely related to the domestic cult were paintings and statuettes. There is a marked difference in attitude and pretension between the mythological paintings in the rooms open to visitors and *lararium* paintings installed in service areas, although they were often done by the same painters (Fröhlich 1991: 93–106; Wallace-Hadrill 1994: 38–44). *Lararium* paintings often follow a rather strict pattern with a defined number and type of elements, as is shown for instance at the House of the Vettii (VI 15.1): the central figure of the togate *Genius*, the living spirit of the *pater familias*, is framed by the Lares, two dancing youths holding each a *rhyton* of wine; below there is a huge serpent to which most likely a protecting and evil-averting function was attributed (Boyce 1937: 54 no. 211; Fröhlich 1991: 279 L70). Thus, the scene is not at all tied up with traditional mythology but is entirely Roman: the *Genius* takes on the type of a Roman priest whereas the Lares seem to be a genuine Roman invention, influenced by neo-Attic types like the *calathiscos* dancers.

The main features of the imperial domestic cult go back to the reform of the cult of the Compitales initiated by Augustus in 7 BC. Each of the 265 city districts (*vici*) was allotted a Compital shrine for which members of the *collegia compitalicia* were held responsible, slaves acting as *ministri* and freedmen as *magistri*. The central cult figures were statuettes of the Lares and the *Genius*, as is documented on several official monuments in Rome; at the same time, they referred to the emperor himself by transmitting the idea of the imperial cult and thus ensured loyalty toward the emperor (Hölscher 1988: 390–400; Zanker 1987: 132–40).

An equally important role was assigned to slaves on the domestic level inasmuch as they had their own household shrines centered on the Lares and the *Genius*. Still, in the Vesuvian cities interesting differentiations according to social levels can be observed, as Thomas Fröhlich pointed out (Fröhlich 1991: 28–48). In the servants' quarters the domestic shrine consisted, as in the House of the Vettii, of a painted representation of the Lares and the *Genius*, eventually enlarged with some cult assistants, whereas in the area of the *dominus* the main focus was on three-dimensional figures of the Lares, the *Genius*, and other gods, called Penates, according to his own preferences.

While the servants' household shrines all appear to be restricted to the Lares and the *Genius*, there seem to be hardly any rules as far as the *lararia* in the reception rooms are concerned. Thus, for instance, in the so-called House of a Priest (V 4.3) the household shrine of the *dominus* installed in the *atrium* consisted of a niche framed by eight painted gods – Bacchus, Venus Pompeiana with Cupid, Fortuna, Jupiter, Mercury, Victoria, Hercules, and Minerva – while the statuettes originally put up in the niche were, at the moment of the volcanic eruption, being stored away in a cupboard of the adjoining room. There were a pair of Lares, a *Genius* (all three of bronze), a marble Venus, and three amber figurines: Cupid, a seated woman, and a hippopotamus (Boyce 1937: 39–40, no. 118; Adamo Muscettola 1984: 26; Fröhlich 1991: 271–2, L 52; Kaufmann-Heinimann 1998: 218, GFV 23). Of course, we do not know whether all the components of this inventory had really been placed in the *aedicula*, but it is not the only case where items which to our understanding do not have any religious connotation are to be found in such a context. In any case we must not forget the whole field of amulets and superstition undoubtedly present in the house, too.

Some slightly different evidence is preserved in the House of the Red Walls (VIII 5.37), where, on the rear wall of the *aedicula* installed in the *atrium*, the *Genius* and the Lares are painted, whereas six bronze statuettes were set up: a pair of Lares, two different statuettes of Mercury, Apollo, and Hercules (Boyce 1937: 77 no. 371; Adamo Muscettola 1984: 15–20; Fröhlich 1991: 291–2 L 96; Kaufmann-Heinimann 1998: 222 GFV 37; fig. 14.5). The group illustrates some features common to many other *lararium* groups: there is no unity of size, style, or number within one specific *ensemble*. Actually this is not surprising if we take into account that household shrines existed over generations. Old, venerable statuettes were preserved and new ones added, according to the house-owner's needs and preferences.

If the *lararium* paintings displayed in the servants' quarters always refer to their religious function, things are different with regard to sculptural works like statuettes.

Figure 14.5 *Lararium* of the House of the Red Walls (VIII 5.37) at Pompeii. Normally, painted *lararia* are typical of the servants' quarters, whereas the more expensive statuettes stood in shrines belonging to more representative rooms. In this one case the two are combined: a rather modest painting of the Lares and the *Genius* on the back wall and six bronze statuettes of the Lares, Mercury, Apollo, and Hercules standing in the *aedicula* (photo: Deutsches Archäologisches Institut, Rome. Photo Labor, Neg. D-DAI-Rom 1971.1114).

A statuette could be of value as a work of art – if we remember for instance Novius Vindex and his art collection – and as a cult object. Moreover, the fact that small-scale sculpture was movable must not be underestimated; several authors mention the talisman-like function of statuettes (Plut. *Sulla* 29.6; Amm. 22.13.3; Apul. *Apol.* 63.2).

It is not surprising that, when looking for evidence of the domestic cult outside the Vesuvian cities, hardly any *in situ* evidence is to be found. Still, isolated imported statuettes found in early Roman camps, and groups of statuettes often preserved in the latest destruction layers of a Roman provincial town, suggest that the domestic cult was brought by the Roman army to the provinces and spread through local society. However, the social differentiation met with in Pompeii has not been found outside Italy so far; this may be due to the generally rather poor state of preservation of paintings (Kaufmann-Heinimann 1998: 186–95).

The domestic cult in the shape given by Augustus must have been extremely popular mainly during the first century AD, as an enormous quantity of bronze statuettes of the Lares, presumably made at this time, are to be found nearly all over the empire. In the later centuries they maintained their important position within the domestic cult, which explains why a Theodosian edict of AD 392 explicitly prohibited secret veneration of the Lares, the *Genius,* and the Penates (*CTh* 16.10.12).

Summary

The main obstacle to understanding religion in the domestic realm is probably the prevailing, ubiquitous inconsistency. There is no clear-cut line between sacred and secular objects and decoration. Strictly speaking, only the main figures of the domestic religion – the Lares and the *Genius* – in their painted or three-dimensional form can be judged as unmistakably religious objects. All the other media consist of different layers of meaning which often cannot be neatly separated.

FURTHER READING

There is no comprehensive study of the subject so far, but several aspects are treated separately. As far as sculpture is concerned, Eugene J. Dwyer (1982) presents the contents of five Pompeian houses, whereas two recent publications about the terrace houses of Ephesus cover the whole range of interior decoration of two dwelling units (Lang-Auinger 2003; Thür 2005). Antonella Coralini (2001), on the other hand, takes one divinity, Hercules, as a starting point. Bettina Bergmann (1994) analyzes the paintings of the House of the Tragic Poet in Pompeii with respect to the art of memory. Three volumes of conference proceedings on Roman housing (Gazda 1991; Laurence and Wallace-Hadrill 1997; A. Frazer 1998) contain papers dealing with different aspects of the subject; see, amongst others, Elizabeth Bartman (1991) and Richard Neudecker (1998) on sculpture collections and Sarah Scott (1997) on late Roman mosaics.

PART III

Symbols and Practices

CHAPTER FIFTEEN

Roman Cult Sites: A Pragmatic Approach

Ulrike Egelhaaf-Gaiser

Subject Matter and Disposition

This chapter deals with the structure, function, and perception of Roman cult sites and their integration into a profane environment, as well as several forms of religious architecture and monumentalization. The focus will be on the pragmatics of cult sites and cult images, in both an everyday environment and the celebration of rituals. The systematic introduction in the first four sections will concentrate on Italian precincts and those in the city of Rome dating from the late republic to the middle imperial period (second century BC to second century AD), which are exceptionally well documented. To verify our findings, we shall then look at three specific examples: the extra-urban grove of Anna Perenna, the monumental temple of Apollo on the Palatine, and the Fortuna Augusta temple near the forum in Pompeii. These were chosen because of their diversity of shape and spatial structure, but they are comparable in terms of their common Augustan background. There are several arguments in favor of this very narrow time window: it is a period of political upheaval, and its far-reaching political change from the republic to the principate had an impact on all spheres of life. It is hardly surprising, therefore, that upon closer inspection, the Augustan "cultic restoration" turns out to be a highly innovative reform program. Since the religious landscape of the Augustan age is very well known, thanks to the wealth of information available, the evaluation and classification of the individual examples within their contemporary context are eased considerably.

Basic Concepts

The concept of "cult site" includes any space that has been designated for worship. Roman antiquarian literature distinguishes between *templum* and *aedes sacra* (Fridh

1990): the *templum* is a ritually defined area; it could refer to a section of the sky selected by the *augur* for the observation of auspices from the flight of birds, with an augur's staff and a spoken formula, or a dedicated cult site that may or may not have been architecturally enhanced. The *aedes sacra*, on the other hand, refers to the temple building as the seat of the gods, which could be erected in the cult precinct. As the rightful inhabitants of the building, the gods were entitled to the rear, offset part of the temple interior (*cella*). Wide doorways allowed them an unhindered view of the open-air sacrificial altar (*ara, mensa*), where the food was placed.

The sanctity of the site depended solely on the status of the land it stood on. Ownership of the land was transferred to the deity in a ritual act (*consecratio*), which also released it from all public claims and removed it from secular access. Once consecrated, cult sites and their furnishings are protected for all time; potentially damaged cult items and votive offerings must be stored or buried in the cult precinct. Inscriptions therefore sanction the short-term removal of votive offerings for restoration purposes, or the removal of dead trees from a sacred grove, or the felling of trees as part of the annual festival of sacrifice (*CIL* 1².366; 9.3513).

Architectural uniformity on the sacred grounds is of secondary importance: in general, the main room forms the center of the precinct. It closes off the open square in front of it and is axially aligned with the entrance. The visual perspective guiding the eye is reinforced by framing porticos, water fountains, and symmetrical staircases and ramps. But the characteristic architectural configuration – the free-standing temple on a high *podium* with a stepped approach at the front and an altar protruding at right angles (on the typology of Roman temple architecture see Kähler 1970) – is joined by chapels and sanctuaries, roadside and domestic shrines, burial sites, *mithraea*, *isea* and *serapea*, synagogues and clubhouses. Even simple, "natural," open-air cult sites, such as mountain peaks, caves, groves, and springs (Edlund 1987: 30–43, 126–46), are generally shaped by man, be it in the form of a separating wall, an altar, and a permanent cult image, or pits for votive deposits in the ground.

Depending on the cult, the deities were worshiped in aniconic or anthropomorphic shape (Gladigow 1994). The dialectic of the potential omnipresence of the gods and their desired association with one particular location is mirrored in the contrast between movable and permanent cult objects (*simulacra, signa, effigies*). The latter guaranteed the visitor accessibility of the deity, and the city (in the case of city gods) its special protection. Cult transfer and the establishment of subsidiary sites were accomplished via the transfer of cult images. According to the foundation legends, the deities expressed their desire to relocate through a sign or a spontaneous appearance at the new site. A prominent example is the removal of the Magna Mater and her sacred stone from Pessinus in 204 BC (Livy 29.10.4–29.14.14; Ov. *Fast.* 4.247–348). The idea of the animated cult image is found in the prodigy lists and autopsy reports on talking and moving, laughing and crying, perspiring and bleeding statues (Caesar, *Bellum civile* 3.105.2–6; Livy 23.1.10–12). An enlightened critique of religion could start with cult images; the accusation of idolatry or, rather, the anthropomorphic depiction of the gods (Lucilius frg. 490–5 Krenkel; Varro ap. Aug. *Civ.* 6.5) aims at the more fundamental inquiry into the relationship between deity and image.

Especially immovable cult images – as temple buildings (Favro 1996: 150–5) and interiors (Mattern 2001) – were subject to a general tendency toward increased luxury and monumentalization. The replacing of small-sized archaic wooden and terracotta images with imposing marble-and-gold ivory statues was justified with a religio-aesthetic argument: precious materials (gold, ivory, variegated marble) and colossal dimensions lent expression to the gravity, the power, and the "beauty" of the deity. To enhance the aesthetic value, statues by renowned Greek artists seized in war were often re-used as cult images in Roman temples. The group of statues in the Palatine temple of Apollo are an instance of this (see the section below on the sanctuary of Apollo Palatinus).

The "furnishings," on the other hand, constitute the functional equipment of the cult precinct and temple buildings – water basins and wells, kitchens, benches and tables, wooden cabinets and shelved niches. In addition to the permanent fixtures there are movable pieces of furniture and instruments such as crockery, lamps, cushions, and sun sails, which could be brought as needed. Representative temple architecture in particular, however, makes it difficult to separate the functional furnishings from "decorative" elements such as wall paintings, mosaics, marble paneling – since both functions are often combined. Colorfully woven curtains and temple doors adorned with metal fittings could be intended as eye-catchers and at the same time serve as boundary markers, floor tiles of variegated marble could be both embellishment and insulation, statues were placed in the *cella* as votive gifts but also displayed as works of art.

The religious ordering principle – the separation between sacred and profane ground as well as the ideal west–east orientation of all temples (Vitr. 4.5.1) – was in practice often compromised by pragmatic interests and spatial constraints. For instance, the Fortuna sanctuary at Pompeii (see the section below on the temple of Fortuna Augusta), which was integrated into an existing urban structure, had to follow the street pattern and the borders of adjoining private properties. In the course of the comprehensive restoration and reorganization of Rome's vast urban space, Augustus introduced for every district a local cult for the *lares* and the *Genius* of the *princeps*, whose modest shrines (*compita*) were found at crossroads (Favro 1996: 135–40).

Spatial Order and Functionality

Archaeological research has often neglected the documentation of cult realia (see, e.g., Baldassare 1996: 35–41) in favor of architectural and stylistic analysis. The less than spectacular, minimal solutions of practicing religions are recorded only in exceptional cases: perhaps one place of worship was indicated simply by a statuette in a wall niche, or a wall painting on a street corner (Bakker 1994). An outdoor altar could at any time be erected from dug-out patches of grass, and a modest sacrificial meal could be prepared with the help of a portable brazier, earthen crockery, and knives: the water necessary for cleaning could be taken from a public running well or the cistern of a neighboring house or grave-owner. A former cult place may therefore at times be identified only from paint residue on the plastering, a burnt layer, or a waste-disposal pit containing charred remains of fruit kernels and bones. These observations should remind us not to infer from the building of a monumental site the establishment of a (perhaps much older) cult or, vice versa, to conclude from the destruction or dilapidation of a cult site the simultaneous cessation of all cult activity (rather than a conceivable change).

At complex cult sites, the functional differentiation between cult building and auxiliary rooms is marked by differences in the layout of the rooms, their dimensions and arrangement. The size, ceiling height, and monumental character of the central building(s) were intended to impress the visitor, and therefore reserved for the representative areas open to public access (entrance portals, temples, open squares, porticos, or dining rooms). The subsidiary rooms, by contrast, are often found on the periphery, inserted under staircases and into dead corners, even if that made them less than user-friendly: kitchens, storage rooms, and latrines were badly lit and exceedingly cramped – the comfort and safety of his workforce and his slaves were of little consequence for the benefactor keen on external representation.

In the late republican era, visitors ascending the stairs and ramps of the imposing terraced sanctuaries experienced a graded spatial hierarchy, from the storage rooms and shops at the bottom via the representative structures (porticos, theaters, fountains, and gardens) to the crowning temple (Scheid 1995). However, spatial differentiation does not automatically presuppose monumental size: even a small cult space could present a highly complex sign system, demarcating various levels of sacredness by way of visual axes and orientation guides. Spatial borders, symmetry, and direction played a prominent part not only within the sanctuary but also in relation to the urban environment of the cult site.

Nature and spring sanctuaries, which marked the city boundaries, also saw their status raised during the Augustan period. The most prominent example is that of the sacred grove of the Dea Dia (Scheid 1990): from the Augustan reforms onward, the Arval Brethren responsible for the cult of the goddess were recruited from the highest circles of the elite.

In the city, by contrast, outdoor cult sites with few or no architectural markers had already disappeared as a result of the uncontrolled private building activity in the late republican era. Within the sanctuaries, too, tree plantations were increasingly encroached upon by grandiose temples and their extensions, as in the case of the Vesta shrine, where the natural grove was taken over by the spacious residence of the priestesses, only to be replaced by a man-made landscape garden and sacral-idyllic wall paintings in the reception rooms. At the same time the members of the elite sought to enhance their prestige by incorporating into the extensive grounds of their villas little decorative garden temples or caves with marble images (Coarelli 1983); correspondingly, in the representative open squares of the Latin sanctuaries (Gabii, Tibur), there is evidence of similar plantations with artificial irrigation (Coarelli 1989: 14–20).

The permeability and reciprocal convergence of religious and profane architecture are reflected in the multi-functional nature of late republican cult compounds. Closely intertwined with their secular environment, these compounds formed an intricate spatial complex (Stambaugh 1978: 580–8): temple buildings in the city of Rome were used as assembly rooms of the senate, as museums, treasure chambers and archives, trading places and markets, as a unique meeting-place and representative backdrop for diplomatic receptions. Suburban sanctuaries offered lodgings and a bath to travelers; indeed, by virtue of their libraries and theaters they evolved into supra-regional cultural centers.

Spatial Perception and Movement

The spatial experience intended by religious architecture emerges from the principles propounded by the Augustan architect Vitruvius: temples should be erected with the best possible view of the city in mind, or be aligned with streets and rivers to impress the passer-by (Vitr. 4.5.2). For the purpose of augmenting the dignity (*auctoritas*) of public buildings, the architect may resort to costly materials – marble, first and foremost – to shape the space aesthetically; among the measures mentioned are the spacing of columns, symmetry, and proportions (Vitr. 3.3.6–9).

The ornamental decor and the shapes and forms of religious architecture, their power to influence the visitor's behavior, are of crucial importance in religious practice. As a socio-psychological construct, "space" is defined by the way it is being experienced (Zanker 2000: 206). Possible parameters for the perception of space are, for instance, its (colossal) size and height, distance or proximity, as well as order and structure. Space is comprehended, measured, and experienced in a pacing motion. Orientation is gained from visual impressions: walls block, portals guide the eye. Eye contact with the cult image encourages interaction and communication (Gladigow 1994: 15–17), facilitates the coordination of movement and conduct within a given space. Conversely, the curtailing or removal of visual clues (through a complete darkening of the room or reduced lighting) leads to a loss of orientation, but it can also focus the eye and heighten the attention – a technique that was used for spectacular performances of ritual acts in mystery cults. Archaeological as well as literary sources emphasize the distance and desired proximity to the deity. Temple doors were normally closed; thus curtains were used in the *cella*, all indoor cult images were hidden from view, and access was granted by the temple's guardians (*aedituus*) on request only (Egelhaaf-Gaiser 2000: 407–17). Inside, bars and fences prevented the visitor from straying into areas only cult specialists or those initiated into the mysteries were allowed to enter (*cella, adytum, penetrale*). Steps on the cult podium, however, gave the temple officials access for ritual ablutions and the clothing of the gods.

At transitions and points of contact between different visual spaces, the perception of the sauntering passer-by and the casual onlooker (Zanker 2000: 216–22) is especially stimulated by the formal vocabulary of the architecture: entrances to cult precincts seek to capture the visitor's attention with portals, inscriptions, and decorative elements. Temple doors are given prominence in the literature and in devotional reliefs as large image carriers; doors opening spontaneously could, in addition, deliver the will of the gods in prodigies (Obsequens 13). Peripheral areas and spatial borders will by their very nature effect a change in behavior. However, the visitor's socialization must also be taken into account. Unlike today, cults in classical times were almost exclusively celebrated at an open-air altar. This open environment had a direct impact on the conduct of the participants: unrestrained jubilation and loud exclamations of joy were permitted, even welcomed (Apul. *Met.* 11.17.4). Presumably, a more stringent code of conduct would have been in place for the exclusive group of high-ranking members of the priesthood who were being served collectively in the closed dining halls (*triclinia*) than for the festive community at the improvised open-air banquet on the lawn outside.

Space and movement are of central importance in conjunction with the dimension of time. Human memory requires spatial concepts: objects or spaces gain a history of their own only through prolonged, continual use. This is why, in a larger circle of participants, places and their ornamental attributes have a stabilizing effect on the group; they help create a sense of identity. Venerable statues and cult objects reaffirm the cult community's distinctive tradition; its creation is associated with specific locations. The history of a local cult can be (re)constructed from signs and monuments, sometimes a mere place name will suffice (Varro, *Ling.* 5.152). A complex sacred landscape is established from the combination and comprehensive spatial correlation of specific local features. Its history is memorized and renewed in rituals and processions. The memorial landscape of *necropoleis* and graves is a special case: grave markers, steles, and grave inscriptions have a deictic function and secure the memory of the dead. The mausoleums and rivaling memorial columns can transform the entire Campus Martius into a landscape of deification.

In extreme cases, the authority of the imperial building programs was invoked to "overwrite" older visual spaces and their connotations with new sign systems (on the special case of Augustan Rome see Livy 4.4.4; Favro 1996). Sacred locations in particular were occupied symbolically by rivaling memorial communities as a means to win prestige. Religio-political memorial sites, therefore, do not only refer to the (mythical) past but also point out present claims to future power. Acts of memorization and continuous care by the community do not simply maintain established sacred landscapes: fresh spatial structures are deliberately created and propagated through the dedication of new religious buildings, as in the case of the Apollo sanctuary on the Palatine, which will be considered below. More common than these planned changes, however, are instances of gradual shift – cult sites that are continually being shaped and reshaped, extended and amended over centuries. The multi-layered problems of cult continuity and change are exemplified in the suburban grove for the local deity of Anna Perenna, which will also be examined below.

Cult Sites in Everyday Life

Rituals performed before the cult image are a means of religious communication and of tending to the gods: cult images are "woken" in the morning (Apul. *Met.* 11.20.4–5); they receive regular meals, are perfumed and clothed, even have their faces painted, their bodies embellished (*CIL* 2.3386, 14.2215), and are "entertained" with outings and processions, musical and theatrical presentations (Gladigow 1994: 19–24).

Such routines before the cult image are a characteristic example of the growing integration of cult practice into everyday life in imperial times.

Regardless of their size or the deity worshiped, all cult precincts must provide for certain basic needs without which normal cult practice is impossible: a water supply is necessary, firewood for sacrifice and feast must be available. Questions as to whether permanent solutions for these requirements would be sought, what shape these would take, and which modalities would be deemed practicable were decided on a case-by-case basis. It is a primary aim of this chapter to document the organizational flexibility in the establishment of cult sites and the resulting diversity of spatial solutions: because of the integration of cult sites into the urban environment, religion could become a part of everyday life, for example as a sacrifice offered in the course of daily meals, or at roadside sanctuaries and crossroads. Equally, everyday life could become part of religion. At complex cult sites (Stambaugh 1978; Egelhaaf-Gaiser 2000: 258–71), the intensity with which certain areas were used may have been inversely proportional to the amount of prestige these facilities could (and did) claim: at the Apollo sanctuary on the Palatine (see below) the porticos, courtyards, and libraries may actually have seen more "traffic" than the temple itself, which would only have been open during religious festivals.

The adjoining subsidiary rooms were instrumental in the smooth operation of the cult rituals and festivities. The workshops, back rooms, and shops of the porticos sold sacrificial meat and flower wreaths; bread was baked and meals were cooked; damaged utensils were repaired and crockery was produced. Archives were managed, financial transactions completed, and mobile furniture including cushions and blankets was stored here. The responsibility for these cult activities lay with the numerous cult personnel (priests, archivists, visitors' guides, gardeners, night-watchmen, slaves and craftsmen; see Egelhaaf-Gaiser 2000: 407–25). However, rarely can we make a positive spatial identification from permanent furnishings. Smaller items were removable. This makes it impossible in many instances to be absolutely certain whether an object truly is part of the archaeological context or whether it has been "imported." The problem is compounded by the fact that all-purpose rooms were occupied by different groups of people, depending on time of day, calendar date, or irregular occasions. A portico, for instance, could be an office or a shop by day, and be used as a place to sleep by night. In synagogues, the dining hall was perhaps turned into guest accommodation; temples not only housed the cult image, but were also used for sessions of the senate and, as museum galleries, were open to tourists at certain times.

On the other hand, movable finds provide an indispensable "reality check" on the ideal images of complex locations reconstructed from the architecture, its decor, and stylistic observations. Even a cursory examination of the work and utility equipment shows that the storage rooms were at quite a distance from where those objects would actually be used. In a cult precinct many rooms could in the course of the celebrations be used by different social groups for a variety of purposes. Thus the strict separation and hierarchy between spatial functions and different social groups suggested by decor, topography, and the network of access ways proves to be a theoretical idealization, which in reality could hardly have been adhered to with all its consequences.

To exemplify these preliminary assumptions, we shall now look at three sites that were either founded in the age of Augustus or saw a significant transformation during the period.

Cult History at the Grove of Anna Perenna

Compared to the much more widely known sanctuary of Dea Dia, the extra-urban grove of Anna Perenna, situated at the first milestone of the Via Flaminia, close to the Tiber, is a highly informative case study in the history of archaeological finds as well as in the history of religio-historical research. If the grove of the Dea Dia is today one of the best-explored extra-urban cult areas (Scheid 1990), this success is above all based on the detailed stone-carved records of the Arval Brethren, which were instrumental in reconstructing the cult community's tasks and composition, and in identifying building structures that were excavated over a span of several centuries. With the cult of Anna Perenna, however, scholarship has continued to speculate about the "origin" of the deity and the provenance of her name. This one-sided interest can be explained from the dim view we take of the most detailed record on the cult: compared to the never-doubted authenticity of the inscribed Arval documents, Ovid's literary description of the origins of the cult and the goddess (*Fast.* 3.523–710) seemed less reliable; it has even been, in part, regarded as poetic fiction (e.g. Bömer 1958: 179–92).

Ovid's descriptions of her festival were more widely credited: at least the given date of March 15, confirmed by an entry in the calendar (*fasti Vaticani*) and the characteristics mentioned – an outdoor banquet held in tents and foliage huts, with men and women toasting each other and asking for a long life – seems to point with reasonable plausibility to an archaic ritual celebrating the old beginning of the year. The rustic flavor of the festival was taken in support of that theory, and its theme of fertility made it rather easy to link the cult to another similarly "popular" day of celebration, the Liberalia on March 17. Ovid's multiple etiological explanations, though, for the name and origin of the goddess did not meet with approval. In particular, the mythical connection of Anna Perenna with Dido's sister Anna, and her apotheosis in the Latin river of Numicus, seemed highly suspect: the competing imitation of Virgil's *Aeneid*, the popularity of the mythical motif of a heroine apotheosized by a river deity, and last but not least the suspicion of an all too simple folk etymology – deriving Anna Perenna from *amnis perennis* – gave rise to the assumption that Ovid's tale was nothing but playful scholarly invention.

This negative appraisal has only been reversed after a recent accidental find (Piranomonte 2002). During the construction of a parking garage in the winter of 1999/2000, a well system was discovered, its masonry dating from late antiquity. An altar and two marble bases from the second century AD were built into its front part. The inscriptions record dedications to the "sacred nymphs of Anna Perenna," clearly identifying the cult site. The four lead pipes which connected the well to a cistern behind it point to a long period of use for this facility, before it was abandoned and filled up between the fifth and sixth centuries AD. The following objects were found in the cistern:

- 549 coins (Augustan period to the end of the fourth century AD);
- 70 oil lamps, unused – therefore probably dedicated as votives (first half of the fourth century);
- cylindrical containers, figurines, and thin lead sheets with ritual curses (fourth century);
- organic and botanic residue, which would indicate cult and sacrificial activity (egg shells, pine nuts), or rather the planting of the grove (fig, peach, hazel, and almond trees, willows and elms, oaks and chestnuts, ivy and vine).

With the help of Ovid's literary testimonial, we can identify three phases of cult practice:

- *Augustan age:* spring cult of Anna Perenna, coin sacrifices (presumably in the walled-in spring, cf. Pliny, *Epist.* 8.8.2 on the *Clitumnus fons*); a one-day annual festival of men and women carousing in the sacred grove.
- *Second century AD:* spring cult, coin sacrifices, annual festival with contests and dedication of the victors. Since an inscribed base was erected on April 5, AD 156, it is highly likely that the repeated victory of the husband and wife mentioned as donors in the inscription (as well as the dedication of a freedman and his victorious patron) refers to the festival's date of March 15.
- *Fourth century AD:* new brickwork, rebuilding of the well system with inclusion of inscriptions as decorative element; coin sacrifices, miniature votives associated with magic rituals.

All further conjecture on the topographical context of the spring is purely hypothetical: a grotto with three small, artificial alcoves that was unearthed some distance away has been interpreted as a nymph grotto because of its perceived similarities with a Sicilian cave cult of Anna and the *paides*. In the masonry discovered opposite the grotto (sixth century BC to the imperial period), generally believed to have belonged to an aristocratic villa, the excavator claims to have found the cult center of the sanctuary (Piranomonte 2002: 78). Her primary piece of evidence is a terracotta antefix (late fourth century BC) in the shape of a river deity, which she identifies as Acheloos, according to Greek mythology the father of the nymphs. Summing up her findings, she posits the theory that the cult of Anna Perenna has its roots in an "age-old" fertility festival, whose religious symbolism is expressed in the numinous character of the grove and spring, and the chthonic, magical quality of the sacrificial gifts and libations.

It remains to be seen whether the ingenious reconstruction of a complex cult site in existence since archaic times will be confirmed by future excavations. The fact remains that even though a pre-Augustan cult phase seems plausible for Anna Perenna, we cannot be certain until and unless the religious function and the connection between the locations are resolved. Ovid's literary testimonial, for instance, calls into question the assumption of a centuries-old, "natural, archaic religiosity" in the countryside: it is a homogeneously urban population that flocks to the extra-urban grove of Anna Perenna for the celebration of the new year. The city dwellers compensate for the lack of comfort out of doors by setting up sun sails and foliage huts for the shade, the supporting tree trunks worthy substitutes for the marble columns of Augustan temple architecture. The Greek drinking vessels (*cyathi, crater*) mirror the refinement of a Hellenistic symposium. The cultivated festival community take their inspiration from the lifespans of Nestor and the Cumaean Sibyl, whose number of years they are vowing to match in cups of wine. And in their intoxicated state, the revelers do not burst into merry rustic chants. Instead, they imitate fashionable songs and dances from the Augustan stage of the day. On their way home late at night, the drunken crowd becomes itself an entertaining spectacle in the city streets.

How can the topographical relationship between city center and periphery, so strongly accentuated by Ovid, be gauged in religio-historical terms? One possible model would be to assume that in the Augustan period, the old Italic cults, which had long been forgotten in the city and only preserved in the independent sanctuaries of the periphery, were caught in the maelstrom of the metropolis. The urbanization of an archaic spring cult then had to be explained as "alienation" or "cult transformation." The existence of an archaic religion in the countryside, whose cult centers were autonomous and without urban connections, however, is a scholarly opinion for which as yet no evidence has been found in the sources (North 1995). Alternatively, it could be argued that the groves and spring sanctuaries of the periphery were from their inception oriented toward the center, Rome. In that case, the urban *habitus* of the festival community would merely be the expression of a strong center–periphery dependency, which ought to be present in other areas as well – in the cult organization, for instance, or in the construction of the local myth. This theory is confirmed in a comparison with the cult of the Arval Brethren, which was revived under Augustus. As evidenced by the inscribed records, the rites performed at the extra-urban precinct were complemented by sacrificial acts at the *magister*'s city residence. The traditional bond between the Augustan priesthood and Rome was strengthened by mythical references to the city's founder Romulus as the progenitor of the Arval Brethren (Plin. *Nat.* 18.6).

In this mythical construct, which ties a border sanctuary to users from the city of Rome, we find a constellation similar to Ovid's description of the festival of Anna Perenna. Ovid's literary revelers concur with the intended reading audience of the etiological cult myths: in the urban, cultivated festival community which frequents the nearby grove of Anna Perenna every March 15, the poet has created his ideal readership. To them he addresses the learned cult *aition* of the first outdoor banquet commemorating Anna's apotheosis in the Numicus, near Aeneas' hometown of Lavinium, thus incorporating the Augustan rituals into Rome's mythical prehistory. Typically, this tale of origins is not presented *in situ*, for instance as a ritual song, but outside the festival context in the artificial style of a Hellenistic epyllion.

The Sanctuary of Apollo Palatinus as a Cult(ural) Center

Unlike the newly discovered nymph's spring of Anna Perenna, the sanctuary of Apollo Palatinus is one of the best-known cult sites of the early Augustan period (Zanker

1983; Lefèvre 1989; Wiseman 1994; Balensiefen 2002). The primary reason for this is the outstanding political significance of the site: vowed by Augustus after the successful naval battle of Naulochos against Sextus Pompeius in 36 BC, the temple was then dedicated in 28 BC as a victory monument three years after the naval battle at Actium, which had foreshadowed the outcome of the civil war against Marc Anthony.

The cult precinct (fig. 15.1) is instructive in that it combines religious, political, and cultural functions as well as several architectural elements and options of the visual vocabulary into a new and highly complex architectural ensemble. Placing it on the southern slope of the Palatine established a symbolic historical connection between the new temple and the old Roman memorial sites nearby (the Hut of Romulus, the Scalae Caci). As a triumphal site blending religious functions with the proud display of looted art, the Apollo sanctuary harks back to the temple dedications of the second century BC on the Field of Mars, with which the Roman commanders used to commemorate their victories in the east. The spatial connection (R, r) between Augustus' private residence, the adjoining temple of Apollo, and a public library was borrowed from Hellenistic palace architecture (Pergamum, Alexandria); in this, too, Augustus was preceded by the members of the late republican elite (Lucullus, Pompeius, Caesar), who pursued the sacralization of their private homes as part of their political rivalry. With its imposing facade, the upper and lower levels separated visually and by function but joined by the monumental temple staircase, the Palatine precinct followed the tradition of the terraced sanctuaries of the republican era.

On the lower level, the peristyle was connected at its western side (D) to the house of Augustus, with representative dining room and private library (Balensiefen 2002: 112–16). Next to the eastern peristyle (D') stood the public library (C) with separate reading rooms for Greek and Roman literature, which were also used for meetings of the senate and poetry recitals. The fact that the different components of the private, public, and religious architecture were perceived by the contemporary viewer as the mark of an intentional hierarchy is documented by the Augustan poet Propertius, who describes the Apollo sanctuary through the eyes of a visitor ascending the temple stairs (Propertius 2.31). The formal occasion for the poem was the completion of the lavish south portico (F), by which the lower terrace was brought to a close, a number of years after the dedication of the temple (Balensiefen 1995). Built from precious variegated marble in yellow, red, and black, the two-storey hall served as a museum-style colonnade. The top level, supported by the water-carrying Danaids, now offered an unimpeded view of the front of the marble temple (A) opposite, with the *quadriga* of Sol as its crowning embellishment on top of the roof. Also visible from above were the figurative images on the ebony doors, which would have been hidden from the view from below by the high temple podium – if the staircase was barricaded, as was indeed the custom in many places. Presumably in the center of the lower level (E), amid famous depictions of animals by the Greek sculptor Myron, a colossal statue of the victorious Apollo Actius stood in the pose of a cithara-player pouring an offering from a sacrificial cup. In the *cella*, though, the lyre-playing Apollo was worshiped in conjunction with his sister Diana and his

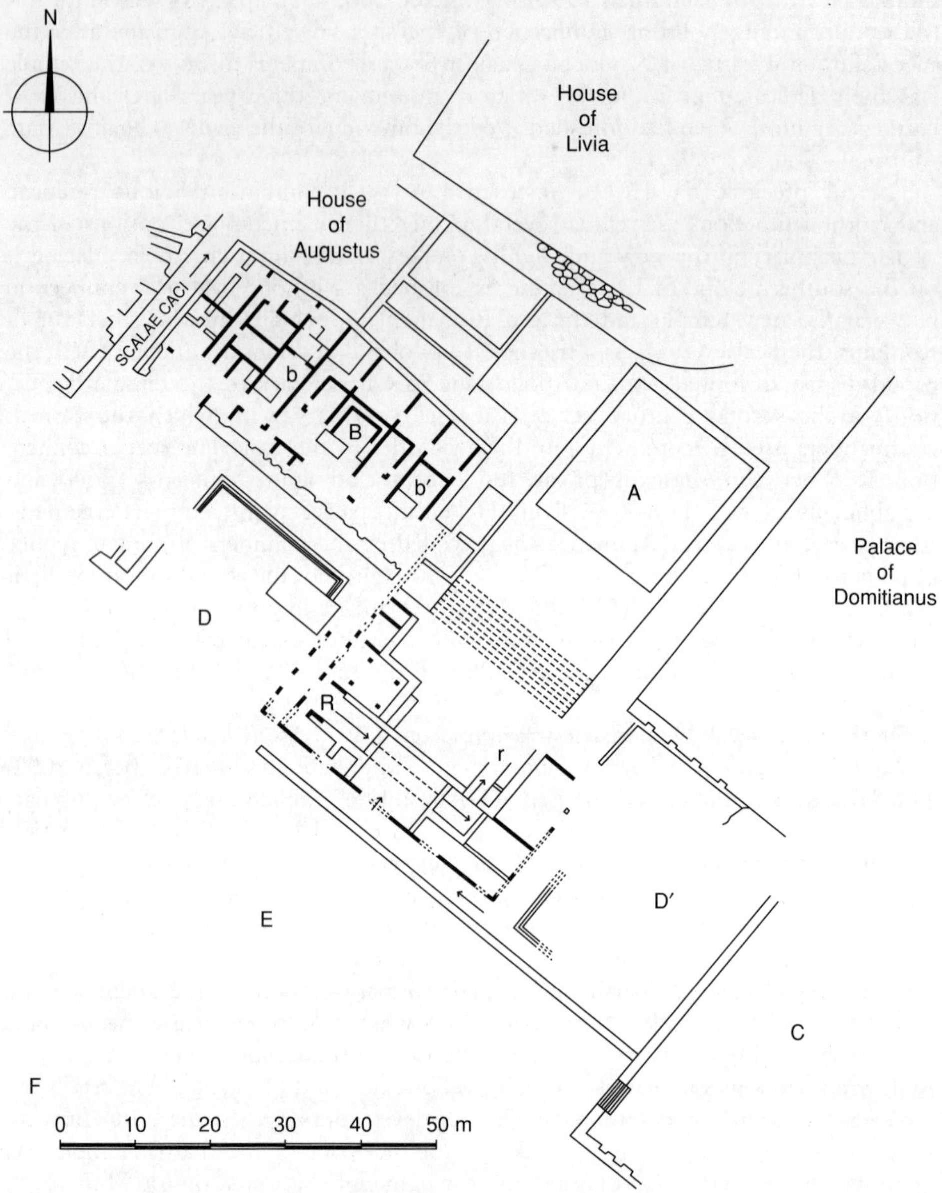

N

House
of
Livia

House
of
Augustus

SCALAE CACI

b

B

b'

A

Palace
of
Domitianus

D

R

r

E

D'

C

F

0   10   20   30   40   50 m

A	Temple of Apollo	D, D'	Peristyle
B	Dining room	E	Terrace
b, b'	Private library	F	Portico of the Danaides
C	Public library	R, r	Underground ramp, leading from the house of Augustus to the temple

Figure 15.1   Temple precinct of Apollo on the Palatine (based on Zanker 1983: 22).

mother Latona; originally separate works of art by three different classical Greek artists, the statues were now combined into one cult image (Plin. *Nat.* 35.5.24–5, 32).

Searching for a political message to compensate for the impression of an arbitrary, eclectic array of compositional art in the cult precinct, scholars have often pointed to the leitmotif of transgression and retribution, which gives a mythical dimension to the civil war situation: the Danaids of the south portico, who are suffering for the murder of their brothers; Hercules' seizing of Apollo's tripod on a decorative clay relief; and, finally, the repelling of the Celts' assault on Delphi and a mourning Niobe on the temple doors. However, this poses the question whether such an intended statement would not have been diluted by the multitude of myths and materials, and the mingling of styles among the works of art, and whether perhaps it might not be more persuasive to see in the visual decor a multi-layered semantics, which contains the thoroughly ambivalent qualities of the god: apart from his role as the relentless avenger and gifted musician, the Palatine Apollo also appears as a wise oracle-giver. This aspect is not only demonstrated by the monumental tripod at the portal of the temple doors, but is also crucially reflected in the representative, administrative, and religious functions that are cumulated in the cult precinct. In its gradual change, throughout the Augustan era, from a symbolic to the factual power center of the capital, the original occasion for the dedication of the Apollo sanctuary fades into the background: the monument commemorating a victory becomes the administrative center of the *princeps*, which in turn has an impact on the cult organization at the sanctuary.

The development can be traced in the textual and visual testimonies: even if no other Augustan cult complex has enjoyed literary prominence approaching that of the temple of Apollo Palatinus (Virg. *Aen.* 8.714–28; Hor. *Odes* 1.31; Propertius 2.31, 4.6; Ov. *Trist.* 3.1.33–68), at first the cult was overshadowed by the civic reality of an enormous triumphal and representative building in the center of the city. Roman citizens, in their day-to-day lives, may indeed have frequented the porticos, courtyards, and libraries more often than the temple itself. As an eminent cult center the Apollo temple is first presented within the context of the Secular Games (17 BC): in the inscribed records of the games (*CIL* 6.32323), the Apollo temple, now a public site for cult and sacrifice, is granted the same status as the temples of Juno and the Capitoline Jupiter. The festival was conducted in person by the *princeps*, who was the *magister* of the *quindecimviri*, the priestly college in charge of the Sibylline Books.

However, Augustus did not implement any radical topographical reforms until he took on the office of *pontifex maximus* in 12 BC. Contrary to the religious traditions which required that the high priest live in the house next to the Vesta sanctuary, Augustus had a shrine to Vesta installed in his residence on the Palatine, thus tying one of the most prominent "state cults" – famously, the priestesses of Vesta tended the sacred fire and the venerable cult image of Athena, the Trojan guardian goddess, saved by Aeneas from her burning city – to the person and the household of the *princeps* (Ov. *Fast.* 6.417–60). At the same time the Sibylline oracles, which had been housed in the temple of Capitoline Jupiter, the highest deity of the Roman state, were moved to the Apollo sanctuary and, after having been thoroughly censored, they were placed in two golden drawers in the base of the statue of Apollo (Suet. *Augustus* 31.1). The utilization of a cult statue's base as a storage space for cult objects was by no means unusual. However, since in a marked difference to a year-round oracular activity, the Sibylline Books were consulted only in exceptional circumstances and in a complex procedure (Scheid 1998a), their transfer to the Palatine was hardly motivated by considerations relating to cult practice. Rather, with this symbolic act the "young" Apollo temple became part of the traditional history of the Greek oracle excerpts – which would normally be revised only through the selection and interpretation of the priests.

This intended elevation of the shrine's status to that of a supra-regional cult center is reflected in an Augustan base from Sorrento (Balensiefen 2002: fig. 135 = Lefèvre 1989: fig. 28): the Palatine cult sites of the Magna Mater, Vesta, and the Apollonian triad are shown on three complementary display sides of the base. The new topographical association of the Sibylline oracles with Apollo Palatinus is visualized by a monumental tripod in the background of the image and a Sibyl with a *sitella* (urn for drawing lots) sitting at the feet of the lyre-playing god. The difference in the semantics of art and literature is remarkable: the early Augustan poets had always presented the oracle-giver Sibyl in the Greek cult tradition as the inspired seer (*vates*), proclaiming Rome's brilliant future in *oral* prophecies. By contrast, the visual symbol of the urn is more in keeping with the experience of a contemporary beholder, who would associate the consultation of an oracle with the Italic cult practice of receiving one's answer on a lot, in *writing* (Champeaux 1990).

The Temple of Fortuna Augusta in Daily Urban Life

The Apollo sanctuary on the Palatine has served as an example of a shrine that was originally conceived as a victory monument, but which was then systematically built up by the "highest power" into a multi-functional cult center and cultural center. The temple of Fortuna Augusta at Pompeii offers an insight into the necessary flexibility in the everyday business of a cult site, as well as its legal and purpose-oriented integration into the urban environment (L. Richardson 1988: 202–6; Eschebach 1993: 272). Because of its exclusive location on the Palatine, Rome's most affluent residential area, the Augustan Apollo sanctuary was far above the hustle and bustle of the Forum, the harbor, and the market. By contrast, the temple of Fortuna Augusta at Pompeii (fig. 15.2), located at a busy intersection immediately north of the Forum and opposite the Forum baths (7), participates fully in the daily life of the city.

The identification and dating of the building (1) to before 3 BC has been confirmed by inscriptions found on site (*CIL* 10.820–8). A full view of the layout shows that the wall of the sanctuary did enclose a two-storey staff building (3) south of the temple. The irregular floor plan with the projecting hall (F) is a result of the legal situation: an inscription (*CIL* 10.821), found in a section of the road next to the temple, marked the border between sacred and private land. There was no source

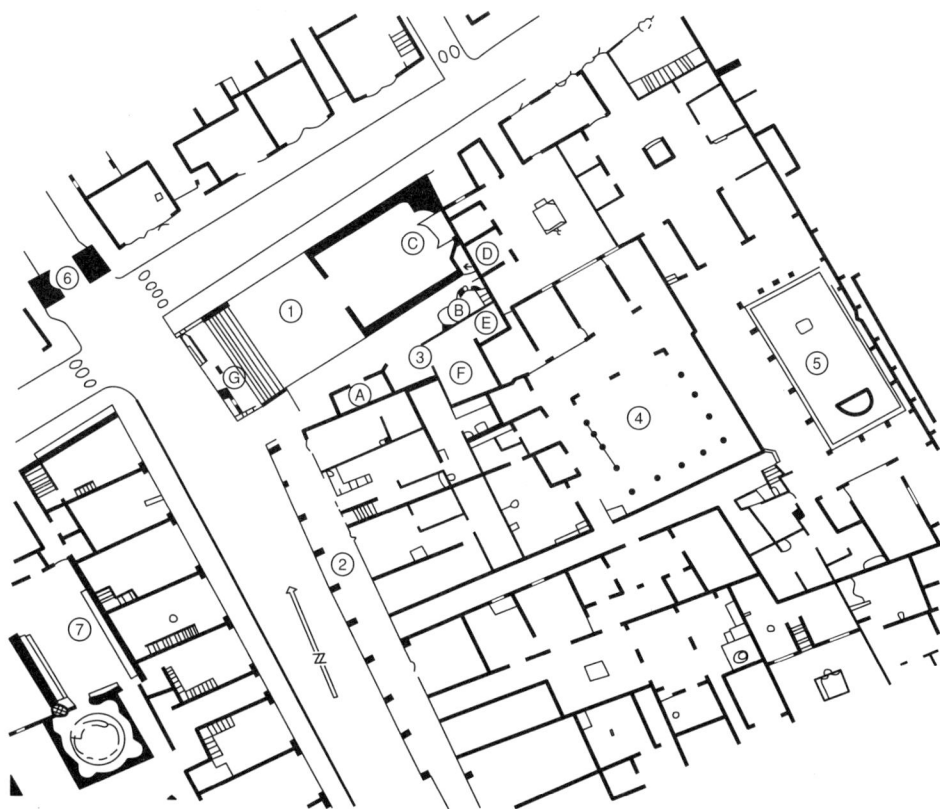

1	Temple of Fortuna Augusta	A	Workshop
2	*Porticus Tulliana*	B	Kitchen/latrine
3	Staff building	C	Niche of the cult statue
4, 5	Private houses of the *gens Tullia*	D	Passageway/corridor
6	"Arch of Caligula"	E	Living room
7	Public baths of the Forum	F	Dining room
		G	Altar

Figure 15.2 Sacred precinct of Fortuna Augusta in the urban context of Pompeii (based on Eschebach 1993: detail of the city-map).

of water in the temple precinct; it had to be fetched from the running well built into the "Arch of Caligula" (6) at the nearby intersection.

According to the representative marble inscription, the founder of the temple, M. Tullius, was the holder of multiple important municipal and religious offices. A politically active member of the municipality seeking to increase his prestige by honoring the emperor with the donation of a temple was the norm: the founding of cult sites associated with the imperial family was not, as a rule, initiated by the central government. Instead, the city council or distinguished citizens did it to raise their own status. It is hardly surprising, therefore, that in spite of the limited space, Tullius' temple donation turns out to be quite ambitious. With all available means it tries to attract the attention of passers-by: along its northern street side, the precinct is accented by the tiles of the pavement for the entire length of the temple podium. The full width of the frontal marble staircase overruns the pedestrian walkway, even extending into the street. The *Porticus Tulliana* (2) south of the temple also cuts into the walkway, albeit to a lesser extent. The columns of its facade blend in with those of the public buildings in the Forum, which are fronted by similar colonnades.

The central location, guaranteeing the privately financed temple a large number of visitors, did have its price: since the limited space did not allow for a front area, the altar (G) was incorporated into the stairs. The sacrificial ceremonies were conducted in an extremely confined space – almost out on the street: cult officials and audience had to stand on the steps around the altar. In order to offset the temple at least minimally from the busy street, an iron fence was erected around the stairs, with only two small doors on both sides of the altar. The two corners facing the traffic in the street were protected by large bumper stones.

An outward-jutting half-niche (C) was added to the rear wall of the *cella* in a later modification. Its marble shrine was intended for the cult image of Fortuna. Like many other buildings, the temple of Fortuna Augusta was damaged severely in the great earthquake of AD 63, and had not been repaired by the time of the eruption of Mount Vesuvius in AD 79. As can be deduced from the unfinished marble blocks in the area of the workshop (A), masonry work for the neighboring *cella* was carried out here. Cult activity would not have been suspended for such a long period: the utterly uncharacteristic placement of the founder's inscription inside the niche, where it would not have been visible to the public, lends support to the assumption that temporary solutions were applied. Obviously it was expected that the restored temple *cella* would be back in use before the external work was finished, and the inscription had therefore – temporarily – been put up inside.

From AD 3 onward, a four-member *collegium* was in charge of organizing cult activities. According to the rules of their association, the *ministri* – in the majority, wealthy slaves – were required to dedicate statues in the *cella* upon the accession of a new emperor. For their meetings and communal meals, the *collegium* may have used the hall (F) of the attached residential building. This would explain not only the investment of a permanent kitchen (B), but also the narrow stonework ledges on its outer wall, most likely the foundations of a hot plate, where food could be kept warm for a short time. The interior of the kitchen contained the usual combination of a stove with a vaulted pantry and a latrine. A staircase led to the upper level, which may have served as a living quarters for the service personnel.

The close relationship between functional ancillary rooms and the representative temple is underlined by the narrow corridor (D) that had originally been a passageway between the rear wall of the temple and the neighboring house (4), granting unobtrusive entrance to cult personnel, as well as easy access for deliveries from the northern main road. As a result of the changed design for the *cella*, the back entrance was then closed, and two arches were inserted between the *cella* and the neighboring house to support the niche protruding from the rear wall: the light-less corridor now became a storage room. The stipulation found in legal documents that there be no common wall between sacred and private buildings was ignored here (and possibly quite often elsewhere) for reasons of practicality.

Regardless of the functional merging of sacred cult space and secular urban space, attempts were still made to at least provide visual clues to the subordinate status of the ancillary buildings: the podium temple probably surpassed the two-storey staff building in height. Moreover, as a representative religious building, with its perron extending into the street, the temple virtually pushed itself into the visual field of every passer-by, while the attached staff house was set as far back as possible. Despite the extreme spatial restrictions dictated by urban structures such as roads and building patterns, there was a desire to meet, in the sensible, practical furnishing of the house on Tullius' private property, all requirements relating to the proper operation of the cult site. At the same time, efforts were also made, with all available visual means of religious architecture and decor, to optimize the external representative appearance of the cult precinct.

FURTHER READING

The technical terms of Roman cult sites in the antiquarian and legal sources are annotated by Fridh (1990). An introductory, easy-to-understand survey of the multi-functionality of Roman cult sites is offered by Stambaugh (1978); a good example of grave-side cult practices is provided in the archaeological excavation guide of the necropolis on the Isola Sacra (Ostia) by Baldassarre (1996). Specifically on the republican temples and the problem of looted art, see Ziolkowski (1992); on the spatial experience, furnishings, and typology of individual building types see Kähler (1970) (temples), Bollmann (1998) (clubhouses), and Hänlein-Schäfer (1985) (Augustan imperial cult sites). Mattern (2001) focuses on the decor and function of temple interiors. H. Martin (1987) presents the archaeological findings on late republican cult images. Sanctuaries in the Italic countryside are examined by Edlund (1987); specifics of the sacred groves are discussed in the volume of proceedings on the Bois Sacrés colloquium (Bois Sacrés 1993). North (1995) critically assesses the religious links between the city and its extra-urban periphery and the concept of rural religiosity; see also Egelhaaf-Gaiser (2000) (contextualization of the cult of Isis) and Rieger (2004) (sanctuaries at Ostia).

CHAPTER SIXTEEN

Complex Rituals: Games and Processions in Republican Rome

Frank Bernstein

Within the discipline of comparative religions, festivals are regarded as the ideal type of complex rituals because rituals are differentiated in terms of the degree of deliberate sequencing of ritual components, and the expenditure and duration included (Gladigow 1998a). In ancient Rome it was precisely the festival known as the games, the *ludi*, among the numerous other Roman festivals, which best meets the above ritual criteria. However, modern perspective on the games is largely based on the games of the imperial period, which were opulent extravaganzas staged by the *principes*, and on images of the frenzied masses in the amphitheater and circus. Even when we consider the bloody persecutions of Christians, the procedure for martyrdom itself seems to have been determined by an appetite for entertainment and public amusement. Of course the games also fulfilled other functions in imperial Rome, such as helping to maintain public order. Still, we must not forget that the Roman games were originally an integral part of the program of public festivals which contributed to the *res publica Romana*'s worship of the gods. In order to clarify the original role of the games this chapter will focus on the period of the republic.

Even from an early date, the *ludi* were held for the sake of the city, which is why they may be regarded as *ludi publici*, as public games (Cic. *Leg.* 2.22, 2.38). The clearest expression of such a role was the introduction of games staged regularly on fixed days in the year, the *ludi stati(vi)* or *annui* respectively, in the festival calendar, where they were shown as public holidays, as *feriae publicae* of the Roman community. Thus the gladiatorial combats (*ludi funebres*), first held in 264 BC in the course of funeral ceremonies in Rome (e.g. Val. Max. 2.4.7), fall outside the category of *ludi publici* for the period of the republic, since they were not connected to fixed public holidays but preserved their private character until the end of the republic. True examples of *ludi publici* can be found in the chariot races held in the Circus Maximus, later also in animal hunting, as well as in the performance of dramas on the stage. Cicero confirms this differentiation of public games into *ludi circenses* and *ludi scaenici*: *ludi publici, quoniam sunt cavea circoque divisi* (*Leg.* 2.38).

Finally, the fact that the origins and development of the *ludi publici* are closely interwoven with the general history of the Roman republic must be emphasized. The array of public games which presents itself on the eve of the principate, including numerous types of spectacles directed to the worship of various deities and a wealth of forms and rites with diverse functions, was by no means the result of a consistent process of emergence from original simplicity developing toward final complexity. Rather, the development of the games was constant, but by no means consistent, running parallel to the development of the Roman state in its rise to hegemony right up to its ultimate dissolution.

Emergence and Expansion of the System of Public Games

The system of public games was not a clearly defined state institution created *ad hoc*, but the result of gradual development beginning in the archaic period, when horse races were staged regularly which were later to find their way into the festival calendar as annual celebrations and were related to the deity Mars. (The double celebration of these *Ecurria/Equirria* on February 27 and March 14 is connected with the change in the dates set for the Roman New Year's Day, since the horse races were originally intended to provide ritual accompaniment to the turn of the year.) However, the Etruscan kings of Rome are thought to have played a formative role in the history of the *ludi publici*, giving the promotion of games in the city of Rome a fundamental shape.

Annalistic tradition attributed the institution of the *ludi Romani*, and the construction of the Circus Maximus for horse and chariot races in the valley between the Aventine and Palatine, to the Tarquins (e.g. Livy 1.35.7–9, 1.56.2). This can be accepted as essentially credible, because this late written evidence corresponds to a highly developed Etruscan games culture that is far more reliably attested by archaeological monuments. The *ara Consi*, the altar to the old harvest deity Consus, existed earlier in the Circus valley. Thus in the Etruscan period, the *Consualia*, long since held annually by the *pontifices* on August 21 and December 15, were extended ritually to include horse and mule races. The new spectacles inaugurated by the Tarquins, though, were neither votive games nor *ludi* that were linked with the triumph, as would be consistent with Theodor Mommsen's widely accepted thesis (1859). These pre-republican games had their actual origin in the Iuppiter cult, the worship of that deity who, as Iuppiter Optimus Maximus, gained a special importance for the Roman polity in the sixth century BC. Key clues to their true origin can be found in the construction and the dedication of the exceptional temple to Iuppiter on the Capitol, so that we can conclude that the rite of the procession, the *pompa*, which opened the *ludi* also points back to the later archaic period. After all, Iuppiter had to be transported from his temple to the venue of the games being held in his honor, that is, to what was known as the Circus valley, where sacrifice was made to him before the beginning of the games proper. With these circensian forms of ritual established in Rome in the archaic period by the Etruscan kings – the combination of procession, sacrifice, and horse or chariot races – an organized staging of the games for the state had come into being, the most noble component of which consisted in the cult of Iuppiter Optimus Maximus.

This decisive link between the holding of public games and public religious observance was adopted by the *libera res publica* and emphasized by the patricians who now headed the Roman community. This ruling elite integrated the rite of the *ludi* into the new state's most important annual celebration, the solemn Capitoline festival of the highest and almighty guardian deity of the republic. From the dedication of the Capitoline temple to Iuppiter around the years 509 to 507 BC, the *ludi maximi/Romani*, as we should initially call them, were held annually, and gradually further days for games were linked with September 13, a date that adopted the day of the sanctuary's foundation. These first *ludi publici stati(vi)* were the expression of the small central Italian power's diligence in the cult of the community's highest deity. The magistrate giving games was thus entitled to ride on a *biga*. Like Rome's Etruscan kings, he escorted the deity in solemn procession to the place of worship, where he made sacrifice to it, and gave the starting signal for the horse and/or chariot races. This duty at the games was actually vested consistently in the chief magistrate. He himself saw to the staging of the entire event and, from time to time, he or other patricians took part in the *circenses* as charioteers.

However much these permanent *ludi maximi/Romani* also laid the basis for further development, the staging arrangements for the early Roman games still followed their own laws, as the votive games held optionally by the chief magistrate alone make clear. As the name suggests, they were based on a vow made during military campaigns in order to attain victory. At the same time they were addressed to Iuppiter Optimus Maximus and are described as *ludi magni/votivi* by the annalists (e.g. L. Coelius Antipater, *FRH*² 11 frg. 57 = Cic. *Div.* 1.55; Livy 2.36.1). Admittedly, ancient reports on these spectacles do not merit any credibility for the content of the evidence handed down. It can only be stated that the military commanders of the fifth and fourth centuries BC also made vows and staged, as well as equipped, games on their own responsibility, whereby they probably availed themselves of the booty they had acquired. But let us return to the permanent games of the young *res publica Romana*.

With the settlement of the "Conflict of the Orders" between patricians and plebeians of 367/6 BC, more complex forms of organization came into being through a differentiation of the magistrates' responsibilities. The development of a kind of supervision by the senate of the staging of public games was one outcome of that significant settlement. As a result of a comprehensive reorganization of responsibilities for the *ludi maximi/Romani*, the chief magistrate's management of the games was intended to be limited to a single *praesidium ludorum*. Now the burden incumbent on him was eased by the newly appointed *aediles curules*. As the *curatores ludorum*, these magistrates were not only responsible for the tasks of keeping order within the framework of the expanding games operations, but the general preparation and staging of the spectacles were probably also delegated to them. The expenses incurred in connection with the preparation, the *impensae ludorum publicorum*, that had been previously imposed on the chief magistrate were now completely reorganized, and from then on were probably split up among the *praesides* and *curatores ludorum*. An enormous expansion and elaboration of the *ludi publici* followed these organizational changes.

With the introduction of the *ludi scaenici* soon after 367/6 BC, the system of public games, which had assumed its first clear ritual and organizational forms in the archaic and early republican periods, entered into a new phase of its development, the enormous dynamism of which was to last into the first half of the second century BC. Not only were the canon of the optional and permanent *ludi publici* and the circle of divine dedicatees considerably expanded, the forms of the cult of the games were also elaborated. The ritual became subject to increasing Hellenization.

In 364 BC, through Etruscan mediation, the stage play was introduced into the old *ludi maximi/Romani* (Livy 7.2.1–12), an elaboration of the "liturgy" that was initially restricted to quite modest performances, but was to usher in a major development. Only gradually, following the example of the impromptu play in Magna Graecia, did a kind of pre-literary theater develop in Rome. Greek influence was to continue to be decisive for the system of games in the city of Rome. When organizing the extraordinary *ludi Tarentini* of 249 BC, the senate, the institution responsible for the introduction and Hellenization of the public games, made use of the Sibylline Books, thus employing an instrument – which appears clearly from the sources for the first time (Varro, *GRF* frg. 70 = Censorinus 17.8; [Acro], *Scholia Hor. carminis saecularis* 8 p. 471 Keller) – that ensured the *ritus Graecus*. Under the impression of that catastrophic year in the First Punic War, the nobility attempted to meet the crisis by taking over and elaborating a gentile cult of Dis Pater and Proserpina without games – without suspecting that in days to come a changed appreciation of these games would bring about the *ludi saeculares*, the most famous and influential celebration of which Caesar Augustus staged in the year 17 BC. The new nocturnal *scaenici* were thus tantamount to a crisis measure of religious policy, a functional role that had already formed the basis for the *ludi magni* for a fairly long time.

The senate had probably already taken up the votive games, originally organized by the military commanders of the early period (see above), in the years around 300 BC as a cultic way of restoring the *salus rei publicae* in critical situations. This was necessary because Rome's increasing military enterprises in Italy, then overseas, were facing defeats and reversals which it was essential to overcome with the help of the highest state deity. Thus when it appeared necessary, the senate would delegate the vowing of *ludi magni* for Iuppiter Optimus Maximus to the holders of *imperium*, that is to say to the consuls or praetors, if necessary also to the dictator. And soon that assembly would have made clearly defined public funds available to the magistrates for the system (Q. Fabius Pictor, *FRH*[2] 1 frg. 20 = Dion. H. 7.71.2; Livy 31.9.10), by means of which a financing model had been established that would be applied to the other *ludi publici* in the following period. But when Rome directed its attention increasingly to the Greek east, the new votive games even served for the preparation of war. However, not only did the extraordinary games for the sake of the state experience a remarkable upswing, but new *ludi publici stati(vi)* were also put alongside the only hitherto regularly celebrated games, the *ludi Romani*. In the space of less than 50 years, the nobility were to incorporate five further annual games into the festival calendar of the *res publica Romana*.

The *ludi plebeii* and the *ludi Ceriales* were not established in the early republic, but on the eve of the Hannibalic war (218–201 BC). The plebeian aediles, the old heads of the sanctuary to the plebeian deity Ceres on the Aventine, did not exercise a *cura ludorum publicorum* ("care for public games") either before or after the settlement of the "Conflict of the Orders" of 367/6 BC. For the time being, they were to play a secondary role to the curule aediles in this respect. It seemed necessary, in view of the impending confrontation with Carthage, to propitiate Iuppiter Optimus Maximus with further games and to prepare the population of the city of Rome for the coming exertions. The *ludi plebeii* thus established essentially followed the "liturgy" of the *ludi Romani* and were staged from 220 BC onward in the Circus Flaminius, in the grounds newly laid out by the censor C. Flaminius on the Campus Martius (Varro, *Ling.* 5.154; Livy, *Per.* 20). Similar policy considerations probably caused the nobility to also expand the old cult of Ceres in 220 or 219 BC by adding games, particularly as a famine made the worship of the deity of vegetation indispensable, and breakdowns in supplies through the war were to be expected. So the new games, which were apparently limited to dramatic plays, were linked to the *Cerialia* that had been celebrated since the archaic period (Pseudo-Cyprianus, *De spectaculis* 4.4). Admittedly, by doing so, Rome trod a new path. The change in cult initiated with the introduction of the scenic rite in 364 BC became narrowed down in the case of the new games of the following decades to these Greek forms.

The *ludi Apollinares* recommended by the *Xviri sacris faciundis* and celebrated in the years 212–209 BC as extraordinary votive games did certainly contribute toward countering a widespread religious uncertainty. Incidentally, these were the only games among the early ones that were held not by aediles, but by the *praetor urbanus*. Already in 208 BC, this spectacle under Delphic influence was made permanent (Livy 27.23.6–7). Above all, however, these scenic games for Apollo were intended to demonstrate Rome's affiliation to the Greek cultural community, a matter of concern that must have appeared urgent in view of the ominous course of the war. For this reason, the nobility had already brought the cult of the Mater Magna to Rome in 204 BC. The domiciling of the tutelary deity of the Trojans and their descendants flanked Rome's policy of alliances in the Greek east. However, when, during the armed conflict with Antiochus III of Syria (192–188 BC), anti-Roman prophecies called that affiliation into question, the senate replied to this, as it were, psychological warfare by instituting the permanent *ludi Megalenses* (Valerius Antias, *FRH²* 15 frg. 41 = Livy 36.36.3–4). For the *ritus Graecus* of these games held since 191 BC before the Palatine sanctuary of the Great Mother of the Gods, the *scaenici* and also the *sellisternium*, copied from a specific variant of the Greek *theoxenias*, proved Rome's profound religious and cultural rooting in the Greek world. And if we can conclude that it was considered possible to ward off a bad harvest and pestilence with the establishment of the *ludi Florales* (Ov. *Fast.* 5.295–330; Livy 41.21.10–11, 42.2.6–7), then it must be clear that the *ludi publici* indeed fulfilled diverse functions, a phenomenon that requires closer consideration.

The early introduction of a pre-literary stage play into the "liturgy" of the public games, and the increasing use of optional spectacles launched by the senate, served as religious-political measures of the first order for coping with both internal and external crises. Only the *pietas* ("loyalty") owed to the gods, only the conscientious *religio* ("scrupulous observation") that was understood as a deliberate *cultus deorum* ("cult of the gods") in order to work toward a lasting *pax de(or)um* ("propitious attitude of the gods"), could lead to any manner of success, according to deep Roman conviction. The insight that everything, no more and no less, was directed by the work of the *numina* (e.g. Cic. *Har. resp.* 19) was firmly rooted in Roman thinking. Military defeats, setbacks and losses, serious breakdowns in supplies, as well as occasional internal discontent and widespread uncertainties among the people were considered to be the consequences of a *religio neglecta* ("neglected cult"), and the expression of an *ira de(or)um* ("anger of the gods") provoked by this. Such difficulties could therefore be interpreted as mere unfortunate intervals on an ultimately victorious and successful way which it was essential to tread purposefully under the protection of the gods, who had been put into a well-disposed and gracious mood by the games. Thus the canon of the extraordinary and also regular public games and the circle of the deities being worshiped were simply enormously expanded. At the same time the "liturgy" of the spectacles was decisively elaborated, when the Punic Wars and the confrontations with the Hellenistic east presented the greatest challenges to the rising Roman state and its society. The choice of the divine dedicatees, and the form of the expanding games that shaped public life far more than the other rites to appease the gods, were now determined by Greek concepts of gods and ritual forms. This upswing in the array of public games in the age of the Punic Wars and overseas expansion, this dynamic development, coincided with the rise and self-assertion of the nobility, who discovered enormous possibilities for functions in the essence of the games, in the singularity of their ritual, and elaborated them decisively.

The Nobility and the Elaboration of Public Games

The dynamic shifts in the process of development in the system of public games were closely linked to the nobility's shifting conception of itself, especially as this office- and achievement-oriented ruling elite was characterized by a fundamental receptiveness to Greek influences. However, through Rome's wars in southern Italy and Sicily, close contacts with Greek culture also resulted for broader sections of the citizenry. The highly developed theater system in particular had left a lasting impression on the troops. Thus the introduction of dramatic performances after the conclusion of the First Punic War did not come about just by mere chance when, in 240 BC, the poet and actor Livius Andronicus produced Latin versions of Greek dramas for the first time (Cassiodorus, *Chronicon* p. 128 Mommsen [mistakenly for the year 239 BC]).

With this cultural and political decision, the nobility was quite certainly reacting to the Roman citizens' interests. At the same time, it managed to impart Greek mythology and culture to wide circles in an impressive and effective manner. Not only the myth about Troy, which the ruling elite had already taken up some time before, employing it for their political goals and using it to shape the Roman "national awareness" (Gruen 1992), but also other myths were now brought onto the stage in imitation of the Attic tragedy, with the objective stated. Nevertheless, right from the outset, specific Roman attitudes were linked with the reception of Greek theater culture. The comedy never attained Aristophanes' causticity. Above all, however, the *fabula praetexta*, the drama with a serious and Roman content, brought mythological, historical, and contemporary topics onto the stage (Manuwald 2001). To name one example: when *metus Gallicus* and *metus Punicus* combined to form an enormous complex of fear in 207 BC, with the *praetexta Clastidium*, Naevius produced an *exemplum virtutis* that was intended to contribute to coping with the psychological crisis (Bernstein 2000).

The changes in the opening rite of the *ludi* in the Second Punic War must come as no surprise. The *pompa* was based closely on the Greek processions, as a detailed ancient description shows us (Q. Fabius Pictor, *FRH*² 1 frg. 20 = Dion. H. 7.72.1–13). The *pompa* was opened by the magistrates who held the games and by Roman youth who were presented as fit for military service, because the junior team was subdivided in accordance with census classes. First rode up the sons of those who held the census as equestrians, that is, the sons of the *equites*, they were followed on foot by the sons of the *pedites* (foot-soldiers), thus the sons of the lower propertied classes. The youth thus embodied the entire *populus Romanus*, which was manifestly being integrated into the public games in this way. In addition, the junior team was intended to make foreign visitors keenly aware of Rome's military strength. However, the Roman people was integrated into the procession far more, as shown above all by the dancers in armor who were accompanied by flautists and cithara-players. The dance performed while wearing armor undoubtedly had a long tradition in the Italic area, but these dancers were now rather under Greek influence, because they performed the *pyrrhiche*, a specific form of the dance in armor which was an important element in the Panathenaic festival. In Athens, the pyrrhichists were divided into three age groups (*IG* 2/3².2.2311, l. 72–4). Significantly enough, the description corresponds with this grouping: it was a matter namely, as it states, of "choirs of dancers in three sections (first men, then youths and finally children)." However, generally speaking in Greece, the dance at the festivals was above all a matter for the citizens. For Athens we know that only certain citizens wearing armor took part in the procession of the Great *Panathenaia*. This example was probably followed in Rome: there, selected citizens or future *cives Romani* were allowed to perform as dancers in armor. In this way, however, the *populus* was being actively involved in the procession in representative form. The Roman pyrrhichists apparently portrayed the *peditatus* (arranged according to *classes* [?]) in full armor, who demonstrated his discipline on the basis of a certainly subtle choreography.

Something specifically Roman was linked with the Greek elements in all these procession participants' presentation. The appearance of the Satyrs who now followed after the choirs of dancers in uniform, mimicking their dance in armor by the so-called *sikinnis,* did admittedly underline Rome's deep rootedness in the Greek cultural community. On the other hand, a group of musicians followed them, before censers and other implements were carried past. These heralded the central element and concluding climax of the *pompa*: the parade of the gods who were also borne along as statues in the procession. Actually, a Greek pageant is described by Fabius or Dionysius, because the line of images of deities is opened by the Twelve Greek Gods. Undoubtedly, the invitation, in particular, of the Twelve Gods to the public games proved Rome's religious and cultural relationship with the Greek world.

The opening rite of the *ludi publici* was intended to emphasize "Roman Greekness," precisely because foreigners were received at Rome's public games, as Fabius and Dionysius expressly prefaced their report. The reorganization of the *pompa* in accordance with Greek models during the Second Punic War underlines the fact that, exactly in those years, there was an attempt to achieve even deeper rootedness in the Greek cultural community. A self-confident representation of the *res publica Romana* linked with the Greek shaping of the procession was emphasized by the conspicuous presence of the Satyrs and the Twelve Gods. The characteristic components of Greek processions were interlinked with emphatically Roman elements, as the hierarchical order of the procession proves. The youth represented the *populus Romanus* and at the same time its military potency, something that was additionally emphasized by the inclusion of the dancers in armor following. However, the deciding factor in involving the youth and the dancers was probably much more the intention of involving the *populus* in the happenings.

Precisely the parade of the pyrrhichists supports this view, as they were recruited from the lower propertied classes and thus represented *hoi polloi.* So the *pompa* must have had an integrating effect to a particular extent in terms of internal politics and community cohesion. Just so the games were already regarded as a central civic event which the *civis Romanus* attended, lining the route the procession took, thus recalling, so to speak, the Roman state as a whole and creating an area in which the community assembled. The *res publica Romana* also included, most importantly, the gods when they determined the procession as *pompa deorum.* They stood, so to speak, above the state; however, they protected it, in return for being invited to the games. Thus the games were, to use Livy's words, a *coetus quodam modo hominum deorumque* (2.37.9). The ritual of bloody animal sacrifice that followed the procession and preceded the chariot races in the circus or the dramatic performances in the theater confirms the perception of the gods being present at the games in the form of their statues (Q. Fabius Pictor, *FRH²* 1 frg. 20 = Dion. H. 7.72.15).

The "Greek" games undoubtedly promoted the formation of Roman identity on a broad level. The reservation of additional days for the *ludi scaenici* and the establishment of new permanent games, in which dramatic performances predominated, prove that the nobility attached extraordinary religious and cultural political importance to the *ludi publici* – despite all the difficulties which an extension of the festival calendar entailed for public life. The development of the length of the permanent public games cannot be described in detail on account of the lack of evidence. However, we do know from the epigraphically attested festival calendars from the closing years of the republic and the imperial period that the *ludi Romani* were ultimately to extend from September 5 to 19, the *ludi plebeii* from November 4 to 17, the *ludi Ceriales* from April 12 to 19, the *ludi Apollinares* from July 6 to 13, the *ludi Megalenses* from April 4 to 10, and the *ludi Florales* from April 28 until May 3.

The public games represented an important instrument in the nobility's internal and external policy, which is why the nobility encouraged their extension and elaboration. However, the Roman ruling elite also discovered new potential in the games as a forum for self-representation. For, in contrast to other expressions of the state religion, it was possible to shape the *ludi publici* in form and in content in a special way without impairing the sensitive relationship between ritual and cult. The *nobiles*, who, on account of the way they saw themselves, were pressing for possibilities of self-presentation, had here found a field of activity offering scope to translate their capability and preparedness to perform into ritual, and to demonstrate the same to the public.

Thus the introduction of new permanent games is to be explained by the interest which the nobility took in them from their own motives. Finally, additional annual games extended the reference framework of an elite dependent on proving their dignity and gaining recognition when they concentrated their activities on religion, and individual nobles entered into competition with one another in this connection. Nevertheless, a considerable explosive force lay in the individual claim. An ambivalence of functions was basically present and so an extended understanding of the *ludi publici* would establish itself. The attempts by the senate, that institutional center of the aristocracy, to exert an influence in a sanctioning and regulatory manner on the dynamic conditions in the system of games only managed to hold up a particular, highly consequential development temporarily. As the guarantor of collective discipline, the senate attempted, above all, to cut down the *ludi votivi*, staged at growing expense by military commanders thirsting for glory, because they served for their self-presentation. These votive games, which, since 205 BC at the latest, were once again vowed and given on one's own responsibility (Livy 28.38.14, 28.45.12), stand out particularly in the records and are an early symptom of the process of disintegration in the Roman ruling elite.

The generals giving games stand at the beginning of a development which was to lead to the conditions in the late republic when the magistrates responsible endeavored to outdo one another in the staging of the public games, in the *apparatus ludorum publicorum*. After all, the curators could decisively promote their career by this. The aedile could build on the electorate's vivid recollection of particularly magnificent games when standing for the post of praetor. Thus a compulsion to take action prevailed. This, at times, could escalate into actionism, as is shown particularly clearly in the display of splendor in the temporary stage installations, the *venationes*, beast hunts, conducted with great enthusiasm. Despite the immeasurable pageantry and uninhibited instrumentalization of the games in the late republic, the religious-cultic dimension of the *ludi publici* was by no means abandoned. And yet the amply familiar process of disintegration of the Roman ruling elite was also reflected by the further development of public games.

Sulla, Caesar, and the New Public Games

The new public games of the late republic owed their existence to the ambitions of the great individual personalities Sulla and Caesar, the dictators who probably made their mark most lastingly on the old *res publica Romana*. Thus it was not old state deities for whom still more *ludi publici stati(vi)* were now established. Instead it was one of those cult personifications that had conquered the Roman pantheon with the rise of the nobility: the goddess of victory, who was ultimately to develop from a *Victoria populi Romani* into a personal tutelary goddess.

After Sulla had defeated the Italians at the Colline Gate on November 1, 82 BC, he probably soon brought about a recommendation by the senate on the establishment of the *ludi Victoriae*, the center point of which was to be marked by that memorable date (Velleius 2.27.6). Already in the following year, *scaenici* and *circenses* were given by the praetorian *curator* Sex. Nonius Sufenas (*RRC* 1.445 no. 421.1), a "classical" program that probably conformed with the usual "liturgy," with a procession and sacrifices. However, the dictator had deliberately avoided apostrophizing the goddess of victory as Victoria Sullana. After all, the new public annual games were intended to contribute toward the acceptance of his restoration of the *res publica Romana*. Thus the *ludi Victoriae* celebrated the victory of the *populus Romanus*. However, this victory could hardly have been achieved without the future reformer's leadership, so we find Victoria appearing as a deity personally standing by the commander. Her annual games, which were ultimately to extend from October 26 until November 1, thus became permanently associated with the dictator's person and indirectly turned into a celebration of thanksgiving for the well-ordered Roman state, organized for the tutelary goddess and her protégé. This ambivalent, all in all rather suggestive concept of Sulla, trusting in the success of his reform work, and influenced by the Greek-Hellenistic *agones* in honor of outstanding persons, made the way free for Caesar. This level of instrumentalization and politicization of the *ludi publici* in an individual's interest had been previously unattained.

Caesar's frequently extolled skill in the political use of symbols and rituals was concentrated to a considerable extent in the suggestive forms and traditions of the public games. Thus his *ludi Victoriae Caesaris* and the honors shown to him within the scope of the public games bring us to the threshold of the imperial period. The medium of the *ludi*, which were effective as publicity and easily manipulated, was decisively employed by Caesar for his own objectives. Already his institution of the new permanent public games shows the dictator's political skill. Before Pharsalus, Caesar vowed a sanctuary to Venus Victrix (App. *Civ.* 2.281), that goddess to whom Pompey had dedicated his theater temple in 55 BC (Tert. *Spect.* 10.5). Caesar let the great impression which the former had made with this building complex, and, in particular, with the magnificent dedication games, waste away in the shadow of his brilliant celebrations in the year 46 BC. Coupled with his fourfold triumph, he staged a sweeping festival of the *gens Iulia* and its successful scion. He dedicated the promised temple to the victorious Venus as Genetrix on the Forum Iulium, and consecratory games, such as had never previously been seen, were intended to let Pompey be completely forgotten (Cass. Dio 43.22.2–23.5). However, the public games, held from July 20 to 30 (permanently so from 45 BC), and entrusted to a *collegium* of organizers, were not entered into the festival calendar of the Roman state as *ludi Veneris Genetricis*. The *ludi Victoriae Caesaris*, as they were called instead according to the evidence of precisely these festival calendars, made most notable reference to the games instituted by Sulla, though they were modified in their function, as the epithet of the goddess of victory alone revealed. As Caesar's rise and extraordinary position proved, Victoria had long since concentrated her favor on this one man. Her second permanent games, inaugurated by her sole protégé, were intended to surpass the existing ones by being linked with the date of the foundation of her old sanctuary (August 1), while preceding it. The celebration of victory now observed annually by games sustained the recollection that it was Caesar's victories that the *res publica Romana* commemorated henceforth. The fact that in it the *dictator perpetuo* to be was the first man then also emphasized the honors connected with the public games.

The honors made use of the wealth of forms rooted in the state cult of the gods and developed over centuries, and substantiated in a quite subtle manner Caesar's outstanding position. The vestments adopted for all the spectacles, the *vestis Iovis Optimi Maximi* and the laurel wreath, as well as the right to give the starting signal at the *circenses*, showed the dictator as the *praeses omnium ludorum publicorum* (Cass. Dio 43.43.1, 43.14.5; cf. above). The participation of his decorated statue in the *pompa circensis*, as well as the heightening of this distinction by decreeing a *tensa* ("chariot") and a *pulvinar* ("couch") of his own, and finally the award of the golden chair and wreath for the dramatic performances, implied Caesar's inclusion in the "liturgy" of the *ludi publici*, bringing him closer to the gods (Cass. Dio 44.6.3, 43.45.2; Suet. *Caesar* 76.1; Cic. *Philippicae* 2.110). In sum total, the basis for the phenomena of the imperial period was laid with Caesar's interference with the venerable system of games of the Roman republic.

Religion and Politics

As an integral part of the public cult and festival order, the *ludi publici* were intended to secure the favor and assistance of the gods. However, at the same time, the nobility developed the public games into a universal instrument of their internal and external policy. The assimilation of Greek models, above all the adoption of the drama and reorganization of the procession, with the simultaneous emphasis on specifically Roman forms and contents, served, not least, the Roman aristocracy's interests in education and public order. When the games gathered the senate and people of Rome, they inculcated the nobility's claim to leadership, and nonetheless strengthened the sense of solidarity between the community's head and its members that was indispensable in the case of all military involvement, and in the face of threats of any kind. Especially the lavish but carefully arranged processions promoted the necessary self-confidence, because they served as an image and a show of the powerful Roman community determined to act under the protection of the favorably disposed gods. In such a way, the *ludi publici* committed the people to the pre-eminence of the nobility and to their objectives. This ruling elite made the games into a comprehensive means of political influence, because they were at the same time intended to help the community to become aware of itself, and to accentuate and sustain its identity. The *ludi scaenici* were of the greatest importance for the development of the consciousness of one's own roots and the destiny of Rome directed by the *numina*. The dramatic performances dominating the appearance of the games represented a propaganda medium capable of being shaped and effective for the huge public. They imparted the great "national" topics and binding values to the people, told of Rome's heroic past, and pointed to a brilliant future ahead. As they cut Greek mythology and culture to Roman conditions and scales, the "Greek" games, for all their differences, did prove that Rome belonged religiously and culturally to the Greek world, fulfilling an urgent foreign policy requirement and facilitating attempts to form contacts and alliances. However, the political functions of the *ludi publici* were not limited to that.

The public games also offered the nobility undreamed-of possibilities of self-presentation, which must have been welcome to the individual in his strivings for public offices. The constantly growing expenditure by the competing magistrates in providing the decor and costumes for the performances involved no risk of offending the sensitive cult order. The gods were in every respect unrestrained, and so a greater quantity of their worship was also always a higher quality, so long as the ritual forms hallowed by tradition were not thwarted. At no point in their development can there be talk of a "secularization" of the *ludi publici*, although certain trends toward secessionism by individuals away from the unity of the political elite also became apparent in the array of public games. The senate, the custodian of collective discipline, was at the most able to slow the process of disintegration of the Roman ruling elite spreading to the *ludi publici*. However, sanction and regulation were unable to prevent the far-reaching consequences. All in all, the nobility smoothed the way for the great individual personalities in this respect, too.

The new *ludi publici* of the late republic, as games in honor of a personal tutelary deity, accompanied Sulla's restoration, supported Pompey's claim to recognition, and demonstrated the extraordinary position of Caesar, who ultimately controlled the fortunes of the Roman state. The new age, which Caesar Augustus was then to establish, was heralded in by the permanent victory games. However, only their deep religious character, their dedication to the *Victoria populi Romani* or subsequently to the *Victoria Caesaris*, made their eminently political exploitation by the dictators possible. In their respective way, these *ludi publici* also established an identity. No doubt Sulla's and Caesar's interference with the traditional system of games did anticipate phenomena of the imperial period and make the future rulers' promotion of games, as well as their subjects' incessant demand for *panem et circenses*, more comprehensible. But the *ludi publici* were already included among the *arcana imperii* long before.

FURTHER READING

The literature on the games in the imperial age is legion. For guidance one might just mention Coleman (2000). For all questions connected with the games of the archaic period and, in particular, of the republican period, as well as the interpretation of the *pompa* presented here, see Bernstein (1998), as well as separately on the enigmatic *Ecurria/Equirria* Bernstein (1999), then also on the long-lasting and constantly newly accentuated *Consualia* Bernstein (1997). Degrassi has edited and commentated the festival calendars (1963); Rüpke (1995a) has presented a seminal study.

Humphrey (1986) has examined the layout and gradual extension of the circuses; Hanson (1959) is still to be recommended for the development of theater construction. Thuillier (1985) decisively promoted understanding of the Etruscan games culture that is documented above all archaeologically. Numerous studies have been published on the divine dedicatees of the games and concepts of the gods forming the basis of this: particularly on Iuppiter cf. Fears (1981a), still Le Bonniec (1958) on Ceres and Flora, Gagé (1955) on Apollo, Borgeaud (1996) on Mater Magna, Fears (1981b) on Victoria, as well as Long (1987) on the Twelve Gods in Greece and Rome.

Hölkeskamp (1987) has made a more profound understanding of republican Rome's unique ruling elite, the nobility, possible. The discussion on the role of the drama in the formation of historical tradition (and also Roman identity) has been given decisive impulses by the reflections of Wiseman (1998).

CHAPTER SEVENTEEN

Performing the Sacred: Prayers and Hymns

Frances Hickson Hahn

Religious rituals were a favorite subject for Roman sculptors and painters; we possess countless images of processions and sacrifices, but only a very few that explicitly show a worshiper in the act of praying. This is not surprising given both the difficulties of portraying and characterizing speech and by contrast the unambiguous and visually more interesting scenes of ritual action. In any event, sculptures and paintings are mute: we do not hear the sound of the pipes or the priest dictating the prayer formulae or the magistrate repeating the solemn words. And yet, all sacrifices and offerings were accompanied by prayers, most simply defined as words addressed to divine powers. Clearly prayer was the most ubiquitous form of religious ritual in Rome, since it not only accompanied all ritual acts but could stand alone as an independent speech act. This chapter attempts to restore the voices to those silent images. After opening with a consideration of the potency of ritual words, I analyze a series of prayers illustrating the different varieties of prayer and characteristics of their performance. The chapter concludes with consideration of the role of prayer in the socio-political life of ancient Rome.

The Power of Ritual Words

Answering the question "do words have any potency?," Pliny the Elder responds that "a sacrifice without prayer is thought to be useless and not a proper consultation of the gods" (*Nat.* 28.10). But the choice of the correct form of prayer was crucial. As Valerius Maximus writes: "following ancient tradition . . . one must use a prayer of petition when entrusting something for protection, a vow when making a request, a prayer of thanksgiving when fulfilling a vow, an inquiry when divining the will of the gods" (1.1.1). This was a significant aspect of the Roman emphasis on formulaic language, handed down and preserved by religious specialists in books, which unfortunately no longer survive. So important was precise duplication of formulae that magistrates recited prayers following a priest's dictation. Such precautions were especially important in situations where the archaic language of a traditional prayer might even mean that the priests themselves did not understand it, as Quintilian remarks of the ancient Salian hymn to Mars (*Institutiones* 1.6.40). Failure to follow the prescribed format was thought to impair the effectiveness of a prayer, as shown in an incident described by Livy (41.16.1). At the annual Latin festival, when the magistrate from the town of Lanuvium neglected to name the Roman people in the list of beneficiaries of divine favor, it was necessary to perform the ceremonies over again.

Scholars have often interpreted such emphasis on words to be indicative of a magical quality in certain ritual behaviors, in that the effectiveness of the ritual seems to be dependent on human technique rather than on divine power. But magic is no longer seen as a useful hermeneutic category, for its distinction from religion, frequently informed by polemical ends, is difficult or impossible to define with any fixity. It also seems hopelessly bound to a positivistic view privileging modern religions over so-called primitive magic. A more productive approach focuses on the techniques by which language acquires efficacy.

The Latin word *carmen* crystallizes the Roman understanding of the power of words. Romans applied the term to both prayers and hymns, but also to magical incantations. Putnam (2001: 133) defines the word's original sense as "a verbal utterance sung for ritualistic purposes." The dominant feature is a style of expression characterized by formulae, redundancy, and rhythm. So prominent was the rhythmical quality that by the late second century BC the word *carmen* referred primarily to poetry. Closely related to the root of the verb "to sing" (**can*), the word *carmen* frequently appears with verbs based on that root (Ernout and Meillet 1959–60: 101). For the Romans, at least formally, there was no distinction between prayer and spell and poetry and song; all were intimately linked to one another.

Prayer as Performance

Austin's theory of performative language provides a fruitful approach to understanding the ancient emphasis on the power of ritual words. In Austin's sense of the word, prayers are performative, that is, speech acts that perform actions. Roman prayers were not simple locutionary acts, addressing statements to the gods or describing the human position vis-à-vis the gods. Rather, prayers were the performance of petition or promise or thanks based on an accepted convention in ritual contexts. This performative quality is perhaps most clearly understood in prayers of thanksgiving. In saying the words "I give thanks that," the worshiper explicitly performs the act of thanksgiving. While a gift or sacrifice often accompanied the prayer, the function and efficacy of that offering was dependent on the words of thanks. Furthermore, it is significant that prayers of thanksgiving always made mention of the divine act that merited the offering of thanks. This is the act of praise that is so closely bound up with thanksgiving. To say "I give thanks that" is to thank and praise. The utterance in and of itself has force or power. Similarly, to say "I vow" is to perform the act of committing oneself to a future action; the promise comes into existence only through and at the moment of the speech act. The phrase "I swear" or "I summon witnesses" is the essence of oath-taking. Likewise, to say "I pray and entreat that" is to perform the act of petition.

Prayers may also be termed performative in the sense of dramatic performances, since they involve actors and an audience, a set-apart space and time, and conventional words and movements. In this dramatic sense, any Roman prayer other than an individual's lone address distinguishes between actors and human audience. But even that individual typically spoke prayers aloud, like an actor soliloquizing on an empty stage. Unlike the common Christian practice, there was no collective prayer in which all present participated verbally. In the private religion of the family, a single individual, most often the *pater familias*, offered prayers on behalf of the group, while other family members stood quietly by. Similarly in public religion, typically a single designated speaker addressed the divine, while the citizen audience stood watching silently. On official occasions, the speakers of prayer were usually either magistrates or priests, although children or women might be specially selected to perform a hymn. In another characteristic shared with dramatic performances, music, often played on pipes, accompanied public prayers. Choral performances would have seemed even more dramatic in their use of multiple instruments and in the frequent addition of movement. On certain occasions, choruses walked in a solemn manner in a ritual procession reminiscent of Greek cult practices and the closely related dramatic performances. The Arval priests performed a three-step dance while reciting the words of their ancient hymn to Mars (*CIL* 6.2104 = *CFA* 296). In a similar fashion, the Salian priests of Mars danced while processing through the city and singing (Dion. H. 2.70.1–5). Even non-choral prayer included some movement, generally the lifting of arms toward the heavens (e.g. Sall. *Bellum Catilinae* 31.3; Livy 5.21.15).

There's a Time and Place

Roman prayer, like other rituals, was distinguished by set times and places. Each setting had its own characteristic prayers, be it home, cemetery, temple, forum, or battlefield. For each of these places, there were regular times for ritual performances: meal-time, birth, death, festival, inauguration, battle; and each of these times had its own characteristic prayers. This is not to say that there was an invariable form for every performance. While the public prayers of magistrates and priests typically followed set forms recorded in books, the private prayers of individuals were more open to variation in structure, language, and content.

The home was the primary setting for worship of protective deities of the family. Every day before the primary meal, offerings accompanied by a brief prayer were made to the household deities at the hearth or at a portable brazier. Birthdays were also set apart as times for offering and prayer at the household shrine, which stood in the central living area of a house (*atrium*) and often resembled a miniature temple with pediment and statuettes (see chapter 14). Funerary rituals took place in the home, as well as at the place of burial, as did annual ceremonies on behalf of deceased members of the family. Within the grounds of an estate, there were several other locations where prayers and sacrifices were regularly made: at boundary stones, springs, groves, and fields. In his second-century BC treatise *On Agriculture*, Cato the Elder preserves four traditional prayers to be offered before sowing, harvesting, and pruning a grove or for purifying an estate (*Agr.* 132, 134, 139, 141).

Of course, temples and shrines are the most familiar scenes for religious ritual, which took place in front of the building, where the altar stood, not out of sight behind closed doors. There priests observed annual festivals on the day of foundation, which served as the deity's feast day. In times of crisis, the senate sometimes decreed public days of prayer, on which the whole citizenry, men, women, and children, went from temple to temple throughout the city praying for divine aid (*supplicationes*). In turn, a favorable outcome of such prayers often led to public days of thanksgiving, on which the citizen body gave thanks for their deliverance. Some sacred buildings and altars also provided the setting for regular clan rituals aimed at securing the well-being of the larger groups of families (*sacra gentilicia*). Although private individuals might offer prayers at any place, many chose to visit temples or shrines where the presence of the deity seemed especially close. Countless votive tablets proclaim answered prayers for aid in childbirth or sickness and protection on journeys. These worshipers often stood before the statue itself to make their prayers heard. In addition, there were numerous roadside shrines, where passers-by paused to salute deities with word and gesture.

Of the many temples in the city of Rome, the best-known was that of Jupiter Optimus Maximus, Juno, and Minerva on the Capitoline hill. This large and ancient edifice served as the stage for grand public rituals before great crowds of citizens assembled to observe their magistrates and priests address the chief gods of the Roman state. On the day that consuls entered office, their first act was to offer sacrifice and prayers at this temple. When a commander set out on a military expedition, he first ascended the Capitoline to make a vow for the successful outcome of his mission. If successful, and the senate decreed a triumph, the triumphal procession wound its way through the city to come to an end at the same temple, and the commander offered prayers and sacrifices of thanksgiving to the same gods to whom he had made his vows. And yet even in this great temple of the Roman state, individuals offered personal prayers. Seneca mocks those who come to the Capitoline to "ask the gods to put up their bail and those who present their legal briefs and expound their cases" (Aug. *Civ.* 6.10).

Not all prayers were spoken in settings that we would identify as sacred. Anywhere that public business took place could be the scene for prayer. When the centuriate assembly met for electoral purposes in the Campus Martius, the consul prayed for divine blessing: "that this business turn out well and propitiously for myself and my pledged magistracy and for the Roman people and plebs" (Cic. *Pro Murena* 1.1). At the close of the census, again in the Campus Martius, the censor prayed, at least until the latter half of the second century BC, that the gods "make the possessions of the Roman people more prosperous and extensive" (Val. Max. 4.1.10). Taking the auspices prior to any public business involved specialized prayers offered wherever the magistrate took his place for observation.

The battlefield had its prayers too. After taking the auspices, the commander offered vows for the successful outcome of the battle, as he might again if the battle did not go well. Our sources tell of numerous campaigns when the general prayed to the patron deities of cities about to be attacked, asking those gods to change sides (*evocatio*). Take, for example, Livy's account of the prayer that Camillus made before leading troops against the city of Veii: "Queen Juno, who now dwell in Veii, I pray that you follow us as victors into our city, soon to be yours, where a temple worthy of your greatness will receive you" (5.21.3). There were also special prayers by which the commander could devote himself and the enemy troops as sacrificial victims to the chthonic deities (*devotio*), as Decius Mus did in war against the Latins: "I consecrate the legions and auxiliaries of the enemy together with myself to the divine dead and the goddess Earth" (Livy 8.9.8). Finally, peace treaties also required sanctioning with sacrifice and prayer that Jupiter punish any violators of their terms.

Each of these many occasions and settings had distinctive paradigms of prayer. As noted above, the Romans made very careful distinctions among ritual performances: petition, vow, oath, thanksgiving. Although relatively few extant prayers represent genuine cultic texts, nevertheless, by analyzing those in combination with literary versions, we are able to describe fairly well the characteristics of Roman prayer, at least formal, and its varieties. The following sections treat the varieties of performance by examining exemplary texts.

Petition

Cato the Elder preserves this prayer for the purification and protection of a farm, which provides an early model for the structure and wording of a traditional petitionary prayer:

> Father Mars, I pray and beseech you to be favorable and propitious toward me and my family and household; wherefore I have ordered this sacrifice of a pig, sheep and bull to be led around my farm, land and estate, so that you may prohibit, avert, and ward off diseases seen and unseen, barrenness and devastation, destruction and intemperate weather, so that you may permit the produce, grains, vines, and bushes to grow large and flourish, that you may keep safe the shepherds and sheep, and that you may grant health and wellness to me, my family, and household; wherefore, for the purpose of purifying and making pure my estate, land and farm, as I have spoken, be honored with the sacrifice of this suckling pig, sheep, and bull. Father Mars, for this purpose, be honored with the sacrifice of this suckling pig, sheep, and bull. (*Agr.* 141)

A petitionary prayer such as this, a simple request of the gods, is the most common type in extant sources. In fact, the verb *precari*, which is typically translated "to pray," essentially means "to request" and may refer to requests of humans as well as of gods. These petitions are represented by numerous prayers for cures, protection, blessing, and aid found in texts of all genres.

The structure of Cato's petition is typical of Roman prayers of all types. It opens with an invocation of the god ("Mars"), including honorific epithets ("father"). Here could be added descriptive phrases to more carefully identify or praise the deity. Next follows a verb or verb phrase that identifies the objective of the prayer; in this passage the words "pray and beseech" mark this as a prayer of petition. The primary part of a petitionary prayer consists of the request itself. Beyond that specific request, petitions frequently include, usually at the end, a more general appeal for the favor of the invoked deity, without which no prayer could be effective ("that you may be favorable and propitious"). An essential component of any petition was an exhaustive listing of the beneficiaries of the request ("me and my family and household"). Finally, petitionary prayers commonly make some reference to the reason that the deity should respond favorably, most often, as here, a reference to present or future offerings.

Cato's prayer also illustrates the typical style of prayers, which is characterized by redundancy. Most obvious is the use of synonyms ("prohibit, avert, and ward off"), which may reflect anxiety about the use of proper terms, but is more likely simply a rhetorical device to increase the prayer's efficacy. A related phenomenon appears in the listing of the component parts of an object ("produce, grains, vines, and bushes"). In these metonymic lists and elsewhere, there is a tendency to use alliteration ("shepherds and sheep"), another form of repetition. The speaker also repeats entire statements ("be honored with the sacrifice of this suckling pig, sheep, and bull"). Over all, the various lexical, syntactic, and rhythmic patterns would have facilitated memorization and correct recitation. More importantly, however, the repetitive patterns of sound and rhythm gave persuasive power to the ritual words.

Vow

In addition to the simple petitionary prayer, a common variant is the vow, a petition expressed in the form of a condition, promising a gift to the deity if the request is granted. Myriad inscriptions referring to the fulfillment of vows testify to the commonness of this practice, particularly in public cult. One well-preserved inscription of the Acts of the Arval Priesthood represents the annual vow taken on January 3 for the health and safety of the emperor and his household. In the year AD 81, the Arval priests prayed:

> Jupiter Optimus Maximus, if the emperor Vespasian . . . and his son Domitian . . . , whom we intend to name, live and their household will be unharmed until the third day of January which will be next for the Roman people of the Quirites, the state of the Roman people of the Quirites, and if you will have kept that day and them safe from dangers, if there are or will be any dangers before that day and if you will have granted a favorable outcome as we intend to say and if you will have preserved them in that condition in which they are now or in a better one, and if you have accomplished these requests thus, then we vow in the name of the college of the Arval Priesthood that we will offer you two oxen with gilded horns. (*CIL* 6.32363.45–52 = *CFA* 48)

Like Cato's prayer for purification and protection of a farm, this prayer opens with an invocation, here to the chief god of the Roman state. The petition for the welfare of the imperial household, which constitutes the primary objective of the prayer, is stated in the form of a series of conditional clauses. Each of these is a repetition of the basic request for health and safety, expressed in different ways and accordingly similar to the references in Cato's prayer to the different aspects of the prosperous operation of an estate. What characterizes this prayer as a vow is the inclusion of a promise to make a sacrifice to Jupiter in the future if the petition is favorably answered. By contrast, Cato's prayer refers only to the sacrifice that accompanies the prayer. A striking addition to this imperial prayer is the phrase "we intend," repeated in two variants, which calls attention to the speaker's interest in avoiding possible misunderstandings caused by a poor choice of words. A similar concern for precision appears in the careful specification of the temporal framework of the petition and in the naming of the Roman people. Particularly noteworthy is the addition of the phrase "or in a better state," so as not to restrict the possible blessings of the god.

In both of these petitionary prayers there is throughout a sense of religious anxiety before the dangerous powers of the gods, who brought both good and evil. Further evidence of that worry appears in the cautionary formulae frequently appearing at the conclusion of a vow and detailing the conditions under which the vow would be considered fulfilled. The petitioner would name various situations that might potentially invalidate the discharge of the vow and declare that these factors would not affect the validity of the vow's fulfillment. In this way, a traditional prayer for the self-sacrifice of a commander concludes with the words "at that time whoever should accomplish this vow and wherever, let it be properly done with three black sheep" (Macr. *Sat.* 3.9.11).

Oath

Livy offers a vivid description of the ritual for ratifying a treaty in his description of the preparations between Rome and Alba Longa before the battle of triplet warriors:

> Then after the terms had been read aloud, [the *pater patratus*] said: "Hear Jupiter; hear *pater patratus* of the Alban people; hear you Alban people. Just as those words have been recited publicly from first to last from those tablets of wax without evil intent and just as they have been here today most correctly understood, the Roman people will not be the first to violate those terms. If they will have violated them first with evil intent and official deliberation, then on that day, Jupiter, may you strike the Roman people, as I here today strike this pig; and may you strike them with as much greater force as you are able and powerful." (1.24.6–8)

This passage illustrates another important variant of petitionary prayer, the oath, a prayer requesting that a divine power witness a statement or action and (usually) inflict a punishment on the party who lies or misbehaves – supplementing the incapability of the human parties to immediately test the truth or effectively sanction the failure of a promise. This form of prayer appears in a wide variety of contexts, not only civil, legal, and military, but also private, primarily as a means of affirming the truthfulness of a statement. Thus the parties to a betrothal took an oath to finalize their promises, just as the parties to a treaty solemnized their agreement with an oath ceremony.

The history of Livy provides a good idea of the structure and content, if not a verbatim record, of treaty oaths performed by the Fetial priests, whose domain included the rituals for declaring war and ratifying treaties. This passage contains all of the elements characteristic of an oath in its fullest expression: the invocation of witnesses, statement to be affirmed, references to intent, and self-curse. Here the Fetial priest in charge of the ritual, the *pater patratus*, addresses the Fetial priest and citizens of Alba Longa as well as Jupiter, the Roman god most frequently invoked in oaths. This dual audience, human and divine, points to the primary function of oaths as a means of affirming the truthfulness of a statement made to others. Without this social context, there would be no need for an oath. Not surprisingly, of all forms of prayer, oaths share the greatest similarities with legal texts. Of particular note in this example are the two references to the intentions of the parties involved, a concept early enshrined in the Roman legal code, that is, that without intent there is no crime. The priest refers to the recitation of the treaty terms "without evil intent" and the potential violation of those terms "with evil intent." In the latter reference, the priest also adds the phrase "and official deliberation," to preclude the possibility of individual violations. The oath recalls the cautionary language of vows with their various escape clauses. In the conclusion, the priest prays for Jupiter to punish the Roman people if they should violate the treaty – first. Some form of self-curse appears in all complete oaths, but is often missing from briefer literary or colloquial oaths. Still, the presumption of divine punishment in the case of perjury always looms as the effective force of an oath.

Thanksgiving

Although prayers of thanksgiving were certainly a very common form of address to the gods in both the public and private spheres, we do not possess any complete prayer of thanksgiving representing an authentic cultic text. Nevertheless, numerous prayers of gratitude in the comic writers, as well as references to such prayers in historiographical writers, give us some idea of their character. Like petitionary prayers they open with an invocation. There follows, instead of a verb of "praying," a phrase meaning "to give thanks." Most importantly, the speaker offers a brief description of the divine blessing for which thanks is given. For example, in Plautus' play *Poenulus*, Hanno prays "All you gods and goddesses, I deservedly give great thanks to you, since you have blessed me with this very great happiness and these joys, that my daughters return to me and into my possession" (1274–6).

The idea of reciprocity is an important aspect of any prayer, but notably of thanksgiving; the prayer, usually coupled with an offering, is considered to be a necessary response and exchange for a divine act. As in this Plautine prayer, the word for thanks is *gratia* or *grates,* the origin of our modern word "gratitude." Etymologists (Leumann 1937: 35; Moussy 1966: 49–56) associate the Latin terms closely with the act of praise. In fact, the words *gratia* and *grates* are often coupled with *laudes* ("praise"), as in this expression of thanksgiving in another Plautine play, "we offer great praise and thanks" (*Asinaria* 545; for the seminal study of Plautine thanksgiving prayers see Fraenkel 1922). Although sometimes interpreted as a synonymous pair, the collocation points to the linking of words of praise with acts of sacrifice in the ritual of thanksgiving (Moussy 1966: 53–4). By naming the deities and recounting their deeds, the speaker praises divine power, an appropriate and necessary exchange for a favor. For this reason, Hanno uses the term "deservedly" (*merito*) to describe his thanksgiving. And yet his prayer is not a mercenary or legalistic act of exchange, but rather a heartfelt act of happiness and joy. Therefore the English terms "thanks" and "gratitude" are not inappropriate to describe this response.

Hymns

One of the most ancient prayers still in existence is one performed by the Arval Priesthood and preserved in an early third-century AD inscription. Despite the lateness of the inscription, its spelling and vocabulary attest its antiquity, dating at the latest to the fourth century BC:

Enos Lases iuuate,
<e>nos Lases iuuate,
enos Lases iuuate!
Neue lue rue Marma<r> sins in currere in pleores,
neue lue rue Marmar <si>ns in currere in pleores,
neue lue rue Marmar sins incurrere in pleores!
Satur fu, fere Mars! Limen <sa>li, sta berber!
Satur fu, fere Mars! Limen sali, sta berber!
Satur fu, fere Mars! Limen sali, sta berber!
<Sem>unis alternei aduocapit conctos,
semunis alternei aduocapit conctos,
semunis alternei aduocapit <conct>os!
Enos Marmor iuuato,
enos Marmor iuuato,
enos Ma<r>mor iuuato!
Triumpe, triumpe, triumpe, trium<pe, tri>umpe!

Lares, help us, (3 times)
and Marmor, do not allow disease and destruction to attack the multitude. (3 times)
Fierce Mars, be satisfied; leap the threshold and stay?. (3 times)
You (pl.) shall invoke all the Semones in alternate turns. (3 times)
Marmar, help us. (3 times)
Triumpe! (5 times)
(*CIL* 6.2104 = *CFA* 296)

While all of the prayers previously considered were spoken by an individual Roman, sometimes on his own behalf, sometimes on behalf of a community, the category of prayer here classified as hymns is distinguished through their performance by a group. The body singing a Roman hymn did not consist of the entire congregation of worshipers, but rather of a select group of priests or a citizen chorus, who addressed the gods on behalf of the larger community. For the performance of this hymn, the priests recited words from rolls kept by public slaves and brought out just for the occasion. While singing, they also performed a three-step dance. Like most other Roman hymns, the primary objective of this hymn was apotropaic. It is characteristic of many Roman deities that they possessed power for both good and ill and therefore had to be placated as Mars is here. First the priests address the Lares, protective spirits of the land, then Mars in his guise as a wild and potentially destructive power, who can afflict crops with disease. The series of petitions is interrupted by what appears to be an instruction to the priests to invoke by turns the Semones, agricultural spirits. In the last full verse, the priests again request Mars' favor. Finally, the hymn concludes with a fivefold repetition of the word "triumph," possibly a prayer for divine manifestation (Versnel 1970: 11–55).

This hymn contains many features characteristic of other prayers, but adapted and magnified for its particular purposes. Most striking is the redundancy, which appears frequently in other prayers, but not to this extent, namely that the priests repeat each of the verses three times and the lines themselves are written out three times in the inscription. Similarly the hymn concludes with repetitions of a single word, again repeated in the inscription. What appears in the text as three divine names (Marmar, Mars, Marmor) are actually variants on the name of a single deity. Furthermore, there is considerable recurrence of consonantal and vocalic sounds such as *lue rue* ("disease and destruction"). Finally, the Arval hymn employs repetition in a metrical sense, a simple form of verse based on lines with a fixed number of syllables. The impression is unavoidable that the structure and wording themselves are considered powerful and effective devices in the achievement of the petition.

In addition to the regular performance of hymns by priestly groups, the Romans also commissioned hymns to be composed for extraordinary occasions and sung by non-priestly choruses. We know of several occasions when consultation of priestly experts following an androgynous birth resulted in ritual expiations including the performance of hymns by choruses of unmarried girls. The first known occurrence of such an event took place in 207 BC; the pontiffs advised that 27 maidens process through the city to the temple of Juno Regina singing a hymn composed by the poet Livius Andronicus (Livy 27.37.5–15). There are at least another seven instances recorded (MacBain 1982: 127–32).

Other occasions for hymns included the Secular Games, intended originally to occur only once in the memory of any living person. The only extant choral hymn from the pre-Christian era is that of the Secular Games presented by Augustus in 17 BC; the lyric poet Horace composed the hymn, which was inscribed together with an account of other ritual activities (Hor. *Carmen Saeculare*, Schnegg-Köhler 2002). The lengthy hymn, sung by a chorus of boys and girls, begins thus:

> Phoebus Apollo, Diana, queen of the forests,
> O deities the glories of the sky,
> Most worthy to be worshiped, grant, we pray,
> Our prayers in the sacred season.
> Now is the time the Sibylline Leaves ordain
> That the chosen maidens and pure young men should sing
> The poem written in honor of the gods
> Who favor the Seven Hills.
> (Hor. *Carmen Saeculare* 1–8, trans. David Ferry)

Horace's hymn unites the poetic and religious strains of Latin *carmina*, deftly manipulating the repetition and rhythm characteristic of both. Unlike most hymns, the *Carmen Saeculare* is not apotropaic in nature. "It is a hymn to confirm by incantation the glory of the Roman status quo" (Putnam 2001: 98; Feeney 1998: 32–8).

Performing Politics

It is the nature of performance that there be both actors and audience. In the home or on the estate, the ritual actor was the *pater familias* or his substitute; the audience, the family or larger household. In the public arena, the actors were typically magistrates and priests; the audience, the citizen body or some segment thereof. In either context, the ritual performance marked the social status of actors and audience. Just as the *pater familias* was the head of the family, so the magistrate was head of the state. In the public sphere, social and political prominence were for the most part co-extensive; magisterial positions were held by members of a small but powerful elite. Furthermore, the same elite group regularly provided the personnel for priestly offices, which could be held at the same time as civil offices. It was unavoidable therefore that public prayers, like public religion, were inextricably intertwined with politics. Beyond the elite personnel, we have already seen that many occasions for prayer were also political in character, from election and inauguration of magistrates to the preparations for wars.

The prayers themselves also speak of political concerns. It is the protection and blessing of the state that is the primary objective of every public prayer. Accordingly, the annual republican vow for the state, which served as a model for subsequent prayers for the emperor and his family, requested protection from dangers, together with the preservation or growth of the state. Petitionary and gratulatory prayers on the occasion of war addressed similar issues of safety and success. Interestingly, comparison of these wartime prayers to debates in the senate over the award of triumphs reveal parallel issues. Senators raised issues concerning the general's meeting of requirements for a triumph: his authority, the number of enemy killed or Roman lives lost, the conclusiveness of the victory, and the return of the army to the city. The prayer that best illustrates this content is a Plautine parody, in which a slave gives thanks for the success of his intrigue, using the language of a thanksgiving offered by a triumphing general:

> The enemy has been conquered, our citizens are safe, the state quiet, peace accomplished, the war over, the state's business well done, the army and garrisons safe. Since you Jupiter and all the other heavenly gods have prospered us, I express my gratitude to you, because I have rightly avenged my enemy. (*Persa* 753–7)

While some political themes are to be expected in official prayers, the extent to which these dovetail with debates over whether or not a particular elite commander was deserving of the honor of a state-sponsored triumph is striking.

Given the close links between prayers and the activities of the political elite, it is reasonable to ask whose interests were served by the system of public prayer. The prayer of the triumphant general, in combination with the triumphal procession, which it verbally mirrored, suggests some possibilities. In this specific case, the prayer served in part to justify a triumph by calling attention to the commander's fulfillment of requirements, and therefore promoted the prestige and influence of the individual commander. At the same time, the prayer provided a justification for the war itself through the proclamation of victory and its rewards. In this way, the prayer benefited not only the individual commander but the senatorial class, which had the primary responsibility for foreign relations. The triumphal thanksgiving also recalled prior petitions for the safe return of the army, which bolstered public confidence that divine assistance was available.

Turning to the broader system of public prayer, the pattern is similar. Clearly, individual priests and magistrates benefited from the starring roles they played in public ritual. Significantly, the wording of public prayers typically employs the first person singular of verbs of prayer. When considered as a system, however, what stands out is the virtual monopoly of public religion and prayer by the elite class. There was a recurring theme in Roman politics that the welfare of the state was dependent on divine favor shown especially toward the ruling class, a theme voiced in the conflict over the admission of plebeians to magistracies and priesthoods. The highly visible roles of the elite in public ritual, in particular the recitation of prayers, served to construct and reinforce their political domination. Priests and magistrates performed as mediators between gods and citizens, and just as divine favor was necessary for continued prosperity of the state, so the religious services of the elite were represented as equally necessary.

Beyond reflecting and maintaining the traditional socio-political hierarchy, prayer could serve as a medium for initiating and legitimating change as well. The most obvious examples of this process are prayers surrounding the transition from republic to principate, which employed conventional formulae and presentation to lend an aura of tradition to innovative practices. One feature of the transition was the attribution to the ruler of a special divine gift of good fortune in war (*felicitas*). A major vehicle for representing this divine favor was the public thanksgiving for victory traditionally offered in the name of the victorious general, but under Julius Caesar and his successor in their names as well. Augustus' Secular Games also involved major modification of rituals and prayers to reflect the new era. As Putnam (2001: 98) has eloquently argued, the accompanying secular hymn incorporated numerous innovations, including a change of emphasis from apotropaic petition to preservation of the current state of blessing. In its ritual context, the hymn reflected the present period of civil harmony, but also served to legitimate Augustan rule by evoking divine favor toward the new state of affairs. A final example of the use of prayer to establish and support imperial rule is found in the annual prayers for the welfare of the emperor and his family, preserved in the Acts of the Arval Priesthood (see above). These are clearly modifications of republican prayers offered annually for the safety and prosperity of the state. Now, however, the state's welfare is represented as dependent on that of the emperor. The new prayers served to communicate this novel state of affairs but also, through the power of ritual, to establish it as convention.

Conclusions

While scholars of Roman religion have paid considerable attention to festivals and ritual acts, they have for the most part neglected the study of prayer in its own right. This neglect belies the significance of prayer in the actual practice of religion. Although sacrifice was certainly the heart of Roman ritual, sacrifice without prayer, as Pliny the Elder commented, was useless. Without words of prayer to identify the purpose of rituals, neither the divine recipients nor the human audience could understand what was happening. As in those mute paintings and relief sculptures, there would be no clue whether the intent was petition, oath, or thanksgiving. The term "supplication" (*supplicatio*) illustrates this problem well. The Romans used the same word to identify public days of prayer and offering for propitiation, expiation, and thanksgiving (Halkin 1953: 9–13). The only distinguishing factor was the content of the prayers of magistrates and people.

Prayers merit close attention not just to identify the immediate objective of a ritual but to gain insight into the mentalité of Roman religion. The content of prayers points to a predominant interest in the physical world of the here and now, not in a personal afterlife or morality. Prayers seek health and safety, success and prosperity. Furthermore, no area of life was devoid of prayers, from politics to war to family life. While cynics may question the religious quality of the public prayers of magistrates, literary texts and votive inscriptions attest the many aspects of private life where individuals sought divine aid: birth, illness, journeys, business. All these prayers demonstrate concerns about the lack of control and predictability of daily life, as well as a fundamental belief or hope in the power of supernatural beings to affect that condition. In addition, there is a noticeable anxiety before the great power of divinities for good or ill, seen in the variety of cautionary statements in vows and oaths.

The study of public prayers also contributes to the understanding of Roman society. They demonstrate the intermingling of religion with the political concerns of the elite. Similarities between issues voiced in official prayers and senatorial debates underscore that junction. The personalization of prayers, which spotlights the elite mediators of divine favor – magistrates, commanders, emperors – served to construct and preserve elite domination. Prayer could also bolster public morale in times of crisis and support optimism in good times. Public prayer thus met needs of both upper and lower classes. While spontaneous prayer at public temples provided an outlet for fear and joy, the institutionalization of that practice protected public order and focused attention on the beneficent and necessary role of the state's leaders.

Even more important than the need for more scholarly attention to the prayers themselves is that for a more integrated approach to the study of ritual, including both word and deed. For the most part, the tendency has been to divorce the study of prayer from the study of ritual actions, with prayer texts left behind for the dissection of philologists, while historians of Roman religion focus on the details of procession and sacrifice. Of course, this very chapter perpetuates the false dichotomization of speech and action. Such scholarly compartmentalization artificially separates elements originally fused. Thus an important direction for future research will be the reintegration of prayer into the study of Roman ritual.

It is good news that there has been in recent years a resurgence of scholarly interest in prayer. In 1997 there appeared under the auspices of the Society of Biblical Literature a critical anthology, including translations and commentaries of prayers from the Hellenistic world, directed primarily to students of classics and theology (Kiley 1997). In addition, a scholarly group in Strasburg formed to promote "Recherches sur les Rhétoriques Religieuses," directed by Freyburger and Pernot, has already published an anthology of Greco-Roman prayers with commentary and an analytical bibliography (2000) and further volumes. These texts provide an excellent starting point for future research and promise new projects on the near horizon. To conclude these prefatory comments as did Livy: "If it were our custom also, as it is for poets, we would gladly commence with good omens and vows and prayers to the gods and goddesses that they grant a propitious outcome to this considerable undertaking" (*Praefatio*, 13).

FURTHER READING

Appel (1909) is the fundamental collection of texts and citations of Roman prayers and their performance; Chapot and Laurot (2001) offers an extensive selection of texts with translation, brief commentary, and bibliography. Halkin (1953) is a comprehensive collection of gratulatory supplications together with detailed description of performance in the republican period. Alan Watson (1993) offers an analysis of fetial formulae for waging war and a comparison to legal procedure. A lexicographical study of the language of petitionary prayers is to be found in Hickson (1993). Versnel (1981b) addresses several questions including methods for making the gods listen to petitions and the rarity of prayers of thanksgiving.

CHAPTER EIGHTEEN

Music and Dance: Forms of Representation in Pictorial and Written Sources

Friederike Fless and Katja Moede

Music and dance are central elements of Roman religious rituals. Musicians like flute-players (*tibicines*) and lyre-players (*fidicines*) (figs. 18.1 and 18.3) take part in many processions and sacrifices. Players of brass instruments (*aeneatores*) (figs. 18.2 and 18.3), playing either horns (*cornicines*) or two different kinds of trumpets (*tubicines* and *liticines*), are in addition participants in both religious and military parades. Moreover, specialized musical instruments are reported for cults that were transferred from the Greek east, like the cult of Magna Mater (Cybele) or Isis: the cymbals (*kymbala*) and shallow drums (*tympana*) of the cult of Cybele and the rattles (*sistra*) of the Isis cult. The instruments dominated the outward perception of these cults so strongly that they came to symbolize the cults both in written and in depicted tradition.

Dance performances were also characteristic of many Roman cults. Ancient written sources claimed that especially armed dances had a long tradition dating back to the royal period. This is paralleled by the long tradition of flute-playing in cults. Music and dance were considered by ancient sources as traditional and noteworthy elements of Roman ritual, while being changed over time with the introduction of new cults. The potential of research to describe the specific qualities of music and dance in Roman culture is, however, limited. Neither the rhythm, melody, and sound of the instruments nor the choreography of the dances can be reconstructed for the different rituals. Our sources simply do not contain that kind of information, even though single instruments were either discovered or reconstructed after depictions.

Even if the religious-aesthetic dimensions of music and dance are not accessible to us, some specific questions such as the organization and social position of musicians and dancers can be examined. Furthermore, on the basis of the written and

Figure 18.1   Marble relief of a triumphal arch after the triumph of Marcus Aurelius in
AD 176. Rome, Musei Capitolini, Palazzo dei Conservatori (photo: Anderson, Fotothek des
Archäologischen Institutes der Freien Universität Berlin).

pictorial evidence, it is possible to describe for which sequences of rituals musicians
and dancers are mentioned. The analysis of the specific qualities of media like texts
and images could give an insight into the function, importance, and relevance of
music and dance for specific rituals. In the end, we know all rituals only through
the mirror of their contemporary representation.

Thus, this chapter will concentrate on the analysis of the transformation of elements of Roman ritual practice into written and pictorial representations. The function and importance of music and dance in the depiction of specific ritual sequences
can thereby be reconstructed. The inclusion and omission of certain elements of the
ritual in these different media are an expressive testimony to the specific perception
of the ritual and thereby also of music and dance as part of the ritual.

Figure 18.2 Marble relief of a triumphal arch after the triumph of Marcus Aurelius in AD 176. Rome, attic of Constantine's arch, south face (photo: Anderson, Fotothek des Archäologischen Institutes der Freien Universität Berlin).

Figure 18.3 Fragment of a marble frieze from the temple of Apollo Sosianus (c. 20 BC). Rome, Musei Capitolini, Palazzo dei Conservatori (photo: Roma, Musei Capitolini, Archivio Fotografico dei Musei Capitolini).

This chapter will be limited to the musicians and dancers directly involved in processions and rituals and reflected in monuments and sources from Rome itself. Cultic songs or music and dance as part of theatrical performances and musical contests will not be included, even if these were part of public cult, too. The focus of this chapter is a discussion of the forms of antique reflection on music and dance in ritual for a better understanding of the function of these elements in the rituals described.

Musicians and Dancers: Duties and Organization in Rome

Roman religion knew not one type of cult specialist who led or carried out the ritual actions, but a huge number of such people who were involved in the success of the ritual. One of those was the (cult) musician whose competence in playing his instrument was necessary for his ritual duties.

The cult musicians were organized in *collegia* comparable to the priesthoods. The oldest *collegium* among the musicians was that of the flutists, which was said to date back to the time of the second Roman king, Numa Pompilius (traditionally dated 716–673 BC). This was the high age of cultic flute-playing, which was supposed to have been adopted from the Etruscans. A common *collegium* of the flutists and the lyre-players is attested for the first time in the early second century AD, even if the musicians were already active together before. For *aeneatores* different forms of organization are known. There were military musicians, a *collegium* active in state cult, and another playing in funeral rituals.

Whereas the organization of cult musicians in *collegia* comparable to the *collegia* of priests seems to suggest a high social status, this is not necessarily the case. After all, people of different professional, religious, or social status were organized in *collegia*. For the *collegia* of cult musicians, however, a generally high reputation is reported. For instance, trumpet-players in public cult (*tubicines sacrorum publicorum populi Romani*) were considered priests (*sacerdotes viri speciosi*) according to some sources (Festus 482 L; Fless 1995: 85). Citizens, even knights, were members and office-holders in this *collegium* and were tasked to lustrate the trumpets at the celebration of the Tubilustrium. Flutists were allowed to have a meal on the Capitol in Rome and perform a procession.

The link of duties and reputation is especially well documented by a monument of the Roman emperor cult that was excavated in 1992–3 at the foot of the Palatine hill, toward the Colosseum (Friggeri 2001: 75–7). In a sacral area with a small, four-pillared temple, remains of two inscriptions were discovered. One (*CIL* 6.40334; *AE* 1996, 247) was found on the bronze covering of a base that once carried a statue of the later emperor Tiberius. Because of the titles mentioned in the inscription, the monument is dated before the adoption of Tiberius by Augustus, that is, before AD 4. The consecration of the monument was performed by the *[aeneator]es: tubicine[s] / [liti]cines, cornicines / Romani*. The same group of trumpet- and horn-players are also found as consecrators on the second inscription (*CIL* 6.40307; *AE* 1996, 248). Here also parts of a base are preserved, which shows how the *aeneatores* successively expanded and modified their consecratory function according to the political climate, in the time between the first Roman emperor Augustus and the last member of the Julio-Claudian dynasty, Nero. Even if the topographical situation of the region before the drastic changes in Rome after the fire of AD 64 made by Nero cannot be reconstructed, the location of this temple close to the political center of Rome documents the importance of the *collegium* that was able to erect such a monument for the emperor cult.

The organizational structure of dancers is less clear. Only the priests of the Salii and the Arval Brethren were organized in *collegia* (Estienne 2005; Scheid 2005d). Both priesthoods – and sources speak of a long tradition of these cults – performed dances in various rituals. During a ritual lasting several days and containing multiple elements, the Arval Brethren sang in a grove sacred to the Dea Dia a ceremonial song and danced the *tripudium*. This is documented by Livy (1.20.4) also for the Salii, who are involved in the service of Mars: Numa had instructed the Salii to carry the holy shields and to proceed through the city singing ceremonial songs and dancing in solemn *tripudium*. According to ancient authors the name "Salii" is derived from their activity, according to Varro (*Ling.* 5.85) *ab salitando*. The boys that performed the Lusus Troiae at the Campus Martius in Rome, however, often named as armed dancers in antique sources (Suet. *Caesar* 39), were part of a military-style organization.

Dancers are also documented in other contexts of the Roman public cult without any mention of their organization or socio-political position. Dionysius of Halicarnassus (7.72.5–10) describes in his *Roman Antiquities*, published in 7 BC, choirs of armed dancers and satyrs for the first *pompa circensis*, said to have taken place in 490 BC (see next section). The armed dancers might have been organized and appeared in military formation, just like the boys leading the procession of the *pompa circensis*. Dionysius (2.71.4) further mentions that armed dancers named *ludiones* or *lydiones* led the processions. He gives only conflicting information about the position of these dancers in the procession, but none of their organization.

The organization in *collegia* served first of all as a professionalization, guaranteeing a correct performance of the ritual. The ritual itself was defined by strict rules, on adherence to which rested the success or failure of the cult observations. Each part of the ritual needed to be performed perfectly, to fulfill the hopes and expectations connected with this sacrifice. The *collegia* not only guaranteed the correct performance of these acts through professional specialization, but also ensured the conservation and proliferation of the necessary knowledge. They offered a framework for the theoretical and practical education of these specialists. From this tradition probably stems the high self-esteem of the *collegia*, documented in monuments.

Translation of Rituals into Literary and Pictorial Representations

The fundamental problem in reconstructing the forms, functions, and significance of music and dance in Roman ritual rests with the characteristics and intentions of the sources that depict music and dance either in literature or in fine arts. Therefore there are quite a few contradictions between written and pictorial sources. One example of these contradictions is the armed dancers, called *ludiones* or *lydiones* in the context of the *pompa circensis* by various authors and the *pompa triumphalis* by Appian (*Libyke* 66). The armed dancers of the *pompa circensis* are described in detail by Dionysius of Halicarnassus (7.72.5–10):

> The Dancers were dressed in scarlet tunics girded with bronze cinctures, wore swords suspended at their sides, and carried spears shorter than average length; the men also had bronze helmets adorned with conspicuous crests and plumes. One man who gave the figures of the dance to the rest, taking the lead in representing their warlike and rapid movements, usually in the proceleusmatic rhythms, led each group. This also was in fact a very ancient Greek institution.

In pictorial representations of the *pompa triumphalis* and the *pompa circensis* there are quite a few figures that exhibit the features described for the armed dancers of literary tradition. However, similar figures occur in completely different contexts. For instance, figures equipped with shield, helmet, and a short lance or herald's staff (caduceus) depicted on coins are described by others as either heralds or dancers (Fless 1995: pl. 11, figs. 2–4; 2004: 39f., nos. 18–22, pl. 11, fig. Rom 21). Equipped with a short tunic, a shield, a staff, and no helmet, but displaying long hair, similar figures occur in depictions of triumphal processions and a procession honoring the tenth anniversary (*decennalia*) of Antonius Pius (Gnecchi 1912: 2. pl. 46, fig. 1; Fless 2004: 40, no. 22). The outfit of these figures closely resembles that of the bearers of incense burners and signs (*tituli*) (Fless 1995: pls. 7–8). Therefore these shield-bearers were interpreted as accompanying participants in the procession. Similar procession attendants are described in texts. For instance, *mastigophoroi* are mentioned as participants in the procession and stewards of the theater in an inscription found in Oinoanda in Asia Minor (Wörrle 1988: 11, l. 63–5; Fless 2004: 57, no. 128). They carry shields, confirming their function as armed custodians.

Regarding the written description of shield-bearers and its context, several interpretations are possible. One has to emphasize that none of the shield-bearers on official monuments is actually displayed dancing. This, however, does not necessarily mean that there is no pictorial formula for the representation of the armed dance. There is a long tradition of depicting armed dancers in Greek and Etruscan art that was adopted by the Romans (Shapiro et al. 2004: 314–17 (M. Lesky), 337–40 (K. Giannotta). Usually these armed dancers hold a shield in their raised left hand while carrying a weapon in the right and moving on tiptoe with an implied rotation. These armed dancers are especially found on monuments of decorative art dating from the early Roman imperial period, that is, decorated bases or other representations in relief (Schneider 1990). The fundamental methodological problem here is to decide whether those images represent correct portrayals of contemporary rituals or archaizing or historical imagination. The archaizing style of certain images, some iconographic peculiarities, and the specific context suggest separating those images of armed dancers from the so-called historical reliefs. It is a separate class of images that also contains dancing figures of Bacchic *thiasos*.

Why is a similar imagery absent from depictions of armed dancers in historical reliefs? The discrepancies between written function and visual representation of the Salii might represent a way to address this issue.

The prime task of the Salii in the cult is to carry the holy shields and to perform the sacred dance during a procession. Livy (10.20.4) uses the word *tripudium* to describe this dance in Latin, a term not used by the authors Plutarch and Dionysius of Halicarnassus (2.70–1), both writing in Greek. The Latin reader probably readily understood the meaning of this word and associated the appropriate form of movement with it. Livy (38.17) himself also uses this word in order to describe the war-like appearance of barbarians, characterized by war chants and *tripudium*. Roman authors refer to the Salii if they compare dances that involve stomping, or directly use the word *tripudium*.

Plutarch (*Numa* 13.4) writes that the Salii performed a lot of rotations and turnarounds with great strength and dexterity in a fast, vivacious rhythm. Dionysius of Halicarnassus (2.70–1) mentions that their dance is attended by "much leaping and capering" and compares it with the dance of Greek Curetes, thereby linking the dance of the Salii to the images and form of the Greek dance. The Latin word does not evoke the dexterity and vivaciousness of Plutarch's description, but a different form of dance. By the different forms of translation of the same dance into written language, associations with diverging aesthetic dimensions are created.

Independent of these nuances of the translation of this dance into texts, it has to be mentioned that the few visual representations usually identified as processions of the Salii generally depict males carrying multiple shields shaped like a figure eight on a pole (Schäfer 1980: figs. 20–4; Shapiro et al. 2004: 339, nos. 355–9, pl. 80). An actual dance, however, is never shown. There is, in accordance with the written description of Dionysius of Halicarnassus, an Augustan relief-fragment which displays the Salii's servants carrying shields on a pole and accompanied by *togati*, but no image of the dancing Salii, who were necessary to perform the ritual (Schäfer 1980: figs. 22–3; 1989: pl. 24, figs. 1–2). Could it be that the depiction of the dance itself was avoided, because the dance movement would contradict the conventions of a depiction of a ritual procession and the associated ideals of movement and connected values?

In countless procession images of the early Roman imperial period one can observe that while the different priests participating in the procession are depicted, they are not shown performing their characteristic rituals and not in their specific garb, but in the *toga* of a Roman citizen or official and walking gracefully (Kleiner 1992: figs. 71–80; Fless 2004: 52–3, no. 100, pl. 13, fig. 100). The Ara Pacis offers examples. Here, participants in rituals that require the presence of some or all priesthoods are depicted, but not the performance of the ritual of all these priesthoods. Furthermore, in Roman images priests and their function are usually referred to by showing the specific sacral instruments (*instrumenta sacra*). The relief fragment containing the procession of the Salii was part of the decorated official chair (*sella curulis*) of a Roman official. Both facets of the official functions of the man for whom the monument was erected were visualized. The procession points to his function as a priest, the *sella* to his function as a magistrate. Both are positive elements, indicating the social rank of this person.

All this, however, does not explain the absence of the typical dance of the Salii. Images of processions, independent of the medium, usually combine dynamic and static elements, standing and walking figures. This is demonstrated by a relief fragment displaying parts of a triumphal procession (fig. 18.3 above; Fless 1995: pl. 10, fig. 2; 2004: 48, no. 72). Next to striding *tibicines* and a *fidicen* standing facing almost directly outward are captured barbarians walking and shield-bearers standing facing outward. These shield-bearers are striking in their motionlessness. This combination of standing and striding figures allows the combining of visual prerequisites: the clear presentation of figures and their attributes (as in the shield-bearers) and the demonstration of the movement of the procession. Rapid movements only rarely occur in these depictions, emphasizing the passing of the procession and thereby strengthening the impression of authenticity in the eye of the beholder. This holds true for images like the relief displaying war booty of the Arch of Titus, depicting the passing through the triumphal arch and evoking a sense of movement (Kleiner 1992: fig. 155; Fless 2004: 49, no. 78). The bearers of burdens on the Arch of Titus and the rest of the Salii's procession on the relief fragment are depicted in profile and in slightly bowed posture. The absence of the dance movement seems to be in accord with ancient visual conventions.

In images, standing or graceful striding is usually emphasized. In literary sources, time is an important facet of the characterization of procession participants. Hastiness and rushing at the *adventus*, that is, the ceremonial of the arrival of the emperor in Rome, are negatively noticed in the case of Vitellius (Tacitus, *Histories* 2.89.1). By contrast the serenity and quietude of Trajan – he adapted his pace to the mass of spectators – were noted positively by Pliny (*Panegyricus* 23.3). In both sources speed was used to characterize the emperors and their behavior during the ritual, one positively and one negatively. Similarly the specific visual representation of the emperor in the ritual has the purpose of demonstrating the correct and ideal performance of the ritual, by presenting a dignified movement and a focus on the actions of the emperor. The depiction of a dance with fast rhythm or excessive gestures is not exactly suitable to emphasize the qualities of dignity and serenity. This might be strengthened by the apparently ambivalent position of Romans toward dance in various sources. Dance is a traditional and central element of Roman cult that is viewed positively. However, there are also more critical appraisals of dance, for instance the Christian apologist Lactancius (*Instutiones* 1.21.45: *qui inhonesto saltatu tripudiant*) criticizes not only Roman religion, but also dance and *tripudium* in particular. Furthermore, there is a lot of critique concerning dance outside the framework of cult. The avoidance of depicting dance as a form of movement in processions which are mentioned in literary sources as containing dances might be linked to a sense of inadequacy when it comes to depicting the movements of a dance in a Roman cult. Other images were deemed more significant to the intended message. This may be confirmed by the exceptions that actually depict dancers.

More extreme dance movements in the context of public cult are probably depicted on a fragment of a frieze in the Palazzo degli Conservatori in Rome (Ronke 1987: fig. 43). It contains four figures dressed in either a *tunica* or a high-girded toga dancing with wide steps and gestures and a rotating movement. These images are probably part of a larger frieze depicting a procession. Because of the ornament completing this frieze block, one can imagine a monument comparable to the triumphal frieze of the temple of Apollo Sosianus (fig. 18.3 above; Kleiner 1992: 84, figs. 63–4; Fless 2004: 48, no. 74). However, it remains unresolved to which ritual this dance is related. The image demonstrates the typical form of recording a dance in a bowed, gesture-rich choreography, which we can find in other genres, such as murals or stucco reliefs or reliefs found in rural cities outside of Rome. There dancing figures are part of the imagery even in reliefs from an official context. They are found in numerous images of magisterial and sacral acts characterized by a specific mode of depiction that varies from that of official monuments of the city of Rome.

A relief of a monumental tomb from the early Roman imperial period in Chieti (Kleiner 1992: 148–9, fig. 124; Schäfer 1989: cat. C 53, pl. 106, fig. 1, pl. 122) depicts a scene that at first in its symmetrical structure and its frontality reminds one of late antique tribunal scenes, such as the small frieze of the Arch of Constantine in Rome (Kleiner 1992: 444, figs. 406–13). The symmetrical structure suggests the order and concentration of the participants in such an official act, which contains elements not only of a tribunal scene but also of a funeral procession, such as musicians and mourners. This impression is disrupted if the scene is observed more in detail. The symmetrical order is dissolved into numerous groups of figures that, wrapped in conversation, seem to turn from the event, moving quite vigorously and gesticulating wildly. The figures appear almost loquacious and un-concentrated. This narrative tool is also used in the imagery of boisterous, almost dancing movements in processions, such as in the depiction of an entry into a theater in a relief from Castel S. Elia (Ronke 1987: figs. 15–19; Schäfer 1989: cat. C 59, pl. 103, fig. 1) and of the cult of Isis on a relief from Arriccia (Rüpke 2001: 103, fig. 10; De Angelis d'Ossat 2002: 266f.). The latter depicts dancing men and women using rattles. The women are shown in movement, bending their knees, thrusting out their buttocks, turning around, waving their arms in the air with extensive gestures, and with heads thrown back.

The pictorial representation of dance as part of Roman ritual seems to depend on the context and specific type of the imagery. Depictions of rituals on monuments in the city of Rome mostly refrain from showing dance, since the specific intention of these monuments stands in contrast to the imagery of rituals. Here the intention is the depiction of significant moments, the visualization of the ritually correct sequence of events, and a graceful representation of the participants.

Another form of translation of ritual is documented by the illustrations of sacrifices at the altar (e.g. fig. 18.1 above). They demonstrate first of all how closely the Roman sacrificial ritual was linked with music. This is demonstrated in well-known archaeological images, if one remembers how often *tibicines* are displayed standing behind the altar. If the image is not combined with elaborate and expansive ritual sequences, the representation of a religious ritual is usually limited to the central act at the altar. The basic elements of this depiction are the *togatus capite velato* at the altar or tripod performing the sacrifice. Sometimes assistants holding the *acerra* or bringing tankards and cups to the altar support him. If both assistants are omitted, *tibicines* behind or next to the altar are always part of the scene. These images demonstrate that the double flute played by the *tibicen* must have been the most important instrument of Roman cult. They also show that the sacrifice itself was closely linked – both temporally and spatially – to the musical accompaniment. This fact is strengthened by literary sources. Here flute-players are mentioned time and again in context with sacrifices of wine and incense; the musician is standing behind or next to the altar. In order to describe this, Pliny uses in his *Naturalis historia* (22.11) the formula that is fixed in Roman literature: . . . *immolasse ad tibicinem foculo posito.*

The imagery is at the same time universal and specific. If it appears on an altar, consecrated in the sanctuary of a god, there is no doubt that the sequence depicted was part of the ritual honoring the specific god. The specific meaning was gained either through the inscription or through the context of installation. The image itself, however, was multi-functional; it could adequately represent the ritual in different circumstances. The sacrifice on the altar itself was a ritual necessity, while processions and feasts could be performed with different degrees of extravagance or not performed at all. Altar, sacrificing *togatus capite velato*, and *tibicen* are therefore the most basic, universally valid image of ritual action. They could be used to represent all religious rituals containing the sacrifice at the altar as a central element. At the same time, this depiction doubtless underlines the importance of music in the form of flute-playing in this phase of the ritual (Suet. *Tiberius* 70.6). The musician is even part of this reduced imagery of religious action. A sacrificial ritual without music was unimaginable to the ancient creator or beholder of these images.

More detailed depictions of ritual action are possible. A pre-sacrifice was to be performed at more elaborate animal sacrifices. In its ritual sequence it corresponds to the libation, the pouring of liquids. Thus, their visual representation is the same. By the inclusion of cult personnel, sacrificial animals, and other elements the altar scene is stretched out into the phase of the actual animal sacrifice. Because of this combination of non-synchronous ritual sequences, such universal images become the characteristic representations of Roman rituals. The peculiarities of visual art made it necessary to amalgamate non-synchronous moments of a coherent sequence into one unified scene. The contemporary beholder was able to relate the elements to the ritual sequence familiar to him. Thus, unlike modern viewers, he was not tempted to view these images as documentation of an actual performance of the ritual.

What was the function of the flute-player? One has once more to resort to literary sources: Pliny (*Nat.* 28.11) assigned the ability of drowning out all disturbing noise by his play to the *tibicen*. Thereby the function of the flute-player could correspond to the function of the herald, requiring silence at the beginning of the sacrifice. Besides the fact that, apparently, the flute-player did not play during the whole time of the ritual, as is confirmed by images uniting non-synchronous moments of the cult, there is another problem in the tradition.

Flute-playing was said to have been introduced during the early Roman royal period, a time beyond written record. Pliny, however, explains this element of the ritual five hundred years later. Is Pliny's explanation valid for the time of origin or can it serve as a general model for all those five hundred years?

In any case, Pliny offered an explanation plausible for his time. Such a procedure is well attested for authors of the late republic or early Roman empire, who, with great antiquarian scholarship, offered new explanations for old rituals or even created a specific meaning for a ritual with their explanation. Therefore we should do better to concentrate on the structuring and aesthetic function of the elements of the ritual.

Function of Music and Dance in Structuring the Ritual and Creating Emotions

Discrepancies between visual and written depictions are the result of the mode of visualization and the basic difference of the media text and image. While texts allow the description of a sequence of events, images compose what seems to be only a snapshot of a moment. Written descriptions can be very detailed in the description of the temporal structure of an event, while an image produces a definite accent, marks unequivocally the main protagonists and items, even if it does not say anything about the temporal sequence of events.

The complexity of rituals in general makes their reproduction in imagery quite difficult. On the other hand, the complex structure allows a variety of forms that can be used to visualize a ritual and its sequences. It is almost impossible to generate a narrative within a single picture. Because of this, specific markers, which definitely describe a situation and are linked to a ritual or ritual sequence, are needed. The phenomenology of religion determined certain repetitive basic elements within the variety of religious activities that can be considered atoms of the ritual. These may be objects or actions that are the core of a simple ritual or generate in combination the sequence of events of a more complex ritual. According to Wallace (1966; see also Cancik and Mohr 1988), in addition to gestures of touching, sacrifices, sermons, prayers, repeated washing, and specific clothing and posture, songs and chants, dances and music are important elements of religious rituals. These elements have an important role in structuring and generating the rhythm of a ritual. The specific elements of a ritual demonstrate to the participant, or to the beholder of a depiction of a ritual, which phase of the ritual is presented. For the participant, the continuous sequence of events has to be structured into discernible units so that he can identify the different ritual actions and adapt his behavior accordingly. Music and dance are here important indicators, since clear accents in sound and movement can introduce a new phase of the ritual. On the other hand, these elements can evoke and control emotions, describing the character of the ritual to the beholder.

Both aspects are found in depictions of religious rituals in ancient Roman art. Pictures of the Roman triumph show clearly how music was used to mark an event and to draw the attention of the viewer. In modern analysis of the Roman triumph the political aspects are usually considered in great detail; however, it is easily forgotten that the Roman triumph is first and foremost a religious ritual, whose prime sacral purpose was the fulfillment of the *vota* before the start of the war on the Capitol. In its depictions the religious aspect of the Roman triumph was made unequivocally clear. This starts in the selection of sequences that was captured in the image. Quite often only the sequence of the procession is found in the images. No other sequence

characterizes a ritual more clearly. According to literary sources, a triumphal procession can be subdivided into three greater sections. The first section moves in front
of the *triumphator* and illustrates the victory (e.g. Josephus, *Jewish War* 7.5–6). Here
loot and arms, but also images of the landscape and conquered cities of the enemy,
were displayed. The battle sequences and the display of the enemy's generals to give
the audience an impression of the battle must have been an especially spectacular
sight. The sacrificial animals followed, white bulls that were to be sacrificed to Iuppiter
at the Capitol. They marked the end of the first section.

The carriage of the *triumphator* made up the second section of the procession,
immediately following the sacrificial animals. The carriage was led by *lictores* in red
coats, carrying *fasces* entwined with laurel. They, together with the officials, marked
the border between first and second sections and announced the victor.

In the third section the soldiers followed in military formation. They were decorated with laurel, unarmed, and displaying their military decorations. They must have
brought an acoustic element to the spectacle, since they sang either mocking or
praising songs about their general.

Various visual stimuli competed for the attention of the spectator. Acoustic signals,
coming from the trumpets leading and accompanying the procession, gave contour
and structure to the event. One example here is the frieze of the so-called temple of
Apollo Sosianus (fig. 18.3 above; Kleiner 1992: 84–6, figs. 63–4; Fless 2004: 48,
no. 71). Here, the barbarians carried on *fercula* and the decorated sacrificial animals
following clearly indicate that this frieze represents a triumphal procession, although
the whole procession is not conserved. The two different groups – vanquished enemies and sacrificial animals – are separated by a trumpet-player. An Antonine relief
panel in the Palazzo dei Conservatori with a depiction of a triumphal procession
also clearly shows that a single pictorial unit of the *pompa triumphalis* may be accompanied by a musician (Kleiner 1992: 288–301, fig. 261). On the rectangular field,
the triumphal procession is limited to the *triumphator* on his *quadriga*. Contrary to
the first example, neither sacrificial animals nor subjugated enemies are part of the
image. Only a trumpet-player strides in front of the *quadriga*, announcing the
triumphator while passing the arch with his music. Numerous examples of Roman
historical reliefs could be cited, confirming this specific use of music in depiction of
Roman ritual. The so-called Altar of the *Vicomagistri* (Kleiner 1992: 147, fig. 122),
however, confirms, while the specific ritual depicted in this monument remains
unclear, that music was not only used during the ritual of triumph. In this monument as well, a religious procession is depicted, in which different groups are separated by powerfully playing musicians. Three trumpet-players lead the procession
of sacrificial animals and priests even here, clearly marking the following sacral unit
of the procession.

In images the musician functions as a marker to the beholder delineating a new
or specific part of the procession. In reality they probably had a similar function of
structuring and accentuating the procession. According to written sources, the display of subjugated enemies resulted in an emotional response of the audience that
included mockery and vituperation. It is probable that a musician would follow
this part of a procession. His playing would silence the shouts from the spectators,

drawing the audience to the following sacrificial animals and evoking a more appropriate, sacral, and solemn behavior.

The musicians' role, however, was not alone that of structuring the ritual and of calling attention, according to the sources. The music also evoked a certain mood, as described for the triumphal procession of Aemilius Paulus by Plutarch (*Aemilius Paulus* 32.2–34.4): "On the third day, as soon as it was morning, trumpeters led the way, sounding out no marching or processional strain, but such a one as the Romans use to rouse themselves to battle."

Only a few sources, however, describe the mood associated with music. One exception is the procession for Isis in Apuleius' *The Golden Ass* or *Metamorphoses* (11.2–16). In this text from the second century AD, Lucius, turned into an ass, is in a heightened emotional state because of the expectation of his impending re-transformation into a human. Therefore he experiences the prospect of redemption very vividly. The music and explicitly plastic description of the exotic procession serve to literarily describe an emotional state, which fulfills a specific function in the text, but also allows a glimpse of the aesthetic quality of such a procession. Apuleius (*Met.* 11.9) tries to generate a visual and acoustic image of such a procession in his reader: "After that sounded the musical harmony of instruments, pipes and flutes in most pleasant measure. Then came a fair company of youth appareled in white vestments and festal array, singing both meter and verse with a comely grace."

Equally expressive are texts that use music in cults as comparison. Cultic music is used to describe the mood in non-cultic events. The Augustan poet Propertius (2.7.11–12) mentions that a *tibia*, used to serenade a loved one, sounded more mournful than *tibicines*. His contemporary Horace characterizes in his first book of satires (6.42ff.) one Novius, who has won an election because he shouted louder than the horns and tubas of three funeral processions.

Roman literature uses the qualities of music and musical instruments in rituals as a metaphor. Cult music was a suitable encapsulation, because it was known to everyone and had a fixed form. Something similar can be observed for dance. The *tripudium* of ritual can be used as a reference in literature to describe completely different dances and their impact.

This utilization of the music and dance of Roman ritual in literature causes one of the basic methodological problems of modern research. For Romans, the rituals accompanied by music and dance were – thanks to their constant repetition – part of daily life, and structured the spatial impression of the city and the temporal experience of the year according to the festival calendar. Year after year the city was filled with rituals accompanied by music and dance – either in processions moving through the city during specific festivities, or in cultic performances at the various temples. Music, in all rituals, formed an acoustic background, the forms of which were widely heard and engraved in the memory of every Roman, and could thereby be used as a reference in literature. Dance, effectively disrupting the ideal of solemn and graceful walking, could only be observed by actual spectators. Both elements, together with the burning or distribution of scents, the illumination and decoration of the procession path or the cultic place, and the decoration of the participants, formed an aesthetic framework for the ritual. Not all facets of this performative aspect of the ritual are suitable for a visual representation of a ritual or for a written description.

FURTHER READING

A recent treatment of the topic is given by the contributions in Brulé and Vendries (2001) for the Greco-Roman world; Péché and Vendries (2001), like Baudot (1973), concentrates on the Roman world. Wille (1967) offers a more synchronic account of Roman music, based on the literary sources. Fless (1995) and Moede (2004) analyze and present the evidence on Roman reliefs.

CHAPTER NINETEEN

Sacrifices for Gods and Ancestors

John Scheid

Sacrifice was at the heart of most acts of cult worship. Depending on the context and on the divinities being honored, there was great variety in the way a sacrifice was performed, in its use of incense, liquid libations, vegetal offerings, or animal victims. The particulars of a sacrifice were equally influenced by the ritual context of all the great religious ceremonies.

The Sacrificial Rite

Sacrifices took place in an open space, in front of the community concerned. In the realms of civic worship, it was celebrated in front of the temple, near a raised altar within the cult space. In the domestic setting, this altar, either permanent or temporary, was installed in one of the communal spaces of the house, the *atrium* or the peristyle. By contrast, for sacrifices of divination and *defixiones*, which were intended to be secret, more isolated, unfrequented surroundings were sought, either a remote area or a burial site. The sacrifice was offered by those who held authority within that particular community: the father, as head of the family, in the domestic sphere, the head (*magister*) of a college, the annual magistrates, or the public priests within a city. The sacrificer was assisted by freeborn young men, porters, and slaves who took charge of the practical arrangements.

Whether it concerned the public religion or private cults, the sacrifice usually began at the start of the civic day, at sunrise, on the edge of the cult area. By contrast, sacrifices considered "magic" were celebrated at night, far from all civic participation. The sacrificers and assistants bathed or washed themselves beforehand. In the "Roman," that is, "traditional," version of the rite, the official dress was the toga, which indicated a citizen, draped in such a way as to leave the arms free and form a kind of hood or veil covering the head (*cinctus Gabinus*; see Dubourdieu 1986). In the "Greek" ritual, the sacrificer was bare-headed and often wore a laurel wreath. The animal victims, always domestic animals (cattle, sheep, swine, more rarely goats), were washed, dressed with ribbons and bands of wool in either white or scarlet, their horns gilded and sometimes decorated with a disc (in the case of cattle), while the backs of pigs and cattle were covered with a fringed coverlet (*dorsuale*; see Krause 1931: fig. 12.4).

In the Roman ritual, the male gods received castrated male animals (with the exception of Mars, Neptune, Janus, and the *Genius*), and the goddesses received female victims (see Krause 1931). The age of the victim varied according to the social status of those making the sacrifice and the hierarchy among the divinities. In principle, adult victims were more suitable for public worship. The gods above received white victims, those below or connected with the night received victims with dark hides, while Vulcan and Robigo received red. In certain sacrifices to Tellus or Ceres, pregnant cows were offered. Sows were generally used in cases of expiation or funerary rituals. Other animals were used for special rites, like the horse in the *October equus* (October 15), the dog in the Robigo sacrifice (April 25), or the white cockerel in the cult of Aesculapius. Remains found on altars in Pompeii and some scholarly records tell us that birds and fish were equally likely. In the domestic context, other kinds of victims could be used according to family custom. Finally, for sacrifices associated with ritual spells, the ingredients varied according to the aim and the particulars of the rite, in which exoticism always played a part.

Fruit, grain, or dairy offerings were carried by assistants in baskets, liquid offerings in jugs, and incense in boxes. We do not know how the offerings of produce were selected and prepared. They could include, for example, spelt (*far*), barley-meal porridge (*polenta*), leavened bread, dry figs, cheeses, spelt porridge (*alica*), sesame, and oil. A salted flour called *mola salsa*, which was used in most public sacrifices, was prepared by the Vestal Virgins for the Lupercalia (February 15), the Vestalia (June 9) and the Ides of September (September 13; see C. Koch 1932). We do not know if the *mola* prepared by the Vestals was used in all sacrifices, or just in the public sacrifices in Rome. We know almost nothing about the particulars of public sacrifice in the colonies and *municipia*, since texts on this topic, describing the precise manner of the rites, are few. Therefore, the presumption that the ritual there was the same as that in Rome is pure conjecture. The gradual elucidation of this question now rests with archaeological study.

Once the preparations were in order, a procession made its way toward the altar of the divinity to be honored. Surrounded by his assistants, the sacrificer approached the altar. The sacrifice began with the sound of a flute, sometimes also a lyre. It started with the offering of incense and wine in the fire of a circular, portable hearth (fig. 19.1). The hearth used to transmit the offering to the deity represented, to some extent, the identity of the person performing the sacrifice, and so too the community involved. We do not know what the rituals were for lighting the altar fires. On the whole, the sources do not specify which divinities were honored in this opening ritual (the verb used is *praefari*). In the sacrificial instructions of Cato, the preliminary libation is addressed to Jupiter, Janus, and Vesta while in other cases,

Figure 19.1 Initial libation at a portable altar (so-called Altar of Angera, Scott Ryberg no. 101, *ThesCRA* 1, pl. 48, no. 105) (photo: by permission of the Civiche Raccolte Archeologiche e Numismatiche del Commune di Milano).

we see that the divinity concerned with the sacrifice is also included. The rite was doubtless addressed to a number of interested divinities, from which those sacrificing sometimes extracted a particular figure that was more directly relevant. We might suppose that it involved a summary of the rites which were to follow, by which the intention was also expressed. As such, libation is one of the key subjects in images of sacrifice, and comes to signify "*pietas*."

After this introductory ritual, the sacrificer proceeded to the immolation (*immolatio*) of the victim (see Latte 1914). In the "Roman" rite, he scattered the back of the victim with salted flour (*mola salsa*, from which the term *in-molatio* is derived), pouring a small amount of wine on the animal's forehead, and, finally, passed the knife over its back. From the prayers that accompanied immolation and the comments of Roman scholars, we can conclude that this ritual signified the consecration of the victim. In the "Greek" variant of the ritual, the sacrificer sprinkled water over the victim, cut a hair from its brow, and scattered the animal with cereal grains (*ritus Graecus*; Scheid 1995, 2005c: 87–122). With these exchanges complete, the sacrificer gave the order to a ritual executioner to "act" (*agere*). In the case of cattle, this meant stunning the animal then bleeding it. Smaller animals simply had their throats cut. In theory, the victim was required to show its consent, usually by nodding its head, and it was often attached to a halter running through a ring at the base of the altar, so its head could make, with the aid of the sacrificer, the gesture of acquiescence. All signs of fear and panic by the victim, as well as any disturbance, were not allowed during the ceremony, since they were regarded as unfavorable *omina*.

With their throats cut, the animals were turned onto their backs and opened up. With the help of his assistants, especially the *haruspex*, the sacrificer confirmed that the offering had been accepted by the divinity (see Bouché-Leclercq 1882: 862, 893ff.). The god's approval (*litatio*) was signified by the normal appearance of the *exta*, which, at the end of the republican period, were seen as comprised of five internal organs: the liver, the lungs, the gall-bladder, the peritoneum, and the heart. If the sacrifice was approved, the rites continued. If the *exta* contained any abnormalities, the sacrifice was annulled and the rites had to start over again with other victims (*instaurare*), and possibly repeated until approval was obtained (*usque ad litationem*). In certain types of sacrifice, the *exta* were inspected, following the Etruscan practice, in order to make predictions of the future (*haruspicatio*).

The Offering and the Banquet

Once this stage was completed, the victim was divided up. The parts due to the divinity (the *exta*, the vital organs) were set aside to cook in a pot (in the case of cattle victims) or roasted on a spit (sheep and pigs). It was for this reason that the temples always contained a kitchen area. After cooking, the sacrificer turned out the divine portion, duly sprinkled with *mola salsa* and wine, onto the sacrificial fire which burned on the altar. Offerings to aquatic deities were plunged in water. Those for chthonic deities (for example, the Lares) or those connected with the Underworld, were thrown onto the ground, where they were cooked on the earth or in a ditch. All of these gestures were accompanied by prayers which explicitly stated who was making the offering, who was receiving it, and who would reap the reward for the ritual; thus, in public sacrifices, the prayer always contained the formula "for the Roman people" (Paul. *Fest.* 59 L).

Sacrificial rites were often much more complicated than these basic gestures. The offering could include other parts of the victim; and some of the offering could be cooked in a more elaborate way and laid out on a table inside the temple. These additional elements should be seen in relation to the ritual of *lectisternium* (Nouilhan 1989). In this ritual, the statues of the gods or of their attributes were placed on dining couches in order to "consume" the ritual offerings on the table before them, while the goddesses "dined" seated in chairs (*sellisternium*; see Schnegg-Köhler 2002: 34–42 and commentaries). This method of celebration became more widespread, and from around the first century AD appeared in a more simplified form as the permanent display of padded couches (*puluinaria*) in the majority of public temples. It is from this period that we also find in temples the tables on which the additional offerings were made.

Thanks to the instructions of the *Fratres Arvales*, we know that the banquet for the divinity was sometimes more elaborate. It involved, at least on certain occasions, two courses (*mensae*); a meat course and a second course of sweetened wine and cake, in the manner of a *symposium*, during which the statue of the divinity was crowned and daubed with perfume (Scheid 1990: 623–30). If it is presumed that, in the cult space and ritual practices, one deity was often associated with other divinities, and that parts of the "banquet," perhaps those that came from the additional sacrifices (with victims of an inferior status), were offered to the divine guests of the titular deity of the place, then we may also suppose that a sacrifice took a good deal longer than the laconic formulae of the epigraphic or historical documents might often suggest. During this phase of the sacrifice, the officials consumed nothing (Scheid 2004). The divinity was always the first to receive her share of the sacrificial offering and did this either alone or with divine companions. During these proceedings, the sacrificer, his aides, and other assistants had to wait. In certain cases, the communities (for example priests, or even the Roman senate during the votive sacrifices at the beginning of the year) made use of this waiting period by organizing discussions concerning the cult or decisions to be taken within that particular group (for example, the election of the president of the sacerdotal college or the preparation of the formula for new vows to be announced after the completion of the votive sacrifices).

When the sacrificial offering had been consumed by the flames, thrown into a stream, or disposed of in a pit, the rest of the victim was touched by the sacrificer and so rendered fit for human consumption. The same procedure held for liquid offering and, without doubt, for offerings of produce (porridge, cakes, bread, etc.). Through these gestures, the sacrificer announced that he was not consuming a sacred food, but one that the divinity had, in a sense, agreed to share with him, or had granted to him, according to the principle of reciprocal gift-giving between men and gods. We see, however, that in minor sacrifices, offered in the course of a meal, the order was reversed: in such cases, it was the gods who received a share of the mortals' food (see below).

The victims offered to the gods of the Underworld were burnt up completely (holocaust), since the living could not share food with the patron divinities of the world of the dead. "Magic" sacrifices, offered in order to influence a divinity, often employed holocaust, since they were generally aimed at Underworld gods. In light of the particular results expected from these rites, the offerings and the general context differed from those of the everyday rituals.

The consumption of meat (accompanied by bread and mixed wine), or of liquid offerings, by those performing the sacrifice presents a complex problem, since there was a vast array of different procedures. The single overriding principle which governed sacrificial banquets was that of hierarchy and privilege. Those overseeing and carrying out the sacrifice generally ate their share straightaway, at community expense. During certain festivals, executive groups banqueted at public expense (*publice*) in particular cult spaces. And so, at the time of the *Epulum Iouis*, the great sacrifice to the Capitoline triad on September 13 and November 13, the senators took part in a sacrificial banquet on the Capitol, under the gaze of the three divinities of the Capitoline temple. For those participants not in a privileged position, the rules were different. With few exceptions – for example, at the altar of Hercules – most citizens did not take part in "public" sacrificial banquets held at public expense. No doubt they had to buy their share, either during the rite itself or from the butcher, unless a benefactor offered them some of the meat and the bread and wine that went with it. At many of the public sacrifices in Rome, there was room only for a banquet restricted to the celebrants. In smaller communities, for example the immediate neighborhood, the college, or the family, the relationship between sacrifice and banquet was more immediate: the sacrifice that was offered was eaten there and then, or at least divided and distributed in order to be taken away, or its equivalent value in money. Sacrifices at the Great Altar of Hercules, in the Forum Boarum, were unusual. They began, like all sacrifices, in the morning and included a first banquet bringing together the sacrificers, and perhaps also the senators (at least on the major occasion, August 12). In the evening, a second banquet took place, to which all citizens, with the exception of women, were invited. These banquets were famous, since none of the meat from the sacrifice was allowed to remain at the end of the day, and none of it could be removed from the cult precinct.

One particular, but very common type of sacrifice was that offered during a public or private meal. Between the first and second course, incense and wine were offered, along with a share of the banquet or other special offerings. This sacrifice was probably the most common of those performed in the domestic context. At all banquets, a sacrifice of this type was addressed to the Lares, to the Penates, and, from the first century BC onward, to the *Genius Augusti*. These sacrifices clearly highlight the connection between the ritual and food: the sacrificers reclined on dining couches (*triclinia*) during the offering, and shared their banquet with the gods.

During certain special rituals like the great *lectisternia* that were introduced in Rome in 399 BC, all the heads of household would celebrate banquets in their homes, to which they invited neighbors and passers-by: in this way they proclaimed their hospitality, which they also offered to the gods they were intending to thank or appease. A sacrificial meal seems to have been required in the cult of Mithras in the imperial period, because the locations designed for Mithraic cult practice appear in the form of a large *triclinium* with an altar at the far end. The initiates banqueted, and water and bread were offered as well as wine. The blood sacrifice was almost certainly performed outside the ritual "cavern." Recent studies of a *mithraeum* have begun to uncover the first remains of these sacrifices and banquets (see Martens 2004a, 2004b; R. Turcan 1980, 1989: 227–34). From what we know, a part of the public rites celebrated during the *Ludi Megalenses*, in honor of the Great Mother (April 4–10) consisted of closed banquets: the great families of Rome formed sodalities in order to dine, no doubt with the goddess, on the festival's high day, April 4, at great banquets called *mutitationes* ("dinner invitations"). Besides the *mutitationes*, a magistrate offered a public sacrifice. "Phrygian" sacrifices performed by the goddess's own priests will not be discussed here.

We know that the cult worship of Syrian gods involved sacrifices, but we do not know how these were performed. In light of certain religious regulations, we might suppose that they included rules for particular levels of purity. Judging from the equipment found in cult spaces sacred to Isis, it appears that sacrifice was performed there too. We also know of libations of water and offerings of incense. But the details of the services are largely unknown. In the case of all the cults imported to Rome, the processions and spectacular rituals of *ecstasis* and self-mutilation are better attested in the sources than the sacrificial rites are, most probably because these practices did not deviate to any great extent from the traditional Roman sacrifices.

Human sacrifice is not entirely unheard of in Rome. As part of a ritual repeated several times in the course of the last two centuries of the republic, Roman authorities offered to the gods of the Underworld representatives of the enemies of the Roman people: a pair of Greeks and a pair of Gauls, who were buried alive. It was in a similar manner that Romans solemnly dedicated besieged towns to the gods of the Underworld, or even, in the private sphere, with the rituals of *defixio*, their personal enemies. These examples clearly show that, on occasion, the Romans resorted to human sacrifice in order to shift the balance in the relationship between mortals and immortals, by granting to the latter absolute power over other mortals.

Great sacrificial liturgies often concluded with games (*ludi*), either theatrical performances or circus races, which often bore the name of the festival. And so the Roman Games or the Plebeian Games were in fact the conclusion to the *Epulum Iovis*. According to the sources, the *epulum* of Jupiter was preceded by nine days of theatrical *ludi* and followed by four days of chariot racing in the Circus Maximus.

Current archaeology has begun to bring to light the remains of sacrificial rituals (Legouilloux 2000 (Hecatomb in Paestum); Jouin and Méniel 2001; M. Robinson 2002; Van Andringa 2003). Interpreting these finds is not always easy, and the difference between the remains of banquets and of sacrificial offerings is still difficult to distinguish on the ground. But already new questions are being raised, and stages of development are becoming apparent, for example in the Celtic provinces where sacrificial practices seem to have changed during the Roman period, from disposing of victims' remains in pits to burning parts of the animal on an altar.

The Interpretation of Sacrifice

According to ancient sources, the offerings made in the course of the initial libation of a sacrifice, the incense and unmixed wine, were closely connected with the nature of the gods. The act of offering was one of reverence, the incense to the immortality and supremacy of the gods, the wine to their divine sovereignty. By doing so, the sacrificers ritually proclaimed the immortality and superiority of the gods. It was, therefore, primarily a sacrificial ritual which did not involve the *sharing* of food. In a sense, it involved offering to the gods the food which was reserved for them. Because of this, a libation of incense and wine could constitute an act of worship in itself.

In times of danger or celebration, for example after a victory, Romans, wearing wreaths and carrying laurel branches, made a tour of the cult sites with their wives and children, in order to "supplicate" the gods. They threw themselves on their knees before them in order to beseech or thank them, in a manner indicating their submission. Incense and wine were offered and matrons knelt down to sweep the steps of the temples with their hair. This supplication dramatized the initial ritual of libation at a sacrifice, which was a solemn address to the gods, extending it, in a spectacular and "realist" way, to all the gods in Rome.

The study of known rituals (which is generally concerned with public rites), ritual vocabulary, and those comments gleaned from ancient sources show that Roman sacrifice was, to ancient eyes, first and foremost, a banquet. To sacrifice was to eat with the gods, conforming to the principles of reciprocity which governed ancient society. To sacrifice was to divide food into two parts, one of which was returned to the gods, the other given to mortals. A sacrifice established and represented, through the sharing of food between gods and men, the superiority and immortality of the former and the mortality and pious submission of the latter. The traditional Roman sacrifice did not commemorate a particular event (as, for example, some rites of Ceres, Mithraic sacrifice, or the Christian Mass), it did not symbolize complete subjection to the god, nor did it attempt to incarnate the divinity. A sacrifice was a banquet, which offered men the opportunity to become familiar with their divine counterparts, to define their respective qualities and status, and, together, to address the matters in hand. Men could take advantage, for example, of the meeting to apologize for an accidental or unavoidable insult to the protecting role or dignity of the divinity (expiation), to make a request or give thanks (supplications), or even to contract agreements (*vota*). Epigraphic and archaeological evidence reveal that this practice was widespread and that it consisted, in most cases, of a promise for a sacrifice to a god in return for a favorable outcome. Unless they are themselves the object on which the agreement is recorded, votive offerings generally indicate the fulfillment of a votive promise, and thus divine benevolence.

Funerary Sacrifices

During Roman funerals, the separation between the living and the deceased was also marked by a sacrifice, and even, from the beginning of the first century AD, about which we have the most information, by several sacrifices. According to the sources, it appears that as soon as the body of the deceased was carried to the necropolis, the funeral rites proper began with a sacrifice (see Scheid 2005c, forthcoming a). Up to the time of Cicero, a sacrifice of a sow was made to Ceres in the presence of the corpse, and then divided between the goddess, the bereaved family, and the deceased. The portion assigned to the deceased was placed on a stake and cremated along with the body. The portion allotted to Ceres was burned on an altar and the family ate theirs on the spot. The offering was, in principle, a sow, but customs varied according to the date, the particular region in Italy, or the social milieu. For more modest funerals, a simple libation of wine, incense, and fruit or crops was sufficient. How these libations were divided between the participants is not known. However, the principle of the sacrifice was no doubt the same: the deceased had not yet entirely left his earthly community, and so could receive a share of a sacrificial victim with Ceres, who was not a goddess of the Underworld, and with his family.

Once the ashes or the body of the deceased were laid in the tomb, and as soon as the eight days of mourning were complete, the family gathered near the tomb to celebrate a second sacrifice. This one was addressed to the Manes of the deceased. As a consequence, the victim was burnt in its entirety on the ground. It appears that the family offered another sacrifice, to the Penates, which then gave way to a large sacrificial banquet at home, to which all the family, neighbors, and, in the case of grand funerals, the people of the local district or even the whole citizen body were invited. Whereas the first sacrifice established the first degree of separation between the deceased and the living, and because it ritually stated that the deceased could no longer eat his share around a table alongside the living, the second sacrifice was the definitive mark of their separation. From this point on, the living and the domestic gods could no longer share a sacrifice or food with him, and moreover, the deceased had now himself become the beneficiary of a sacrifice, in as much as he now formed part of the collective divinity, the Manes. And it was doubtless this sacrifice of separation and the sacrifice to the Penates that were repeated during the annual festival of the dead.

From archaeological study, more is known about funerary sacrificial rites than other kinds of sacrifice, since the remains of these rites are easier to identify than those in a temple or banqueting space. These remains reveal the great variety in these practices (see Fasold et al. 1998; Fasold and Witteyer 2001; Heinzelmann et al. 2001; Ortalli 2001). Some communities continued to perform animal sacrifices at funerals and the subsequent periodic funerary rites, while others seem to have replaced them with libations. Many things are still uncertain, but progress in current research should, in the not too distant future, provide a clearer picture of the variations between Rome, Italy, and the provinces.

FURTHER READING

Starting points for the study of Roman sacrificial ritual are some more detailed descriptions. For private sacrifices: Cato, *De agricultura* 83, 132, 134, 139. For the public vows *pro salute reipublicae* and problems during the ritual: Livy 41.14.7–15.4; for the sacrifice *Graeco ritu*: Dionysius of Halicarnassus, *Roman Antiquities* 7.72.15–17; Schnegg-Köhler (2002: 34–43) (Secular Games, sacrifices *Graeco ritu*, and holocausts). A general description of the sacrifice and the evidence is given in: Wissowa (1912: 409–32); Latte (1960: 375–93); Scheid (1990: 326–36; 441–676; 2005c). For a comparative study of sacrifice in the ancient world: Reverdin and Rudhardt (1980); Grottanelli and Parise (1988); Georgoudi et al. (2006). For iconography of the sacrifice: Ryberg (1955); *ThesCRA 1.2.a.* figs. 76–254.

For the problem of the sacrificial banquets and sharing of sacrificial meat: Kajava (1998); Santini (1988); Scheid (2005c: 213–54); for interpretation of Greek sacrifice: Detienne and Vernant (1979); for interpretation of Roman sacrifice: Scheid (1990: *passim*); *ThesCRA 1.2.a.* 190–2; for ancient speculations about Roman sacrifice: Prescendi (forthcoming).

(trans. Jane E. A. Anderson)

PART IV

Actors and Actions

Religious Actors in Daily Life: Practices and Related Beliefs

Nicole Belayche

Religious practices offer us an echo of the place of religious matters in Roman daily life. Most scholarly research either focuses on public cult practices or separately investigates votive rituals and others – like superstitious or forbidden ("magical") practices – as if they refer to different conceptions of reality or satisfy different religious needs. When they are scrutinized together, one may realize that the whole range of ritual ways betrays a coherent conception of the world and answers similar needs in day-to-day life, however diverse it may appear; but each ritual was performed in a particular social context (Rüpke 2005a, English edn).

"Humanity Born for Pains" (*natum in curas hominum genus*) (Tibullus 3.4.9)

Three reasons might explain the academic partition within studies of Roman religious life. Daily homage paid to the gods was largely not spectacular; even blood sacrifices used small animals in the main, as is demonstrated by the statistical data available (M. Jameson 1988). Two late testimonies assume this fact. A law of 392 that forbids pagan practices lists them by the ways they were performed: "venerate his Lar with fire, his *Genius* with wine, his Penates with fragrant odors; he shall not burn lights to them, place incense before them, or suspend wreaths for them" (*CTh* 16.10.12.4–6). These gestures are depicted for an annual festival in Mamre, Palestine (Sozomenus, *HE* 2.4.5). Such modest offerings did not leave many traces. The visibility of ritual practices to modern observers is thus related to devotees' social and economical status (Juvenal 12.10–14). Attention is thus primarily focused on public celebrations, for their remains are indeed more available. The rule admits exceptions, however: in 293 BCE, at the most critical point of a battle, a general promised only a libation to Jupiter, instead of vowing a temple to him as usual (Livy 10.42.7). In daily life, religious acts should not be described as if they concerned only private or domestic behaviors (De Marchi 1896–1903). A partition between *publicus* and *priuatus* is only legitimate when the issue is to qualify ceremonies' status from a juridical viewpoint, and to pinpoint consequently who are the religious actors (magistrates and public priests for the state religion), and which budget finances them (the city for the state religion). As far as Roman religious anthropology is concerned – that is, according to a world representation assuming the existence of superior beings with whom communication is managed through rituals (Brodersen 2001) – principles and means of communication were similar whatever the juridical status (Scheid 2005c: 125–8).

Ritual procedures using solid materials (writing on stone or lead, and terracotta offerings), or displaying such impressive ceremonies in times of crisis that they are reported in historiography (e.g. Livy 26.9.7 during the Second Punic War), have lasted better over time. During dramatic periods or when social and political competition was at its climax, invocations to gods used to include practices as excessive as was the panic, or as unique as was the challenge. They were generally labeled as *superstitio* or "magic," thus condemned by law and authorities (e.g. Livy 25.1.6–12 in 213 BCE), as if they betrayed more irrational behavior. We shall have to be more cautious after comparing a few rituals.

Scheid (1985b [2001]: 17) offers another key for those wishing to account for the academic classification. His limpid overview of Roman piety, setting the standard from now on, shows that collective cult, in particular public cult, was the "essence of Roman religion." Roman religion was a civic one: (1) individuals felt concerned in it as members of the *res publica*; (2) the rituals performed related to the group, and violations that occurred had consequences for the group. The *populus Romanus quiritium* played its part as a ritual actor either as a whole, the state, through ownership of public responsibilities, or through its various components. These were: (1) associations or *collegia* based on professional, social, or religious links (Rüpke 2004a); (2) families (the basic collective entity) acting through the father as chief of the family or through his representative (e.g. Cato's *uillicus*, *Agr*. 139); and (3) individuals. All members of the community, men and women alike, acted ritually, that is, engaged themselves in a relationship with the gods, following a common ritual range to that end, according to contexts, circumstances, and needs.

Our modern minds are trained in the Abrahamic tradition, whose core is that the religious relationship is a personal one (faith in God), even if the faithful belong to communities (whether the "people of Israel," or the church as *corpus Christi*, or "the faithful community" for Muslims). Therefore it is hard to gather how far the religious activity of individuals, families, or associations could be as deeply socialized as it was in ancient Rome. The *res publica*'s calendar gave a framework to fields that we are used to considering as belonging to private domains, for instance the cult of the dead. Such a highly conservative authority as Cicero could thus say in his treatise on *Laws* (2.30) that "private worship may not be satisfactorily performed (*religioni priuatae satis facere*) without the assistance of those in charge of the public rites (*iis qui sacris publice praesint*); for the people's constant need for the advice (*consilio*) and authority (*auctoritate*) of the aristocracy helps to hold the state together." When Cicero, speaking as a *pater familias*, a lawyer, and a rhetorician as well, pleaded for his house back after it had been confiscated by Clodius, he defined the citizen's house in the same words as Camillus had when he was defending the *Vrbs'* location three centuries and a half earlier (Livy 5.52): "Within its circle are his altars, his hearths, his household gods, his religion, his observances, his ritual" (Cic. *De domo sua* 109). And yet, when the context was a private one, and mainly within competitive situations, which are one of the biggest issues of relationships in such hierarchized societies as was the Roman one, the range of practices might be enlarged, for instance in calling for supernatural beings as auxiliaries for action. The way these practices worked out, however, was not that different (see *infra*).

"Every Living Soul Trusts to Heaven" (*omnes mortales dis sunt freti*) (Plautus, *Casina* 348)

The interweaving between individuals and the civic community as a whole is obvious when considering places where ceremonies were held. They often combined public temples and private houses. During the festivities performed by the Arval Brethren, sacrifices took place at Dea Dia's *lucus*, five miles away from Rome, where the goddess's sanctuary was located, and in the house of the *magister* who presided over the priestly college (*CFA* 55, 59–61, in 87 CE; Scheid 1990: 506–8).

Two feasts illustrate perfectly this intricate relationship between individual and collective levels. The *ludi saeculares* (Secular Games) and the *Parilia* were periodical festivals. They were to insure felicity for the Roman community for a more or less distant future, from a year at the *Parilia* up to a *saeculum* for the Secular Games, performed in each 100- or 110-year cycle. This festival is exceptionally well attested: we can confront literary descriptions (mainly Zosimus *Historia Nova* II, 5) with epigraphic reports of the ceremonies (Schnegg-Köhler 2002) and monetary issues engraved with depictions of a few sequences (Scheid 1998e). Ceremonies lasted during three days and nights, from May 31 to June 2. They began after a few days busy with preparatory purification that took place in private houses and in various sites in the city. During this time prior to the feast, citizens dressed in togas received the items required to purify their own houses: *suffimenta* in Latin, *ta katharsia* in Greek. Proceedings were the duty of the *quindecemuiri sacris faciundis*, the priests in charge of sacred ceremonies performed according to a Greek rite, while seated on a podium at the Capitol and on the Palatine, as for any public distribution. The involvement of all members of the state in the *Ludi* was also proclaimed on the first day when public heralds (*praecones*, *kérykes*) ran throughout the city in order to call for participation in the festival (Zosimus, *Historia Nova* 2.5.1). During the three festive days, the whole Roman people had a part within diverse groupings depending on the moment or the ritual. Sacrifices were the duty of public priests. Supplications were the task of *matronae*, as the guardians of the family values upon which the civic community was built (Freyburger 1977; van Straten 1974 for gesture). Hymns were sung by *matronae* and groups of children, who symbolized the Roman people to be (Feeney

1998). Besides the whole range of actors, the arrangement of the ceremonies itself contributed to an expression of the people's entireness.

On April 21, the anniversary of the foundation of the city of Rome coincided with the *Parilia* festival (Ov. *Fast.* 4.747–82). It was an annual time for the fumigation and purification of citizens' houses. Just as two days earlier, when the festival in honor of Ceres was closing (Ov. *Fast.* 4.393–416 on April 12–19), or when the *lustratio agri* (purification of the fields) was performed (Tibullus 2.1.1–26), the whole population, in both town (Athenaios, *Deipnosophistae* 8.361ef) and country, offered sacrifices, walked in processions, performed dances with songs (Virgil, *Georgics* 1.338–50). All these rituals aimed at providing expiation in case of offense to the gods, and calling for a life's space and time free from troubles and life-giving for earth and flocks. During the *Parilia*, the prayer addressed to Pales ended with a formula which sums up the ordinary relationship between men and gods: "*Quae precor eueniant et nos faciamus ad annum grandia liba Pali*" ("May my prayer be granted and we will year by year make great cakes for Pales") (Ov. *Fast.* 4.775–6). The votive relationship was the nucleus of the communication system, a contractual relationship built on *ius* (the men's right) and *fas* (the gods' right) and respectful of both.

"When the Gods are Propitious to a Man, they Throw Money in his Way" (*quoi homini di sunt propitii lucrum ei profecto obiciunt*) (Plautus, *Curculio* 531)

The Romans, like the Greeks before them, conceived the superior world – we sum it up as "the gods" – as being peopled by many beings, so numerous that they might be infinite in number (Petronius 17.5). "The world is full of gods" (*omnia quae cernerent deorum esse plena*), Cicero repeated (*Leg.* 2.26), many centuries after Thales had said it. The polytheistic conception was a subtle way to share all fields of activity between diverse extra-world referees (Scheid 1999a). Such a diffusion, rooted in a world representation that isolated the many areas of peculiar competence, enabled this conception to embrace the whole world, however infinite it might be. Ritual was established as a relationship strategy with this world. According to that kind of representation, divine beings were expected to be influential at any moment of life, just as they were held to cause large natural phenomena. The emperor Maximinus Daia said as much to the city of Tyre in 311 (*apud* Eus. *HE* 9.7.7–8). Rationalizing the world along these specific lines leads to many practical consequences. Religious acts have to be performed before any activity, public and private as well, in order to feel confident of the gods' goodwill – what the Romans called *pax deorum* – or, on the contrary, to be vigilant for any kind of hostility detected through codified signs (Val. Max. 2.1.1). "I go out with clear auspices, with a bird on my left (*aui sinistra*)" (Plautus, *Epidicus* 183f.).

Gods are considered as supporting human projects or not. Success, sanction, or failure being interpreted as a legitimization (or not) by the powers that had been invoked, ritual procedures were planned in order to make those powers propitious and have them as allies. Care for the gods, the very meaning of *religio*, had therefore to go through life, and one might thus understand why Cicero wrote that religion was "necessary." Religious behavior – *pietas* in Latin, *eusebeia* in Greek – belonged to action and not to contemplation. Consequently religious acts took place wherever the faithful were: in houses, boroughs, associations, cities, military camps, cemeteries, in the country, on boats. "When pious travelers happen to pass by a sacred grove or a cult place on their way, they are used to make a vow, or a fruit offering, or to sit down for a while" (Apuleius, *Florides* 1.1). All these topographical or institutional places have not left the same number of remains; they vary with place and period.

Individuals had their own private protectors, a *Genius* for men and a *Iuno* for women; they were favorable when honored rightly (Plautus, *Captivi* 290; Tibullus 2.2.1–10). The passing of ages and stages in life was devoted to specific divine beings as well. There were those who accompanied mothers and newborn children, and young boys wore a *bulla* around their neck to be used as an apotropaic amulet. Once they had grown up to the age of *iuuentas*, by the time they could put on the *toga uirilis*, they offered the *bulla* to protecting, domestic deities, the Lares (Néraudau 1979: 147–52), before going to the Capitol for a sacrifice, and to the temple of Mars Ultor from the time of Augustus onward (Dio 55.10.2). Once the bride had crossed over her new home's threshold without touching it (Plautus, *Casina* 815–17; Catullus 61.166–8), specific deities attended to the wedding night, up to Pertunda, who cared for penetration and who was therefore fiercely denounced by Augustine (*Civ.* 6.9.3). Domestic Lares and the Penates were referees and attendants for the whole *familia* at home (Tibullus 1.3.34; Juvenal 12.87f.; see Fröhlich 1991). The lady mistress honored them in the various sequences of the month (Cato, *Agr.* 143.2; Orr 1978). During meal-times, offerings called for these deities' benevolence: "once the first service was over, people were used to keep silence until the food portion that was reserved as an offering (*libata*) was taken to the altar and thrown into the fire, and a child had said that gods are propitious (*deos propitios*)" (Servius, *Aeneis* 1.730). In both country and town, the Lares of the crossroads (*compitales*) represented a similar guardianship principle (Ov. *Fast.* 2.616), providing stability and cohesion. They were supplemented with a strategy of political control when closely linked to the imperial order from the Augustan reform onward (Ov. *Fast.* 5.129–48; Fraschetti 1994: 272–6; in Puteoli, Steuernagel 2004: 43f.). On a larger geographical scale, neighbors might meet in regional cult places, which could belong to a private owner: "Many affairs are dealt (*multae res aguntur*), vows are made and discharged" (Pliny, *Epist.* 9.39.2; Scheid 1997: 249f.).

A relationship with the supernatural world might only be undertaken once the faithful had delineated its conditions, that is, once the divine beings had been recognized as superior powers. The ritual construction had to settle them as possible partners. The faithful had to call the deity they invoked by the proper name: ritual address was an invocation and identification of the power concerned as well. If the person ignored the right theonym (the personal name), or the name the god preferred, he could use a periphrasis approved as being welcome and advised by pontiffs (Gellius 2.2): *si deus, si dea* (Alvar 1985). He might also use a formula that was previously familiar to the Grecks (Aeschylus, *Agamemnon* 160): *siue quo alio nomine te appellari uolueris* (Servius, *Aeneis* 2.351). Such caution was the rule within every context, either votive or magical. A lead tablet aiming at a rival's destruction called for the nymphs *siue quo alio nomine uoltis adpellari* (*CIL* 11.1823). Is that the reason why, in late antiquity, a magician practiced at Anna Perenna's temple (Piranomonte 2002)?

Saying the deity's name represented the slightest, first step in theological definition, for it defined the deity as a superior being and attributed to it a power within a circumscribed field. For similar reasons, the theonym was frequently accompanied by cultural epithets (epiclesis) that drew explicit limits to the deity's field of action. Jupiter is *optimus maximus*, Mars is *pater* or *uictor* (Belayche et al. 2005). When a sacrifice was performed, the *praefatio* (introductory rite) consisted of an incense and wine libation on an altar with a fire (*ThesCRA 1*. 203–4). It was an equivalent through gesture to the address by the name. It expressed a preliminary homage, "the solemn salutation of the gods" (Scheid 2003: 109; 2005c: 44–50). Being introduced to the gods required observance of concrete conditions, too; scholars are used to referring to them as ritual purity (Veyne 2005: 448–9). Entering the deities' area – the sacred (*sacer*) – demanded a few qualities from cultic actors and the space and time of the ceremony (Cic. *Leg.* 2.24). There were set behaviors, gestures, and festive surroundings throughout, all more or less demonstrative according to the ritual's status. Place (temple and altar), actors, and sacrificial animals adorned with garlands and crowns regularly figured on great public sacrifice reliefs (Ryberg 1955), and ritual operators washed their hands in running water as a preliminary. Festive time itself was declared as set apart from profane time, available for human activity. After participants had been required to keep silent (*fauete linguis*), music created a symbolic separation from daily life. Flutists (*tubicines*) belonging to one of the city's *ordines* were called for public rituals. Within private ceremonies, the faithful could rent a lyre-player for a sacrifice (*rem diuinam faceret*) performed at home (*domi*) in order to thank a god once, say, one's son had come back safely (Plautus, *Epidicus* 314–16, 414–16). The whole range of dispositions was more complex and punctilious in the case of "magical" rituals, because the divine power was summoned to come and to proceed to action (*PGMtr* IV.55–7).

All these preliminary rites co-occurring at the meeting with superior beings are compelling, because the relationship between the two partners is unbalanced on the ontological level. And yet, however almighty and immortal the gods might be, they had rights and duties within the Roman community like any of its members (Scheid 1985b [2001]: 69).

"Men were Used to Protect Themselves (*muniti essent*) by Dedications against Shocks of Fortune (*aduersus fortunae impetus*)" (Servius, *Aeneis* 4.694)

Actions and decisions were regulated by vows throughout daily life. Religious relationships were defined as an engagement between two partners, the *uotum*, for they were first rooted in justice, and not in affective links with the gods, even if such a contractual approach did not prevent feelings. The formula that went with the offering, "*ut tibi ius est*" ("according to your right/as you must get on the basis of your right"), assumed this fact, as much as the gesture of putting one's hand on his heart to express fairness when the vow was made. The rite was built up with words and gestures, both following precise rules that left no place free for imagination or improvisation, in "magical" contexts *a fortiori*. Gestures were in accordance with divine beings' personalities. During the *deuotio*, which offered the enemy people in a vow, the general who devoted himself "touches the earth while saying Tellus, and raises his hands toward heaven when pronouncing the name of Jupiter" (Macr. *Sat.* 3.9.12).

From the smallest individual prayers up to the state's safety, however grave or important the request might be, all vows displayed the same structure, which can be summed up by the formula "*do ut dem*," "give to me and I shall give to you (back)." "One who had gained his prayer would with his own hands bring the honey-cake, his little daughter following with the pure honeycomb in hers. O Lares, turn the bronze javelin away from me . . . and <as thank offering for my safe return shall fall>" (Tibullus 1.10.21–6). In Rome, women "whose prayer has got an answer (*potens uoti*)" went up to Nemi at the temple of Diana, the goddess concerned with birth, already crowded with ex-votos, and "carry from the city burning torches, while garlands wreathe her brows" (Ov. *Fast.* 3.267–70). The epigraphic protocols of the Arval Brethren perfectly testify to the structure of a votive relationship. For instance, the vow pronounced on March 25, 101, "for safeness, return, and victory" of the emperor Traianus provides us with a model of its architecture (*CFA* 62, 23–36, *passim*):

> The Arval Brethren uttered the vows in these words, written below: "Jupiter best and greatest, we ask, beseech, and conjure you that you make the emperor Caesar, the son of divine Nerva, Nerva Trajan Augustus Germanicus . . . return well and lucky and safely as a victor from those places and provinces that he visits . . . if you do this as we vow, we vow that then a gilded ox will be yours in the name of the college of the Arval Brethren. Queen Juno, in the words by which we have today sworn to Jupiter best and greatest for the well-being and return and victory of the emperor Caesar . . . , if you do the same, we vow in the like formula that a gilded ox will be yours in the name of the college of the Arval Brethren." (trans. Rüpke)

Most votive offerings (*ex uoto* or *uotum soluit* in Latin, *euchèn* or *kat' euchèn* in Greek) were made for the safety (*pro salute, hyper sôtèrias*), well-being (*pro incolumitate*), or good health (*pro ualetudine, hyper hygeias*; Plautus, *Amphitryo* 1–16) of living people or institutions (MacMullen 1981; Veyne 2005: 425–8). In 174 BCE, a harmful plague decided the Roman people to vow a two-day festival and a *supplicatio* (Livy 41.21.11). On every January *calends*, *Salus publica* received a vow in terms of caution and anticipation for the year. Vowing was used as a regular means to keep control of the future, as was the case through the *Navigium Isidis*, intended to open the sea for safe sailing each March (Apul. *Met.* 11.16.7; Alföldi 1937). Other vows might last for a longer period, ten or twenty years for a *taurobolium* (*ILS* 4153.12 = Duthoy 17). The emperor and his *domus* received periodical, official vows as well. They were decreed for Augustus by a *senatus consultum* (*Res Gestae* 8); on January 3, annual vows are recorded on calendars like that of the *XX cohors* in Dura-Europos (Beard et al. 1998: 2.71) and in the Arval Brethren's *commentarii* (Scheid 1990: 298–309). The faithful made vows for their own safety alike, for instance for that of their eyes (*TAM* 5.1.332), and for that of their relatives (Cato, *Agr.* 141.2). The rite was so common that it was frequently written down only in an abbreviated formula (*P S S S = pro salute sua [et] suorum*). Good health was for sure a priority within societies that interpreted illness as a sign sent by the gods (Horstmanshoff and Stol 2004). Vows were pronounced for properties and crops as well. Those for oxen's good health (*uti ualeant*) are advised by Cato, who informs his dependent about the appropriate ritual expenditure (*Agr.* 83). They are often attested to in epigraphic documentation coming from the Greek-speaking part of the empire (*euxamenos hyper tou boos*, *TAM* 5.1.509; *hyper probatón sôtèrias*, Drew-Bear et al. 1999: no. 336). In rural, imperial Phrygia, votive epigraphs were frequently accompanied by a relief depicting the family who dedicated it (fig. 20.1). Votive processes went with all risky moments of life like birth, professional projects, travel for men (Plautus, *Captivi* 922) or goods (*ILS* 4751), and war. Pliny somewhat ironically reports

Figure 20.1 Votive epigraph from imperial Phrygia (Drew-Bear et al. 1999: no. 166) (photo: Museum of Anatolian Civilisations 17.1.64).

the practice of writing down vows on columns and walls at the Clitumna Springs (Pliny, *Epist.* 8.8.7).

Not all dedications that we can still read explicitly tell us what the nature of the contract was. The majority only publish it after its fulfillment (*uotum soluit, euxamenos*), making the offering once the vow has been satisfied. A certain Tullia offers the counterpart for her vow after her hair has been recovered (*CIL* 11.1305). Other inscriptions more or less clearly record despair, fear (*ILS* 3411), pain (*paschousa* in Greek), or dangers from which the faithful escaped safely (*IG* 10, 2.1.67: *sôtheis ek megalou kindunou tou kata thalassan*; Veyne 2005: 518–19). Other devotees, who were saved from shipwreck (*ultimum uotum*, Petronius 103–4), or who have been abandoned by doctors (*ILS* 3513: *derelictus a medicis*), thank the gods the more warmly the more they were considered by men as lost. The gods took care of a faithful person's bodily health even without his visiting specialized curative sanctuaries (cf. *infra*). During festivals, sacrificial meat that was shared by participants once the god had got his part (the *exta*) was welcome to enrich the ordinary diet, as such *feriae* were expected to be times of good cheer (Plautus, *Curculio* 532). Last but not least, gods played a role as guarantors for property, temples being used as deposit banks (Plautus, *Bacchis* 306–13). Except during the night, when they were closed (Plautus, *Bacchis* 900–1), they remained open all the time for the most anxious of the faithful. Seneca, who had an abstract idea of the divine as a Stoic, considered as *dementia* (folly) and *furor* (deluded madness) the way some devotees undertook an intimate relationship with cult statues: "There are men who summon the gods to give bond for them, and some who offer them lawyers' briefs and explain their case" (*De superstitione, apud* Aug. *Civ.* 6.10; Lactantius, *Institutiones divinae* 2.2.14; see Estienne 2001). In Florence, a devotee called for Isis to recover a tax unduly paid to the imperial *fiscus* by his city (*RICIS* 511/0208).

To put it shortly, the votive relationship was a ritual product of routine and universal preoccupations, like desire for well-being and apprehension about the future, even without a specific expected wish or trouble. A devotee of the Magna Mater declared he had performed a *taurobolium* "for happiness' sake" (*symbolon eutychiès*) (Duthoy 1969: no. 33.4). Gods were thus invoked as "*custos*," "*conservator*," "*adiutor*," "*salutaris*"; "*sôter*" in Greek. Religious issues embraced the worldly conduct of life; they aimed at negotiating possible critical steps (*discrimina* in Latin, Juvenal 12.24) as best they could, and feeling secure with peaceful promises. One of the most famous cases of political negotiation through a *uotum* is that of Camillus, in 367 BCE: after he had been created a dictator in the midst of a harsh conflict between patricians and plebeians, he promised to dedicate a temple to *Concordia* (Plutarch, *Camillus* 42). From a sociological analysis, the votive relationship offered a supernatural legitimacy for decisions or actions. From a psychological approach, it entailed being assisted and reassured, through the forwarding of hopes or disappointments, anger or contentment, to superior powers (Versnel 1981b). Whatever topographical or functional competency each power had according to each occasion, their whole community could appear as a possible alternative. We can easily find epigraphs calling for the whole pantheon (*dis deabusque omnibus*, in Greek "to X kai tois allois theois*") or to the peculiar gods of a community, for instance "the Twelve

Gods" or "the Roman people's gods" (*tous dèmou Rhômaiôn theous*) (*TAM* 5.1.423). All the gods could be seen as protectors, even YHWH, to whom Jews made public vows "for the emperor's sake" (*CIJud* 972). In that respect, mystery cults or so-called oriental cults were no different. Epigraphic and literary documents they have left demonstrate that they are votive in the majority (Apul. *Met.* 11.9.5; Belayche 2000), and that the expected salvation was first and foremost a terrestrial one (Bianchi and Vermaseren 1982; Burkert 1992: 23–38).

Ordinary testimonies of votive relationships consist of graven dedications on stone and contracts painted on *uotiuae tabellae* (Cic. *Nat.* 3.37.89, at the Samothracian gods' sanctuary; Tibullus 1.3.27f.; Juvenal 12.27f., 100f.). They were very similar to offerings hung as mere gifts or thanksgivings (de Cazanove 1993). Votive objects by the thousand were unearthed in Italian sanctuary deposits (*fauissae*), a practice that came to an end during the second century BCE (*CstipiVot*; Bouma 1996; *ThesCRA* 4. 226–8); but the habit remained in the Greek-speaking Mediterranean (van Straten 1981; Schörner 2003). These "*ex-votos par destination*" (Morel 1992) were figurines, showing a veiled head like that of ritual actors, and miniature objects molded as anatomic ex-votos figuring parts of the body, either external ones (arm, leg, eye, penis, etc.) or internal organs (uterus, belly; Gladigow 1995: 353–9; *ThesCRA* 1. 359–68) for the most part. They were quite similar in all sanctuaries, notwithstanding local or chronological peculiarities. They show day-to-day images of a society as summed up in the title of a book that presents ex-votos in modern contemporary practices: *Le miracle et le quotidien* (Cousin 1983). The objects were produced on a quantitative level that we may qualify as "industrial" for the time. They were then sold in shops settled by sanctuaries or inside *temenè* themselves, where the faithful could choose the one fitting their own wishes. In Rome, roads going to Aesculapius' temple on Tiber Island were lined with shops of that kind. Excavations at the springs of the river Seine have brought many of these sculpted, wooden ex-votos to light (Deytz 1983). In Rome, the votive deposit of Minerva Medica's temple on the Esquiline dates back to the fourth century BCE. The goddess's epiclesis, written on a vase, attests to her curative function (Gatti Lo Guzzo 1978). Further to the east, in Lydia, stone dedications show side by side a text telling the matter of the vow and its figuration: "for the good health of my feet" going with a carving of two legs; "for my breasts" (with relevant depiction; *TAM* 5.1.323–4). Consequently the "marketplace of religions," to quote North when defining the polytheistic conception, was a lucrative economic market as well (Dignas 2002). At the temple of Artemis in Ephesus, small silver models were sold as reproductions of the temple itself, hence the jewelers' riot against Paul of Tarsus when his preaching denounced these hand-made objects as mere stuff (Acts 19.23–8).

In terms of structure, the votive relationship is a voluntary and dynamic one, because it weaves a reciprocal link. The faithful usually initiated communication, but the engagement of both parties was constrained. When the faithful person had gotten satisfaction, when he was *uoti compos* (*CIL* 6.402), he became *damnatus* or *reus uoti* (Livy 39.9.4); that was the starting point for the *Bacchanalia* affair (see also Servius, *Aeneis* 4.699; Macr. *Sat.* 3.2.6; Turlan 1955). Fulfillment was regularly made public in an abbreviated written formula: *V S L M* (*uotum soluit libens merito*). Divine signs received during the vow could provide the faithful with their first information about its reception. The *litatio* performed on the dead sacrificial animal gave a clue about the gods' dispositions toward the human will, either favorable or hostile (Tibullus 2.1.25–26; *ThesCRA 1.* 228–30). If rationalistic thinkers were dubious about false dreams, which "fill affrighted souls with false alarms" that are propitiated at dawn thanks to an offering (Tibullus 3.4.7–10), the majority used the *Oneirocriticon*, written by Artemidoros of Chalcis, as a "*technique d'existence*" (Foucault 1984: 17) for interpreting dreams. Epigraphs record quite frequently that the faithful made their consecration by divine order (*ex iussu, ex epitagès* in Greek), after a vision (*ex uisu*) considered as being premonitory (*ex monitu*), after a dream (*kat' onar*; van Straten 1976; Veyne 1986). Reliance on divine justice and its benevolent power – which is the very meaning of ancient "belief" (*fides* in Latin and *pistis* in Greek) – assumes gods are *epèkoos* (listening), a theological quality frequently honored in the imperial period (Weinreich 1912). The faithful could also choose to have ears or footprints depicted on the dedicated stone as a symbol of divine care, or to consecrate a monumental, sculptured foot in order to portray the godly presence. We may thus catch the reason why Nemesis, who undertakes divine judicial power, is invoked as *exaudientissima* at Apulum in Dacia (*CIL* 3.1126).

The devotee got back divine anger if he neglected to fulfill the vow once it had been satisfied. Even public legislation recalled the fact (*Digest* 50.12.2: *De pollicitationibus*). In Lydia, a devotee promised (*euxeto*) a stele if his son recovered good health "without spending money at the doctor's." The vow was indeed listened to, but he did not offer the stele in return; after the father had been punished, the deity "accomplished the vow for his son" (Petzl 1994: no. 62). Otherwise, the votive engagement had to be renegotiated. The historian Livy records many of these public debates upon fulfillment of vows (e.g. the vow made to Apollo during the siege of Veii, Livy 5.23, 25), and allows us to follow the stages from the *uer sacrum* vow pronounced in 217 up to its fulfillment in 195 (Livy 22.10; 33.44; Scheid 1998c). If the divine being had not satisfied the vow, the faithful were released from it. Therefore the deity had to respect the contract in order to get his return. For all these reasons, votive processes logically lasted for a long period, even if travelers' vows ("to go and return," "*pro itu et reditu*") were probably fulfilled in the middle of the trip. A temple to Mars Ultor was vowed by Octavian before the battle of Philippi in 42 BCE, and the dedication by Augustus occurred 40 years later (Suet. *Augustus* 29.2). When vows are regular ones, the periodicity is fixed: one year for the *vota publica* on January 1, for the *Parilia* vows, or for vows for the health of oxen, according to Cato (*Agr.* 83: *Hoc uotum in annos singulos . . . uouere*). Thus Varro (*Ling.* 6.60) could imagine that the verb *nuncupare* (to pronounce a vow) had been formed on the epithet *nouus* (new <vow>).

Fulfillment of a vow might be accompanied by gratulatory ceremonies that were not part of the contract strictly speaking (*habere gratias, eulogia, eucharistón*, and the lexicon of the same family in Greek). A Plautus character declares: "Seeing I have managed this affair well, I must go in the temple here and pray (*in fano supplicare*)" (*Curcullio* 527). These thanksgiving rites are similar to honorific ones (see chapter 17).

Searching for More Insurance for the Future through Preliminary Expiations and Curses

The votive relationship already encompasses an anticipatory component for what is to be, when periodical vows are pronounced. As for more hypothetical risks or unknown destiny, Romans had other, no less voluntary, means.

Pietas, depicted on coins by cult objects or as a female figure sacrificing over an altar with a fire (Siebert 1999; *LIMC*, s.v. "Pietas"), had such an importance in Roman daily life that possible faults, hence impiety, were a permanent matter for carefulness (Cic. *Leg.* 2.22). Expiatory rites were a means to prevent unconscious intrusions into the gods' realm, while keeping nevertheless the largest possible area free for action: for instance when a peasant wanted to clear part of a sacred grove (Cato, *Agr.* 139), or a sacred grove had to be cleaned out (*CFA* 94, II.7–8). These *piacula* worked as a guarantee for the current action, in the same, although inverse, way as curses could stamp an action as an impious one *a priori*, through the ritual context. Many of these curses come from imperial Anatolia; they aimed to protect the integrity of tombs against any material spoliation or undesired inhumation. According to each curse, possible violators of these memorial places had to pay a penalty to the imperial *fiscus*, and/or the community (Strubbe 1997: nos. 113, 125, 72ter), and/or the main local temple (nos. 121, 114), at least. More dramatically, divine anger was called down upon them in order that they would be destroyed: "may he not know the pleasure of children and of life, may the earth be not accessible and the sea not navigable, but may he die with all sufferings, childless and destitute and deformed" (Strubbe 1997: no. 285; 1991). These recurrent formulae are highly informative. Scholars have rightly underlined that the declaration by itself plays a performative role, recalling procedures usually coined as "magical," mainly *defixiones* (Gager 1992).

Versnel (1991) magisterially demonstrated that these texts are a ritualized form of "the appeal to justice." The issue is not to get assistance from superior powers in a contest with a rival to be superseded or destroyed; it is to call on the gods as "judges and witnesses" (Cic. *Leg.* 2.16), relying on a belief in their perfect justice. Oaths were taken for a similar purpose, and perjurers had to reckon with divine punishment. In the middle of the first century CE, the juridical power, Nemesis, who had kept her Greek name, had a statue on the Capitol in Rome, close to Jupiter, the god of oaths, and to Fides as personification of good faith (Plin. *Nat.* 28.22). Already back in the second century BCE, Plautus (*Curculio* 268–9) made fun of so many perjurers praying Jupiter Capitolinus to protect them. Funerary curses were intended to make active in advance the equal justice of the gods, and they likewise used contract formulae: "They will pay back (*apodôsousi*), retaliate with blood and death" (Strubbe 1999: no. 127). This might explain why public fines were supported by a cosmic sanction.

Appeals to divine justice were even more frequently made in the whole empire in cases of anonymous aggression, mainly from thieves. These prayers are different from *defixiones* (Versnel 1991). They are better classed with *deuotio*, for they appear as a contract with an auxiliary deity. A coat was stolen: *Deuoueo eum qui caracellam meam inuolauerit* (Cunliffe 1988: no. 10.5–7). The deity invoked for justice was to get part of – or the whole of – what had been stolen: "To the god Nodens. Silvanus has lost his ring. He has given half his value to Nodens. Do not allow good health among those who possess the name of Senecianus until he brings it right to the temple of Nodens" (Audollent 1904: no. 106; Ogden 2002: 219–22). The wish for respect for justice turned to a call for the gods' revenge (Cunliffe 1988: no. 35), when it was suspected that an untimely death happened after a criminal action (Cumont 1923; Graf 1997a: 174–5). And yet, curse procedures were built on the same contractual structure as the votive relationship.

Towering over Competitive Situations through the Activation of Ritual Powers

Curses and occult practices, intended to be maleficent toward someone or to constrain him within a social or affective relationship, were means of another kind to face specific problems in competitive relationships (Graf 1997b). Pliny considered that "there is indeed nobody who does not fear to be spell-bound by imprecations (*diris precationibus*)" (*Nat.* 28.19); and he lists a range of behaviors encompassing superstitious actions (e.g. breaking eggshells), apotropaic practices (e.g. writings with words reputed as being powerful), ritualized, protective formulae (*carmina*), and magical charms for agonistic or love issues. When a situation was critical, a civic community itself could be tempted to search for solutions with *magoi*. During a plague (*loimos*) that happened in Antioch (Syria), the city consulted the Delphic oracle, which demanded the sacrifice of a citizen's child. "The lot fell upon the son of the mage (*tou magou*). The mage promises to stop the plague, if they leave his son alone" (Libanios, *Declamatio* 41 [*Magi repulsa*] *Incerta*, Foerster 7.367). The famous rhetorician Libanios had to persuade his fellow citizens to refuse the proposition.

This contribution does not have to do specifically with what has been labeled as "magic" in antiquity and through historiography (Phillips 1991b; Graf 1997a; J. Smith 1995; Jordan et al. 1999: esp. 55–66). It just has to underline a point that has already come to light: votive relationships do exist in some practices defined as "magical." If we examine the *deuotio* of ancient *imperatores* (Livy 8.9.5–8) from the point of view of its architecture, it recalls many parallels in daily life, except that the ordinary devotee does not send himself to death with his rival. Lead tablets have vows to bestow an opponent upon superior powers in order to get rid of him: "I hand over, I dedicate, I sacrifice to your divine power" (*CIL* 11.1823 = Audollent 129; Graf 1997a: 148–51). And yet, some points distinguish the two types of practice, votive and "magical." First, each of them refers to a peculiar context. It was a public one when the relationship was votive, a secret one or performed in the shadows, at night for instance, for "magical" processes (MacMullen 1981 [1987 edn.]: 89–90). "Men, even when they offer silent prayers and vows, have no doubt that the gods understand them" (Cic. *Div.* 1.129). Some religious ceremonies required secrecy, for instance when dead souls (the Manes) had to be appeased every February 21 at the Feralia. The rite consisted in binding the dead souls in order to be protected from them:

"We have bound fast (*uinximus*) hostile tongues and unfriendly mouths" (Ov. *Fast.* 2.569–82, quotation 581). However "magical" it could be – that is, putting constraint on some power – the Feralia ritual was part of the religious state calendar. Other needs might call for the use of charms. For instance, Cato advised the cure of dislocations through "formulae" (*Agr.* 160: *cotidie cantato*). But all these acts were performed openly. The simple fact of rituals being performed secretly (not *libera luce*, *CTh* 9.16.3.7, in 319), as if they were clandestine, aroused much more suspicion than the kind of procedures they followed (Kippenberg 1997: 150–7). A second difference stands in the purpose of both ritual actions. Wishing to influence the orientation of coming events, magical practices rely not on respect for the rights of both orders, human and divine, but on the principle of a sympathy between nature (this world) and the supernatural (the Under- and upper worlds) (Graf 1997a: 231–2). This is attested by the ritual pinning of nails into representational figures (Louvre, Paris, inv. E 27145 A, Rüpke 2001 [2007]: fig. 17). These practices call on divine powers, even those of the traditional pantheon, not as partners in a contract, but as auxiliaries in, or agents for, an action. This is Delphic Apollo's task on a magical papyrus (*PGMtr* 2.1–10, 139–40).

Political ambitions were often suspected of calling for such obscure practices, when rivalries for power grew harsher. Under Tiberius' reign, Calpurnius Piso was accused of poisoning Germanicus: rumor said that "spells (*carmina*), curses (*deuotiones*), leaden tablets engraved (*plumbeis tabulis insculptum*) with the name of Germanicus" had been found (Tacitus, *Ann.* 2.69.3). Such suspicions and affairs mainly flourished when emperors faced opposition, like Nero in the first century, or Constantius II three centuries later, when he put Barbation on trial in 359 (Amm. 23.5.10; see Funke 1967). Public legislation was very attentive to the prevention of such actions, from the Sullan law *de sicariis et ueneficiis* in 81 BCE up to late antiquity. Generally, all competitions arising from social life could lead to the desire of using these practices (Gager 1992): games, even poetry competitions (Aug. *Conf.* 4.2(3)), love (Ogden 2002: 227–42), justice, and professional challenges (Ogden 2002: 210–18, 274). As early as the fifth century BCE, in the Twelve Tables of law, we read this warning: "No one may make incantations against another's crop (*fructus excantassit*)" (*apud* Seneca, *Naturales quaestiones* 4.7.2; Ogden 2002: 275–86). The African rhetorician Apuleius of Madaura, who had married a very wealthy widow, had to defend himself against an accusation of *magica maleficia* (*Pro se de magia*; Hunink 1997). Two centuries later, Libanios, who suffered from a chronic disease, attributed it to the maleficent charm of a chameleon hidden in his classroom (*Life* 248–50; Bonner 1932; Graf 1997a: 191–2). He himself was accused of performing forbidden rites (consulting *goèteis* and astrologists, performing sacrifices to the dead; *Life* 43, 63, 98). In his *Oratio* 36 (*Peri tón pharmakôn*, Foerster III.27f.), he lists the possible authors of such accusations: his fellow citizens, local senators, his colleagues, either advocates or professors, his pupils; in short, the whole civic society; and he decided on contemporary sophists longing for his professorship. These stories and others offer us a good illustration of the competitive ambience that prevailed in relationships among members of civic elites, and of how much the "magic" label could be instrumentalized.

The drawing up of all written charms follows the same model. They call for one (or more) power(s) for winning superiority or victory for the operator's sake, for instance in judicial matters: "Holy and strong, mighty and great-powerful Name, give favor, glory, victory to Proclus whom Salvina bore, before the *dux* of Bosra in Arabia, before Pelagius the assessor . . . in order that he might be justifiably or unjustifiably victorious in any judgement before any judge . . ." (Kotansky 1991). Love magic and agonistic *defixiones* are the most attested to in terms of numbers. Competition in chariot races was so sharp that a law of 389 condemns to death charioteers who would make use of magical means (*CTh* 9.16.11). A defixion from Carthage gives a ritual spell able to destroy the adversary's team: "I call for you, demon who lives here: I offer you these horses *ut deteneas illos et inplicentur nec se mouere possent*" (Audollent 1904: 233, cf. also 247, 286, etc.). A tablet found in Berytus (Syria-Phoenicia) helps us to visualize the ritual gestures that go with the spell (fig. 20.2). The first line, "*Katochos hippón kai hènikôn*" ("Bound for horses and charioteers"), sums up the domain within which the rite is efficient and proclaims the ritual modality, a link (*defixio, katadesmos* in Greek) which is the core of "magical" practices. Next, powerful names embrace the picture of a man whose body is wrapped and his legs crossed. Enclosed thus, he is stuck with pins, according to a common ritual of correspondences. Then the text gives the expected, paralyzing effect (ll. 15–21): once retained and bound, thrown into confusion, the Blues' horses and their charioteers too will be turned upside down, massacred, and interred. A similar scenario is narrated at a chariot race in Gaza (Syria-Palaestina) in the fourth century CE (*hi avolant, illi praepediuntur*; Hieronymus, *Life of Hilario* 11.11); but, in that case, paralysis is provoked by some water blessed by a holy monk. This last anecdote testifies that these practices crossed over all religious communities (Meyer and Smith 1999; Sfameni Gasparro 2002).

These sort of actions, to which a secret ritual attributed a reputation of effectiveness, could work finally as a way out from dissatisfaction within, or in hopes for, one's present life. In the third century, an "emigrant," probably a slave, made a curse against the Italian land and Rome's gates, for he longed to go home to his native country (Jordan 1985: no. 129). Since hostile forces could operate at every moment of life, people were accustomed to protect themselves in advance; they wore apotropaic amulets portraying powerful deities, like the Egyptian ones (Plin. *Nat.* 33.12.41), and written phylacteries: "Protect Alexandra . . . from every demon and every compulsion of demons and from demonic (forces?) and magical drugs and binding-spells" (Jordan 1991; Gager 1992: 218–64).

Conclusion

As far as it is possible to reconstruct Roman religious needs from the remains, most of them ritualistic, that are left, those needs appear as mainly terrestrial and pragmatic: health, happiness, success, whatever might be the ways to get them. Assistance called from the gods, either by a contract with them or in summoning up supernatural beings reputed to be powerful, was rooted in the belief in their

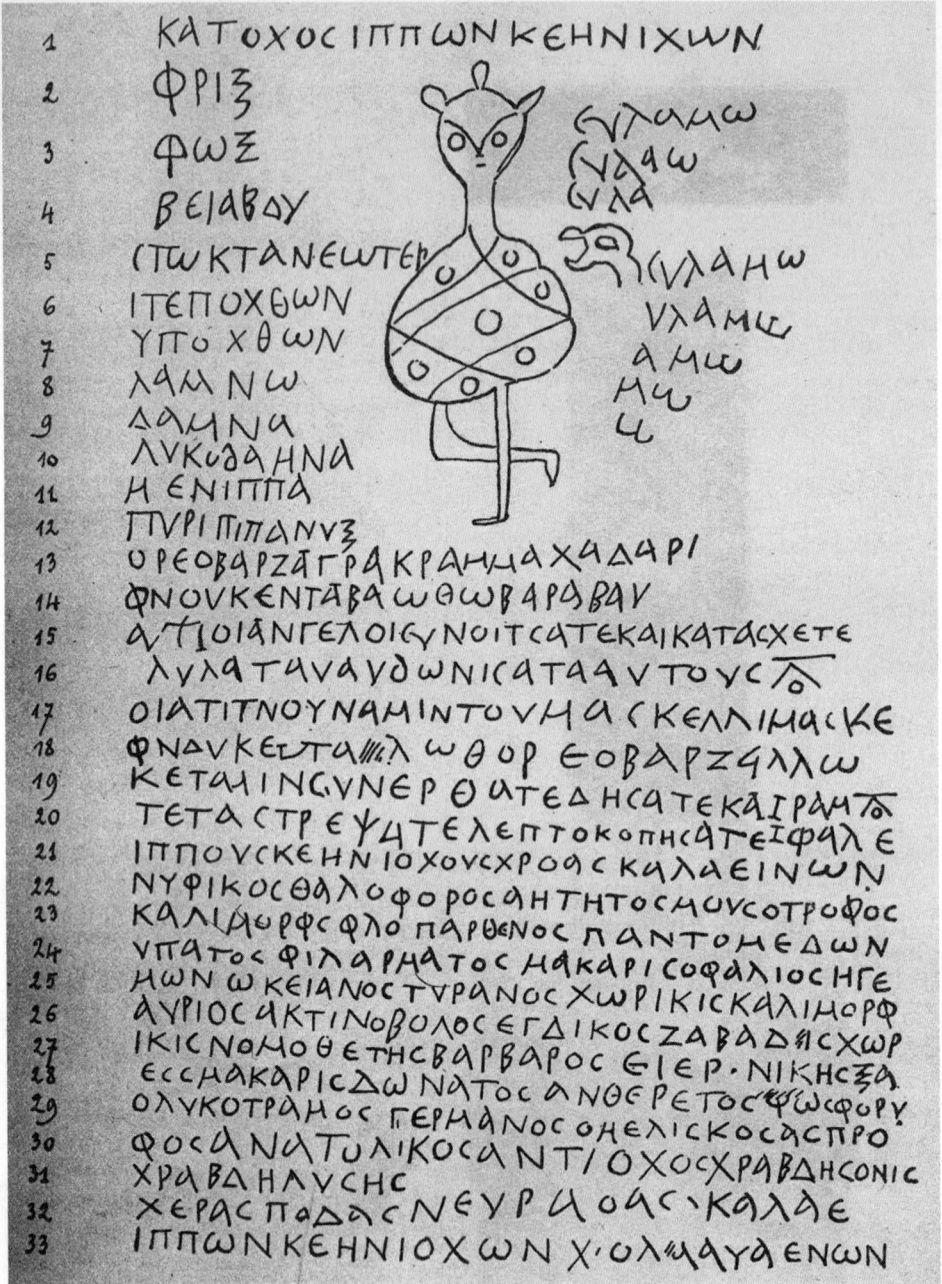

Figure 20.2 Charm on a tablet found in Berytus, Syria-Phoenicia (*SEG* 40, 1990, 1396; Mouterde 1930: pl. III, no. 34).

ever-presence and almightiness within the world. Consequently, divine figures could serve as extra-world referees taking the part of the faithful in social procedures of negotiation and legitimization. Relationships with the divine realm were defined within a strictly ritualistic frame. Ritualism does not go necessarily with a utilitarian, cynical relationship, as the comic author Plautus depicted that of some devotees in order to make the audience laugh. Nor does it imply a "cold" or "blasé" relationship, as dominant historiography portrayed it for long, because it was influenced by a spiritualistic experience (e.g. R. Turcan 1989: 23–31). Ritualism is *the* relational procedure that goes coherently with the way Romans conceived the respective places of men and gods within the world. In that respect, becoming a devotee in so-called oriental cults did not signify a mental "revolution." It was another, supplementary way of living one's relationship with the gods (Veyne 1986). If some of these cults might have proposed a life of beatitude *post mortem*, fear of death is first a reality for *hic et nunc* life, as Burkert calls it (1992: 32) after Plato (*Res publica* 330b). Cumont, who still stands as an authoritative scholar for historians of religions, analyzed the diffusion of "oriental religions" as filling a psychological gap and satisfying new spiritualistic needs (1929: 24–40). Closer investigation of a later generation has brought many corrections to that picture. In an Apuleius novel, Lucius was so curious about magical practices that he was changed into an ass. The greater profit he gets when joining Isis' cult is to be rendered to his human form, as if he was born again: "Verily, he is blessed and most blessed that by the innocence of his former life hath merited so great grace from heaven" (Apul. *Met.* 11.16). Theories on religion or gods concerned speculative issues. Cicero attests to the fact when, in his treatise *On divination*, he explores the two different ways of considering divination: from a political point of view and from a conceptual one. Intimate attitudes, existential questions, or ethical preoccupations, like those of Cicero in his philosophical works, Seneca in his *Letters to Lucilius*, Marcus Aurelius' *Thoughts for himself*, or later authors, belong to intellectual and philosophical thinking, and not to religion.

FURTHER READING

A general account of the importance of ritual in ancient religion is given by Scheid (2005c); see also Veyne (2005). A shorter account of domestic religion is given by Orr (1978); Bakker (1994) lists and analyzes the findings for the city of Ostia; Steuernagel (1999) adds the religious activities of associations; see Veyne (1989) for the private use of the public religious infrastructure. Magic as a technique for the problems of everyday life is described by Graf (1997a) and – with ample evidence – by Mirecki and Meyer (2002); Lane Fox (1986) demonstrates that such findings are valid for Christians, too. The mentality of the conditional gift to the gods, the vow, is analyzed by Pleket (1981) and van Straten (1981).

CHAPTER TWENTY-ONE

Republican *Nobiles*: Controlling the *Res Publica*

Veit Rosenberger

The senate was the dominant political power in the Roman republic: senators held the highest offices, almost all political issues were decided in the senate, not in the assemblies, and the major priestly colleges consisted largely of senators. Within the senate, the *nobiles* formed an elite. *Nobiles* were the members of the few extremely successful families who had reached the consulate, the highest office in the republic, over several generations. Nonetheless, the *nobiles* were not a homogeneous group: the most successful family were the Claudii, reaching the consulate in every generation over a period of four centuries; even the emperors from Tiberius to Nero belonged to this family. During the republic, there existed on the one hand a wide consensus within the senatorial aristocracy. Roman *nobiles* acted within a dense network of structures and mechanisms guaranteeing, reproducing, and sanctioning both the vertical and horizontal integration of classes, groups, and individuals. Their identity manifested itself in a rich repertoire of rituals and other symbolic forms of (self-)representation, such as triumphs and funeral processions (Hölkeskamp 2004: 112–13). On the other hand, senatorial competition, which ultimately led to civil wars and to the end of the republic in the first century BC, seems to have threatened the consensus within the Roman nobility since at least the time of the First Punic War (264–241 BC); the problems were probably much older and inherent in the republican system (Bleckmann 2002: 243).

An important field of action for Roman senators was divination. In Roman thought, divination could be classified in two ways: artificial versus natural divination and solicited versus unsolicited divination. Artificial divination is based on knowledge and requires interpretation, for instance the augural discipline, prodigies, astrology, or oracles given by lots. The opposite, natural divination, relies on divine inspiration and is conveyed intuitively, for example through dreams, ecstatic utterances, and oracles (Cic. *Div.* 1.12). Divination by solicited signs comprises all techniques which were used to ask the gods at a specific moment; most *auspicia* belong to this category. Unsolicited signs were the *auspicia oblativa*, signs occurring without being asked for and usually indicating divine assent or dissent for a concrete undertaking; prodigies also belong to this group. Although this classification does not stand closer investigation – dreams, for example, were far from being self-evident and flocks of professional dream-interpreters made their living from this; the distinction between solicited and unsolicited auguries may depend on the situation – it gives an impression of the variety of divination techniques used in the Roman world. The two most important types of public divination during the republic were prodigies and auspices.

Prodigies

Prodigies may be defined as unusual events signifying the wrath of the gods and a disruption to the *pax deorum*, the "peace" with the gods. Thus, a *prodigium* – the Romans also used the terms *portentum* or *ostentum* – was always a bad sign. Prodigies did not occur on a special day in the year, did not point at an individual, but at the *res publica*, did not foretell the future, and were expiated by Roman officials usually at the beginning of the new year. As prodigies were classified, for example, lightning striking important buildings or sites, monstrous births like children with two heads, speaking animals, wild animals entering the city of Rome, eclipses, meteors, comets, and rainfalls of blood, milk, meat, or stones.

Although no ancient author gives a detailed description of the procedure that turned an unusual event into a prodigy, the following model can be reconstructed with some degree of certainty. First, the unusual sign had to be announced to a magistrate, usually a consul or a praetor (*nuntiatio*). The magistrate would then report the sign in the senate, in some cases taking a witness with him (*relatio*). The senate had the right to accept or to refuse the sign. Once a prodigy was accepted (*susceptio*), the senate had the power to decide which ritual to perform to expiate the *prodigium*. Usually, the senate would hand over this task to specialized priests: the pontiffs, the decemvirs (since Sulla, a college of 15 priests), and the *haruspices*. Usually, only one of the three priesthoods was asked for its opinion. The priests retired to consult their holy books, which contained ritual texts, not prophetic utterances; the pontiffs used the *libri pontificum*, the decemvirs the Sibylline Books, and the *haruspices* the *libri rituales*. The powers of these priesthoods were narrowly defined. The senate could accept, refuse, re-interpret, or amplify the advice of the priests. Since the colleges of the pontiffs and the *decemviri* consisted solely of senators, the senate held ultimate control of the prodigies. The priests functioned as subcommittees of the senate. Because Roman religion was by no means as rigid and unchangeable as believed in publications until almost the end of the twentieth century, but open to change, this model might be subject to modifications over time. Thus it is not clear whether prodigies were debated and interpreted immediately after they were reported or at the end of the old year.

Our sources for Roman prodigies are rare and often brief to the point of obfuscation. Livy mentions prodigies, and sometimes their expiation, at the beginning or at the end of a year. Iulius Obsequens, an author probably of the fourth century AD, compiled a list of prodigies based on Livy. Cicero deals with prodigies in his work *On Divination* (*De divinatione*). Other authors mention prodigies only occasionally. Examining the sources for prodigies proves to be a thorny problem. In Livy's narrative prodigies are isolated phenomena. It is widely accepted that Livy had his information about prodigies, probably with the historian Valerius Antias as intermediate, from priestly lists, especially the *commentarii pontificum*, published every year in the whitened board (*tabula dealbata*) of the pontiffs and finally published as *annales maximi*. Andreas Bendlin pointed out the weaknesses of this theory. First, it does not explain the prodigies expiated by priesthoods other than the pontiffs, and secondly, the contents of the *tabula dealbata* are highly debatable and might not include prodigies and/or their expiation. Therefore, it is plausible that the information about prodigies was handed down in a list kept by the senate. Even so, constructions of prodigy reports for political or literary reasons are always to be reckoned with (Bendlin 2005: 88–9). Thus, in the search for a coherent general structure much is plausible but not definitely verifiable.

The beginnings of regular expiation of prodigies are difficult to assert. Between 250 and 50 BC, prodigies are mentioned every second year on average. The first prodigy in Livy's account is a rain of stones in the Alban hills during the reign of Tullus Hostilius (Livy 1.31.2–4). Although every recorded event at such an early time in Roman history should be doubted, Livy's notice may at least indicate that prodigies were expiated before 249 BC. What changed in the middle of the third century BC was the frequency and the political quality of prodigies.

Some types of prodigies occurred only in relatively short periods. Seventeen *prodigia* concerning celestial lights occurred between 113 and 100 BC, nine cases of miscarriage occurred in 98–90 BC, weapons in the skies only in the second half of the second century BC, statues of gods sweating only in the first century BC, bee prodigies exclusively 118–111 BC. Once a strange event had been accepted by the senate as a *prodigium*, it was likely that another sign of the same kind would soon be related. At the same time, such signs seem to lose their divinatory quality after some years. Not every earthquake or lightning became automatically a *prodigium*. Why a sign was accepted as a *prodigium*, why others were not, and how many signs were rejected during a year is beyond explanation, because of the scarcity of the sources. What remains is a few cases of pragmatism.

Two cases may demonstrate the pragmatic attitude of the senate. After the reporting of numerous earthquakes in 193 BC, the consuls announced that on any day on which an earthquake had been reported, no one should report another earthquake (Livy 34.55.4). In 173 BC, a plague of locusts was expiated together with further prodigies by sacrifices and a supplication. When immense swarms of locusts invaded Apulia the following year, a designated praetor was sent to Apulia to organize collecting the locusts (Livy 42.10.7–8). Thus, the locusts of 172 BC were not regarded as a prodigy. Although the senate held ultimate power in the process of expiating a prodigy, it would be missing the point to interpret the Roman prodigy system as having been controlled by cynical and unscrupulous senators leading the dumb masses. Prodigies were not expiated because of the superstitious masses; prodigies communicated subtle messages.

Prodigies and Communication

Of the three priesthoods to propose an expiation rite, the *decemviri* were prominent in the period to the end of the second century BC. Thereafter the senate asked the *haruspices* more frequently. Pontiffs played a marginal role. Since the *decemviri* and the pontiffs consisted of senators, these colleges offered the *nobiles* an additional, although limited, field of influence. Only in a few cases do our sources note concurrence and disagreement between the priesthoods (Livy 42.20.1–4). It has been pointed out that the prodigy notices seem to be very specific violations of particular norms (Jason Davies 2004: 30). Unfortunately, the scarcity of our sources permits only speculation: if mules giving birth are reported only from Reate and no other town, this might be due to a special connection between Reate and Rome; for example, a senatorial family might have had strong ties to that city. Scientific explanations of the prodigious events, as put forward by Krauss (1930), do not help our understanding of the phenomenon. To some degree, prodigies articulate fears – earthquakes or military defeats, when turned into a prodigy, are catastrophic by nature. A number of prodigies can be interpreted by analogy: if the sacred spears of Mars in the Regia moved of their own accord this might be taken as a sign indicating war. Miscarriages may have symbolized problems in the system of procreation, fundamentally threatening a society based on agriculture. Other prodigies, such as mules having offspring, may as *adynaton* (impossibility) represent fears of an abstract loss of order. Many prodigies can be interpreted with the concept of liminality. Hermaphrodites are a transgression of the boundary between male and female, a boy with the head of an elephant is a mixture of human and animal, wolves entering the city of Rome violate the boundary between wild and civilized.

Since the prodigies were a violation of a border, boundaries were reinforced by the expiations. Most expiatory rites can be classified in the following system.

1   The removal of the prodigious event:
   (a)   *From Rome:* In 135 BC, an owl, which was heard first on the Capitol and then about the city, was caught and burned (Obsequens 26); in 101, a strange and rare scapegoat-ritual was performed: priests led a she-goat with its horns on fire through the city and expelled it through one of the gates (Obsequens 44a).
   (b)   *Inside the city:* This group includes the burial of lightning-bolts as well as the live burial of Vestals who had been convicted of unchastity. The two unchaste Vestals of 216 were buried within the walls at the *porta Collina*, the farthest possible spot from the forum (Livy 22.57.2).
   (c)   *Outside Rome:* Androgynes, for example, were not killed in Rome, but drowned by the *haruspices* in the sea (Livy 27.11.1–6) or in a river (Obsequens 27a).
2   The restoration of borders through rituals:
   (a)   In a *lustratio*, priests led a procession around the city walls, thus ritually restoring the boundaries and the safety of Rome.

(b)   In a supplication, the entire population went to the open temples and made
      sacrifices wearing wreaths in their hair and carrying laurel-twigs in their hands.
      The aim was the restoration and redefinition of the borders between gods
      and humans, namely boundaries between groups of Roman society. At the
      lectisternium of 217 BC, celebrated after the defeat at lake Trasimene, the
      statues of the 12 Olympian gods were ritually served food for three days
      (Livy 22.10.9). Such a sacral dinner community symbolized both the close
      connection and the difference between the gods and the Romans.

By transgressing the boundaries between senators and the rest of the Roman citizens, by celebrating rituals together, prodigies and their expiation were a means of
defining Roman identity. Only a few and rare rituals do not fit into this system, such
as a ritual fast in honor of Ceres, recorded only for 191 BC (Livy 36.37.4).

The same type of prodigy would not always be expiated with the same rituals.
The only exception is a rain of stones, regularly expiated by a *novendiale sacrum*,
feriae for nine days, during which work and lawsuits had to cease. Plagues were
expiated by games (*ludi*) from 364. When lightning struck in the city of Rome, the
bolt was buried and the place enclosed. For all other prodigies, the Romans used a
variety of rituals which can be classified as elements of regular cults performed outside the regular order, such as processions, supplications, *vota*, and sacrifice. Even
if the same type of prodigy recurs over centuries, the priests seem to have been
consulted by the senate every time. Sometimes, it seems, one ritual could suffice to
expiate several prodigies. In 93 BC, if Iulius Obsequens is to be believed, 13 prodigies
were expiated by lustrations (Obsequens 52).

For the senators, prodigies and the highly performative expiation rituals were a
means of communication. First, the senate, endowed with secular and religious competence, functioned as an interface between humans and the gods. Senators interpreted the signs and took care of their expiation. Second, expiating prodigies was
a means of coping with disaster and of strengthening identity and cohesion within
the Roman *res publica*. Prodigies did not foretell future disasters or the end of Rome.
On the contrary, the Romans were always able – such is the overall image we get
from reading the sources – to successfully expiate the signs. Therefore, the reporting of prodigies did not lead to fear or panic. Only the Romans had to deal with
such terrible signs, but the gods communicated them only to the Romans, thus legitimizing Rome's domination. If we accept that the whitened board (*tabula dealbata*)
of the pontiffs contained a constantly updated list of the prodigies of the current
year and if we accept that the list was accessible to everybody – our sources are highly
ambiguous about this – its result would not have been fear or panic; it would have
communicated that everything would be handled by the consuls in due course.

It is therefore plausible that the number of prodigies and the extent of expiation
rituals increased during times of crisis. This can be demonstrated in Livy's treatment
of the Second Punic War. Although we always must take into account his literary
strategies (Davies 2004: 12–52), it is worth examining the prodigies and expiation
rituals of 207 BC, a year about which Livy's notes are particularly detailed. At the
beginning of the year, a rainfall of stones had been expiated by a *novendiale sacrum*.

Other prodigies from Italian towns were reported: lightning struck the temple of Iuppiter at Minturnae and at Atella the city wall and a gate, a river of blood was seen at Minturnae, at Capua a wolf had entered the city and killed a guard. These prodigies were expiated by sacrifices and a one-day *supplicium*. Then again a rain of stones led to another *novendiale sacrum*. After that, a four-year-old hermaphrodite was discovered at Frusino and expiated according to the advice of the *haruspices*: it was put into a chest, carried out to the sea and drowned. But this was not enough. The pontiffs declared that 27 maidens should sing a hymn during a procession through the city of Rome. While they were learning the hymn in the temple of Iuppiter Stator, the temple of Juno Regina was struck by lightning. In order to expiate this prodigy, the matrons resident in the city of Rome or within 10 miles thereof brought a con-tribution from their dowries. This was made into a golden basin as a gift and carried to the temple of Juno Regina by 25 matrons. Then the decemvirs appointed the day for another sacrifice to Juno Regina: a procession went from the temple of Apollo through the *porta Carmentalis* into the city to the temple of Juno Regina on the Aventine hill. Livy describes a route containing a number of landmarks, such as the forum and the *forum boarium*. The procession halted in the forum and, passing a rope from hand to hand, the maidens advanced and accompanied their singing of the hymn by stamping their feet (Livy 27.37.7–15). As a result, the procession did not take the shortest way from the temple of Apollo to the temple of Juno Regina. The advant-age of this route was that the procession lasted longer and that a larger part of the city was covered: more people could watch the procession and thus take part in it.

The expiation rituals of 207 lasted an extraordinarily long time: the two nine-day rituals, the supplication in between, and the one-day procession all added up to at least 20 days. If we take into account the fact that the priests needed some time to find the appropriate rituals, there must have been a substantial delay. According to Livy, the consuls waited with all other business until the rituals had ended. And they had good reason to wait. In 209, when a hermaphrodite was reported for the first time, no rituals were performed. Two years later, in 207, the Romans came up with a religious innovation due to the potentially problematic domestic situation. The two new consuls, Gaius Claudius Nero and Marcus Livius Salinator, were enemies. Furthermore, Marcus Livius Salinator, consul for the first time in 219, had been exiled after quarrels over the distribution of booty from a successful war with the Illyrians: in 207, the outcast, consul again, had to be re-integrated into society. The rituals can be interpreted as a representation of harmony between the consuls and between Salinator and the people. Besides, the military situation was giving some cause for alarm: in early 207 the Carthaginian general Hasdrubal was on his way to Italy in order to bring fresh troops to his brother Hannibal. Performing the rituals might have provided the time to find the fitting strategy to deal with Hasdrubal. If this hypothesis is correct, the delay had been worth it. The two consuls defeated Hasdrubal in the battle at the river Metaurus in the same year and weakened Hannibal's position in Italy.

About 50 percent of all known prodigies happened in Rome. Almost all remain-ing prodigies occurred in Italy, most of them in towns along the important roads, for example along the Via Appia and Via Latina between Rome and Capua. Only a few prodigies were expiated in the places where they had happened; for instance, the hermaphrodite found at Ferentinum in 133 BC was drowned in the local river (Obsequens 27a). The status of the territory on which a prodigy had occurred was not crucial. The Romans took care of many prodigies happening on *ager peregrinus*, on territory not directly belonging to Rome (Rasmussen 2003: 219–40). Therefore, dealing in Rome with prodigies from cities outside Rome was an important means of communication. While the Romans showed that they cared for the other cities, they also underlined Rome's position as the high court to deal with matters of religion. Even if we do not know if other Italian cities used the category "prodigy" at all – the concept of prodigy may have been exported by the Romans – the expiation of prodigies at Rome helped to create a common identity. About 80 percent of Italian prodigies were announced from cities located in a stretch between the area of Caere in the north and that of Capua in the south, between the sea in the west and the Apennines in the east. This region corresponds to the extension of Roman territory in the middle of the fourth century BC; it was densely populated with Roman citizens. Therefore the importance of prodigies as a means of communication with the Etruscan *socii*, allegedly a reason why the Etruscan cities sided with the rebellious Italians during the Social War (91–89 BC), only shortly before the end of the conflict if at all (MacBain 1982: 60–81), has to be revised. The centre at Rome used prodigies mainly to communicate with its citizens outside the *urbs*, not with the *socii*. After the end of the Social War, when Roman citizenship had been granted to all Italians, prodigies were not needed any longer to symbolically differentiate cities with Roman citizenship from the *socii*. This is one of the reasons for the decline of the prodigy system during the first century BC – the practice of reporting and expiating prodigies declined significantly after the Social War and ended in the early empire. Another factor in this highly complex phenomenon is the rise of individual generals to power: while they attempted to control divine signs, they suppressed the constantly negative prodigies and preferred positive signs signifying divine favor. As a group, the *nobiles* lost influence.

Augurs, Magistrates, and Auspices

Augurs did not foretell the future, they only expressed the approval or disapproval of the gods. Thus, augury is comparable to the interpretation of prodigies. In his classic article on the augural law, Jerzy Linderski (1986) distinguished between the individual augurs and the college of the augurs, composed, to be clear about this point, of the individual augurs. The number of the college of the augurs was constantly increased: from three to nine members in 300 BC, to 15 by Sulla, and 16 by Caesar. The task of the college of the augurs was observation and explication of the auspices and *auguria*. When a *vitium* occurred, the college of the augurs was consulted. *Vitium*, a mistake in the performance of a ritual, could happen at the elections, at the legislative assemblies, or especially in connection with military operations. As in the case of a priestly college offering explanation of a prodigy, the senate was free either to accept or to reject the advice. When Marcus Claudius Marcellus was about to enter upon his consulship in 215 BC, there was a clap of thunder. The senate consulted the augurs and declared that he was *vitio creatum*, that is, that there was a defect in the election. The senate agreed and Marcellus had to abdicate (Livy 23.31.13). But there was another reason why he had to step down: for the first time in Roman history, both consuls were plebeians. Marcus Claudius Marcellus accepted the verdict of the augurs, but he reacted in a peculiar way. From that time on, whenever he planned an important undertaking and did not want to interfere with the augurs, he traveled only in a closed litter (Cic. *Div.* 2.77). In this way he could not be seen and he could not see any signs occurring outside: bad omens would not concern him. The college also acted on the day the magistrates took up their office, at decisions of the assemblies, and at the start of a war (Linderski 1986: 2159–62).

While the college of the augurs acted only when consulted by the senate, individual augurs acted on their own initiative. Only the individual augurs held the auspices or observed the sky (Cic. *Leg.* 2.20f.). Of all Roman priests, the augurs had the most prominent position. Cicero claimed that the highest and most important authority was that of the augurs because they had the power to grant or refuse permission to hold an assembly, to declare null and void the acts of assemblies, and to force consuls to resign their offices (Cic. *Leg.* 2.31). Notwithstanding Cicero's garrulousness and self-confidence, and notwithstanding the fact that Cicero was an augur himself, his judgment is correct. Once an augur had perceived a bad sign, he could close a session of the assembly with the formula *alio die* – "at another day." Any business already begun was abandoned. Such a procedure would buy time to debate important issues again and to influence decisions. Generals of the late republic, for example Mark Antony, proudly referred to their augurate in their coinage.

Auguria had no time limits and were performed only by the augurs. If a magistrate was inaugurated, the *augurium* would last for a year. In the case of a priest it would last for his entire life and if a temple was inaugurated there was no time limit at all. The most prominent example is the *augurium salutis*, an annual prayer, which had fallen into oblivion and was revived by Augustus – the augurs asked the gods if it was permissible for the magistrates to pray for the safety of the people (Vaahtera 2001: 133–6).

In contrast to *auguria*, auspices were valid for one day only and could be held by anybody. The result of an *auspicium* was a divine "yes" or "no"; interpretation was not required. Again, the Romans were quite practical about divination: if an *auspicium* did not lead to the expected divine approval of an intended undertaking, it was repeated the following day. Auspices primarily meant signs from the observation of birds, but thunder and lightning could also be important. Festus, a lexicographer of the second century AD, knew of five different categories of signs: from the sky (thunder and lightning), from the flight of birds and from the sounds produced by birds, from sacred chickens (*tripudium*), from quadrupeds (given by animals), and from unusual, threatening occurrences (Festus 316 L). Auspices from the flight of birds require the magistrate to go to the place of observation before sunrise, to define his *templum*, the religious delimitation of a specific area, and to wait for the sign. As soon as the magistrate had received the sign he had been waiting for, the session was over and the business could be started. Auspices regarding the *res publica* were held only by the magistrates or the individual augurs and were performed before important decisions: assemblies, elections, and war.

The basic form of magisterial auspice was the *tripudium*: when chickens, brought especially for that purpose, ate their food in such greed and haste that part of the food fell from their beaks, this signified divine assent. A magistrate could influence such behavior by letting the chicken starve or by taking care that the fodder was dry, so it would fall off better (Cic. *Div.* 1.27f.). If this ritual was not public – our sources are unclear about this aspect – it was reduced to a dialogue between the magistrate and his assistant, who had to watch the chicken. The *tripudium* was performed before the start of an expedition and at the beginning of the day of a battle. When Publius Claudius Pulcher, consul in 249 BC, intended to start the naval battle against the Carthaginians at Drepanum, the chickens refused to eat. Instead of complying with the divine sign, the consul ordered the chickens to be thrown into the water, adding: "If they do not want to eat, they may drink" (Suet. *Tiberius* 2.2). Publius Claudius Pulcher lost the battle. His impious action ruined his career. When he came back to Rome, he was heavily fined. Roman authors, especially Livy, constructed Roman defeats along the same lines: Roman defeats result from the neglect of divine signs.

If the interpretation of a sign turned out to be wrong, a Roman would not blame the divination system, but himself: the mistake must be in the ritual or in the interpretation. Anthropological research reveals the same phenomenon in other civilizations: there might be doubts about the quality of a diviner, but never doubts about the system of divination. Nevertheless, divination was not uncontested. Cicero's work *De divinatione* reflects the problems connected to divine signs during the late republic. In the first book, Cicero's brother argues that divination is possible, while in the second book, Cicero himself maintains that almost all sorts of divination, except for the types important for the *res publica*, are bogus. At the end of the work, Cicero leaves the reader to decide. Although it is unclear if Cicero was the first to articulate doubt, and although Cicero relied heavily on Greek philosophers, it is obvious that the discourse about divination contained some skepticism.

Although seers and prophets were a part of the Roman construction of the mythical past – the first augur, Attus Navius, who was contested by one of the Roman kings, had more powers than other augurs (Livy 1.36) – they do not occur as public priests in republican Rome. Apart from the public augurs, there were also private seers meeting the ever-present demand for divine help in decision-making. In contrast to the public diviners, they could be treated with disdain. Astrologers were occasionally banned from Rome. Cato's saying that a *haruspex* was forced to laugh on meeting another *haruspex* (Cat. *Agr.* 5.4) refers to *haruspices* working for money. The *haruspices* who were asked to find a ritual to expiate a prodigy came from the upper class of Etruria. They were also specialists in extispicy, the examination of the entrails of sacrificial victims (North 1990: 51–61).

Individual Politicians and the Power of Divination

Omens reported to have happened to a given person, in most cases prominent politicians at a turning point in their careers, differ from prodigies. Omens are the only signs said to foretell the future. Many omens are favorable signs; negative omens were never expiated by the *res publica*. While prodigies might actually have occurred in one way or another, omens were definitely constructed. The first Roman senator regarded as having direct contact with the gods was Publius Cornelius Scipio Africanus, who defeated Hannibal at Zama (202 BC) in the Second Punic War and who used to sit in the temple on the Capitoline hill. He neither confirmed nor denied rumors that he conversed with Iuppiter (Livy 26.19.5). During the lifetime of Scipio, the consensus within the senate was still strong: Scipio, the most famous man and therefore the politically most dangerous man of his time, spent the last decades of his life in exile outside Rome.

Although divinatory practices had great importance in the Roman republic, abuse can scarcely be diagnosed. Obstruction as a means of political struggle was used only in the late republic. Even then only elections, not laws, were blocked. Generally, obstruction was not used to influence the masses, but to control the members of the senatorial elite. Since the priests dealing with the signs came from the Roman nobility, their interpretation expressed the consensus within the Roman elite. Obstruction was a means of delaying a decision, not completely revoking it. Thus, premature decisions were avoided (Rüpke 2005a: 1450).

Negative signs were constructed in order to display the unlawfulness of a political adversary and to demonstrate that the gods were his enemies. One of the first death omens (*omen mortis*) concerns the politician Tiberius Sempronius Gracchus, who had made many enemies by his attempt to enforce agrarian reforms. On the day he was killed, he hurt his foot severely on leaving his house; ravens threw a stone in his way (Plut. *Gracchus* 17). These signs gave the clear message that it would be better for Gracchus to stay at home. Our sources are too scant to decide if the signs were constructed by the enemies of Gracchus in order to show that he was doomed or if his supporters adorned his last day with divine signs. Another sign, this time concerning his brother Gaius Sempronius Gracchus, is clearer. In 121 BC, a pack of wolves was said to have scattered the boundary stones which had been set up during the division of properties by Gaius Gracchus (Obsequens 33): an unequivocal hint from the gods that they were not pleased with the division of land planned by Gracchus. Finally, Gaius Gracchus was slain and the division of land abandoned.

A particular case of the uses of interpretation for personal advantage can be studied in Cicero's speech *De haruspicum responso* of 56 BC. During Cicero's exile (59–56 BC), his personal enemy, P. Clodius Pulcher, ensured that Cicero's house in Rome was demolished and the site was dedicated to the goddess Liberty. On his return from exile, the site of his house was given back to Cicero, who planned to rebuild it. In the same year, the senate declared a strange rumbling noise outside Rome a *prodigium* and asked the *haruspices* to interpret it. According to the *haruspices*, divine anger was provoked because, inter alia, games had been celebrated without enough care and thereby polluted, envoys had been slain against all faith and right, and sacred and holy places had been profaned (Cic. *Har. resp.* 9). This untypical answer, which goes far beyond the usual advice of the ritual for restoring the peace with the gods, seems to have been evoked by the critical political situation. And the answer was used by both sides: while Clodius referred the response of the *haruspices* to Cicero's plans of rebuilding a private house on sacred ground – for Clodius clearly a sacrilege – Cicero delivered a speech to prove that the sign referred to Clodius' crimes. Finally, Cicero had powerful friends for a time and rebuilt his house. Although he somehow doubted divination in his work *De divinatione*, he talks about a dream he had during his exile: the long-deceased general Gaius Marius approached him in this dream and asked him why he was so sad. When Cicero lamented his exile, Gaius Marius told him to cheer up and to go to the temple of Honor (*honos*) and Virtue (*virtus*). Cicero claimed that the senate met in that very temple when it decided to recall Cicero from his exile (Cic. *Div.* 1.59). By publishing this dream – it is not unlikely that Cicero talked about it long before his works were published – Cicero allied himself with the tradition of another famous Roman who had been exiled and who had returned in triumph.

Generals of the civil wars accepted only positive signs and they had private seers, thus documenting their ability to communicate with the gods: the boundary between "private" and "public" divination disappeared. In the war against Jugurtha (111–105 BC), Marius had his personal soothsayer (Plut. *Marius* 8.4); Sulla had a *haruspex* who turned a Roman soldier killed by lightning during the siege of Athens into a favorable sign (Obsequens 56b). Publius Cornelius Lentulus Sura took part in the conjuration of Catilina, and Lentulus felt called upon to do so by a prophecy of the *quindecimviri* that the next ruler of Rome would come from the family of the Cornelii (Cic. *In Catilinam* 3.9). A number of positive omens are reported about Caesar. Signs foretold his victory at decisive battles; on precisely the day when he defeated Pompey at Pharsalus (48 BC), the statue of Victoria in the temple at Elis in southern Greece turned toward the door; at Pergamum drums sounded in the temple; at Tralles in Asia Minor a palm tree, symbol of victory, grew within a few hours in front of the statue of Caesar (Caesar, *Bellum civile* 3.105). During the last decades of the Roman republic, signs became personalized. We also know of omens foretelling Caesar's death. His wife Calpurnia dreamed that she was holding her dead husband in her arms (Plut. *Caesar* 63).

In the case of Augustus, positive signs abound. When he first entered Rome after the death of Caesar, the sun shone on him and produced a rainbow (Obsequens 68), an obvious indication of divine favor. In 42 BC, three suns were seen merging into one during a sacrifice (Obsequens 70), which prophesied that the power of the triumvirs would be inherited by one person – Octavian/Augustus. Signs were told about the critical points of his life: at the beginning of his political career at Rome and at important battles. It seems plausible that the signs were not just inventions of later historians and biographers, but were communicated during the important events. During the reign of Augustus, prodigies turn up only in 17 and 16 BC. The prodigies of 17 BC did not just happen anywhere, but took place in the villa of Livia, Augustus' wife (Obsequens 71), and seem to have been welcome in the context of the Secular Games (*ludi saeculares*) taking place in the same year. The following year, the day after Augustus had left Rome to travel to Gaul, the temple of Iuventas burned down, a wolf killed some people in the Forum Romanum, the Forum was swarming with ants, and at night torches wandering from south to north illuminated the sky. As expiation the citizens offered prayers for the safety of the emperor (Dio 54.19.7).

The burning down of the temple of Iuventas (= Youth) could be interpreted as foretelling a catastrophe in the system of reproduction, the wolf and the ants in the Forum as strangers invading Rome, the torches as signs of war: by leaving Rome, the prodigies seem to say, Augustus had stripped the city of its defense. The prodigies illustrate the close connection of the emperor to divine signs. After Augustus, only few prodigies were expiated. The process of personalization and monopolization of divine signs ended with Augustus – signs were reserved for the emperor. Later biographers would narrate omens at the birth, death, and other significant turning points in the lives of the emperors. The end of the republican prodigy system and the political decline of the senate were two facets of the fundamental transformation of power at Rome between 60 BC and AD 14.

FURTHER READING

The fundamental study of ancient divination is still Bouché-Leclerq (1879–82), a massive work in four volumes. The slim volume of Bloch (1963) is also helpful. MacBain (1982) studies the relation between Rome and the Italian cities and offers a list of prodigies. Rosenberger (1998) interprets prodigies as violations of boundaries which were restored by the expiations. Rasmussen (2003) approaches Roman divination from a sociological point of view and offers a list of prodigies. On augurs, see the immensely learned article by Linderski (1982) and Vaahtera (2001). Essential for our understanding of the political processes in the Roman republic is Hölkeskamp (2004).

CHAPTER TWENTY-TWO

Emperors: Caring for the Empire and Their Successors

Peter Herz

The Mental Situation

Like most people in antiquity the Romans of the last centuries BC loved stability and security in all parts of their life. It made no special difference if this applied to their private life or to the state in which they lived. *Res novae* or new things were equivalent to unwanted and dangerous changes or even the enforced ruin of the existing order. On the other hand the glorified past of their own state and their own society was looked upon as ideal.

The Romans knew very well that those common and desirable goals "stability" and "well-being" could not be achieved or secured by their own abilities. Achieving and securing those things were the direct result of the social and political behavior of the whole Roman state, where everything was done according to the will of the gods of the Roman state.

The aim of all these efforts was the creation of a harmonious situation that one could describe as consensus between human beings and gods (*consensus deorum hominum*). The Romans themselves were proud that they were the people that paid most attention, when it came to the point, to fulfilling all obligations to the Roman gods. This was a special kind of behavior that the Romans themselves called *religio*. Therefore Cicero was very proud when he declared the Romans the most religious people that existed on earth (*populus religiosissimus*). The visible result was that the Romans had become the masters of the whole world with the gods on their side.

This fundamental attitude was additionally emphasized because there existed no difference between secular and religious authority in Rome. On the contrary, each political or military competence was firmly connected with religious demands and religious authority. The symbiosis of these two parts is still reflected in the expression "right to order with the right to consult the gods" (*imperium cum auspiciis*), which described the official power of all higher Roman magistrates (Linderski 1995). Therefore every representative of the Roman state was obliged to ask for the permission of the Roman gods for all his planned activities before he was allowed to perform any official act in public (e.g. before organizing elections). If he omitted the obligatory consultation of the gods or continued with his plans even though the gods had already demonstrated that they disliked his doings, the project was legally invalid from the beginning.

The same strict categories were applied by the Romans if it came to the separation of things belonging to the gods (*sacrum*) or to human beings (*profanum*). Under the Roman interpretation, even an unwitting violation of this divine order had to have grave consequences that endangered the single citizen as well as the Roman state as a whole. The disturbance of the former harmony between gods and human beings was usually revealed by a series of catastrophes. This included natural catastrophes like an eclipse of the sun, earthquakes, a stroke of lightning, but also defeats of the Roman army.

The Religious Situation at the End of the Republic

This basic religious attitude of the Roman population had been intensified by the collective experiences of the last chaotic century of the Roman republic. Bloody civil wars, catastrophic defeats in wars against foreign enemies like the Cimbers and the Teutons, and social unrest like the slaves' war under Spartacus had afflicted not only the Roman people, but the whole world that was ruled by the Romans. In this way a mental situation had been created in which humans felt abandoned and punished by the gods. The poet Horace (*Epodes* 16) declares that the civil wars are a direct result of Romulus' fratricide. That means Rome and its population are doomed from the foundation of the city by Romulus and Remus. Horace, who had lived through the civil war between the followers of Caesar and his murderers, feels so desperate that he has only one final piece of advice for his fellow-citizens: leave this doomed land and follow me to a land far away without war and bloodshed.

The unpleasant feeling that they lived in a final time and were close to a catastrophic end of the whole world was not only widespread among the Roman population, but was common knowledge among nearly all people that lived in this time. That mankind existed indeed on the eve of the final destruction was corroborated by a multitude of oracles and ominous prophecies. Closely connected with the fear of a catastrophic end of the world and mankind was the hope that the looming catastrophe had to occur but that it did not mean the final end for the whole world. For there existed also a widespread conviction that after such a catastrophe there would be a new beginning for mankind, one could say a second chance. The guarantee of the new beginning was usually identical with the appearance of a divine being or at least of a human being who had been sent by the gods. With the friendly assistance of this person a new beginning would be possible.

These messianic expectations could assume quite different forms. For the people in the east of the Mediterranean world, this messiah was of course identical with the person who would free these nations from the oppression and injustice of the Roman domination, and bring back older and therefore better times. This holds true for the expectations that the Greeks connected with the policy of Mithradates VI (120–63 BC), but also for the messianic hopes of the Jews, who expected first of all, contrary to the Christian interpretation, a Jewish messiah with political aims. The Romans themselves expected especially the appearance of a man who would bring the nearly endless succession of civil wars and political upheavals to a fortunate and final end. In this case, too, the expected condition of the new world that would emerge was identical with the return to an older and therefore near paradisiac time.

The great poet Virgil voiced the hopes of many of his contemporaries in one of his poems (*Eclogue* 4). Virgil, too, was convinced that mankind had reached the final period of its existence, but that after the catastrophe a new generation would be sent from heaven and a new golden era would start again. Virgil had no specific idea who would accomplish this redemption of mankind and make the new golden era a reality. When he wrote this poem he only hoped for a child that would be sent from heaven. This "child" has to be understood as a symbol of something new and innocent, something that had not been tainted by past guilt. This poem was the expression of a widespread sentiment, not a political manifesto with a clear agenda. Every politician who responded to the feelings of the population could be regarded as the heaven-sent savior.

The Response of Augustus to the Problems

In the reality of political life after the murder of Gaius Iulius Caesar it soon became obvious that Gaius Iulius Caesar Octavianus, the adopted son and heir of the murdered dictator (since January 16, 27 BC, honored with the title *Augustus* = "the sublime"), was the best qualified to respond adequately to these not very specific expectations. Octavian took up these vague expectations of a divine savior, but he transferred these ideas onto his own person and made them politically useful for himself (Ramsey and Licht 1997).

Certainly it was very helpful for him that in the eastern parts of the empire the concept of the divine benefactor (*euergetes*) and savior (*soter*) was much more firmly established than in Rome. The Greek east already had a long religious tradition of how to deal with such divine rulers, dating back to the time of Alexander the Great. Therefore Augustus only had to step into the role of the Hellenistic kings and the whole system of religious honors that had evolved around their person. Sacrifices, temples, competitions, statues, identifications between ruler and god represented a well-established religious system challenged by nobody.

Thus Augustus could use without hesitation all the religious and ideological opportunities that were offered to him by the precedents of the Hellenistic world. Very soon the tradition was formed that Augustus had been conceived by his mother Atia when she visited the temple of Apollo in Rome and that his real father was Apollo himself. Besides the message to the public that the new ruler of Rome was a demigod and therefore capable of achieving more than ordinary humans, Augustus thus placed himself in a long-established tradition going back to the time of Alexander the Great. According to the so-called *Alexanderroman* the great king had been fathered by the god Zeus-Ammon himself.

This was a narrative that not only ranked Alexander amid such illustrious persons as Hercules and Dionysus, borne by mortal mothers but with the supreme god Zeus as their father. It was also an indication of things to come. At the end of his human existence Alexander had become a god. By adapting his own policy to the image of Alexander the Great, Augustus indicated what he expected at the end of his life: he would become a god himself.

The Acceptance of the Emperor Cult

While in Rome Augustus was compelled to respect the sentiments of the senate, and had to accept a political compromise that did not allow him to establish a real cult for his person during his lifetime, outside Italy things looked quite different. In Rome and Italy a cult that addressed the emperor directly was impossible; therefore people preferred to establish cults for divine qualities that were closely connected with the person of the emperor. To this group belonged the cult of the imperial peace (*pax Augusta*) or the fortunate destiny of the emperor (*fortuna Augusta*). In this case divinities that before the empire had been the property of the whole Roman state were redirected to the emperor and privatized.

This is proved by the so called calendar-decree of Asia. The provincial council of Asia had announced a competition to find the best way to honor the emperor Augustus. The best proposal was to let the New Year's Day of the local calendar coincide with the birthday of Augustus (September 23). Parts of this decree have been conserved on inscriptions and allow us a glimpse into the sentiments of the population:

> Because Providence that dispenses divinely over our lives by employing labor and energy has looked for perfection in life by procreating Augustus whom she equipped with excellent qualities because of the well-being of mankind. Just as she had sent him as a savior for us and our offspring. A savior who brought the war to an end and set every thing in order. By his appearance Caesar surpassed the hopes of everybody who received good news (*euangelion*) before us. He did not only surpass everybody who had been a benefactor (*euergetes*) before him but he did not leave any hope for those (benefactors) who will come in future times.

The winner of the competition, the Roman governor of the province of Asia, was characterized as a man who had been sent as "a benefactor of the province by the hand and the spirit of the god (= Augustus)." In a later part of the decree the provincial council declared, "He (Augustus) has given a new face to the whole world, a world that with the greatest pleasure would have plunged itself into the abyss had not the greatest common good of every human being, that is, Augustus, been born."

The decree for the province of Asia has been handed down to us by mere chance. The parallel decrees for the isle of Cyprus, where during the reign of Augustus people twice renamed all 12 months to honor Augustus and his family, have unfortunately been lost (Samuel 1972).

Under those circumstances it comes as no surprise that it soon became the case that, in the imagination of many contemporaries, the personal security of the emperor and his domination (*securitas imperatoris*) was equated with the security and the well-being of the whole empire (*securitas imperii*). You could even say that the Roman empire could only continue to exist and function properly if the emperor and his government were not questioned.

This ideological concept becomes evident in an inscription from the city of Assos in western Asia Minor (*Syll.*³ 797 = *IGRR* 4.251 = *Inschriften von Assos* no. 26). The inscription informs us of a certainly routine affair: the beginning of the reign of the emperor Caligula (spring 37) and the oath-taking of the city of Assos. Interesting is the introduction of the text, which describes the action in religious language:

> Because the beginning of the reign of emperor Gaius Caesar Germanicus Augustus has been reported who is expected by all human beings with prayers and as the whole world in no way can find a limit for her joy and each city and each nation hurries to see the face of the god just as if the most blissful time for mankind were near, the city of Assos has decided . . .

At the end of the text we are informed that the city had dispatched five envoys to Rome, who prayed for the well-being of the emperor and offered a sacrifice to Iuppiter Capitolinus in the name of their home city. Certainly hundreds if not thousands of comparable legations crowded Rome in this year to see the emperor and offer sacrifices to the supreme Roman god on behalf of Caligula.

The religious language developed and fostered by the existence of the imperial cult permeated nearly completely the official language of the empire, at least in the east. Therefore the simple fact that the emperor Caligula had consented to become the honorary leading magistrate of the city of Kyzikos in Asia Minor, and had granted his old friends, the Thracian princes Rhoemetalkes, Polemon, and Kotys, the right to succeed their ancestors in their territories, resulted in a decree of the city (*Syll.*³ 798 = *IGRR* 4.145). The decree is about contemporary with the oath of Assos and was published in exuberant and completely religious language:

> As the new sun, Gaius Caesar Augustus Germanicus, intended to enlighten with her rays even the kingdoms that are subjected to the domination of the emperor to demand even more veneration for the splendor of her immortality, he appointed the children of (king) Kotys, his early friends Rhoemetalkes, Polemon, and Kotys, to the kingdoms that were due to them from their fathers and ancestors, without giving the kings a chance to find the appropriate thanks for the benefactions of such a god even if they had intended to do so. Now they enjoy the superabundance of the divine grace and are greater in this respect than their predecessors, because these received the dominion in the succession of their fathers, while they were appointed as kings thanks to the grace of Gaius Caesar to be co-rulers with such gods. Acts of grace from the gods differ from human succession by inheritance like day from night, immortality from transitoriness.

The identification of the emperor with Helios, the Sun-god, has been total. Caligula is the "new sun," who is physically completely removed from the sphere of ordinary humans and has no obligation to bother herself with the sorrows of the humans. But because of her philanthropy she showered the "superabundance of her divine grace" (*charis*) on the human beings. In this context the idea of "mercy" or *charis* means that the emperor was not obliged to do anything positive at all for humans. It was the result of his divine benevolence (*indulgentia*) and originated from his divine friendliness to the poor, plagued people (*philanthropia*). This concept points to an ideological development originating in Hellenistic times, when *philanthropia* was a central virtue of a ruler. As a result of such imperial acts of grace pouring down from heaven, ordinary people were obliged to worship the emperor in order to ensure that this dispensation of the splendor of the emperor's divine immortality could be guaranteed. The whole concept tended to emphasize the inferiority of ordinary humans face to face with the power and the exalted status of the emperor.

The Emperor and the Population of the Empire

How did the population of the empire perceive the emperor? Certainly people regarded him as a person endowed with extraordinary (i.e. divine) abilities and powers. That was a definition most people could embrace without difficulty. But was the emperor a visible god (*theos epiphanes*)? Here we encounter difficulties. For the western parts of the empire where the necessary religious traditions were lacking, I am skeptical. The eastern provinces had a completely different religious tradition in dealing with rulers and cultic honors, and for them things are completely different. Here we find the widespread perception that the emperor was not only endowed with special, super-human abilities, but that he was indeed a visible god.

We have a very illuminating example of this belief from the little town of Akraiphia in central Greece (*ILS* 8794 = *Syll.*[3] 814). The inscription reports the local reaction to a declaration of liberty for the whole of Greece that had been announced by the emperor Nero during a visit to Greece. The local population reacted to the act by establishing an official cult dedicated to "the liberating Zeus Nero, for all eternity." In this case Nero represents a special aspect of the supreme god, his ability to free people.

Most ruler cults known from the Hellenistic kingdoms represent the religious reaction of the population to positive achievements by a ruler that had already become reality. Besides the fact that these cults were limited to a city or a nation, things in the world that was ruled by the Roman emperors were completely different. In this world such cults were in many cases established immediately after the beginning of the reign. This means people reacted at a time when the new emperor had achieved nothing at all, if we disregard the fact that he had succeeded in assuming government, which in earlier times had justified such a cult. Therefore it is legitimate to say that these religious honors are a public recognition of the extraordinary political position the future emperor would have in this world.

In addition, these honors aimed also at the position of the emperor as a mediator between the gods and the humans, and hopefully at the benefits that could be effected by his future government for the whole empire and his population. In the conception of those people the emperor was still a mortal human being, but a very special one, who had been endowed by the gods with important qualities and powers that were only accessible to him and that were necessary for him to achieve his task on earth. Many people probably even identified the emperor as a god who had revealed himself only for a certain time before he returned from the earth to the rest of the gods in heaven (*theos epiphanes*).

The Emperor as Guarantee of Peace and Security

How the beneficial work of the emperor was perceived by most members of the population is nicely demonstrated by an episode from the last days of Augustus, in AD 14. Near Naples the emperor's ship met a ship from Alexandria. When the crew and the passengers recognized the imperial vessel and the emperor, they changed their clothes and put on their white garments destined for religious service, put wreaths on their heads, offered sacrifices with incense to the emperor, and acclaimed him with the words "Because of you we are living, because of you we can travel the seas, because of you we enjoy liberty and wealth."

Under those circumstances it comes as no surprise that in some parts of the empire the emperors could appear as miracle-workers and heal sick people. Thus we have the story that Vespasian (AD 69–70), the founder of the Flavian dynasty, during a visit to Alexandria healed sick people by only laying his hands on them. The interested public interpreted this immediately as a sure indication that he had been elected to his office by the gods.

As a rule imperial cult did not mean presenting an individual declaration of faith; such a perception is clearly influenced by the Christian tradition of religion. Imperial cult meant the individual was expected to take part in collective religious acts. Each human being under Roman rule was obliged to participate in such religious activities not as an individual but as a member of the citizenship of his home town, a soldier in a military unit, a member of a local city council, or a member of the Roman senate.

The most illustrative examples come from the city of Rome. The imperial capital was divided into 265 blocks (*vici*) (Plin. *Nat.* 3.66f.), which constituted a kind of *collegium* with its own magistrates, the so-called *magistri vici*, who were each year elected from the local inhabitants. They were supposed to offer regular sacrifices to the imperial *Genius* and the guardian spirits (Lares) of the imperial household, which were worshiped in a small chapel on their block, as well as to organize festivities and represent their community within the city of Rome. The *Genius* is best understood as a personal guardian spirit each male human being owned. The female equivalent was the *Iuno*.

The Propagation of the Imperial Theology

One of the great problems for those dealing with the imperial cult is the question of how the "theology" of the cult and the information were disseminated. In this context a papyrus from Egypt offers valuable information. The text has preserved part of a play that was staged at the local theater. The god Phoebus Apollo himself appeared on stage to announce to the audience that he had just accompanied the emperor Trajan, with his carriage drawn by white horses, to heaven. But then he announces the good news that the new emperor Hadrian has just entered office, who is characterized with the words "whom all things obey because of his virtue and the *Genius* of his divine father (= Trajan)."

The superhuman appearance of the emperor and his core family could quite effectively be transmitted by the minting of coins (see chapter 11). Of course coins could not replace the written message of an honorary inscription and an official oration praising the divine achievements of the emperor, but certainly coins were much more widely disseminated within the empire. Coins used a pictorial language with a concentrated and simplified message that could be immediately understood, at least by the population of the cities. A coin with a picture showing the supreme god, Jupiter, handing a small statue of the goddess of victory to the emperor transmitted a definite message: the emperor has received his power and his ability to be victorious from the supreme god himself.

Only a very small minority of the Roman population had the chance to meet the emperor at least once during their own lifetime. The emperors only rarely left Rome or Italy – the traveling emperor Hadrian (AD 117–38) is clearly an exception – but the desire to enjoy the personal presence of the emperor was very great. Under these circumstances the fabricated image of the emperor was of enormous importance, because it could be used as a substitute for his person. You could address the image of the emperor when you offered sacrifice to him; the picture of the emperor was present if you took an oath and invoked his name to confirm the validity of your statement. A slave who felt tortured by his master could flee to the statue of the emperor and find a kind of asylum, because the shelter offered by the image of the emperor was as valid as the emperor himself.

The conviction that the statue of an emperor was as powerful as the living emperor himself was much more than an expression of a primitive popular belief. It represented a kind of belief that was also shared by the higher ranks of the political hierarchy. Therefore the picture of the emperor could be used even during diplomatic encounters to represent the authority and power of the emperor if he could not attend the meeting. When the Armenian king Tiridates met Domitius Corbulo, the Roman supreme commander who had conducted the war against him, the reigning emperor Nero (AD 54–68) was far away in Rome. Tacitus (*Annales* 15.28) has described the ceremony that took place in AD 63.

The Roman and Armenian armies, arranged in battle order, were watching. In the center of the Roman army a *tribunal* had been built, on which the seat of a magistrate (*sella curulis*) with the image of Nero had been placed. After victims had been sacrificed king Tiridates approached this image, took the diadem from his head, and placed it in front of the image. Afterward Tiridates traveled to Rome to receive his appointment from Nero himself. The presence of the emperor's image during this ceremony has a double meaning. First of all the image had the function of sub-stitute for the emperor, but then it also emphasized that Corbulo, the leading Roman magistrate in the place, was licenced to act as the representative of the emperor.

As in the eyes of the people the emperor and his well-being were an indispens-able precondition for the well-being of the empire as a whole, the subjects too had to contribute their share so that the other gods supported and protected the emperor. The legal aspects of the problem that we can grasp in the imperial oaths were not sufficient.

Therefore people had to turn directly to the gods to win their assistance for the security of the emperor. This was accomplished by regular prayers and sacrifices for the security of the emperor, but also by collective actions, when the population publicly offered vows (*vota*) for the security of the emperor. Each year on January 3 the so-called "taking of vows" (*nuncupatio votorum*) took place. It was a public and collective ceremony during which the assembled population took a solemn vow in front of the images of the gods and the emperor.

Thanks to the testimony of Pliny (*Epist.* 10.100f.) we know quite well the words of such a vow as it was usually made in the reign of emperor Trajan. Pliny, as the governor of the province of Bithynia and Pontus in what today is Turkey, was obliged to organize such a ceremony and recite the words of the vow, which were repeated or at least confirmed by the people, who had to take part in this ceremony. To take part in such a publicly performed ceremony did not mean that people were expected to make an individual confession of their creed – such a problem faced only the Christians with their very strict monotheistic creed – but they had to take part as citizens of the Roman empire or as members of a group.

Changing Attitudes to the Emperor

From the late second century AD we encounter more and more a peculiar religious formula, especially in official inscriptions. This formula declared that an individual or a group of persons had dedicated themselves to the divine power and the majesty of the emperor (*devotus numini maiestatique eius*). The concept is quite revealing for the mentality of a large part of the population. Certainly it is more than a mere confirmation of loyalty to the emperor. It implies the old Roman concept of *devotio*. *Devotio* means that an individual offered himself to the irate or still undecided gods as a substitute to avert the evil that endangered other persons or the Roman state. The best illustrations of this religious conviction are the famous *devotiones* of the Decii Mures during the early republic (fourth/third centuries BC). The Decii Mures sacrificed their own lives in battle to secure the victory for the Roman state.

It is possible to identify comparable and especially spontaneous promises at a very early point during the empire. Already in the year 27 BC the tribune of the plebs Sextus Pacuvius or Apudius (Dio 53.20.2–4) pledged his life for Augustus' ("according to the habit of the Iberians"). In AD 37, during a life-threatening illness of the emperor Caligula (37–41), other men declared that they would give their lives in exchange for the health of the emperor. While Augustus had declined the offer of his enthusiastic follower, Caligula insisted after the recovery from his illness that the vows had to be fulfilled.

In the eyes not only of the Roman public but also of the provincials, the stability and security of the empire were determined by the situation of the emperor's family. An emperor without children could guarantee the security of the empire only for the period of his own earthly existence. The quality of his preceding personal reign was of no avail in such a situation. Should an emperor die and the question of his succession not have been definitely decided, that could endanger the whole of the Roman empire and its existence. In such a situation there was nearly no chance of preventing fierce factional conflicts and as a result even a civil war between the warring factions, as the bloody civil wars after the death of Nero, the last emperor of the Julio-Claudian dynasty (AD 54–68), showed. The collective memory of the Roman people during the early empire was very much influenced by the recollection of the civil wars that had led to the establishment of the Augustan system of government.

Therefore it was a near-divine obligation for a reigning emperor to provide offspring, if possible male, who could follow their father and take over his reign. If for various reasons such a solution was not possible, the emperor was obliged to find at least a political construction that could guarantee a smooth transition of power to a qualified person. A daughter could marry the possible successor. That was the method applied by Augustus, who used his only daughter Julia in this way. Julia was given successively, just like a trophy, to three men (Marcellus, Vipsanius Agrippa, Tiberius) each of whom was at that particular moment the most likely successor to Augustus. If even this alternative was not available, any other female member of the imperial family could marry the future successor. This was the system under the early Antonines: Trajan adopted Hadrian, who was already married to a niece of Trajan. Hadrian himself first adopted Aelius Verus and, after Aelius' unexpected death, Antoninus Pius. Pius' daughter Faustina II was subsequently married to Marcus Aurelius, one of the two adopted sons of Antoninus Pius.

As the marital union between Faustina and Marcus Aurelius produced a real crowd of children, among them some potential successors to the throne, it was no longer necessary to adopt sons in order to secure the succession within the family. Unfortunately the problems returned after a while as Commodus, the successor to Marcus Aurelius, was married but without children. At the same time he was plagued with five married sisters and consequently five brothers-in-law who all aspired to become emperor. If even the extended family failed to produce any fitting successor, the emperor could take any suitable man and adopt him as his son and successor. This was done by Nerva. He could only evade enormous political pressure by the surprising adoption of Trajan at the end of AD 97.

The decision of the reigning emperor to choose such a solution was to a certain extent regarded as inspired by the gods. The great altar of the imperial providence

(*Providentia Augusta*) in Rome was founded in memory of such a decision. But we can see how the original concept of *providentia Augusti* as a quality of the emperor expanded very fast (J.-P. Martin 1982). First the work of providence transgressed the realm of planning the succession and was expanded to guard the emperor against plots. And finally even the providence of the emperor for the well-being of the Roman state became a firm element. Already in the year 31, when Seianus, the mighty prefect of the praetorians, was overthrown, people recognized the salutary work of imperial providence.

The inscription of an altar from Interamna in Umbria is quite revealing for this development (*CIL* 14.4170 = *ILS* 157). The altar was dedicated "To the constant imperial security and the public liberty of the Roman people" (*Saluti perpetuae Augustae libertatique publicae populi Romani*) and continued "To the providence of Tiberius Caesar Augustus, who was born for the eternity of the Roman name, after the most pernicious enemy of the Roman people had been removed" (*Providentiae Ti. Caesaris Augusti nati ad aeternitatem Romani nominis, sublato hoste perniciosissimo p(opuli)R(omani)*). Here already the ideological identification of the well-being of the emperor and the security of the whole Roman people has been accomplished. At the same time the near-messianic position of the emperor who had been born to secure the eternal dominion of the Roman people by employing his divine providence is clearly recognizable.

As the number of children in the imperial family was never very high (the exception to the rule is the marriage between emperor Marcus Aurelius and Faustina II), each birth was of political importance. Most revealing is the birth of twin boys in the year AD 23. They were the grandsons of the reigning emperor Tiberius, who regarded their birth as a kind of divine blessing. This information was conveyed to the public by coins that showed the two little boys just emerging from two *cornucopiae*. The political message was very simple: the succession of the emperor has been secured by the birth of these two boys, and because of this the future of the empire will be splendid.

The Emperor as a God-Sent Person

The importance of securing a smooth transition between the different imperial reigns shows that even the emperor's near-godlike power did not overcome the realization that he was a mortal human being and his time on earth was limited. But even this sorry fact did not stop the religious phantasy in developing an explanation that gave a deeper meaning even to the death of an emperor. If people could perceive the birth of an emperor or at least his assuming imperial responsibility as the descent of the emperor from heaven (or, less elaborately, his being sent by the gods), the death of the emperor could not mean the end. Therefore a widespread perception understood the death of the emperor as his return to the gods – matching the model of descent. Parallel to this model there was the more challenging interpretation that the emperor had been a mortal being but had been endowed with extraordinary divine powers to accomplish his work on earth. If he had been successful, his death marked only the end of his earthly existence, and the transition to a new existence and his reception by the gods in heaven.

This religious model was very old and reaches back to the demigod Hercules, who had spent his whole life on earth fighting monsters and evil powers that endangered mankind. The removal of his body from the burning pyre and its subsequent transposing to heaven, where he was received by Zeus, the supreme god, was identical to becoming a god. By the quality of his past achievements Hercules had earned the right to become a god. The example of Hercules presented a kind of blueprint for gods to come. In historical times the first Roman to become a god was the dictator Iulius Caesar. In the version of the poet Ovid (*Metamorphoses* 15.840–50) it was Venus herself, the divine ancestress of the Julian family, who was ordered by Iuppiter to descend from heaven to take Caesar's soul and bring it back to heaven. On its way to heaven Caesar's soul transformed itself into a fiery comet that conveyed the message to the world that Caesar had become a god.

Beginning with Augustus a kind of routine for imperial burials and the aftermath developed. After Augustus' burial a senator confirmed under oath that he had seen Augustus' soul ascend to heaven. This was a statement that prompted the Roman senate to declare that Augustus had indeed ascended to heaven and therefore was entitled to receive the appropriate honors that the Roman state and the Roman citizens owed a god: a temple, a priest, sacrifices, etc. Augustus now became *divus Augustus* (god Augustus). From now on till the fourth century most emperors received comparable honors after their death. In many cases these divine honors were extended to cover their dead spouses (Augustus' wife Livia became *diva Augusta*). In some cases even minor members of the imperial family were declared gods (Nero's baby daughter Claudia became *diva Claudia virgo*, the "divine virgin Claudia," after her premature death).

The underlying "theology" of becoming a god, or apotheosis, may be sketched as follows. The decision to remove the emperor's soul from his mortal remains came from the supreme god himself, who dispatched his messengers to bring the soul to him. This act of removal was symbolized for the public by releasing an eagle that rose into the air. The mythological model was Zeus' eagle that had carried away the Trojan prince Ganymede, who had been destined to become Zeus' cup-bearer.

Most people had no difficulty in accepting the extraordinary position of the emperor. Only two groups offered fierce resistance to the imperial cult. The Jews were convinced that only one god existed, their national god YHWH, who was at the same time the real king of the Jewish people. Here religious and political issues were amalgamated and led to open resistance against the Roman rule. The case of the Christians was at the same time different and more complicated. The Christians, too, followed a monotheistic belief, but they were convinced that the rule of the Roman emperor was legitimized by the decision of their god. Unlike the Jews they did not object to the emperor himself, but only to the reality of the imperial cult. They deplored especially the fact that the emperors had not yet recognized the true faith and accepted the fact that not Jupiter but the Christian god was the real cause of their rule. Therefore, the Christians offered no fundamental opposition to ruler cult but only to the realities of a still pagan world. When the emperors had become Christians and accepted the Christian god as the supreme source of their power, many features of the old ruler cult were easily adapted to the new reality and lived on.

FURTHER READING

There exists no solid monograph covering the whole field of emperor cult. Clauss (1999) is far too one-sided to fulfill expectations. For the mental situation at the end of the republic compare the studies by Alföldi, collected in Alföldi (1997). For the beginnings of the young Augustus and his efforts to legitimize his rule see Ramsey and Licht (1997). A real mine of information on a lot of important aspects is provided by a series of important studies by Fishwick (1987–2004). As Fishwick concentrates on ruler cult in the western part of the empire, the eastern or Greek part is less than adequately treated. This deficit is partly covered by the study of Price (1984), who concentrates on Asia Minor.

For the mental situation, see Herz (2000). For the concept of the divine election of the emperor, Fears (1977) is still valuable. An exemplary study of the concept of the close connection of divine abilities and the emperor is J.-P. Martin (1982). For the organization of the ruler cult in Rome see Lott (2004). Useful for the adaptations of the calendars to fit the purposes of ruler cult is the compendium of Samuel (1972).

CHAPTER TWENTY-THREE

Urban Elites in the Roman East: Enhancing Regional Positions and Social Superiority

Athanasios Rizakis

From the late Hellenistic period, leading citizens of Greek cities played a central role in the conduct of political affairs, thanks to the support of Rome, and served as mediators between their own communities and the central power. As such, they attempted to avoid any possible unfortunate consequences of Roman rule, while also actively seeking the benefits which were to be won by the creation of bonds with Roman notables. These bonds, facilitated by the importance accorded by Roman aristocrats to Greek *paideia* ("education," "culture"), formed the basis of Roman rule in the Greek world under Augustus and his successors. The relations between Greeks and Roman aristocrats extended and deepened after Actium. Moreover, the imperial administration, seeking to improve the government of the provinces, now applied a policy of integrating Romanophile elites within the Roman system by means of the citizenship (*civitas*). These leading citizens subsequently completely assumed civic power and, acting in agreement with the Romans, they took the initiative of introducing the imperial cult, whose priesthoods they performed. From the first century, AD, the imperial cult became a dominant part of the civic landscape and created a bond between aristocratic families and the emperor. This privileged link increased their own prestige and that of their families within their local context. This is reflected in the honors that they received for their generosity and their mediation with the emperor on the part of their city.

Local Patriotism and Euergetic Activities

Nevertheless, such devotion to Rome and the emperor did not distance the provincial elites from the traditional cults of their cities, which they occasionally administered as a hereditary duty, nor did it diminish their attachment to their place of birth. In fact, such an attachment was particularly strong for those engaged in intellectual activities, as, for example, M. Antonius Polemo, Flavius Arrianus, Claudius Charax, Herodes Atticus, and Plutarch. The last is the most firmly rooted of all in the soil of his small native city of Chaeroneia, which he wished to serve through inclination as much as through conviction. In his *Life of Demosthenes* (2.1–2), he states that he decided to live in Chaeroneia, so that an already small town would not become smaller still.

This inconstant faithfulness, so to speak, to their place of birth remains unshaken even when leading citizens leave their homeland to take up responsibilities at a provincial or even imperial level. In fact, this temporary distancing actually strengthens their bond with their homeland and with it the desire to spend the rest of their life in the place of their birth, assume local civic duties, and indulge in considerable euergetic activity. Dio, orator or philosopher, or both at the same time, is a typical case of these cosmopolitan patriots who remain deeply attached to their tiny native cities and engaged in the affairs of their own homeland or of the province. On more than one occasion he reminds his audience of the benefactions made to Prusa by members of his family and especially by himself: "I have performed for you the greatest liturgies, in fact no one in the city has more of them to his credit than I have. Yet you yourselves know that many are wealthier than I am" (*Oration* 46.5–6). After his return from exile (AD 96), all his speeches are preoccupied above all with schemes to beautify his modest city of Prusa (e.g. *Oratio* 45.12–13). From his first speech onward, he is ready to offer his services as the city's "guiding light." He desires, he says, the expression of love by and the esteem of all, not that statues, honors, or public proclamations be proposed for him. He does, however, make a point of recalling the honors bestowed on his father and all his family, which are signs of prestige sufficient to ensure him a respectful audience (Dio, *Oratio* 44.2–5).

The social behavior of the elite is motivated by the culture of distinction that can be summed up by the word *philotimia*, that is, the "love of honor." This together with patriotism (*philopatria*) are the most important virtues of the leading citizens who are praised by authors during the first and second centuries AD. At the same time, inscriptions offer numerous witnesses to the zeal displayed by elite members on behalf of their *glyketate patris*, their beloved country. In particular, honorific decrees give some indication of the importance assumed by euergetism in the outlook of the elites in their relations with both the ruling power and the masses. The generosity displayed by elites is manifested in various ways, particularly when they have the opportunity to exercise local, provincial, or religious offices or perform costly civic liturgies. To traditional euergetic activities, familiar from the past – such as the perpetual problem of maintaining cities' vital supplies – are now added new types of euergetic activity. These new activities assume a new scale and are mainly concerned with the public distribution of various goods, feasts, and games, but chiefly with the erection or completion of public buildings, temples, galleries, athletic facilities, such as the *gymnasia*, *stadia*, and cultural establishments that embellished and monumentalized civic centers. It is not surprising that the energetic activities of most senators included large public works, which usually involved the erection or completion of public buildings. The most spectacular example of this kind of great *euergetes* (benefactor) is Atticus and his son Herodes, who, although Roman senators, performed the various higher offices of their own home city in the first half of the second century and spent considerable sums on building and feasts on behalf of their city (Athens), the cities of the province of Achaea, and sometimes far beyond these narrow limits. Philostratus (*Vita Sophistarum* 2.1) tells us that Herodes Atticus spent 4,000,000 *denarii* on an aqueduct at Alexandria Troas and that his generosity was more appropriate for an emperor than a private citizen.

A parallel case from the Greek world, albeit on an entirely different scale, is provided by C. Iulius Eurycles Herclanus L. Vibullius Pius (mid-second century). He was a senator, drawn from Sparta, and a descendant of the Eurycles who, to display his support for the emperor, undertook the construction of a stoa at Mantinea (AD 136/7) dedicated to Antinoos (*IG* 5.2.281 = *Syll.*³ 841). Similarly important is the euergetic activity of equestrians and other local aristocrats. The most interesting example of this comes from the cities of Asia Minor, where benefactors like the millionaire Opramoas of Rhodiapolis in Lycia (*IGRR* 3.739 = *TAM* 2.3905) can be compared to Atticus.

This euergetic behavior remains constant throughout the high empire, although a change in outlook is to be seen from the early third century AD. There is a change in material culture and in the manner of self-presentation by the elite. Agoras, the old centers of public life, are abandoned, whilst public display moves as a whole to the imposing *viae colonnatae* and to places of athletic activity. Thus public building as a major indication of status is gradually replaced by other euergetic activities, such as the introduction of new sacred games (*hieroi agònes*), that is, by games that are "panhellenic and iselastic." This privilege, accorded by the emperor, enhanced the regional position of the cities, linked them with Greek tradition, and also improved the social image and position of the members of the local elite, to whom the cities had entrusted their fate. Among the many cases of this there is, for example, that of Saoteros of Nicomedia, favorite of Commodus (c. AD 180), who, on the evidence of Cassius Dio (72.12.2), caused his city to profit from his influence, so that, thanks to Saoteros, the people of Nicomedia "received from the Senate authorization to celebrate a festival and to build a temple to Commodus, which seemed to imply a neocoria" ("office of temple-warden"). It was at that moment that Commodus, a great friend of the people of Nicaea, gave permission to the city to institute a *hieros agon*, entitled *Commodeia*.

Elites' Cosmopolitism, Hellenic Identity, and Personal Ambition

The peace and tranquility prevailing in the second century, and the renaissance of Hellenism in the eastern part of the empire, offered cities new opportunities to widen their contacts and offered to the civic elites a new arena for a great deal of activity. Indeed, now cultural exchanges between cities on both sides of the Aegean sea increase, whilst old institutions, such as that of foreign judges, are revived. There is great mobility on the part of athletes and artists, who take part in games and competitions, which constantly increase in number. Likewise, sophists travel more to other cities and give public demonstrations of their knowledge or talent, both during large panhellenic gatherings and at every local festival. Some of them spend long periods in various cities and occasionally offer them their services or make benefactions, in return for which they are granted honors and even hold the eponymous magistracy. The real reasons for such visits are not always clear. In some cases, antiquarian interests may have stimulated such travels by lettered Greeks, the best examples of such being Pausanias, Charax, and Lucian.

Other literary-minded members of the civic elite seek to investigate ancestral bonds between their city and the metropolitan cities of Hellenism. The habit of searching for ancestral links with certain renowned cities, such as Sparta, Argos, and Athens, goes back to Hellenistic times, a period that enjoyed works on genealogy, the origins of cities, and intercity ties of kinship. From the second century, however, this tendency assumes enormous dimensions. The activity of Publius Anteios Antiochus, the historian and orator of Aigeai, in Cilicia, illustrates this phenomenon. A letter from the Argives, addressed to the council and people of the Aegaeans of Cilicia, indicates that Antiochus succeeded in getting recognition of the *eugeneia* of his homeland in Cilicia with the Argives, subsequent to his prolonged stay in Argos. The authorities of Argos address a letter to those of Aigeai, communicating the text of an honorific decree containing the account of Antiochus concerning Perseus and the parentage between the two cities, which Argos is ready to accept (*SEG* 41, 1992, 283). The activity of Antiochus on behalf of his city, when viewed in the context of the Panhellenion, is clearly intended to prove its Greek origins and thus to distinguish it from its neighbor and rival, Tarsus, which also claimed an Argive origin.

If certain candidate cities were not genuine Greek foundations, then it was the job of "mythographers, orators and local poets" to create such ties. They attempted to link their town to the most prestigious Greek communities, whose fame continued to be considerable under the empire. This is the case of Sparta, whose ties with the Ptolemies, during the days of their thalassocracy in the third century BC, and whose later high standing with Rome, may have enhanced the prestige of a Spartan ancestry and pushed many cities, as Cibyra for example, to establish a *syngeneia* (kinship) link with Sparta. On the other side, thanks to the initiative of local notables, cities try to create between them bonds of friendship and understanding, sometimes celebrated by honorific coins. It was probably the personal initiative of Aelius Heracleides, a member of the Smyrnaean elite, that was responsible for the striking of the *homonoia* coinage, in the reign of Commodus, celebrating the relations of Smyrna with Athens and with Sparta, and likewise that of Antonius Polemon between Smyrna and Laodicea.

The creation of the Panhellenion, in the second century AD, was the most important manifestation of this spirit of Greek values and cultural tradition. Membership of this league offered both an incentive and a prestigious outlet for the *philotimia* of upper-class Greeks, who were unsparing of their efforts in their attempts to reach their goals. Thus the visit and the activity in Sparta, Athens, and Platea of Tiberius Claudius Andragathos Attalos of Synnada are clearly to be connected to the desire on the part of his city to lodge its candidature with the Panhellenion. Andragathos and his brother Claudius Piso Tertullinus, members of the aristocracy of Synnada under Hadrian and Pius, were probably the ambassadors who brought (AD 140–1) the decree of Synnada found at Athens (*IG* 2².1075 with *IG* 3.55).

Serving their Cities and their Own Career

However, cities frequently faced various problems and so were led to enlist the help of their great men, particularly when it was a matter of settling serious political or economic questions that involved the future and the prosperity of the *polis*. These problems offered the elite the opportunity for an audience before the governor, the senate, or even the emperor, in order to press the interests of their homeland (Dio, *Oration* 44.12). Such circumstances also offered the city in question the opportunity to express its appreciation of the effectiveness of the approaches made by the elite and consequently to award them honors in recognition of their services. In fact, this task was not new. Already from the beginning of Roman involvement in the Greek east, eminent citizens of Greek states exploited their friendship with the commanders of Roman armies to ensure the safety and advancement of their own and other communities. These relations became stronger after Sulla. The entourage of Pompey contained several Greeks, of whom Theophanes of Mytilene was the best-known. These individuals cooperated with Rome, thus helping their individual native cities. However, it is during the empire above all that these relations especially increased. In fact, patronage was indispensable to the system. This was partly because no formal bureaucratic mechanisms existed for bringing candidates to the emperor's attention. It was also because the Romans conceived the merit of officials in more general and moral terms than we do today. Thus the degree of subjectivity was greater, as was the degree of latitude of what was acceptable in terms of patronage. Plutarch, who himself enjoyed friendships with many notable Romans, suggests that his compatriots should look for protection from among the Romans. Creating relations with the powerful is, in his eyes, justified only by the desire to serve collective interests (Plutarch, *Moralia* 815 C). In fact, although such personal friendships were of vital importance for cities facing problems, they were not always without their dangers, since these bonds might be utilized either for the common good or for personal advancement, although the latter was the more common course of action, in the view of Plutarch. However that may be, such use of patronage connections must have been common, since Dio of Prusa (*Oratio* 45.8) was able to boast of having refrained from using his influence with the proconsul and the emperor to personal advantage in quarrels at Prusa regarding the election of decurions. In an oration delivered in Prusa, Dio (*Oratio* 43.11) defends himself against the charge of employing his personal connections with the proconsul of Bithynia during local political struggles to have his enemies tortured and exiled. It is difficult to show how far the accusations against Dio were true or not. It is obvious, however, that relations with the governor allowed members of the elite, even more than the city itself, to profit, a practice that was extremely well known.

The theoretically unlimited extent of the authority and the omnipotence that governors apparently enjoyed vis-à-vis the cities naturally caused members of the local elite to turn to them to seek help and support, which, under certain conditions, they were eager to offer, since the Roman authorities were convinced that good provincial government rested upon the smooth cooperation between the proconsul and the local ruling class in provincial cities. Over the first two centuries, the local elites worked with provincial governors in a balanced and mutually satisfactory fashion. Needless to say, this cooperation, far from being conducted on equal terms, was very one-sided. Both politicians and moralists openly state that real power resides at the seat of the governor. The governor was all-powerful. Thus a successful local career for a member of the local elite depended very much on the quality of his relationship with each of the governors, as did promotion to the equestrian and senatorial order, since governors recommended leading provincials for high offices appointed by the emperor. This did not mean that a notable had to be a friend of the current governor. Rather, it meant that he had to have access to the appropriate network of friends at Rome. Fronto, an African senator, tells us that, as soon as his friendship with Arrius Antoninus, *iuridicus per Italiam regionis Transpadanae*, became widely known, he "was approached by many desiring the *gratia* of Antoninus." The letters addressed to him by Fronto (2.174, 176, 188) show that these people were local notables who had been directed toward Fronto by mutual friends with requests concerning local administration. Fronto thus functioned at Rome as a channel of communication, through whom such requests were routed. Similarly, Libanius (fourth century AD) tells us that when he was on good terms with the governor, large numbers of those laboring under various injustices would approach him and request his help so that the governor would put an end to their sufferings (*Oratio* 1.107).

Mediators between Rome and the Cities: Diplomatic Activities

Fortunately, the cities were not dependent solely upon the goodwill of the provincial administrators. In some cases, they preferred to apply directly to the highest authority, that is, the Roman emperor, their intention being thereby to overcome any objection on the part of the governor. The business was then confined to the local aristocracy, who either carried out a diplomatic mission to the senate or the emperor himself or addressed a *petitio*, both of these means of communication being frequently mentioned in the epigraphic records. What motivated cities was the hope of acquiring, by means of embassies, greater prestige than their rivals at the smallest possible expense to themselves. The arguments and appeals employed by ambassadors were various and adapted to the aim of their particular mission, although certain arguments are repeated, and may thus be considered to belong to the rhetorical *koine* of the time. During the Severan period, appeals are frequently made to the loyalty (*nomimophrosyne*) and benevolence displayed by the city toward the Romans. Frequently, however, cities that were unable to employ such means attempted to draw upon the arsenal provided by their historic past, their greatness and beauty, and the fact that they were a historic cultural center. Such speeches fit well into the cultural milieu of the period, the Second Sophistic. This culture is characterized by rivalry, sometimes feverish, over the leading position of cities, the *proteia*, a demand which largely rested upon the glories of the cities' past. The most detailed reference to the success of a diplomatic mission to the emperor is to be found in an inscription from Caria, which was dispatched after a catastrophic earthquake (Pausanias 8.43.4).

A fundamental task of embassies was the maintenance of rights and privileges that had been granted by the Roman authorities to Greek cities. Ambassadors usually defended the interests of their own community, their own *patris*, although occasionally they promoted the interests of a different community, or of an *ethnos*, or of a provincial *koinon*, or even of an international union (such as the Amphictiony). The rights and privileges were inscribed on stones displayed in public areas, the most spectacular example being the so-called "Archive Wall" in Aphrodisias. This comprises a selection of a large number of such documents highlighting the city's privileges. Often the powerful individuals who, thanks to the relationship that they have established with the Roman authorities, have helped their city are praised.

Embassies were dispatched precisely to express the concerns felt by cities regarding measures taken by the emperor that might do damage to the economic life of their province. Communities applied to the emperor in order to gain approval of measures, at city or provincial level, regarding trade, economy, financial support, judicial and administrative matters, and, in particular, border disputes between neighboring cities and taxes. In cases of extreme necessity, such as natural disaster or fire, the cities issued appeals for financial help. In some exceptional cases, leading citizens took the initiative to make a personal appeal to the emperor without waiting for an embassy to be arranged. A typical example of this kind of intervention is that of Aristeides in favor of his own city of Smyrna, damaged by a terrible earthquake. He sent a letter to Marcus Aurelius, in emotive and rhetorical terms, who did not wait for an embassy from Smyrna to arrive but asked the senate to vote immediately money for restoration (Dio, *Oratio* 32.3; Philostratus, *Vita Sophistarum* 2.9; Aristeides, *Oratio* 19).

Furthermore, questions were submitted to the emperor regarding the organization of markets and the dates of religious and sporting festivals. For example, in 29 BC, Pergamum received permission to found a temple of the Goddess Rome and Augustus, so becoming a center for the imperial cult. It founded games, the *Rhomaia Sebasta*, which included a trade fair of three days' length. Later an embassy obtained from Augustus a grant of *ateleia* for the period of the games. This *ateleia* held good in particular for the trade fair but also for the port of Pergamum, Elaea. The *ateleia* in question was probably immunity from the provincial tax, that is, the taxes collected by the *publicani*. Imperial intervention was also requested in relation to a number of internal matters, such as the recognition by the imperial administration of a city as the seat of the *conventus*, to which smaller cities were then obliged to pay certain special taxes; the definition of the number of members of the local *ordo*; the improvement of its politico-judicial statutes; and finally the permission to create a *gerousia*.

The most crucial and difficult cases, born of and nurtured by the spirit of rivalry between members of the local elites and between cities themselves, concerned territorial disputes or the struggle for the acquisition of titles and first place among neighboring cities. Their mutual jealousy earned from the Romans the ironic term *hellenika hamartemata* (Dio, *Oratio* 38.38): "In truth such marks of distinction, on which you plume yourselves, not only are objects of utter contempt in the eyes of all persons of discernment, but especially in Rome they excite laughter and, what is still more humiliating, are called 'Greek failings'!" These struggles, rather than concerning important things, involved trivial affairs, fights over names, *peri onomatôn*, or over *ta proteia*, for primacy (Dio, *Oratio* 38.24). The best-known example of this rivalry over the *proteia* – that is, the possession of the titles *metropolis* (capital city), *neokoros* (warden of the temple of the Augusti), and *protetes Eparchias* (first place in the province) – was that between Nicomedia and Nicaea, which inspired Louis Robert (1977) to give it the eloquent title of "the glory and the hatred."

These rivalries frequently caused the proconsul and the imperial administration great difficulties, because large cities that struggled with each other were supported by smaller cities, with the result that the province occasionally split into two opposing camps, a fact which had negative consequences when the time came to take decisions at the *koinon* or by the governor. This was an important reason why, when differences arose, provincial elites' members tried to reconcile opposing sides and bring about *homonoia*, "concord," the creation of which was celebrated with the issuing of commemorative celebratory coins. Such attempts were reinforced by intellectuals, such as Dio (*Oratio* 40 and 41) and Aristeides (*Oratio* 23f.), who, in their analysis of interstate relations, rejected every sort of *stasis* (internal strife), promoted *homonoia*, and urged cities with differences to return to a state of *homonoia*. If reconciliation proved impossible, then the emperor was forced to intervene. Imperial authority was required to put an end to great differences between cities and it was the emperor who gave the final judgment. Thus Nicaea, after its support of Pescennius Niger through hatred of its neighbor, Nicomedia, which was allied to Septimus Severus, was deprived of the titles.

The elite played a decisive role regarding the interests of the cities, since rivalries between them were not always devoid of real content. For example, the *proteion* or first place was no empty honor, following Dio's own words (*Oration* 38.26), which seem to negate the disparaging reference immediately preceding. The title imposed the first place of the city in the procession of embassies at the *Koina Bythinias* (provincial assemblies of Bithynia) and indicated that it was the strongest and most brilliant of all the cities in the province: "I may have said already that their doings were not mere vain conceit but a struggle for real empire – though nowadays you may fancy somehow that they were making a valiant struggle for the right to lead the procession, like persons in some mystic celebration putting up a sham battle over something not really theirs" (Dio, *Oration* 38.38). The *proteion* also indicated that the city was the center for the *Synedrion* and, as center of the imperial cult, raised taxes from the lesser cities of the province (*Oratio* 38.26) and was visited more than any other city by the proconsul. Through such visits, the city hoped to gain support against its rival cities in the province. This perhaps explains why the quarrel between

Nicaea and Nicomedia, which started under Tiberius, continued at least until the fourth century AD.

Elites as Bearers of Civic Ambition

Cities placed their hopes in their leading citizens, because these missions required financial support that cities frequently could not provide and because notables alone possessed the necessary intellectual and moral qualities. In some cases, attempts were made to send individuals descended from royal families, local dynasts, or at least the oldest families, who enjoyed the widest network of links. As the success of a mission depended on their devotion to Rome and to the emperor, it is therefore not at all surprising that those who undertook to carry out these contacts were above all the leading men of the province, that is, the high priests of the imperial cult. However, such personages certainly did not have a monopoly on such missions. If some members of the civic elite enjoyed the possibility of more direct access to the Roman administration, thanks to their personal relations with noble Roman families, or if they had the requisite eagerness and, in particular, the rhetorical abilities to impress the senate and the emperor and so succeed in their mission, this made them ideal candidates for undertaking such delicate missions, whose nature could vary so widely.

Josephus (*Antiquitates Iudaicae* 15.2.3–5) relates that Agrippa confirmed the rights of the Jewish communities of Asia Minor thanks to an oration of Nicolaus of Damascus pronounced before him and a council of Roman office-holders (14 BC). A story in Philostratus' *Vitae Sophistarum* (1.25) regarding the Smyrniot sophist, Polemon, shows despite its anecdotal character the great stress laid by cities on the struggle for the *proteia* and the contribution made by intellectual members of the elite to an outcome successful for the city: "Smyrna was contending on behalf of her temples and their rights, and when he had already reached the last stage of his life, appointed Polemon as one of her advocates." Unfortunately, Polemon dies before being able to complete the mission with which his native city has entrusted him. Nevertheless, the emperor reads the speech of Polemon and is completely convinced by his arguments, "and so Smyrna carried off the victory and the citizens departed declaring that Polemon had come to life to help them."

An inscription from Ephesus, in honor of a lawyer who was sent to represent Ephesus before the emperor Macrinus and his son, Diadumenianus, and to defend the *proteia* and other demands made by his homeland, provides us with another case of a successful embassy. Similarly an inscription from Side, in Asia Minor, reminds us of the services of an illustrious citizen "in whose time the city was victorious in all the cases before the most divine emperor." Q. Popillius Pytho, of Beroea in Macedonia, is honored (*SEG* 17, 1960, 315) for having requested from Nerva the right for Beroea alone, the birthplace of Popillius Pytho, to hold the titles of *metropolis* and *neokoros*. The inscription in the theater must have been erected after the death of Nerva, although Pytho must have made his request some time between AD 96 and 98. Beroia had probably become *neokoros* of the *Sebastoi*, like Ephesus, for the first time under

Domitian. Likewise, Antonia Tryphaina, of Cyzicus, thanks to her connections with Gaius, helped Cyzicus in many ways, especially over the acquisition of the title of *neokoros* of the family of the emperor Gaius. A decree in her honor (*Syll.*[3] 366), erected by the *boule* and *demos* (city council and all citizens), express their gratitude for that and other benefactions.

Local Rivalries and Popular Complaints against Elites' Members

The activities of the local elite did not always receive a positive response from the provincial administrator or from rival politicians or, more generally, from the people of the cities. The sources indicate that quarrels broke out that sometimes led to open civic strife (*seditio, stasis*). Plutarch gives a description of the chief manifestation of such strife, which broke out when there were differences and conflicts between members of the local elite, who were represented by the *boule* and the *gerousia* (council of the elders), and the rest of the citizens, who constituted the *demos* and the majority in the assembly, which met in the theater or the stadium. Thus lack of wheat or barley, for example, could sometimes lead to a great civic crisis and open *seditio*, which threatened the peace of the province and required the immediate intervention of the proconsul. Dio became the target of the citizens of Prusa. They accused him (*Oratio* 46.9) of having stockpiled corn, of practicing usury, and of investing in speculation in real estate. Such accusations were highly serious and certainly made the position of the proconsul extremely difficult, since the members of the elite directed their appeals for support and help to him, in the hope of defeating their rivals. In some cases, the governor reacted positively to the appeal by nobles who requested his support. The friendly stance of the governor is to be explained by the fact that the good administration of the province and, in particular, the prosperity and order of the city rested upon his close cooperation with members of the local elite. In a recently published document from Beroea, the proconsul L. Memmius Rufus is recorded as issuing an edict under Trajan or Hadrian regarding the funding of the *gymnasion* of the city, which was closed from time to time because of financial problems. He was supported in his effort by the *honoratiores*. As Pliny (*Epist.* 9.5) says, the work of the governors involves treating his charges with humanity, but the "most important part of this quality was to respect inequalities and not to attempt to level everything." The proconsul presumably managed in this fashion to ensure that the euergetic activity and *philonikia* ("competitive outlook" or "behavior") of the elite were not lessened. In extreme situations, when the governor managed to reconcile the warring parties, the reconciliation was celebrated as a manifestation of *homonoia*.

His position was undoubtedly worse when there were cases of maladministration and fraud on the part of the local elite. In the case of fraud, a notable might lose his position as a privileged ally of the governor, become a scapegoat, and face accusation in particular of having proposed ambitious construction projects that led to the economic ruin of the cities and individuals. Such an example, given by Dio, concerns his own pet project, conceived after his return from exile (AD 96), of embellishing his native city, Prusa (*Oratio* 45.12–14). The project has been welcomed by the people of Prusa and sponsored by one or more proconsuls, as well as by Trajan himself, but later Dio is being attacked, by his opponents, on the charge of impiety and lack of local patriotism and as being chiefly concerned to serve his personal pride and ambition (*Oration* 47). To restrain misconduct and prevent financial chaos, governors might intervene in the case of extravagant projects undertaken by small cities, a common feature of the second and third centuries AD. Cassius Dio (52.30.2–4) was *logistes* of Pergamum and Smyrna and so was well aware of the socio-political problems of Greek cities. He therefore advises that any waste of money over expensive public buildings and games in which cities involved themselves in the attempt to outshine their neighbors should be forbidden, as such activities led to financial ruin. The excessive expenditure in which certain notables engaged, such as Atticus and his son Herodes, brought but ephemeral glory, in the view of Plutarch (*Moralia* 821 F), who categorically rejects such expenditure. "Offering theatrical perform-ances, distributing money or producing gladiatorial shows are like the flatteries of harlots, since the masses always smile upon him who gives them and does them favors, granting him an ephemeral and uncertain reputation."

Local Aristocrats as Models: Civic Honors and Imperial Awards

The euergetic activities of the members of the local elite and the various services that they offered to their homeland had a positive effect upon the social position and prestige of the benefactors and their families, especially if their euergetic activ-ity was considerable or if they had a privileged relationship with the proconsul or emperor (Dio, *Oratio* 44.12, 45.2–3) or if their intervention had contributed to the solution of city problems. Generally speaking, Greek cities were faithful to their elite, from whom help was often requested. In return, they repaid the various services rendered by the elite with honors, offices, and titles (e.g. son of the city, father of the city, etc.) The placing of the honorific monuments in the city center with inscrip-tions commemorating magistracies, priesthoods and benefactions ensured publicity and the promotion of the honorand, together with his status as a role model for the rest of the citizenry. Cities attempted, with the bestowal of honors expressing their gratitude, to oblige *euergetai* to continue their activity and to encourage others to do likewise.

Rome, for its part, honored them, initially with citizenship, which constituted the highest possible honor for provincial *peregrini* and which the members of the local elite were proud to acquire. When T. Statilius Lambrias, of Epidaurus, died, some time between AD 40 and 42, the Athenians, in marked contrast to their earlier atti-tude, described him as being honored by possession of "that great gift, renowned among all men, Roman citizenship." The award of a high priesthood was an equally great honor and the choice of candidates was made according to extremely strict criteria that may be summarized as follows: wealth, social position, good relations of the individual in question and his family with the imperial milieu or with the emperor himself. A high priesthood was the highest possible recognition, in one form, of life-long services rendered to the city, to the province, but, above all, to Rome. Despite the heavy financial burden involved, the prestige of the family that undertook this office was enormous, as is evident from the titles bestowed on them, such as "first in the province," "first in Asia," or "first of the Greeks" (= *primus Acheon*). The exercise of the priesthood could serve, sometimes, as a stepping stone for those ambitious individuals who were not yet senators or knights, but it was not a "boost" for a career in Rome. In fact many other activities of the members of the local elite, in both a civic and provincial context, gave them the opportunity to display their generosity, their abilities, and their devotion to Rome. The participation of the most influential members of the local elite in the game of diplomacy and, above all, in the success of a diplomatic mission was, in addition to being an ornament needed for a successful career, the only area in which members of the local elite could indulge in political activity. Success in an embassy offered the hope of acquiring Roman citizenship, if it had not already been acquired, and the expectation of rising to equestrian rank.

After the reign of Hadrian, the Panhellenion opened a new area of activity for ambitious aristocrats, since contribution to the preparation of the candidature dossier and then participation in the administration of the League was a great honor, in that all its important officials were rich Roman citizens and some of these, or some of their descendants, had had senatorial or equestrian career. The prestige inherent in serving in the League arose from the close association of the Panhellenion with the ruling power. Service in the Panhellenion might also be a means of furthering one's career. It offered members of the local elite the opportunity of contact with a Roman institution at a time when, although the senate and the equestrian order were open to provincials, the places available in these orders were severely limited. By their actions that did such good to their cities, these personages invested in their future and strengthened the chances of ensuring a successful career for their descendants, since it was the privileged political and judicial status of local families that brought future knights and senators to the attention of the Roman authorities. The case of M. Apuleius Eurycles shows how an ambitious officer of the Panhellenion, originating from Aizanoi in Asia Minor, was able to exploit his association with the League in connection with his ambitions for his future career. Eurycles was honored by the Athenian Areopagus with a public statue and portrait as well as their writing a flattering testimonial to him (*OGIS* 2.505). Five or six years after his term as Panhellene, in AD 162 or 163, he held the post of *curator* to the Ephesian *gerousia* and thus entered into contact by correspondence with Marcus and L. Verus (*Hesperia*, suppl. 6, 1941, 93–6, no. 11). An inscription from Aphrodisias shows that later Eurycles served twice as high priest of the Asian *koinon*, and, at an earlier date, he was appointed, probably directly by the emperor, to the post of *curator* of the free city of Aphrodisias.

The eagerness displayed by the cities in their respect and in the honors voted by the city, the people, and the council to these exceptional persons naturally reflected their rank and privileged status. These persons owed this privileged position to their wealth and to their ascendancy, and the characteristic pair of words found in honorific decrees passed in their honor, "by family and wealth" (*genei kai plouto*), is extremely explicit. Of such personages, distinguished by their superior education, that is, by their *paideia* and their moral virtues, the great majority are members of third or fourth generations of "talent and wealth combined." Thus in many cases the family had acquired Roman citizenship many generations ago, if it did not descend directly from the Roman colonists who had settled in Greece in republican times and after. In most of these cases, the father of the knight had discharged various municipal and religious offices, of which the most important was the priesthood of the imperial cult. One example of this, which is by no means the only one, is provided by Lycia, where the members of the local *ordo* attempted to exploit their position to attract the attention of the governor and of the emperor himself (Opramoas: *IGRR* 3.739). Lyciarchs were usually drawn from this elite, but the progress of these *novi cives Romani* toward the highest imperial positions occurred only gradually. No member of the first generation of *cives* was honored with equestrian or senatorial status during the course of the first century AD. Promotion to equestrian rank occurs in the second generation, at the beginning of the second century AD, whilst it is only the third generation, under Trajan, that provides the first consul. The honors that the cities bestowed upon them in certain cases raised them far above the level of their peers, let alone that of common mortals. An example of this is the use of the title of *ktistes* (founder but frequently, in imperial times, benefactor or restorer), reserved for the emperors up to the time of the Flavians, or even the building of a *heroon* and the instituting of a cult or establishing funeral games of a heroic character, to be held at regular intervals. Bearers of similar titles were usually rich citizens, who had pursued a successful career in the context of the *imperium Romanum*. As equestrians or senators they were exploiting their highly placed contacts to win privileges for their native cities. When they returned to their birthplace, they engaged in such lively euergetic activity that they were deservedly granted the title of *ktistes* or "New Themistocles" or "New Epameinondas." The very few who received heroic honors held equally high social positions.

Conclusion

The members of the local elite in this period are notable for their twin attachment to Rome and to their homeland. Firmly rooted in the reality of their times, they fully accepted Roman authority, whose benefits they recognized. The political integration of the elites via the *civitas* into the imperial system, and the promotion of various of its members to the equestrian and senatorial orders, are the counterpart at the individual level of the changes that took place in the social structure and the conduct of affairs of cities that justify, in the eyes of some scholars, the claim that political Romanization, with an aristocratic coloring, existed. The members of the local elite now completely ensured the functioning of traditional social and political institutions, particularly in the area of cultural and agonistic life, in the form of banquets, festivals, and games. They were appointed as mediators to function between their city and the Roman administration – in the words of Renoirte (1951), "agents de liaison" between two worlds – in the domain of both cultural life and political realities.

Benefactors attempted to perpetuate the influence of their families by establishing perpetual foundations, to anticipate and administer distribution of food or the holding of banquets. These habits were particularly common in Asia Minor and the Aegean world. The recognition by their fellow citizens is expressed in honorific decrees that maintain the civic memory of benefactions performed by the families of the elite by means of the continuity of the political duties assumed by the *euergetes* (benefactor), and by their continuing and increasing social role. It is the sign of an eternal familial faithfulness, reflected in the notion of "ancestral benefaction." Civic honors and distinctions awarded in the past or in the present legitimated the rank of the family, its power, and its high social status in general. A *euergetes* was not merely a social or political personage. He was the model of a civic ethic whose constituent elements are to be deciphered through the eulogies, public laudatory speeches, that the city delivered on the members of its elite who belonged to a long tradition of civic values.

FURTHER READING

There is a very rich literature about elites under the Roman empire; the topic has been extremely fashionable for some decades. But the most profitable reading is the literature of imperial times, especially speeches or writings of famous orators and moralists (Dio of Prusa, Aristeides, and Plutarch), members of the upper provincial class. These sources can be supplemented by modern studies dealing with particular aspects; for instance, the cultural environment of this period and the intellectuals (Borg 2004 b; Desideri 1978; C. Jones 1978; Renoirte 1951; Salmeri 2000; Sterz 1994; Swain 1996; Tobin 1997), the imperial cult (Burrell 2004; Herz 1997; Lozano 2002; Price 1984) and policy (Meyer-Zwiffelhoffer 1999; Millar 1992), the social and political behavior of elites (S. Jameson 1966; Quass 1993; Strubbe 2003; Veyne 1992), and finally the bonds or rivalries between cities for primacy (Curty 1995; Hauken 1998; C. Jones 1999; Merkelbach 1978; Robert 1977).

CHAPTER TWENTY-FOUR

Living on Religion:
Professionals and Personnel

Marietta Horster

The priests of the official pagan cults in Rome, and in Italian and provincial cities organized similarly to Rome, were well-off men, senators, knights, or other citizens with income from landed property, trade and commerce, or handicraft. In some cities of the Greek-speaking part of the Roman empire, priesthoods were sold. These priests sometimes received a personal income out of the purchase of the hides of the sacrificed animals or as part of the fees for sacrifices (Dignas 2002: 251–71). However, even these priests and priestesses did not depend on that priestly income as sustenance. They did not make their living from religion. This income was only a surplus, a welcome addition to the priests' existing wealth and income. It was meant as a recompense for their taking over these sometimes costly duties and the purchase price.

As a rule, in Roman as in Greek cults incoming money, as for example penalties (*multae*) and votives, belonged to the sanctuaries and their gods or heroes and not to the priests. To give "the tenth" (*dekate, decuma*) to a god or goddess (of course not to a priest) was a sign of respect and thankfulness for all kinds of situations in life, like the harvest every year or booty in times of war. In Jewish religion the tenth or tithe was a kind of tax depending on income which had to be paid once a year. In contrast to Roman and Greek cults, the priests and Levites of the temple in Jerusalem, and later also some Christian priests, were sustained by their community, their temple or church (e.g. 1 Maccabees 10. 3, 11. 35; 1 Samuel 8. 15, 8. 17; 1 Corinthians 9. 13–14). The tradition of the payment and sustenance of priests and attendants of the temples or churches is also to be found in Egyptian religion, even in the times of Roman domination. Hence, in different religions and cultic traditions of the orient there existed priests who made their living from religion under Roman rule.

However, priests and priestesses in the city of Rome as well as in Roman and Greek cities all over the empire did not make a gain from their cultic duties, and did not make their living from religion.

Cult Servants of "State Cults" Paid by the Roman State, the Cities, or the Sacrificing Magistrates or Priests

Many of the attendants and servants to the priests and magistrates in the city of Rome were not paid for their specific duties but were taken care of as dependants of the state or of individuals. These servants and attendants were slaves sustained by the state, called *servi publici* or *publici*, or to a lesser extent by their private owners (magistrates or priests); others were freedmen. Both slaves and free citizens could be called *ministri* – servants to the priests. Our sources for these attendants are restricted to a few remarks in literary sources and later lexica, a few funerary inscriptions of *ministri*, and some other inscriptional evidence, as well as reliefs and other monuments depicting scenes of ritual processions and of sacrifices.

Although we know of some of the duties of the different servants and attendants, it is impossible to give exact definitions or detailed descriptions for all of the duties and functions of these *ministri*. The *ostiarius* (janitor) was someone keeping a sanctuary's keys, the *aeditumus* in charge of a temple was a kind of sacristan, *fictores* were bakers of the sacrificial cakes, the *pullarii* were keepers of sacred chickens, the *victimarii* assistants at (animal) sacrifices. The *victimarii* had different functions and names. For example, the one who had to beat the animal-victim with an axe or a hammer was called *popa*. According to the inscriptional evidence of the city of Rome, most *victimarii* were freedmen, but according to late antique literary sources, Isidor and Servius, the *popa* was a public slave. Moreover, we know of dancers and musicians, *tibicines* (flute-players), *fidicines* (lyre-players), *liticines* (players on a *lituus*, that is, trumpeters), and *cornicines* (players on a *cornu*) being all part of some of the cultic processions and other rites (Fless 1995: 79–93; and chapter 18 above). *Vicoministri* were public slaves who assisted the *vicomagistri*, representatives of the quarters or *vici* of the city of Rome, during their ritual performances of the *compitalia*, a festival honoring the Lares, gods of the crossroads.

However, there were not only adult *ministri* but also young ones called *camilli* and *camillae* (boy- or girl-attendants of the *flamen Dialis* and the *flaminica*) or *pueri et puellae patrimi matrimique*, boys and girls with father and mother alive if serving other priests than the *flamen* and his wife. The *camilli* and other boys (and girls only to the *flaminica*, the wife of the *rex*, and the empresses as members of imperial cult service) serving at the sacrifices all seem to be freeborn. The servants' and attendants' sustenance by parents, masters, former masters, the cities, or the city of Rome did not depend on the attendants' specific duties, such as at a sacrifice or procession; their living had to be guaranteed whatsoever duty they had to perform. It is likely that freedmen like the *kalatores* (Rüpke 2005a: 595–6, 1517–36) assisting their former masters were paid or rewarded by their masters for these specific duties, but we have no direct evidence for that.

For the time of the empire, we have evidence of such freedmen as *kalatores* (personal servants of a priest) of the Arval Brethren, the *flamines*, the augurs, the *epulones*, the *pontifex maximus* and the other *pontifices*, the *rex sacrorum*, and some of the *sodales* serving the imperial cult. Reliefs of the first to third centuries depict *camilli* or boys holding the *guttus* (a jug, a narrow-necked vessel; fig. 24.1), the *acerra* (box for incense), and sometimes the *patera* (shallow bowl), which was used in different contexts in the rituals. Many of the *ministri* wore a tunica or toga, and the *victimarius* was dressed additionally with a kind of apron called *limus* (figs. 12.2 and 18.1 above). The attendants carried different vessels for the ritual, of which we know the names (*catinus, lanx*, etc.) but often do not know what they looked like or their exact ritual purpose (Siebert 1999: 25–63). During processions they also carried *canistra* (baskets) and *fercula* (stretchers or trays) filled with the sacrificial cakes (fig. 24.1). The *victimarii* were responsible for the animal-victims during the procession and the sacrifice. They guided the victim (bigger animals like pigs, sheep,

Figure 24.1 Fragment of a frieze of the Trajanic period, now in Copenhagen (Fless 1995: pl. 3.2) (photo: Ole Haupt, Ny Carlsberg Glyptotek, Copenhagen).

cows, and oxen) with a rope or line around its neck to the altar (fig. 12.1 above). Attendants and servants are shown pouring a liquid, the wine, into the *patera* the priest or magistrate is holding. The young *camilli* as well as the elder *ministri*, obviously the *victimarii*, are often presented with the *mantele* (kind of hand-towel) (Fless 1995: tab. 2.1). These attendants assisted the sacrificer in the necessary purification rites with water and towel, as part of the so-called pre-sacrifices with wine, if it was a libation, and with incense. They poured wine over the animal-victim's head before an immolation took place. After those pre-sacrifices it was the *victimarius'* turn. He had a *culter* (knife) with which the sacrificial victim's carotid was cut through and the *exta* (entrails) were cut out (Siebert 1999: 79–84).

Apparitores: Public Attendants of Magistrates and Priests Paid by the State or the Cities

Unlike most of the above mentioned slave-servants, freedmen, or freeborn citizens in ritual contexts, the so-called *apparitores* received a fixed salary and were paid by the state. These *apparitores* served the Roman magistrates in the city of Rome and during their term of office in the provinces. *Apparitores* are also known from *municipia* and *coloniae* in Italy and the provinces. Our sources for the *apparitores* are identical to those for the *ministri*. However, we have more inscriptions (more than five hundred in Rome, Italy, and the provinces) and more depictions, especially of the lictors and their *fasces*, bundles of rods with an axe. In republican times, the fasces had not been just symbols of power but were used for punishment: flogging with the rods and executions with the axe. According to Gladigow (1972) they thus had a sacral function on their own. From late republican times the lictors no longer had the right to punish. The *fasces* were reduced to symbols of power. During the empire, the *fasces* seem to have become such popular symbols of outstanding power that they were often presented on funerary reliefs of magistrates of the cities or municipal priests of the imperial cult, even if these men had lictors only on special occasions or were not allowed to have as many *fasces* as were depicted on their funerary reliefs (Schäfer 1989: 209–21).

Most *apparitores* were freeborn, though some were freedmen-citizens (Purcell 1983: 161–70). They included the *scribae* (professional writers), *accensi* (attendants), *lictores* (lictors), *viatores* (agents on official errands, messengers), and *praecones* (announcers, criers). In the city of Rome, not only did they attend the magistrates to perform their duties and to represent the power of the magistrate, but some of them were also part of the priestly representation and entourage. We know of *viatores* of the senatorial priestly colleges of *augures*, the *decemviri epulones* and the *sodales Augustales* (Rüpke 2005a: 624). Twelve lictors went in front of a consul wherever the latter set his course. They even wore the same cloths as the consul to multiply his presence and representation of power. Lictors were also part of the representation of the *pontifices* and the Vestal Virgins, although they had only one or two lictors.

Apart from the *viatores*, who were agents to some priests and priestly *collegia*, and whose duties were thus connected to religion in a wider sense, we do not know of any active participation by *apparitores* in processions or sacrifices. The *praecones*, the announcers, however, had some very important duties in the context of the cult. It was their task to announce at the beginning of cultic rites, especially of sacrifices, that the people had to be silent (*favere iubebant*, Festus 78 L). The ritual prayer was not to be disturbed; no ominous word should cross the starting prayer, the *formulae*, the sacrifice. The prayers themselves – if not performed by the magistrats and priests directly – were sometimes read first by one of the *praecones* like a prompter. This scene was depicted on reliefs with the *praeco* holding the scroll with the text, the priest or magistrate then repeating the words.

In a narrow sense, neither the *apparitores* nor the state-slaves or *ministri* made their living from religion. The lictors and other agents made their living as freeborn or freed citizens. The *apparitores*, who were organized in colleges, were only paid for during their time of office, hence for their annual duties. However, they did not officiate every year, thus it was not a regular income.

In other cities of Italy and the provinces, the institution of the *apparitores* was modeled on the Roman one, but it was not the same. The salary of the attendants was quite low. Two cities' statutes from Spain, one of the *colonia* of Urso in 44 BC (with later additions) and one of the *municipium* of Irni in Spain from the late first century AD, provide rules for *apparitores* in which the salary of the state-attendants is specified (Urso) or at least general rules to the *aes apparitorium* are laid out (Irni). According to the *lex Irnitana* chapter 73 (trans. González 1986: 193) the members of the city council had to decide which payment was appropriate to each kind of *apparitor*. The salary would then be paid from the common fund of the city. In the *lex Ursonensis* chapter 62 (trans. M. Crawford 1996: 422) the rules are as follows "Whoever shall be IIviri (highest magistrates of the city) has the right and power . . . to have two lictors, one servant (*accensus*), two scribes (*scribae*), two messengers (*viatores*), a clerk (*librarius*), a crier (*praeco*), a *haruspex* [see below], a flute player (*tibicen*). And whoever shall be aediles in the colony . . ." etc. The *apparitores* were exempt from military service throughout the year of their service to the IIviri or aediles. The fee for each of those "who shall serve the IIviri, is to be so much: for each scribe 1200 sesterces, for each servant 700 sesterces, for each lictor 600 sesterces, for each messenger 400 sesterces, for each clerk 300 sesterces, for each haruspex 500 sesterces, for a crier 300 sesterces." The attendants to the aediles (including the flute-players with 300 sesterces) received even less than the ones for the IIviri. According to the next chapter in the city law, they had to serve at least one quarter of the year before they had the right to receive money. Compared to the income of a day-laborer with approximately 3–5 sesterces a day (Duncan-Jones 1982: 54), thus about 700–1,500 sesterces a year, the *apparitores* of the city of Urso were not well off. It is likely that these Roman citizens were only "part-time" *apparitores* and, like the magistrates they attended, had other sources of income than the fees they collected. Some of the *apparitores* later became members of the city council and took over one of the city's magistracies or priesthoods (e.g. *CIL* 9.5190, 12.524, 14.4642). Hence, they had to have a good income and social standing, and, for sure, the income was not based upon their employment as *apparitores* (Purcell 1983: 147–61).

According to the evidence of the inscriptions in imperial times, not every city of the Roman empire had so many and such diverse *apparitores* (Fear 1989). In the cities as in Rome, these attendants were part of the representation and public appearance of the highest magistrates and in Rome of some priests as well. Hence, they were deemed necessary for public rites performed by the magistrates (and priests in the city of Rome) and some, like the *praeco* or the municipal *haruspex*, even took over an active part in these rites.

Haruspices: Specialists in Divination

Divination was used and applied in the Roman world from the first contact of Rome with *haruspices* at the end of the fifth century BC (Livy 5.15) into the early sixth century AD (Haack 2003: 216–21). Divination was meant to interpret the will and attitudes of the gods toward the community and individuals indicated by signs and omens. There was a discussion going on about the origins of the science of divination – Etruscan, Greek, or Sabine – but most of the ancient authors (e.g. Livy, Dionysius of Halicarnassus) thought of divination as an Etruscan ritual and cognitive system. The so-called *haruspices*, men specialized in the Etruscan discipline of divination, were integrated into public and private Roman religion and cult. The Etruscan discipline was thought to encompass three different sections, written down in sacred books describing the different techniques of divination about prodigies (*prodigia*), signs (*monstra*), and marvels (*ostenta*) (Capdeville 1997: 477–95): the *libri haruspicini* (Thulin 1912: 2449–54) concerning entrails of animals, *fulgurales* (1912: 2441–9) concerning lightning, and *rituales* (1912: 2455–68) concerning the rites for founding a city and the like. These books were translated into Latin during the first century BC. Some handbooks are supposed to have retained the Etruscan sacred formulae in their original form combined with an explanatory commentary in Latin (Capdeville 1997: 501–4).

The first *haruspices* in Rome were at the service of the senate and the magistrates (Thulin 1912: 2433; Haack 2003: 51–75). Although most of the stories about the early republican *haruspices* seem to be fictitious in detail and circumstances, these anecdotes are telling in their substance: after the Romans' violent kidnapping of a first *haruspex* in 406/396 BC from the Etruscans (Livy 5.15), we hear next of a *haruspex* explaining to the consuls of the year 340 BC, Decius and Manlius, the meaning of the entrails of the sacrificed victims before a decisive battle against the Samnites (Livy 8.9.1). The inner organs in the victims predicted Decius' death, but in all other respects the signs were favorable. Here, as well as in many other later incidents and anecdotes, the main aim of divination for the Romans can be seen: to learn about the will of the gods, especially to find out whether the gods are favorable to the Romans and are willing to help them and their leaders in case of war. As a rule, the negative interpretation of signs is always reported as having consequences: either magistrates like Fabius Maximus (Livy 23.36.10; 27.16.15) took the right lesson from it – in his case a delay of his marching off in 215 BC and again in 209 BC during the war against Hannibal – or magistrates like Tiberius Gracchus in 212 BC or Marcellus in 208 BC and later even Caesar on the Ides of March 44 BC died because they were not careful enough to pay attention to negative signs (Livy 25.16.1–4; Cic. *Div.* 1.33; Livy 27.26.13f. with 27.27; Caesar: Cic. *Div.* 1.119; Suet. *Caesar* 77; Plut. *Caesar* 63.4). During the second century BC the practice of divination became more personalized and thus sometimes "private." The decision to ask a diviner for his assistance became a question of politics (MacBain 1982; Haack 2003: 51–75). By means of divination, militarily and politically ambitious leaders could present themselves as protected by the gods and thus being more qualified than their rivals in politics. C. Gracchus was on friendly terms with his personal *haruspex* (Val. Max. 9.12.6). Marius (Sall. *Bellum Iugurthium* 63.1; Plut. *Marius* 8.8), Sulla (e.g. Cic. *Div.* 1.72; Plut. *Sulla* 9.6), and later the notorious Verres (Cic. *In Verrem* 2.3.28) had each a *haruspex* of his own. The *haruspices'* duties were to protect their patrons and to add to their success and glory, respectively. However, beside these private diviners attached to political leaders, throughout the last two hundred years of the republic public *haruspices* existed and performed their regular duties, serving the Roman community and its elected magistrates.

At least during the late republic and early empire, there was an *ordo* of 60 *haruspices* (e.g. *CIL* 6.2161–2, 32439, 11.3382; Tac. *Ann.* 11.15; Rüpke 2005a: 591f.), not all of them Etruscans. Romans and men from other Italian regions were members, too. The emperor Claudius stressed that this kind of divination was the *vetustissima Italiae disciplina* (Tac. *Ann.* 11.15). Thus, regional differences between Roman and Etruscan or other Italian traditions seem to have vanished in the mid-first century AD. The emperors, too, could have their own *haruspices*. All these official *haruspices* lived in Rome, and made their living from their knowledge and special ritual techniques. We do not know whether they received regular pay or fees for their duties; however, a salary is quite likely.

We do know that at least some of the *haruspices* in the cities of the Roman empire and those in the legions were paid on a regular basis. But unlike the *haruspices* of the city of Rome, the municipal diviners were integrated into the group of civic attendants, the *apparitores*. The city law of Urso states that the fee for a *haruspex* to the IIviri (see above) was 500 sesterces a year, quite a small sum. Of such *haruspices* of cities in Italy and the provinces more than thirty inscriptions are known (Wiegels 1988: 17–28 and texts later published in *AE*). They all were Roman citizens, most of them freeborn, some freedmen. Some *haruspices* are known from the Roman army, serving in the legions (at least in Numidia). Only one *haruspex* is known as part of the *concilium* of a Roman governor in a province (*AE* 1921, 39).

According to Cicero, there was a time (second century BC?) when the senate sought to protect the accepted and needed professionals of Etruscan haruspicy and divination. The senate's decree made provisions for boys from leading families to be sent to Etrusan communities to study the art, lest – because of the poverty of its members (the *haruspices*) – the art should lose its religious authority and be converted into a means of mercenary gain. (Cic. *Div.* 1.92, cf. Val. Max. 1.1) The state had an eminent interest in the *haruspices*, but poor, freelance, and therefore gain-seeking professionals were not in the senate's interest. Yet "private" *haruspices* – that is, diviners not paid by the state, the city, or a magistrate – existed. They did not hesitate to name their profession on their funerary inscription or in dedications and gifts they offered (e.g. *AE* 1925, 120 Rome; *CIL* 9.2087 Beneventum; *AE* 1966, 220 Bath). These private *haruspices* received their income from fees for every service they rendered. In the eyes of public authorities and of well-educated senators and knights like Cicero, Maecenas, or Augustus, these private diviners belonged to the world of superstition, and had nothing to do with the official ones, who were needed for state reason (Cic. *Div.* 1.92; Dio 52.36.3).

Superstition, a Luxury? – or – He shall Love Her Forever: The Cost of Magic

At the end of the third or beginning of the second century BC a literary character, a certain Periplectomenus, explains in a comedy of Plautus (*Miles* 692–4) why he is inclined not to marry. Women are too expensive; they will ask "for money on the 19th of the month to pay the woman who utters incantations (*praecantrix*), the woman who interprets dreams (*coniectrix*), the inspired prophetess (*hariola*), and the woman who divines from entrails (*haruspica*)." And, he adds, women would not send away the one who observes the sky (*qua supercilio spicit*) without giving her anything. But it was not only female superstition that was a subject of laughter or of concern. Male superstition was also widespread: in his treatise on how to administer and direct a farm (*De agri cultura*), written in the first half of the second century BC, Cato the Elder admonishes his *vilicus* (steward or overseer) that he should not consult a private *haruspex*, a private *augur*, a prophet (*hariolus*), or a magician (*chaldaeus*) (Cato *Agr.* 5.4). We may assume that in Cato's eyes the money one had to spend on these "experts" was not worth it.

In the mid-second century AD, Apuleius (*Apol.* 26.6) gives a "vulgar" (*more vulgari*) definition of the people who earn their living with magic: "a magician is someone who, because of his community of speech with the immortal gods, has an incredible power of spells (*vi cantaminum*) for everything he wishes to." What did people desire a magician to do? Love spells and the notorious love-philters most often were the province of old women (e.g. Propertius 4.5). But these spells or magic tricks did not always work the way they should: there are anecdotes like the one about the senator L. Licinius Lucullus. He was given a love-philter by one of his freedman – to the effect that he was reduced to the state of helplessness (Nepos, *De viris illustribus* 74.8; Plut. *Lucullus* 43.1–2; Plin. *Nat.* 25.25.1). Not only harm or love but also illness and death were thought of as appropriate subjects for magic and for magicians, who would be paid for their efforts and spells. People believed in healing charms and the power of magical formulae and incantations (Versnel 2002). Although Pliny the Elder derides many such formulae as ridiculous (*Nat.* 27.267), he confesses that some of these incantations were tested by experience and were in fact powerful (*Nat.* 28.29). In contrast to most of Pliny's stories, one told by Apuleius in one of his novels (*Met.* 2.28–30.9) might record a magical trickery. He sketches a man from Larissa who asked an Egyptian prophet and priest to revive his dead son. After being paid, the prophet raised the boy from the dead. Celsus, the famous writer of medical treatises, is supposed to have compared Jesus Christ's miracles with those of the sorcerers (*goetes*) and the "Egyptians," that is, magicians and prophets (Origen, *Contra Celsum* 1.68, 3.50). Spells, love-philters, and healing charms were part of Roman magic and thus of superstition, as were the driving out of demons, the raising of the dead, but also the selling of sacred doctrines for a little money.

Although, from 81 BC (see Modestinus in *Digesta* 48.8.12; Paulus, *Sententiae* 5.23.15), the *lex Cornelia* imposed penalties on those who made evil sacrifices, performed impious sacrifices, or carried out sacrifices at night in order to bewitch or to put a spell on someone, sorcery and magic practices seem not to have been forbidden in general. The Roman authorities took some action against astrologers and others. Nevertheless, diviners, sorcerers, and magicians could be found in the Roman *forum* or Greek *agora*, in the temples and near the circus, places where prostitutes or beggars could be found as well (Dickie 2001: 233–6 with references).

The Latin word *superstitio* (Greek *deisidaimonía*) is very close to the word *religio*, especially in the poems and treatise of authors of late republican times until the first century AD (Calderone 1972). Moreover, the word *sacra* is used quite often in the context of magic and sorcery, and thus it does seem to be part of the world of religion and cult, even if not of the official Roman one. However, quite often in Roman texts and poems there are differences between Roman religion on the one hand and superstition on the other hand as part of foreign religions, of non-official religious sentiments and beliefs.

The context of foreign cults, the concern for the preservation of religious practices and the state's interest, and the fear that "religious" professionals could make profit from the poor (as simple-minded) and superstitious people are the reasons for the many expulsions of astrologers, magicians, etc. from Rome and Italy in republican and imperial times. For example, the practices the former praetor Vatinius in 50 BC is accused of are called *sacra*, that is, part of religious dealings, but they are new and not according to the Roman traditional rites, and he had dared to criticize parts of Roman religious customs: "after engaging in wicked and unheard of rites (*inaudita et nefaria sacra*), and after being in the habit of summoning up spirits of the Underworld, after honoring the Gods with the entrails of boys, he is so insane and morally degenerated as to treat the auspices undertaken by the augurs on behalf of the Roman state with contempt" (Cic. *In Vatinium* 14; trans. Dickie 2001: 137).

Intellectuals like Cicero and Seneca and poets like Horace want us to believe that *superstitio* was an insanity, an illness of the mind (e.g. Hor. *Sermones* 2.3.79f.; Seneca, *Epist.* 123.16). However, it was widespread and deeply rooted in Roman society. "Superstition" seemed to be restricted neither to the early Romans nor to women or poor people. Romans classed as unfortunate the days immediately following the calends, *nones*, and *ides* of each month. Unlucky days were termed *dies atri*, because they were marked in the calendar with black charcoal, the lucky ones with white chalk. There were also days which were thought especially favorable for martial operations, but the anniversary of a national misfortune, the defeat of the Romans by the Gauls near the river Allia, July 16, 390 BC, was given a prominent place among the black days of the calendar. But not every general was influenced by such beliefs. When some officers advised Lucullus to lie still just as he was going to cross the river Tigris because that day was one of the unfortunate ones which they call "black days," for on it an army engaging with the Cimbrians was destroyed, "Lucullus answered with the memorable words: 'Verily, I will make this day a lucky one for the Romans'" (Plut. *Lucullus* 27.7).

Superstitio, magic and the practices described could be expensive. Philostratus tells us a story about cities in the region of the Hellespont (*Vita Apollonii* 6.16). In the mid-first century AD, after there had been earthquakes, magicians, Egyptians, and Chaldeans promised they could calm the gods with sacrifices and prevent the cities suffering more such earthquakes, but would not start with the necessary rites unless the sum of 10 talents was deposited. The sage Apollonius, hero of Philostratus' account, saved the cities from paying such an enormous sum and drove out the impostors and quacks. Then he himself divined the causes of the earthquakes, made the necessary offerings, and received only small amounts of money from the cities.

Sacrifices and prayers for a good fortune and future were not the province of magicians and sages only. They were the aim of usual and official sacrifices and prayers, too. Obviously, the conviction that more could be done was widespread, although a belief in the spirits of the dead or in demons was not necessary: the wearing of amulets and lucky charms, the avoidance of unlucky days for important dates like weddings, were part of the life of Romans (and Greeks, modern English people or modern Germans, etc.). Senators like M. Servilius Nonianus and C. Licinius Mucianus worried about losing their sight and therefore wore lucky charms to prevent them from going blind (Plin. *Nat.* 28.29). Lucky charms were apotropaic objects. To have an apotropaic sign on the threshold was also quite common, and a dead owl nailed to the door of a house was supposed to avert all evil (that it supposedly had earlier caused). To know that a dead owl was needed and to have it at hand might have needed a specialist, who was paid for his knowledge and his prayers and spells. Soothsayers and dream interpreters like Artemidorus, who published a book on dreams, were welcome to superstitious people and were able to make a good living from their abilities and their knowledge.

But the cost of *superstitio* could be not only money but also life. Several anecdotes about Roman senators have to do with magic. In one of the stories, M. Scribonius Libo Drusus, a relative of the emperor Tiberius, was accused in AD 16 of aiming for the throne. According to Tacitus (*Ann.* 2.27–31) the senator Firmius Catus, an intimate friend of Libo's, had

> prompted the young man, who was thoughtless and an easy prey to delusions, to resort to astrologers' promises (*chaldaeorum promissa*), magical rites (*magorum sacra*) and interpreters of dreams (*somniorum interpretes*), dwelling ostentatiously on his great-grandfather Pompeius, his aunt Scribonia, who had formerly been wife of Augustus, his imperial cousins, his house crowded with ancestral busts, and urging him to extravagance and debt, himself the companion of his profligacy and desperate embarrassments, thereby to entangle him in all the more proofs of guilt.

In the end Libo Drusus had to commit suicide. Although Tacitus does not mention money at all, without doubt Libo Drusus had to pay for the different services – and perhaps Firmus had paid for them in advance. In that case, the astrologers and dream interpreters would have cashed in twice. In the aftermath of the alleged conspiracy of Libo Drusus, the senate expelled astrologers and magicians (*mathematicis magisque*) from Rome and Italy and at least two of them were executed (Tac. *Ann.* 2.32; Dio 56.25, 57.15). According to the chronicle of the late antique Codex Calendar of 354, 45 sorcerers and 85 sorceresses were even executed under Tiberius. Another political affair took place during the reign of Nero and is reported to some extent by Tacitus (*Ann.* 16.21, 23, 30–3). The senator and former consul Barea Soranus was facing trial in AD 66. His daughter Servilia wanted to help him and hence gave money to some magicians (*magi*) to know the future. His daughter's dealings became part of the accusation, as the accusers imagined that the magicians received money not for a simple consultation but to put a spell on Nero or to help Soranus out by magic. During the cross-examination before the senate, Servilia had to confess that she had spent a lot of money on these magicians and even had to sell her jewels and precious clothes in order to pay them.

Professional astrologers, soothsayers, prophets, dream interpreters, and magicians could be very expensive. Obviously, in Rome and Italy as well as in the provinces such professionals in divination and magic of different sorts existed – impostors as well as sages and trained experts. There were old women making magic spells for a little money, food, or wine, and there were high-class magicians and dream interpreters whose services were quite expensive. Not only did illiterate women or peasants believe in their ability to know the future, to make life easier and a destiny better, but also members of the highest classes called on their service – and paid for it.

FURTHER READING

Purcell (1983) wrote a thorough survey of different aspects of the public attendants to magistrates of the city of Rome and of other cities in the Roman empire. He collected all sources known until c. 1981 and discusses the *apparatiores'* social antecedents, their duties, their organization, and their advancement in society.

Dickie (2001) gives an excellent and well-written introduction to the different aspects of magic and "superstition" in Greek and Roman societies from classical to late antique times. He cites his sources in English translations.

A collection of inscriptions concerning the professionals and their attendants does not exist. Many of the *haruspices'* inscriptions are quoted at full length (but without translations) in Wiegels (1988: 17–28). Purcell (1983: 171–3) has an appendix with inscriptions on *apparitores* (Latin, no translations). Cicero's *De divinatione* is available in the Loeb Classical Library collection (trans. W. A. Falconer). Linderski (1982) gives an introduction to Cicero's views on Roman divination and explains Cicero's sometimes diverging positions on *religio* and *superstitio* in different publications, mainly *De re publica* and *De divinatione*.

PART V

Different Religious Identities

CHAPTER TWENTY-FIVE

Roman Diaspora Judaism

Jack N. Lightstone

Methodological, Conceptual, and Theoretical Issues

Scope of this chapter and methodological considerations

Topical scope

To understand the scope of this study is to understand many of the methodological issues and problems regarding the evidence for such an inquiry. This chapter focuses on the religion and ethno-religious community of the Jews in Roman antiquity as it manifested itself not only in the city of Rome but also in the Greco-Roman Diaspora (from Greek meaning "dispersion"). Geographically, this includes the lands of the Roman empire *outside* of the territory in the southern Levant which the Jews called "the Land of Israel," or simply "the Land," and which, until the mid-second century, Roman authorities called "Judea" and thereafter "Palestine." This study examines Judaism as a case study of an ethnic, minority religion and community within imperial Roman society – more properly deemed Greco-Roman society east of the Italian peninsula.

Temporal frame

This chapter's account holds in general terms for the latter half of the first century CE through the first quarter of the fifth century CE, with the most robust body of evidence representing the third, fourth, and early fifth centuries CE. To be sure, Jews were already well established in Rome in noticeable numbers by the time of Cicero (in the first half of the first century BCE) and in major Hellenistic cities of the eastern Mediterranean basin by as much as 150 to 200 years earlier. However, the archaeological, inscriptional, and Roman legal record for Greco-Roman Diaspora Jews begins to burgeon in the late Roman period, near the end of the second and beginning of the third century and onward (see, for example, Levine 2000; Frey 1936–52; Noy 1993–5; Noy and Horbury 1992; Noy and Bloedhorn 2004; Noy et al. 2004; see also Linder 1987). Moreover, a good deal of what may be gleaned from the literary evidence for the preceding century, for example, from the earliest Christian literature, Philo, and Josephus (all c. mid-first to the early second century CE), can still be safely applied to the third through early fifth centuries, while the opposite is not the case. Finally, any relevant evidence from the early rabbinic movement comes from a literary record which begins at the end of the second century only.

The nearly-four-centuries-long span of this study covers a period during which the pagan imperial Roman power was at its height in western and southern Europe, the Mediterranean basin, and adjacent Near East under Claudius' successors. The period ends before the mid-fifth century CE after the reign of Theodosius II, the sponsor of the first great codification of Roman law, with an increasingly divided empire – east and west – and with the latter succumbing to Visigothic/Gothic encroachment. Pagan Greco-Roman religious cults thrived for more than two-and-a-half centuries of this nearly four-century span, among them Hellenized and Romanized versions of Middle Eastern and Egyptian religions, and the imperial cult reached its zenith. At the beginning of this period Christianity was but a smattering of small, relatively insignificant communities meeting in the private homes of patrons in the Levant and in some of the larger mercantile centers of Asia Minor. After the first quarter of the fourth century CE, under Constantine and his successors, Christianity ascended to the status of a state-promoted religion, displacing the imperial cult and ultimately wiping out the public practice of pagan religion.

For the most part, Jews and Judaism in the Greco-Roman Diaspora thrived and developed as long as Greco-Roman pagan religions were in a healthy state, as the aforementioned burgeoning of evidence during the late Roman period indicates. The two disastrous rebellions against Rome by Jews in the Land of Israel, the Great Revolt, which resulted in the destruction of the Jerusalem Temple and the permanent cessation of its cult in 70 CE, and the Bar Kochba rebellion, put down in 135 CE, had little negative, lasting impact upon Greco-Roman Diaspora Jews and Judaism. Neither did a limited rebellion of Diaspora Jews in several Mediterranean cities c. 115 CE. As we shall see, the main structures and institutions of the Jews' community and their Judaism were well established and flourishing before the Great Revolt, and minor setbacks aside, continued to flourish during the nearly four centuries under study.

However, the first decades of the fifth century mark a turning point, as Roman legislation and policy increasingly mention Jews, pagans, and Christian heretics in the same breath (Linder 1987: 63). While Jews and Judaism in the Roman world did not suffer the fate of paganism under Christian Roman rule, the first decades of the fifth century are characterized by increased systematic intolerance of Judaism and the annulment of centuries-long privileges of members of the Roman Jewish communities (Linder 1987: 63–76). For example, long-standing exemptions from imperial services, and from civic liturgies and magistracies for those Jewish decurions who are heavily involved in service to the synagogue and Jewish community (see below, "Constituent roles and institutions within the synagogue/community"), are withdrawn in the early fifth century, and by the beginning of the sixth, Jewish decurions must perform civic duties, but they may not receive the honors and privileges due members of the curial class (Linder 1987: 76). Roman law permits existing synagogues to be maintained, but prohibits the building of any new synagogues. In 418, Jews are expelled from the imperial administration by Honorius, and expressly forbidden to serve as imperial executive agents, guards, or soldiers (Linder 1987: no. 45). In 527, Justinian criticizes officials for not strictly enforcing this policy (Linder 1987: no. 56). In 425, Valentinian II bars Jews from the legal profession (Linder 1987: no. 51). In 423, Theodosius II bans entirely the ownership of non-Jewish slaves by Jews (Linder 1987: no. 48). In essence, the first half of the fifth century marks the beginning of quite another period for Roman Diaspora Jews and Judaism.

Socio-cultural compass

As we have stated, our interest is to contribute to an understanding of *minority* religious social constructs within Roman society, specifically by offering a case study of Jews and Judaism in the Greco-Roman Diaspora, that is, outside the Land of Israel. As we shall see later in this chapter, Jews and Judaism in the Greco-Roman Diaspora – more specifically, of the Italian peninsula, Greece-Macedonia, Asia Minor, the northern Levant, and Roman north Africa – share so many traits, structures, and institutions, all within so similar a context, that it is useful to see them as adherents of a single religion, despite what must have been varying degrees of local variation. All these Jews shared the experience of living as (1) an ethnic-religious minority, (2) in a (so-called) pagan urban environment, which (3) had been substantially Hellenized with an overlay of Romanization over a Hellenistic foundation. In fact, Schwartz has argued (1998) that east of the Italian peninsula, Rome, more so than the Hellenistic kingdoms it replaced, promoted Hellenization, rather than "Latinization," as a means of uniting the empire (see also MacMullen 1984). Indeed, the inscriptional evidence for Roman and Italian Jews during the Roman period indicates that while some Jews or Jewish communities may have functioned in Latin in their "inner-group" lives together, most did not. In this period, Greek seems to have been the "insider" language of the vast majority of even Roman and Italian Jews for social, cultural, and religious purposes (see Noy 1998). As to the ancestral language of the homeland, Hebrew, it is limited to a few vestiges in utterly formulaic usages, such as wishes at the end of funerary inscriptions, otherwise devoid of Hebrew, that *shalom* ("peace") be bestowed upon the departed.

With the retention of Greek for "insider" social, cultural, and religious communication came the sharing among Greco-Roman Diaspora Jews of well-established cultural products, such as several "standard" translations of the biblical scriptures into Greek, of which two seem to predominate – one attributed to a translator named Aquilas, the other known as the Septuagint, the "translation of the seventy" – a "family" of texts likely *not* identical to the church's Greek Old Testament. In addition to sharing scriptural texts, I have little doubt that Greco-Roman Diaspora Jews shared liturgical compositions, as well as a number of extra-canonical works, again circulating in Greek.

Finally, as we shall discuss at length below, Jews across Italy, Greece-Macedonia, Asia Minor, the northern Levant, and Roman Africa seem to have *formally* organized their lives together as a community in much the same fashion (M. Williams 1998; see also Rutgers 1998: 171–98). They did so in service of what appears to be much the same ends, and they required and received from non-Jewish authorities much the same social, cultural, and legal "space" to so organize their lives together. Writing at the close of the first century CE, Josephus argues this point extensively throughout *Antiquities 14* by reproducing (or forging – it matters little for our purposes) edicts from Roman authorities at the end of the republic and beginning of the imperial period. He thereby intends to help assure that this "space" will continue to be there. Sanders (1999: 2) summarizes the list of rights and privileges which, according to *Antiquities 14* (cf. *Antiquities 16*), were granted Roman Diaspora Jews by Roman edicts. Moreover, he documents the number of times each right or privilege is mentioned. These include the right: to gather and have a place, that is, a synagogue, in which to do so (five times); to observe the Sabbath, including dispensations from Roman and or civic service to do so (five times); to have appropriate ("ancestral") food, including shops offering meat not only from "clean" species and appropriately slaughtered, but also from animals that do not come from the pagan-temple-based cattle market (three times); to administer themselves, that is, to have their own councils and to be subject to their decisions (twice); and, lastly, to levy taxes for communal use and services, as well as to send to the Land of Israel (twice) (Smallwood 2001: 133–43; Suet. *Caesar* 42.3; Jos. *Antiquitates Iudaicae* 14.213–16, 241–6, 256–64; see also 14.235, 16.27–57, 162–5, 172f.; Philo, *Legatio* 158.)

In sum, there is ample reason for seeing Greco-Roman Diaspora Jews and Judaism as a relatively coherent and consistent social construct with respect to social and communal organization, culture, and religion, inevitable local variation notwithstanding (see Kippenberg 1995). And it is upon this larger general common construct that this chapter focuses.

Drawing the general from the particular

As has just been intimated, there is an attendant methodological difficulty in our proposed examination. Such an exercise will involve trying to draw *general conclusions about a broad spectrum of communities.* How much local distinctiveness must there be to invalidate generalizations? To what extent does a general description mask idiomatic local constructs? There are no cookbook answers to these questions. How one proceeds is a matter of scholarly taste and judgment. And the exercise is made more difficult by the fact that our evidence is episodic, diverse, and grossly incomplete. If one had nearly comprehensive evidence for Jews and Judaism from each of a significant array of the Greco-Roman Diaspora communities, generalizations would be better founded, even while local distinctiveness would stand out in sharp relief. But such is not the state of the evidence for any of these communities, indeed, is hardly ever the case in the study of peoples and societies of antiquity or late antiquity.

It also follows from the aforementioned that any account of Judaism and Judaic life in the Greco-Roman Diaspora *must of necessity end up being a "composite."* That is to say, often evidence from one locale must be brought together with evidence from another. How do we know whether such composite descriptions are *mere* creations of the scholar in accordance with some preconceived image, preconceptions of which the scholar himself or herself may not be aware? The answer to this problem is at best partially satisfying. First, the scholar must exhibit awareness of the problem to begin with, before proceeding to deal with the evidence. Second, she or he will have demonstrable warrant for bringing pieces of evidence together from different communities or geographical areas – again a matter of taste and judgment. Such awareness and warrants are founded (1) on understanding the idiomatic character of the different types of evidence in hand, and (2) upon the articulation of the conceptual or theoretical models which inform the use of the evidence. Therefore it is to these matters that I now turn.

The evidence

I should like briefly to give the reader some notion of the type of primary evidence in hand for elucidating Jewish life and Judaism in the Greco-Roman Diaspora. The list which follows is far from exhaustive and comprehensive. Nor in a chapter such as this can I discuss in detail the value and limitations of the various types of evidence. Rather, the account serves to illustrate the variety, diversity and (indirectly, at least) limitations of the witnesses.

Archaeological evidence

Archaeological evidence for Jews and Judaism of the Greco-Roman Diaspora is of several types. Excavations especially of ancient synagogues and of tombs abound across Italy, Greece-Macedonia, Asia Minor, and the highly Hellenized northern Levant and north Africa. Some sites are earlier than the turn of the third century; many more are third century and later, but stand on sites of earlier synagogues. Many are simply third century and later (see Levine 2000; Strange 2001). Of the 115 known ancient synagogues in the Greco-Roman world, 75 are attested by archaeological remains or inscriptional evidence, and 13 of the 75 are attested by both (see Rutgers 1998: 127–30). In addition to what is gleaned from architectural features and site locations of synagogues within their respective urban environments, mosaics and other art and inscriptions provide valuable evidence (see Fine 2005). Synagogue inscriptions and epigraphic remains (Frey 1936–52 [1975]; Noy 1993–5; Noy and Horbury 1992; Noy and Bloedhorn 2004; Noy et al. 2004; Tcherikover and Fuks 1957–64; Lüderitz 1983) more often than not inform us of benefactors and benefactions, and of honors bestowed on Jews, on non-Jewish patrons, and on the imperial house and its representatives. These inscriptions give honorific and formal-functional titles for benefactors, giving us some notion of formal roles and institutions within the community (see Harland 2003).

Tomb inscriptions and funerary art are frequent. They proffer information about names, family relationships, and formal titles, again, giving evidence of formal community roles and offices (Frey 1936–52 [1975]; Noy 1993–5; Noy and Horbury 1992; Noy and Bloedhorn 2004; Noy et al. 2004; see also Tcherikover and Fuks 1957–64; Lüderitz 1983; Goodenough 1952–65).

Some (few) inscriptions in whole or in part from or about Jews place them in, or show their support for, institutions outside the synagogue and Jewish community, for example, in the amphitheater and theater (e.g. in Cyrenaica, Lüderitz 1983: 70f.; in Miletus, Frey 1936–52 [1975]: no. 748), giving us some notion of Jews' presence and participation in patterns of benefaction supporting the local city's institutions (see Barclay 1996: 236f.; Harland 2003).

Narrative literary works by Jews

Narrative literary works by Jews purporting to describe and/or interpret important events regarding Jewish life in the Greco-Roman Diaspora are invaluable, despite their tendentious and apologetic character. Of chief importance are writings by Philo of Alexandria, especially *Embassy to Gaius* and *Against Flaccus* (dating from the reign of Caligula near the mid-first century CE), and of Josephus, principally *Antiquities of the Jews* and *Wars* (from the last third of the first century CE). They provide the most direct evidence for Jews and Judaism as a minority ethno-religious construct in the Greco-Roman Diaspora.

Other literary works by Jews

A plethora of other literary works in Greek by Jews of the Greco-Roman Diaspora promote faithfulness to Judaic life within a dominant, pagan, Greco-Roman world. These range in genre from the "philosophical-allegorical" works of Philo (first half of the first century CE), through the "Jewish" Sibylline Oracles (compiled in the sixth century from materials dating from the second century BCE through first century CE), to 3 and 4 Maccabees (first century BCE to first century CE), to name a few.

Pagan Greek and Latin authors

A number of so-called pagan Greek and Latin authors mention and characterize Jewish life in the midst of their cities. I shall name a few by way of example. We have already noted passing remarks made by Cicero (especially in his trial defense of Flaccus, former proconsul of Asia) and the literary compositions of Ovid, Horace, Martial, and Juvenal (particularly in their more satirical works). Roman historians and biographers like Tacitus and Suetonius proffer information about Jews in the empire, and Jews figure in the correspondence of Pliny the Younger with his imperial master while the former administered Rome's affairs in Asia Minor in the second century (see M. Stern 1974–84).

Roman legal edicts

While dating almost exclusively from the mid-second century CE on, with the highest concentration dating from the late fourth and early fifth centuries (under the Valentinian-Theodosian emperors), Roman legal edicts are invaluable corroboration of much that is only hinted at in earlier evidence concerning the organization of Jewish life within, and the participation of Jews in the institutions of, the pagan (and later, Christian) cities of the Greco-Roman Diaspora. Conveniently, each edict is referenced by the Roman codes by calendrical date, the emperor(s) promulgating the edict, and the Roman authority to whom the edict is directed for implementation. And while the codifiers undoubtedly made errors – sometimes with respect to dates, sometimes in conflating more than one edict – the chronology is accurate enough for our purposes. The principal sources for the 64 legal edicts concerning Jews and Judaism are the *Code of Theodosius II* (438 CE) and its associated *Novels* and *Interpretatio* (end of the fifth century), the *Code of Justinian* (534 CE) and the associated *Digest* (533 CE), and the *Breviarium* of Alaric II (506 CE) (see Linder 1987: 27–53).

New Testament and patristic writings

Early Christian sources, both New Testament (latter half of the first century CE and early second century) and patristic writings (early second century CE and beyond), provide a wealth of information about Jews and Judaism in the Greco-Roman Diaspora, notwithstanding their own tendentiousness in dealing with Jews and Jewish institutions, the archetypical "other" for most early Christian authors.

Writings of the early rabbis

The writings of the early rabbis, a religio-professional guild that emerged in the Jewish community of late second-century Palestine, also proffer information about Jewish life and Judaism in "Mediterranean provinces," namely, the lands of the Roman Mediterranean outside of Palestine. However, the relevant passages in rabbinic literature (turn of the third century CE through the late sixth or the turn of the seventh centuries) are decidedly episodic and usually rabbi-centric; that is to say, early rabbis assume (or presume) a prominence and authority in these Diaspora communities, an authority which no evidence corroborates (see Levine 1998a: 98–138).

Biblical literature

As mentioned, Greco-Roman Diaspora Jews possessed and revered (Jewish) biblical literature (which they read and studied in Greek); they possessed as well an expansive supplementary set of documents which the church later collected in what it came to call the Apocrypha and Pseudepigrapha of the Old Testament. These texts shaped the Diaspora Jews' perceptions and social constructions of their reality, and proffered authoritative norms, laws, religious rites, and festivals, which had to be adapted to Diaspora settings, but which they could not ignore (see Sanders 1999: 5).

Imagining (Greco-)Roman Diaspora Jews and Judaism: conceptual and theoretical issues

Evidence does not select and organize itself. Nor does evidence interpret itself. For any phenomenon studied our prior notions of *how phenomena such as this one work* inform our selection of salient evidence, our classification and organization of the data, and our articulation of what the evidence selected and so organized means. These notions comprise one's theoretical or conceptual models – one's "take" on the evidence.

The upshot of the foregoing is that different accounts of the same phenomenon are inevitable. Some accounts will be complementary, others contradictory; some more satisfying by standards of scholarship, some less so. Complementary accounts highlight different aspects of the phenomenon under analysis. Accounts which arguably ignore or patently distort salient and pervasive evidence must be deemed deficient.

Not being able to articulate and, when called upon, to defend one's conceptual or theoretical models, one's "take," is problematic. Moreover, one's "take" must be open to refinement, ramification, or abandonment, should the evidence so indicate. This constitutes a norm which distinguishes scholarly conceptual and theoretical models from doctrinaire stances. Again in a chapter such as this, one cannot provide a complete rendering of one's conceptual and theoretical models and of their appropriateness over against others. Permit me, however, in summary fashion to give an account of the principal elements which comprise this chapter's "take."

My conceptual and theoretical framework is informed from three complementary venues. The first stems from the social-anthropological insight that all humans live in shared, socially constructed "worlds" and that the elements or various spheres that comprise these worlds must "hang together" sufficiently. In other words, these elements must be sufficiently congruent and mutually re-enforcing so as to give the whole an air of "self-evidence" for the social actors (see especially Berger and Luckman 1966; Douglas 1973, 1975). Moreover, those elements which hang together and mutually reinforce one another have both synchronic and diachronic dimensions. In other words, elements which exist *at the same time* (syn-chronic) reinforce one another by replicating in sphere after sphere the same basic patterns. For example, in biblical Judaism, about which we shall speak at greater length below, the mapping of territory, the social caste system with its marriage restrictions, the purity laws, to name just several socially constructed spheres constituting the Jewish Bible's "world," all exhibit the same general pattern; the rules governing *each* sphere define concentric circles of gradations of holiness, with the most holy, protected, "powerful," or authoritative at the center. The social actor, experiencing the same basic patterning in sphere after sphere of his or her life, comes to experience that pattern as simply *the way things are*, as *nature-like*. However, especially in pre-modern societies, the elements of one's socially constructed world must also be perceived to have *continuity over time* (dia-chronic) *with an authoritative past, even if matters have in reality changed, sometimes significantly over time.* In large part this requisite is a defining element of "traditional societies." Sometimes this is achieved by focusing attention in formal practices and processes on what is preserved of the past; sometimes the record of the past is rewritten to accord with the present. The biblical authors engage in the latter, when they put into Moses' mouth teachings characteristic of a much later period. As regards the former, witness Rome's consistent attempts during the imperial Roman period to portray itself as operating in direct continuity with Roman republican norms and institutions; the imperial system gives the senate a formal role reminiscent of a level of authority it in fact no longer has. At the same time, the early emperors' powers are defined with reference to republican legal institutions, notwithstanding the fact that the emperor wielded a level of authority over a time-frame unimagined in republican law. It is because of this aforementioned air of "self-evidence," created by such synchronic and diachronic repetitions and consistencies, that the "worlds" which human communities construct for themselves are experienced by their "inhabitants" as being as immutable and "given" as the natural and biological world (see Douglas 1973).

Especially in pre-modern times (and still for many in modern times), what we call religion was (and is) an integral part of these humanly constructed, shared "worlds"; religious phenomena did not constitute some distinct realm of belief and activity apart from others. Among other things, these religiously informed "worlds" comprise: (a) shared perceptions of how things really are; (b) shared definitions of social roles and institutions, (c) shared norms and rules for how people (and supernatural beings) should interact; (d) shared stories that account for how things are and who people are; (e) and shared rituals which celebrate and re-enact salient elements of that story and components of the "world" (see Geertz 1966; Berger 1967). In the following sections of this chapter, these descriptive and analytic categories cut across the themes by which this study deals with the evidence at hand.

Second, I am informed by sociological and anthropological perspectives on minority communities in complex, pluralistic, or quasi-pluralistic societies. Minority communities must have, to some significant extent, shared "worlds" which the social actors in question must reasonably perceive as particular unto themselves. These minority social constructs must support and perpetuate the group's continued existence as a distinct community with its own identity. However, unless the minority community advocates for its members a radically sectarian existence, cut off as much as possible from social interaction and commerce with others, shared worlds constructed by minority communities must permit a requisite degree of *participation in and acceptance by* the host society.

In some sense, therefore, successful minority-community worlds must become particularistic instances or variations of the host society's socially constructed "world." That is, *at one and the same time*, the social norms and institutions of the minority community must: (1) serve the community's needs for perpetuating a distinctive social grouping, with particular norms, institutions, and roles; (2) be so conceived as to appear to reflect, and be experienced in some serious sense as reflecting, those of the host society; and (3) because of this partial overlap and/or mirroring of minority and host-society constructs, permit and facilitate a significant degree of participation by minority members (as individuals and/or as a community) in the host society (and at times vice versa).

Finally, my "take" on the evidence for Jews and Judaism in the Roman Diaspora has been significantly shaped by the results of recent case studies focusing on the "struggle for success" of ancient Jewish, early Christian, and so-called pagan religious communities in specific urban settings of the late Roman Mediterranean world. First and foremost, one must recognize that Greco-Roman Diaspora Jewish communities and their Judaism were decidedly urban phenomena. Second, the inhabitants of Greco-Roman cities, of whatever religious or ethnic stripe, lived "cheek by jowl" with one another in crowded urban environments. Consequently, the social segregation which one usually associates with sectarian-minority religious behavior was difficult (if not impossible) to achieve and for the most part socially dysfunctional in such settings. Third, not only are Greco-Roman cities "close" affairs because of their crowded physical traits (synagogues, beside churches and pagan temples, all near common civic space like the basilica and marketplace, and with domiciles and shops of various communities adjacent to or interspersed with one another), Greco-Roman cities also demanded of their inhabitants (of means) mutually upholding systems of benefaction and civic service. The "honor" bestowed and received in return for such benefaction and civic service (in the form of magistracies and service as a member of the local curial class) made the city and its constituent elements function, served to cement the patron–client relations so much a part of Greco-Roman social and economic life, and provided recognized means of social integration and acceptance. Benefaction and civic service made the city work and maintained its infrastructure and principal institutions. As such, benefaction and civic service were for the Roman authorities an essential element of governance, peace, and order throughout the empire, because Roman imperial government relied heavily upon quasi-autonomous urban government and organization as its basic and principal substrate of governance.

Greco-Roman Jews were not apart from and outside this urban system; they could not be. Those (relatively few) Diaspora Jews who would have attempted to define for themselves a life which minimized social and cultural participation in (primarily) pagan urban life would have had to follow a more hermetic and ascetic or monastic-like life (see e.g. Philo, *The Contemplative Life*, on the *therapeutae*). The overwhelming body of evidence points in the other direction, and so invites the use of models of minority integration and participation in the local host society and culture, within the limits which permit the maintenance of a significant and meaningful ethnic-religious community and culture.

Roman Diaspora Judaism: An Adaptation of Late Biblical Judaism for Life as a Minority Community within Greco-Roman Urban Settings

Our account of Greco-Roman Diaspora Judaism is organized under five thematic headings: (1) Roman Diaspora Judaism's continuities with, dependence upon, and appropriation of biblical literature and late biblical Judaism; (2) discontinuities and disjuncture between Roman Diaspora Judaism, on the one hand, and biblical literature and late biblical Judaism, on the other; (3) Roman Diaspora Judaism's repatterning of key aspects of the biblical-Judaic "world"; (4) the synagogue as both the institution *par excellence* of the Roman Diaspora and a typical Roman civic institution; and (5) constituent roles and institutions within the synagogue and community.

The first two themes deal with Roman Diaspora Judaism's general appropriation and adaptation of late biblical Judaism and that biblical literature upon which late biblical Judaism is founded and in which it finds legitimacy. In so dealing, we explore the *diachronic* dimension of Roman Diaspora Jews' social construction of a "plausible" "world" for themselves. As we shall see in the first section below, the evidence for and from Roman Diaspora Judaism indicates, on the one hand, that its dependence upon late biblical Judaism is profound and provides the foundation of their religious-ethnic identity and practice.

On the other hand, we argue (in the second section below) that the core patterning of biblical Judaism's "world" is significantly at odds with the synchronic requirements of Roman Diaspora Jewish communities for a religion and way of life the patterns of which not only sustained their ethnic and religious identity as a minority but also reflected the dominant normative patterns of the host urban societies in which they had significantly to participate, and be accepted as significant participants. But, as we shall argue, biblical Judaism's social "mapping" places non-Jewish nations at its periphery and Jews exclusively at its center, hardly a recipe for a viable minority social and cultural construct. The last three of our five themes examine those constructs which together served to create these synchronic homologies. The section on our third theme shows that Roman Diaspora Judaism radically recontextualizes those elements that it appropriates from late biblical Judaism. We shall see that Diaspora Judaism imagines a world in which non-Jews are ubiquitous, in which Jewish communities "dot" the essentially non-Jewish social map, and in which Jews meaningfully participate in non-Jewish society – albeit within certain limits, for example, by continuing to practice endogamy or by avoiding *direct* participation in, or support of, pagan cults. The sections on our fourth and fifth themes, therefore, deal with the principal, characteristic institutions and roles by which Diaspora Jews and Judaism organized and effected their religious-communal life together in the "pagan" (later Christian) cities of the Roman Mediterranean. These institutions were central to these Jewish communities' response to the requisites of social formation and the construction of a "new" context in which their array of appropriated and adapted elements of late biblical religion could be melded with elements of their own invention. Equally important, they mimicked normative forms of urban social organization and governance in Greco-Roman cities of the period, and even permitted "crossover" activities; Jews as groups and as individuals could be benefactors of urban institutions, and, at times, pagans acted as benefactors and patrons of Diaspora Jewish institutions.

Before proceeding to the exploration of these five themes, it is worth stressing one point. Although the evidence for Roman Diaspora Judaism, particularly the archaeological and inscriptional evidence, dates in large measure from the third century CE and later, the literary evidence, especially from pagan writers, early Christian literature, Josephus, and Philo, indicates that all of the main features of Roman Diaspora Judaism were already well established during or before the first century CE. These Diaspora Judaic constructs were not a response to the destruction of the Jerusalem Temple in 70 CE and the consequent demise of late biblical Judaism. Nor were they the innovations of the early rabbinic movement, who in popular contemporary Jewish imagination are understood as the group that "saved" Judaism by formulating a

religion without a Temple and sacrifice in the aftermath of the Temple's destruction. Rather Roman Diaspora Judaism developed in, and in response to, the social
and cultural context outside the Land of Israel, while late biblical Judaism still thrived
in the Land.

Roman Diaspora Judaism, biblical literature, and late biblical Judaism: continuities, dependence, and appropriation

I have proffered the view that an important element in any socially constructed world
experienced by its inhabitants as plausible and self-evidently appropriate is the shared
perception of continuity with an authoritative past. Without a doubt, biblical
literature and late biblical Judaism, in the main constructs of the Land of Israel,
provided the principal elements of that continuity for all Jews in the Roman era,
whether living in their "homeland" or in the Diaspora (see e.g. Sanders 1999).

We can be confident that Jews in the Greco-Roman Diaspora read, principally in
Greek translation, the biblical literature, which had been composed in Hebrew with
some few Aramaic texts, and promulgated and accepted as authoritative in the Land
of Israel during the second Temple Period (late sixth century BCE to late first
century CE). Like the Jews of the Land, Greco-Roman Jews understood that this
biblical collection comprised three parts or classes of documents: the most holy was
"the Torah of Moses," rendered in Greek as "the Law of Moses;" the second part
was the collected writings of the biblical "prophets" (which included the bulk of the
biblical narrative dealing with Joshua's career through the destruction of Solomon's
Temple and the demise of the monarchy in Judah); the third was a collection of
supplementary "sacred writings." I will not here rehash debates about the process
of canonization of the biblical traditions or about probable regional differences as
to what was to be included in the second and third divisions of the tripartite collection of the bible (see Lightstone 2002). Certainly a substantial body of supplementary literature in Greek circulated with the biblical tradition (much of which
was later classified by the church as the Apocrypha and Pseudepigrapha to its Old
Testament). Whether or not in any one locale any of these supplementary documents
were considered part of the biblical collection of "sacred writings" does not matter
for our purposes.

Later we shall discuss the synagogue as a principal institution of the Greco-Roman
Jewish communities. Evidence for Hellenistic Egypt shows that synagogues are well
established there as early as the mid-third century BCE (see Levine 2000; Rutgers
1998: 127–30), presumably as a place of assembly and prayer, as the designation
proseuche in use among Hellenistic Egyptian Jewry indicates. The literary evidence
for the first century CE indicates that synagogues are ubiquitous in the Greco-Roman
Diaspora Jewish communities. At this juncture, however, it is important to note that
Greco-Roman Diaspora communities kept sets of the sacred scrolls in the synagogue
for use during public readings of scripture, followed by a sermon-study session
elucidating their meaning, again a practice well attested in the literary evidence from
the first century (e.g. Book of Acts). This activity constituted a (or the) core element
of communal prayer services on Sabbaths and festivals (and, perhaps, twice additionally during the week, as in the Land of Israel).

That not only was the content of the scrolls deemed holy, but also the scrolls themselves were perceived as holy objects, is indicated by architectural elements in excavated synagogues of the Roman period. Increasingly through the late Roman period, an elaborate niche in which the scrolls were kept (or placed during communal prayer) becomes the architectural feature around which and toward which the synagogue assembly hall was oriented (see Levine 2000). And such Torah niches seem often to be framed by representations of Temple cult symbols, such as the Jerusalem Temple seven-branched candelabra. It is as if communal prayer were directed *through* the niche in which the scrolls are placed, a conduit to heaven, as it were, likened to the Jerusalem Temple.

In the Land of Israel, the tripartite biblical tradition was probably perceived as three concentric circles of holiness: the Torah of Moses, at the center, was the most holy, ringed about, in turn, by the "prophets" and the other "sacred writings," as if the outer domains protected the inner. In fact, this shared perception of "the way things are ordered" – concentric circles with the most sacred, holy, and authoritative at the center, protected by successive encompassing domains – is replicated time and time again in sphere after sphere in the Torah of Moses' prescriptions for the religious cult and social organization of Judaic life in the Land of Israel. This model of the "world" is at the heart of the Torah's own perception of the world as communicated in its narrative and especially its legal content. And we must understand this model in order to appreciate Greco-Roman Diaspora Judaism as an ethno-religious minority phenomenon in Rome's empire in the Mediterranean lands outside the Land of Israel.

The Torah established YHWH, the creator, as the unique and only deity of Israel, with whose ancestor Abraham, YHWH, according to this Torah, made a covenant to follow God's law (later revealed to Moses) so that through Abraham's descendents "all the nations of the earth shall be blessed" (Genesis 12. 3). Biblical Judaism, grounded in *the* Torah, believed wholly to have been revealed to Moses, ordained a Judaic world, at the center of which was the Holy of Holies, surrounded by the Sanctuary and Outer Courts of YHWH's *unique and only* Holy Temple, in YHWH's only chosen Holy City, Jerusalem, bounded by the holy Land of Israel, beyond which lay the "lands of the nations." In the biblical articulation of matters, YHWH's "name" "dwelled" in the Holy of Holies in Jerusalem. Elaborate purity laws and rites ensured that "uncleanness" made no ingress into that dwelling place, lest YHWH's "name" or "presence," allergic, as it were, to uncleanness, depart. (Uncleanness was produced and released by many things, chiefly corpses, running or bleeding sores, venereal diseases, and menstrual blood.) In this view, such a departure by YHWH's presence from his only "dwelling place" in this world meant the dissolution of divine order on earth, characterized as war, pestilence, famine – in the biblical text's language, "and they will not die in their uncleanness, having rendered unclean My sanctuary which is in their midst" (Leviticus 15. 31).

Biblical purity law and rites of purification were intended to produce the requisite degree of purity in the Land of Israel, so as to maintain a higher degree of purity in Jerusalem, allowing the maintenance of a more elevated degree of purity in the Temple, permitting the utmost degree of purity to be guaranteed in the Holy of Holies. The classical rabbinic rendition of this essentially biblical view of matters is stunningly articulated in Mishnah Tractate Kelim 1: 6–9.

1:6

1   There are ten [levels] of holy [territory]:

2   The Land of Israel is more holy than all of the [other] lands.

3   And what is [the nature of] its holiness?

4   [In] that they bring from it[s produce the offerings of] the *omer*, the first fruits, and the two loaves,

5   Which they do not thus bring from [the produce of] the other lands.

1:7

6   Cities surrounded by a wall are more holy than it [the Land of Israel].

7   [In] that they send forth the leprous.

8   And they parade [in cortege] around within [the city the bier of] a dead person as they wish.

9   [But once] it [the dead person] leaves [the city], they do not return it [back within the city walls].

1:8

10   [The territory] within the walls [of Jerusalem] is more holy than them [the territory within the walls of other walled cities].

11   [In] that they eat there lesser holy things and second tithe.

12   The Temple Mount is more holy than it.

13   [In] that men with a flux, and women with a flux, and those who are menstruating, and women who have recently given birth do not enter there.

14   [Within] the rampart is more holy than it.

15   [In] that Gentiles and one unclean with corpse uncleanness do not enter there.

16   The Women's Court [of the Temple] is more holy than it.

17   [In] that one who has immersed that self-same day [and is waiting until the next to bring a purification offering] does not enter there.

18   And they [who unwittingly transgress this interdiction] are not liable on account of it for a sin offering.

19   The Court of [male] Israel[ites of the Temple] is more holy than it.

20   [In] that one [who has completed all other rites of purification but] who lacks [i.e. does not yet have] his atonement sacrifice [brought on his behalf] may not enter there.

21   And they [who unwittingly transgress this interdiction] are liable on account of it for a sin offering.

22   The Court of Priests is more holy than it.

23   [In] that [clean] Israelites enter there only at the moment [required to fulfill] their sacrificial needs,

24   [i.e.] for the laying on of hands [upon the sacrifice to confess one's sins], for slaughtering [of the sacrifice], for the waiving [of portions of the sacrificial meat before the altar].

1:9a

25   [The Area] from the Vestibule [of the Sanctuary] to the Altar is more holy than it.

26   [In] that [temporarily] blemished [priests and priests] whose head is uncovered do not enter there.

27   The Sanctuary is more holy than it.

28   [In] that only those [priests] whose hands and feet are [first] washed may enter there.

29   The Holy of Holies is more holy than it.

30   [In] that only the High Priest enters there [and only] on the Day of Atonement at the moment of the *avodah* [service]. (Mishnah Kelim 1:6–9a, translation my own)

According to the late biblical tradition of the Land of Israel, the maintenance of these concentric circles of holiness required, as well, the organization of the People of Israel in a hereditary caste system, again in concentric circles of holiness: at the center the high priest, the chief officer of the Temple; the members of the priestly families, who performed the rites of the Temple; supporting clans of the Levites, a caste of Temple workers and officials; surrounded and supported by the caste of Israelites, the remainder of the nation. Upon each caste were incumbent different levels of purity maintenance, and since these castes were hereditary, endogamy and rules about who might marry whom were of the utmost importance.

Beyond the Israelites were the other nations of the earth, who did not acknowledge YHWH or practice his laws of purity, and therefore, unbeknown to themselves, endangered the very continued welfare of the world, because they let the powers of uncleanness run rampant. In other words, if uncleanness was kept away from the center, YHWH's life-giving and world-maintaining power could flow out of it to the world, albeit diluted and dispelled by uncleanness as it reached areas in which the necessary purity rites were either unknown or not practiced. In this sense, all of the people of Israel (in their Land) constituted "a kingdom of priests and a holy nation" (Exodus 19. 6) for all nations.

It is clear that the biblical tradition, inherited and revered by the Diaspora Greco-Roman Jewish communities, replicated in sphere after sphere the same basic patterning – both in human life and activity, and in the perceived spatial ordering of earthly territory. In all these spheres one encounters the model of concentric spheres of increasing holiness – the whole intended to maintain at the center a kind of "life-giving," world-ordering "machine."

It is also clear that Roman Diaspora Jews (1) understood their identity in terms of the biblical tradition's basic narrative, (2) inherited the late biblical tradition's monotheism, and depended upon biblical law for (3) family law, (4) life-cycle rites, (5) dietary law, and (6) their calendar of weekly Sabbaths and festivals. The biblical literature, and especially the Psalms, (7) provided the texts for prayer. And the biblical tradition lay at the center of (8) Diaspora Jews' continued relation with and support for the institutions of the Land of Israel, especially the Jerusalem Temple until its destruction in AD 70, although, as we discuss at length below, Diaspora Jews had especially to reconceptualize and recontextualize their "world's" relationship to the Jerusalem Temple, as defined in biblical Judaism.

Permit me to note those elements of biblical-inspired law, teaching, and tradition adopted or adapted by Greco-Roman Diaspora Jews for which evidence is most abundant and explicit (see Sanders 1999).

Diaspora identity and the biblical narrative

There is ample evidence that Jews of the Greco-Roman Diaspora understood themselves to be that people with whom YHWH made a covenant via the agency of Abraham, their common ancestor, and to whom YHWH revealed completely and finally his law (Torah/*nomos*) via the agency of Moses. From the biblical narrative they understood the Land of Israel to be their homeland. And the biblical account of the people's liberation from Egyptian bondage again by the agency of Moses (and Aaron) figured prominently in their identity. Pagan Latin (e.g. Tac. *Hist.* 5.1–13) and especially Greek authors (e.g. Apion as cited in Josephus, *Against Apion*) appear to know that these elements were at the core of the identity of the Jews they encountered (see M. Stern 1974–84: I. nos. 163a–77). And, as we know from Philo (e.g. *Special Laws, Allegorical Interpretations, Moses, Questions and Answers on Exodus, Creation, Abraham*, etc.), and Josephus (*Antiquities, Against Apion*, and *Life*), Diaspora Jews felt compelled to defend the integrity of the biblical narratives against pagan detractors (like Apion) who sought to delegitimize the Jews by mocking or attacking these narrative elements.

Biblical monotheism among Diaspora Jews

The question of what monotheism did or did not mean to Jews in (late) antiquity is complex; it is not a subject to be dealt with at length in this chapter. On the basis of their biblical tradition, Greco-Roman Diaspora Jews understood that their allegiance was to one God, and one God only, YHWH. Certainly many, perhaps even the overwhelming majority of, Diaspora Jews (and Jews of the Land of Israel) understood no other gods to exist; this conception of monotheism is entirely consistent with biblical Judaism's reading of the biblical literature and with the view of the final redactors of the Torah of Moses in the fifth century BCE (see Kugel 2003). This YHWH-alone tendency is a highly salient (and perhaps the least understood) characteristic of Diaspora Jews for their pagan neighbors. Inveterate critics of the Jews among pagan Latin and Greek authors characterize Jewish monotheism as atheism, since the reality of "the gods" seems to them to be denied by the Jews among them (e.g. Tac. *Hist.* 5.13; Dio 67.14.1–2; Barclay 1996: 312).

Moreover, the matter is not one of belief and theology alone. The fact that Jews did not offer sacrifices even to YHWH in their synagogues may have reinforced the grounds for characterizing Diaspora Jews as atheists. More important still, Jews did not (directly) participate in the civic cultic rites of their cities, including the imperial cults as they emerged in the late Roman, pre-Christian empire. Since pagan festivals and cults, on the one hand, and athletic games, on the other, were sometimes related, many scholars, such as Barclay, for one, conclude that Roman Diaspora Jews would have avoided the amphitheater and stadium and their games, further emphasizing their "otherness" on the religious and civic fronts simultaneously. But the arguments adduced by Barclay (1996: 236–7), for example, are problematic. He concludes that when the formal Jewish community of Cyrenaica in the first century CE support "the amphitheater" and vote to have dedicatory inscriptions placed therein (Lüderiz 1983: 70–2; see also Harland 2003), a Jewish communal building is probably designated, not the civic structure of Cyrenaica. But Barclay must admit that such a designation for a Diaspora Jewish communal building would be unique in all the extant evidence for Greco-Roman Diaspora Jews and Judaism.

More significant still, evidence is far from univocal on Jews' alleged avoidance of athletic games and theatrical performance and their civic venues. Philo seems to have acquired a thorough gymnasium education, which would have included training as an *ephebe* in the appropriate athletic contests. And as Barclay himself points out, Philo's "familiarity with theatrical and sporting events (chariot races, boxing, wrestling and pancratist contests) indicates that he enjoyed the regular entertainments of Alexandrian citizens" (Barclay 1996: 114; see esp. Philo, *Providence* 2.58, *Freedom* (*Probus*) 26; see also L. Feldman 1993: 58–67). Yet Philo's theological monotheism is unimpeachable, as is his expressed loyalty to what he understands to be the norms of the Law of Moses. And the Jewish community of first-century CE Cyrenaica supported and had dedicatory inscriptions placed in the city's amphitheater. Thus some Diaspora Jews, as individuals and as communities, seem to have been able to make the distinction between direct and indirect participation in activities dedicated to pagan deities, and in so doing bolstered their participation in civic life and its services.

As much as detractors may have criticized Jews for their non-participation in the pagan cults of their respective cities, Roman authorities recognized and accepted this non-participation and regularly provided dispensation from the pagan-cult involvements. Moreover, synagogues were tolerated, even respected, as cultic sites in the civic landscape of temples and could be located in prime civic space – the synagogue of Sardis being the most stunning example. Early Christian churches, by contrast, did not enjoy the same privileges.

However, this does not mean that Greco-Roman Diaspora Jews did not admit of the existence of other supernatural beings, both malevolent and benevolent. As was the case for their brethren in the Land of Israel, late antique Jews in the Diaspora understood their world (heaven and earth) to be populated by myriads of unseen entities. Some worked evil and brought disease (namely, demons) and others (angelic or good spirits) could be called upon (or compelled) to help thwart these evils. Curiously enough, among the names found in lists of angels in *Sefer Harazim*, a late antique Jewish text of theurgy (or "white" magic) are the names of some classical Greek gods, such as Helios, Aphrodite, and Hermes (see *Sefer Harazim* 4:60ff, 1:176ff, ed. Margolioth 1966; see discussions in Barclay 1966: 122, and Lightstone 1984).

The incantations and theurgic rites of *Sefer Harazim* resemble many collected by Preisendanz in *Papyri Graecae Magicae* (*PGM*) (1973–4 [1928–31], 4: 1169–226, 3009–85, 13: 335–40, 22a: 17–27, 22b: 1–26, 25: 1–42; see also Betz 1986), a number of which have been identified as "Jewish" and many others of which have been deemed to have been influenced by Jewish practices. "Angelic" beings are called upon or compelled by incantations, votive rites, potions, and amulets to assure health, love, and success or to counter the suspected malevolent wishes and spells of others (see *Sefer Harazim* 1:28ff, ed. Margolioth 1966, for incense offered to angels; see also Barclay 1996: 119–23; Lightstone 1984; Goodenough 1952–65: 2. 153 207). Preisendanz also included in his collection (*PGM*) a more extended Greco-Roman Jewish text, the Leiden Papyrus, which can only be characterized as a hermetic-like cosmological-cosmogenic treatise, "The Eighth Book of Moses," in which the Jewish God effects matters in the cosmos through a pantheon of associated supernatural figures (McBrearty 1986). Finally, Goodenough (1952–65: vol. 2) has collected many amulets of Jewish origin.

One cannot dismiss such evidence by asserting that such Jewish theurgists operated at the fringes of the Diaspora Jewish community or under condemnation from Jewish authorities. The anti-Judaic sermons *Against the Jews* of John Chrysostom (late fourth century CE) indicate otherwise. Chrysostom warns his Gentile Christian parishioners not to frequent Jewish holy men *operating in the local synagogue* to seek incantations, amulets, and potions (Meeks and Wilken, 1978: 85–127). All of this seemingly flies not only in the face of biblical Judaism's more radical monotheism but also in the face of explicit biblical injunctions against sorcery (Leviticus 19. 31, 20. 6, 20. 27; Deuteronomy 18. 11).

Biblical family law

Our evidence will not allow us to identify the full extent to which biblical family law was adopted or adapted by Greco-Roman Diaspora Jews. While we might safely presume that much (like the biblical prohibitions against adultery and consanguineous marriage) was practiced, we have little or no way of knowing about other aspects (like levirate marriage). The key element of biblical family law for which Diaspora Jews were conspicuously known by their non-Jewish neighbors was endogamy. Jews married other Jews (by birth or by conversion). Again, we know that this was one of the more salient, observed features of Diaspora Jewish life, because it engendered comment and criticisms from those pagan writers critical of Jews and Judaism (e.g. Tac. *Hist.* 5.1–13, esp. 5.5.1–2). For the latter, Jews "stuck to themselves" or were out-and-out misanthropes. Since we know that Jews did indeed participate extensively and intensively in the life of their urban settings (a point to be discussed at length later), I believe the charge of misanthropy to largely reflect the Diaspora Jewish penchant for endogamy.

Furthermore, there is sufficient evidence to suggest that Jews continued to do what was necessary to continue to perpetuate the priestly caste (and presumably the levitical caste as well) – yet another instance of some sort of observance of biblical family law. Paul encounters members of the priestly caste in Asian Jewish communities, including the sons of one "chief priest," Sceva. Both Sceva and his sons, it seems, *qua* members of the priestly caste, enjoyed elevated status and authority (and, according to Acts 19. 12–20, were perceived by others to possess some degree of theurgic power).

As a matter of note, Jews in the Greco-Roman Diaspora seem to have practiced monogamy (like their Latin and Greek neighbors), although biblical law permits polygamy, which some Middle Eastern Jews continued to practice.

Biblical life-cycle law

As with family law, we do not know the full repertoire of biblically inspired life-cycle rites practiced by Greco-Roman Jews. However, male circumcision figures prominently in a variety of evidence at hand. Again, pagan writers critical of Jews and Judaism harped regularly on circumcision as an abominable mutilation (Juvenal 14.103–4; Tac. *Hist.* 5.5.1–2; Mart. 7.30.5, 7.35.3–4, 7.82.5–6, 11.94; M. Stern 1974–84: I. nos. 240, 243, 245; Barclay 1996: 282–319).

Diaspora Jews in the Greco-Roman world practiced not only infant (male) circumcision, but also circumcision of adult male converts and of their (non-Jewish) male slaves serving Jewish households. To be a non-Jewish slave in a Greco-Roman Diaspora Jewish household seems to have presumed a process of conversion (see Linder 1987), since upon manumission former slaves joined the local Jewish community as free members and pledged to support the synagogue of their former owners (van der Horst 1999: 22, 33–34; see Frey 1936–52 [1975]: I. nos. 683, 690).

Whether Roman Jews supplemented biblical life-cycle rites with others is less clear. We do not know whether specific rituals marked boys or girls achieving the age of majority; nor is it clear whether biblical-related rites were complemented by pagan ones such as celebrations of birthdays or rites of attaining physical maturity, which for non-Jewish Roman youth was marked by the donning of the *toga virilis* around their sixteenth birthday. However, it is difficult to imagine that Roman Jews did not adopt many rites of their host society, when such rites did not run afoul of specific Judaic prohibitions. Since many male Jewish figures in frescos of the Dura-Europos synagogue (third century CE) are clearly depicted togate (see Goodenough 1952–65: illustrations throughout vol. 11), indicating that some strata of Greco-Roman Diaspora Jewish society wore togas on at least some occasions, one suspects that some rite existed in Jewish circles too marking the first donning of the *toga virilis*.

Biblical dietary prescriptions

That Greco-Roman Jews respected biblical prohibitions regarding eating certain species of animals – most notably, abstaining from eating pork and refraining from eating food which had been dedicated to a pagan god – is widely and clearly attested in the body of evidence. Pagan critics of Greco-Roman Diaspora Jews ridicule Jews spurning pork (e.g. Juvenal 14.96–106; cf. Tac. *Hist.* 5.5.1; Plut. *Quaestiones conviviales* 4.4.4–6.2; see M. Stern 1974–84: I. no. 258). And Paul and Peter must deal with the question of whether, as some early Christians maintained, Gentile Christians, *like Jews*, must refrain from eating species and meats deemed unfit or unclean by biblical Judaism (Acts 10. 9–16, 11. 3–10, 15. 19–20). Furthermore, among the privileges afforded the Greco-Roman Diaspora Jews in Roman edicts Josephus proffers in *Antiquities 14* as genuine is the instruction to a city council to ensure that food which Jews may consume is available in the city marketplace.

Sabbath and biblical calendar of festivals

Biblical literature preserves several festival lists in Exodus (34. 16–26), Leviticus (23), Numbers (28, 29), and Deuteronomy (16). Biblical Judaism conflated these lists, to which it added the Feast of Esther and Hannukah. Evidence for Greco-Roman Diaspora Judaism's calendar of festivals clearly reflects the conflated list promulgated by biblical Judaism. Early rabbinic literature (e.g. Tractate Rosh Hashannah in Mishnah, Tosefta, and Bavli) enjoin that legates from the Land of Israel, operating under the authority of the rabbinic-Patriarchal courts (*shaliah bet-din*), travel throughout the Diaspora setting the calendar and its festivals on the basis of astronomical observances and calendrical intercalations made in the Land. As with so many early rabbinic injunctions, it is difficult to know whether these are merely theoretical portrayals or contrived narratives, not uncommon features of this literature. The only clear instance of a "festival letter" sent from the Land of Israel to a Diaspora community is that contained among the Elephantine Papyri (Lindenberger 1994: nos. 30a, 30b) from Persian-period Egypt. Therein Jerusalem Temple authorities write to the Elephantine Jews regarding the celebration of Passover. We know that (before 70 CE) Temple agents were sent throughout the Greco-Roman Diaspora to collect annual levies for support of the Temple; later, in the third, fourth, and early fifth centuries CE, the Palestinian Jewish Patriarch did the same. It is a reasonable hypothesis that these same agents played a role in coordinating the Jewish calendar of the Greco-Roman Diaspora communities with that in the Land of Israel. Finally, there is no clear evidence for the period under study that the Diaspora communities practiced two sacred days for every one celebrated in the Land in order to account for astronomical differences across Mediterranean and Middle Eastern Lands, as enjoined in early rabbinic literature. The rabbinic injunctions about the same, called *yom tov sheni shel galuyot*, were certainly in force throughout the Diaspora during the Islamic period. Nor can we say that the earliest rabbis' normative use of a lunar calendar extended even to other Jewish inhabitants of the Land of Israel, let alone the Greco-Roman Diaspora (see S. Stern 2002).

As to the enumeration of years, the later Jewish practice of counting in *anno mundi* is not the regnant practice of Jews in the Roman period, even in the Land of Israel or among rabbinic circles. Rabbinic texts refer to the enumeration of years in formal documents as *minyan shtarot* (enumeration [for] writs), which counted years from the founding of the Seleucid dynasty. No comparably specific, normative practice emerges in the evidence for Roman Diaspora Judaism outside the Levant, but one may suppose, on the basis of Levantine Jewish practice, that Roman Diaspora Jews shared no specifically "Jewish" scheme for the enumeration of years.

For non-Jews in the Greco-Roman world, Jews refraining from work on the Sabbath (and other holy days) and the inauguration of Sabbaths and festivals with the lighting of lamps is one of the obvious and conspicuous traits of Greco-Roman Diaspora Jews (Ov. *Ars* 1.75f., *Rem.* 219–30; Hor. *Sermones* 1.9.60–78; Juvenal 3.10–18, 14.96–106; Mart. 4.4; Seneca, *De superstitione apud* Aug. *Civ.* 6.11; Tac. *Hist.* 5.1–13, esp. 5.4.4; Plut. *De superstitione* 8, *Quaestiones conviviales* 4.4.4–62; M. Stern 1974–84: nos. 256, 258; Suet. *Augustus* 76.2; see Barclay 1996: 282–319). For inveterate critics of Jews and Judaism among pagan Greek and Latin authors, abstention from work is labeled as idleness. Some Latin authors complain that even non-Jews have adopted the practice of lighting Sabbath lamps and the observance of some Sabbath restrictions.

The Torah ordains the celebration of three pilgrimage festivals, Passover, Pentecost, and the Feast of Booths. The Book of Acts (6. 5), for example, attests to the presence in Jerusalem of many Diaspora pilgrims in first-century-CE Jerusalem during these festivals; indeed some Diaspora communities and their expatriates living in Jerusalem constructed synagogues in Jerusalem. The earliest Christian communities in Italy, Greece-Macedonia, Asia Minor, the Levant, Egypt, and north Africa all relied on local Jewish authorities' determination of the dates of Passover for their Greco-Roman Jewish communities in order to establish annually the date for Easter. Later, when this manner of determining Easter was declared unseemly for Christians, some Christians continued to determine the date of Easter with reference to local practice by Jews of Passover (a Christian heresy, of course).

The observance by Greco-Roman Diaspora Jews of the holy days of the biblical Day of Remembrance and Trumpeting (later renamed "New Year") and the Day of Atonement is also well attested, although the best evidence is from the late empire. John Chrysostom, when a presbyter in late fourth-century Antioch, admonishes his (Gentile) Christians who are wont to go to the local synagogue(s) to celebrate with the Jews the New Year, the Day of Atonement, and the Feast of Booths (Meeks and Wilken 1978: 85–127).

Celebration by Diaspora Jews of the Feast of Esther, commemorating the story narrated in the biblical Book of Esther, is also attested. However, again evidence from non-Jewish sources dates from the century following the Christianization of the Roman empire (Linder 1987). Roman authorities (now Christian) perceive a possible mocking of Christ in the Jewish practice of hanging effigies of Haman (the arch-villain of the story) during the feast.

The biblical literature and communal prayer

The Torah's mode of communal service to YHWH is sacrifice in YHWH's one and only Temple in Jerusalem. With few notable exceptions (for example, the temple of Onias in Greco-Roman Egypt), Diaspora Jews observed the interdiction against sacrificing to YHWH outside of the Jerusalem Temple. As synagogue prayer services developed, it is evident that the biblical texts functioned as sources for these developments. I have already noted the public reading of the Torah and prophets in Greek translation, and a sermon-study session explicating the readings of the day formed one cornerstone of the synagogue ritual on Sabbaths, festivals, and other occasions. As I stated earlier, the Book of Acts (see 13, 14. 1, 15. 21, 17. 1–2, 18. 4, 18. 24–6, 19. 8) maintains that Paul exploited this practice to preach the Gospel to the Jews; according to Acts, as a visiting Jewish sage attending Diaspora synagogue rites, he would permit himself to be honored by acceding to requests to deliver the sermon-study session. Whether or how often this happened we cannot say; perhaps, it is part of Acts' *Tendenz* that the Gospel was first offered to, and rejected by, the Jews before being offered to the Gentiles. But the Book of Acts, nevertheless, assumes that scriptural readings from the Torah and Prophets, followed by a scriptural lesson, form a cornerstone of Greco-Roman Jewish synagogue rites.

Much later in the sixth century, the now-Christian Roman emperor had to intervene to ensure the Diaspora Jews' right to use Greek and Latin in the public readings of scriptures in the synagogue (and in prayer), as Palestinian or Palestinian-oriented Jews had begun advocating the exclusive use of Hebrew (Linder 1987: no. 66)

Since the formal reading of scriptures in the synagogue service took place in Greek, it is safe to conclude that public prayer was conducted in Greek as well, drawing heavily on biblical texts to fashion the liturgy. The Psalms, originating from, and in

use in, the Temple service itself, and poetic texts from the biblical prophetic literature provided – in Greek, and perhaps in some locales in Latin, translation – a ready-
made, authoritative repository for synagogue prayer. The *sanctus* of the Latin and
Greek Mass is obviously based on the *keddushah* of the Jewish prayer service, itself
highly dependent upon biblical texts, particularly Isaiah. It is probable that the
sanctus relies upon Greek and/or Latin versions of the *keddushah* in use in Diaspora
Jewish liturgy.

Biblical support for attachment to and support for the Jerusalem Temple

The Torah of Moses envisaged a society in which members had regular access to
the Temple cult. As the occasion demanded or devotion so inclined, one brought
to YHWH's Temple purification offerings to finalize purification from uncleanness,
guilt offerings to expiate transgressions performed unwittingly, peace offerings,
votive offerings and thank offerings, first fruits, second tithe, the *omer* offering, and
the Passover offering. Three times a year one was enjoined to make pilgrimage to
Jerusalem and the Temple on the principal agricultural festivals. Such ready access
to the Temple was impossible for Diaspora Jews, indeed impossible for most Jews
in the Land of Israel not living in the immediate vicinity of Jerusalem. The Temple
cult as imagined in the Torah of Moses also imagined a city-state-sized society (as
it probably had been during the period of Ezra and Nehemiah and their immediate
successors at the beginning of the Persian period, until perhaps the time of
Alexander the Great).

Still on the strength of the norms of the Torah, Diaspora Jews continued to have
an affinity for, and consistently supported, the Jerusalem Temple until its destruction in 70 CE. As we noted earlier, while the Temple stood, Diaspora Jews with the
required means attempted to make pilgrimage to Jerusalem for one of the great
festivals – however infrequently this might be for any one individual in his or her
lifetime. Individuals also sent money to have sacrifices offered on their behalf or to
support the regular daily offerings. Diaspora communities collected an annual poll
tax, on the strength of laws in Exodus 30. 11–16 concerning the half-shekel, and
sent these amassed sums to Jerusalem's Temple – this despite Roman legislation which
seemingly barred such massive transfers of funds across provincial borders. Rome apparently chose to look the other way, with the exception of one Flaccus, proconsul of
Asia in Cicero's time. Flaccus was tried for his confiscation of these funds amassed
by the Jews of the province of Asia. After the demise of the Temple, Rome had this
same tax collected and remitted to the Roman authorities to support the pagan
temple to Jupiter built on the site of the Temple to YHWH. With the establishment of the Palestinian Jewish Patriarchate as a Roman-sanctioned administrative entity
in the Land of Israel in the latter part of the second century CE, Diaspora Jewish
communities similarly collected and amassed revenues that were sent to the Land of
Israel to support the functions of the Patriarchy; a practice stopped early in the fifth
century by the Christian Roman emperors (Linder 1987).

Further with respect to the centrality of Jerusalem in Diaspora Jews' consciousness, Philo of Alexandria describes Jerusalem as the mother city of the many

Diaspora communities, which Philo describes as "colonies" of Jerusalem, a concept which Roman authorities (and all Hellenized peoples) would immediately understand (*Legatio* 281f.). In Roman legal terms a "colony" was a municipal entity with its own constitution enjoying full "Latin rights," *as if* they were on Italian soil. Thus Philo seeks to portray Diaspora Jewish communities vis-à-vis Jerusalem and the Land of Israel. As we shall see, such a portrayal of matters was a fiction; Diaspora Jews were patently not able to implement many of the provisions of their constitution, the Torah, *as if* their communities were on the soil of the Holy Land.

In sum, the biblical literature and chiefly the Torah of Moses provided the authoritative basis – in its narrative, in its family, social, and cultic laws and injunctions, and in its cultic and prophetic poetry – for many constructs at the core of Roman Diaspora Judaism. On the synchronic dimension, (1) it provided the basis for perceptions of a distinctive ethno-religious identity; (2) it allowed all Diaspora Jews to see themselves as part of one single people; (3) it fostered the perception that they were the same *ethnos* as those who lived still in the Holy Land. Moreover, on the diachronic dimension, Diaspora Jews' biblical heritage (4) permitted them to live a life deemed to be in continuity with Jews (Judeans/Israelites) of the past. However, Roman Diaspora Jews' appropriation of biblical Judaism and biblical literature also set up significant barriers to various forms of social interaction with non-Jews, and to participation by Jews in activities and functions by which the host city expressed and reinforced civic identity and solidarity within a larger social construct, the Roman empire, an important requisite as well on the synchronic dimension. Later I shall discuss how Diaspora Jews and Judaism overcame the latter barriers and forged the requisite mechanisms for social integration and solidarity with their host cities and the empire. At this juncture, however, I turn from Roman Diaspora Judaism's continuity with biblical tradition to its opposite: the principal and serious areas of disjuncture with the scriptures which they inherited, read, studied, and revered.

Roman Diaspora Judaism, biblical literature, and late biblical Judaism: discontinuities and disjuncture

I have argued that the biblical literature served as an authoritative "source book" for much of the social identity, social structures, and a distinctive ritual and cultic life which gave expression and reinforced these structures among Diaspora Jews. Now I point to the opposite. What is most often highlighted in this respect is Diaspora Jews' distance from the Jerusalem Temple, the only site, according to biblical Judaism's understanding of the scriptures, where the cult of YHWH, an almost exclusively sacrificial one, may be practiced. As noted, the Jewish temple of Onias, in the region of Leontopolis in Greco-Roman Egypt, is the notable exception which undoubtedly proves the rule, since to our knowledge, no other Greco-Roman Diaspora Jewish communities availed themselves of this option. I do not wish to understate the importance of physical distance from Jerusalem and the biblical interdiction against sacrificing elsewhere in describing transformations of biblical Judaism devised and/or adopted in the Diaspora – in particular, the emergence of the synagogue, and a cult of scriptural readings and scriptural lessons, and of prayer – as normative alternatives to the sacrificial cult in the Jerusalem Temple. Indeed, with the destruction of the Temple, and with the realization that the opportunity to re-establish that Temple was a remote eventuality (confirmed by the failure of the Bar Kochba rebellion), these normative institutions of the Diaspora became the norm for Palestinian Jews as well. In fact, ample evidence shows that these institutions – synagogue, public reading of scriptures and scriptural lessons, and prayer – had taken hold in the Land of Israel by the first century CE, before the Temple's destruction in 70. Moreover, as I have remarked earlier, the adoption of a cult without sacrifice, but *exclusively* of words, not only distinguished Diaspora Jews from their brethren in the Land of Israel (at least before 70); it also was an oddity in the urban settings of the Roman Mediterranean as a whole, another factor perhaps in some Latin and Greek authors' assertions that (Diaspora) Jews were atheists, since these Jews seemed not to practice a sacrificial cult of even their own national god, YHWH.

All this being said, the disjuncture between the socially constructed world enjoined by the scriptures and the circumstances of Jews in the Roman Diaspora is much more profound than the challenges presented by distance from Jerusalem and scriptures' interdiction of sacrifice to YHWH anywhere other than the Jerusalem Temple. This challenge is simply symptomatic. Biblical literature's most basic patterning of things will have been experienced as fundamentally problematic for Greco-Roman Diaspora Jews. Measured against the basic world view of the Torah of Moses, Diaspora Jews lived outside *the* Land in the unclean lands of the nations, far from the Temple, for which purity maintenance served to create guarded and bounded concentric circles of holiness, and from which YHWH's life-giving and ordering power flowed. The further from the source, as we have seen above, the more diluted that power by forces of uncleanness. Yet it was in this more diluted, remote territory that Roman Diaspora Jews lived. Moreover, apart from this fundamental patterning and the sets of meanings and perceptions conveyed by them, to what end was the observance of the Torah's injunctions and prohibitions serving to maintain the Jews as a "people apart," observing cultic festivals and rites serving to keep YHWH's life-giving presence in his Temple? In other words, Diaspora Jews might appropriate many of the particulars enjoined by Torah law and see their identity as reflected in the Torah's narrative, but the particulars no longer "fit" into the whole of which they are constituent elements. This, not the inability to worship YHWH via sacrifice as enjoined in scriptures, constituted the fundamental problem and challenge for Greco-Roman Diaspora Jewry's construction of a "self-evidently" appropriate and "plausible" world understood (both by Diaspora Jews and by their Jewish brethren in the homeland) to be legitimated by the authority of the Torah of Moses. What Roman Diaspora Jews gleaned from the Bible and biblical Judaism, as well as non-, post-, or para-biblical institutions, such as the synagogue, scriptural readings, scriptural lessons, prayer, and others which we shall discuss later – all these had to fit within some *new* or *other* "whole," some novel, overarching perception of the shape and nature of their "world." After I have articulated briefly this new whole, I shall discuss such institutions as the synagogue and prayer, and other phenomena characteristic of Roman Diaspora Judaism, as elements of this typically Diaspora "world."

Roman Diaspora Jews' repatterning of the biblical "world"

Fundamentally, Roman Diaspora Jews and Judaism seem to have perceived the architecture of their "world" in a manner which at one and the same time resembled both (1) the cultural patterns of their contemporary "pagan" neighbors and (2) ancient Israelite culture. By the latter I mean Israelite culture of the period prior to those radical centralizing tendencies which inform the redaction in the early Persian period of the Hebrew scriptures in their current form (see Lightstone 1984, 1988). Let me first expand upon the latter assertion, before returning to the former.

Following the lead of an earlier effort in the seventh century BCE at radical centralization, which did not survive the death of its royal sponsor, King Josiah, the Persian-period radical centralizers, for whom Ezra and Nehemiah were key leadership figures, vilified, among other things, the ancient Israelite practice of engaging in cultic activity "on [every] high place and under every spreading tree" (Deuteronomy 12. 2). The aspects of these centralizers' program may be characterized by the following list: the worship of YHWH alone; cultic practice at the Jerusalem Temple only; the singular authority of the Torah wholly revealed to Moses; strict endogamy and maintenance of caste distinctions; strict application of purity maintenance for and in the Temple cult. These centralizers rejected what appears to have been a normative, shared construction and perception among ancient Israelites of their "world" – unfortunately called "syncretistic" by Morton Smith (1971). "Syncretistic" in fact misses the unity and coherence of this ancient Israelite mapping of the "world," in which access to the divine, and to its gifts, benefits, and powers, could be had at a multiplicity of propitious locations and via a range of mediating figures, human and supernatural.

These gateways of access between heaven and earth were identified as such in tribal and clan stories and traditions. Many of these traditions have been preserved, ironically, by the centralizing framers of the extant Hebrew scriptures. For example, Jacob's dream (Genesis 28. 11–23) of a ladder connecting heaven and earth upon which angels, God's agents, ascend and descend, serves to justify the location of an Israelite cult at Bethel. Moreover, according to Genesis 35. 6–8, on his return years later from Padan-Aram, Jacob is said to have buried his wet-nurse "under the altar" which he himself had previously erected at Bethel. Similarly, Shekem, the traditional burial site of the tribe/clans of Joseph, is itself a principal ancient Israelite cultic site. It is as if the co-location of cultic altar and ancestral tombs at the same site enhanced the locale's efficacy as a conduit of communication and exchange between heaven and earth – anathema to the later framers of scripture, who see the tombs of the dead, even of the most holy and revered dead, as sources of virulent uncleanness, from which the central Jerusalem Temple must be protected.

In ancient Israel, not only were there a multiplicity of propitious locations where access to heaven and God's blessings could be had, but also there were a variety of holy persons, living and dead, who could effect beneficent exchange between heaven and earth: priests, local levites, ecstatic judges/heroes, prophets and prophetesses, even the spirits of the dead, and others labeled and vilified by scriptures' framers as witches and necromancers.

Roman Diaspora Jews opted similarly to construct and to perceive their "world" as dotted with multiple locations where privileged communication with YHWH could be had; they too recognized a variety of persons as holy and as such able to access the life-giving, healing blessings of YHWH via prayer, amulets, potions, and incantations (some of which involved rituals in which votive offerings were probably used).

As we have seen, John Chrysostom, in his two famous sermons *Against the Jews*, clearly attests that Jewish holy men, operating within the precincts of the synagogue(s) in Antioch, dispensed remedies, amulets, and incantations; he castigates his Christian congregants for seeking the services of these Jewish holy men and is among the first to articulate the notorious vilification that Jews are in league with the devil and consequently that Jewish (holy-men) healers heal by the devil's power (see Meeks and Wilken 1978: 85–127). The occasion which incited Chrysostom to compose these two sermons is noteworthy, and we have had occasion to refer to it earlier. The Jewish High Holy Days (New Year, which he calls Trumpets, and the Day of Atonement) were approaching, and Chrysostom was acutely aware that many of his (Gentile!) Christians had in the past gone, and imminently intended to go, to the synagogue to celebrate, pray, and fast with the Jews. Thus Chrysostom takes the opportunity to attempt to convince his Christian congregants not to frequent Jewish healers/holy men either or to use Jewish courts to settle their disputes, both of which he clearly indicates operate out of the synagogue.

Some of the holy persons accessed by Roman Diaspora Jews were deceased, as in the case of famous martyrs, ancestors, or those who had been perceived to be exceptionally holy or learned in life. Their tombs were particularly efficacious sites for personal prayer, and their spirits could be enjoined in prayer to intercede with God and the angels on behalf of the supplicant (see Lightstone 1984). The Maccabean martyrs (Hanna and her sons) were such a case; their alleged tombs in Syria were the site of veneration and pilgrimage. At some later date these remains were re-interred under the floor of a synagogue in Antioch, which was subsequently annexed by Christians as the church of the Maccabean Martyrs (now effectively Christian saints) (see Bikermann 1951). And, of course, not even the Jerusalem centralists dared expunge pilgrimage to and prayer at the traditional site of the tombs at Hebron of the ancient Israelite Patriarchs and Matriarchs, and the tomb of Rachel near Bethlehem. So important were the Patriarchs' tombs as a holy site that when Herod rebuilds the Jerusalem Temple, he fashions around the tombs at Hebron walls, large sections of which still stand, that architecturally replicate the outer retaining wall of the rebuilt Temple described in Josephus (see *Bellum Iudaicum* 5.184–243; *Antiquitates Iudaicae* 15.380–425). Anyone seeing these walls will draw the appropriate analogy.

Of course, chief among those holy places which dotted Roman Diaspora Jews' "world" was the synagogue. As stated earlier, clear evidence for the existence of synagogues comes from Hellenistic Egypt almost two centuries before the Roman conquest of Egypt in the first century BCE (Tcherikover and Fuks 1957–64). Literary evidence from the first century CE, such as the writings of Philo (e.g. *Flaccus*, *Legation*), Josephus (e.g. *Antiquities*), and the early Christian community (e.g. Acts), indicates that the synagogue is a ubiquitous and the central institution of Jewish communities throughout the Mediterranean basin, including the Land of Israel. In part, the synagogue was holy because the sacred scrolls of scriptures (the relic of YHWH's word) were kept there. John Chrysostom (*Against the Jews*) clearly attests that such a view was rampant not only among the local Jews, but among many of his Christian congregants as well (see Meeks and Wilken 1978: 85–127). And, in part, the consistent use of the location as a place for *communal* prayer and the *public* reading of scripture seems to have made the synagogue holy (Fine 1997). Of course, no synagogue could rival the Jerusalem Temple in holiness and in efficacy as a nexus between heaven and earth. And even after the Temple's destruction, the location on which it had stood remained the most holy site for all Jews. But our point has not to do with the perceived *relative* holiness of one site versus another, or even of the persistent importance of the site of the Jerusalem Temple for Roman Diaspora Jews. Rather, the matter herein being emphasized has to do with fundamental patterning and perceptions of the world. In one such patterning, namely by the centralizers who redacted, promulgated, and promoted scripture, the world was ordered around one holy place, the Jerusalem Temple. According to another patterning evident among Roman Diaspora Jews (and seemingly shared with many ancient Israelites), the world had a multiplicity of such places, even if some were far more holy than others.

None of this is to say that Roman Diaspora Jews explicitly and self-consciously rejected the biblical Judaism of the radical centralizers' scriptures in order to rehabilitate an ancient Israelite model soundly criticized in scriptures. Nothing could be further from the truth. Rather they repatterned the scriptures' world precisely in order to appropriate scriptures' narratives, teachings, rituals, and social injunctions in a Diaspora setting.

As stated earlier, the basic patterning of the world by Roman Diaspora Judaism is not only reminiscent of ancient Israelite religion; it is also thoroughly Greco-Roman. The urban landscape of Roman Italy, Greece-Macedonia, Asia Minor, north Africa, and the upper Levant was dotted with temples and altars to both local and other gods. Some were Hellenized and Romanized versions of pre-Roman or pre-Hellenistic "indigenous" deities; many were imported deities from Greece and Rome; others were "foreign" deities from Egypt, the Near East, and, of course, Judea (YHWH). To these one must add the increasingly important cult of the Roman emperors practiced in cities across the empire. Moreover, the activities of many of the private and quasi-private voluntary associations and professional guilds involved some cultic and/or liturgical performance. Pagan (and Christian) holy men too dispensed potions, amulets, and incantations that enlisted the powers of the supernatural good against the supernatural evil that brought disease, family strife, and unhappiness, as the Greek magical papyri demonstrate (Preisendanz and Henrichs 1973–4; Betz 1986). Jews simply had their own means of doing the same, their own set of holy persons and saints, their own common holy site and institution, the synagogue, in all very Greco-Roman – with the sole major exception that Jews would not participate in the religious institutions of their non-Jewish neighbors. This aside, Roman Diaspora Jews could perceive their religious life and institutions as entirely consistent with the "best practices" of their host society, whose basic patterning of reality was not entirely dissimilar from their own, even while Diaspora Jews accorded themselves the basis for their distinctive social identity as Jews.

The synagogue as a typical Roman civic institution

To this point, I have discussed the synagogue as a holy place for communal prayer and the public reading of scriptures – in Greek (and perhaps for some congregations in Rome and Italy, in Latin). In passing, I have noted that Jewish holy men/healers operated at least some of the time out of the synagogue premises and that the synagogue council and the Jews' courts usually sat in the synagogue. It is clear, then, that the synagogue was not simply a place for communal religious functions. Just as the synagogue was much more than a "place of prayer" (*proseuche*, the designation preferred among Jews in Egypt) offered in service and devotion to YHWH, so too it was much more than the Roman Diaspora Jews' counterpart to the other temples in the urban landscapes. Rather, as an edifice, the synagogue's use overlapped, even if it did not entirely coincide, with the typical functions of a number of public buildings in the city; for example, the basilica (a general-purpose civic building); the gymnasia (a place for education); the civic council building (*bouleuterion*, or in Rome, the *curia hostilia*); the city's treasury building; the city archives; the place where the city's justices held judicial proceedings (sometimes in the basilica, sometimes elsewhere, like the *forum/agora*). Clearly the synagogues were for Roman Diaspora Jewish communities the Jewish civic building(s) *par excellence*, the seats of the "corporate" functioning of the Jewish communities within their host cities (Smallwood 2001: 139–41, 225f.; Barclay 1996: 65–71). Even more important, as the foregoing (and partial) list of civic institutions having some parallel in the synagogue indicates, the functions and institutions associated with the synagogues resemble in structure and function the principal civic institutions and functions of a typical Roman imperial-era city.

Permit me to expand upon this assertion, since it is key to understanding the "fit" between the two "worlds" in which the Roman Diaspora Jews lived simultaneously as an ethno-religious minority in Roman imperial urban society: (1) a "world" particular to the Jewish minority; and (2) a "world" shared with other non-Jewish inhabitants of the city, in the life of which the Jew must meaningfully participate and be accepted as a meaningful co-participant. I repeat the basic point, because of its importance. Precisely in their most parochial setting, the Jews replicated quite stunningly patterns and institutions characteristic of their host society. This pattern of imitation and replication in the parochial setting of that which is typical, normative, and valued in the host, non-parochial society is, as far as I can see, a primary strategy of Jewish ethno-religious success, persistence, and identity (re)formation in the Roman Diaspora. In socio-anthropological terms this parallel between inner-community institutions, roles, and structures, on the one hand, and extra-community civic institutions, roles, and structures shared with non-Jews, on the other, allowed Diaspora Jews to experience their communal life as Jews as "normal" and self-evidently "appropriate," as it reflected normative civic life and society. At the same time, many of the structures and institutions of non-Jewish civic life could be experienced by Roman Diaspora Jews, not only as having the normative force of the majority host society behind them, but as "fitting" in light of how Jews organized their own religious and ethnic affairs.

In sum, the Roman Diaspora "synagogue" is not simply a Jewish civic building (let alone a Jewish cultic building only); the synagogue is the umbrella institution *par excellence* of the Jewish community. The "synagogue of the Jews" is almost a synonym for the "community of the Jews" (Barclay 1996: 236; Lüderitz 1983: 72; Rajak and Noy 2002). There is no comparable institution in the Roman urban landscape, other than "the city" itself (Rajak 1999; Fitzpatrick-McKinley 2002). It is true that in many respects the synagogue looks like a typical Greco-Roman voluntary association (P. Richardson 1996; Harland 2003). And I do not dispute that often Jews, their non-Jewish neighbors, and even Roman authorities may have perceived them that way. But it seems equally clear that the structures and functions "umbrella-ed" under the aegis of the synagogue make it resemble, I repeat, "the city" itself. (And this may be true of other associations in the urban landscape.) This "semblance" provides in socio-anthropological terms a basis for the Jewish community's claims to be fully part of the urban landscape and to participate in the city's public life (Harland 2003). Moreover, it provides the basis for non-Jewish civic authorities and patrons to recognize the place of the synagogue, and its associated services, functions, and functionaries, in the larger urban community and to participate in synagogue life by benefaction and the resulting receipt of honors, as, for example, in the cases of one Claudia Severa in Asia (Rajak 1999; Rajak and Noy 2002; also Fitzpatrick-McKinley 2002) or one Marcus Titius son of Sextus in Cyrenaica (Lüderitz 1983: 71, discussed by Barclay 1996: 236).

Constituent roles and institutions within the synagogue/community

Literary and inscriptional evidence concerning the "government" and "administration" of the synagogue communities provides a remarkably consistent array of functions and titles across the Roman Diaspora (see Rutgers 1998: 24–7). Following is a list of the some of these titles from a sampling of the sources:

- patriarchs, not to be confused with the Patriarch of the Land of Israel (e.g. Linder 1987: no. 9);
- elders (*presbyter*, e.g. Linder 1987: no. 9; Noy 1993–5: 1. no. 157; Rutgers 1998: 144; Epiphanius, *Panarion* 30.11.1–4; Levine 1999: 90);
- priests (*hiereis*, e.g. Lüderitz 1983: 72; Acts 19. 13–20; Epiphanius, *Panarion* 30.11.1–4; Levine 1999: 90);
- "heads" of the law or judges (see e.g. John Chrysostom's two sermons *Against the Jews*, Linder 1987: no 28);
- fathers of the synagogue (e.g. Linder 1987: no. 9);
- mothers of the synagogue (e.g. Noy 1993–5: 1. no. 5);
- rulers of the governing council (*gerousiarch*, e.g. Noy 1993–5: 1. nos. 18, 23, 76, 163; 2. nos. 86, 130, 189, 354, 554);
- scribes (*grammateus*, e.g. Noy 1993–5: 2. nos. 85, 114, 188, 266, 547);
- rulers (*archontes*, e.g. Lüderitz 1983: 70, 71, 72) [of the Jewish community or corporation (*politeuma*)];

- rulers of the synagogue (*archisynagogues*, e.g. Noy 1993–5: 1. nos. 4, 14, 20; Epiphanius, *Panarion* 30.11.1–4; Levine 1999: 90); and in the Levant,
- *hazzan*, a sort of treasurer-administrator *fonctionnaire*, perhaps (Epiphanius, *Panarion* 30.11.1–4; Levine 1999: 90).

Many of these titles designate authoritative roles and functions in the synagogue community, and, therefore, may be time-limited designations ending with the cessation of tenure of office. Some, like "mother" or "father" of the synagogue, seem to be honorifics bestowed on individuals in recognition of persistent or major benefaction, or in recognition of long service (see Rajak and Noy 1993).

Notwithstanding the plethora of titles listed, two institutions appear fundamental throughout the Diaspora: the authority of a governing council (*gerousia*), and the centrality of the ruler(s) of the synagogue (archisynagogues) (Rajak and Noy 1993).

In Philo's first-century CE Alexandria, where multiple synagogues functioned, we have evidence for the existence of a council of synagogue councils, an overarching *gerousia* for all synagogues, and of a "ruler" of this superintending body. Although we have no such explicit evidence for a superintending Jewish council in other Diaspora cities, such as Rome, where there were numerous synagogues, one cannot rule out the possibility, even probability, of the existence of a council of councils in these other urban settings (M. Williams 1998).

Inscriptions strongly suggest that membership in the *gerousia* and assumption of the role of ruler of the synagogue were the privileges (and the burden) of a hereditary aristocracy, the trans-generational socio-economic elite within the Jewish communities (see Rajak and Noy 1993). In this sense, these council members and "rulers" constituted a class of Jewish "decurions," a Jewish communal counterpart to the decurions upon whose shoulders rested the administration of the cities of the Roman empire. This emergence of a Jewish communal nobility parallel to, and perhaps overlapping with, the civic curial class explains how, for example, a child deceased at the age of three years and three months could be called an *archisynagogos* on his tomb inscription (Noy 1993–5: 1. no. 53), or a 12-year-old carry the title *grammateus* (Frey 1936–52 [1975]: no. 284).

Indeed, Roman legal texts make the explicit link between Jewish communal and civic curial functions (see Linder 1987: 76). How so? Consistently until the fifth century, Roman law granted certain levels of exemption from the curial burdens of civic magistracies to leaders of the synagogue, because it assumed that their personal resources and time would have been greatly exhausted within the context of the synagogue community. From this we learn not only that many Jewish leaders were of the curial class generally, and were regarded as such by Rome, but also that Roman law itself recognized magistracies and liturgies served within the synagogue as a form of "alternative service" for civic magistracies and civic and imperial liturgies. In this regard, three edicts (Linder 1987: nos. 7, 9) from Constantine, one issued in 321 CE and two from 330 CE, seem to represent and confirm what he or his officials considered already long-standing imperial policy. Interpolations in square brackets are my own:

We grant to all the curias [i.e. city councils] in a general law that the Jews shall be nominated to the curia[l offices, if they qualify as decurions]. But in order to leave them something of the ancient custom as a solace, we allow them [i.e. the Jews' decurions] in a perpetual privilege that two or three [Jewish decurions] in every [civic] curia shall not be occupied through any nominations [to civic magistracy offices and civic liturgies] whatever. (Constantine, *CTh* 16.8.2; trans. Linder 1987: no. 7, p. 127)

Those who dedicated themselves with complete devotion to the synagogues of the Jews, to the patriarchs [the term "patriarch" appearing in such context designates a local synagogue official; it is unrelated to the Patriarchate in the Land of Israel] or to the presbyters, and while living in the above-mentioned sect, it is they who preside over the law [of the Jews], shall [if they qualify to be decurions] continue to be exempt from all liturgies, personal as well as civil; in such a way that those who happen to be decurions already shall not be designated to transportations of any kind, for it would be appropriate that people such as these shall not be compelled for whatever reason to depart from the places in which they are [and so be unavailable to serve the synagogues]. Those [aforementioned synagogue officials] who are definitely not [yet named as] decurions, shall enjoy perpetual exemption from the decurionate. (Constantine, *Codex Theodosianus* 16.8.2; trans. Linder 1987: no. 9, pp. 134–5)

. . . to the priests (*hiereis*), archisynagogues, fathers of the synagogue, and others who serve in the same place: we order that the priests, archisynagogues, fathers of the synagogues, and others who serve in synagogues shall be free from corporeal liturgies. (Constantine, *CTh* 16.8.4; trans. Linder 1987: no. 9, pp. 134–5)

It follows, then, that as an anti-Jewish measure, the Byzantine Christian Roman empire eventually canceled these exemptions from civic magistracies and liturgies for Jewish *decuriones* serving synagogue-based magistracies.

In sum, the evidence supports a clear and incontrovertible picture of Roman Diaspora-synagogue-community administration characterized by a remarkably consistent set of institutions and functions sustained by an interlocking system of honors, benefaction, and service in magistracy-like roles. The purpose of this system was to provide communal infrastructure, to define and enforce important norms for orderly Jewish life in public and private Jewish spheres, to maintain the public cult of YHWH through public scriptural reading, study of scriptures, and prayer, to ensure the education of Jewish youth in the particulars of Jewish life and responsibility; to care for the economically underprivileged, to heal the sick, and to bury the dead. The principal "players" in this system were a socio-economic elite, who, in essence, comprised a quasi-hereditary Jewish aristocracy and plutocracy. Their authority and responsibility were vested in a synagogue/community "council," to which they were essentially harnessed (probably for life) by status and wealth, and ultimately by birth.

As I stated, I do not wish to enter the debate as to whether the Diaspora synagogue community was a voluntary association. Clearly, in many important respects the synagogue community looked and functioned like a typical voluntary association (see Harland 2003). The foregoing paragraph, however, impels one to restate another, quite different analogy; the synagogue communities (and perhaps other voluntary associations in the cities as well) looked and functioned remarkably like the Greco-Roman cities in which they were situated. And, in my view, this would have been as apparent to a non-Jewish city dweller looking at the synagogue community, as it would have been obvious to a member of the Jewish synagogue community. To the Jew, the city's structure and institutions would be experienced as "natural" and "self-evidently appropriate" in light of his or her experience within the structures and institutions of the Jewish community. Moreover, to that same Jew, the synagogue community's structure, institutions, and roles would seem completely "normal" in light of his or her experience of the city's institutions of governance. Finally, it would have been the expectation of the Jewish community that their non-Jewish urban neighbors and the urban authorities would themselves perceive the analogy at least at the implicit level.

The experience of this homology by both Jews and non-Jews is in my view expressed indirectly when Jews singly or as groups engage in public acts of benefaction in their host cities (see Harland 2003), and especially when prominent non-Jewish city dwellers act as benefactors of the synagogue and the Jewish community and receive appropriate honors. We have had occasion to note above the cases of Claudia Severa and Marcus Tittius. The former is honored in an inscription as the provider of a building and property to serve as the synagogue. She is mentioned in the same breath as prominent members of the Jewish community who subsequently provided the means to renovate the synagogue in a subsequent phase of its development (Rajak 1999, see also Rajak and Noy 2002). The case of Marcus Tittius (Lüderitz 1983: 71, discussed in Barclay 1996: 236) is even more instructive; his benefactions to the Jewish community of Cyrenaica were recognized in an inscription which pledges to honor him not only at each meeting of the Jewish community or its representatives, but also by an inscription in the city's amphitheater. This same Jewish community honors another non-Jewish benefactor, Decimus Valerius Dionysius, for his contribution to the Jewish community (*politeuma*). What contribution? He paid for repairs, made in the *Jewish* community's name, to the civic amphitheater (Lüderitz 1983: 70, again discussed in Barclay 1996: 237). He too was to be honored at regular gatherings of the Jewish community and by an inscription in the amphitheater paid for by the Jewish community. These are fascinating and instructive instances of "crossover" benefactions and honors, between Jews and a non-Jewish patron, and in the cases from Cyrenaica, between Jewish communal and civic institutions. They serve to highlight that Jews' actions effectively represented their own and the city's institutions as somehow alike, and they portray how in some locales these actions reinforced such perceptions in others by confounding Jewish and civic benefactions and honors. These examples notwithstanding, I do not claim that the homologies between the synagogue and the city were often or always explicitly acknowledged and communicated; rather I maintain that they usually are implicitly communicated in the "homologous shape of things," and, perhaps, they are all the more powerful in their effects for remaining at an implicit level of communication.

Final Remarks

An exhaustive discussion of Roman Diaspora Judaism is not possible in a chapter such as this. Nevertheless, the foregoing has attempted to reconstruct in general terms the Judaism which characterized Jewish communities in the urban settings of the Greco-Roman Diaspora from approximately the mid-first to the mid-fifth centuries CE. In more recent scholarship, much has been written about Diaspora Jews, their literature, social history, and cultural traits, and their relations with non-Jewish authorities – based on the plethora and wide variety of evidence which has come to be available. However, few, if any, scholarly attempts had been made since the mid-1980s to describe what we may safely assert about the shape and character of their Judaism, or about that Judaism's place in Diaspora Jewish communities' struggle for social success and social continuity as a religio-ethnic minority in the Greco-Roman urban landscape. This chapter has attempted to begin to fill that void.

The precise constructs adopted by Roman Diaspora Judaic society and culture to address this dual problematic have enjoyed considerable longevity, from late anti-quity through medieval and into modern times. So normative did these constructs become that rabbinic Judaism, well before it became dominant in Mediterranean Jewish societies sometime near or following the rise of Islam, had no alternative but to adopt these constructs as their own, to "rabbinize" them when they could, and to pro-mote them as part of the rabbis' version of the Torah of Moses. Indeed, if one looks at forms of Jewish communal organization in today's highly secularized Jewish communities, it is easy to see much more than mere vestiges of Roman Diaspora synagogue/communal patterns of organization and authority still at work – with a contemporary version of a Jewish curial class, benefaction, and honors once again reflecting other contemporary non-Jewish patterns (see e.g. Weinfeld 2002).

FURTHER READING

For a general political and to some extent social history of Jews in the late republican and earlier imperial Roman period, one may turn to Smallwood (2001). Three relatively recent and very readable works do a good job of tackling the complex evidence from and about Greco-Roman Diaspora Jews. They are: Barclay (1996), Gruen (2002), and Rutgers (1998). With respect to the development of the ancient synagogue, the reader will find a compre-hensive and engaging account in Levine (2000).

ACKNOWLEDGMENT

This chapter was written in the academic year 2004–5 during a leave of absence granted by Concordia University (Montreal QC Canada). It was completed in the winter and spring of 2005 while I was a visiting research fellow at the Miller Center for Contemporary Judaic Studies at the University of Miami. The research for and writing of this chapter were aided by a grant from the Social Sciences and Humanities Research Council of Canada to support my research on the impact of urbanization and the urban environments during the Roman imperial period on the development of ancient Judaism. I am grateful for the support of all of these parties.

CHAPTER TWENTY-SIX

Creating One's Own Religion: Intellectual Choices

Attilio Mastrocinque

Substitutes for State Religion

In the first century BC, Cicero's treatises *De natura deorum* and *De divinatione* witness the creation of a systematic rational inquiry into religion in the Latin language. Varro, in his *Antiquitates rerum divinarum*, distinguished among a theology of poets, one of the state, and a philosophical theology, which he called *theologia naturalis*,

> on which the philosophers have transmitted us many books, in which they ask who the gods are, where, what their gender, whether or not they have always existed; whether they consist of fire – as Heraclitus believed – or of numbers – according to Pythagoras – or of atoms – as Epicurus said. That and other things could be easier listened to inside in a school as in a public square. (frag. 8 Cardauns)

Varro emphasized the legend of Numa as a pupil of Pythagoras perhaps because he wanted to demonstrate that Roman religion was already aware of the philosophical level at the beginning of its life (Varro, *Curio de cultu deorum* I, 35f. Cardauns = Aug. *Civ.* 7.34f.). Cicero too was looking for the true bases of religious beliefs among the main philosophical streams, such as the Platonic Academy, the Stoa, or the Epicurean Kepos.

However, it was not only *theologia naturalis* that opened new fields of inquiry to the cultivated Roman upper class of the late republic. Many of them were attracted by mystic and secret rituals, by forms of religiosity that common people could not understand. These forms could not replace public religion. Neveretheless, in taking up elements of religion that had been known to many Greek cities much earlier, these intellectual choices further broadened a religious spectrum that was adding exotic cults, astrology, archaizing Augustan inventions, and emperor worship to more traditional forms of public religion.

New Ways Toward a Scientific Religion: The Democritean Way

As an empirical classificatory means one can distinguish between two main forms of a rational reflection on religion: a Democritean and, on the other hand, a Pythagorean, Chaldean, and Stoic one. The first form was moving from the Democritean and Epicurean approach to the study of nature. In Cicero's *De natura deorum* 1.18ff. the Epicurean religious attitude is exposed by the senator C. Velleius: the mere existence of the gods is accepted because it is a belief of every human mind, a natural concept (a *prolepsis*, according to Epicurus), and therefore a well-founded belief. The gods are free from any passion and have to be venerated by mankind but not feared. Diseases and every other accident in life are provoked by movements of atoms, not by gods, demons, or divine providence. Cultivated people such as the poet Lucretius or Lucianus's friend Celsus, rich families such as the Pisones of the villa at Herculaneum, were attracted by Epicureanism. Many funerary inscriptions of the imperial age testify the spread of Epicurean beliefs also among the common people. Formulae such as *non fui, fui, non sum, non desidero* ("I was not, I have been, I am not, I do not want": *CIL* 8.3463) were so frequently used that they were abbreviated. For instance *NF NS NC* signifies *non fui, non sum, non curo* ("I was not, I am not, I do not care": Cagnat 1886: 291). A Latin inscription from Rome reports a Greek text in which is unveiled the truth about the afterlife: "Do not go forth nor pass along without reading me; but stop, listen to me and do not leave before you have been instructed: there is no crossing ferry to Hades, nor Charon the ferryman, nor Aeacus holding the keys, nor the dog Cerberus" (*CIL* 6.14672 = *IG* 14.1746). Such skeptical ideas were supported by Epicureanism.

Epicurus had been following the path which Democritus, in the fifth century BC, had opened with his theory on atoms. Epicurus was not interested in divination, whereas Democritus was, as Cicero states in his *De divinatione*, and this fact could have been a starting point for creating a tradition of Democritus as an ancient teacher of divination in a scientific form.

In the second or first century BC some writings were published under the name of Democritus, but they had been written by the Pythagorean Bolos of Mendes, in Egypt (Stephanus Byzantius, s.v. *Apsynthos*; Suda, s.v. *Bôlos*). Not all of Democritus' apocrypha were the work of Bolos; for instance, the "sphaera of Democritus" quoted in a magical papyrus (*PGM* 12.352ff.) could have been the work of an astrologer aimed at forecasting good or ill; the alleged Democritean book *Physika kai mystika* could be a work of the imperial age (Wellmann 1928: vii). The seminal writings of Bolos merged the Greek scientific tradition of Democritus and Theophrastus (an ancient leader of the Aristotelian school) with the oriental tradition of the Magi and Chaldeans, which had been interested for many centuries in the study of occult properties of stones, plants, and animals and their relations with the stars. According to the Chaldeans, for instance, "the stones had some religious associations and we are told of their affinity with the stars" (Plin. *Nat.* 37.100). These two traditions were used, for instance, in order to transform the color of metals and other substances, and that represented one of the most ancient forms of alchemy. The major antecedent for such a syncretism was offered by the tradition according to which Democritus was a pupil of Ostanes, Xerxes' Magus during the Persian invasion of Greece (e.g. Diogenes Laertius 9.34f.), and of Pythagoras (Greek scientist, philosopher, and theologian of the end of the sixth century BC) or of a Pythagorean scholar (Diogenes Laertius 9.38). Thus Hippolytos (*Against the Heresies* 1.11) wrote: "And Democritus was an acquaintance of Leucippus. Democritus, son of Damasippus, a native of Abdera, conferring with many gymnosophists among the Indians, and with priests in Egypt, and with astrologers and Magi in Babylon, (propounded his system)." Bolus Mendesius himself formulated this (*Book of Democritus for Leucippus* 2.53f. Berthelot):

> "Be aware, Leucippus, of what is reported in the books of Persian prophets about that Egyptian procedure; I have written a book in common Greek, because such a matter could be better dealt with in that language. It is not a common book; in fact it reports ancient enigmas and the health-giving things that the ancestors and the kings of divine Egypt have granted to the Phoenicians . . . That treatise includes whitening and dyeing yellow, the softening and boiling of copper ore."

Bolos' aim was the knowledge of sympathies and antipathies which joined or separated each substance, plant, or animal to or from others. This kind of research was the first step toward a construction of scientific knowledge of the whole cosmos and the gods. Indeed the religion of the Chaldeans and Magi was founded upon a supposed scientific and empirical knowledge of the cosmos. Bolos' discoveries and methods allowed later learned theologians to control the substances and produce supposed miracles. Similar researches had been produced, in the same late Hellenistic period, by other scholars, such as Metrodoros of Scepsis, friend of Mithridates Eupator, and Zachalias of Babylon; they explained many of the secrets of substances, their relations with the stars, and the concrete use of them.

Anaxilaos of Larissa was a Pythagorean Magus and follower of Bolos' teaching; he wanted to bring to Rome the science of substances as the basis of a new religious attitude. He was expelled by Augustus in 28 BC (Suet. frag. 81 Reifferscheid). Simon Magus and Marcus, a magician follower of the Gnostic Valentinus, used the gimmicks of Anaxilaos' repertory in order to perform miracles (Förster 1999). The study of substances in both a Democritean and a Magical (that is, of the Persian Magi) tradition was the basis of the knowledge of the cosmos for many scholars of Hellenistic and imperial times, such as Pamphylos (c. AD 60) or Neptunalios (second century AD). This was also the starting point of the cosmological and theological system of the apocrypha of Ostanes and Zoroaster, the most influential representative of Iranian theology and of the doctrine of the Magi. The Democritean approach to knowledge of the world could produce indifference to religion or, on the other hand, a new knowledge of the gods through the secrets of nature.

The Pythagorean Way

A similar and related approach to a new rational religion, that is, to the *theologia naturalis*, was that of the Pythagorean thinkers. In the late republic many learned men resorted to the Pythagorean tradition as a higher form of religion. They were mostly members of the Roman upper class, often senators and members of the opposition to popular leaders. As Ferrero (1955) maintained, after the Gracchan period and because of the crisis of aristocracies, the work of many intellectuals had to take up a position in the high towers of a secret and refined wisdom and leave the field of free divulgation. After the rise of the principate the *plebs* gladly chose the emperors' rituals, whereas several aristocrats preferred forms of elite religions.

One of the main features of late republican Pythagoreanism in Rome was its closeness to the doctrines of the Chaldeans and Magi (see Humm 1996). It is also noteworthy that contemporary Stoicism – above all that of Poseidonius – was deeply interested in the same oriental doctrines, which were teaching how the stars moved, how they influenced earthly life, how substances in the world were related to each other and to the gods.

One eclectic scholar in Rome was Alexander Polyhistor, a Greek from Anatolia, Sulla's freedman, and Octavian's teacher. He merged elements of Pythagoreanism, Stoicism, Platonism, and Aristotelianism. He was one of the most ancient witnesses of Pythagoras' alleged apprenticeship at Zoroaster's school. He accepted the Stoic theory of a world's intelligence, and also Pythagorean numerology, but preferred the traditional conception of an afterlife in the kingdom of Hades to Pythagorean metempsychosis or immortality in the sky for perfect men.

The Pythagorean science of numbers and geometry was a theological means to know the secret laws of both cosmos and gods. "The number is the creator's means of judgment and the paradigm of creation" (Syrianus, *in Aristotelem, Metaphysics* 1080b 16 = Hippasus, frag. 11 Timpanaro Cardini). "The Pythagoreans were studying numbers and lines, and gave them to the gods as presents. They called one number Athena, another one Artemis, and likewise another Apollo; in a similar way another one was called Justice, and another Temperance. They are dealing likewise with geometric figures" (Porphyry, *De abstinentia* 2.6.1).

The geometrical figures were the rules that gave forms to everything and also were the means which the gods used to create anything, for they were the forms of the gods themselves. The Chaldeans, too, knew the numerical value of each god and were famous for their mathematical and geometrical skill, and in that respect also their doctrine could be conflated with Pythagoreanism. Another major feature of both Pythagorean and Chaldean doctrines was the theological dimension attributed to the sky, and by this means too they were fatally attracted by each other. Astrological mysticism was said to have been conceived by Pythagoras himself (Diogenes Laertius 8.27) or by Alcmaeon the Pythagorean (Cic. *Nat.* 1.27) and was transmitted to late republican Neo-Pythagoreanism also through the Pseudo-Platonic *Epinomis*. The Pythagoreans believed in the salvation of the perfect soul and in its return to heaven, that is, to the gods; their highest form of knowledge was that of the heavenly laws; they conceived the theory of planetary harmony as a music produced by the planets.

Late republican philosophers and theologians tried to conceive a rational theological system from these philosophical bases, often merged with Chaldean and Stoic doctrines.

The most influential exponent of Roman Neo-Pythagoreanism was Nigidius Figulus (see Della Casa 1962). Suetonius (frag. 84 Reifferscheid) defined him as *Pythagoricus et Magus*, Augustine (*Civ.* 5.3) as *mathematicus*, that is, astrologer. Nigidius had studied in Asia Minor, was a close friend of Cicero, and fought with Pompey against Caesar, who never revoked his exile. Many Roman members of the upper classes were adherents of his religious, philosophical, and political *sodalicium* (Pseudo-Cicero, *In Sallustium invectiva* 5.14; Scholia Bobiensia in Ciceronem, *In Vatinum* p. 317 Orelli). Here, probably, the books of Pythagoras and Orpheus, the mythical musician and theologian, were read (cf. Servius, *Bucolica* 5.10). Nigidius was looking for new forms of divination, and therefore resorted not only to Etruscan haruspicy but also to Chaldean horoscopes and even boy mediums who uttered prophecies by means of his spells and rituals ("Fabius had lost 500 *denarii* and went to consult Nigidius, who, by means of spells, induced an utterance from some boys, who told where a bag had been buried with a part of the sum and to whom the other moneys had been given": Apuleius, *De magia* 42). His reputation as a caster of horoscopes was increased thanks to his forecasting of Octavian's rise to power (Suet. *Augustus* 94; Cass. Dio 45.1.3–5) and of the sad destiny of the Pompeian faction (Lucanus, 1.639–72).

A Roman from Sora, Valerius Soranus, showed great freedom of mind in dealing with theological matters. He chose the party of Marius, and Pompey put him to death. Some verses of his in which he defines Iuppiter as both male and female were famous: *Iuppiter omnipotens regum rerumque deumque/progenitor genetrixque deum, deus unus et omnes* ("Almighty Iuppiter, father and mother of kings, of things, and gods, only god and all gods"). Varro (Aug. *Civ.* 7.9 = *FPL* frag. 3 Morel = Varro, *Curio de cultu deorum*, I, p. 35 Cardauns), in his commentary on these verses, interpreted them as meaning that Iuppiter was the world in which he himself spreads and also receives his own seed. Valerius Soranus could have taken up an Orphic idea of divine androgyny (*Orph. fragm.* 81 Kern) and of the identity of Zeus with the totality (frag. 21 Kern). Cleanthes the Stoic's *Hymn to Zeus* presents similar speculations on the nature of this god. The poet Laevius likewise maintained that Venus was both female and male (Macr. *Saturnalia* 3.8.3). Granius Licinianus, a contemporary scholar of Varro, in his *De indigitamentis* maintained that Minerva was the moon (in Arnob. 3.31). These learned theologians were researching into the true nature of the gods and, as in the Pythagorean tradition, they identified them with heavenly bodies, with the natural elements, or with numbers and geometrical figures.

Nigidius and Varro were interested in the religions of oriental peoples, and Varro also studied Jewish monotheism. He noticed that the Jews admitted no image of their god, whom he identifies with Iuppiter, and that the Romans too, in the beginning and under Numa, had worshiped their gods without any idol (frag. 38 Cardauns).

Varro (*Antiquitates rerum divinarum*, esp. frags. 8, 23 Cardauns) aimed to discover the precise relation between gods and nature. He often followed the Stoic path, for instance in his belief in the *anima mundi*, which he identified with fire and with our own life's principle (frag. 23 Cardauns = Tert. *Nat.* 2.2.19). He tried to infer the nature of a god from his name, as the Platonic *Cratylus* had earlier attempted to do, and accordingly to give him his domain in the world. Varro adhered to the Stoic view of the philosopher Dionysius in maintaining that there were three kinds of gods: the visible ones, like Sol and Luna; the invisible, like Neptune; and deified men, like Hercules (Tert. *Nat.* 2.2.14–20 = frag. 23 Cardauns); and he believed in three doors leading to the heavenly afterlife: in Scorpio, between Leo and Cancer, and between Aquarius and Pisces (Servius, *Georgica* 1.34). This was a variation on the Pythagorean doctrine of the two doors. Varro wanted to be buried according to Pythagorean forms, in a clay sarcophagus with leaves of olive, myrtle, and black poplar (Plin. *Nat.* 35.160).

Nigidius acted as a private theologian; Varro gave the support of his erudition to Pompey and later to Caesar; Cicero acted as a statesman and wanted to give new theological foundations to public religion. Cicero picked up many elements from Platonism, Stoicism, and Pythagoreanism and explained his most important views in the *Somnium Scipionis*, where a heavenly afterlife is promised to benefactors of the republic. Like the Stoic Cleanthes he conceived the cosmos as a great temple, where the earth was at the center and the gods appeared as mystic visions; he believed in the Pythagorean harmonies of heavenly spheres and in the Pythagorean and Chaldean order of the planets, with the sun in a central position as a leader of the other heavenly bodies. The human soul was conceived as a god:

> Strive on indeed, and be sure that it is not you that is mortal, but only your body. Know, then, that you are a god, if a god is that which lives, feels, remembers, and foresees, and which rules, governs, and moves the body over which it is set, just as the supreme God above us rules this universe. (*Somnium Scipionis* in *De republica* 5.24, 26)

The likeness of men to gods is stressed also when he says: "There is really no other occupation in which human virtue approaches more closely the august function of the gods than that of founding new towns or preserving those already in existence" (*De republica* 1.12).

Germanicus, Tiberius' adoptive son and author of an astrological work, believed in the divine nature of stars and planets, and consequently did not admit the Stoic idea of *ekpyrosis*, that is, the destruction of the whole cosmos, after which it will start afresh in a new cycle of time. By means of his astrological knowledge he looked for the secrets of gods, as the Chaldeans and the Pythagoreans did.

In the age of Nero, the philosopher Cornutus, probably a Stoic, composed a theological handbook (*Theologiae Graecae compendium*, ed. C. Lang, Leipzig 1881), in which the allegorical interpretation of gods as elements or powers of nature is developed.

Conflation of Rational Theology and Revelations

After Varro, the most important Roman theologian was Cornelius Labeo, probably a Neoplatonist of the third century AD. He often followed the ways of Varro. The *Etrusca disciplina* was again proposed as a serious form of ritual and divination; etymology in a Platonic form was a good means to know the nature of gods; but an oracle of Apollo could also provide us with unquestionable answers even about the Jewish god Iaô (YHWH) and his identification with the sun and with Greco-Roman gods (frag. 15 Mastandrea = Macr. *Sat.* 1.18.19–21). In the second half of the third century Porphyry wrote the *De philosophia ex oraculis haurienda* (fragments ed. G. Wolff), in which the oracles were evaluated as the main source of theology. The theological oracles *par excellence* were the Chaldean ones.

Pythagorean, Democritean, and Chaldean doctrines were supposed to be scientific means to know the gods, but the Roman theologians of the imperial age had to face the revealed verities and often resorted to syntheses of both forms of knowledge: rational argumentation and revelation. Starting from the end of the republican age a number of prophets, sibyls, and divine men of the eastern Hellenistic world came into contact with Roman civilization, and their influence grew more and more. The most influential were the heretical Jews, among whom many thaumaturgists, exorcists, givers of apocalyptic prophecies, and followers of Solomonic wisdom were able to persuade a number of Romans to believe in their doctrines.

Both pagan thinkers such as Apollonius of Tyana (Philostratus, *Vita Apollonii*) or Alexander of Abonouteichos (Lucian, *Alexander*), and Christian Gnostic leaders such as Marcellina the Carpocratian (Irenaeus, *Adversus haereses* 1.25.6) or Marcus the Valentinian, also resorted to Pythagoreanism in order to give a greater authority to their philosophy, to their supposed miracles, or even to their Gnostic Christian faith. The Pythagorean legend of Helen was used by Simon Magus in a new form of heretical Judaism. The ways of reshaping the Greco-Roman religion and mythology were many and the possibilities offered by such syncretisms were virtually endless.

In the same period, that is, by the end of the republic and especially in the imperial age, works on substances, stars, and gods circulated in the Greek and Roman world under the signature of Zoroaster, Ostanes, and other famous Magi and pretended to unveil the secrets of both the material and heavenly worlds. The Jewish apocrypha, on the other hand, were rooted in the Jewish religion, in its orthodox or heretic form, and the Persian ones were perhaps connected with Mithraism. Even the Christians produced a few works on the occult properties of substances and animals, such as the *Physiologus* or the *Kestoi* of Iulius Africanus (ed. J. R. Vieillefond) or on astrology, such as the *Hermippus* (eds. G. Kroll and P. Viereck). A large majority of Chaldean, supposedly Persian, Christian, and Jewish heretical theologians agreed that the sun was the leader and guide of all heavenly bodies (a Pythagorean, Chaldean, and Stoic theory), and that a supreme, spiritual, and unknowable god manifested himself in the form of a spiritual and shining Man (a Mesopotamian, Jewish, Christian, Gnostic, and perhaps Mithraic belief), similar to the sun, or in the form of a polymorphic creature (according to Orphic, Egyptian, and several Gnostic traditions).

Pagan Literature on Revelations

The Greco-Roman world reacted to the offensive of Jewish and Christian prophecy – which was often hostile to pagan gods – by producing revelations in the same style. The literary production that we know as Hermeticism gathers a number of books devoted to the science of plants, minerals, animals, man, heavenly bodies, and the gods. That knowledge was not supposed to be empirical, but rather a revelation by Hermes Trismegistus or by the supreme god to Hermes himself in the form of a dialogue between a spiritual and initiatory teacher and a pupil.

Ancient Orphism was also used to present revelations by gods about substances, stars, and planets or about the gods themselves. These revelations took the form of Orphic pseudepigrapha, like the Orphic *Lapidarium* or the *Book of Eighty Stones*, the *Astronomia*, or the *Physika* that Suda ascribes to Orpheus.

In the second half of the second century AD a seminal collection of oracles was produced by two Chaldeans both named Iulianus, the second of whom was considered the founder of Theurgy. Their doctrines about the first and supreme god, his divine manifestations, and Hecate, the intermediate goddess between god and world, were expounded in the form of inspired utterances in *Chaldaean Oracles*, one of the most influential theological holy books in late antique paganism.

Another means to know the gods was recognized in a new approach to inspired poets. Plato despised the mythology of ancient poets and his judgment perhaps contributed to its derogatory treatment by Varro. But in the Pythagorean tradition there was a stream of allegorical interpretation of mythology, which allowed the acceptance of it as a high level of knowledge and a confirmation of Pythagorean doctrines, as in the case of the rape of Helen, which was interpreted not as a deception of her husband, but as an allegory of the abode of the soul in the moon, for Helen was construed as Selene. The Neoplatonists (followers of Plato starting from Plotinus) accepted such a way to rehabilitate the poets as prophets of theological truths, as one can read in Porphyry's *De antro nympharum*. In the verses of Homer images of a divine reality could be recognized, as in the case of the Homeric Proteus' transformations, which became the forms of the heavenly king according to one magical papyrus (*PGM* 4.941 = Homer, *Odyssey* 4.458). Verses of Virgil were used as a divinatory device: the *sortes Vergilianae* (Scriptores Historiae Augustae, *Hadrian* 2; *Alexander Severus* 14). We know series of Homeric verses were used in the same way (*PGM* 7.1–148), or simply to avert a storm (Kotansky 1994: no. 11) or the evil eye (*SGG* 1, no. 390).

With the changing modes of legitimizing religious authority and growing demands on the functions and coherence of "religion," the central problem was the foundation of a true, ethical, and logical religion, which could satisfy humankind better than traditional public religion. Egyptian, Mesopotamian, and Orphic theological traditions (or what were supposed to be these) were inquired into for prophetic books with which to supply this new foundation of Greco-Roman paganism.

Theological Literature or Sects' Holy Books?

A number of arguments have been raised about the existence of religious sects and religious rituals related to Hermeticism, late Orphism, or Theurgy. Did they exist only as literary phenomena or also as religious communities? The problem ought to be set into the framework of the foundation (on sound bases) of beliefs in the old gods, and of the reaction to the challenge of the Epicureans and Christians and to public religion dominated by imperial cults. A first example proves negative. Theurgy was a very high form of knowledge which could be attained only by few, very cultivated men, and was often beloved by late Neoplatonic philosophers, such as Jamblichus and Proclus. Many of them used magical instruments and performed particular rituals. Their doctrine was transmitted in a private and restricted vein, as in the case of Proclus:

> Asclepigenia, Plutarch the thaumaturgist's daughter, let Proclus know the tradition of the great Nestorius' mysteries and all theurgic doctrine which she had inherited from her father. From then on the master (Proclus) used mostly Chaldaic rituals in order to purify his soul; he was entertained by nocturnal visions of Hecate and used Hecatic *sistra* and *rhomboi* (instruments whirling on a string) in order to give water or dryness to Attic land. (Marinus, *Vita Procli* 28)

We are told about the miracles, the ascetic life, and the doctrine of several theurgists in many pagan works of late antiquity, such as the *Lives of Philosophers* by Eunapius or the *Life of Isidorus* by Damascius.

Even more questionable is the existence of Hermetic or Orphic religious communities. No doubt the authors and many readers of Hermetic and Orphic books performed the normal pagan cults but shaped their beliefs in an intellectual form. The emperor Julian prayed to Hermes in secret at home (Amm. 16.5.8); a late antique head of this god has been discovered in a private house at Messene: these facts suggest that Hermes was privately worshiped at home. Hermeticism was produced strictly by non-Christian theologians, but the Hermetic books were studied also in some Gnostic circles, that is, by believers who merged forms of heretical Judaism with Christianity. Fragments of a Hermetic *Discourse on Eight and Nine* (a treatise on the theological meaning of the numbers) have been found in the Gnostic library at Nag Hammadi, in Egypt. The Hermetic books influenced the beliefs of Gnostics and other believers about salvation of the soul (Arnob. 2.13). A strong Hermetic influence is shown by an initiatory Egyptian ritual which allowed a man to travel to the highest heavens and consult the god Mithra (*PGM* 4.679–829). Some verses of an Orphic poem are written on an alabaster cup covered by reliefs representing a winged divine snake worshiped by 16 members of a sect, probably a Gnostic sect.

Even from these examples it is evident that there is a problem in connecting Hermetic, Orphic, and Theurgic literature with socially real and well-defined religious sects or communities. On the other hand, another problem will be faced if we ask what the Mithraists read as theological literature of their own: maybe the Zoroastrian apocrypha, but there are reasons to suppose that they also read theurgic literature. A Mithraic leader like Maximus, Julian the Apostate's counselor, was also a theurgist (Eunapius, *Vitae philosophorum* 476) and performed rituals to Hecate, one of the major Theurgical divinities (ibid., 475; Johnston 1990). Firmicus Maternus (*De errore profanarum religionum* 4), in a passage devoted to Mithraism, relates that the Magi knew of a male and a female nature of fire, and the female was represented as Hecate. Dedications to her (*CIL* 3.1095) or her statues (*CIMRM* 84f., 486, 1187) in several *mithraea*, as well as mentions of priests or initiatory priests of both Hecate and Mithra (*CIL* 6.733, 500, 504, 507, 510f., 1675, 31940; *ILS* 1264; *AE* 136; cf. *CIL* 6.846, 1779, 31118; 13.3643) allow us to suppose that Theurgical doctrines about Hecate and the related Chaldean oracles were discussed in the *mithraea*.

From Private Theology to Magic

The one main stream of theology which always wanted to be different from ritual efficacy was orthodox Pauline Christianity, and this opposition contributed to a new definition of both magic and Christian orthodoxy.

With the exception of the Christian attitude toward "magic" (Thee 1984) and its consequent ancient Christian (and modern) definitions, the Romans produced no precise definition of what magic was and what was not. Even the arguments adduced by Apuleius' *De magia* are too controversial to give us a clear and unequivocal definition. The only safe information is that of Pliny the Elder (*Nat.* 30.8–11), according to which magic was the religion inherited from the Persian Magi. A Jewish and a Cypriot form of the same magic also existed. The definition by the later philosopher Eusebius of Myndus (fourth century AD) is also interesting: magic is the study of the several powers of the substances (Eunapius, *Vitae philosophorum* 474–5) carried out by some lunatics.

We are used to placing under the heading of magic many mysterious doctrines, images, words, and rituals, a series of magical papyri (the *PGM* and their supplements), *lamellae*, and gems, and we are often satisfied with such a definition (see Dickie 2001). The learned magicians who conceived recipes, amulets, or spells, however, were inspired by the most influential holy texts of different religious streams, such as Gnosticism, Solomonic wisdom, Chaldean theology or Theurgy, the pretended Persian religion of the Hellenistic Magi, Hermeticism, Egyptian religion, etc. The heading "magic" has to be better clarified according to these more precise and concrete headings. One cannot assume that magic did exist in the Roman empire as an autonomous religious stream, because the magicians referred to the main contemporary religions.

In the case of many religious traditions it is difficult to recognize the many different levels leading from the great theologians, such as Pythagoras or Julian the Theurgist, to the communities which performed in daily life some rituals related to the theological bases, and to the private or magical use of the religious beliefs. For instance, we know the complex doctrine of Marcus, the follower of Valentinus, who was active in Gallia, a Christian Gnostic who pretended to have found the secrets of the Father and of Jesus the Son in the name of Jesus himself, in the alphabet's secret harmonies, and in the religious value of numbers. He was actually playing on Pythagorean patterns; he performed for his numerous pupils and rich sponsors rituals inspired both by Christianity and the magical recipes or gimmicks of Anaxilaos, the Pythagorean. The Christian heresiologists Irenaeus (second century AD) and Hippolytus (third century AD) describe several of these rituals. On the other hand we know a magic *lamella* (Dupont-Sommer 1946), that is, an amulet, whose text seems to merge doctrines similar to that of Marcus and to that of the Peratae, a Gnostic sect passionately addicted to astrology.

At an inferior social and cultural level the common people resorted to magical practices that, after all, descended from complex theological theories. For instance, Ammianus Marcellinus (29.2.28) narrates that under emperor Valens "in the baths a young man was seen to touch alternately with his fingers of either hand first the marble and then his breast, and to count the seven vowels, thinking it was a helpful remedy for a stomach trouble." Perhaps the youth did not know the ancient Pythagorean theory of the harmonies of stars and of the seven vowels as tunes of the planets; maybe even the practitioner of magic arts who prescribed the remedy did not know its origin, because the Pythagorean theories had been adopted by many religions and were spread in a thousand beliefs. The learned magicians resorted rather to contemporary theological literature, such as the works of Porphyry or Jamblichus, the most influential Neoplatonic thinkers of late antiquity.

Whereas few Roman theologians were concerned with a reappraisal of the Etruscan divinatory tradition, many others followed Nigidius' way and looked for other forms of revelation, which were, in many cases, accessible only to initiates to secret knowledge practicing a spiritual style of life. The magical papyri (*PGM* 3.187–96) and Ammianus Marcellinus (29.1.29–32) inform us that some learned men organized consultations of Apollo's private oracles, with a home Delphic tripod, a divinatory instrument reproducing the cosmos, on which the performer, clothed like an Egyptian priest, by means of particular rituals selected the letters composing the divine answer. Two triangular bronze tables for private divination have been discovered at Pergamum and Apamea; they are related to the cosmology of the myth of Er in Plato's *Republic* and to Theurgical doctrines on Hecate. The Theurgists were able to make the gods appear by turning magical instruments called *iynges* (Damascius, *De principiis* 2.95 Ruelle; Psellus, *Opuscula* 38, *Philosophica minora*, 2.133 O'Meara; cf. also Marinus, *Vita Procli* 28). Other kind of magicians were described in many of the recipes of the magical papyri as making the god prophesy or appear in private séances.

Many learned and religious men of the imperial age studied and commented on the *Oracula Chaldaica* or Orpheus' ancient theology or the supposed archaic treatises of Hermes. We should not conceive all of them as practicing only Pythagorean sacrifices, that is, bloodless offerings, or even only silent mental prayers and contemplation of god. Many cultivated philosophers and theologians took part in public religious life, and also animal sacrifices. Some of them resorted to private rituals which we usually refer to as magic, exorcism, or initiatory rituals, as we can read in Eunapius' *Lives of Philosophers*, in the works of Proclus, or even in the *Biography of Plotinus* by Porphyry.

The Main Concerns of Theologians during the Late Imperial Age

The learned pagans, before surrendering, resorted to the highest forms of theology they ever had produced. First of all, Neoplatonism took increasingly the form of theological speculation; Porphyry and, even more, Jamblichus were engaged in the study of the gods, the cosmos, and the existing religions of the empire. Already middle Platonism (Platonic philosophers from the late republic to the age of Plotinus) had speculated on the phenomenology of religions; for example, Noumenios made his contribution to new interpretations of Mithraism and Jewish religion. On the other hand, the second- to third-century leading figures of Gnosticism, Mithraism, Theurgy, Hermeticism, and other traditions resorted to Plato's doctrine to conceive their cosmology, myths of creation, concept of the soul, and many other features of their doctrines. The highest god (or gods) were placed on a hyper-cosmic level and their nature fit with that of Plato's ideas. Platonism was more suitable than Stoicism for the difficult task of harmonizing pagan and Christian doctrines. The Stoic gods were living in everything within the cosmos; they were the lords of nature; but the Christians hated the cosmic gods and equated them with bad demons. Platonism, however, allowed the theologians to conceive of the supreme gods as separated from the material world and only thinkable by men, like Platonic ideas or Pythagorean geometric figures and numbers. The supreme god was defined as the One, the Good, the unknowable God, and the first manifestation of himself was a divine entity conceived as pure form, or the sum of every form. Gnosticism, Mithraism, and other religious streams were concerned with the distinction of a male and a female manifestation of the unknowable God. One of the main concerns of late antique theologians was to understand how the spiritual, highest God was in touch with the material world and by means of which divine mediators he acted in the world. These mediators were the gods of the ancient polytheism and a polymorphic compound of astrological divinities, angels, and demons of the material world that the theologians had to organize into a system.

The Intellectual Choice of Julian the Apostate

Among both intellectuals and common people the idea of a higher, supreme, spiritual god was increasingly taking root, and therefore the main problem was to reshape public religion in order to get in contact with him. Arnobius (*Adversus nationes* 2.13, 62, 66) describes, at the beginning of the fourth century, three ways often chosen in order to let the human soul come back to the supreme god, from which it had come down to the earthly world (Mazza 1963): (1) that of the know-all, probably the Gnostics, consisting in separating the soul from the material world; (2) that of the Magi, who used prayers or spells by means of which they were able to overcome the bad divinities which barred the going back up to the Father God; and (3) that of the Etruscans, whose doctrine taught how to give the soul immortality by means of certain sacrifices to certain gods.

Public religion was sometimes able to purchase some benefit from the emperor, but it could hardly purchase the soul's salvation for individuals. Therefore a new general religious system had to be borrowed from a great theologian and adopted by the empire.

During the tetrarchic period, at the end of the third century, Porphyry's theology became the most accredited in the state religion. The emperor Julian the "Apostate" was the latest theologian in Roman pagan history to propose to reshape public religion in order to secure both salvation in the afterlife and the benefits a man could expect in his private and social life. His theology was admittedly indebted to Jamblichus' works. Before his untimely departure from this world, he produced three major works, *Against Heracleium* and the discourses *On King Helios* and *On the Mother of the Gods*. The two discourses, together with *On Gods and the World* by his friend Salustius, were meant to be the catechism of the empire.

The higher domain of gods was reshaped above all according to the Neoplatonic and Mithraic conceptions, with an unknowable god, the "One" or the "Good," who manifested himself as the god Helios, from which other immaterial gods were produced, the most important of which was the Mother of the Gods. The cosmic gods, led by the heavenly Helios, were conceived of according to the Stoic theories, and the divine emanations affected everything as a providential rain of benefits to earth and humankind. Since everything is created by the gods, the different civilizations and religions of the empire are related to the nature of the supreme gods of every people, among which also the Jewish god is taken into account by Julian in his work *Against the Galileans*. The evil in life is related to human impiety and atheism.

This theological system was indebted to the philosophical readings of the emperor, to his frequenting of *mithrea* and Mithraic leaders such as the Theurgist Maximus, but also to his conception of Roman history, for he wanted to recreate the alleged piety of the times of Numa and of the glorious Roman past. Philosophy, theology, and also astronomy taught Julian the laws of heaven and, since "the divine mind is the supreme Law" (Cic. *Leg.* 2.11), he wanted to reproduce the divine law in the laws of the Roman empire. In his endeavor Plato's *Laws* gave some help. Once he went to Cappadocia and noticed that "many people did not want to perform sacrifices whereas a few did want to but did not know how to perform them" (*Epist.* 78). Consequently one of his first concerns was the celebration of many sacrifices. His paganism was not at all innate; he knew it through philosophical and theological literature or pagan initiations, for he was educated as a Christian. The intellectual emperor was seen by the pagans themselves as a maniac for bloody sacrifices (Amm. 21.12.6ff.). In fact he distinguished between the cult to inferior divinities, which were pleased with incense and sacrificial smoke, and the hyper-cosmic gods, whose cult was practiced by philosophers and initiates to mystery religions, such as Mithraism, the cults of Cybele and Attis, or Theurgy. Only the most cultivated believers could unveil the secret messages of religious truths that the ancient poets had transmitted under the mask of mythology, as Julian explains in his *Against Heracleium*.

In his short reign (361–3) and in the subsequent decades the creation of the *mithraeum* of Hawarte (Syria), many inscriptions related to the cult of Cybele, mostly from the Roman Phrygianum near the Vatican, and other evidence show that, thanks to Julian's religious politics, the mystery religions enjoyed new favor, even if only among the pagan cultivated elites. At his court both Etruscan *haruspices* and Platonizing Theurgists were active, because Julian wanted to be in touch with both cosmic and hyper-cosmic gods, whose opinion was known through sacrificial divination and Theurgical rituals or also through privileged dreams (see Briquel 1997). Such a religion was hardly understandable and acceptable to the common people, and in any case it was not given the time to take root more firmly.

Between the end of the fourth and the beginning of the fifth centuries two late pagan intellectuals, Martianus Capella and Macrobius, produced works in which the theology that had been blossoming under Julian was proposed again, even if in the form of entertainment. Quite surprisingly to us, the *Wedding of Mercury and Philology* by Capella was still interested in the Etruscan pantheon, and Macrobius' *Saturnalia* still stuck up for heliocentric theology, which was peculiar to the pagan empire from Elagabalus to Julian. In his *Commentary to the Somnium Scipionis* Macrobius clarifies his inclination toward Platonism and Pythagorism. The choice of these two intellectuals was quite singular and elitist in an age when philosophers and learned people were taking on the office of leaders of the Christian church, and the few pagans were limiting themselves to non-religious topics, as did Ausonius, the teacher of the young prince Gratianus. It is true that one of the latest pagan philosophers, the learned Hypatia, did dare to represent the municipal community of Alexandria in front of the imperial government, and to pass from the private speculative level to a public one; but she was lynched by the Christians in AD 415.

FURTHER READING

The most important texts, mostly available with English translations in the Loeb library, are: Cicero, *De natura deorum* and his *Somnium Scipionis*, in *De republica* 6; Lucian, *Alexander, the False Prophet*; Philostratus, *Life of Apollonius of Tyana*; Porphyry, *On the Cave of the Nymphs* (ed. R. Lamberton, Barrytown, NY, 1983); Julian the Apostate, *Hymn to King Helios*; Sal(l)ustius, *De deis et mundo* (ed. A. D. Nock, Cambridge, 1926); Eunapius, *Lives of the Philosophers and Sophists: The Greek Magical Papyri in Translation* (*PGMtr*) (ed. Hans D. Betz, Chicago, 1986 [1992²]).

For solar theology see Cumont (1909 b). Festugière (1944–54) offers the fundamental edition, translation, and commentary of the Corpus Hermeticum. The best overview of Roman Pythagoreanism is given by Ferrero (1955). Lewy (1978) analyzes the late antique practices of Theurgy and the Chaldean oracles. Mastrocinque (2005a) offers a substantial introduction to Jewish Magic and Gnosticism; ancient magic in general is dealt with by Graf (1997a, 1997b). Roman intellectual efforts are analyzed by J. Barnes and Griffin (1989). The history of Roman religion by Liebeschuetz (1979), leading from the republic into late antiquity, remains thought-provoking.

CHAPTER TWENTY-SEVEN

Institutionalized Religious Options: Mithraism

Richard Gordon

Attracting Attention

If the sun is the source of all life, the contrast between light and darkness is one of the most basic natural provocations to the human imagination. Greek and Roman "civic religion" made extensive use of it for a variety of symbolic statements. Civic sacrifice was performed typically soon after dawn; the Olympian gods, tokens of an ordered universe, shimmered and gleamed; light connoted life, ordered normality, and salvation; darkness suggested unreason, disorder, fear, mystery, trickery, death. But perhaps no ancient cult made more overt use of the contrast than the Roman cult of *Sol Invictus Mithras*, Mithras the unconquerable sun. Christian apologists such as Firmicus Maternus scoffed that his adherents worshiped a Sun-god *speluncis abditis . . . obscuro tenebrarum squalore*, in hidden-away caves, in pitchy darkness (*De errore* 5.2). Such a paradox caught the eye, and the imagination. What is the point? Well, come in and find out.

Paradox – mild, easily resolved paradox – is an attraction for a cult not anchored in the secure and familiar framework of the annual calendar of celebrations imposed by civic religion. Like the cults of Cybele and Attis, of Isis and Harpocrates, of Jupiter Dolichenus, of Sabazius, the Roman cult of Mithras paraded its exoticism. For example, whereas Greco-Roman religion, having no acknowledged history, acquired its authority through the weight of tradition, some Mithraists at least claimed that their cult had been founded by the prophet Zoroaster (Porphyry, *De antro nympharum* 6). Instrumentalizing the Stoic, and later Platonic, claim that the religion of certain "civilized barbarians" – the Egyptians, the Phrygians, the Brahmins, the Persians – offers insight into the paradigmatic religious beliefs of primitive man, they claimed that the cult of Mithras possessed greater authenticity than civic cult.

By the same token, they could claim that Mithraism, like the Egyptian cults, and that of the Jews, was far older than Greek and Roman religion, since the chief debate about Zoroaster was whether he had lived five thousand years before the fall of Troy or six thousand years before Xerxes' invasion (Diogenes Laertius, proemium 1.2). Mithras may have been new and strange in the empire – Lucian quipped that, with his Median sleeved tunic and tiara, he could not even speak Greek (*Deorum concilium* 9) – but his cult claimed to be of hoary antiquity.

There were other self-conscious distances, too. Whereas the classical temple had a distinctive architectural form appropriate to its function as the home of a cult statue, the Mithraic temple, at least in towns, was often a room in a rented space inside a larger building, a *horreum* or an *insula*. It fused three functions kept separate in civic cult: a house for a cult image, a sacrificial site, and a meeting-place for a dining group. As such, it was indeed similar to, say, the *andra* (cult dining rooms used by men only) known at Palmyra, Dura-Europos, and other Syrian sites. We may also think of the cult's non-classical iconography, its promotion of a hero, Mithras, extravagantly dressed in Persian cap, trousers, and a billowing cloak, subduing a grown bull with his bare hands and then stabbing it to death; its use of the bas-relief, with all its narrative possibilities, in preference to the normative cult statue; the plethora of unfamiliar figures and scenes that crowd these reliefs, demanding to be interpreted by some knowledgeable exegete. Then again the striking rituals: the veiled, lamp-carrying male-bride (Nymphus) greeted with the words "[See (the)] Nymphus, hail Nymphus, hail new light!" (Firmicus Maternus, *De errore* 19); or the initiation scene on a ritual vessel found in the *mithraeum* at Mainz, showing a Father, the senior member of a Mithraic congregation, seated on a chair and aiming an armed bow at a terrified initiate, entirely naked, whose arms are bound in front of his chest (cf. Beck 2000). Except possibly for the whipping scene in the Villa dei Misteri at Pompeii, whose documentary status is quite uncertain, nothing comparable is known from any other cult of the Greco-Roman world – except from the *mithraeum* at Capua, to which I shall return. Exceptional, too, are the references everywhere in the archaeological record to non-casual astral/astrological lore (for example the "houses" of the planets, or, in the *mithraeum* on the island of Ponza in the Gulf of Naples, to the Pole constellations, cf. Beck 2004: 151–231), references that in number and quality far exceed those known from any other widespread ancient cult; and the Mithraists' determined, indeed conscientious, rejection of women. In the second-century Roman marketplace of cults, such sophisticated self-distancing evidently appealed to a relatively wide assortment of men both in Italy and in the provinces.

Sol Persicus Mithra

Some preliminary observations are in order. Since it became fashionable in the 1970s–80s to think of the Mithraic cult image as a sort of star-map (instaurating the allegorical turn of the high and late Renaissance), an entire literature of decipherment has grown up on the topic, and not merely in the wackier corners of cyberspace. Indeed, hardly a week passes but someone claims to have unlocked the secret of its meaning – it has become a sort of pastime. In view of that willful reduction of Mithraism to this one "mystery," it may be as well here to insist right away that there is plenty else to say about this cult of the "Persian Sun" (Dracontius, *Romulea* 10.538), and to announce that I shall be ignoring astrology and star-maps completely.

Just a word, too, about neologisms. In my view, it is best, where possible, to avoid the term "Mithraism," since it falsely suggests that the cult was somehow a separate religion. This is one aspect of the older view of the "oriental religions" that supposedly exposed the failure of traditional civic cult (the term "oriental religions" now survives only as a docket-name for classifying artifacts in Roman provincial archaeology). At least in later antiquity the cult was known as the mysteries of Mithras. Porphyry, for example, in the mid-third century, explicitly names it *ta tou Mithra mysteria* (*De abstinentia* 2.56, 4.16), and frequently mentions both initiands and the process of initiation. This term was used earlier, in the 180s, by the anti-Christian writer Celsus (*apud* Origen, *Contra Celsum* 6.22). It is, however, mainly a Christian term, being first found in Justin (*1.* 66; *Trypho* 70, written under Antoninus Pius). Both Christians and Neoplatonists had their own reasons for highlighting the initiatory aspects of the cult. Although expressions denoting "worshiper of . . ." were common in antiquity (e.g. *Hermaistai, Poseidoniastai, Hercolei* at Delos, *Mercuriales* at Rome, *Martenses* at Beneventum), Mithraists preferred to give themselves a different name, based on a ritual gesture, the hand-shake: they called themselves by the Greek word *syndexioi,* those bound by the hand-shake. It would be absurd for us to follow them on this point; but I only fall back on "Mithraism" where the most neutral term, "the Roman cult of Mithras," would be intolerably clumsy. It would, however, be pedantic to object to another common neologism, "*mithraeum,*" in the sense of a cult room or complex dedicated to Mithras. The proper Mithraic word was *spelaeum,* cave, with reference to Mithras' act of killing the bull, though they often spoke neutrally of *templum.* Anyway, "*mithraeum*" is at least calqued on the Greek word *mithreion* used by the fifth-century church historian Socrates. Finally, I detest the word "tauroctony" (which denotes the image of Mithras killing the bull), since it is so clearly part of an academic tendency – admittedly difficult to resist – to use what look like technical terms but are often falsely reassuring reifications or simplifications; but it is sometimes unavoidable.

A net has been defined as a series of holes with string round them: an apt metaphor for any story about the Roman cult of Mithras. Mithra (in ancient India Mitra) was the Indo-Iranian god of the contract. His cult was introduced into Anatolia by the Achaemenids after Cyrus' defeat of Croesus of Lydia (546 BC). As a result the god's name was known in Greece during the classical period, to Xenophon for example, but, as far as we can tell, without any details of his cult (notoriously, Herodotus thought he was a goddess [1.131.3]). With Alexander's conquest of the Persian empire, the *raison d'être* of Iranian cult, the symbolic reinforcement of Persian rule, was removed; no grand temple to Mithra survived into the Hellenistic world; his cult seems to have continued there only within particular Iranian families and in numerous, but isolated, localities. It is unlikely that there will ever be enough evidence to bridge the gap between Iranian Mithra, known mainly through the Avestan hymn (*Yašt*) in his honor, composed c. 450–400 BC, and the Roman cult of Mithras/Mithrēs. Many have tried – this is one of the neuralgic points of Mithraic scholarship – but there is no genuinely and incontestably relevant evidence.

Archaeologically, the cult of Mithras first appears in the Roman world in the Flavian-Trajanic period, when traces of it (inscriptions, *mithraea*) are suddenly found at several widely separated sites, in Rome, Germania Superior, Raetia/Noricum, Moesia Inferior, Judea. The contexts are those we might expect: the military, the provincial toll system, harbor towns; the big surprise is Alcimus at Rome, the rich slave-bailiff of Tiberius Claudius Livianus, praetorian prefect from AD 102 (*ILS* 4199). No less striking is the fact that the first clear literary reference dates from the same period: the poet Statius refers to Mithras, identified with solar Apollo, "twisting the recalcitrant horns in a Persian cave," *Persaei sub rupibus antri/indignata sequi torquentem cornua Mithram* (*Thebaid* 719f.), a passage probably written in the mid-80s. This early evidence suggests that the cult already presented many of its later features – Mithras identified as Persian, as a Sun-god and as bull-slayer; the contrastive torchbearers; the death of the bull as the guarantee of agricultural fecundity.

A few years ago it became briefly fashionable to argue that the Roman cult was created in Italy (Vermaseren 1981; Merkelbach 1984; Clauss 2000). The early archaeological finds do not support this claim; neither do they point to an origin in Anatolia. However, the fact that key terms of Mithraic language are Greek and were translated into Latin implies an origin somewhere in the eastern Mediterranean. On the basis of not unreasonable assumptions about the rate at which a private cult of this kind might spread, it has recently been suggested that such an "explosion" presupposes a century and a half of archaeologically invisible growth, which would date the initial foundation to the mid-first century BC, uncannily close to the Cilician pirates' secret *teletai* of Mithras on Mount Olympus in Lycia-Pamphylia mentioned by Plutarch, *Life of Pompey* 24 (based on Poseidonius). However, those who cling to this detail generally prefer to remain silent on the question of how a Lycian mountain-top cult of Mithra could have become a Roman cult celebrated in underground "caves" (the fountain-head of this error is Cumont 1902, rightly criticized by Francis 1975a; but even Francis seems to be unaware of the location of this Olympus, since he continually speaks of "Cilician pirates," and wrongly assumes that *en Olympô* could mean "in caves on Mount Olympus"). More recently still, the excavators of the double cave-*mithraeum* at Dolichene/Dülük in Commagene, just west of the Euphrates, have claimed that their site supports a late Hellenistic/early imperial date for the foundation of this temple (Schütte-Maischatz and Winter 2004). Given its location, this would be of the greatest importance if true, and is not inherently implausible; but the evidence, a coin of the Seleucid Antiochus IX Cyzicenus (114–95 BC) and a very few sherds of high-quality pottery datable to the first century BC/AD, all found in infill, is not strong; nor does the rock-cut image of Mithras killing the bull appear anything other than standard; moreover the archaeologists themselves suggest that the cave was earlier used as a limestone quarry. At present, it seems most likely that the entry of the cult into the western empire is to be connected with the Flavian organization of the Euphrates frontier.

Whatever its origins, the Roman cult seems to have been successful mainly in Italy, in the northwestern provinces, especially Germania Superior, and in all the Danubian provinces. Elsewhere, in north Africa including Egypt, Spain, western Gaul, Britain, and throughout the east Mediterranean, it is uncommon and extraneous – associated predominantly with military sites and harbor towns. In Germany, the focus of early excavation upon the *limes* suggested that there, too, it was primarily a military phenomenon. But recent discoveries on non-military sites (e.g. Biesheim on the Rhine near Colmar; Wiesloch near Heidelberg; Mündelsheim and Güglingen near Heilbronn; Sechtem near Bonn; Gellep near Krefeld) now suggest that unpretentious *mithraea*, sometimes made of wood or even turf, which would have been irrecoverable by older archaeological procedures, were to be found in many minor settlements, often on the outskirts of town, well away from the recognized sites of civic cult, and sometimes surrounded by a fence (as at Forum Claudii Vallensium/ Martigny near Lake Geneva).

Such structures could only have accommodated small numbers. But there are several larger temples – the *cella* of the largest known *mithraeum*, recently discovered in the grounds of what was probably the summer villa at modern Els Munts (on the Costa Dorada, north of Tarragona) of the governor of Hispania Tarraconensis, and presumably used by the slaves and freedmen of his household (*familia*), measures 30 by 8.7 meters, giving a usable area, excluding the kitchens, of 260 square meters. In light of this discovery, if confirmed, it is worth speculating on the likely size of the *mithraeum* that is known to have existed inside the imperial *domus* on the Palatine AD 209–11 (*ILS* 4270); the *mithraeum* beneath the Baths of Caracalla measures 23 by 9.70 meters, that is, 223 square meters, without the side rooms. Such *mithraea* had correspondingly large congregations: an important inscription found at Virunum in Noricum, originally intended to record the names of the 34 men who contributed to repairing one of the *mithraea* there in AD 183, was afterwards used to record the names of new members, 64 of them over the following 18 years, varying in number from eight in the years 184 and 192 to one in the years 186, 190, 194, 196, and 201 (*AE* 1994, 1334). Some of these later members seem to have decided in AD 201 to go off and found a new *mithraeum*, presumably (caution: suspiciously few deaths are recorded for this period) because the old one was too crowded (*AE* 1994, 1335).

The social composition of this *mithraeum* is also instructive, because it seems to confirm what we can infer from the evidence at Ostia: apart from a small number of locally fairly eminent members, the great majority are freedmen from the main local families, or rather their descendants. There is one *peregrinus*, one slave, and no women. At *Pons Aeni*, a *mithraeum* at the important crossing of the Salzburg– Augsburg road over the Inn, one of the local potters, Ma[rt]inus or Ma[tern]inus, dedicated a *sigillata* vessel that he had carefully decorated with an image of Mithras in barbotine technique, expensive because time-consuming (Gordon 2004: 270, fig. 8). The impression of a relatively self-conscious, relatively prosperous, group is supported by the inference from caches of sacrificial bones buried within or near several *mithraea*. At Quintana/Künzing on the Danube in Raetia, for example, the great majority of bones were those of suckling pigs and chickens, quite different from the beef mainly consumed by the garrison of the local fort (von den Driesch and Pollath 2000). In one of the shopping-lists from the *mithraeum* at Dura, the largest single outlay, 28 *denarii* 11 *asses*, was for wine, then meat, ?19 *denarii* (*CIMRM* 65, AD 240–53).

Ostia, as a port town, also provides a microcosm of the cult's further history. (Much more could have been said had the Fascists' excavations been conducted with proper attention to stratigraphy; as it is, in order to present the imperial Roman past in time for the planned world exposition, they irreparably destroyed a massive amount of evidence, above all for the site's later history. The same applies, of course, *mutatis mutandis*, to almost all excavations undertaken before 1945.) The earliest of the 15 *mithraea* known from the town dates from c. 160. Over the next thirty years a further three were founded, followed by seven more in the long Severan period (193–235). The remaining four all date from the mid-third century. It is now thought none of them was violently destroyed; all seem to have been quietly abandoned during the fourth century as the center of Ostian life shifted to Portus, which was made an independent community by Constantine. None of the Ostian *mithraea* has kitchens or storage rooms, and we have to assume that, as at Dura, food, including meat, was bought in. In the provinces, especially the northwest of the empire, however, such additional rooms are an important feature of Mithraic temples, and underscore the central role played in the cult by communal meals. In some, such as the temple at Riegel in the Schwarzwald, large quantities of high-quality cups, plates, and jars have been found (Cämmerer 1986). The most striking recent discovery, however, is the *mithraeum* of the Roman *vicus* at Tienen in Gallia Belgica (Belgium), where the remains of a large-scale party were discovered in three specially dug waste-pits (Martens 2004a, 2004b). All the pottery, locally produced cooking pots, lids, plates, and incense burners, and beakers imported from Trier, each to the number of at least 88 items, had been deliberately smashed before being thrown, together with food refuse, into the pits. The small wooden temple here, just 12 by 7.5 meters, could never have held so many people. From the age of the mainly piglet bones, it could be calculated that they were all killed in late June/early July; it appears therefore that in the period AD 260–80 – the period of the "third-century crisis" and the Gallic empire – the Mithraists in Tienen, perhaps at a summer solstice, perhaps on the occasion of the rededication of the temple, held a magnificent celebration with their friends and relations and then disposed of all the utensils in a ritual act paralleled elsewhere in northern Gaul – one of many indications of the extent to which the cult was adapted to local needs and usages.

Identity

The provision of an organized space for private ritual meals, of an independent and locally variable calendar of sacral events, of a non-standard site of memory co-associating sights, scents, particular actions, and experiences, was of course not peculiar to the cult of Mithras. In the Greco-Roman world, the boundaries of civic cult were by no means coterminous with those of religious life *tout court*: all the myriad private religious associations, of the traditional gods, the *dendrophori* attached to the cult of Cybele, the *pastophori* of Isis, offered something generically similar. What distinguished the "universal" private cults was the degree to which they were able to construct a distinctive – not alternative – religious identity for their worshipers. Imaginative essays in such construction are familiar from Catullus' *Attis* poem (*Carmen* 63) or the final book of Apuleius' *Metamorphoses* (11), but we have nothing similar for Mithras. There are no Mithraic *stelae* advertising the god's wonders, no aretalogies, no famous oracles. A sketch of a distinctively Mithraic identity has to be pieced together from scraps of incoherent information. This section, and the three following, are intended as contributions toward such a sketch.

The focus of each *mithraeum* was the cult image. This image could be simple or complex. The simple form, in relief or statuary, is the plain tauroctony: the god killing the bull in a cave, flanked by the torchbearers Cautes and Cautopates, and with the dog, snake, scorpion, raven, Sun, and Moon in standard places. Although an action is taking place, the sole narrative hint is the ear(s) of grain emerging from the dying bull's tail. Otherwise Mithras is disengaged from the implied sequence of actions. The simple tauroctony thus takes on the function of a theophany, making the god available for contemplation. The complex form, by contrast, highlights narrativity. It is divided into three main phases: (1) the birth of Mithras from the bare rock, and its antecedents; (2) the heroic performance: the "water miracle," the manifestation of the bull from the Moon, and its pursuit by Mithras, a hunt that turns into a sacrifice; (3) the sequel: the enlistment of the Sun (*Sol*), the shared feast, Mithras ascending to heaven over the Ocean in Sol's chariot. This complex form is to be understood as an elaborate commentary upon the central scene of sacrifice, partly verbal-descriptive but mainly as the reference point of "imitative ritual." The narrative represents the bull's death as the First Sacrifice, followed by the First Meal, the bull's flesh eaten by Mithras and Sol, accompanied by unmixed wine. Mithraic ritual meals commemorated this primal sacrifice; the charter function is dramatized by those cult reliefs, which could be spun round on their axis to reveal the First Meal on the reverse. The cult thus subverted the usual Greco-Roman rationale of sacrifice as a gift for the gods. Other elements of the narrative commentary, for example the "enlistment of Sol" (to which I return below), provided a charter for initiation; others, such as Mithras carrying the bull, provided the basis for ethical self-modeling and so one means of personal identification with the heroically steadfast god. Another index of the density of the relation between cult image and ritual performance is the habit of making dedications in the *mithraeum* to inanimate entities from the narrative, for example *Fonti perenni*, to the Never-failing Stream (*CIL* 3.15184[24], 10462) and *Petrae genetrici*, to the Generative Rock (e.g. *CIL* 5.8657 = *AE* 1985, 454; *CIL* 3.4424; *ILS* 4244), as though they were themselves divine and could hear, like the nymphs and healing divinities to whom such dedications are more normally made.

In addition to the inscription of ritual practice into the code of myth, the cult of Mithras modeled the ritual lives of its initiates in a highly original manner by creating a set of hierarchically arranged grades of membership, from lowest to highest, in Latin: *Corax* (Raven), *Nymphus* (male bride), *Miles* (Soldier), *Leo* (Lion), *Perses*

(Persian), *Heliodromus* (Sun-runner), *Pater* (Father). These names, in this order, are certainly attested at Santa Prisca on the Aventine in Rome (say AD 200), and the sequence confirmed in the Mitreo di Felicissimus at Ostia (c. AD 250). In both temples the hierarchy is correlated with the planets, thus forming a notional "ladder" from Here to There, which, according to Celsus, was the path taken by the soul (Celsus *apud* Origen, *Contra Celsum* 6.22). How widespread the grade organization was outside central Italy is uncertain; the cult vessel from Mainz mentioned earlier shows at least Miles, Heliodromus, and Pater walking in a procession; and the numerous wall-graffiti at Dura, insofar as they have been published, repeatedly mention all the grades except Heliodromus (cf. Francis 1975b). My own view is that they were usual if not universal. But their significance in constructing a specifically Mithraic ritual and moral identity, as well as a post-mortem hope, cannot be overestimated. In the *mithraeum* of the Castra peregrinorum in Rome we find the wish: *Leo vivas cum Caedicio patre*, "Best wishes on becoming a Lion under Caedicius as Father!" (*AE* 1980, 49f.). Tertullian (though I prefer generally not to use Christian, because usually polemical and hence potentially distorting, evidence) mentions a ritual in which the Miles has to reject a proffered crown because "my crown is Mithras" (*De corona* 15); and Porphyry tells us that when the Lions were made to wash their hands in honey they were instructed to "keep their hands pure from everything that causes pain, is harmful and morally offensive"; and then they had to cleanse their tongues "of everything sinful" (*De antro* 15). In placing such emphasis upon personal ethical demands the cult of Mithras is clearly part of the revolution in religious sensibility generally referred to as "the second paganism" (Versnel 1981b; Veyne 1989, 1999). In this connection a very recent find at Huarti/Hawarti near Syrian Apamea is of great interest. Just beside the cult niche of the *mithraeum*, dating from the later fourth century, is a fresco of part of a city wall, surmounted by several ghastly, grimacing, decapitated heads, each pierced by a spear (Gawlikowski 2004). Nothing comparable has ever been found in a western context, and in my view the likeliest explanation is that this scene represents the contract-breakers and sinners, demonic and human, whom Mithra slaughters in the *Mithra-Yašt*. That is, hearing of Sasanian Persian religion through, say, Nisibis brought late antique Roman Mithraists for the first time into contact with genuine Iranian traditions relating to their god. Much must have been incomprehensible to them; but the Mithraic tradition of moral purity meant that they could recognize at least the motif of the destruction of the wicked.

Nilsson suggested in 1950 (Nilsson 1988: 667–79) that the cult of Mithras, like the later religion of Mani, was created by an individual of genius, working from rituals and myths derived from one of the Anatolian cults of Mithra(s) and blended with astrological theory and Greek ideas about initiation. Even if that, or something like it, were true – and we shall never know for certain – the case of Huarti/Hawarti makes clear that innovation was always possible, and welcome. Moreover, Origen observes that "among them [the Persians] are rituals of initiation (*teletai*) which are interpreted rationally by the erudite, but enacted directly by the common, rather shallow people" (*Contra Celsum* 1.12). "Rationally" here means allegorically, and wherever allegory is institutionalized, we can expect to find a wide variety of interpretation and understanding. That just such a luxuriant divergence existed in Mithraic circles is clear from the disagreements cited by Porphyry over the meaning of animals represented in the mysteries (*De abstinentia* 4.16). Nevertheless, the miniature cult images in Danubian style that have been found in German, Judean, and Roman *mithraea* support the belief that the cult maintained an overall coherence despite these pressures toward interpretive diversity.

Communication

I have pointed out that Mithraic congregations were relatively exclusive. At Ostia, it has been reckoned that, allowing a half-meter per man, the 14 now locatable *mithraea* might have held on average 35 people: the smallest 18, the largest 40 or 42. Selectivity of membership was evidently important. There is no question of evangelism, if by that we mean the lust for indiscriminate conversion projected by the pious literature of early Christianity. Individual Mithraists must have sought to convince selected members of their own circle of acquaintances of the merits of Mithras. Pre-existing groups, slave *familiae*, the agents of the *portoria*, the *familia Caesaris*, and military units were ideally suited to this sort of "internal conversion," based upon friendship, common experience, and shared goals. By the reign of Commodus, for example, the *procurator castrensis*, the head of the entire organization of the domestic side of the imperial palace, was a worshiper of Mithras; at latest by 209–11, probably much earlier, there was an official Mithraic organization inside the palace (see above). Although the cleft between life before and life after initiation cannot be compared with that of the claims of Christianity, the moral and psychological demands led to a sharpened sense of separation from the world of common experience, as well as the more obvious consciousness of privileged access to a divinity strong to save (*deus praesens*: *AE* 1980, 52; *praestantissimus*: *AE* 1976, 411b; 1991, 1301). It was this sense of belonging to a moral elite that fueled the process of Mithraic missionizing.

We may assume that the original nucleus of such congregations was formed by a very small group of men, perhaps often just a single individual, who had moved to another town, or slave *familia*, or military camp, from elsewhere. The basis of such men's knowledge of the cult would have been another existing community. In the absence of explicit evidence we have to use inference. For example, the sole known Mithraic dedication at Aosta is by a *circitor*, an itinerant customs inspector, of the *XL Galliarum* (*AE* 1989, 334). Again, Firmidius Severinus, a veteran of the vexillation of *VIII Augusta* seconded in AD 185 to Lugdunum (Lyon), made a dedication *deo invicto genio loci*, "to the unconquered God, spirit of this place," at Geneva in 201 (*CIL* 12.2587). Since he refers to his 26 years of service, but still calls himself *miles*, he had probably made the move from Lugdunum fairly recently; the very unusual title *genio loci* suggests a *mithraeum* or cult room here, presumably founded by Severinus. An analogous process, that of contact-conversion, is clearly implied by the foundation texts of the first Dura *mithraeum* (*CIMRM* 38/39; 41, cf. Dirven 1999: 260–72): Ethpeni, the commander of the *numerus Palmyrenorum* long stationed in Dura, who dedicated the first cult relief there in AD 168, must have been stimulated to found his *mithraeum* – a small affair in a private house – by contact with the troops of L. Verus in the period AD 162–6.

It seems unlikely that the individual Mithraist needed to bring with him more than the memory of a relief of Mithras killing the bull, and his own experience of initiation. An actual tauroctony, simple or complex – a number of easily portable examples are known – would simply have been a bonus. The moments of Mithras' "biography" required for cultic purposes were few in number and easily memorable. The minimal architectural requirements of a temple, when it came to be required, could hardly have been simpler: an aisle, with two lateral podia. The layout of the cult niche was optional, as was the extent to which temple and image provided information about other elements of the *hieros logos*, and stressed local or individual interpretations. Evidently, too, one could name the god as one pleased: for example, among the six inscriptions certainly or probably from the *mithraeum* in the house of the *tribuni laticlavii* in Aquincum (Aquincum V) where the name of the god survives, we find, in their likely historical order, *Sol Invictus, Invictus Mithras, D(eus) S(ol) I(nvictus) M(ithras), Sol Invictus Mithras* (twice), and *Invictus Mythras Nabarze* (*AE* 1990, 817, 820, 814, 818f.; *ILS* 4260).

Similar considerations apply to the question of whether the mysteries employed normative written texts that could have served as the basis for standard rituals and have been a main means of reliable colportage. Individual congregations certainly did possess texts of some kind: fragments among the graffiti of the second and third phases at Dura, and the discrete verses of the lower layer of *dipinti* at S. Prisca in Rome, make this certain. But of what scope? And what status did they have?

The key factor must have been the degree of literacy of the founder(s) of each community. In any given instance, the basic narrative material encoded in the complex cult image, the *hieros logos*, need not have been committed to writing. But it may often have been, especially in Italy. The existence of written texts is well documented in other telestic cults. The authority of the book in general – not necessarily, but plausibly, a Mithraic one – is acknowledged in a Mithraic context by the well-known images of "Magi" on the faces of the piers of the cult niche at Dura, phase III (c. AD 240). Such images of scrolls served as emblems of membership in the cultivated class: they imply a claim to rhetorical, legal, or technical education (one Mithraic dedicator at Speyer in Germany was a public *haruspex*, diviner: *AE* 1990, 757; another, at Martigny, was a *flamen* and former *duovir*: *AE* 1998, 867). In the narrower context of Mithraism, the images allude to arcane, esoteric – in that sense "bookish" – wisdom. For example, a tantalizing reference at Dura on the Syrian frontier to *pyroton asthma*, fiery breath, as the "baptism of (the) holy ones" (*niptron hosion*), is said to be a doctrine of the Persian Magi (*CIMRM* 68), which implies a whole gamut of speculation unknown to us from western evidence; and that in a *mithraeum* apparently used exclusively by "simple soldiers."

As for S. Prisca, the literary quality of the painted verses does leave something to be desired (Vermaseren and van Essen 1965: 187–240). But it is rather the effort to express oneself in a literary mode, in a *carmen sacrum*, a ritual hymn, that should attract our attention. I see no difficulty in taking these *dipinti* as excerpts from a *carmen sacrum*, or perhaps rather from more than one, presumably composed by the Father, in the Severan period. The fragmentary line 21, *reddite cantu*, "rehearse in song," suggests that it was sung, either on a particular occasion or regularly. The topics range from cosmological description, through epiclesis of inanimate objects that had key roles in the story of Mithras (in this case, the stream that Mithras caused to flow out of a rock) and moral exhortation linked to Mithras' deeds (such as carrying the entire weight of the bull heroically on his shoulders), to the allusion to the Lions cited below. The formulation is personal to the composer; but the thoughts themselves draw upon the common body of Mithraic belief. The very existence of such compositions suggests, what is anyway obvious from the iconography, that there was a considerable body of exclusive lore current in Mithraic circles that commented upon both mythical event/example and ritual practice. The resolve to "give an account" is typical of the "universal cults" under the empire.

Patronage and Deference

The cultural horizon implied by the use of written texts suggests another issue connected with status claims: that of patronage. If individual Fathers provided cult furniture at their own expense, their reward did not simply lie, as they piously claimed, in heaven. These men must have been in many ways the driving forces within Mithraic congregations: their knowledge and enthusiasm were crucial to the continued existence of such small religious groups, ever liable, as we know from the archaeological record, to fail for one reason or another. In return for that outlay of expense and effort, the Fathers as a group expected deference. At Ostia, for example, one Diocles dedicated his brick altar faced in marble to Mithras *ob honorem C. Lucreti Menandri patris*, as a mark of respect to the Father of the congregation (*CIMRM* 225). A Mithraic *symbolon*, a secret utterance belonging to the sacred "property" of an initiation cult, addresses the initiate as *syndexie patros agauou*, "hand-shaker" of an illustrious Father (Firmicus Maternus, *De errore* 5.2), the genitive case suggesting an unspecifiable relation of dependence. The best-preserved lines at S. Prisca request that the *sanctus Pater*, the reverend Father, should "receive the Lions as they offer incense," *accipe thuricremos . . . accipe Leones* (lines 16f.). All this suggests that we should think of relations within Mithraic congregations at least partly in terms of patronage.

It is a truism that the society of the empire was articulated not merely by legal, economic, cultural, and geographic differentia but also by patronage networks. If the grand central patron was the emperor, who found his moral and political justification in its exercise, his very capacity to act as patron within the empire, at the level of hundreds of individual cases, was brokered by individual senators and equestrians. "Grand" patronage is thus the indispensable grease that oils the machinery of a society of legally differentiated orders. As a mode of social interaction, it simultaneously confirms the necessity and propriety of the unequal distribution of power and wealth, and gives the impression that the distribution of those social goods is subject to the intervention of rational goodwill. It has thus an important masking effect. At the same time, it offers a powerful model for social interaction through-out the society.

We can trace the descent of patronage networks down through the structures of local city government to the micro-level of the patrons of professional corporations. Yet anyone in a position to accord or withhold favors, distribute rewards or sanc-tions, can act in the manner of a patron at the micro-level. In so doing, he asserts his (temporary) social power, fulfills the possibilities of his social position, and acquires the profit *par excellence* that consists in the feeling both that one's existence is justi-fied and that one is *comme il faut*. At any rate, in the procession of the seven grades at S. Prisca in Rome, the Father sits by himself on a throne, dressed as Mithras, his hand raised as though he were a patron greeting his clients. The demand for deference is but one aspect of a claim to high status within the congregation: the number of inscriptions referring to *patres*, which far outweighs references to all other grades put together, is another. At S. Prisca, again, the dignity of the Fathers is apparently one that spans the world: *Nama [Patribus] ab oriente ad occidentem*, "Hail to the Fathers, from east to west" (Vermaseren and van Essen 1965: 155, 179). In all these respects, the seriousness with which the notion of Fatherhood was taken in Mithraism far outstrips the rather perfunctory use of the theme in the context of other corporations, professional and religious.

Specialized private religious structures like Mithraism naturalize the model of the patron–client relationship; but they also idealize it. What remains is the desirable essence, generous altruism, service of the other world. The religious act decently masks its contribution to the reproduction of social relations of inequality.

The Suffering Body

Patronage and deference were, however, only one aspect of Mithraism's naturaliza-tion of key social values. There is also the use of fear and intimidation. I have already mentioned the initiation scene on the ritual vessel from Mainz. Much more striking is the series of panels, now seriously deteriorated, that were painted c. AD 225–40 on the revetment walls of the podia of the *mithraeum* at Capua Vetere near Naples (Vermaseren 1971: 24–48). Only seven of an original 12 or 13 can now be deci-phered, all of them apparently depicting initiation scenes in which a naked, often blindfolded, man is subjected to intimidation or threat. The clearest cases are a man enduring a burning torch pushed into his face (R II), another apparently having his arms singed (L III), and a prone man with a scorpion directly above his bare back (L II). In each case there is a clear distinction between the initiator, a man dressed in a quasi-military fashion, with helmet and flowing cloak, the mystagogue, dressed in white, who exhorts or teaches the initiand, and the wretched subject. These scenes seem to explore the implications of one of the key narrative scenes, after the bull's death, in which Mithras seems to threaten Sol, who kneels before him (the "enlist-ment" of Sol).

Distantly in the wake of Michel Foucault and Norbert Elias, ancient historians have explored the symbolic functions of violent spectacle in antiquity, both in the *théâtre de terreur*, the spectacle of public execution, and in the history of gladiatorial combat. The Roman principate strikingly confirms their account of the symbolic value of the body in pre-industrial state repression. Indeed, the explicitness, inventiveness, memorability, and expense of Roman ceremonies of degradation, the apparently unlimited ability of the judicial system to produce "worthless bodies" (in Latin: *vilis sanguis*), the centrality of the spectators' consent and desire (*Occide! Verbera! Ure!*, "Kill him, thrash him, burn him!": Seneca, *Epistulae* 7.5) – all these serve to make the principate the example Foucault must have wished he had thought of.

Placed in this context, the initiation rituals at Capua are suggestive. Although they have no direct connection with the apparatus of state power, their images of subjection, degradation, and suffering imply an *imaginaire* based on the same premises as the *théâtre de terreur*, namely the ingenious multiplication of forms of humiliation, the use of physical suffering to underwrite the triumph of Power, a heightened interest in the reactions of the implied spectator. Capua boasted the second largest amphitheater in the entire Roman world, built in the late Flavian/Trajanic period over the republican amphitheater (where Spartacus had trained), and was the center of an important gladiatorial training school. Of course these Mithraic panels depict voluntary sufferings and humiliations, performances rather than tortures, of roles assumed and played out. But we cannot deny the evidence that the performances were not "mere" play-acting: they were accompanied by the intentional infliction of pain, to say nothing of terror and humiliation. Rather, the Mithraic teletarchs saw in that real-world violence a symbolism appropriate to their own ends, the production of a Mithraic body "fit for the job," a body that could under no circumstances be female.

We may conclude that the primary intention of the degradation of the Mithraic body at Capua is to image, both to the subjects and to the spectator, the superiority of constituted Power, the legitimacy of authority, and the mystic connection between masculinity, hierarchy, and salvation. The initiate was induced to believe that he could only attain the desired identification with Mithras by accepting the right of beneficent Authority to inflict pain and terror for his own good, not once, but repeatedly. Whether this was understood in the manner of popular Stoicism as learning to endure the buffets of Fortune, as proof of the superiority of the race of men over that of women, or more specifically as punishment for sin, as the Lions' purification with honey would suggest, Authority is presented and experienced as controlling the sole road to the higher end. It was not for nothing that the tetrarchs at Carnuntum in November 308 recognized Mithras as *fautor imperii sui*, upholder of their empire (*ILS* 659).

FURTHER READING

Classic is the English translation of Cumont (1902). But it is now more than a century old and hopelessly outdated: more than 54 Mithraic temples have been discovered since World War II, 33 of them since 1965; in this chapter, I have deliberately referred to as much recent material as possible. Better introductions are provided by Clauss (2000), which has an additional recent bibliography in English, and the excellent remarks of Beard et al. (1998), via the index. Recommended too are the relevant sections of Alvar (2007). The standard corpus of the archaeological material, by Maarten J. Vermaseren, *Corpus inscriptionum et monumentorum religionis Mithriacae* (*CIMRM*) (1956–60), is, like Cumont, seriously out of date. The S. Prisca texts, whose reading is often doubtful, were published by Vermaseren and van Essen (1965) but can most easily be found in Betz (1968; trans. in Beard et al. 1998: 2. no. 12.5(h)). The Tienen excavation and reports of other recent discoveries can be found in Martens and De Boe (2004, extensive bibliography) cited above. Recent archaeological finds can be consulted through the Archaeological Reports of the electronic *Journal of Mithraic Studies* now under transfer to the Classics Dept., University of Canterbury at Christ Church, New Zealand (www.clas.canterbury.ac.nz/ejms).The best astronomic/astrological account is Beck (2006).

CHAPTER TWENTY-EIGHT

The Romanness of Roman Christianity

Stefan Heid

Growth and External Perception

When Paul was planning his journey to Spain, a country new to Christianity (Romans 15. 20–4), he knew that he would encounter an established Christian community during his stay in Rome along the way. This community was, however, marked by tensions between Jewish and pagan Christians. He recommended that it remain loyal to the state (Romans 13. 1–7). The Christians became the talk of the town in AD 64 when Nero held them responsible for the fatal conflagration which spread from the Circus Maximus through large parts of the city. He then had a "considerable number" executed during circus games at his villa on the Vatican hill (Tac. *Ann.* 15.44; *1 Clemens* 6.1). This shows that the Christians were already perceived by Roman society as an autonomous group, which had ceased to benefit from the legal protection of the Jewish religion. In practice these are likely to have been staged executions in which the condemned represented a mythical character or a mime with a deadly ending. It may be that executions in the form of living torches referred to the myth of Hercules; those being torn apart by hounds may have recalled the myth of Actaeon.

Christians residing in the capital of the empire had to face the state's demand for loyalty more so than those in the provinces. Their belief in the only god of Jesus Christ caused them to withdraw from participating in those public occasions which incorporated pagan religious ceremonies. They did not live in a ghetto, nor did their external appearance set them apart from others in the city (*Epistula ad Diognetum* 5). Like the Jews, however, they were regarded as outsiders because they kept themselves aloof from the cults of other deities and thus in practice from most activities around which public life was organized. This was true of the *cursus honorum* but also of membership of numerous professional and funeral associations, and of participation in such significant public events as *spectacula, certamina, pompae,* and *epula publica* (Min. Fel. 12.5). Christians may also have been reluctant to rely on the public distribution of grain, because of its connection to the cult of Ceres and Annona. This distancing from the outside world allowed, and in fact rendered it necessary, for the community itself to develop as such in a rapid and comprehensive manner.

Instead of participating in pagan sacrifices and festivities, the Christians celebrated the Eucharist on the first day of every week (1 Corinthians 16. 2; Acts 20. 7; Iustinus Martyr, *Apologia* 1.67.8); initially connected to a communal meal (Agape), which was soon arranged separately. It had a charitable and social function, especially since Christians avoided the public feasts. The Eucharist ("Thanksgiving") continued to be not only a sacrificial ritual, but a constant of caring for the poor every week, a task which became centralized as early as during the second century (Iustinus Martyr, *Apologia* 1.65.6–7). Those responsible for both services and care were the bishop, presbyters ("superintendents" presumably refers to both), and deacons (Iustinus Martyr, *Apologia* 1.65.5). Under bishop Soter (traditionally dated 166–74) we hear of a well-organized care system for the poor among the Roman congregation, which extended well beyond the city itself (Eus. *HE* 4.23.10). In the middle of the third century the community was so prosperous that it was able to support a clergy of over 155 individuals (bishop, presbyter, deacons, sub-deacons, and others) and 1,500 registered recipients of support (*HE* 6.43.11).

Devotional Spaces in the City

The Christian Justin, a resident of Rome, wrote around 160 that all Christians who lived in towns or in the country held a Eucharistic "congregation at the same place" on a Sunday (Iustinus Martyr, *Apologia* 1.67.3). This was surely meant to convey to the pagans that the Christians did not engage in a conspiracy, moving from one location to another. Rome's particular problem lay more in its size than its multi-ethnicity (we hear of dogmatic and discipline-related, not ethnic, divisions). It is most likely that a number of meeting-places offered room for ritual and other acts of Christian communal life. There were logistical reasons for always holding services at the same time and same place every Sunday. It is unlikely that rented flats served as meeting-places, more likely privately owned houses (*domus*; see Romans 16. 5), which were not open to view from the outside and whose addresses were not made available to the general public.

Probably Christians from surrounding quarters congregated in each of these, although it is unlikely that there were fixed geographical divisions. Deacons carried the Eucharist to the sick (Iustinus Martyr, *Apologia* 1.65.5); apparently they were familiar with their quarter and had access to corresponding lists of names. Even the social tasks, which consisted mainly in distributing the goods that had been brought to the Eucharist, required a stable organization and fixed bases. Therefore meetings did not escape the attention of those outside. Rumors about severe irregularities spread, but other "secret cults" faced similar accusations. In any case the Christians did not follow a route of secrecy and explained the sequence of their meetings to a willing public in an easily intelligible manner (Iustinus Martyr, *Apologia* 1.65–67; Min. Fel. 9). The inclination of the Roman Christians toward openness to the public is illustrated by the fact that Justin appeared as teacher in the gown of a philosopher (*pallium*), gave public lessons, and claimed the freedom of speech accorded to teachers.

Our understanding of Rome's first centers for services and the first house churches (*domus ecclesiae*) is limited (cf. Hist. Aug. *Alexander Severus* 49.3). It is uncertain whether they were absorbed into the so-called titulary churches of the fourth and fifth centuries. Even if these titulary churches may often be connected to private *domus* we can only suspect that their predominant usage was liturgical (S. Clemente, Ss. Giovanni e Paolo, S. Crisogono). It is also unknown whether in pre-Constantine Rome any churches were owned communally, that is, meeting-houses established specifically for services, which could be recognized as such by pagans (cf. Porphyry, *Contra Christianos* frag. 76). It is, however, reasonable to assume that spacious centers for the cult existed despite the fact that not even an episcopal church is known; it is telling that the Lateran church built by Constantine did not continue any earlier Christian building on the same spot.

This sobering archaeological situation means that we cannot conclude from the later titulary churches that Christians were divided into factions, with at first only isolated groups of them living in Rome as if on islands (Lampe 1989: 301–7). A strong sense of unity stood against any separation. Paul already wrote without reservation "to all that be in Rome . . . called to be saints" (Romans 1. 7), which presupposes a community unified in principle and able to hear his letter at its meetings. In Rome there were not only individual Christians but the "church in the area of the Romans" (cf. Ignatius, *Ad Romanos proemium*). The exclusion of splinter groups in the middle of the second century (Marcion, Valentine, etc.) proves that the Roman congregation was in effect already unified at that time. Other instances are the dispute around the Easter celebrations under bishop Victor (189–98), the establishment of a parish cemetery probably under bishop Zephyrinus (198–217) (Catacomb of Callixtus), and the notable organizational differentiation of the community in the middle of the third century. This real unity and social effectiveness explain the strong action taken by the authorities during the Decian and Valerian persecutions of the Christians, which resulted in special consequences in Rome, culminating in the execution of the reigning bishops.

Suburban Funerals and Obsequies

Pietas toward the ancestors had already been a fundamental aspect of traditional Roman culture, and the Christians emulated this. Their care for the dead was based in the first instance on the family as in the Roman tradition. In those cases where family connections had been disrupted as a consequence of converting to Christianity, for example with slaves, foreigners, or the persecuted, the community also became involved (Aristides, *Apologia* 14.3; 15.6; Tert. *Apol.* 39.6). In so far as honoring the dead within the family called for religious rites, these practices led to the development of a Christian type of funeral and a corresponding commemoration of the dead. These include funerary prayers and from a certain point in time also celebration of the Eucharist. In general the Christian approach to funerals was not markedly different; it only omitted what was considered to be unacceptable. For the long procession from the city to the cemetery – Roman law only allowed burials outside the city walls – the Christians dispensed with the *pompa funebris* and wreaths, so that their funerals were criticized for their plainness (Min. Fel. 12.6, 38.3–4). This did not preclude carrying martyrs before the city "in great triumph," as is confirmed by Cyprian for Carthage (*Acta proconsularia Cypriani* 5).

Christians wore mourning dress and held a funeral feast. Otherwise funerary prayers and Mass gave a Christian character to the cultic elements of commemorative celebrations, which traditionally consisted of prayers, sacrifices, and processions. The annual commemoration was celebrated no longer on the person's birthday but at the date of death or burial (*dies depositionis*) – noted on epitaphs with the abbreviation *DP* or *DEP*. This practice is in accordance with general trends connected to funerary banquets (Carletti 2004), but is also linked to external necessities. In most cases it was the family who remembered the birthdays of its dead. Therefore the memory of the birthdays of those Christians whose faith had severed the connection to their family could be lost when they died. In such cases in particular the community arranged their funeral, and the "day of commemoration" (*dies natalis*) of those who had passed away could only be celebrated at the day of their death or burial (*Martyrium Polycarpi* 18.3; cf. Ignatius, *Ad Romanos* 6.1).

During the first two centuries Christian burials are sometimes found in pagan cemeteries above ground. Since the turn of the second to the third centuries, exclusively Christian communal cemeteries were established underground at a time of rapid expansion of the Christian community. These were financed by the Roman bishop (Catacomb of Callixtus) or by affluent Christians (Catacomb of Priscilla, Domitilla, Praetextatus, Calepodius, and Novatian). Underground burials were not invented by Christians, but so far the Romans had only known relatively small family *hypogea* in which Christians belonging to that particular family could also be buried. Christians, however, also developed intensively used communal cemeteries which could be expanded. During the third century, burials there still took place in a uniform manner, in succession, dispensing with monumental self-representation and expressing their feeling of religious communality and of solidarity beyond family boundaries, a feeling rooted specifically in the hope of resurrection from the dead. The general trend toward interring the body and thus – to limit space and costs – toward burial in subterranean facilities was received positively by Christians, apparently for social (leveling of class boundaries) and religious reasons (belief in the resurrection), and further developed in the aforesaid manner.

It has been conjectured that the bishops of Rome led the Eucharistic services and commemorations for the dead during the time of persecution, in order to assemble the whole community around themselves on different days and in different places. This would constitute the origins of the later stational liturgy in which the popes assembled the city's congregation in different churches (*stationes*) (Baldovin 1987:

146). Such a practice is, however, impossible to imagine in terms of organization before Constantine and cannot be proven. A stational liturgy in the city did not exist before the sixth century (cf. below). There are, however, indications that the sub-urban graves of the martyrs were already frequented on certain days during the third century. Not only was it easier to assemble larger crowds outside the city, it was also easier to organize these congregations, since the date (of death or burial) and place (the respective cemetery) were fixed.

The Development of Martyr Cult

The sad fate of prisoners from the provinces who were brought to the capital to be executed during Roman games was shared by Christians. A prominent example is bishop Ignatius of Antioch (probably around 110), who had been convicted *ad leones*. He wrote to the Christians in Rome during his journey as a prisoner:

> Rather, charm the beasts that they become my grave and leave behind no part of my body, lest I become a burden to anyone when I have been put to rest (in a tomb). Then I will truly be a disciple of Jesus Christ when the world will not see even my body (i.e. tomb). Implore Christ on my behalf that through these means I will become a sacrifice for God. I do not command you like Peter or Paul. They are apostles, I am a condemned man, they are free but I am now a slave. (*Ad Rom.* 4.2–3; Eus. *HE* 2.25.7 speaks also of showing/seeing the body/tomb of Peter – both are meant by *tropaion*)

Ignatius attempts to dissuade the Roman Christians from preventing his martyr-dom: when I am thrown to the lions they will devour me completely, and thus there will not be a body which you must bury and a grave to look after so you can show it to "the world." The Roman community therefore cared for the martyrs' mortal remains and their burial. Such piety was normal and was afforded all Christians, but even more so a bishop. But Ignatius insists that "the world" should not even see his body in future. Why should the world wish to see his body? Evidently because the tombs of the martyrs were visited! Ignatius is thinking in particular of the graves of Peter and Paul, which were sought out by Christians from around the world. Ignatius by no means wishes to question their worship or even have them understood as a burden to the Roman congregation. He therefore immediately adds that he was not issuing a command like Peter and Paul, since they were apostles and thus placed above him. For himself, however, he declines being honored with a tomb.

One would thus like to assume that the tombs of the apostles in Rome were already being shown around 110. Ignatius appears to presume this, and not surprisingly so. As early as the late first century the gospel of St. Mark and the first (and second) letter of St. Peter bear witness to the apostle's authority beyond his death (Knoch 1991). The spiritual-religious conditions for a cult centered on the grave lay in the Jewish martyrs' cult (Horbury 1998; Frankfurter 1998b: 99–225). It is possible to go further and to discern a commemoration of martyrs in the celebration of the Eucharist (Ignatius, *Ad Romanos* 6.1; cf. *Martyrium Polycarpi* 18.3). For Ignatius

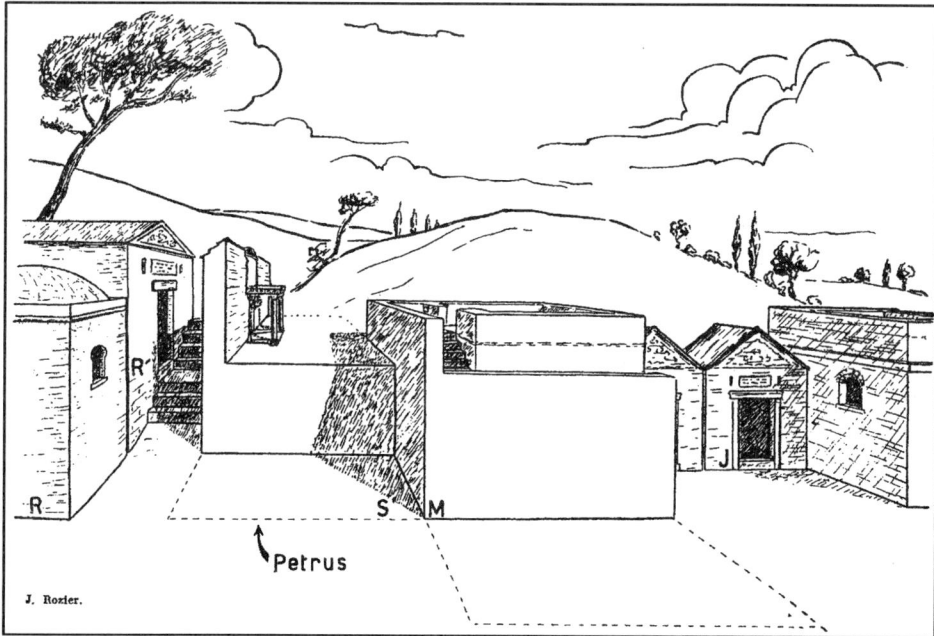

Figure 28.1 Reconstruction of the·*memoria* of Peter at the Vatican during the second half of the second century (Fiocchi Nicolai 2001: 13). R, R′, S, M, J = tombs.

describes his sacrifice in the arena, in which the Christians too should participate in order to encourage the lions, as a Eucharistic service in which he himself becomes the sacrificial offering (Brent 1999: 231–3).

Archaeological evidence exists around 160 for the "victory monuments" of Paul on the Via Ostiense and of Peter at the Vatican, which were already "shown" to foreigners (Eus. *HE* 2.25.7, cf. 4.22.2–3) (fig. 28.1). In the mid-third century we hear of Christian "cultic sites," amongst them the *coemeteria* (*HE* 7.13). This could also refer to those spots in cemeteries where martyrs were venerated (Rebillard 2003a: 16). When bishop Sixtus II arrived at a *coemeterium* with four deacons during the Valerian persecution of Christians despite an interdict (*Acta proconsularia Cypriani* 1; Eus. *HE* 7.11.10), it was surely in order to commemorate a martyr (Cyprianus, *Epist.* 80.1).

The burials of the martyrs under, and partly above, ground were neither separate nor privileged. Nevertheless the bishops assumed authority over these graves (and later on the complete cemeteries) because of their public interest. For this reason they kept lists of those confessors who were threatened with a martyr's death, not only to appeal to the public authorities on their behalf but also in order to return the bodies of exiled witnesses to Rome (Hippolytos, *Refutatio* 9.12.10). The fact that epitaphs on the martyrs' tombs display only the name of the individual – as in the *depositio martyrum* (list of martyrs) – likewise points in this direction: the martyrs were separated from the family (*gens*) and handed over to the whole church to be venerated (*ILCV* 1.953–6, 958, 960–1, 1996, 2001).

Some martyrs' graves from the period around 250 until the shift under Constantine have been proven, or rendered likely, by archaeology. According to the *depositio martyrum*, the church in Rome had begun to celebrate the days of the martyrs at their tombs from the first half of the third century at the latest. Open meeting-places were sufficient for congregations above ground to commemorate the dead and the martyrs, thanks to the mild climate. They were protected by arcades and porticos similar to the so-called *triclia* underneath S. Sebastiano, which served the fervent veneration of Peter and Paul by Christians from Italy and overseas (Africa?) from about 240–60 (258 according to the *depositio martyrum*). The graffiti of the *triclia* show that feasts for the dead (*refrigeria*) in honor of Peter and Paul were "promised" or "arranged," that is, banquets and meals for the poor were provided in honor of the apostles. Presumably Christians could accept the church's ban on participating in *epula publica* by legitimating their feasts for the dead as celebrations of the martyrs.

The Constantinian Shift

When Constantine surprisingly achieved an overwhelming victory over his rival Maxentius at the Milvian Bridge on October 28, 312, he was convinced that he owed it to the Christian god. His triumphal *adventus* in the city on October 29 ended at the foot of the Capitol by the *Tria Fata*, a memorable place where once martyrs had refused to ascend the Capitol to avoid having to sacrifice to Jupiter (Fraschetti 1999: 239). Christianity now fully entered into the public sphere. Without delay Constantine had imposing churches built and endowed them richly: inside the city the Church of the Savior at the Lateran as early as 312–13 (later also S. Croce in Gerusalemme), on the suburban cemeteries – where documented, each related closely to the location of martyrs – St. Peter (Vatican) around 319–22, St. Paul (Via Ostiense), St. Laurentius (Via Tiburtina), St. Marcellinus and Petrus (Via Labicana), probably the anonymous basilica on the Via Praenestina, and likely as one of the first the "Basilica of the Apostles" *ad catacumbas* (Via Appia), later called St. Sebastian.

Constantine erected some of these churches on imperial land above the catacombs. His role as *pontifex maximus* allowed him to override the sacral property law, which protected graves. Thus he leveled the cemetery of the Vatican in favor of the tomb of St. Peter and dismantled the graves underneath the "Basilica of the Apostles." First of all Constantine wished to honor the martyrs, not only with the basilicas of Peter and Paul on the overground cemeteries of the Vatican and the Ostian and Appian Ways, but also with the "circus-shaped" basilicas above the catacombs. Even if all these edifices contained many graves right from the beginning, it is unlikely that their primary function was to create covered cemeteries. This would not have required their exceptionally rich decoration and endowments. Rather, they were real *martyria*; since they were, however, located in cemeteries, space for burials was created at the same time. The cult of the martyrs required room above ground because the tightly confined holy tombs in the catacombs could not be made accessible to the public at large; this became possible only once subterranean routes for pilgrims had been constructed under Pope Damasus (366–84).

In erecting the churches, Constantine continued the tradition of imperial building programs and aimed to attest to the fullness of his power, supported by the Christian god, and to perpetuate it. He followed a clear program with a shifting focus: on Rome after his victory over Maxentius, on Jerusalem following his defeat of Licinius. A number of the Constantinian martyrs' basilicas outside the gates of Rome were linked to imperial mausolea. This is surely due to the desire to associate members of Constantine's family with the Roman church's official commemoration of the dead at the martyrs' shrines (Brandenburg 2004: 18, 89–91). However, this is the dynastic extension of a claim to power, which first had to be secured in more immediate ways. The dynastic commemoration of the dead at the suburban *martyria* would only succeed if the Christian religion managed to establish itself across society.

Therefore, Constantine also had to win over the capital in intellectual and political terms following his military victory. For this reason he interpreted his victory not as a victory over Rome, but over Maxentius on behalf of Rome: he did not conquer Rome but liberated it (*CIL* 6.1139; cf. *Panegyrici latini* 12 [9].2.4; Eus. *HE* 9.9.2). Constantine's honorary monuments and major buildings in the years after 312 were meant to proclaim just this. They were nothing but memorials of his victory to bind the Romans, pagans as well as Christians, to himself. In this sense his churches were more "Roman" than would be expressed by the notion of a purely imperial commemoration of the dead.

A key document is the programmatic speech which Constantine "wrote," that is, apparently had delivered by a messenger (Const. Imp. *Or. ad sanct.* 1.1), to the church's officials and friends in Rome one Easter. It is disputed whether it has been transmitted only in a reworked version. Looking back at his conversion, Constantine turns toward his new task of spreading the Christian faith across the empire (*Or. ad sanct.* 11.1), and comes to a reckoning with Maxentius in political as well as religious terms. He thematizes his victory and reveals its political and religious implications for the city of Rome. The speech almost provides a late response to the pressing question of the pagan encomiast of 313, as to which god Rome owed its liberation from a hopeless situation (*Panegyrici latini* 12[9].2.4–5, 26.1). The memory of the battle of the Milvian Bridge is still fresh, which provides one reason besides others to assume an early date for the speech, such as Easter 315 or 316 (Edwards 2003: xvii–xxxiii).

Constantine's speech thus belongs in the context of monumentalizing his victory over Maxentius. He now equates the "divine inspiration" (*instinctus divinitatis*) of which the arch of honor erected in 315 speaks (*CIL* 6.1139; cf. *Panegyrici latini* 12 [9].11.4) more concretely with Christ (*Or. ad sanct.* 26.1), which is not surprising after the edict of Milan. What is, however, remarkable in the speech and applicable only to Rome is Constantine's intention of honoring the apostles and martyrs and apparently of erecting "temples" for them (*Or. ad sanct.* 19.9, cf. *ICUR NS* 8.20752). For the sacrifice of the Eucharist was being offered, and hymns, psalms, acclamations, and praise of God were being sung, in honor of the Christian heroes (*Or. ad sanct.* 12.4–5). Constantine does in fact give the Roman church splendid ecclesiastical interiors, some of them built on the property of Maxentius. These churches become magnets which attract the Christian Romans and visitors to the city (cf. Eus. *Theoph. syr.* 4.7, 5.49).

The Martyrs' Basilicas as Trophies of Constantine

Victory monuments (*trophaea, tropaia*) served as propaganda tools: communicating an imperial ideology of victory to a public whose sympathies were being sought. Constantine had to silence doubts: patriotically minded Romans asked whether with his victory over Maxentius he would also question Maxentius' notion of Rome. Maxentius had re-established the significance of the ancient metropolis of the empire not only through propaganda but also through an almost Augustan building program (Aur. Vict. 41.17). At the same time the Christians had to be convinced of the genuine nature of Constantine's conversion, following years of persecution and uncertainty over the religious intentions of Maxentius (Eus. *HE* 8.14.1). Constantine addressed both concerns in his victory monuments.

In 315 the Roman senate and the people of Rome dedicated precisely that honorary arch which commemorated Constantine's act of liberating Rome to him. It was placed in a prominent position by the Flavian amphitheater ("Colosseum") along the route of the triumphal processions of late antiquity. Even though this had been a victory in a civil war, the imprisoned Dacians who crowned its columns signaled what appeared to be a victory over barbarians. The senate also gave the nearby basilica of Maxentius, now the *basilica Constantini*, to Constantine. A large-scale statue of him seated on a throne and holding a standard resembling a cross as a sign of victory over his adversary was erected here at the "most frequented place in Rome" (*Panegyrici latini* 12 [9].25.4; Aur. Vict. 40.28; Eus. *HE* 9.9.10; Libanius, *Laud. Const.* 9.8).

While honorary arch and colossal statue were aimed at the city's public, the churches were specifically meant for the Christians of Rome. Constantine chose locations whose *Genius loci* was suited to conveying his imperial-religious propaganda. As early as 312–13 he ordered the destruction of the barracks of the equestrian guard, which had acted as Maxentius' personal guard during the decisive battle. He then donated the land to the church to erect the Lateran basilica, and thus a victory monument for himself which kept alive the memory of its founder as a *basilica constantiniana*.

By distinguishing the *tropaia* of the martyrs, their graves, through the suburban basilicas, Constantine erected other trophies to his victory over Maxentius besides the honorary arch and the colossal statue (Const. Imp. *Or. ad sanct.* 22.1; Eus. *HE* 2.25.7, 10.4.20, *Theoph. syr.* 4.7). He perceived the victory of the Roman martyrs as closely related to the defeat of the "tyrant," who had let the "bodies of the saints" be tortured (*Or. ad sanct.* 22.2–3). The "bodies" of the martyrs held particular significance for him, as a special power resided in them (*Or. ad sanct.* 17.4; Eus. *Vita Constantini* 2.40). By honoring the persecuted church of Rome in the martyrs, he once again defeated the persecutor Maxentius. The festive cult of the martyrs served as a foil to his imperial message of victory, and this cult caused the basilicas to become privileged places of burial right from the start.

The "Basilica of the Apostles" serves as a particularly good example. It stood on the Via Appia above the so-called *triclia*, where Peter and Paul had been venerated since the mid-third century. This was a place where the persecuted church had sought solace in the apostolic martyrs (cf. Piétri 1976: 376–80). It was precisely for this reason that Constantine wished to endow it with greater, monumental significance, by reflecting the functions of the *triclia* in important elements of the architecture of the new building (Tolotti 1982: 171–88). It is likely that he engaged the company of builders which had still been employed on Maxentius' villa on the opposite side of the road to construct the circus-shaped "Basilica of the Apostles" (Brandenburg 2004: 63–4, 68–9). In this way he gave the lie to Maxentius' imperial claim, which had been expressed in his *heroon* with a circus. The day of remembrance of the two apostles on June 29 may have been meant to counter the celebration of Rome's founders, Romulus and Remus (Cracco Ruggini, 2001: 387–92). If this was so, the apparent triumph of the pair of apostles *ad catacumbas* over the self-proclaimed Romulus Maxentius (cf. *Panegyrici latini* 12 [9].18.1) now illustrated it in a surprising way.

The basilica of Peter which lies alongside the Via Triumphalis (Hieronymus, *Viri illustres* 1.6) finally gives unmistakable expression to the idea of victory in its inscription. On the arch between nave and transept it read: "Because with you as our leader the world rose to the stars, Constantine the victor in triumph founded this hall for you (Christ/Peter)" (*ICUR NS* 2.4092–5; cf. Const. Imp. *Or. ad sanct.* 25.5).

The Martyrs as the Glory of Rome

The ideology of Rome also played a role. The persecutors of the Christians lost the battle and brought disgrace to Rome (Const. Imp. *Or. ad sanct.* 24). On the Arch of Constantine Maxentius was declared an illegitimate ruler, who had deliberately usurped Rome and had raged there with contempt for all morals (Eus. *HE* 8.14, *Vita Constantini* 1.33–6; Aur. Vict. 40.23–5). Constantine, on the other hand, freed Rome from the tyrant with the help of the sign (of the cross) which brought salvation and he "restored" the city, Romans, and senate to their former splendor and nobility (Eus. *HE* 9.9.11, *Vita Constantini* 1.40.2; Rufinus, *HE* 9.9.10–11; cf. *Panegyrici latini* 12 [9].1.1). He executed *damnatio memoriae* on Maxentius and his followers only for satisfaction's sake, but spared the city itself (*Panegyrici latini* 12 [9].20.3–4). The true foe of Rome was Maxentius (Lact. *DMP* 44.8), even if he had propagated an ideal Rome and restored the city as his permanent residence following the years of the tetrarchy's division of the empire.

Constantine seized the Roman ideal which Maxentius had newly proclaimed in order to make it his own (Curran 2000: 54, 77, 80, 114), not without adding a moral-religious dimension. Constantine presented himself as the preserver of old Roman virtue and religiosity and projected this on to the church and its martyrs. For the martyrs of Rome were the city's glory (Const. Imp. *Or. ad sanct.* 22.2). The new basilical monuments of victory functioned even more as such since they stood like a majestic rampart before the gates of Rome (for a later testimony, see *ICUR NS* 2.4107), where god had led Maxentius – it was none other than he who had raised the Aurelian city wall to almost double its former height! – to seek battle and lose (*Or. ad sanct.* 22.2; Eus. *Praeparatio evangelica* 13.11.1–2, *HE* 9.9.4; cf. *Panegyrici latini* 12 [9].15.1). Eusebius gushed about "royal Rome," whose resting places of the martyrs made the city on the mountain rise like a single monument of victory at the center of the globe (Eus. *Theoph. syr.* 4.7).

Large-scale monuments of victory were the pride of a city (see in general McCormick 1986), and every visitor to Rome wished to see them. Ideologically Constantine's monuments belong to the period before 325, when it was yet impossible to envisage relocating the capital away from Rome to Constantinople with lasting effect. As imperial monuments they expressed Rome's claim to be and remain the imperial city *par excellence*. For Constantine the church now became the vehicle precisely of this restoration. By honoring his divine companion in battle and the martyrs, the church brought fortune and victory to Rome (cf. Const. Imp. *Or. ad sanct.* 26). While it had so far maintained a watchful attitude toward the Roman state, the church was now set on the way to becoming itself the carrier of the idea of Rome through Constantine's massive intervention. Rome's church entered into this new task in the most visible and effective manner through the cult of the martyrs.

The church was sustained by conservative values and thus could not resist the idea of a Christian Rome. It was precisely this which facilitated the entry of the Roman aristocracy into the church. The quick spread of Christianity amongst the Roman upper classes can only be explained by the fact that the aristocracy's conservative values were shared by the church. The veneration of the martyrs contained key Roman ideals. The martyr is of noble birth (*Or. ad sanct.* 12.4). He faces struggles and suffering safe in the knowledge of victory and pays no heed to wounds and setbacks (Dörries 1954: 134–5). A sense of morality and prudence renders the martyr strong (*Or. ad sanct.* 17.3–4). Eusebius' encomium on the wife of Rome's prefect, Sophronia, who committed suicide in order to escape the attentions of Maxentius, provides an obvious example of the transference of the strict morality of ancient Rome to the Christian notion of martyrdom (Eus. *HE* 8.14.16–17, *Vita Constantini* 1.34).

The Annual Cycle of Victory Celebrations

The emperor's portrayal of victory required public demonstrations, as frequent and regular as possible, in addition to eye-catching monuments. Contests in the arenas were most successful in presenting this image of the invincible emperor, and they secured lasting memory within the cycle of annual celebrations (Curran 2000: 223). The emperor was able to establish new festivities and games at will in order to keep the myth of his victory alive. The athletes gained victory through his favor. His victory in turn was the victory of Rome. Constantine employed this tool to reach at least the pagan population. He renovated the Circus Maximus, possibly also because the spectators at the games, which had been held for Maxentius on the day before the decisive battle, had chanted "*Constantinus invictus*" (Lact. *DMP* 44.7; cf. *Panegyrici latini* 12 [9].15.4, 26.5). Thus Constantine also celebrated his victory after his triumphant entry into the city with games in the Circus Maximus.

By erecting the martyrs' churches Constantine wished to reach the Christians of Rome through popular celebrations of victory, since the annual assemblies honoring the martyrs were held there. The "basilicas" were considered to be official public buildings and served to hold Mass in honor of the Christian god who had been accepted by the emperor. All services included a prayer for the emperor. It could be seen as a disadvantage that the martyrs' churches were sited on the periphery; yet the desire to celebrate the particularly Christian kind of victor in the martyrs held greater importance (Const. Imp. *Or. ad sanct.* 12.3). Nothing could elevate the victor Constantine more than being commemorated as the imperial founder of the churches during the martyrs' commemorations. These were celebrations of victory during which light-colored clothes were worn as a sign of joy: the appropriate framework for soliciting the Christians' loyalty to one's own claim to rule through setting in context the victory.

Rome possessed more martyrs than other cities, which could only help to promote the myth of Constantine's victory. The list of martyrs of the calendar of 354 displays around 35 names of martyrs who were venerated at the respective catacomb on almost 20 days during the year on their name-day, although the calendar appears to have omitted a number of martyrs. Together with the *depositio episcoporum* (list of bishops) it apparently lists those days on which the bishop of Rome, with his clerics and the city's congregation, met every year at each martyr's cemetery (on days of more than one martyr a choice had to be made). The list continues a practice which had been established from at least the mid-third century, but in its present form it may have been compiled as late as under bishop Miltiades (311–14) or Silvester (314–35), as festive celebrations of Mass in the cemeteries, which in principle were open to all, had become possible under Constantine.

It is striking that the Easter calendar of the Chronograph of 354 begins in the year 312. Constantine, who saw in Christ the "brighter sun" and the truly invincible god (*Or. ad sanct.* 1.1, 15.4) and rejected pagan celebrations, appears to have been the driving force behind the calendar of martyrs (cf. Eus. *Vita Constantini* 4.23). Since the martyrs' calendar starts with Christmas on December 25, its beginning coincides with the (new?) pagan celebration of the invincible Sun-god. This gave the martyr's calendar the character of a true cycle of celebrations: the day of the invincible Christian god, which was celebrated in St. Peter with good reason (Ambrosius, *De virginitate* 3.1), thus became the founding celebration of the victorious martyrs. It may be that Constantine himself introduced the celebration of Christmas with this intention (cf. Wallraff 2001: 182).

Maxentius created the circus at the Via Appia where he resided. Constantine surpassed him by establishing halls of victory for the martyrs along the main routes in and out of Rome. He also endowed them richly, allowing the poor to receive food on the commemorative days of the martyrs (cf. Const. Imp. *Or. ad sanct.* 12.5), in the same way as the decorative images on the Arch of Constantine proclaimed his *liberalitas* (distribution of money to the Roman public). The seven silver altars together with the numerous vessels of the Lateran Basilica are likely to be connected to such an endowment by the emperor (Piétri 1997: 866). While the Roman public suffered from famine under Maxentius (*Panegyrici latini* 12 [9].4.4, 16.1; *Chronica minora* 1.148; Eus. *HE* 8.14.6), the church now arranged public meals at the places of victory in honor of the imperial founder, who thus participated in the victory of the martyrs who were being venerated. The myth of the martyrs' victory elevated that of Constantine to divine heights. By honoring the martyrs in its new basilicas, the victorious church honored the tyrant's vanquisher.

Liturgy and Munificence

Those martyrs whose tombs were located in the vicinity of the new basilicas were venerated there on their anniversaries. This allowed a connection to be made to those more modest celebrations which used to take place in the cemeteries before 312. Both the time (the martyrs' *dies natalis*) and place (their *coemeterium*) were fixed for the celebrations. For this reason a stational liturgy for the martyrs developed almost of its own accord, in that all Christians of Rome came to their graves on their anniversaries, even if not in the form of a procession. This liturgy of the martyrs, which had its origin in the Roman notion of victory, is captured in the *depositio martyrum*, which may be seen in some respect as the earliest papal stational calendar.

The development of such a calendar of saints (*Sanctorale*) and its importance to the Roman service has to be seen as an innovation. In any case the services inside the city which were led by the presbyters on Sundays did not serve to commemorate the martyrs. The development of a martyrs' calendar which spanned the year was at least indirectly a consequence of Constantine's ecclesiastic program. It surely was one of the most successful tools to secure not only Constantine's imperial dynasty but also the Romanization of the Christians of Rome. Significantly, the *depositio martyrum* and the *depositio episcoporum* have been inserted into the manuscript collection of the calendar of 354. The Christians are the only religious group with their own lists of celebrations, an indication that many celebrations listed in the Roman calendar framework (*Fasti*) with their corresponding *spectacula* would soon become obsolete.

Constantine's partisan attitude toward Christianity as expressed in the church buildings could not be mistaken. It appears to have caused a wave of Christianization in Rome, as proven by the rapid growth and extension of the catacombs (Fiocchi Nicolai 2000, 2001). Parts of the prosperous upper class also turned to the new faith, as is illustrated by the increasing number of sarcophagi with Christian imagery (Dresken-Weiland 2004). Presumably a significant number of these sarcophagi were placed in the new martyrs' churches, which served as privileged places of burial. These noble families had villas close to the green belt of Rome and in the Campagna, and such an arrangement met their need to present themselves in a suitable way. Sarcophagi which celebrate the passion of Christ, as well as of Peter and Paul in the sign of Constantine's *tropaion* or *labarum* (imperial banner), belong to the time of

Constantine (Deichmann 1967: nos. 61, 212; cf. Const. Imp. *Or. ad sanct.* 1.1, 11.4–6).

It goes without saying that members of the emperor's family frequented the cemeteries as well, in particular at the celebrations of martyrs which developed into opportunities for social contact amongst the Roman upper class (Mratschek 2001). If the big mausoleum of the "Basilica of the Apostles" (St. Sebastian), which lies on the southern side and forms an integral part of the church building, was indeed designed for a member of the emperor's family, then Constantine invited the nobility to emulate him. Soon mausolea were indeed placed around all these martyrs' churches like satellites. Senators and noble families did not erect isolated mausolea on their own land as they had done during the early empire. Instead they put their representative burials on display in the communal Christian cemeteries at the graves of the martyrs. The money of the upper class which was becoming Christian noticeably flowed to the *necropoleis*; the external perception of the Christian faith literally moved outside the city.

The munificence of the senatorial class, which had always found its expression in games and temple festivities, discovered the church's rituals. The aristocracy played an important role at the anniversaries of the temples; in most cases they were linked to games in which it could prove its generosity (Salzmann 1990: 184–8). There is no reason not to believe that the Christian aristocracy took on this role of providing assistance to the martyrs' basilicas and founded additional churches. It supported special supplies of food to the people (cf. Amm. 27.3.5–6; Paulinus of Nola, *Epist.* 13.11) and financed the establishment of new communal cemeteries on their extensive suburban properties.

The Circus-Shaped Martyrs' Basilicas

The desire to emulate, indeed to surpass, the games in celebrating the martyrs may find its expression in one peculiar characteristic of Roman ecclesiastical architecture of the Constantinian and post-Constantinian periods. The suburban martyrs' basilicas, and only these (apart from St. Peter and St. Paul), are based on a ground-plan resembling a circus (fig. 28.2). In addition to those mentioned above, the Basilica of Mark on the Via Ardeatina and that of Agnes on the Via Nomentana belong to the late or post-Constantinian basilicas with ambulatory. The latter was dedicated to the "*Victrix Agnes*," according to the inscription that records its consecration (*ICUR NS* 8.20752). The anonymous ambulatory basilica on the Via Praenestina and the "Basilica of the Apostles" (St. Sebastian) were erected at imperial villa complexes containing a stadium (the church of St. Peter also lay at the site of an abandoned circus).

The seemingly circus-shaped ground-plan of the basilicas with ambulatory can hardly be understood by referring to a cosmological symbolism of eternity. It is more likely that the martyrs' basilicas are to be placed in the context of the heroes' cult of imperial times. This cult was connected in particular to places of athletic contest, in so far as Hercules was regarded as the patron of athletes. The Christians accordingly publicized their heroes, the martyrs, in circus-shaped churches (La Rocca 2002).

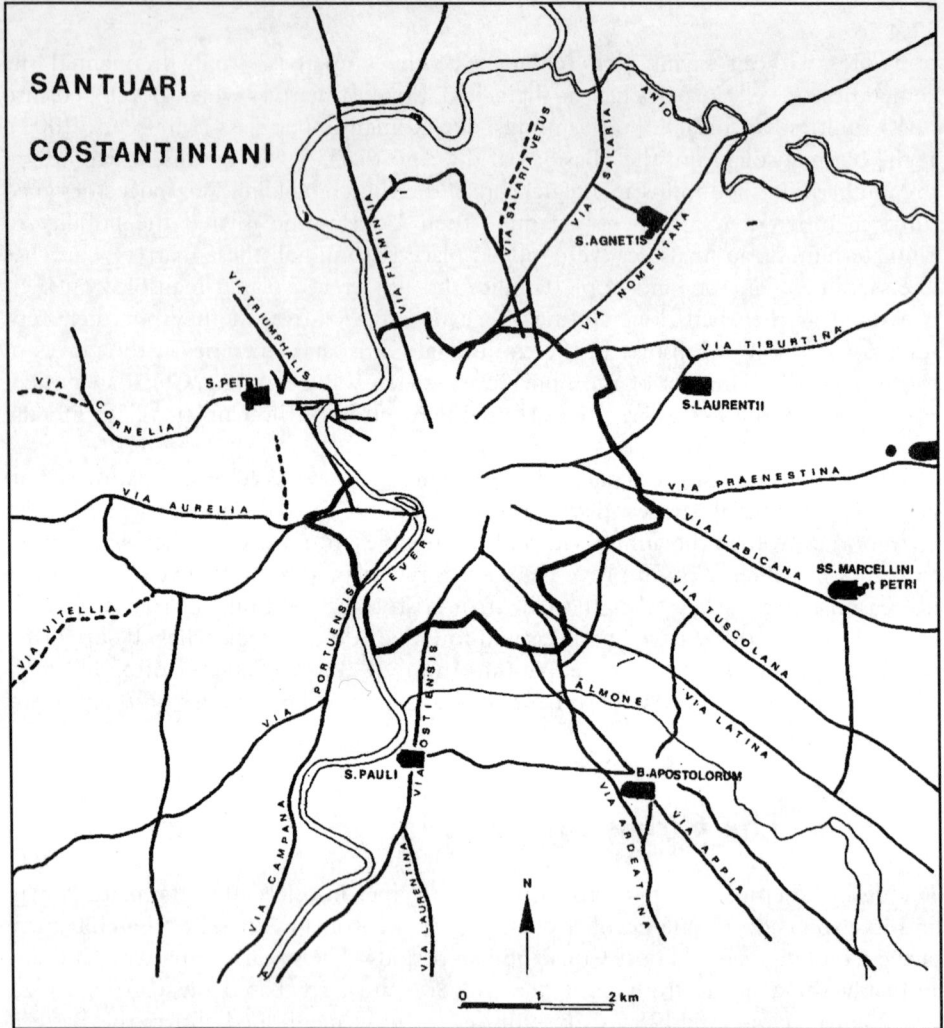

Figure 28.2 Constantinian church buildings outside the gates of Rome (Pani Ermini 1989: fig. 4).

Such Christian borrowings from the heroes' cult cannot, however, be proven. The basilicas in honor of the martyrs were without doubt intended as architectural expressions of triumph. All of Constantine's churches express this also in architectural, and monumental, terms: the Basilica of Peter through the canopy (*Ziborium*) above the martyr's tomb, the Lateran Basilica through the so-called *Fastigium* – a gable monument in between nave and altar room, which carried the statues of Christ and the apostles (fig. 28.3) – and the other basilicas on precisely these circus-shaped ground-plans.

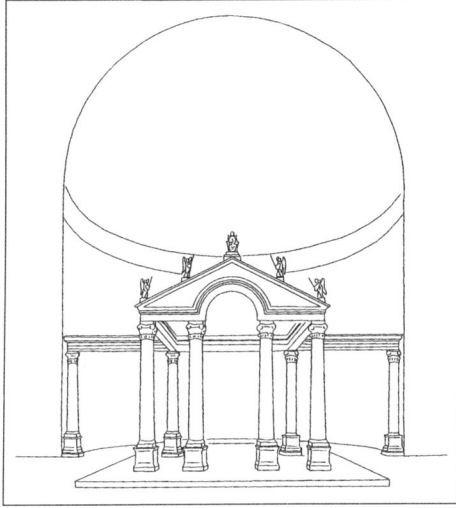

Figure 28.3 Reconstruction of the presbyterium of the Constantinian Lateran Basilica (Bisconti 2000: 186).

The circus as location of victorious athletes and the basilicas as celebratory spaces for the martyr-athletes led to the idea of erecting the new churches on the ground-plan of a circus. Such a play with architecture was not unusual (Torelli 2002). The playful nature of this approach explains also why, while the entrance wall of the basilicas was placed at an angle to the main body of the building, like the section of a circus which contained the starting gates, it was at varying angles, just as this aspect was handled at will in pictorial representations of a circus.

If nothing else, this playfulness indicates a certain understanding of martyrdom. The martyr as victorious athlete had been a *topos* of Christian publicity from the start. "Athlete of Christ" and "Athlete of the Faith" became regular descriptions of martyrs and confessors from the third century, especially when they were paraded during circus games. The first letter of Clement, which was composed in Rome around 96, writes of the athletes of Nero's persecutions of the Christians, who had fought the *agon* of life and death in the arena (*1 Clemens* 5–7). The apostle Peter endured many "pains," bore witness, and reached the place of glory he merited, which in this context refers to the staging of the victor's ceremony. Paul is also mentioned – echoing 2 Timothy 3. 10–4. 8 – whose missionary activity takes on the appearance of a contest, in that he is repeatedly taken prisoner and tortured, but finally obtains the victor's prize.

The Martyrs as Athletes of Christ

Many more such examples exist. However, what is important is that Constantine introduces the metaphor of contest precisely at the point in his speech of 315 (316?)

in Rome when he speaks of services in honor of the martyrs. The apostles (the "wise men") provide a lasting example for those who were prepared to be martyred because of the divine power against which no one can do battle. God, to whom they nobly bore witness, awarded them the victor's wreath. Henceforth the heroes deserve continuing commemoration and eternal glory, by celebrating the sacrifice of the Eucharist for them (*Or. ad sanct.* 11.5–6, 12.2–5). Therefore the martyrs were honored as athletes in the churches of Rome. Amongst those who were persecuted under Maxentius and Maximius, Eusebius mentions in particular the *agon* of the women who gained the prizes of victory for their heroism in Rome (*HE* 8.14.14). He speaks as a matter of course of the "*agon* of martyrdom," of the holy and great *agon* in different kinds of sport, especially because of those martyrs who had to battle naked against the animals (*Antiquorum martyrorum collectio* 1, *HE* 8.2.3, 3.1, 6.5, 7.1).

The martyrs of Lyon and Vienna who suffered in the amphitheater are portrayed by Eusebius as combatants for the faith whose sufferings are inscribed on lasting *stelae* which will proclaim their *tropaia*, their victories over the demonical adversaries, and their wreaths forever (*HE* 5, *praefatio* 4). He continues that the stadium of these combatants lies in Gaul (*HE* 5.1.1), by which he refers to the amphitheater but also the locus of martyrdom *per se*, insofar as the "stadium" here becomes synonymous with the battle of martyrdom. In this sense the athletes of the faith everywhere suffered martyrdom during the persecution of Severus. But in particular the athletes of God from all over Egypt and the Thebaid were sent to Alexandria in order to undergo diverse types of combat, so to speak in the greatest stadium, and finally to gain the wreath of victory from God (*HE* 6.1.1). Martyrdom itself may therefore be termed a stadium or arena. A considerable number of legends note that the confessors entered into the stadium of martyrdom. The different contests, that is, series of tortures, which they underwent are termed stadiums or arenas. Even the martyr's church itself becomes a stadium (Aug. *Civ.* 8.27, *Sermo* 280.2.2; Basilius, *In Gordium martyrum* 1; Pseudo-Basilius, *In Barleam martyrum* 2; *BHG* 1477b).

Therefore it surely would have been possible to conceive of the idea of developing for martyrs' churches a triumphal architecture based on a circus-shaped ground-plan in Rome, in particular since it is likely that people assumed that the martyrs had achieved their victory over death and the devil precisely there, outside the gates of Rome.

Martyrs' Celebrations and the Days of the Games

It is difficult to tell what effect this had on the liturgy. Many of the prayers for Mass contained in the Roman sacramentaries of the seventh and eighth centuries were meant for the "*agon*," "contest" and "victory," of the martyrs. We may therefore assume that such metaphors had long become a common feature of martyrs' celebrations. Furthermore, it ought to be investigated whether the celebrations contained special acclamatory elements (cf. Const. Imp. *Or. ad sanct.* 12.4), known from the circus. Similar exclamations may have entered the martyrs' liturgy. The sarcophagi of the late fourth century certainly often portray Christ or the Constantine *labarum* in the center, with rows of apostles to their left and right acclaiming them.

In the martyrs' liturgy of the Constantinian and post-Constantinian period, Christ definitely still remains at the center of attention as divine victor and author of the victory of his athletes: the wreaths of victory gained by the martyrs are his due. As the victorious athlete in the circus owes his victory to the emperor, so the individual martyr is subsumed in Christ. For the liturgy it is important only that the martyrdom took place, not how. Also of importance are the actuality and eternity of the victory celebration, which shows the martyrs' victory to be a divine one. Any historical interest is lacking, in favor of a public and triumphant consciousness of victory itself.

It was not Constantine's intention to replace the Roman games with the circus-shaped basilicas and the liturgy in honor of the Christian athletes that were celebrated in them: the games had to continue. The calendar of celebrations containing 177 days of games (of which 66 were *ludi circenses* in the Circus Maximus) survived even after his death. Likewise the martyrs were celebrated, in the extensive *Suburbium*, preferably not on days which would have kept the Christians away from the games in the circus and amphitheater. For the martyrs' days of the *depositio martyrum* were subject not to conscious planning, but to historical chance. The enormous extension of the suburban martyrs' stations in the fifth and sixth centuries, as shown in the Roman calendar of the *Martyrologium Hieronymianum* and the formulae of the Sacramentary of Verona, likewise does not point toward any desire to oust the games. Not even half of about one hundred new celebrations took place on the days of the games.

Little is known about conflicts. After the shocking pillage of Rome by Alaric from August 24 to 27, 410, the Romans immediately went to the circus games and derided the martyrs whose tombs had been unable to protect the city (Aug. *Sermo* 296.7.8; Orosius 1.6.4). Fewer and fewer Christians attended the annual thanksgiving service, so that Pope Leo said, probably on September 6, 442, during the *Ludi Romani* (which lasted a number of days): "The pagan idols are honored more than the apostles. Foolish games are frequented more than the churches of the holy martyrs. Yet who has raised up again this city so richly blessed? Who has liberated its inhabitants from imprisonment? Who has saved them from a massacre? Was it the circus games or the care of our saints?" (*Sermo* 84.1). Leo appears to have had in mind the circus games of August 28, which seemingly again proved very popular. On the other hand he hoped to supplant the significant *Ludi Plebei* from November 12 to 16, with their public meals, with the celebrations of the great charitable collect (*Sermo* 6–11).

Apart from the formulae in the prayers of the martyrs' celebrations the Roman church did not employ this set of tools, which had been familiar to the Byzantine and north African church since the fourth century and which allowed these celebrations to compete with the games. There the martyrs' celebrations were indeed turned into veritable games and athletics of the faith. Sermons were designed as "encomia of the athletes" and the *Passio*, which was termed a true *athlesis*, was read as part of the liturgy. Cycles of paintings of the martyrs in the churches were understood as images honoring victorious athletes. Augustine as well as the Byzantine preachers (Gregory of Nyssa, Gregory of Nazianz, Basil of Caesarea, John Chrysostom) consciously used the idea of presenting the celebration of a martyr as a sportive spectacle as an overarching theme for sermons and the (biblical or legendary) report of the passion, in order to redirect the popularity of the games toward the celebrations of the church. On the day of St. Cyprian in Carthage, Augustine complained about the wild celebrations that took place in the martyr's church during the night: "We do not celebrate games with the demons here, but the feasts of the martyrs; we do not leap about here, but sing" (*Sermo* 311.5–6, 335D, drawing on Matthew 11.17; cf. Paulinus of Nola, *Carmen* 27.573).

In Rome, reading out the *Passiones* was prohibited by the church (*Decretum Gelasianum*). This prevented the martyrs' celebrations from turning into replacements for the circus games. The notion of the *agon* only played a minor role in the Roman *Passiones* and sermons on the martyrs. Eastern influences came to the fore only from the sixth century onward through the Byzantines in Rome. The Greeks in particular appear to have found the games in Rome objectionable (Theodoretus, *HE* 5.26). It is no coincidence that complaints were voiced precisely by those who venerated St. Anastasia at the church of the Byzantines, which lay right next to the Circus Maximus. They objected to the Roman church's prohibition on reading out the *Passiones* of the "athletes of the Lord" during the service, which drove the faithful to displays of diabolical boxing matches (de Gaiffier 1964). The celebration of St. Anastasia on December 25 coincided with a traditional day of games. The Greek legend about her, which was likely composed in Rome itself, accordingly pictured the saint's martyrdom in terms of a contest throughout (*BHG* 76z).

The dangers which the wars against the Goths and the Byzantine reconquest posed to the *Suburbium*, as well as the noticeable depopulation of the city, led to a profound change of the suburbs from the mid-sixth century. Burials there continued in spite of the establishment of cemeteries inside the city, and the martyrs' shrines continued to be visited by pilgrims into the seventh and eighth centuries. The stational liturgy of the martyrs, however, was reduced, concentrating mainly on churches close to the city (Gregorian and Old Gelasian Sacramentary; *Comes* of Würzburg). On the other hand, the titular churches inside the city were integrated into a system of stational services, in particular over the weeks leading up to Easter (*Quadragesima*), in which the pope and the urban population took part. The classical Roman stational liturgy of the early Middle Ages was now developing.

The circus-shaped basilicas were doomed by this shift of focus from services held at the periphery right into the center of the city. The martyrs' basilicas of St. Boniface and St. Sophia outside the gates of Rome continued to be mentioned as worthy of their contest, yet without in all likelihood referring to any concrete architectural feature (*BHL* 1413, 1415; *BHG* 1637y). The titular churches inside the city benefited instead. They now established connections with named martyrs, since a church that did not commemorate a martyr, and indeed possess relics, now became inconceivable (fig. 28.4). The Roman legends (*gesta martyrum*) were being composed from about the sixth century in order to establish this connection between the titles and the Roman martyrs, and to render the choice of new churches for the stational liturgy inside the city plausible. In this way the commemoration of the martyrs now became linked to the liturgy inside the city. This itself had been made possible by extending the city's liturgy from Sundays to weekdays.

Figure 28.4 Stational churches of Rome during the sixth century (Baldovin 1987: 274).

Other Aspects of Romanization

My argument has focused on the veneration of the martyrs and the lasting influence which Constantine exerted on it. His initiative in erecting buildings and establishing celebrations was crucial in initiating the Romanization of Roman Christianity. A second wave of a very different kind was caused by Pope Damasus (366–84). This is the high point of the Latinization of the church, whose most significant precursor had been Hieronymus (d. 419/20), who had been completely imbued with Roman literature. The church switched from Greek to Latin as the language for the liturgy, which found its expression in the elevated Latinity of the *Canon Romanus*. Hieronymus revised the existing Latin renditions of the Bible for the most part according to linguistic criteria (*Vulgata*). Damasus placed splendid inscriptions in "heroic meter" in praise of the martyrs in the catacombs, which Dionysius Filocalus, the editor of the calendar of 354, had chiseled in square lettering resembling classical models (Hieronymus, *De viris illustribus* 103.1). The verses elevate the martyrs to "Roman citizens." The authors of epic paraphrases of the Bible sought formal beauty, and the epigrams likewise adopt the traditions of Virgilian poetry. Hieronymus had already been inspired by Virgil's verses during his visits to the martyrs' tombs on a Sunday (*Commentarium in Ezechielem* 9.5–13). All these examples show the desire for the church to become the pillar and agent of renewal for "classical" Latinity. This conjured up the former greatness of Rome, which was now defined entirely in terms of the church.

FURTHER READING

The research into Rome in the late classical period has made significant progress since World War II, due to the intensive cooperation by those academic institutions participating in the Unione internazionale degli Istituti di Archeologia, Storia e Storia dell'Arte in Roma (cf. its *Annuario*). This progress is evident in the publication of numerous journals and conference proceedings edited in Rome. The fertile connections between classical and Christian archaeology and historical research are a key characteristic. Charles Piétri's *Roma christiana* (1976) offers a first attempt to write a history of Rome in the late classical-early Christian period on this basis (see also Inglebert 1996). Topographical inquiries inside and outside Rome are now becoming ever more detailed. This means it becomes even more unlikely that a comprehensive history of the city of Rome will be produced. A central concern in investigating the development of Christian Rome, given what has been said above, is the establishment of the city churches (*tituli*) and their patronages during the fifth to seventh century. Older research which takes textual evidence on face value is now outdated. The hagiographic texts from Rome, both Latin and Greek, have to be interpreted strictly as texts dating from the fifth to seventh centuries and mined for evidence concerning the church. Jost (2000) is helpful in this. The "Book of the Popes" (*Liber Pontificalis*), whose earliest version contains the biographies of the bishops of Rome until the sixth century, repays renewed attention, particularly as an English translation is now available for the first time (Davis 2000). Here, too, research so far has not advanced beyond studies of detail (*Mededelingen van het Nederlands Instituut te Rome* 60/1, 2001/2).

PART VI

Roman Religion Outside and Seen from Outside

CHAPTER TWENTY-NINE

Exporting Roman Religion

Clifford Ando

This chapter examines the spread of specifically Roman cults to the provinces. Its argument proceeds with two concerns foremost in mind. First, I concentrate on the religious life of Roman citizens. For it is among communities of citizens that we should expect Roman cults to have spread first, both because Roman religion was first and foremost a religion of and for a juridically defined community of citizens (Scheid 1985b: 47–76; 1985a), and because, naturally, it is through the movement of adherents that cults must in the first instance themselves move.

Second, I seek to problematize the very assumption that what cults do is spread or, perhaps, that what the religious do is proselytize. For historical reasons – some, indeed, quite powerful – this expectation both governs and complicates the study of religion in the ancient Mediterranean as perhaps nowhere else. The latter part of this introductory section and the conclusion to the chapter both take up this issue.

Bracketing that problem for the moment, the chapter falls into two parts. The next two sections examine the topic empirically, by considering in turn the religious life of two types of communities principally in light of provincial evidence. The first of these sections studies colonies of Roman citizens, who were thought to remain in some fashion in the *populus Romanus* and whom one might expect, therefore, to remain participants in the Roman people's religious life. The following section turns principally to municipalities, and seeks to characterize the degree of control – and extent of autonomy – granted them in religious life. In both sections I argue for a high degree of change over time in Roman and local practice. Indeed, at a high level of abstraction, perhaps the chief way in which local practice mirrored Roman practice was in its sheer fluidity.

The second half of the chapter turns to Roman theory or, perhaps, Roman theology, and argues above all that there were substantial structural impediments to the spread of Roman cults. (The historical origin of the question why we should expect cults to spread is examined below.) I concentrate there on two bodies of evidence: first, the bodies of religious law concerned with geographic aspects of priestly action and authority and, second, Roman historical accounts of their own attempts to move cults. Such actions are often described, as we shall see, as attempts to move the god himself or herself; their success is therefore seen as contingent upon the willingness of the god to move and, often enough, concurrently to accept not just any, but quite particular, new worshipers. However we might wish to redescribe those concerns in light of our own theoretical postulates, the framework within which Romans conceived the spread of cults and adhesion of individuals to them is clearly radically different than our own.

This reflection returns us to the problematic expectation on the part of Christian and post-Christian scholars that religions spread, an expectation that exists within the study of religion more generally, and within the study of Roman religion more specifically, largely through the influence of two related forces. The first of these is the awareness that the Roman empire provided a context for the diffusion of many religions, most famously the so-called oriental or mystery cults. This view of the empire's religious history has itself a long tradition. For the most famous of those mystery cults was, of course, Christianity, and the Christians developed very early a theory of history by which to understand relations between religion and empire. Their most significant move was to assent to imperial propaganda in equating the accession of Augustus with the foundation of the empire. By ignoring, in other words, the long history of the empire's acquisition and privileging instead the constitutional change from democracy to imperial monarchy as a historical nodal point, the Christians could associate in time and therefore in causation the establishment of the empire and the birth of Christ. God himself had so provided, the argument ran, in order that the new religion might spread more rapidly in a unified world (Melito of Sardis, *Apologia* frag. 1; Eusebius, *Triakontaeterikos* [*Tricennial Oration*] 4.2 and 16.5–8; see Ando 2000: 48; see also Momigliano 1987: 142–58).

There were of course those who dissented from this view, and contexts in which the arguments for it seemed less cogent, but this is not the place to review the history of that debate. Its contours are relevant here because it was that debate, together with the ecclesiastical histories that adopted its framework, which naturalized the proposition that what religions do is spread.

The second force contributing to the prominence of this proposition in religious historiography derives from the early modern experience of empire, as well as from the historical and polemical literatures to which it gave rise. These urged that empires were agents of cultural change, and that pre-eminent among their ambitions – or, perhaps, their instruments – was the imposition of their own law, language, and religion (Pagden 1995). Empires, in other words, should have a *Reichsreligion*, an imperial religion, whose furtherance might constitute an important part of some imperial project, even as it contributed directly to empire's justification. For late medieval, Renaissance, and early modern Europe, of course, that religion was Christianity. But the theories of empire that developed in those periods and later did not regard Christianity's role in European imperialism as novel. On the contrary, they connected it directly with the providential role assigned the Roman empire in the original success of Christianity itself (see, e.g., Engelbert of Admont's "On the rise and end of the Roman empire," esp. chs. 15 and 18).

On this understanding, the Roman empire presents something of a paradox. For the empire did witness an extraordinary efflorescence of religious activity, particularly among utopian cults, and there can be no doubt that the political stability and social order provided by the empire contributed very directly to that phenomenon. But neither the imperial government itself, nor the empire's governing class, contributed in any concerted and sustained way to the propagation of any particular religion. The only exceptions might be imperial cult, on the one hand, and on the other the intensification of public displays of loyalty through oath-swearing that followed upon Caracalla's grant of universal citizenship, the most famous of which took place under Decius (Rives 1999; Ando 2000: 206–15). But these are not true *comparanda*, for reasons that will emerge across this chapter and which I revisit in its conclusion. Thus might it be said, not untruthfully, that the Romans gave the Mediterranean world all religions but their own.

Colonies

Roman citizens existed in Italy before the Social War, and in the provinces before the Constitutio Antoniniana, in a number of configurations, some formal, others not. Although traders and soldiers were normally the first Romans to enter and, indeed, to settle in new territories (see e.g. Hatzfeld 1919), it is to colonies that scholars have traditionally turned in seeking concentrated populations of Roman citizens self-consciously seeking to replicate the forms and institutions of a specifically Roman culture (exemplary essays drawing on scholarship of this kind are Millar 1990 and Edmondson 2006). Although it would be misleading to suggest that such scholars have no evidence for this understanding of Roman colonialism, they do as a group rely heavily on the heuristic value of a single *imperial* text, by which to interpret the abundant but tessellated evidence from the middle and late republic. That text is the concluding paragraph of a chapter in Aulus Gellius' *Attic Nights*, in which Gellius reflects on the difference between *municipia* and *coloniae*, and himself refers to 'a speech of Hadrian in which the emperor touched on just that topic.

> But the relationship of colonies (to Rome) is different. For they neither come into citizenship from without, nor do they grow from their own roots, but they are developed as offshoots of the citizen body, as it were, and have all the laws and institutions of the Roman people, not those of their own devising. This condition, although it is more constrained and less free (than that of municipalities), is nevertheless thought preferable and more prestigious because of the greatness and majesty of the Roman people, of whom colonies seem to be little images, as it were, and sort-of representations (*propter amplitudinem maiestatemque populi Romani, cuius istae coloniae quasi effigies parvae simulacraque esse quaedam videntur*). At the same time, the rights of municipalities have become obscure and largely forgotten, and hence out of ignorance they are not able to be exploited. (Gellius 16.13.8–9)

In reading this passage, scholars have tended to concentrate solely on the phrases "little images" and "sort-of representations," and have not been urged to caution by Gellius' final lament, that the relevant bodies of law had by his day become "obscure and largely forgotten." The ignorance Gellius identifies is a product not simply of changes in public law under the principate, but of the changing ideology of colonization itself. It is by no means clear that the small maritime colonies of the early third century BC, the much larger colonies north of the Po and west of the Alps of the early second, and the abundant triumviral and Augustan veteran colonies of the second half of the first century BC can be understood as in any way conceived along similar lines (Ando forthcoming a: ch. 3). In other words, to the extent that Gellius' framework is meaningful, it is so in an avowedly high imperial context, by which time the foundation of colonies *ex nihilo* had long since ceased (for a list of post-Augustan colonies see Brunt 1987: 589–601). Awareness of that fact only heightens the irony of understanding republican colonialism in light of Gellius, for the speech of Hadrian that aroused Gellius' interest concerns exactly two already extant cities, both *municipia*, seeking precisely to "come into citizenship from without."

Rather than take the purpose and form of colonies for granted, we need to test precisely whether they did, in fact, "have all the laws and institutions of the Roman people." Not that it is obvious what it would mean for them to do so! For example, in a speech to the people in 63 BC, opposing a proposal to establish further colonies in Campania, Cicero told them of a visit he had made to a then recently founded colony at Capua:

> First, as I have said, although in other colonies the chief magistrates are called *duumviri*, (at Capua) they wish to be called praetors. If the first year in office brought this desire to them, don't you suppose that in a few years they will seek the title of consul? Then, two lictors preceded them: not with staffs, but with *fasces*, like those who precede the urban praetors here! The greater victims were located in the forum, to be approved on consultation by those praetors from the tribunal as is done by us consuls; the victims were then sacrificed, to the accompaniment of a herald and musician. (Cic. *Leg. agr.* 2.93)

Cicero here argues that it was very precisely the continuance of the colonists' Roman citizenship – their remaining within the *populus Romanus* – that should have precluded Capua's becoming an *effigies parva populi Romani*, with strictly parallel institutions, priesthoods, magistracies, and rituals.

As it happens, the first and in some respects the only period of Roman colonization when practice and theory are well and equally attested is that which followed shortly upon the death of Cicero and lasted into the reign of Augustus. For in that period not only were many colonies founded – whose sites have yielded important archaeological, numismatic, and epigraphic evidence regarding their initial occupation – but many works of social, religious, and political history were written, in which the foundation of cities and the expansion of the *populus Romanus* were both theorized and described (regarding literature on religion of this period, see C. Koch 1960; Momigliano 1984; Beard 1986). Nor can there be much doubt that the work performed in these arenas influenced each other.

Consider, for example, the foundation of Rome by Romulus. Most Augustan and post-Augustan accounts of that act urge that he established the religious boundary of the city – its *pomerium* – using the "traditional" Roman method of delineation by plow, a method some Romans understood themselves to have inherited from Etruria (Dion. H. 1.88; Ov. *Fast.* 4.819–36; Plut. *Romulus* 11; dissenting in one respect or another, Livy 1.44.3–5, and Virg. *Aen.* 1.419–26, 5.750–8). But they can have had little if any evidence for that event. It is no doubt significant that Cato the Elder in the second quarter of the second century BC regarded the drawing of city boundaries by plow as customary.

> For the founders of cities used to yoke a bull on the right and a cow on the inside; then, clad in Gabine fashion, that is, with part of the toga covering one's head and part cinched, head covered by part of the toga, they took up a curved plowshare, so that all the turned-up soil would fall inside, and with a furrow so drawn they designated the place for the walls. They picked up the plow at the places for gates. (Cato, *Origines* 1, frag. 18 Peter = Servius ad Virg. *Aen.* 7.755)

It is likewise significant that Varro in the age of Cicero ascribes the ritual to Etruria and, by etymological sleight of hand, argues that all *urbes* – all cities – were necessarily so founded; hence, he concludes, "all our colonies are described in ancient writings as cities, because they were founded in the same way as Rome" (Varro, *Ling.* 5.143). But Varro himself knows of pomerial boundary stones from only two sites – Rome and Aricia. It is rather from the *next* generation – from the Caesarian foundations at Capua in Italy and Urso in Spain, and the early Augustan foundations in southern Asia Minor – that we have evidence for the widespread use of plows in colonial foundations (Capua: *ILS* 6308; Urso: *Lex Ursonensis* c. 73; Asia Minor: Levick 1967: 35–7). If, therefore, the practice pursued in these late colonies was notionally modeled on that at Rome, we should probably regard it as modeled on a self-understanding achieved in light of antiquarian research and no small amount of invention.

The foundation of a Roman city required several further official actions beyond the drawing of the *pomerium*. These are attested in various configurations in late republican texts – none, alas, produced by witnesses to the rituals of foundation, at least so far as we know. The closest thing to such testimony now extant is a dedication in honor of Titus Annius Luscus, one the triumvirs dispatched by the senate to settle supplementary colonists in Aquileia in 169 BC:

> *T(itus) Annius T(iti) f(ilius) tri(um) vir.*
> *Is hance aedem*
> *faciundam dedit*
> *dedicavitque, legesq(ue)*
> *composivit deditque,*
> *senatum ter coptavit.*

> Titus Annius (Luscus), son of Titus, triumvir (for the settlement of colonists). He provided for the construction of this temple and dedicated it; he composed and delivered laws (to the colony); and three times he enrolled its senate. (*AE* 1996, 685)

Dispatched to settle new colonists in an already established but fragile colony, Luscus will not have needed to draw the *pomerium*. He did, however, perform three acts, each presumably essential to, and often well attested at, other foundations: he dedicated a temple; he gave the community its laws; and he enrolled its senate and so gave its social structure juridical force and permanence. What role did these actions play in establishing the Romanness of local religious life?

As it happens, the organization of public spaces, and the positioning of temples (and basilicas) in relation to them, are one area in which Roman theory and Roman practice not only harmonize, but harmonize across the centuries. This is as true of early colonies as of later western ones; and Roman ideas about the proper organization of public spaces came to have very considerable influence in the gradual development and occasional *de novo* rebuilding of Greek city centers in the east, where Roman practice diverged quite strongly from Greek (Hesberg 1985; Gros 1988; 1996a: 17–269; 1996b; Hölscher 1998). What is more, in describing early in the reign of Augustus the principles according to which "sacred buildings, the forum, and the other public spaces" were to be apportioned, Vitruvius famously gave pride of place to the Capitoline triad: "For the sacred buildings of those gods who seem especially to exercise guardianship over the city – to Jupiter, Juno and Minerva – plots should be assigned in the loftiest location, from which the greatest part of the walls might be seen" (Vitr. 1.7.1).

But it is not clear that Vitruvius intends a strictly normative statement. One might advance three cautions against reading him in that way. First, he acknowledges throughout that cities perforce develop in response to geographic, demographic, and political contingencies: in this very chapter, he allows that principles of temple placement vary if the city has no harbor, or gymnasium, or amphitheater. Second, in the books he later devotes to the situation and design of temples, he as much as acknowledges that while Rome offers exemplars of particular architectural styles, it does not offer exemplars of all; what is more, it cannot, by virtue of its long development, in any way serve as a paradigm of city planning. Third, it is by no means obvious that the tutelary deities of all colonies were – or could be – the same. Not surprisingly, then, Capitolia are rather less well attested in early and mid-republican colonies, but proliferated in the western provinces in the imperial period (Capua, many times colonized, acquired a Capitolium only under Tiberius: Suet. *Tiberius* 40) and there often served as loci for state rituals, not least the empire-wide prayer-oath commanded by Decius (Barton 1982; Ando 2000: 207–8). As with the *pomerium*, so with Capitolia, it may be that practice homogenized around a particular ideal in response to cultural changes at work in Rome in the late republic and early principate.

Titus Annius Luscus also gave to Aquileia its colonial charter, its *lex*. The charter of Aquileia does not survive. But even before we lament that loss, we must recall that the very possession of a charter in itself distinguished colonies from Rome, which famously resisted the codification of what the Severan jurist Ulpian called *ius publicum*, the body of law governing its public affairs – its magistracies, priesthoods, and rites (Ando 2006). The attempt by the center thus to fix the structure of colonial life, and to overdetermine any deliberations regarding innovation, was thus both ahistorical and, after a fashion, untrue to Roman experience.

That said, we do possess extensive clauses of the *lex coloniae Iuliae Genetivae* – the colonial charter of ancient Urso, near modern Osuna, in Spain (*ILS* 6087; *FIR Bruns* 28; *FIRA²* 21). Urso was founded in 44 BC, by an unknown magistrate; the charter itself repeatedly cites the authority and authorship of Julius Caesar. Its religious clauses have recently been subjected to careful scrutiny (Rüpke 2006b), and constraints of space permit me here to gesture only to two important conclusions of that reading. First, the charter assigns to the *duumviri*, in consultation with the decurions, the task of determining "which days will be festal, and how many, and what rites will be performed publicly, and who shall perform them" (*Lex Ursonensis* c. 64). Second, the charter provides for the institutionalization of two priesthoods, *pontifices* and *augures*, but, remarkably, assigns them virtually no powers or responsibilities whatsoever (*Lex Ursonensis* c. 66–8). That is, although the charter provides for the replication in the colony of the two most prestigious colleges of priests at Rome, it seemingly removes from them all significant functions held by their counterparts at Rome, in particular, the pontiffs' control of the calendar and the augurs' power to stop public actions through *obnuntiatio*. One effect is to transfer control over public religion in a very limited sense to the public: in comparison with Rome, significant authority is removed from life-long priests and transferred to elected magistrates and the city council.

The degree of autonomy granted the decurions at Urso is perhaps best revealed by comparison with another centrally produced document, the Feriale Duranum, the calendar of the auxiliary *cohors XX Palmyrenorum*, produced early in the second quarter of the third century AD for a military unit stationed in Mesopotamia. To be sure, it was directed at a military and not a civilian body. Nevertheless, it commends to them the celebration of an enormous number of specifically Roman holidays, and precludes all possibility of local variation beyond the capacity to celebrate the "birthday" of their unit. In particular, neither the ethnic origin of the unit, nor the religious landscape in which it served, makes any impression upon its official celebrations (*P. Dura* 54 = *Roman Military Records on Papyri* 117).

Against such normative documents as charters and army calendars must be set an astonishing array of evidence for local diversity and, often enough, for careful replication of Roman institutions (fine particularized studies include Rives 1995; Belayche 2001: 108–219; 2003). These might even go hand in hand. Two particularly fascinating examples of this phenomenon include the inscription of a *lex sacra* at Carthage (Ennabli 1999) and the worship of Mater Matuta at Beirut (Kaizer 2005). The *lex sacra* concerns public cult (Ennabli frag. 3, line 3), directed to a variety of deities in a number of locations. Almost all the names of the gods are lost, though one set of rites is to be performed at the Capitolium (Ennabli frag. 7), and the identity of other gods can be conjectured with considerable confidence from the words that do survive. These name an astonishing variety of specialized offerings, and occasionally specify the structures, even temporary structures, in which they should be made; and both the offerings and structures have parallels at Rome and in central Italy. What is novel is the inclusion of Abaddir (Ennabli frag. 5, line 2): in Roman eyes, evidently a local god, but more likely in origin a Punic baityl. Mater Matuta's worship at Beirut is known from an imperial dedication by a woman with

Latin, Greek, and Semitic names (*CIL* 3.6680 = *ILS* 3490). As its most recent read-
ing points out, the dedication confronts us with a number of questions. Did Flavia
Nicolais Saddane's use of the name "Mater Matuta" point in some unproblematic
fashion to the same deity as was worshiped in Rome? Almost certainly not: Mater
Matuta was likely to have been the local *interpretatio* of the Greek goddess
Leucothea, who may herself have been identified with a local (Semitic) god.

About both these texts we should like to know when – and whence – the worship of their problematic gods began. How soon after the foundation of the colonies
did the worship of indigenous deities by Roman citizens begin? Through whose agency?
Was it the result of intermarriage? The importation of deities by the newly enfran-
chised? These texts are examples only, of a phenomenon widely attested in colonial
life. Some such dedications and *leges sacrae* may well reflect developments in local
religion away from whatever framework was imposed at the moment of foundation.
But we should be not therefore conclude that the developments to which they attest
amount to deviance, or a falling away from some ideal, for two reasons. First, the
one extensive colonial charter in our possession makes specific allowance for local
initiative; and, second, Roman religion at Rome was not static either.

Municipalities

As with colonies, so the legal and political frameworks defining the communities known
as *municipia* (municipalities) changed over time. The category emerges with some
distinctness in the legal landscape of the fourth century, though it has clear
antecedents in earlier arrangements between Rome and its neighbors. Its defining
characteristics at that time may be described as consisting in autonomy in matters
of self-governance for the community as a whole, together with a set of rights and
obligations attached to its citizens, in particular the obligation to serve in military
units in support of Roman campaigns, and the right to attain Roman citizenship
upon migration to Rome (Sherwin-White 1973; Humbert 1978). For our interests,
the subsequent history of the *municipium* has two principal turning points. The
first was the Social War, whose settlement issued in the enfranchisement of the
population of Italy but the classification of its communities as *municipia* (or, to
be precise, all its communities that were not already colonies). Second, starting at
the very end of the second century BC and continuing into the high empire, Roman
magistrates arranged for grants of municipal status to provincial cities. This latter
process seems to have achieved regular form in the reign of Augustus, when a model
charter was written that, in one form or another, was deployed throughout the western provinces (Galsterer 1987). These developments extended the concept of the
municipium in two potentially contradictory ways: the settlement of the Social War
made concrete what had theretofore been merely potential, namely, the existence of
communities consisting entirely of Roman citizens but which nevertheless maintained
distinct traditions at the level of public law (including religion), while the drafting
of a model charter certainly had the potential to constrain the autonomy that once
served as the municipality's distinguishing characteristic – precisely the issue upon
which Gellius remarked (see above). What in fact do we find?

In point of fact, much surviving evidence, early and late, points to considerable interest in local cults on the part of Romans at Rome and in provincial communities. But its interpretation is problematic. For example, nearly the earliest significant evidence for official Roman state interaction with cults outside Rome – at least, evidence contemporaneous with the events it describes or, as in this case, the events of which it is a product – records radical action against local manifestations of the cult of Bacchus (*ILS* 18; on this event see North 1979; Cancik-Lindemaier 1996; de Cazanove 2000b; and cf. de Cazanove 2000a). The extant *senatus consultum* of 186 BC raises concern on two grounds relevant here. First, it explicitly embraces non-citizen communities in its effects; indeed, the one extant copy was found in southern Italy, outside Roman territory. And yet our major literary source for this episode – Livy, book 39 – concentrates on the arrival of the cult at Rome and the disturbances it caused there. The second cause for concern is that Roman priestly law as it emerges in antiquarian writings of the first century BC explicitly excluded non-citizens from its ambit, and there are good reasons for thinking that reconstruction appropriate (see the section on "*Reichsreligion*," below). On what religious or political grounds did the Romans interfere in the religious life of alien Italians?

One answer arises from detailed consideration of the content of the *senatus consultum* itself, especially in light of what we learn from Livy (see also Ando 2003: 5–11). That answer harmonizes with some considerably later Roman attempts to reconstruct mid-republican practice, as well as with imperial evidence for Roman interference in the institutions of social life in provincial towns; and this evidence is up to a point self-reinforcing. In particular, the senate's decree orders no changes in the forms of ritual practiced by cult members, beyond commanding that no man shall be a priest. But Livy records – on what evidentiary basis, we do not know – that the cult had only recently admitted men to its priesthood; and it may be that the senate's action should be understood in that light. If this is correct, then the senate was acting in particular against the behaviors of cult members in relation to each other, and not in relation to the god: Rome wished, therefore, to preclude the possibility that cults could serve as vehicles for achieving local solidarity. Regarded in this fashion, the action taken against the Bacchalia can be read against the very considerable evidence under the empire for official disapproval of *collegia* – a term that embraces guilds, fraternities, and other private clubs (Pliny, *Epist.* 10.34; *Digestae* 47.22).

This reading of the senate's action against the worshipers of Bacchus should be compared with the fate of Fregellae, a colony of Latin status established in 328 where the Liris emerges from the Apennines into the plain (Livy 8.22.2). Fregellae revolted from Roman dominance under mysterious circumstances in 125 BC (evidence for the revolt and punishment is sparse: Cic. *De inventione* 2.105 and *De finibus* 5.62; Livy, *Per.* 60; Asconius p. 17.17–22 Clark; *De viris illustribus* 65.2). Writing a little over a century later, the Greek geographer Strabo described Fregellae in his day as "just a village, but it [was once] a noteworthy city, which held in attribution many of the surrounding cities": "now those cities come together at Fregellae, to hold markets and perform certain rites" (5.3.10). As with the controls imposed upon the cult of Bacchus, the Romans appear in Fregellae ostentatiously (and perhaps piously) to have allowed or insisted upon the continuation of cult even when

they worked to dismantle the civic framework that almost undoubtedly had made
that cult meaningful.

The cults of Fregellae thus constitute an extreme variant upon what the second-
century AD lexicographer Festus calls *municipalia sacra*, "municipal rites": "Those
sacra are called *municipalia* which a people had from its origin, before receiving
Roman citizenship, and which the *pontifices* wanted them to continue to observe
and perform in the way in which they had been accustomed to perform them
from antiquity" (Festus 146 L). Festus here as elsewhere draws upon the historical
and taxonomic efforts of late republican and Augustan scholars, notably Marcus
Terentius Varro and Verrius Flaccus. Bracketing for the moment changes in their
ideological and intellectual contexts, their efforts are united by a desire to render
the vast and variegated data of Roman religious history comprehensible. The respect
accorded to non-Roman cults in a new, Roman context – a context framed by the
presence of citizens but not by some extension of the Roman state – is thus notable.
It suggests the convergence of two quite different histories, one in which foreign
cultural practices were domesticated through their inclusion in the norms of Roman
law, and another in which imperial expansion forced a broadening in Rome's own
cultural and anthropological awareness (Ando forthcoming a: ch. 6).

As we move out to the provinces and forward to the principate, we must recall
the significant differences in the legal framework that shaped the development
of provincial municipalities under the principate in contradistinction to that of
the municipalities of Italy in the years after the Social War. Most importantly, the
municipalities of the empire were not composed exclusively of citizens. Rather, the
communities had what was known as "Latin status," which meant above all that their
magistrates obtained Roman citizenship upon their departure from office. What is
more, significant grants of municipal status to provincial cities began only under the
principate. In other words, it followed upon the theoretical and historical work of
Roman intellectuals and jurists of the late republic. It therefore represents, if anything, a self-aware development not so much upon historical practice in Roman Italy
as upon the particular understandings of that practice achieved in the latter half of
the first century BC.

With that caution in mind, let us turn to the provinces. There we find, in addition to a host of evidence in the form of dedications, titles of priests, and the like,
one remarkably well-preserved normative text, namely, the *lex Flavia municipalis* –
a municipal charter drafted at Rome for the cities of Spain, to which area in its entirety
Vespasian granted Latin status (fragments have been located in several cities;
González 1986 provides a composite text and translation, of which Galsterer 1988
provides a useful overview). Any cities therein that had previously been alien and
tributary were thus raised to municipal status. But the imposition of a uniform charter in itself draws attention to the paradoxical and limited nature of the autonomy
that in the public law tradition remembered by Gellius had been the municipality's
distinctive characteristic. For as the empire grew and interactions between Romans
and aliens increased exponentially, it became more and more in the central government's interest to standardize the scope and, indeed, the particulars of local
autonomy. As a result, the range of issues in both public and civil law left to local

decision-making had become by the Flavian era highly restricted (Humbert 1978). What of religion in this scheme?

Unfortunately, the composite text of the Flavian charter commences with the nineteenth chapter, and it is overwhelmingly likely that public rites and priesthoods were treated in the missing chapters (Galsterer 1988: 79). But the actions of magistrates in the Roman world almost always had a religious component, and much can be reconstructed from extant clauses on public finances, games, and judicial business about the nature and form of public religion under the charter. I single out three conclusions of particular importance.

First, allowance is made for the continuance of cult from the community's life before it became a colony. This is revealed by a chapter on the arrangement of spectators at public spectacles:

<LXXXI> Rubric. Concerning seating at games.

People should watch the games given in this municipality in the same seats in which their class sat at spectacles before this charter, so long as it is in accordance with a decree of the decurions or *conscripti*, and so long as it is in accordance with past and future plebiscites, *senatus consulta*, edicts and decrees of the divine Augustus, Tiberius Julius Caesar Augustus, Tiberius Claudius Caesar Augustus, Imperator Galba Caesar Augustus, Imperator Vespasian Caesar Augustus, Imperator Titus Cesar Augustus, and Imperator Domitian Caesar Augustus. (*Lex Flavia municipalis* ch. 81)

The chapter clearly envisions a continuity of practice before and after the change in status. Admittedly, no specific provisions are here made regarding the identity of the gods honored at the spectacles, nor has any constraint regarding the maintenance of pre-Roman cults been preserved. But in light of the power granted even to colonies to control their pantheon and calendar through majority decision of their council, and in light of Festus' claims regarding so-called "municipal rites," it seems prudent to grant that power to the Flavian municipalities.

Second, the councils of Flavian municipalities appear to have had control of their calendar and, as a consequence, of their pantheon, analogous to that granted to colonies, as illustrated in the Caesarean charter of Urso. For in the clauses regulating the conduct of legal affairs, judicial business is explicitly prohibited

on those days which it is or will be appropriate to have and regard as festal and holy for the sake of honoring the imperial house, or on those days on which games are given in the municipality in accordance with a decree of the decurions or *conscripti*, or on those days on which a meal or distribution of meat is given to the townsmen or dinner is given at municipal expense to the decurions or *conscripti*, or on those days in which assemblies are held in the *municipium*, or on those days on which in accordance with this law, public business is postponed for the sake of the harvest or vintage. . . . (*Lex Flavia municipalis* 92)

Again, the clause regarding the establishment of games by the council of the municipality seems to rely upon an earlier clause that, on the analogy of the charter of

Urso, will have granted the magistrates the power to fix a religious calendar – to decide, in other words, what gods would be honored publicly, and when – in accordance with a majority decision on the part of the council.

Third and last, the worship of certain gods and performance of specific religious actions were stipulated by Rome. We have already seen that the charter set aside certain days "for the sake of honoring the imperial house." In addition, it orders magistrates to swear their oaths of office (separate oaths were taken when entering and exiting public office) "openly in an assembly, by Jupiter, the divine Augustus, the divine Claudius, the divine Vespasian Augustus, the divine Titus Augustus, the *Genius* of Imperator Caesar Domitian Augustus and the *dei Penates*," that they would act, or had acted, in accordance with the law and in the best interest of the town (*lex Flavia municipalis* ch. 26; cf. ch. G, 59, 69, and 73). The insinuation of a divine role for the deified and current emperors is scarcely surprising. But the presence of the *dei Penates* is; all the more so, the absence of the Capitoline triad. Regarding the last, our analysis is hampered by the absence of an immediately contemporary colonial charter; the absence of the triad there would be even more surprising. As it stands, we cannot fix an explanation along a range, one pole of which attributes the absence precisely to the municipal rather than colonial status of the town, and the other to the replacement of the Capitoline triad by the imperial house. The first explanation esteems the conservative nature of Roman public law, and relies upon the fact that municipalities, no matter how many Roman citizens they contained, were nevertheless not wholly and integrally subsumed within the *populus Romanus*. The second points us toward that moment, visible in Christian martyr acts, when Roman magistrates might say to Christians: "We, too, are religious. Our religion is a simple one: we swear by the *Genius* of our lord the emperor and we offer prayers for his health, something that you, too, should do" (*Passio S. Scillitanorum* 3, 14; cf. Tert. *Apol.* 24.9; see Ando 2000: 385–98; cf. Rives 1999).

Reichsreligion

The presence of the *dei Penates* in the municipalities of Spain causes some surprise, for two reasons. First, the Penates were understood to be the household gods of Aeneas, which he transported from Troy to Rome. By that standard metonymy which identifies the household of the king with the polity he rules, the Romans came to regard Aeneas' Penates as the common and peculiar gods of the *populus Romanus*. Their implication in Roman political mythology, and in particular in that reasoning which viewed the power of the consuls as directly continuous with that formerly exercised by the kings, was so great that no magistrate with *imperium* was held to be legitimately installed in office until he had first sacrificed before Vesta and the Penates. For that reason, we might have expected the Penates to appear in oaths in colonies, but not in a notionally alien community – except, perhaps, as an index of just how Roman such communities in fact were. The second reason to be surprised at the Penates' presence in Spain is that we know where they were, and that was not in Spain. They were in Lavinium (Thomas 1990; Scheid 1993; Ando 2003: 220–1, 229–30).

Indeed, Roman legend and political practice together suggest that the residence of the Penates in Lavinium was both odd and well known. For on the one hand, magistrates had to go to them to sacrifice. That is, newly elected magistrates formally left Rome and journeyed to Lavinium, there to sacrifice to the Penates, in order to complete their installation in their Roman magistracy. And not surprisingly, the very considerable lore that grew up around the Penates devotes considerable energy to explaining precisely that fact. It concentrates above all on what is described as their choice to dwell there. In the version related by Valerius Maximus, upon his arrival in Italy, Aeneas founded the city of Lavinium and there installed his household gods. When his son Ascanius subsequently founded Alba, he moved his ancestral gods to the new city. The very next day, the gods were discovered back in their former *sacrarium.* "Since it was considered possible that this had been the work of human hands," the gods were moved again. "They made their will apparent by removing themselves a second time" (Val. Max. 1.8.7).

The stories that circulated around the *dei Penates* – the need to explain their location – gestures toward a problem central to the concerns of this chapter. Simply stated, it is this. In Roman religion, not all gods moved; nor was it always possible to perform cult wheresoever one willed – to say nothing of performing a ritual in two places simultaneously. To observe this is to strike asunder the very expectation that has traditionally motivated the study of our topic. This is not to say that Roman religion writ large did not spread – specific forms of rituals, governing principles, bodies of law, indeed, specific gods moved as their practitioners and worshipers did. What the invocation of the Penates demands is rather some consideration of the constraints internal to Roman religion upon its export.

To illustrate the scope and nature of Roman investment in geographic fixity, for lack of a better term, we might turn to two bodies of evidence. The first concerns gods like the Penates, who consent or refuse to move, as well as the rituals by which their removal was effected; the second concerns those bodies of religious law that regulated borders and the status of land.

Perhaps the best evidence for gods who move – or move Roman-style – is the literature that developed around accounts of *evocatio*, "summoning forth," a ritual in which a Roman commander invites the tutelary deity of a city to abandon its charge and accept equivalent or greater worship at Rome (Le Gall 1976; Blomart 1997; Gustaffson 2000; Ando forthcoming b: ch. 6). Only two lengthy accounts of the rite survive from antiquity: that of Livy, writing in the 20s BCE about the sack of Veii in the first decade of the fourth century (5.21.1–5, 22.3–7); and that of Macrobius, writing in the late 420s CE about the sack of Carthage 560 years earlier (*Saturnalia* 3.9). To these we can add perhaps another three cases for which Romans under the republic provide specific testimony. By the early principate, however, Roman historians and theorists of empire commonly made much more general claims, to the effect that all the gods of the empire had once been summoned, and now were resident at Rome. To that argument I shall return. Livy provides, however, our only narrative of the rite, and he insists not simply that the goddess explicitly assented to the move, but that she expressed her assent through her statue and, indeed, that the transfer of her cult statue from Veii to Rome amounted to the removal of the goddess herself (Livy 5.22.3–7).

Since our interest here is in the movement of gods and cults, and not in imperialism or foreign gods or a specific rite, we can bracket for the moment issues of context and simply adduce several further examples of gods who moved, or declined to do so, in response to Roman requests. Perhaps the most famous such god is Cybele, the Great Mother, an Anatolian goddess whom the Romans were told to bring from her shrine in Asia to Rome in the final years of the Hannibalic War (Beard et al. 1998: 96–8). Two extended literary accounts of her transfer survive, by Livy and by Ovid, and they share several features relevant to this argument. I single out two. First, both authors identify the goddess with her baityl – that is to say, each slips unproblematically between references to "the stone," "the image," and "the goddess" (Livy 29.11.7, 14.10–14; Ov. *Fast.* 4.317). Second, both authors imagine that the adoption of a new cult requires the presence of the god, and each supposes that in this case, at least, the goddess somehow is a particular cult object. As a consequence, we might conclude that the location of the cult object fixes the location of the goddess, and restricts her worship to that site. This would, I suspect, be too narrow a conclusion. But that it is conceivable amounts to an urgent caution against naturalizing the notions attendant upon "spreading": that one can worship a god wheresoever one chooses, regardless of wherever else that god is worshiped; and, for that matter, that gods desire more worshipers, from more places, races, and walks of life.

Comparable in its focus on the will of a god – in this case, on the god's desire not to move – is the story of the god Terminus ("Boundary"), who was asked to leave his temple in order to clear ground for a new temple to Jupiter. The sources differ whether the ritual used was *evocatio* or *exauguratio*, the latter a ritual by which his temple would have been desacralized in respect of him, freeing the land to be rededicated to another purpose. They agree, however, that Terminus declined, and so remained where he was (see esp. Festus s.v. Nequitum 160 L, citing Cato's *Origines* frag. 24 Peter; Livy 1.55). Further examples might easily be adduced; but the point is so far established.

The other substantial body of evidence on Roman religion's commitment to a particular sacred geography derives from Roman writings on religious law. That literature, which must now be reconstructed from scattered allusions and quotations, spans several centuries and embraces what were taken to be several distinct bodies of law, each of which underwent internal change over time and yet differed, the one from the others. Their specific content, and the content of those changes, are not at issue here. I wish only to stress how many were the ways in which those bodies of law figured the city of Rome as ritually and religiously distinct.

So, for example, according to Varro, augural law provided for the division of land into five categories: Roman, Gabine, alien, hostile, and indeterminate (Varro, *Ling.* 5.33). In continuing to provide specifically for Gabine land, augural law appears to have been ossified at an early stage in Rome's development – Gabii was allied to Rome in the early fifth century but more or less disappears from the historical record in the fourth century BC. But what is important here is not so much the specific distinction drawn, but that it was drawn at all. Similarly, for the taking of auspices, it was crucial that holders of *imperium* distinguish between civilian and non-civilian space, a border marked by the *pomerium*. The information gleaned by the taking of auspices was vitiated if the magistrate crossed the *pomerium* (see e.g. Cic. *Nat.* 2.10–12). The *pomerium* functioned similarly in other contexts, to distinguish Roman civilian space as essentially removed from war. So, when receiving embassies, the senate met only those from friendly and allied states within the *pomerium*; those whose status was hostile or unknown were met outside (Bonnefond-Coudry 1989: 137–51).

Perhaps the most trenchant evidence comes from the correspondence between Pliny the younger and the emperor Trajan during the former's stint as governor of Bithynia-Pontus. Pliny several times consulted Trajan on matters of pontifical law, and in every case Trajan demurred, urging that pontifical law did not apply because, in essence, provincial lands were fundamentally not Roman, and so exempt (for better or worse) from the operations of Roman religious law. For example, when Pliny wrote to ask Trajan whether he could safely approve the moving of the Great Mother's temple in Nicomedia, he expressed concern that he could not locate a *lex* – a statute, a written set of regulations – for the temple. He diagnosed the problem as deriving from the fact that "the method of consecration practiced in Nicomedia was *alium apud nos*, different from that practiced among us." Trajan responded that Pliny could be "without fear of violating religious scruple," as the *solum peregrinae civitatis capax non sit dedicationis, quae fit nostro iure*, as the "soil of an alien city cannot receive consecration as it is performed according to our law" (*Epist.* 10.49f.).

In another case, Pliny wrote regarding the desire of "certain persons" to move the remains of their relatives. "Knowing that in our city cases of this kind are customarily brought before the college of *pontifices*," Pliny thought he should consult Trajan as *pontifex maximus*. Trajan responded by suggesting that "it would be a burden to enjoin provincials to approach the *pontifices* if for just reasons they want to move the remains of their relatives from one place into another place" (10.68–9). What Trajan does not explain here, but which emerges from other evidence, is that the authority of the *pontifices* in particular, but that of other colleges, too, was expanding in geographic extent (see e.g. *ILS* 1792 from AD 130, which records a grant of permission by the *pontifices* to transfer a corpse into Italy from without; or *ILS* 4037 from AD 213, which records the restoration of an altar to Circe at Circeii, southwest of Rome, in accordance with a decree of the *quindecimviri sacris faciundis*). An early piece of evidence for this concerns an attempt by the equestrian order at Rome to dedicate a statue to *Fortuna equestris*, Equestrian Fortune. At first they were unable to find a temple to that goddess in Rome. When they did find one, in Antium, *repertum est*, "it was discovered that all the rites, temples and idols of the gods in the towns of Italy were *iuris atque imperii Romani*, under the law and power of Rome" (Tac. *Ann.* 3.71.1). But there progress stopped, the provinces destined forever to remain, as a matter of law, religiously not Roman.

Conclusion

In conclusion, let me concentrate on three issues raised by the material above. These are, first, the problem of concentrating on civic rather than private corporate bodies or, for that matter, individuals; second, the problem of historical change in the conceptualizations that restrained or promoted the spread of Roman religion; and third, the devising of frameworks within which to compare religions that spread with those that don't.

I have concentrated in this chapter upon civic religion – upon the religious practices and institutions performed by elected or appointed magistrates and organized through public law. According to Roman lights, this was Roman religion (Ando 2003: 1–3, citing earlier work; Ando and Rüpke 2006). The practices of individuals, families, and *gentes* were held specific to them, and formed part of private practice. What we tend to call "state" cult was, for them, "Roman," precisely because it was shared: participation in it – one's stake in its validity, performance, and outcomes – was entailed by membership in the Roman community.

It follows, then, that the practices of citizens abroad, whether that of individuals or expatriate communities, might and almost invariably did share in central philosophical, theological, and practical aspects of Roman civil religion, but at the same time they were not expected to do so. They were not understood to be organized in any fundamental or necessary way according to Roman principles, or supervised by Roman priests, or performed by Roman magistrates. That they were a mechanism by which Roman practice became familiar to non-Romans must, of course, be true; but that history must be separately unfolded.

Second, the changes adumbrated above in the ideology of colonization and in the public law framework of municipal autonomy took place alongside changes in religious thought and practice. These are significant in themselves; together, they also form a significant index of developments in the ideology of empire itself. At one point, for example, the poet Virgil describes a battle between Octavian and Mark Antony as mirrored by a battle in heaven between the gods of Rome and those of Egypt (Virg. *Aen.* 8.675–713). In the same era, Livy ascribed to the early fourth-century leader Camillus a speech deploring the possibility that the Romans might desert the recently sacked city of Rome and decamp to the recently acquired and significantly undamaged city of Veii (5.51–4). The passage was no doubt influenced by contemporary rumors that Mark Antony wished to make Alexandria rather than Rome the capital of the empire. But there is more, for what Livy through Camillus insists upon is the peculiarly Roman nature of a religion that can be practiced only at Rome itself.

By the high empire, many Romans looked back knowingly on that earlier prejudice against Egyptian cults (see most pointedly Servius on Virg. *Aen.* 8.698). They also wrote histories of Roman expansion, and of cult practice in that period, in which Rome had systematically brought all the gods of the empire to Rome (see e.g. Min. Fel. 6.2ff.). On the one hand, these histories reflect a substantial expansion in the capacities of Roman self-understanding, and provide one measure of the greater cosmopolitanism of high imperial culture. On the other, it is not so obvious how a religion in the business of importing the gods of others might then conceive the exporting of its own.

This is not to say that some specifically Roman cults and ritual actions did not spread under the empire. The most obvious examples of them are imperial cult and the periodic swearings of loyalty required by the central government. But the concerns of those actions were decidedly locative (cf. J. Smith 1990). That is to say, like more highly localized civic cults, the cults and rituals of the empire made sense only within a specific geographic, political, and historical context, and they aimed to attract and cement the support of the divine in the maintenance of the conditions, institutions, and personalities of the here and now. In that respect, too, the Roman cults of the Roman empire should be distinguished from Christianity, in ambition a truly imperialist cult the empire inadvertently bequeathed to the world.

FURTHER READING

Perhaps the best place to start is the wide-ranging chapter on "Roman religion and Roman empire" in Beard et al. (1998: 1.313–63). The differences in perspective between my chapter and that one should provoke salutary reflection. Gargola (1995) is an exceptionally valuable study of the pragmatics of republican colonization, with insights throughout into the rituals involved in the founding of colonies. Next one might turn to one of several studies of the religious life of particular communities: Rives (1995) and Belayche (2001) concentrate on colonies; Mitchell (1993: vol. 2), and Woolf (1998: 206–37) offer regional studies.

Among the separate foci of this chapter, particular emphasis should be given to the colonial and municipal charters, on the one hand, and to the separate information contained in the so-called *leges sacrae*, regulations governing specific cults. Rüpke (2006b) studies the colonial charter of Urso; the best essay on the "Romanization" of municipal life in the provinces is Scheid (1999b). An empire-wide study of cult regulations is lacking. For the monumental context for Roman and provincial cult practice see Gros (1996a: 122–206).

CHAPTER THIRTY

Religion in the Roman East

Ted Kaizer

Religion in the eastern provinces of the Roman world was not, it seems, what one would have called "Roman." In the larger sites of Greece and Asia Minor the main gods were those known since the days of Homer: Athena and Zeus in Athens, Artemis in Ephesus, and Apollo at his oracles in Claros, Didyma, and Delphi. In the rural areas of Anatolia, deities depicted on horseback, so-called "rider-gods," were especially popular, including the Moon-god Men and a divine couple called *Hosios kai Dikaios* ("the Pious and the Just"; Delemen 1999). Different sub-regions could be characterized by peculiar forms of worship. In Lydia, the so-called "confession inscriptions" emphasize how worshipers attempted to placate the fury of the gods following sinful behavior (Petzl 1998; Rostad 2002). And in Phrygia, peasants' sanctuaries have revealed numerous small votive steles on marble, dedications of inscribed reliefs to local gods such as Zeus Ampeleites ("of the grape vine") and Zeus Thallos ("the young branch"), recording the yearnings and hopes of the inhabitants of the countryside (Drew-Bear et al. 1999). The further east one goes, the more exotic the cults become. In Rome's real orient, the lands of Syria, Mesopotamia, and Arabia, worship often centered on deities with obscure names and attributes: Bel, Yarhibol, and Aglibol in Palmyra, Azzanathkona in Dura-Europos, and Dusares in the Nabataean realm (Eissfeldt 1941; R. Turcan 1996). Sacrifices were made on high places or in indigenous sanctuaries which often followed ancient Mesopotamian plans, before being adapted to Greek architectural models. Rites were conducted by priests with peculiar headgear and dress. According to all outward appearances, religion in the east looked very different from a Roman perspective. Semitic and other non-classical languages (and their respective scripts) were used alongside Greek in the inscriptions documenting the cults. And the gods and their worshipers were often depicted in sculptures and other visual representations in hieratic fashion and with other non-classical features such as a consistent frontality.

"Roman" Religion in the East

That is not to say that "Roman" religion as such was completely absent in the east. There are three main aspects which need to be mentioned in this regard, although the division was maybe not always as clear-cut as we would like. First, with the foundation of a Roman colony came, traditionally, a certain religious export package, in order for the colony to mirror the imperial capital not only in an institutional but also a cultic sense: a set of Roman gods (headed by the Capitoline triad of Jupiter, Juno, and Minerva) and also some specifically Roman priesthoods, such as *pontifices* and *augures*. In the Near East, this process can be traced, for example, at Berytus (present-day Beirut), a city founded as a colony under Augustus which later became famous for its Roman law schools, and at Jerusalem, refounded under Hadrian as the colony Aelia Capitolina, the first part of that name being a reflection of the emperor's family name. Other places in the Near East acquired colonial status only later in the Roman period, simply by imperial grant, without veterans of the Roman armies settling there. In such cases, Roman gods and priesthoods were often hard to find. Thus, at the Syrian desert city of Palmyra, which officially became a colony in the early third century, the indigenous divine world or "pantheon" remained unaffected when the new institutional structures of the colony were implemented.

Secondly, with the one-man rule that came over the Roman world with Augustus, the so-called "imperial cult," in the form of sacrifices and other rituals focusing on the emperor himself "as on a god," swiftly spread over the empire's eastern provinces. The very designation "imperial cult" is something of a misnomer. On the level of the Roman state cult, the living emperor was head of the important college of pontiffs (*pontifex maximus*), but not himself a god. Only after his death could he, if the senate voted so, become a *divus*. On any other level, however, the emperor's subjects could grant him divine honors as they wished (Gradel 2002). That being said, there are of course well-known instances where a request on the part of provincials for worship was turned down, or at least adjusted, by the emperor, in a public show of moderation. Tacitus, for example, paraphrases a speech supposedly given by Tiberius in reaction to an application from the provinces for permission to build him and Livia a shrine (*Ann.* 4.38), and an inscription from Gytheion (on the south Peloponnesian coast) quotes a letter from Tiberius to that city recording his satisfaction with "honors more modest and of a human sort" (*EJ*[2] 102b, with Sherk 1988: no. 31). But in general our evidence overwhelmingly suggests that the living emperor commonly received a cult in the eastern provinces, and the modern question of whether the inhabitants actually "believed" that their emperor was a "real god" is the result of looking through Christianized glasses, and obscures more than it reveals. Contrary to what happened in the western provinces, which seem to have had imperial cult more thrust upon them, the existing civic structures in the Greek east were such that worship of the emperor, both the living one and his predecessors, was incorporated more easily, and also more eagerly, into local religious frameworks (Price 1984). For citizens and provincials alike, treating the emperor in the same way as one would treat a traditional god was one way to accommodate the new power structure to which they were now accountable. Asia Minor was filled with dedications to the ruling emperor, and even as far east as Palmyra in Syria we can find a *Caesareum* or *Sebasteion*.

Possibly our best example comes from the west coast of present-day Turkey, from Ephesus. Here we see how the cult of the emperor is integrated within the civic and religious structures of a city dominated by the famous temple of Artemis. A lengthy inscription, recording substantial donations to the cult of this goddess by a local benefactor named Salutaris, described among other things in meticulous detail how, in addition to images of Artemis, imperial statues were to be carried in a religious procession and to be set up in a central place (Rogers 1991). A ritual that included both the cult of the local Artemis and that of the emperor provided the participants and spectators with a double sense of identity: adherence both to the local community and to the structures of imperial power. Indeed, the coinage issued by Ephesus confirms this, referring to the city's special position as being twice *neokoros* (literally "temple warden"), namely both of Artemis and of the emperor (Friesen 1993; Burrell 2004).

Thirdly, and potentially the strongest vehicle for spreading Roman religion to the outposts of empire, all divisions of the imperial army participated in the worship of those gods who had looked after Rome during its rise to world domination. Soldiers both in the legions and in the auxiliary units (the latter not consisting of Roman citizens, at least not under the early empire) were given guidelines on which sacrifice to perform, on what day, and to whom. Our best piece of evidence of such institutionalized adherence to Roman cults comes from the fortress town of Dura-Europos, located on the Euphrates: the archives of the auxiliary cohort which was stationed here in the third century AD contained a ritual calendar written on papyrus, the so-called *Feriale Duranum* (Welles et al. 1959: no. 54). The soldiers would sacrifice on days of important festivals of the city of Rome, on birthdays of members of the imperial family, and on other days commemorating imperial successes, to the gods who formed part of the Roman state cult, such as Mars the Avenger and Mother Vesta, or to the deified emperors themselves. In fact, the troops which used this calendar at Dura-Europos came from Palmyra, situated c. 200 km to the west in the Syrian steppe, a city whose religious life was not "Roman" at all; but if we had had only their calendar to go by, we would never have guessed their place of origin.

Interaction between "Rome" and the Indigenous Cults of the East

As it happens, we have more sources for the religious behavior of these same Palmyrene soldiers who were recruited under the Roman flag and found themselves stationed at the Euphrates. Unlike the official calendar, other evidence, in the form of inscriptions and sculptures, shows their involvement in a variety of local cults, which is indeed in accordance with the army's behavior throughout the empire at large. There is an abundance of material which shows how Roman soldiers, themselves of course seldom Roman in an ethnical sense as the empire progressed, took part in the worship of indigenous deities. They either continued to sacrifice to the ancestral gods of their hometown, as for example many Palmyrene soldiers who were enrolled in auxiliary units in Roman Dacia (present-day Romania) or north Africa did, or they made offerings to the gods of the locality where they were now stationed. Involvement in local cults took place on all levels, from an ordinary soldier of the fourth legion, based in Syria, who dedicated a small altar at Dura-Europos "to the ancestral god Zeus Betylos of those by the Orontes river" (*SEG* 7.341), to the Roman governor who traveled to Jerusalem to attend a Jewish festival (Josephus, *Antiquitates Iudaicae* 18.5.3 [122]).

When the Roman authorities were called in to act as arbitrators in the event of a clash between city and sanctuary, which happened regularly, their general attitude seems to have been one of sympathy toward the local cults. We can follow some of the stories through epigraphic dossiers, compilations of related inscriptions, often inscribed on the walls of the temples (Dignas 2002). When in the middle of the first century AD, the governor of Asia was called in to mediate between the famous temple of Artemis in Ephesus and those civic authorities who had borrowed money from the temple without repaying their divine creditor, he took sides with the temple in dissolving the administrative controversies. And a later governor of the province acted on behalf of the emperor when in the early second century AD the priests of a local Zeus at Aezani, a minor place situated inland in western Turkey, complained to the Roman authorities that some of the town's citizens held plots which belonged to the sanctuary without paying rent; in this case the governor wrote a letter in which he urged the restoration of the so-called sacred land. However, Rome could easily leave its positive attitude behind when the situation required different politics, especially when a place had backed the wrong horse in a situation of conflict: for example, because Tegea in Arcadia had supported Mark Antony in the civil war against Octavian, the later Augustus, the latter robbed the sanctuary of the town's local Athena of its sacred objects once he was established.

Interaction between local cults in the Roman east on the one hand and aspects of imperial religion on the other can also be encountered on a very different level. Some of the so-called toponymic deities in Syria, gods who were named after one particular locality, were given by their worshipers the epithets "Best" and "Greatest," originally belonging to Jupiter Optimus Maximus, the leading god of Rome, who had his temple on the Capitoline Hill in the imperial capital. In such cases the inscriptions, written in Latin (instead of Greek, which was the common language in Rome's eastern provinces) applied standard abbreviations (*IOM*) to label the gods. The two most famous examples are the local lords of Heliopolis (Baalbek in the Bekaa valley in Lebanon) and of Doliche (now a small village in eastern Turkey), both of whom were also depicted with a very recognizable, nearly canonical iconography. *IOMH(eliopolitanus)* was mostly portrayed as a beardless figure wearing a *kalathos* (some sort of fruit basket) on his head, standing on a plinth flanked by bulls, and enclosed in a sheath which was divided into a large number of sections displaying busts. He held a whip in his right hand and an ear in his left (Hajjar 1977, 1985). *IOMD(olichenus)* stood, characteristically, on the back of a bull, wearing a tiara and a tunic, and wielding an axe in his right hand, in an image which went back to Hittite precedents (Hörig and Schwertheim 1987). The worship of these deities, who both had a huge following in the Roman empire as a whole, above all among soldiers, clearly calls to mind the cult of the main Jupiter from Rome. But they were not the only ones, and the same borrowing of Jupiter's epithets happened in the cult of rather obscure deities such as "the Lord of the Dances," who received dedications at a sanctuary in the mountains near Berytus under the name of *IOMBalmarcod* (*CIL* 3.155), or the otherwise unknown *IOBeelseddes*, who was worshiped at a minor site in Syria called Timnin el-Tahta (*IGLS* 6.2925). By taking over the labels of Jupiter Optimus Maximus, these local gods, even the minor ones, laid claim via traditionally Roman means to a position of the highest cultic power. Simultaneously, key aspects of Roman religion were given the opportunity to penetrate the indigenous religious systems to which these gods belonged.

Greco-Roman Patterns of Religious Culture in Palmyra

It could be argued, however, that the influence of Rome on religious life in the east was traceable also in places which were less obviously permeated by aspects of Roman religion, even places in the orient which seem at best to have undergone the effects of Greek culture, and at worst to have maintained a dominant indigenous character. Let us look in some detail at Palmyra, a city with a unique local religious culture (Kaizer 2002). The inhabitants of its divine world came from various oriental spheres of influence: Bel and Nebu were originally Babylonian; Reshef and Shadrafa had a Phoenician background, Allat and Baal-Shamin were brought to the city by tribal groups, and Yarhibol and Aglibol originated at Palmyra itself. Sometimes the oriental deities are identified with Greek ones in the bilingual (Greek and Aramaic) inscriptions from the city, but in most cases it seems clear that the Greek name is secondary. They were worshiped in sanctuaries which had traditionally been built in mud-brick, centered on a sort of chapel or series of niches with an altar in front of it and set in a sacred enclosure, although, as time went by, most of them were gradually transformed into monumental Greco-Roman temples in the first three centuries AD. That the Palmyrene cults were indigenous and affected by Greek culture ("Hellenism") is certainly true. But that should not blind us to the fact that, simultaneously, Palmyra conformed to at least some of the general frameworks of religious behavior that were in vogue in other, more "typical," cities in the eastern provinces of the Roman empire, such as Ephesus and Antioch, and also the cities of the Syrian Decapolis. I will come back to Palmyra with examples of this soon, but first we will need to sketch briefly the setting of such patterns of religious culture in other places in the Roman east.

　　Whereas in the "culturally bare" western lands of its empire Rome found a reason to introduce its own language (Latin) as the *lingua franca* and its own imperial culture, Greece and (since Alexander the Great) Asia Minor and the Levant had Greek language and culture in common long before the imperial armies arrived on the spot. The Roman authorities could not do better than to take full advantage of the ready-made structures which they found at their disposal, and the eastern half of the Roman empire was therefore in a true sense "Greek." With only few exceptions, namely the above-mentioned colonies and the military sphere, nearly all business was conducted in Greek *koine*, the dialect in use in the eastern Mediterranean in Roman times along-side a variety of Semitic and other non-classical vernaculars. The Roman upper class aspired to be assimilated to Greek culture in general, and to be instructed in Greek mythology in particular (Cameron 2004). Above all, rather than filling the lands with its own imperial officials, Rome managed to rule the enormous subject area in the east through the existing structures of the quasi-autonomous cities and the collab-oration of their leading citizens. Though the final say in all truly important matters (i.e. taxation and military decisions) lay of course with Rome, civic culture in the eastern provinces was Greek, or, as it is usually named in order to accentuate the particular development which the cities' civilization underwent under Roman rule, "Greco-Roman" (Millar 1993b).

In the ideal type of the Greek city of the Roman period, territorial division of the citizen body found religious expression in public cults: each civic tribe had its own representative deity (A. Jones 1940). As regards Palmyra, the social structure of this desert city was built up around large clans and family groups, which we could also call "tribes," but tribes in a non-classical sense. Each of those groups had its own set of specific deities to look after, which makes it often difficult to distinguish between a deity functioning as a civic symbol for the inhabitants of one of the city's districts, and one acting as an ancestral god for a clan. Civic tribes (based on territorial divi-sion) and familial tribes (based on a historical or legendary common descent) are not mutually exclusive, and when Palmyra came firmly within the orbit of Roman power, new civic structures were introduced into the city, including tribes based on classical models, with their own civic cults (Kaizer 2002).

A second pattern of religious culture known from the Greco-Roman cities that can also be encountered at Palmyra is the phenomenon known as "euergetism": the system by which the upper class of the citizen body voluntarily made large dona-tions to the city's public works, among which, of course, were the construction of temples and the maintenance of rituals and priestly functions (Veyne 1990). The symbolic language used in the monumental Greek inscriptions which were erected throughout cities such as Antioch and Ephesus, especially in their public places, served to create a situation in which the benefactors and their descendants would be remem-bered "for ever." As regards Palmyra, the public inscriptions which reflect the city's social life were written not only in Greek, but also in a local dialect of Aramaic, and this "exotic" facet runs the risk of us focusing too much on local peculiarities, for example on the otherwise unknown names of the Palmyrene gods. However, the symbolic language that commemorated individual benefactions to the local cults at Palmyra was very much that of the Greco-Roman world at large.

In the eastern provinces of the Roman empire, the relationship between the human world and the divine sphere found expression in a combination of different sacrificial acts and other rituals, mirroring the various ways in which humans dealt with each other (Veyne 2000). Again, despite a number of local and oriental features at Palmyra (especially with regard to the Aramaic terminology used to describe ritual practice), there was a substantial correspondence between the Palmyrene sacrificial system and the methods of religious observance known from other cities in the Greco-Roman world. Also at Palmyra, the worshiper could reach the god by burning incense (the most common act) or by libation, through sacrifice proper (varying from small birds to large animals), by hosting the deity on a bed with cushions (a rite called *lectisternium* in Latin), or by placing offerings on a table in front of the image (in Greek: *trapezomata*), and above all by "sacred banqueting," dining and drinking in a religious setting under the auspices (or even in the symbolic presence) of the deity (sometimes called *theoxenia*). The complex sacrificial system at Palmyra corresponded thus at least partially to that in vogue in other cities of the Greek east, trading material and immaterial matters between man and god in an empire-wide process that further developed in a world dominated by Rome. Needless to say, these broad Greco-Roman patterns of religious behavior will also have affected the way in which indigenous, non-classical religious aspects functioned in the society of an "oriental" city such as Palmyra (Kaizer 2004). On the other hand, the available sources, especially the inscriptions, often give the impression that on a popular level religious life in the Near East hardly changed under Roman rule (Teixidor 1977). Standard religious formulae, which must have had a bearing on the essence of the act of worship, were applied in the inscriptions in seemingly unimaginative fashion, but that is of course not to say that these formulaic patterns continued to refer to unchanged religious notions.

Mythological and Religious Interest in the Past in the Second Sophistic

There is one source which will always need special mention in a discussion of religious life in the Near East in the imperial period, namely the pamphlet *On the Syrian Goddess*, traditionally ascribed to the famous satirist Lucian, who wrote in the second century AD. *On the Syrian Goddess,* or *De dea Syria* (*DDS*) as it is more commonly known, describes the temple and the cult of the Syrian goddess Atargatis at Hierapolis ("the holy city"), present-day Mabog in northern Syria. It is the only literary text we have that deals in detail with the cult of one particular, and important, temple in Syria under Roman rule, and – as a contemporary account of the cult by someone who claims to be an insider – potentially our best access to pagan worship in the region. However, any interpretation of this invaluable short text is as frustratingly difficult as its contents are fascinating. *DDS* is in the first place the masterly accomplishment of an author – whether indeed Lucian, who claims elsewhere to come from another north Syrian city, Samosata, or whether another, unknown (but equally skilled) literator – who produced on the linguistic level a complicated and nearly perfect imitation of the style of the work of Herodotus (Lightfoot 2003). Naturally, the observation that the author of *DDS* deliberately parodied the technique and fashion of the Greek historian who was known at least since Cicero (*Leg.* 1.5) as "the father of history" has serious consequences for the way in which we can use his text for historical purposes. Can we build any theories on the information about the cult given in *DDS*, for which there is no unequivocally corroborative evidence from Hierapolis outside the text? This is of course a much-debated question. Since *DDS* was, first and foremost, rigorously structured around a Herodotean model, the provision of accuracy with regard to the actual cultic realities at the temple of the Syrian goddess cannot have been at the forefront of the author's mind. Some fantastic exaggerations in *DDS*, for example a reference to columns at the temple's entrance of 600 feet in height (28), indeed hint at an attitude which was rather tongue-in-cheek. However, to make the joke (describing a temple in Roman Syria in the same manner in which Herodotus would have done it) work, the author would have needed to portray at least a *realistic* representation of religious life in the region. And to be able to do so he must have been familiar with many aspects of Near Eastern worship, which is of course what he claims in the opening lines: "I myself that write am an Assyrian" (1). Without giving an accurate or "true" picture of what went on in this specific temple at Hierapolis, *DDS* can therefore still be considered as emblematic of religious life in Rome's orient as a whole.

Viewed from a non-oriental perspective, the text is relevant also on a different level for what it reveals – though in deliberately confusing terms – about common Greco-Roman *perceptions* of what counted as "Near Eastern" (Elsner 2001). Exploring religious and other cultural identities was a very common feature, indeed the main characteristic, in the writings of most authors in this period, which was known as the "Second Sophistic." This label, which originated in antiquity itself, was given to a Greek cultural "movement," or rather the blossoming of a Greek literary culture, which harked back deliberately to the classical age, when Athens had been the center of the world (Bowie 1974; Swain 1996). The mythological interest in the past which is present in *DDS*, for example the listing of five different and contradictory traditions about the foundation of the temple at Hierapolis (12–27), has strong parallels in writings from the same period that cover the Greco-Roman world. Its most obvious exponent was the *Description of Greece*, written by Pausanias, who traveled as a tourist or pilgrim (depending on our definitions) through mainland Greece, where he visited temples and other antiquities from the classical period which were still there by the time he wrote in the second half of the second century AD. Pausanias was above all interested in the various stories which linked certain sanctuaries to specific gods and their various mythologies, and attempted to show a critical attitude toward what he was taught at the different places. In a certain way the Greek religious identity which his work thus helped to (re-)create provided a counterbalance to the domination of the Greek world by Rome (Elsner 1992).

Among other figures of this period that are relevant to a discussion of religion in the Roman east, mention ought to be made briefly of the voluminous writer Plutarch, who, as a local politician and highly educated philosopher, also held a priesthood at the temple of Apollo at Delphi for the last thirty years or so of his life. From his writings, datable to the last decennia of the first and the first decennia of the second century AD, we can distil an image of a man for whom religion was a very serious matter, combining a philosophical approach with professional participation in cultic life (Swain 1996). Simultaneously he investigated religious issues with historical questions in mind, producing works such as *On the Pythian Oracles, On the Decline of Oracles,* and *On Isis and Osiris.* One of the key figures of the Second Sophistic, he interpreted Roman rule as an agent of the divine sphere, and at the beginning of his career as an essayist he even wrote a piece called *On the Fortune of the Romans*, exploring the part played by Fortune and Virtue in Rome's ascent to world domination. Though never showing any clear sign of exasperation with the fact that his beloved world of Greek cities was now under the rule of Rome, Plutarch tended to minimize the empire's role (and also that of the leading citizens of the cities on whom Rome depended for the indirect manner of governing that empire, for that matter) when talking about the natural order, in favor of an interpretation which placed that order in the lap of the gods.

Religious Life in Dura-Europos

Returning from the intellectual level to what actually happened with regard to local cults, it must be emphasized that the framework of Roman rule of course *did* have an undeniable significance for the way in which the religious landscape, or rather landscapes, of the east could develop in the first three centuries AD. To illustrate this, we will finally, having come toward the end of this chapter, return to the fortress town of Dura-Europos on the Euphrates, since this site provides – thanks to the important archaeological findings which by far exceed its position in the ancient world – what is potentially our best case study for religious life in a normal small town under the empire. This "Pompey of the Syrian desert" was founded by one of Alexander's successors in the early Hellenistic period as a Macedonian colony, Europos, on a plateau overlooking the river, at a site called Dura. Toward the end of the second century BC the town came to be part of the Parthian empire. Only in AD 165 did it pass under Roman control, and remained so until the neo-Persian conquest and destruction in AD 256. Although there are some material remains that relate to the earlier periods, it is from the last ninety years of its history, when it belonged to the Roman empire, that most of our sources date.

In this Roman phase, Dura-Europos had a wide, kaleidoscopic spectrum of cults (Welles 1969). Some of these went back to the days when Europos was founded as a colony. Unfortunately, there is hardly any firm archaeological evidence for this earliest period, since the gridiron plan which is so characteristic of the map of the city, and in which most of the temples and other religious buildings were embedded, was implemented only later, toward the end of the second century BC. But an early Hellenistic origin can nonetheless be assumed for some cults. A parchment from AD 180 lists four men who during that year occupied the priesthoods of, respectively, Zeus (under the name of Zeus Olympios the main god for the Seleucids), Apollo (a patron deity for them), the *Progonoi* or ancestors (probably of a Seleucid king), and Seleucus Nicator (one of Alexander's generals and the founder of his own dynasty) (Welles et al. 1959: no. 25). Since by AD 180 Dura-Europos had been under Roman control for 15 years, it may evoke some surprise that these cults, which can all be linked with religious attitudes of the time of the city's foundation, would have survived the centuries of Parthian control into the period of Roman rule. It would be possible, however, to interpret these cults not so much as fossils of the early

Hellenistic age, which had continued their role in the city, but as a sort of reinvention of tradition instead: as a deliberate form of highlighting a Greek past, along the lines of the phenomenon of the Second Sophistic, which we have encountered above.

As regards the period in which Dura-Europos was part of the Parthian empire, we seem to be on firmer ground. Many of the temples still in use when the city was under Roman control, and the gods worshiped inside them, go back to the Parthian centuries. However, not one of them can be viewed as typically "Parthian." A fair number of the gods and their cults who first appeared in Parthian Dura-Europos actually came from Palmyra, the above-discussed Syrian desert city, c. 200 km to the west, which had strong cultural links with Dura-Europos, especially thanks to trade (Dirven 1999). Others came from villages along the Middle Euphrates (for example Aphlad, who is identified in one inscription as "god of Anath, village of the Euphrates"), or were local versions of universally known deities, such as Artemis and Adonis. In the Roman period itself, a further number of temples were constructed, some for deities who had entered the city with the Roman soldiers who were now stationed there. To this category belong a small *mithraeum*, that is, a shrine of the bull-killing god Mithras, and a temple where Jupiter Dolichenus was worshiped. The arrival of the Roman garrison will certainly have had consequences for the clientele of some of the existing sanctuaries. At least a part of the temple of the goddess Azzanathkona, which had been built in the Parthian period, was converted into an archive for the military cohort. But as we have seen above, the soldiers took part also in the traditional religious life of the town.

Dura-Europos is probably best known to the larger public because of its synagogue and its baptisterium, reconstructed in the National Museum of Damascus and the Yale University Art Gallery in New Haven respectively. As regards the synagogue, its extremely well-preserved wall paintings, which depict a series of scenes from the Hebrew Bible, go of course directly against the Jewish prohibition of figurative art. As regards the Christian baptisterium or house church, its unfortunately worn frescos depict instances from both the Old and the New Testament. Both communities seem to have used Greek and an Aramaic dialect alongside each other, suggesting contacts with their co-religionists in west and east. It is often argued that serious religious competition between the various religions and cults *must* have taken place, and that the wall paintings in the synagogue and the baptisterium played a major role in putting up resistance against the otherwise-minded. However, there is no good evidence that in this situation co-existence provoked any religious interference: differentiation of religious choices does not necessarily imply competition. And from our own times we know that preaching exclusiveness on a theological level is one thing, but ecumenical practice, or at least living together in peace, quite another.

Concluding Remarks

The evidence from Dura-Europos has often led to general conclusions about the nature of worship in the normal small towns of the Roman east. In contrast to monumental buildings in cities such as Ephesus, Antioch, or even Palmyra, proper

Greco-Roman religious architecture was absent in places such as Dura-Europos. The fact that here temples often grew out of houses has led some to suggest that the cults of the small town that was Dura-Europos were of a relatively private nature. However, an alternative religious architecture does not automatically exclude patterns of worship known from the Greco-Roman world. There is no reason to assume that the groups of worshipers who assembled in the temples of a small town were more exclusive or private than their counterparts in the grand cities of the Roman east. Instead we are faced with a recurrent situation: towns filled with, and dominated by, varieties of traditional, indigenous, and classical polytheistic cults.

Such was religious life in the eastern provinces of the Roman world. According to the model that I have sketched, it was characterized by a general tolerance not only on the part of Rome toward foreign, non-Roman religions, but above all on the part of the various cults and forms of religion toward each other. This should not surprise us. In a metropolis, a small and fanatical sect could have kept a low profile. In a hamlet, there cannot have been too much religious variation amongst the population anyway. In a middle-sized town, there was probably not that much alternative to a religious attitude of live and let live.

FURTHER READING

A comprehensive monograph on religion in the Roman east in general seems to be lacking. The best overview of the pagan cults in the eastern part of the Roman world is Lane Fox (1986: part one). On Asia Minor (present-day Turkey), see above all the second volume of Mitchell (1993), placing the pagan evidence in the context of a growing Christianity. Dignas (2002) is a detailed study of the financial affairs of temples in Hellenistic and Roman Asia Minor, and of their relationship with cities, kings, and emperors. As regards Syria and the Near East, a very accessible introduction to the religious world is now Butcher (2003: ch. 9), and see also Sartre (2005: ch. 10) for a general overview. Millar (1993a) remains the starting point for an exploration of the religious identities of the different sub-regions. The classic work on how the cults from the east spread through the Roman world is still Cumont (1929), translated into many languages, and not surpassed by R. Turcan (1996). Teixidor (1977) argues from a study of inscriptions that popular religion in the Near East remained unaltered throughout the Roman period. Of great importance is a small book by Bowersock (1990), which convincingly shows the vitality of pagan cults in the Roman east, and which describes the impact of Greek culture on indigenous forms of worship. Palmyra, a city in Syria whose abundant sources make it one of our best test cases for understanding religious life in the Roman east, has received treatment of its patterns of worship by two recent books: Dirven (1999), whose model of religious interaction is built upon a study of the behavior of Palmyrene expatriates in Dura-Europos, and Kaizer (2002), a methodical re-evaluation of the evidence for the city's cults, rituals, priests, and worshipers. Lichtenberger (2003) provides an overview of religious life in the cities of the Syrian Decapolis as a whole, based above all on the numismatic evidence. Last but not least, Lightfoot (2003) is not just a superb commentary on the enigmatic treatise *On the Syrian Goddess*, but simultaneously an in-depth study of Levantine religion.

CHAPTER THIRTY-ONE

Roman Religion in the Vision of Tertullian

Cecilia Ames

The western Christian literary tradition that begins in the second century with the first Latin Christian authors from the north of Africa introduces a vision of Roman religion from a different stance, not just because it does so from another religion, but because it does so from somewhere distant from Rome, a province in the west of the empire. These authors, among whom Tertullian, Minucius Felix, Cyprian, Arnobius, Lactantius, and St. Augustine stand out, in their eagerness to defend, diffuse, and impose Christian religion, concentrate their efforts on attacking Roman religion, in an attempt to discredit its gods and its religious practices. Hence these Christian texts abound with references to Roman religion and its followers, but do so from a new perspective, as elements of a discourse that transforms the traditional image, initiating a way of constructing the other which will become paradigmatic in western literary tradition. These references to Roman religion are most varied and not only embrace the religious practices of Roman citizens, which they mention, describe, and criticize, but also approach the attempts at systematization and theoretical discussions on Roman religion developed by different Roman authors, who are apprehended in a special way and with whom a discussion is established.

This vision of Roman religion that Christians outside Rome bequeath in their writings has two features. On the one hand, it shows a clear perception of the different religious practices in different cities of the empire, as well as local selection in the reception of Roman practices, providing rich material to investigate this religion as a local, regional, and provincial phenomenon. On the other hand, however, what is also present and intimately bound to this is the question of the Christian reception of Roman literature, of the role played by the literary texts containing information on religion for the expansion, knowledge, and diffusion of Roman religion anywhere in the empire. From this perspective, the issue of literary representations and systematization of Roman religion is important, as well as the specific handling of this systematization and representation by the first Latin Christian apologists in the north of Africa, the cradle of a discursive construction that begins with Tertullian, is apprehended and reproduced by Minucius Felix, Cyprian, Arnobius, and Lactantius, and reaches its full development in St. Augustine. Of these, Tertullian is the oldest writer and his apologies, the two books of *Ad nationes* and *Apologeticum*, and *De spectaculis*, constitute privileged texts to observe this procedure, because the references to Roman religion found in them stem substantially from the literary tradition, and hence these works also offer a space for reflection on literature as a means of religious diffusion, reflection, and criticism.

Although the oldest documents in Christian Africa are the first Latin versions of the Bible, which regrettably no longer exist, and the martyr acts, the importance of these apologetic writings by African authors resides in the fact that they are the first Christian works written in Latin that have reached us. For this reason, these works constitute the point of departure for the approach to the vision and treatment of Roman religion by Christians living, observing, and fighting for Christianity against Roman religion outside Rome, though under Roman dominion, that is, in a Roman province of the west of the empire. However, this Latin Christian literature has its precedents in Greek Christian literature. When at the end of the second century the Christian writers in the north of Africa begin writing in Latin, Christian literature, whose language until then had been Greek, already had a consolidated tradition of apologetic works which had begun to appear in the first half of the second century. Greek apologetic works, unlike previous Christian texts, which had been directed to the inner circles of the Christian community for the edification and invigoration of the faithful, were for the first time directed to the outer world, to a non-Christian public, entering the domain of culture, of philosophy, and of the science of the time. Thus, with the aim of refuting the calumnies spread about the empire regarding Christians and responding to the accusation that Christians were a danger to the Roman state, the Greek apologists began a controversy with philosophy, mythology, and pagan religious practices, especially Greek religion and oriental cults. With regard to behavior and practices, the apologists drew attention to the Christians' virtuous way of life and insisted on the fact that faith in one god only was necessary for the preservation and well-being of the world, the emperor, and the state. As regards philosophical argument, they exposed the different religions, the nature of their gods, and the myths of their divinities as absurd and immoral, demonstrating that only the Christians had a correct idea of god.

In this sense, the Africans belong to this Greek-oriental Christian tradition and the first Latin apologies present many of the characteristics common to Greek apologetic works. However, Latin apologies had some important differences, especially concerning Roman religion. Although Greek apologies are formally addressed to the emperor, Roman religion is not an issue in these works. Besides, the reception of Latin texts by Greek authors is very limited and, therefore, unlike the apologies written in Greek, apologies in Latin do not argue as much with Greek philosophers as with Latin authors, so the treatment of systematic representations of Roman religion constitutes the originality of this Christian literature which begins to develop in the west. Two very important Roman writers of the late republican era, Varro and Cicero, have a place here, although many Latin authors are quoted and argued against: Seneca, Virgil, Pliny, Livy, Tacitus, and Suetonius, among others.

African Christian writers dispute with Roman authors by references to representations, systematization, and arguments on Roman religion used by these very authors. Thus this peculiar form of reception of Roman texts is the vehicle for the construction of an image of Roman religion and for the configuration of an anti-Roman discourse, for which these Christian authors use the same argumentative strategies as their Roman adversaries. It was from reading Roman works rather than from observing religious practices that Christians depicted in their writing what Roman religion consisted in, what rites their followers practiced, what the citizens of the empire really believed in, what the nature of their gods was, among other questions. From these writings, a particular image of Roman religion is written from the perspective of Christian intellectuals belonging to a well-positioned social sector in a certain Roman province. From reading these authors, then, a question arises: how did a set of religious practices, which for centuries was considered a religion and which called itself *religio Romana*, become superstition – *superstitio*? Successive discursive strategies led Christian authors to speak no longer of Roman religion or of the religions of the Roman citizens, but rather of "paganism," calling their fellow non-Christian citizens "pagans," without making any sort of distinction. Roman religion, the practices of Roman citizens, soon became "paganism," their gods demons. This rejection of Roman religion constitutes, at the same time, the specific genesis of Roman Catholicism and the mutation of the Christianity that began in Galilee with Jesus' preaching, a process bound to the expansion of Christianity in the west and its eventual Romanization and Latinization. Latin Christian texts testify to this dual process, the genesis of Roman Catholicism and the metamorphosis of Roman religion. Furthermore, an anti-Roman discourse emerges from these writings, an image of the *pagani* and, mainly, a paradigmatic way of building an image of the other and of stigmatizing those who do not share the same beliefs and religious practices (Cancik 1995: 200). Tertullian institutes this form of discursive construction in Latin.

Tertullian

Quintus Septimius Florens Tertullianus (c. 160–220) is the first Christian author that can be located and identified with relative accuracy. Tertullian was born in Carthage, the main city of the Roman province in Africa, which during this period experienced a remarkable urbanistic development which reached its peak at the beginning of the third century. Thanks to its flourishing agriculture, this province supplied Rome with regular shipments of foodstuffs. This intense traffic made Carthage a cosmopolitan trading city with several thousand Carthaginians, Greeks, Romans, and Hebrews.

Wealthy, belonging to the upper social circles, Tertullian's father may have been an officer of the Roman army. Perhaps his family belonged to the *ordo equestris*, a part of the highly Romanized autochthonous social sector whose social evolution is characteristic of the second century (Schöllgen 1984: 176–87). Although in fact there is very little reliable information on his social extraction and activities (T. Barnes 1971: 11–21), certain characteristics of his life and education suggest that he belonged to the upper social sectors. In accordance with this social level, Tertullian enjoyed a thorough education which helped him master Latin and Greek to perfection, as well as literary and philosophical tradition. He was well trained in law and rhetoric and became a prominent lawyer, but he is not likely to have been a jurist. The details of his life that we know from Jerome (_De viris illustribus_ 53) are mostly taken from Tertullian's own works and partly based on misunderstandings. Thus Tertullian's own written work constitutes the main source of knowledge of his life. He spent his life in his native city of Carthage and may never have visited Rome (T. Barnes 1971: 243–5). Both his parents were pagan and we have no date for or details of his conversion to Christianity, since he himself makes no reference to it, but it is generally assumed to have been around 193. From then on, he put all his juridical, literary, and philosophical culture to the service of his new-found religion. With a violent temperament and burning energy, he nursed a fanatic passion for the truth: for him the whole problem of Christianity and paganism was reduced to _vera vel falsa divinitas_; his defense of Christianity and attack on paganism and heresy were the motor of an intense literary work which combines juridical and apologetic discourse. Thirty-one works remain, not all complete, which are classified according to their content as apologetic works, doctrinal and polemic works, dedicated to combating doctrinal errors, and moral and ascetic works on questions of church practice and Christian life. _De pallio_, a short, original piece in which Tertullian defends the reasons why he, as a Christian, has decided to continue wearing the typical philosopher's dress, cannot be comprised in any of these categories, but is generally assigned to the apologetical writings (Price 1999: 107).

Tertullian wrote complicated Latin; his non-classical style has strongly personal connotations and, in turn, documents a specific lexicon, which constitutes the groundwork of the construction of Christian terminology in Latin. Although he is always mentioned as the first Latin writer and the founder of the Latin Christian lexicon, it is necessary to bear in mind that he continued a Christian literary tradition that had begun before him in the north of Africa with the first Latin translations of the Bible and the martyr acts, among other texts (Daniélou 1970; Cancik 1975: 116–19). Among Tertullian's numerous works, we shall focus on _Ad nationes_ and _Apologeticum_. In both works Tertullian makes use of the world of representations of the old culture and of religious criticism, turning the habitual arguments for the defense of paganism into arguments against it. Both the content and the target audience of these two works are key to analyzing Tertullian's vision of Roman religion, the religion practiced by "the others," those to whom the works are directed. However, with regard to the audience of Tertullian's works, it is necessary to clarify that among his apologetic works, those dedicated to non-Christian readers also include _Ad Scapulam_, _De testimonio animae_, _De pallio_, and _Adversus Iudaeos_. Finally we will analyze the critics of the Roman rituals in _De spectaculis_.

Ad nationes

Ad nationes, put together by Tertullian in 197, is the first Christian apology in Latin to have reached us. It consists of two books and was perhaps intended to be an apology directed to the world, unfinished and uncorrected, although other researchers state that it is simply a draft of collected material that would later find its completed expression in *Apologeticum*, a work written shortly afterwards. The kinship between both works is quickly visible, because almost the entirety of the content of *Ad nationes* is to be found once again in *Apologeticum*, albeit with certain modifications and a different structure. This partial repetition of the content has given rise to different interpretations regarding the relationship between the works, and in particular, the status and character of *Ad nationes*. The work survived only in a Parisian codex from the ninth century, the *Codex Agobardinus*, which contains 13 works by Tertullian and which, in spite of its defects, continues to be a generally safe source for the wording of the text.

The first book begins by proving that the juridical process against Christians is irrational and goes against all the principles of justice, pointing out that this iniquity is the fruit of ignorance, since the pagans condemn what they do not know (chapters 1 to 6). In the following chapters (7 to 19) it refutes accusations and calumnies suffered by Christians, which had become commonplace, and proves them false; by *reductio ad absurdum*, the argument shows that the opponents themselves should be accused (*retorquere crimina*), in such a way that even if the accusations against Christians were true, the pagans themselves commit worse crimes, whereby they are not entitled to condemn. Regarding references to Roman religion, it should be noticed that all the concrete data that appear in the work concerning beliefs or religious practices is taken from literary tradition; it always consists of standardized examples from different genres, particularly philosophy, historiography, poetry, and manuals of rhetoric.

Formally, this work is a speech directed to a numerous audience, to "the world"; the second person plural is frequently used. It has no introduction and goes straight to the point:

> One proof of that ignorance of yours, which condemns whilst it excuses your injustice, is at once apparent in the fact that all who once shared in your ignorance and hatred (of the Christian religion), as soon as they have come to know it, leave off their hatred when they cease to be ignorant; nay more, they actually themselves become what they had hated, and take to hating what they had once been. (*Nat.* 1.1)

Although the tone of the first book is defensive rather than aggressive, the opening sentence illustrates the way in which Tertullian builds the "other," the non-Christian audience he addresses. Without a doubt, the "world" to which he directs the work is learned Roman citizens in general, among whom are also those in charge of administering justice, who, although not the direct target audience of the work, Tertullian appears to address when writing the book (Becker 1954: 76). He draws the attention of these learned Roman citizens to their "ignorance," an ignorance related to hatred and their contradictory behavior in the face of injustice. These opening words, then, are a subtle attack on his audience, whom he constructs as ignorant and unjust and to whom, in turn, he announces the theme of the book, which revolves around juridical procedures. Tertullian picks up from, and elaborates on, much of the Greek apologists' material and, in general, does not stray far from the path they set. The

content of this first book is once again almost completely present in the
Apologeticum, although restructured and adapted to the aim of the argument, which
has required a process of selection that has led Tertullian to present the material
more concisely and to exclude some information and explanations present in *Ad
nationes*.

The second book has a more original character. Here, Tertullian undertakes to
criticize pagan religions in general, and in particular attacks Roman beliefs concerning gods, incisively ridiculing them; he explores the concept of god and proves that
pagan divinities are purely human inventions, or are simply men deified after death,
so it is not the gods that have made the Roman state great, nor, therefore, can the
fall of the Roman state be a consequence of abandoning its cult. Tertullian thus responds
to the accusations against Christians. To prove the doctrines concerning their gods
irrational and their morals reproachable, Tertullian resorts to numerous examples and
details taken from historiography, poetry, and philosophy, which are proof of the
thoroughness of his knowledge and mastery of Roman literary tradition. Unlike the
first book, the content of this second book appears more concisely in *Apologeticum*.
The tone of this book is no longer defensive but decidedly aggressive, because from
subtly calling the audience ignorant in the first book, he here calls them *miserandae
nationes*, an overtly offensive denomination: "Our defense requires that we should
at this point discuss with you the character of your gods, O ye heathen, fit objects
of our pity, appealing even to your own conscience to determine whether they be
truly gods, as you would have it supposed, or falsely, as you are unwilling to have
proved" (*Nat.* 2.1.1).

In this case, too, the opening words announce the theme of the book: the gods
of the Romans and the question of truth and falsehood. However, Tertullian's aim
goes beyond the philosophical discussion on the nature of gods. In this first chapter he makes it clear that he will undertake an incisive criticism, embracing not just
the gods but the actual practices of traditional Roman religion, the institutions of
elders, the mechanisms of legitimization:

> It is therefore against these things that our contest lies – against the institutions of
> our ancestors, against the authority of tradition, the laws of our governors, and the
> reasonings of the wise; against antiquity, custom, submission; against precedents,
> prodigies, miracles – all which things have had their part in consolidating that spurious
> system of your gods. (*Nat.* 2.1.7)

To proceed with this objective, Tertullian must move away from the path of Greek
apologists (Becker 1954: 88) and resort to material about Roman gods and practices. This material he finds in the work of Marcus Terentius Varro, *Antiquitates
rerum divinarum XVI libri*. In the first chapter of the second book, Tertullian begins
with a presentation of Varro's system, the entire book becoming a dialogue and discussion with the Roman author. Varro's work is not just Tertullian's starting point
but also the structuring principle of this book, because he presents Varro's system
and proceeds systematically, following it point by point. Tertullian utilizes Varro's
classification (*tria genera theologiae*), which distinguishes gods from philosophers, *genus*

physicum, gods from poets, *genus mythicum*, and gods from nations, *genus gentile*. He introduces the image of adoption in connection with this third type of gods, which corresponds to civil theology, because they are the gods the different nations have chosen and adopted to practice their cult:

> For he has made a threefold distinction in classifying the gods: one being the *physical* class, of which the philosophers treat; another the *mythic* class, which is the constant burden of the poets; the third, the *gentile* class, which the nations have adopted each one for itself. (*Nat.* 2.1.10)

This image of "adoption" that characterizes civil theology introduces to us the way in which Tertullian attempts to seize and understand the status of religions in the Roman empire, to approach the issue of freedom of religious practice and the plurality of cults, which differed from one city to another and which on many occasions were unknown to the Roman citizens themselves, so that as from here Tertullian refers to the complex, contradictory relationship between local religions and universal religion. The concept of "adoption," introduced here and reformulated in *Apologeticum*, he finds useful both to describe the plurality of cults in the empire and to criticize the Roman gods who passively allow themselves to be chosen and, therefore, depend on the contingency and arbitrariness of local decisions, a point Tertullian goes on to develop in chapter 8 when he once again picks up the theme of civil theology. Opposing the opinions of philosophers and the inventions of poets, Tertullian introduces the question of the relationship between truth and place (*Nat.* 2.1.11), and this allows him to go on to disqualify municipal adoption as an election that changes from one place to another, since each town is likely to adopt a different divinity. In the face of this theology, Tertullian presents his own ideas about truth characterized as *certa* (sure) in opposition to the opinions of philosophers, which he describes as *incerta* and *varia* (manifold), as *integra* in opposition to the inventions of poets, which he qualifies as *indigna* and *turpia* (shameful), and *communis* (general) in opposition to local pantheons, which he describes as *passiva* and *voluntaria* (*Nat.* 2.1.14). In the following chapters, Tertullian systematically presents Varro's system, focusing in chapters 2 to 6 on the *genus physicum*, on the *genus mythicum* in chapter 7, and on the *genus gentile* in chapter 8. Here he picks up the issue of municipal adoption, of gods elected not according to the truth but on an arbitrary whim (*Nat.* 2.8.1). And he opposes this to his image of god characterized as *communis*, present and to be venerated everywhere (*Nat.* 2.8.2).

Based on this, Tertullian points out that if those gods that are universally worshiped, such as stars or elements of nature, do not hold up to philosophical testing, much less so can those gods that are sometimes unknown even to the citizens themselves. He illustrates this with a long list of gods (*Nat.* 2.8.3–7), initially containing central divinities from different Roman provinces: the Syrians' Atargatis, the Africans' Caelestis, Varsutina from Mauretania, the Arabs' Obodas and Dusaris, Belenus from Noricum. Then, referring expressly to Varro as his source, he adds a series of unknown gods from small Italic towns (*dei decuriones*): Delventinus in Casinum, Visidianus in Narnia, Numiternus in Atina, Ancharia in Asculum, and Nortia in Vulsinii, ending up with the indication that worshiping municipal gods is limited to within the city walls.

This freedom to adopt gods, enjoyed by the inhabitants of municipalities in the Roman empire, has absurd consequences, which Tertullian illustrates using Egypt as an example, since they deify and worship animals. Following the standard pattern of deifying, he shows that the god Serapis is a transformation of the biblical character Joseph (*Nat.* 2.8–19). Tertullian's argument likens the Roman religious system to an endless sum of local religions, so that Roman religion is nothing but a complex conglomerate of divinities unknown to the very citizens of the empire.

The second part of the book ranges from chapter 9 to 17 and refers to Roman national gods that are either deified men or inventions or personifications. In this he follows the Greek apologists who had already referred to gods as deified men, except that Tertullian uses classical authors, mostly Roman, like Varro, Cassius Hemina, Cornelius Nepos, Tacitus, Diodorus Siculus, and Pliny the Elder. From these origins of the relevant deities Tertullian deduces that it is not the gods that have made the Roman state great, nor, therefore, can the fall of the Roman state be a consequence of its abandoning its cult. In this second part of the second book Tertullian continues the polemic with Roman religion and especially with Varro's system but in another dimension (Rüpke 2005b, 2006a). The object of Tertullian's confrontation is no longer Varro's tripartition, nor civil theology, but Rome itself, the dominant city which legitimates itself as such by means of this theology and spreads absurdity. Here appears the political dimension of theology and its relationship with a system of dominance:

> Since, however, it is no longer to the philosophers, nor the poets, nor the nations that we owe all superstition, although they transmitted it, but to the dominant Romans, who received the tradition and gave it wide authority, another phase of the widespread error of man must now be encountered by us; nay, another forest must be felled *by our axe*, which has obscured the childhood of the degenerate worship with germs of superstitions gathered from all quarters. (*Nat.* 2.9.2)

Returning to Varro, he discusses Varro's distinctions, for example between *dei certi*, *incerti*, and gods of certain or unknown function. Next Tertullian refers to Roman gods as *dei hostiles* and identifies two specifically Roman types of gods: those that derive from men and those simply devised, that is to say, divinities that are the personification of virtues or abstract powers. Once again Tertullian introduces a catalogue of controversial, ironic examples, loaded with sarcasm, in chapters 9–11 quoting such Roman figures as the unsuccessful Eneas, the fratricidal Romulus, and divinities like Sterculus, the *hetaera* Laurentia, the lover Antinous, and the abstract divinities of Varro, of feeding, birth, and marriage, which are ridiculed and reduced to absurdity in chapter 12. But it is not the divinities but the Varronian and Roman classifications that are reduced to absurdity. After detailed proof that Saturn, the oldest god, had been a man, and hence all the later gods share this characteristic, he broaches the issue of the credibility of those who have become gods after death and returns to the controversy with Varro. The lists of divinities seem never-ending:

gods, abstract divinities, heroes, animals, beings of the zodiac, and toponyms. Faced with so many species of divinities with different functions Tertullian wonders: what do the remaining gods have left to do, once the special Roman divinities have taken over all these functions?

This ridiculing and ironizing of the Roman gods, always based on data and examples taken from literary tradition, is a constant element in each detailed catalogue of gods of different categories. It is from here that he eventually approaches the question of the legitimization of Roman dominance, wondering whether Roman political superiority can be based on religious grounds. The detailed description of Roman gods he has already made renders this statement absurd, since gods like Sterculus, the god of excrements, and the whore Laurentia cannot possibly be the origin of Rome's greatness. Nor can the foreign gods adopted by the Romans after conquering other peoples be related to its greatness, since gods who were not able to defend their own peoples could hardly be expected to behave otherwise with the conquerors. What is more, the empire was not a result of Roman religiosity, but rather the opposite, because its very expansion was determined by ruthlessness: Tertullian insists that empires are not determined by their religiosity. The book's closing paragraph reaffirms this idea and leaves no doubt as to the universal perspective of Tertullian's argument: universal kingdoms existed prior to the Romans, and these kingdoms did not fall on account of their religiosity or of their cult (*Nat.* 2.17.18).

It is clear from the content of the second book that philosophical argument – Tertullian's starting point, since he announces at the beginning of the book that he will criticize *error* (*Nat.* 2.1.2) – is not the book's only purpose. The audience of the work Tertullian has in mind leads him to incorporate other elements beyond the philosophical discussion on the nature of gods; hence the references to religious practices, especially in the city of Rome. Choosing Varro is not by chance. Little is said in this scholar's work of the empire's different religions. His *Antiquitates rerum divinarum* is a work dating back to the late republic, arising from the tendencies to reflection and systematization developed in Rome as from the third century as a result of imperialistic expansion and an increased exchange with Greek culture. Responding to this tendency, Varro, on one hand, makes a complete compilation of traditional religious practices, thus documenting them, and, on the other, creates a systematic framework with which to legitimate these religious practices philosophically. The instrument for this is the differentiation of three types of theology, among which civil theology stands out, granting a theoretical status to traditional Roman practices (Rüpke 2005b). Varro admits that cult and divine apparatus are historically contingent, but as a Roman citizen he feels committed to defend what has been legitimated by antiquity and ancestral tradition. This is what Tertullian attacks. This is clearly expressed at the beginning of the second book (*Nat.* 2.1.7) where he criticizes all practices based on traditionalistic arguments. This is the reason for using Varro's works as a structuring principle of the book as a whole.

Tertullian begins by addressing the *miserandae nationes*, but gradually concentrates his criticism and attack on the dominant people, whose headquarters is Rome. This is why his criticism is aimed particularly at the religious practices of the city of Rome, with information taken from Varro. Although all gods are criticized, Tertullian is

remorseless with the gods of the Romans and ridicules them in the extreme, allowing him to attack the notion that Roman superiority is based on religiosity.

Apologeticum

Written shortly after *Ad nationes*, the *Apologeticum* is Tertullian's most important
work, addressed to the magistrates, the leading elite of the Roman empire, whom
he attempts to convince (Price 1999: 109). It is characterized by its careful organization, wealth of arguments, and accomplished rhetoric. It is an allegation, in which
Tertullian starts out by dealing with the irregularities of the proceedings used
against Christians (chapters 1–3) and re-examines the value of the laws adduced against
Christians (chapters 4–6). It then goes on to defend Christians against the accusations of hidden or secret crimes (7–9) and thoroughly refutes the accusations of public crimes (9–39). He then contends that the association of Christians is perfectly
lawful, their doctrine is true, and their behavior is irreproachable (39–45). He ends
up examining the relationship of Christianity with philosophy because it is a truth
revealed by god (46–50).

Apologeticum offers much material from *Ad nationes*, but is not a mere literal
repetition, as the material is often expanded or developed with another purpose,
differently laid out, and responding to a different argumentative structure, and within
this framework many expressions appear more refined and sophisticated. Unlike *Ad
nationes*, it is an organized work following a plan and constituting a unit. In the
opening lines we miss the incisive tone of *Ad nationes*, especially that of the second
book, which was fundamentally an attack on pagans in general and the Romans in
particular; hence the fundamental place given to the reference to Varro's work. In
Apologeticum, on the other hand, the dispute with Varro is no longer the structuring or linking thread, because it mainly defends Christians. Tertullian, returning to
certain lines already posed in the first book of *Ad nationes*, creatively incorporates
elements of Greek apologetics and addresses his work to the magistrates of the Roman
empire, stressing that it is they who are in charge of administering justice. The opening words are indicative of Tertullian's change of attitude: "Rulers of the Roman
Empire, if, seated for the administration of justice on your lofty tribunal, under the
gaze of every eye, and occupying there all but the highest position in the state, you
may not openly inquire into and sift before the world the real truth in regard to the
charges made against the Christians . . ." (*Apol.* 1.1).

With a new discursive strategy, Tertullian addresses the *Romani imperii antistites*,
the bosses of the empire, that is, the sector of Roman leaders in general, whom, at
the end of the work, he will call *boni praesides* (*Apol.* 50.12). This way of addressing his audience is in stark contrast with the direct aggression in referring to them
as *miserandae nationes* in the second book of *Ad nationes*. Undoubtedly, the purpose of Tertullian's discourse is now that of persuasion, demanding the construction of a different audience. This audience will find its counterpart in numerous
expressions throughout the work as a whole; *Apol.* 2.14 is an eloquent example: *hoc
imperium, cuius ministri estis, civilis, non tyrannica dominatio est* ("the power of which
you are servants is a civil, not a tyrannical domination"). This shows not only Tertullian's

change of attitude with regard to the audience, but also his consideration of the Roman dominance system. Tertullian decidedly attacks Roman religion, not the Roman system of dominance, for he shows that he values the empire and insists on the need to abide by the rule of Roman authority.

With all types of arguments, Tertullian requests and demands from these authorities that Christians be granted the freedom to practice their religion, like any inhabitant of the empire, because virtually all the cults of the Greeks, Romans, Egyptians, and other peoples belonging to the empire are a part of Roman religion, even to such a point that the Egyptians were allowed to consecrate animals and to try anyone who killed a consecrated animal. The Jews' religion had the privilege of the status of a *religio licita*. This tolerance of the Roman religious system left out only the Christians. With regard to religious freedom, he again picks up the topic of the "adoption" of municipal and provincial divinities and introduces for the first time this formula: *unicuique etiam provinciae et civitati suus deus est* (*Apol.* 24.8). However, this passage, with its list of provincial gods and unknown Italic towns, differs somewhat from that of *Nat.* 2.8.3. In *Ad nationes* this passage was intended to show up the absurd consequences of the freedom to adopt gods that vary from one city to another, where they end up being ignored by the citizens themselves, while in *Apologeticum* it is used as an argument in favor of religious freedom to show that all but Christians are allowed to practice their own religion (*Apol.* 24.9).

On the basis of the considerations regarding a true and false divinity, he again picks up the theme of the belief that the Romans govern the world because of the gods they worship (*Apol.* 25), making the arguments against the relationship between Roman dominance and religiosity even more pointed. Using irony and sarcasm, he relates ridiculous Roman gods such as Sterculus, Mutunus (suggesting defloration of the bride), and Larentia to the expansion of Roman dominance. Illustrating his arguments with literary episodes, he points to the absurdity of thinking that foreign gods would prefer the Romans, who are strangers. As in *Ad nationes*, he argues against any causality between religion and the greatness of the empire, remembering that kingdoms have not grown on the strength of their religion, nor did those who lost their kingdoms and became part of the Roman empire lose their religion.

After Tertullian has shown that the greatness of the empire is not based on mercy (*Apol.* 25–7), the same argument is used to prove the absurdity of the cult to the gods for the emperor's health, and he tackles the theme of imperial cult and of the relationship of Christians with the emperor (*Apol.* 28–34). Tertullian responds to the reproach of high treason by stating that the Christian form of cult shows loyalty to the emperor. Subsequently he clarifies that Christians invoke the true god for the health of the emperors and proposes a Christian Roman empire:

> For we offer prayer for the safety of our princes to the eternal, the true, the living God, whose favor, beyond all others, they must themselves desire. They know from whom they have obtained their power; they know, as they are men, from whom they have received life itself; they are convinced that He is God alone, on whose power alone they are entirely dependent, to whom they are second, after whom they occupy the highest places, before and above all the gods. (*Apol.* 30.1)

In order to prove that Christians are enemies of neither the state nor humanity (*Apol.* 35–8) and that it is unjust to call their associations illegal, and with the aim of modifying their classification as a sect, he charmingly describes the Christian cult (*Apol.* 39–41). The final paragraphs are devoted to highlighting the superiority of revealed truth and, recalling Roman examples such as Cicero and Seneca, he concludes with a subtle exhortation to martyrdom.

De spectaculis

Tertullian's criticism of Roman religion and of the institutions derived therefrom leads us to pay attention to his observations in chapter 38 of *Apologeticum*, where the two topics he develops in his treatise *De spectaculis* are present. Here, he details the link between public shows and idolatry, and their incompatibility with Christian life:

> We renounce all your spectacles, as strongly as we renounce the matters originating them, which we know were conceived of superstition, when we give up the very things which are the basis of their representations. Among us nothing is ever said, or seen, or heard, which has anything in common with the madness of the circus, the immodesty of the theater, the atrocities of the arena, the useless exercises of the wrestling-ground (*cum insania circi, cum inpudicitia theatri, cum atrocitate arenae, cum xysti vanitate*). (*Apol.* 4)

Although *De spectaculis* does not belong to the apologetic writings, and is therefore not directed to the "others," it is nonetheless interesting for our purpose because Tertullian devoted several chapters to criticizing rituals and Roman festivities, based on a lost work by Suetonius, *Ludicra historia*, and perhaps also on Varro's *Antiquitates*. *De spectaculis* belongs to the third group of writings, that of the practical-ascetic writings, about discipline and morals, and in this work Tertullian condemns absolutely all forms of Roman *ludi*, that is, not just public games in circuses, in arenas, and in amphitheaters, but also fights between athletes and gladiators. Tertullian's severe warning regarding different forms of scenic representations is based on the immorality and crudeness of these public shows and on their close relationship to the cult of Roman gods. The work makes it quite clear that Tertullian is fully aware that attendance at games and other amusements constitutes a deeply ingrained social practice of Roman citizens. Christians from Carthage, as Roman citizens, took part in these instances of Carthaginian urban life, where the theater, the circus, and the arena were important spaces for meeting and communicating; besides, visiting the theater conferred great social prestige (Schöllgen 1984: 58ff.). Hence Tertullian's insistence on changing Christians' habits and on eradicating these social practices traditional in Roman institutions, which he bases on links to rituals of Roman religion.

It is hard to date the writing accurately; no doubt it was written in his pre-Montanist period, between 197 and 200, and some researchers even claim that it was composed before *Ad nationes* (Becker 1954: 348–9). It is directed to the interior of the Christian community, to all those baptized (M. Turcan 1986: 37–45) and not just to the catechumens (*dei servi*), whom he mentions at the start of the work.

Here Tertullian announces the general plan of the work, the prohibition of shows to Christians by faith, truth, and discipline, and, in chapters 2 to 4, he develops the justification of these three points. After this introduction (chapters 1–4) Tertullian devotes the first part of the work, from chapter 5 to chapter 13, to demonstrating that these shows are idolatrous in their origins (5), their names (6), their ceremonial – that of the circus – (7), their venues – a study of the circus – (8), and their techniques – those of the circus (9). Next he develops the theme of idolatry in the theater (10), in the arena (11), and in the amphitheater (12), devoting chapter 13 to his conclusions. The second part goes from chapter 14 to chapter 20, where Tertullian explains that the shows are contrary to Christian discipline. In the third part, chapters 21 to 30, he claims that the shows are incompatible with God and truth (M. Turcan 1986: 35–7).

With regard to his critical view of Roman religion, in the first part of the work Tertullian refers to religious institutions and practices of the Roman state and its derivations, the games (*ludi*), criticizing the rituals and traditional festivities of Roman religion, during which different types of shows and ritual acts were carried out. His references to the Roman authors from whom he has gleaned the information show that he directs his criticism toward the rites of the city of Rome, rather than the rites that his fellow citizens practice in the city of Carthage. In chapter 5, expressly mentioning Varro and Suetonius, Tertullian refers to the origin of the games, showing their close relationship with religion, since many religious festivities derived from the games, and he gives several examples that tend to highlight the relationship between the games and the cult of different Roman gods in their corresponding festivities. Thus the festivity of Liberalia was held in honor of Liber Pater, Ecurria in honor of Mars, and Consualia of Consus.

After treating the origin of the games as more or less legendary, Tertullian goes on to deal with the games of a historical time, whose names have not changed since their foundation, showing the idolatrous nature of their origin because they point to their link with the god to which they have been dedicated. This explains why Tertullian makes no mention of the *ludi Romani* in honor of Jupiter, the most important in Rome, or the *ludi Magni*, or the *ludi Plebei*, because their names do not evoke the religious character of the festivity and, therefore, do not ground the relationship of the games with idolatry. Thus, Tertullian attacks Roman institutions and all forms of games: The games that honor the gods are considered idolatry and the games that honor the deceased are considered superstition:

> You have festivals bearing the name of *the great Mother* and Apollo of Ceres too, and Neptune, and Jupiter Latiaris, and Flora, all celebrated for a common end; the others have their religious origin in the birthdays and solemnities of kings, in public successes in municipal holidays (*reliqui ludorum de natalibus et sollemnibus regum et publicis prosperitatibus et municipalibus festis superstitionis causas habent*). There are also testamentary exhibitions, in which funeral honors are rendered to the memories of private

persons; and this according to an institution of ancient times. For from the first the "Ludi" were regarded as of two sources, sacred and funereal, that is in honor of the heathen deities and of the dead. (*Spect.* 6.2–3)

He also attacks Roman magistracies, since it is the different magistrates who organize the games and he considers every act of a magistrate as such as a commitment to the official religion. When referring to circus pomp, Tertullian extends the model of the city of Rome to the rest of the provinces:

> What high religious rites besides, what sacrifices precede, come between, and follow. How many guilds, how many priesthoods, how many offices are set astir, is known to the inhabitants of the great city in which the demon convention has its headquarters. If these things are done in humbler style in the provinces, in accordance with their inferior means, still all circus games must be counted as belonging to that from which they are derived; the fountain from which they spring defiles them. The tiny streamlet from its very spring-head, the little twig from its very budding, contains in it the essential nature of its origin. (*Spect.* 7.3–4)

After devoting several chapters to circus games, Tertullian focuses on the topic of theatrical representations, *ludi scaenici* (chapter 10), which, because of their origin, their name, and their ceremonial, are akin to circus games. Here he also refers to rituals in the city of Rome held in the sanctuary of Venus. Christians should reject all forms of shows, as well as exercises in arenas (chapter 11) and combats in amphitheaters (chapter 12), because they are all bound to Roman religion. The second and third parts of the work center on Christian discipline. In Tertullian's view, Christians should only witness one show, the final game: the next coming of the Lord.

Conclusion

Tertullian's view of Roman religion displays special characteristics. His selection of sources of information is not determined by the mere quantity or quality of information on religious practices, but by his intentions, the audience, and the reception framework. These writings are undoubtedly not a source of information on beliefs and practices, because the references and the concrete data on Roman religion that appear in them are taken from literary tradition, always cases and standardized examples from philosophy, historiography, poetry, and manuals of rhetoric. There is no doubt that the information selected has a Christian apologetic intention and the examples given show the contradictory, inhuman, or ridiculous nature of Roman religious practice, so that they are functional for his philosophical argument. But this is not Tertullian's only purpose; he also has a clear awareness of the Roman empire's dominance structure, of the city of Rome's role, and of his own provincial position, and hence his controversy is surprisingly related to Rome instead of being related to what, for most of his readers, is his own perceptible environment.

Thus Tertullian, from his position as a provincial, approaches the theme of Roman dominance and within this framework analyzes and ridicules Roman religious practices, showing that Roman gods cannot face up to the challenge of empire because they lack universality. He adopts a universal perspective, viewing the empire in its entirety, and hence location has a decisive role in his argument. He uses the same empty structures that described the way religions were organized in the Roman empire: *provincia*, *civitas*, *municipium*, the populations. The complex relationship between local religions and imperial religion is at the base of it all, hence his dispute with Varro's project of legitimating Roman religious practices outside Rome. Tertullian argues on the basis of place; this is why he criticizes the Roman categories of local religion, provincial religion, and imperial religion, and bases his proposal of a universal religion on this criticism. Yet new categories are not generated. Thus Tertullian, when attempting to impose Christianity, does no more than make it a new Roman religion.

FURTHER READING

A general introduction, with references to specific and updated studies, is to be found in Young et al. (2004), and the origins of Christian literature in particular in Heine (2004: 131–41) and Daniélou (1970); references to Latin Christian vocabulary in Cancik (1975: 116ff.). On the first Latin apologists, see Price (1999) and Fiedrowicz (2000), and especially Rüpke (2006a) on the literary representations of the first Latin apologists on Roman religion. As for the problems in writing a scientific biography of Tertullian, see T. Barnes (1971); Carthaginian social stratification and Tertullian's social extraction are to be found in Schöllgen (1984), Carthaginian religious context in Rives (1995), Tertullian as a provincial Roman citizen in Price (1999: 126). In reference to *Ad nationes* and *Apologeticum*, the works of Becker (1954) and Waltzing (1931) are fundamental; on the dating of both works, see Becker (1954: 33–5); on *De spectaculis* see M. Turcan (1986) and Sider (1978). Basic studies on Varro are Cardauns (1978), Lehmann (1986), and Lieberg (1973); regarding the reception of Varro, Rüpke (2005b) is fundamental. On religion as a cause of the greatness of Rome in *Apologeticum*, see Heck (1987: 22–94); on Tertullian's relationships with the Roman state in general, Klein (1968) and Zilling (2004); on the relationship with pagans, especially the senatorial circle, Klein (1968: 49–80); on the metamorphosis of Roman religion, Cancik (1995). Rüpke (1997) is important for the methodological conceptualization of provincial religion and imperial religion.

Latin texts and translations can be found online at the Tertullian Project (www.tertullian.org; *Ad nationes* trans. Dr. P. Holmes, both *Apologeticum* and *De spectaculis* trans. Rev. S. Thelwall).

Bibliography

Abramenko, A. 1993. "Die innere Organisation der Augustalität. Jahresamt und Gesamt-organisation," *Athenaeum 81.* 13–37.

Ackerman, Robert 1987. *J. G. Frazer: His Life and Work.* Cambridge.

Ackerman, Robert (ed.) 2005. *Selected Letters of Sir J. G. Frazer.* Oxford.

Adamesteanu, D., and Dilthey, H. 1992. *Macchia di Rossano: Il santuario della Mefitis. Rapporto preliminare.* Galatina.

Adamo Muscettola, S. 1984. "Osservazioni sulla composizione dei larari con statuette in bronzo di Pompei ed Ercolano," in: U. Gehrig (ed.), *Toreutik und figürliche Bronzen römischer Zeit: Akten der 6. Tagung über antike Bronzen, 13.–17. Mai 1980.* Berlin, 9–32.

Alcock, Susan E. 1993. *Graecia Capta: The Landscape of Roman Greece.* Cambridge.

Alföldi, Andreas 1937. *A Festival of Isis in Rome under the Christian Emperors of the Fourth Century.* Budapest.

Alföldi, Andreas 1965. *Early Rome and the Latins.* Ann Arbor.

Alföldi, Andreas 1973. *Die zwei Lorbeerbäume des Augustus.* Bonn.

Alföldi, Andreas 1997. *Redeunt Saturnia Regna,* trans. E. Alföldi-Rosenbaum. Bonn.

Alföldy, Géza 1989a. "Die Krise des Imperium Romanum und die Religion Roms," in: Géza Alföldy (ed.), *Die Krise des Römischen Reiches: Geschichte, Geschichtsschreibung und Geschichtsbetrachtung.* Stuttgart, 349–87 (= HABES 5).

Alföldy, Géza 1989b. "Die Krise des Imperium Romanum und die Religion Roms," in: Werner Eck (ed.), *Religion und Gesellschaft in der römischen Kaiserzeit.* Vienna, 53–102.

Alföldy, Geza 1991. "Augustus und die Inschriften: Tradition und Innovation," *Gymnasium 98.* 289–324.

Alvar, Jaime 1985. "Matériaux pour l'étude de la formule *sive deus, sive dea,*" *Numen 32.* 236–73.

Alvar, Jaime 2007. *Mystery Cults in the Roman Empire.* Leyden.

Ando, Clifford 2000. *Imperial Ideology and Provincial Loyalty in the Roman Empire.* Berkeley.

Ando, Clifford (ed.) 2003. *Roman Religion.* Edinburgh.

Ando, Clifford 2006. "Religion and *ius publicum,*" in: Ando and Rüpke (2006: 126–45).

Ando, Clifford 2008. *The Matter of the Gods.* Berkeley.

Ando, Clifford forthcoming, a. *Administration and Acculturation in the Roman Empire.*

Ando, Clifford, and Rüpke, Jörg (eds.) 2006. *Religion and Law in Classical and Christian Rome*. PawB 16. Stuttgart.

Anson, L. 1911–16. *Numismata Graeca: Greek Coin Types Classified for Immediate Identification*. 6 parts. London.

Appel, Georg 1909. *De Romanorum Precationibus*. Giessen.

Appelbaum, S. 1976. "The social and economic status of the Jews in the Diaspora," in: Menahem Stern and Shmuel Safrai (eds.), *The Jewish People in the First Century 2*. Assen, 701–27.

Appelbaum, S. 1979. *Jews and Greeks in Ancient Cyrene*. Leyden.

Ascough, Richard S. (ed.) 2005. *Religious Rivalries and the Struggle for Success in Sardis and Smyrna*. Waterloo.

Athanassiadi, Polymnia, and Frede, Martin (eds.) 1999. *Pagan Monotheism in Late Antiquity*. Oxford.

Atkinson, D. 1914. "A hoard of Samian ware from Pompeii," *JRS 4*. 27–64.

Audollent, Augustus 1904. *Defixionum tabellae*. Paris.

Austin, John L. 1962. *How To Do Things with Words*, eds. J. O. Urmson and Marina Sbisà. Cambridge, MA.

Babelon, E. 1916. *Le trésor d'argenterie de Berthouville près Bernay (Eure)*. Paris.

Bacchielli, L. 1988. *Scienze dell'antichità: storia, archeologia, antropologia 2*. Rome.

Bailey, D. M. 1980. *A Catalogue of the Lamps in the British Museum 2: Roman Lamps made in Italy*. London.

Bakker, Jan Theo 1994. *Living and Working with the Gods: Studies of Evidence for Private Religion and its Material Environment in the City of Ostia (100–500 AD)*. Dutch Monographs on Ancient History and Archaeology 12. Amsterdam.

Baldassarre, Ida 1996. *Necropoli di Porto*. Itinerari dei musei, gallerie, scavi e monumenti d'Italia 38. Rome.

Baldovin, J. F. 1987. *The Urban Character of Christian Worship: The Origins, Development, and Meaning of Stational Liturgy*. Rome.

Balensiefen, Lilian 1995. "Überlegungen zu Aufbau und Lage der Danaidenhalle auf dem Palatin," *Mitteilungen des Deutschen Archäologischen Instituts (Rom) 102*. 207–8.

Balensiefen, Lilian 2002. "Die Macht der Literatur: Über die Büchersammlungen des Augustus auf dem Palatin," in: Wolfram Hoepfner (ed.), *Antike Bibliotheken*. Mainz, 97–116.

Baratte, F. 1986. *Le trésor d'orfèvrerie romaine de Boscoreale*. Paris.

Baratte, F. 1999. "La vaisselle du trésor de Vaise," in: G. Aubin, F. Baratte, J.-P. Lascoux, and C. Metzger, *Le trésor de Vaise à Lyon (Rhône)*. Documents d'Archéologie en Rhône-Alpes 17, série lyonnaise 6. Lyon, 36–79.

Baratte, F., and Painter, K. (eds.) 1989. *Trésors d'orfèvrerie gallo-romains*. Exhibition catalogue. Paris.

Barchiesi, Marino 1962. *Nevio epico*. Padua.

Barclay, John M. G. 1996. *Jews in the Mediterranean Diaspora from Alexander to Trajan (323 BCE–117 CE)*. Berkeley, Los Angeles, and London.

Barnes, J., and Griffin, M. T. (eds.) 1989. *Philosophia togata*. Oxford.

Barnes, Timothy D. 1971. *Tertullian: A Historical and Literary Study*. Oxford.

Barnes, Timothy D. 1993. *Athanasius and Constantius: Theology and Politics in the Constantinian Empire*. Cambridge, MA.

Bartman, E. 1991. "Sculptural collecting and display in the private realm," in: Gazda (1991: 71–88).

Bartman, E. 1992. *Ancient Sculptural Copies in Miniature*. Columbia Studies in the Classical Tradition 19. Leiden.

Barton, I. M. 1982. "Capitoline temples in Italy and the provinces (especially Africa)," *ANRW II.12, 1*. 259–342.

Baudot, Alain 1973. *Musiciens romains de l'Antiquité*. Montreal.

Baudy, Dorothea 1988. *Römische Umgangsriten: Eine ethologische Untersuchung der Funktion von Wiederholung für religiöses Verhalten*. RGVV 43. Berlin.

Baumer, Lorenz, Hölscher, Tonio, and Winkler, Lorenz 1991. "Narrative Systematik und politisches Konzept in den Reliefs der Traianssäule: Drei Fallstudien," *JdI 106*. 261–95.

Bayly, C. A. 1996. *Empire and Information: Intelligence Gathering and Social Communication in India, 1780–1870*. Cambridge.

Beard, Mary 1986. "Cicero and divination: the formation of a Latin discourse," *JRS 76*. 33–46.

Beard, Mary 1990. "Priesthood in the Roman Republic," in: Mary Beard and John North (eds.), *Pagan Priests*. London, 17–48.

Beard, Mary 1994. "The Roman and the foreign: the cult of the 'Great Mother' in imperial Rome," in: Nicholas Thomas and Caroline Humphrey (eds.), *Shamanism, History and the State*. Ann Arbor, 164–89.

Beard, Mary, North, John, and Price, Simon 1998. *Religions of Rome. Volume 1: A History. Volume 2: A Sourcebook*. Cambridge.

Beck, Roger 2000. "Ritual, myth, doctrine and initiation in the mysteries of Mithras: new evidence from a cult-vessel," *JRS 90*. 145–80 (= *Beck on Mithraism*. 2004. Aldershot, 55–92).

Beck, Roger 2004. *Beck on Mithraism: Collected Works with New Essays*. Aldershot.

Beck, Roger 2006. *The Religion of the Mithras Cult in the Roman Empire*. Oxford.

Becker, Carl 1954. *Tertullians Apologeticum: Werden und Leistung*. Munich.

Belayche, Nicole 2000. "*Deae Suriae sacrum*: la romanité des cultes 'orientaux,'" *Revue historique 102/3*. 565–92.

Belayche, Nicole 2001. *Iudaea-Palaestina: The Pagan Cults in Roman Palestine (Second to Fourth Century)*. Religion der römischen Provinzen 1. Tübingen.

Belayche, Nicole 2003. "Les formes de religion dans quelques colonies du Proche-Orient," *Archiv für Religionsgeschichte 5*. 157–79.

Belayche, Nicole, and Mimouni, Simon (eds.) 2003. *Les communautés religieuses dans le monde gréco romain: Essai de définition*. Turnhout.

Belayche, Nicole, Bendlin, Andreas, and de Cazanove, Olivier 2000, 2003, forthcoming. "Forschungsbericht Römische Religion (1990–)," *Archiv für Religionsgeschichte 2*. 283–345, *5*. 297–371, *9*.

Belayche, Nicole, Brulé, Pierre, Freyburger, Gérard, Lehmann, Yves, Pernot, Laurent, and Prost, Francis (eds.) 2005. *Nommer les dieux. Actes des Colloques de Rennes et Strasbourg (octobre et novembre 2001)*. Turnhout.

Bell, Catherine 1992. *Ritual Theory, Ritual Practice*. Oxford.

Bell, Catherine 1997. *Ritual: Perspectives and Dimensions*. Oxford.

Bellah, Robert 1967. "Civil religion in America," *Daedalus 96*. 1–21.

Bendlin, Andreas 1995. "Rev. F. Graf (ed.), *Mythos in mythenloser Gesellschaft: Das Paradigma Roms*," *JRS 85*. 265–6.

Bendlin, Andreas 2000. "Looking beyond the civic compromise: religious pluralism in Late Republican Rome," in: E. Bispham and C. Smith (eds.), *Religion in Archaic and Republican Rome: Evidence and Experience*. Edinburgh, 115–35, 167–71.

Bendlin, Andreas 2005. "Divination, römische II.C.4: Quellen und Interpretationen," *ThesCRA 3*. 88–9.

Benveniste, E. 1969. *Le vocabulaire des institutions indo-européennes*. Paris.

Berger, Peter 1967. *The Sacred Canopy: Elements of Sociological Theory of Religion*. Garden City, NY.

Berger, Peter, and Luckmann, Thomas 1966. *The Social Construction of Reality: A Treatise in the Sociology of Knowledge*. Garden City, NY.

Bergmann, Bettina 1994. "The Roman house as memory theater: the house of the tragic poet in Pompeii," *Art Bulletin 76.* 225–56.

Bernstein, Frank 1997. "Verständnis- und Entwicklungsstufen der archaischen *Consualia*: Römisches Substrat und griechische Überlagerung," *Hermes 125.* 413–46.

Bernstein, Frank 1998. *Ludi publici: Untersuchungen zur Entstehung und Entwicklung der öffentlichen Spiele im republikanischen Rom.* Stuttgart.

Bernstein, Frank 1999. "Die römischen *Ecurria / Equirria* – kriegerische Feste?" *Nikephoros 12.* 149–69.

Bernstein, Frank 2000. "Der römische Sieg bei Clastidium und die zeitgeschichtliche Praetexta des Naevius," in: Gesine Manuwald (ed.), *Identität und Alterität in der frührömischen Tragödie.* Würzburg, 157–73.

Berrens, Stephan 2004. *Sonnenkult und Kaisertum von den Severern bis zu Constantin I. (193–337 n. Chr.).* Stuttgart (= Historia Einzelschriften 185).

Betz, Hans Dieter 1968. "The Mithras-inscriptions of Santa Prisca and the New Testament," *Novum Testamentum 10.* 62–80.

Betz, Hans Dieter (ed.) 1986 [1996]. *The Greek Magical Papyri in Translation, Including the Demotic Spells. I.* Chicago.

Bianchi, Ugo 1978. "Gli dei delle stirpi italiche," in: *Popoli e Civiltà dell'Italia antica, VII.* Rome, 195–236.

Bianchi, Ugo, and Vermaseren, Marteen J. (ed.) 1982. *La soteriologia dei culti orientali nell'impero romano.* EPRO 92. Leyden.

Bidez, J., and Cumont, Franz 1938. *Les mages hellénisés: Zoroastre, Ostanès et Hystaspe d'après la tradition grecque.* 2 vols. Paris.

Bietti-Sestieri, Anna Maria 1992. *The Iron Age Community of Osteria dell'Osa: A Study of Socio-Political Development in Central Tyrrhenian Italy.* Cambridge.

Bikermann, Elias J. 1951. "Les Maccabées de Malalas," *Byzantinische Zeitschrift (B) 21.* 63–83.

Bikermann, Elias J. 1988. *The Jews in the Greek Age.* Cambridge, MA.

Bisconti, F. 2000. "Programmi figurativi", in: S. Ensoli and E. La Rocca (eds.), *Aurea Roma.* Rome, 184–90.

Bisconti, F. 2005. "*Basilicam fecit*: Tipologie e caratteri degli edifici di culto al tempo dei Costantinidi," in: A. Donati and G. Gentili (eds.), *Costantino il Grande.* Milan, 82–91.

Bland, R. F., 1996. "The Roman coinage of Alexandria, 30 BC–AD 296: interplay between Roman and local designs," in: D. M. Bailey (ed.), *Archaeological Research in Roman Egypt.* Ann Arbor, 113–27.

Blänsdorf, Jürgen 1995. *Fragmenta Poetarum Latinorum.* Stuttgart.

Bleckmann, Bruno 2002. *Die römische Nobilität im Ersten Punischen Krieg: Untersuchungen zur aristokratischen Konkurrenz in der Republik.* Berlin.

Bleckmann, Bruno 2003. *Konstantin der Große.* 2nd edn. Hamburg.

Bloch, Raymond 1963. *Les prodiges dans l'antiquité classique: Grèce, Etrurie et Rome.* Paris.

Blois, Lukas de 1976. *The Policy of the Emperor Gallienus.* Studies of the Dutch Archaeological and Historical Society 7. Leyden.

Blomart, André 1997. "Die evocatio und der Transfer fremder Götter von der Peripherie nach Rom," in: Cancik and Rüpke (1997: 99–111).

Boccaccini, Gabriele 2001. "History of Judaism: its periods in antiquity," in: Jacob Neusner (ed.), *Judaism in Late Antiquity 1.2.* Leyden, 285–308.

Bodel, John 1986 [1994]. "Graveyards and groves: a study of the *Lex Lucerina*," *AJAH 11.* 1–133.

Bois Sacrés [de Cazanove, Olivier, and Scheid, John (eds.)] 1993. *Les Bois Sacrés: Actes du Colloque International organisé par le Centre Jean Bérard et l'École Pratique des Hautes Etudes (Ve section).* Naples.

Bollmann, Beate 1998. *Römische Vereinshäuser: Untersuchungen zu den Scholae der römischen Berufs-, Kult- und Augustalen-Kollegien in Italien*. Mainz.

Bömer, Franz (ed., trans., comm.) 1957–8. *P. Ovidius Naso: Die Fasten*. 2 vols. Heidelberg.

Bonnefond-Coudry, M. 1989. *Le Sénat de la République Romaine de la guerre d'Hannibal à Auguste: Pratiques délibératives et prise de décision*. Rome.

Bonner, Campbell 1932. " Witchcraft in the lecture room of Libanios ," *TAPhA* 63. 34–44.

Bonnet, Corinne, Rüpke, Jörg, and Scarpi, Paolo (eds.) 2006. *Religions orientales – culti misterici: Neue Perspektiven – nouvelles perspectives – prospettive nuove*. PawB 16. Stuttgart.

Borg, B. E. 2004a. "Glamorous intellectuals: portraits of *pepaideumenoi* in the second and third centuries AD," in: Borg (2004b: 157–78).

Borg, B. E. (ed.) 2004b. *The World of the Second Sophistic*. Berlin.

Borgeaud, Philippe 1996. *La mère des dieux: De Cybèle à la Vierge Marie*. Paris.

Bouché-Leclerq, Auguste 1879–82. *Histoire de la divination dans l'antiquité*. 4 vols. Paris. Repr. 2003.

Bouma, Jelle 1996. *Religio votiva: The Archaeology of Latial Votive Religion – The 5th-3rd C. BC Votive Deposit South West of the Main Temple at "Satricum" Borgo Le Ferriere*. Groningen.

Bowersock, Glen W. 1990. *Hellenism in Late Antiquity*. Ann Arbor.

Bowie, Ewen 1974. "Greeks and their past in the Second Sophistic," in: Moses Finley (ed.), *Studies in Ancient Society*. London, 166–209.

Boyce, G. K. 1937. *Corpus of the Lararia of Pompeii*. Memoirs of the American Academy in Rome 14. Rome.

Bradbury, Scott 1994. "Constantine and anti-pagan legislation in the fourth century," *Classical Philology* 89. 120–39.

Brandenburg, H. 2004. *Die frühchristlichen Kirchen Roms vom 4. bis zum 7. Jahrhundert*. Regensburg and Milan.

Brashear, William M. 1995. "The Greek magical papyri: an introduction and survey; annotated bibliography (1928–1994)," in: *ANRW II 18.5: 3*. Berlin, 380–684.

Bratož, Rajko 2004. "Die diokletianischen Christenverfolgungen in den Donau- und Balkanprovinzen," in: Alexander Demandt, Andreas Goltz, and Heinrich Schlange-Schöningen (eds.), *Diokletian und die Tetrarchie*. Millennium Studies 1. Berlin, 115–40.

Braund, Susanna Morton 1997. "Virgil and the cosmos: religious and philosophical ideas," in: Charles Martindale (ed.), *The Cambridge Companion to Virgil*. Cambridge, 204–21.

Brendel, Otto 1930. "Immolatio boum," *Römische Mitteilungen* 45. 196–226.

Brent, A. 1999. *The Imperial Cult and the Development of Church Order*. Leyden.

Briggs, Ward W., and Calder, William M. 1990. *Classical Scholarship: A Bibliographical Encyclopedia*. New York.

Briquel, Dominique 1996. "Le taureau sur les monnaies des insurgés de la guerre sociale: à la recherche d'un symbole pour l'Italie," *REL* 74. 108–25.

Briquel, Dominique 1997. *Chrétiens et haruspices: La réligion étrusque, dernier rempart du paganisme romain*. Paris.

Briquel, Dominique, and Gaultier, F. (eds.) 1997. *Les plus religieux des hommes: Etat de la recherche sur la religion étrusque*. Paris.

Brock, M. G., and Curthoys, M. C. (eds.) 1997. *The History of the University of Oxford*. Nineteenth-Century Oxford Part 1.6. Oxford.

Brock, M. G., and Curthoys, M. C. (eds.) 2000. *The History of the University of Oxford*. Nineteenth-Century Oxford Part 2.7. Oxford.

Brodersen, Kai (ed.) 2001. *Gebet und Fluch, Zeichen und Traum: Aspekte religiöser Kommunikation in der Antike*. Antike Kultur und Geschichte 1. Münster.

Brodersen, Kai, and Kropp, Amina 2004. *Fluchtafeln*. Frankfurt.

Brooten, Bernadette 1982. *Women Leaders in the Ancient Synagogue*. Chico, CA.

Brown, Peter 1978. *The Making of Late Antiquity*. Cambridge, MA.

Brown, Peter 1981. *The Cult of the Saints: Its Rise and Function in Latin Christianity*. Chicago.

Bruhn, A.-J. 1993. *Coins and Costume in Late Antiquity*. Dumbarton Oaks.

Brulé, Pierre, and Vendries, Christophe (eds.) 2001. *Chanter les dieux: Musique et religion dans l'antiquité grecque et romaines. Actes du colloque des 16, 17 et 18 décembre 1999*. Rennes.

Brunt, Peter A. 1987. *Italian Manpower 225 B.C.–A.D. 14*. Oxford.

Bruun, Christer 1993. "Herakles and the tyrants. An archaic frieze from Velletri," *Deliciae Fictiles (Acta Instituti Romani Regni Sueciae) 50*. 267–75.

Bruun, P. 1997. "The victorious sign of Constantine: a reappraisal," *Numismatic Chronicle 157*. 41–59.

Buckland, W. W. 1963 [1975]. *A Text-Book of Roman Law From Augustus to Justinian*. 3rd edn., ed. Peter Stein. Cambridge.

Buonocore, M. 1996. "Roma e l'Italia centrale dopo la guerra sociale: amministrazione, territorio e comunità," *Panorami 8*. 19–31.

Burkert, Walter 1992. *Les cultes à mystères dans l'Antiquité*. Paris (English edn. Cambridge, MA, 1987).

Burnett, Andrew M. 1987. *Coinage in the Roman World*. London.

Burnett, Andrew M. 1999. "Buildings and monuments on Roman coins," in: G. M. Paul and M. Ierardi (eds.), *Roman Coins and Public Life under the Empire*. Ann Arbor, 137–64.

Burnett, Andrew M. 2005. "The Roman West and the Roman East," in: Howgego et al. (2005: 171–80).

Burnett, Andrew M. and Amandry, Michel (gen. eds.) 1993–. *Roman Provincial Coinage*. London.

Burrell, Barbara 2004. *Neokoroi: Greek Cities and Roman Emperors*. Leyden.

Burrow, J. W. 1966. *Evolution and Society*. Cambridge.

Burrow, J. W. 1967. "The uses of philology in Victorian England," in: Robert Robson (ed.), *Ideas and Institutions of Victorian Britain: Essays in Honor of George Kitson Clark*. London, 180–204.

Butcher, Kevin 2003. *Roman Syria and the Near East*. London.

Cadotte, Alain 2002/3. "*Pantheus et dii deaeque omnes*: les formules de synthèses divines en Afrique du Nord," *Antiquités africaines 38–9*. 55–72.

Cagnat, René 1886. *Cours élémentaire d'épigraphie latine*. Paris.

Cagnat, René 1914. *Cours d'épigraphie latine*. Paris.

Calder, William M. 1981. "Ulrich von Wilamowitz-Moellendorff: an unpublished Latin autobiography," *Antike und Abendland 27*. 34–51.

Calder, William M. 1981/2. "Research opportunities in the modern history of classical scholarship," *CW 74*. 241–51.

Calder, William M., and Ehlers, Dietrich 1991. "The German reception of J. G. Frazer: an unpublished document," *Quaderni di storia 33*. 135–43.

Calder, William M., and Kramer, Daniel J. 1992. *An Introductory Bibliography to the History of Classical Scholarship: Chiefly in the XIXth and XXth Centuries*. Hildesheim.

Calder, William M., and Smith, R. Scott 2000. *A Supplementary Bibliography to the History of Classical Scholarship: Chiefly in the XIXth and XXth Centuries*. Bari.

Calderone, Salvatore 1972. "Superstitio," *ANRW 1.2*. 377–96.

Cameron, Alan 1968. "Gratian's repudiation of the pontifical robe," *JRS 58*. 96–9.

Cameron, Alan 2004. *Greek Mythography in the Roman World*. Oxford.

Cämmerer, B. 1986. "Riegel, Mithräum" in: P. Filzinger, D. Planck, and B. Cämmerer (eds.), *Die Römer in Baden-Württemberg*. 3rd edn. Stuttgart, 506–8.

Cancik, Hubert 1975. "Christus Imperator: Zum Gebrauch militärischer Titulaturen im römischen Herrscherkult und im Christentum," in: Heinrich von Stietencron (ed.), *Der Name Gottes*. Düsseldorf, 112–30.

Cancik, Hubert 1985–6. "Rome as sacred landscape," *Visible Religion* 4–5. 250–65.

Cancik, Hubert 1995. "*Occulte adhuc colunt*: Repression und Metamorphose der römischen Religion in der Spätantike," in: Hans G. Kippenberg and Guy G. Stroumsa (eds.), *Secrecy and Concealment: Studies in the History of Mediterranean and Near Eastern Religions*. Leyden, New York, and Cologne.

Cancik, Hubert, and Mohr, Hubert 1988. "Religionsästhetik," *Handwörterbuch religionswissenschaftlicher Grundbegriffe* (Stuttgart) *1*. 121–56.

Cancik, Hubert, and Rüpke, Jörg (eds.) 1997. *Römische Reichsreligion and Provinzialreligion*. Tübingen.

Cancik, Hubert, and Rüpke, Jörg (eds.) 2003. *Römische Reichsreligion und Provinzialreligion: Globalisierungs- und Regionalisierungsprozesse in der antiken Religionsgeschichte*. Erfurt.

Cancik-Lindemaier, Hildegard 1996. "Der Diskurs Religion im Senatsbeschluß über die Bacchanalia von 186 v. Chr. und bei Livius (B. XXXIX)," in: Hubert Cancik, Hans Lichtenberger, and Peter Schäfter (eds.), *Geschichte – Tradition – Reflexion: Festschrift für Martin Hengel zum 70. Geburtstag. Bd. II: Griechische und Römische Religion*. Tübingen, 77–96.

Capdeville, Gérard 1997. "Les livres sacrés des Étrusques," in: J. G. Heintz (ed.), *Oracles et prophéties dans l'Antiquité. Actes du Colloque de Strasbourg*. Paris, 457–508.

Carandini, Andrea 1997. *La nascita di Roma: Dèi, Lari, eroi e uomini all'alba di una civiltà*. Turin.

Carandini, Andrea (ed.) 2000. *Roma: Romolo, Remo e la fondazione della città*. Milan.

Carcopino, J. 1941. *Aspects mystiques de la Rome païenne*. Paris.

Cardauns, Burkhart 1960. *Varro Logistoricus über die Götterverehrung*. Würzburg.

Cardauns, Burkhart 1978. "Varro und die römische Religion: Zur Theologie, Wirkungsgeschichte und Leistung der 'Antiquitates Rerum Divinarum,'" *ANRW II.16, 1*. 80–103.

Carletti, C. 2004. "*Dies mortis-depositio*: un modulo 'profano' nell'epigrafia tardoantica," *Vetera Christianorum 41*. 21–48.

Carradice, I. A, 1995. *Greek Coins*, London.

Castriota, David 1995. *The Ara Pacis Augustae and the Imagery of Abundance in Later Greek and Roman Imperial Art*. Princeton, NJ.

Cecconi, Giovanni Alberto 1994. *Governo imperiale e élites dirigenti nell'Itlaia tardoantica: problemi di storia politico-amministrativa (270–476 d.c.)*. Como.

Chadwick, Henry 1998. "Orthodoxy and heresy from the death of Constantine to the eve of the first council of Ephesus," in: Averil Cameron and Peter Garnsey (eds.), *The Cambridge Ancient History. XIII: The Late Empire*. Cambridge, 561–99.

Chadwick, Henry 2001. *The Church in Ancient Society: From Galilee to Gregory the Great*. Oxford.

Champeaux, Jacqueline 1990. "*Sors oraculi*: les oracles en Italie sous la république et l'empire," *Mélanges d'Archéologie et Histoire de l'École Française de Rome 102*. 271–302.

Chaniotis, Angelos 2005. "From communal spirit to individuality: the epigraphic habit in Hellenistic and Roman Crete," in: *Creta romana e protobizantina 1*. Padova, 75–87.

Chapot, Frédéric, and Laurot, Bernard 2001. *Corpus de prières grecques et romaines*. Recherches sur les rhétoriques religieuses 2. Turnhout.

Chassignet, Martine 1996. *L'Annalistique romaine. Tome I: Les Annales des pontifes et l'annalistique ancienne*. Paris.

Chastagnol, André, and Duval, Noël 1974. "Les survivances du culte imperial dans l'Afrique du nord à l'époque vandale," in: *Mélanges d'Histoire Ancienne offerts à W. Seston*. Paris, 87–118.

Chilver, G. E. F. 1985. *A Historical Commentary on Tacitus' Histories IV and V*. Oxford.

Christ, Karl 1982. *Römische Geschichte und deutsche Geschichtswissenschaft*. Munich.

Clauss, Manfred 1999. *Kaiser und Gott: Herrscherkult im römischen Reich*. Stuttgart.

Clauss, Manfred 2000. *The Roman Cult of Mithras*. Edinburgh (German edn. 1990).

Coarelli, Filippo 1983. "Architettura sacra e architettura privata nella tarda Repubblica," in: *Architecture et société: De l'archaïsme grec à la fin de la république Romaine*. Paris, 191–217.

Coarelli, Filippo 1988. *Il Foro Boario*. Rome.

Coarelli, Filippo 1989. *I santuari del Latio in età republicana*. Rome.

Coarelli, Filippo, and La Regina, A. 1984. *Abruzzo, Molise*. Guide archeologiche Laterza, 9. Rome.

Cohn, Bernard S. 1996. *Colonialism and its Forms of Knowledge: The British in India*. Princeton, NJ.

Coleman, Kathleen 2000. "Entertaining Rome," in: Jon Coulston and Hazel Dodge (eds.), *Ancient Rome: The Archaeology of the Eternal City*. Oxford, 210–58.

Colonna, G. (ed.) 1985. *Santuari d'Etruria*. Milan.

Coralini, A. 2001. *Hercules domesticus: Immagini di Ercole nelle case della regione vesuviana (I secolo a. C.–79 d. C.)*. Studi della Soprintendenza archeologica di Pompei 4. Naples.

Corbier, Paul 1998. *L'épigraphie latine*. Saint-Just-la-Pendue.

Corcoran, Simon 1996. *The Empire of the Tetrarchs*. Oxford.

Cornell, T. J. 1995. *The Beginnings of Rome: Italy and Rome from the Bronze Age to the Punic Wars (c. 1000–264 BC)*. London.

Cousin, B. 1983. *Le miracle et le quotidien: Les ex-votos provençaux, images d'une société*. Aix-en-Provence.

Cracco Ruggini, L. 2001. "Pietro e Paolo a Roma nel tardoantico e le tradizioni dell' 'Urbs' arcaica," *Pietro e Paolo* (Rome). 387–92.

Crawford, John S. 1999. "Jews, Christians and polytheists in late antique Sardis," in: *Jews, Christians and Polytheists in the Ancient Synagogue: Cultural Interaction during the Greco-Roman Period*. London and New York, 190–200.

Crawford, Michael H. 1974. *Roman Republican Coinage*. 2 vols. Cambridge.

Crawford, Michael H. 1996. *Roman Statutes 1*. London.

Crawford, Michael H. (ed.) forthcoming. *Imagines Italicae*.

Creighton, J. 2000. *Coins and Power in Late Iron Age Britain*. Cambridge.

Cumont, Franz 1956. *Mysteries of Mithras*. New York (French edn. 1902).

Cumont, Franz 1909a. "Le mysticisme astral dans l'Antiquité," *Bulletin de l'Académie Royale de Belgique, Classe des Lettres et des Sciences Morales et Politiques 1909*. 256–86.

Cumont, Franz 1909b. *La théologie solaire du paganisme romain*. Mémoires de l'Académie des Inscriptions et Belles Lettres 12/2. Paris.

Cumont, Franz 1923. "Il sole vindice dei delitti ed il simbolo delle mani alzate," *Atti della Pontificia Accad. Rom. di Archeologia, Ser III, Memor. I 1*. 65–80.

Cumont, Franz 1929. *Les religions orientales dans le paganisme romain*. 4th edn. Paris.

Cunliffe, Barry (ed.) 1988. *The Temple of Sulis Minerva at Bath*. Oxford.

Curran, J. 2000. *Pagan City and Christian Capital: Rome in the Fourth Century*. Oxford.

Curty, O. 1995. *Les parentés légendaires entre cités grecques*. Paris.

Daniélou, Jean 1970. "La littérature latina avant Tertullien," *REL 48*. 357–75.

D'Arms, John H. 1970. *Romans in the Bay of Naples: A Social and Cultural Study of the Villas and their Owners from 150 B.C. to A.D. 400*. Cambridge, MA.

Davies, Jason P. 2004. *Rome's Religious History: Livy, Tacitus and Ammianus on their Gods.* Cambridge.

Davies, Jon 1999. *Death, Burial and Rebirth in the Religions of Antiquity.* Abingdon.

Davis, R. 2000. *The Book of Pontiffs.* 2nd edn. Liverpool.

De Angelis d'Ossat, M. (ed.) 2002. *Scultura antica in Palazzo Altemps: Museo Nazionale Romano.* Cat. Rome. Milan.

de Cazanove, O. 1993. "La penisola romana prima della conquista romana," in: A. Vauchez (ed.), *Storia dell'Italia religiosa I.* Rome and Bari, 9–39.

de Cazanove, O. 2000a. "Sacrifier les bêtes, consacrer les hommes: le printemps sacré italique," in: S. Verger (ed.), *Rites et espaces en pays celte et méditerranéen.* Collection d'Ecole française de Rome 276. Rome, 253–76.

de Cazanove, Olivier 2000b. "Some thoughts on the 'religious Romanization' of Italy before the Social War," in: Edward Bispham and Christopher Smith (eds.), *Religion in Archaic and Republican Rome and Italy.* Edinburgh, 71–6.

de Cazanove, Olivier 2000c. "I destinatari dell'iscrizione di Tiriolo e la questione del campo d'applicazione del senatoconsulto de bacchanalibus," *Athenaeum 88.* 59–68.

de Cazanove, Olivier 2005. "Le aree interne dal III al I secolo: il quadro archeologico," in: *Tramonto della Magna Grecia: Magnamque Graeciam, quae nunc quidem deleta est (Cic., Laelius de am., 4, 13). Atti del quarantaquattresimo convegno di studi sulla Magna Grecia. Taranto 24–28 settembre 2004.* Taranto, 763–99.

de Cazanove, O., and Scheid, J. (eds.) 2003. *Sanctuaires et sources dans l'antiquité: Les sources documentaires et leurs limites dans la description des lieux de culte.* Naples.

De Grummond, Nancy, and Simon, Erika (eds.) 2006. *The Religion of the Etruscans.* Austin, TX.

De Libero, Loretana 1992. *Obstruktion: Politische Praktiken im Senat und in der Volksversammlung in der ausgehenden römischen Republik.* Stuttgart.

De Marchi, Attilio 1896–1903. *Il culto privato di Roma antica. 1. La religione nella vita domestica. 2. La religione gentilizia e collegiale.* Milan (repr. Forlì 2002).

De Visscher, F. 1963. *Le Droit des tombeaux romains.* Milan.

Dearn, A. 2003. "The coinage of Vetranio: imperial representation and the memory of Constantine the Great," *Numismatic Chronicle 163.* 169–91.

Degrassi, Atilio 1963. *Inscriptiones Italiae XIII: Fasti et elogia 2: Fasti anni Numani et Iuliani. Accedunt ferialia, menologia rustica, parapegmata.* Rome.

Deichmann, F. W. 1967. *Repertorium der christlich-antiken Sarkophage.* Vol. 1. Wiesbaden.

Del Tutto Palma, L. (ed.) 1996. *La tavola di Agnone nel contesto italico.* Florence.

Delehaye, H. 1933. *Les origines du culte des martyrs.* 2nd edn. Brussels.

Delemen, Inci 1999. *Anatolian Rider-Gods: A Study of Stone Finds from the Regions of Lycia, Pisidia, Isauria, Lycaonia, Phrygia, Lydia and Caria in the Late Roman Period.* Bonn.

Della Casa, A. 1962. *Nigidio Figulo.* Rome.

Dench, E. 1995. *From Barbarians to New Men.* Oxford.

Derks, Ton 1998. *Gods, Temples and Ritual Practices: The Transformation of Religious Ideas and Values in Roman Gaul.* Amsterdam Archaeological Studies 2. Amsterdam.

Desideri, P. 1978. *Dione di Prusa: Un intellettuale greco dell'impero romano.* Florence.

Desideri, P. 1994. "La letteratura politica delle elites provinciali," in: G. Cambiano, L. Canfora, and Diego Lanza (eds.), *Lo Spazio letterario della Grecia antica.* Rome, 11–33.

Detienne, Marcel, and Vernant, Jean-Pierre (eds.) 1979. *La cuisine du sacrifice en pays grec.* Paris.

Deubner, Ludwig 1920. "Griechische und römische Religion 1911–1914," *Archiv Für Religionswissenschaft 20.* 411–41.

Devoto, G. 1940. *Tabulae Iguvinae*. Rome.

Devoto, G. 1977. *Le tavole di Gubbio*. Florence.

Deytz, Simone 1983. *Les bois sculptés des sources de la Seine*. Gallia Suppl. 42. Paris.

Dickie, Matthew W. 2001. *Magic and Magicians in the Greco-Roman World*. London.

Dietrich, Hermann, and Hiller, Friedrich von 1994 [1934]. *Usener und Wilamowitz: Ein Briefwechsel*. 2nd edn. ed. William M. Calder. Leipzig.

Dignas, Beate 2002. *Economy of the Sacred in Hellenistic and Roman Asia Minor*. Oxford.

Dillery, John 2002. "Quintus Fabius Pictor and Greco-Roman historiography at Rome," in: Miller, J. F., Damon, C., and Myers, K. S. (eds.), *Vertis in Usum: Studies in Honor of Edward Courtney*. Munich, 1–23.

Dirven, Lucinda 1999. *The Palmyrenes of Dura-Europos: A Study of Religious Interaction in Roman Syria*. Leyden.

Donaldson, Terrence (ed.) 2000. *Religious Rivalries and the Struggle for Success in Caesarea Maritima*. Waterloo, ON.

Dörries, Heinrich 1954. *Das Selbstzeugnis Kaiser Konstantins*. Abhandlungen der Akademie der Wissenschaften in Göttingen. Phil.-hist. Kl. 3, 34. Göttingen.

Dorson, Richard 1968. *The British Folklorists*. Chicago.

Douglas, Mary 1973. *Natural Symbols*. 2nd edn. New York.

Douglas, Mary 1975. *Implicit Meanings*. London.

Dräger, Olaf 1994. *Religionem significare: Studien zu reich verzierten römischen Altäre und Basen aus Marmor*. Mitteilungen des Deutschen Archäologischen Instituts Rom: Ergänzungsheft 33. Mainz.

Drake, Hal 2000. *Constantine and the Bishops: The Politics of Intolerance*. Baltimore, MD.

Dresken-Weiland, J. 2004. "Ricerche sui committenti e destinatari dei sarcofagi paleocristiani a Roma," in: F. Bisconti and H. Brandenburg (eds.), *Sarcofagi tardoantichi, paleocristiani e altomedievali*. Vatican City, 149–53.

Drew-Bear, Thomas, Thomas, Christine M., and Yildizturan, Melek 1999. *Phrygian Votive Steles*. Ankara.

Driesch, A. von den, and Pollath, N. 2000. "Tierknochen aus dem Mithrastempel von Künzing, Lkr. Deggendorf," in: K. Schmotz (ed.), *Vorträge des 18. Niederbayerischen Archäologentages*. Rahden, 145–62.

Dubourdieu, Annie 1986. "Cinctus Gabinus," *Latomus 45*. 3–20.

Dubourdieu, Annie 1989. *Les origines et le développement du culte des Pénates à Rome*. Rome.

Dumézil, Georges 1968–73. *Mythe et epopee*. 3 vols. Paris.

Dumézil, Georges 1970. *Archaic Roman Religion, with an Appendix on the Religion of the Etruscans*. 2 vols. Chicago.

Dumézil, Georges 1974. *La religion romaine archaïque*. Paris.

Dumézil, Georges 1975. *Fêtes romaines d'été et d'automne suivi de Dix questions romaines*. Paris.

Dunbabin, Katherine M. D. 1978. *The Mosaics of Roman North Africa: Studies in Iconography and Patronage*. Oxford.

Duncan-Jones, Richard 1982. *The Economy of the Roman Empire: Quantitative Studies*. 2nd edn. Cambridge.

Dupont-Sommer, A. 1946. *La doctrine gnostique de la lettre waw*. Paris.

Duthoy, R. 1969. *The Taurobolium: Its Evolution and Terminology*. EPRO 10. Leyden.

Dwyer, E. J. 1982. *Pompeian Domestic Sculpture: A Study of Five Pompeian Houses and their Contents*. Archaeologica 28. Rome.

Eck, Werner 1989. *Religion und Religiosität in der soziopolitischen Führungsschicht der Hohen Kaiserzeit*. Cologne, 15–51.

Eck, Werner 1995. *Die Verwaltung des Römischen Reiches in der Hohen Kaiserzeit*, 1. Band.

Eck, Werner 1998. "Inschriften auf Holz," in: Peter Kneissl and Volker Losemann (eds.), *Imperium Romanum: Festschrift für Karl Christ zum 75. Geburtstag*. Stuttgart, 203–17.

Eck, Werner 2004. *Köln in römischer Zeit*. Cologne.

Edlund, Ingrid E. M. 1987. *The Gods and the Place: Location and Function of Sanctuaries in the Countryside of Etruria and Magna Graecia (700–400 B.C.)*. Stockholm.

Edmondson, Jonathan 2006. "Cities and urban life in the western provinces of the Roman empire, 30 BCE–250 CE," in: David Potter (ed.), *A Companion to the Roman Empire*. Oxford, 422–64.

Edwards, Mark 2003. *Constantine and Christendom: The Oration to the Saints. The Greek and Latin Accounts of the Discovery of the Cross. The Edict of Constantine to Pope Silvester*. Liverpool.

Edwards, Mark 2004. "Pagan and Christian monotheism in the age of Constantine," in: Simon Swain and Mark Edwards (eds.), *Approaching Late Antiquity: The Transformation from Early to Late Empire*. Oxford, 211–34.

Egelhaaf-Gaiser, Ulrike 2000. *Kulträume im römischen Alltag: Das Isisbuch des Apuleius und der Ort von Religion im kaiserzeitlichen Rom*. PawB 2. Stuttgart.

Egelhaaf-Gaiser, Ulrike, and Schäfer, Alfred (eds.) 2002. *Religiöse Vereine in der römischen Antike*. Studien und Texte zu Antike und Christentum 13. Tübingen.

Eissfeldt, Otto 1941. *Tempel und Kulte syrischer Städte in hellenistisch-römischer Zeit*. Leipzig.

Elm, Dorothee, Rüpke, Jörg, and Waldner, Katharina (eds.) 2006. *Literatur als Medium und Reflexion von Religion im Römischen Reich*. PawB 14. Stuttgart.

Elsner, Jaś 1992. "Pausanias: a Greek pilgrim in the Roman world," *P&P 135*. 3–29.

Elsner, Jaś 2001. "Describing self in the language of the other: pseudo (?) Lucian at the temple of Hierapolis," in: Simon Goldhill (ed.), *Being Greek under Rome: Cultural Identity, the Second Sophistic and the Development of Empire*. Cambridge, 123–53.

Engel, A. J. 1983. *From Clergyman to Don: The Rise of the Academic Profession in Nineteenth-Century Oxford*. Oxford.

Ennabli, Liliane 1999. "A propos de Mégara," in: Serge Lancel (ed.), *Numismatique, langues, écritures et arts du livre, spécificité des arts figurés*. Afrique du Nord antique et médiévale. Paris, 193–210.

Ernout, André and Meillet, A. 1959–60. *Dictionnaire étymologique de la langue latine: histoire des mots*. 4th edn. 2 vols. Paris.

Eschebach, Liselotte (ed.) 1993. *Gebäudeverzeichnis und Stadtplan der antiken Stadt Pompeji*. Cologne, Weimar, and Vienna.

Estienne, Sylvia 2001. "Les 'dévots' du Capitole: Le 'culte des images' dans la Rome impériale, entre rites et superstition," *MEFRA 113*. 189–210.

Estienne, Sylvia 2005. "Saliens," *ThesCRA 5*. 85–7.

Fabbricotti, E. 1967/8. "Elementi ceramici e fittili vari," in: A. Carandini, F. Berti, C. Gasparri, et al., *Ostia I: Le terme del nuotatore*. Scavi dell'ambiente IV. Studi miscellanei 13. Ostia, 117–18.

Farnell, Lewis R. 1907. "The place of the 'Sonder-Götter' in Greek polytheism," in: *Anthropological Essays Presented to Edward Burnett Tylor*. Oxford, 81–100.

Fasold, Peter, and Witteyer, Marion (eds.) 2001. *Tradition und Wandel im Grabbrauch Rätiens und Obergermaniens während der frühen Kaiserzeit*. Römischer Bestattungsbrauch und Beigabensitten. Wiesbaden.

Fasold, Peter, Fischer, Thomas, von Hesberg, Henner, and Witteyer, Marion (eds.) 1998. *Bestattungssitte und kulturelle Identität*. Xantener Berichte 7. Cologne.

Fasold, Peter, Struck, Manuela, and Witteyer, Marion (eds.) forthcoming. *Körpergräber des 1.–3. Jahrhunderts in der römischen Welt*.

Favro, Diane 1996. *The Urban Image of Augustan Rome*. Cambridge.

Favro, Diane 2005. "Making Rome a world city," in: Galinsky (2005: 234–63).

Fear, Andrew T. 1989. "La *lex Ursonensis* y los *apparitores municipales*," in: Julián Gonzáles (ed.), *Estudios sobre Urso Colonia Iulia Genetiva*. Seville, 69–78.

Fears, J. Rufus 1977. *Princeps a diis electus: The Divine Election of the Emperor as a Political Concept at Rome*. Papers and Monographs of the American Academy in Rome 26. Rome.

Fears, J. Rufus 1981a. "The cult of Jupiter and Roman imperial ideology," *ANRW II. 17, 1.* 3–141, pls. 1–13.

Fears, J. Rufus 1981b. "The theology of victory at Rome: approaches and problems," *ANRW II.17, 2.* 736–826, pls. 1–12.

Feeney, Denis 1991. *The Gods in Epic: Poets and Critics of the Classical Tradition*. Oxford.

Feeney, Denis 1998. *Literature and Religion at Rome: Cultures, Contexts, and Beliefs.* Cambridge.

Feldherr, Andrew 1998. *Spectacle and Society in Livy's History*. Berkeley.

Feldman, Burton, and Richardson, Robert D. 1972. *The Rise of Modern Mythology 1680–1860*. Bloomington, IN.

Feldman, Louis H. 1993. *Jew and Gentile in the Ancient World: Attitudes and Interactions from Alexander to Justinian*. Princeton, NJ.

Felletti Maj, Beatrice 1977. *La tradizione italica nell'arte romana I*. Rome.

Ferrea, Laura 2002. *Gli dei di Terracotta: La ricompositione del frontone da Via di San Gregorio*. Milan.

Ferrero, Leonardo 1955. *Storia del Pitagorismo nel mondo romano: Dalle origini alla fine della repubblica*. Turin.

Ferrua, Antonio 1971. "La catacomba di Vibia," *Rivista di archeologia cristiana 47.* 7–62.

Ferry, David 1997. *The Odes of Horace*. New York.

Festugière, A. 1944–54. *La révélation d'Hermès Trismégiste*. 4 vols. Paris.

Fiedrowicz, Michael 2000. *Apologie im frühen Christentum: Die Kontroverse um den christlichen Wahrheitsanspruch in den ersten Jahrhunderten*. Paderborn.

Fine, Steven 1997. *This Holy Place: On the Sanctity of the Synagogue during the Greco-Roman Period*. Notre Dame, IN.

Fine, Steven 2005. *Art and Judaism in the Greco-Roman World: Toward a New Jewish Archaeology*. Cambridge.

Fink, R. O., Hoey, A. S., and Snyder, W. F. 1940. "The *Feriale Duranum*," *YCS 7.* 1–222.

Fiocchi Nicolai, V. 2000. "Gli spazi delle sepolture cristiane tra il III e il V secolo," in: L. Pani Ermini and P. Siniscalco (eds.), *La comunità cristiana di Roma*. Vatican City, 341–62.

Fiocchi Nicolai, V. 2001. *Strutture funerarie ed edifici di culto paleocristiani di Roma dal IV al VI secolo*. Vatican City.

Fishwick, Duncan 1987–2004. *The Imperial Cult in the Latin West: Studies in the Ruler Cult of the Western Provinces of the Roman Empire I.1.–III.3*. Leyden.

Fitzpatrick-McKinley, Anne 2002. "Synagogue communities in the Graeco-Roman cities," in: John R. Bartlett (ed.), *Jews in the Hellenistic and Roman Cities*. London, 55–87.

Flesher, Paul V. M. 2001. "Prolegomenon to a theory of early synagogue development," in: Jacob Neusner and Allan J. Avery-Peck (eds.), *Judaism in Late Antiquity 2, 3, 4*. Leyden, 121–54.

Fless, Friederike 1995. *Opferdiener und Kultmusiker auf stadtrömischen historischen Reliefs: Untersuchungen zu Ikonographie, Funktion und Benennung*. Mainz.

Fless, Friederike 2004. "Römische Prozessionen," *ThesCRA 1.* 33–59.

Fögen, Marie-Theres 1993. *Die Enteignung der Wahrsager: Studien zum kaiserlichen Wissensmonopol in der Spätantike*. Frankfurt.

Fontaine, Jacques 1989. "Discussion," *ACTES of the 11th International Congress of Christian Archaeology. Pontifical Institute of Christian Archaeology* (Rome) *1*. 152–213.

Förster, N. 1999. *Marcus Magus: Kult, Lehre und Gemeindeleben einer valentinianischen Gnostikergruppe.* WUNT 114. Tübingen.

Forsythe, Gary 1999. *Livy and Early Rome: A Study in Historical Method and Judgment.* Stuttgart.

Forsythe, Gary 2005. *A Critical History of Early Rome: From Prehistory to the First Punic War.* Berkeley.

Foucault, Michel 1984. *Le souci de soi.* Paris.

Fowden, Garth 1998. "Polytheist religion and philosophy," in: Averil Cameron and Peter Garnsey (eds.), *The Cambridge Ancient History. XIII: The Late Empire.* Cambridge. 538–60.

Fowler, W. Warde 1902. "Dr. Wissowa on the Argei," *CR 16.* 115–19.

Fowler, W. Warde 1908 [1920]. "The Latin history of the word *religio*," in: *Roman Essays and Interpretations.* Oxford, 7–15.

Fowler, W. Warde 1911. *The Religious Experience of the Roman People, from the Earliest Times to the Age of Augustus: The Gifford Lectures for 1909–10.* London.

Fox, Matthew 1996. *Roman Historical Myths: The Regal Period in Augustan Literature.* Oxford.

Fraenkel, Eduard 1922. *Plautinisches im Plautus.* Berlin.

Franchi De Bellis, A. 1981. *Le iouile capuane.* Florence.

Franchi De Bellis, A. 1988. *Il cippo abellano.* Urbino.

Francis, E. D. 1975a. "Plutarch's Mithraic pirates," in: J. R. Hinnells (ed.), *Mithraic Studies 1.* Manchester, 207–10.

Francis, E. D. 1975b. "Mithraic graffiti from Dura-Europos," in: J. R. Hinnells (ed.), *Mithraic Studies 1.* Manchester, 424–45.

Frankfurter, David 1998a. *Religion in Roman Egypt: Assimilation and Resistance.* Princeton, NJ.

Frankfurter, David (ed.) 1998b. *Pilgrimage and Holy Space in Late Antique Egypt.* Leyden.

Fraschetti, Augusto 1994. *Rome et le Prince* (Italian edn. 1990).

Fraschetti, Augusto 1999. "*Veniunt modo reges Romam,*" in: W. V. Harris (ed.), *The Transformation of Urbs Roma in Late Antiquity.* Journal of Roman Archeology. Supp. Series 33. Portsmouth, RI, 235–48.

Frateantonio, Christa 1997. "Autonomie in der Kaiserzeit und Spätantike," in: Cancik and Rüpke (1997: 85–97).

Frazer, Alfred (ed.) 1998. *The Roman Villa: Villa Urbana.* First Williams Symposium on Classical Architecture held at the University of Pennsylvania, Philadelphia, April 21–2, 1990. Philadelphia.

Frazer, James George (ed.) 1929. *Publii Ovidii Nasonis Fastorum libri sex: The Fasti of Ovid.* 5 vols. London.

Frey, Jean-Baptiste 1936–52. *Corpus inscriptionum Judaicarum.* 2 vols. Rome (repr. 1975 with Addenda by B. Lifschitz, New York).

Freyburger, Gérard 1977. "La supplication d'action de grâces dans la religion romaine archaïque," *Latomus 36.* 283–315.

Freyburger, Gérard, and Pernot, L. (eds.) 2000. *Bibliographie analytique de la prière grecque et romaine (1898–1998).* Recherches sur les rhétoriques religieuses 1. Turnhout.

Fridh, A. 1990. "*Sacellum, sacrarium, fanum,* and related terms," in: *Greek and Latin Studies in Memory of C. Fabricius.* Göteborg, 173–87.

Frier, Bruce W. 1979. *Libri Annales Pontificum Maximorum: The Origins of the Annalistic Tradition.* Rome.

Friesen, Steven 1993. *Twice Neokoros: Ephesus, Asia and the Cult of the Flavian Imperial Family.* Leyden.

Friggeri, Rosanna 2001. *The Epigraphic Collection of the Museo Nazionale Romano at the Bath of Diocletian*. Milan.

Fröhlich, Thomas 1991. *Lararien- und Fassadenbilder in den Vesuvstädten: Untersuchungen zur "volkstümlichen" pompejanischen Malerei*. Römische Mitteilungen, Ergänzungsheft 32. Mainz.

Funke, A. H. 1967. "Majestäts und Magieprozesse bei Ammianus Marcellinus," *Jahrbuch für Antike und Christentum 10*. 145–75.

Furley, William D., and Bremer, Jan Maarten 2001. *Greek Hymns*. 2 vols. Studien und Texte zu Antike und Christentum 9–10. Tübingen.

Gagé, Jean 1950. *Huit recherches sur les origines italiques et romaines*. Paris.

Gagé, Jean 1955. *Apollon romain: Essai sur le culte d'Apollon et le développement du "ritus Graecus" à Rome des origines à Auguste*. Paris.

Gagé, Jean 1976. *La chute des Tarquins et les débuts de la république romaine*. Paris.

Gager, John G. 1992. *Curse Tablets and Binding Spells from the Ancient World*. Oxford.

Gager, John G. 2001. "New Greek curse tablets," *Greek, Roman and Byzantine Studies 41*. 5–46.

Gaiffier, B. de 1964. "Un prologue hagiographique hostile au décret de Gélase?" *Analecta Bollandiana 82*. 341–53.

Galinsky, Karl 1996. *Augustan Culture: An Interpretive Introduction*. Princeton, NJ.

Galinsky, Karl (ed.) 2005. *The Cambridge Companion to the Age of Augustus*. Cambridge.

Gallini, Clara 1970. *Protesta e integrazione nella Roma antica*. Bari.

Galsterer, Hartmut 1987. "La loi municipale des Romains: chimère ou réalité?" *Revue historiques de droit français et étranger 65*. 181–203.

Galsterer, Hartmut 1988. "Municipium Flavium Irnitanum: a Latin town in Spain," *JRS 78*. 78–90.

Ganzert, Joachim 2000. *Im Allerheiligsten des Augustusforums: Fokus "Oikumenischer Akkulturation."* Mainz.

Gargola, Daniel J. 1995. *Lands, Laws and Gods: Magistrates and Ceremony in the Regulation of Public Lands in Republican Rome*. Studies in the History of Greece and Rome. Chapel Hill, NC.

Gatti Lo Guzzo, L. 1978. *Il deposito votivo dell' Esquilino detto di Minerva medica*. Rome.

Gawlikowski, M. 2004. "Le mithraeum de Haouarte (Apamène)," *Topoi 11/1*. 183–93.

Gay, Peter 1966–9. *The Enlightenment: An Interpretation*. 2 vols. New York.

Gazda, E. K. (ed.) 1991. *Roman Art in the Private Sphere: New Perspectives on the Architecture and Decor of the Domus, Villa, and Insula*. Ann Arbor.

Geertz, Clifford 1966. "Religion as a cultural system," in: Michael Banton (ed.), *Anthropological Approaches to the Study of Religion*. London, 1–46.

Georgoudi, Stella, Koch-Piettre, Renée, and Schmidt, Francis (eds.) 2006. *La cuisine et l'autel: Les sacrifices en questions dans les sociétés de la Méditerranée ancienne*. Bibliothèque de l'école des hautes études, sciences religieuses 124. Turnhout.

Geraci, Giovanni 1971. "Ricerche sul Proskynema," *Aegyptus 51*. 3–211.

Giardina, A. 1994. "L'identità incompiuta dell'Italia romana," in: *L'Italie d'Auguste à Dioclétien*. Collection d'école française de Rome 198. Rome, 1–89.

Gildenhard, Ingo 2003. "The 'Annalist' before the Annalists: Ennius and his *Annales*," in: Ulrich Eigler, Ulrich Gotter, Nino Luraghi, and Uwe Walter (eds.), *Formen römischer Geschichtsschreibung von den Anfängen bis Livius*. Darmstadt, 93–114.

Gildenhard, Ingo, and Ruehl, Martin (eds.) 2003. *Out of Arcadia: Classics and Politics in Germany in the Age of Burckhardt, Nietzsche and Wilamowitz*. London.

Gildersleeve, Basil L. 1896. "Rev. Hermann Usener, *Götternamen*," *AJP 17*. 357–66.

Ginsburg, Judith 1981. *Tradition and Theme in the Annals of Tacitus*. New York.

Gladigow, Burkhard 1972. "Die sakralen Funktionen der Liktoren: Zum Problem von institutioneller Macht und sakraler Präsentation," *ANRW I.2*. 295–314.

Gladigow, Burkhard 1994. "Zur Ikonographie und Pragmatik römischer Kultbilder," in: Hagen Keller and Nikolaus Staubach (eds.), *Iconologia sacra: Mythos. Bildkunst und Dichtung in der Religions und Sozialgeschichte Alteuropas*. Berlin, 9–24.

Gladigow, Burkhard 1995. "*Anatomia sacra*: Religiös motivierte Eingriffe in menschliche oder tierische Körper," in: P. J. Van der Eijk, H. F. J. Horstmanshoff, and P. H. Schrijvers (eds.), *Ancient Medicine in its Socio-Cultural Context 2*. Amsterdam, 345–61.

Gladigow, Burkhard 1998a. "Ritual, komplexes," *Handwörterbuch religionswissenschaftlicher Grundbegriffe 4*. 458–60.

Gladigow, Burkhard 1998b. "Polytheismus," *Handwörterbuch religionswissenschaftlicher Grundbegriffe 4*. 321–30.

Gladigow, Burkhard 2005. *Religionswissenschaft als Kulturwissenschaft*. Religionswissenschaft heute 1. Stuttgart.

Glazer, Nathan 1972. *American Judaism*. 2nd edn. Chicago.

Gnecchi, F. 1912. *I medaglioni romani*. 3 vols. Milan.

Goette, Hans Ruprecht 1986. "Kuh und Stier als Opfertier. Zur 'probatio victimae,'" *Bulletino Comunale 91*. 61–8.

Goldscheider, Calvin, and Zuckerman, Alan S. 1984. *The Transformation of the Jews*. Chicago.

González, Julián 1986. "The *Lex Irnitana*: a new copy of the Flavian municipal law," *JRS 76*. 147–243.

Goodenough, Erwin R. 1952–65. *Jewish Symbols in the Greco-Roman Period*. 12 vols. New Haven, CT.

Gordon, Richard L. 1990. "Religion in the Roman empire: the civic compromise and its limits," in: Mary Beard and John North (eds.), *Pagan Priests: Religion and Power in the Ancient World*. Ithaca, NY, 235–55.

Gordon, Richard L. 2004. "Small and miniature reproductions of the Mithraic icon," in: Martens and De Boe (2004: 259–83).

Grabbe, Lester L. 2001. "Hellenistic Judaism," in: Jacob Neusner (ed.), *Judaism in Late Antiquity 1.2*. Leyden, 53–83.

Gradel, Ittai 2002. *Emperor Worship and Roman Religion*. Oxford.

Graeven, H. 1901. "Die thönerne Sparbüchse im Altertum," *Jahrbuch des Deutschen Archäologischen Instituts 16*. 160–89.

Graf, Fritz 1997a. *Magic in the Ancient World*. Cambridge, MA (French edn. 1994).

Graf, Fritz 1997b. "How to cope with a difficult life. A view of ancient magic," in: Peter Schäfer and Hans G. Kippenberg (eds.), *Envisioning Magic: A Princeton Seminar and Symposium*. Studies in the History of Religions 75. Leyden, New York, and Cologne, 93–114.

Grafton, Anthony 1983. "Polyhistor into *Philolog*: notes on the transformation of German classical scholarship, 1780–1850," *History of Universities 3*. 159–92.

Grandazzi, Alexandre 1997. *The Foundation of Rome: Myth and History*. Ithaca, NY.

Gratwick, A. S. 1982. "Ennius' *Annales*," in: E. J. Kenney and W. V. Clausen (eds.), *The Cambridge History of Classical Literature. II: Latin Literature*. Cambridge, 60–76.

Grodzynski, D. 1974. "Superstitio," *REA 76*. 36–60.

Gros, Pierre 1976. *Aurea Templa: Recherches sur l'architecture religieuse de Rome à l'époque d'Auguste*. Rome.

Gros, Pierre 1988. "Les autels des Caesares et leur signification dans l'espace urbain des villes Julio-Claudiennes," in: R. Etienne and M.-T. Le Dinahet (eds.), *L'espace sacrificiel dans les civilisations méditerraniennes de l'antiquité: Actes du colloque tenu à la Maison de l'Orient, Lyon, 4–7 Juin 1988.* Lyon, 179–86.

Gros, Pierre 1996a. *L'architecture romaine du début du IIIe siècle av. J.-C. à la fin du Haut-Empire. I: Les monuments publics.* Paris.

Gros, Pierre 1996b. "Les nouveaux espaces civiques du début de l'Empire en Asie Mineure: les exemples d'Ephèse, Iasos et Aphrodisias," in: Charlotte Roueché and R. R. R. Smith (eds.), *Aphrodisias Papers 3. JRA* Supplementary Series no. 20. Ann Arbor, 111–20.

Grottanelli, Cristiano, and Milano, Lucio 2004. *Food and Identity in the Ancient World.* Padua.

Grottanelli, Cristiano, and Parise, Nicola (eds.) 1998. *Sacrificio e società nel mondo antico.* Bari.

Gruen, Erich S. 1990. *Studies in Greek Culture and Roman Policy.* Leyden.

Gruen, Erich S. 1992. "The making of the Trojan legend," in: Erich S. Gruen (ed.), *Culture and National Identity in Republican Rome.* Ithaca, NY, 6–51.

Gruen, Erich S. 1998. "Jews, Greeks and Romans in the Third Sibylline Oracle," in: Martin Goodman (ed.), *Jews in a Graeco-Roman World.* Oxford, 15–36.

Gruen, Erich S. 2002. *Diaspora: Jews amidst Greeks and Romans.* Cambridge, MA, and London.

Guarducci, Margherita 1967–77. *Epigrafia Greca.* 4 vols. Rome.

Guidobaldi, M. P. 2002. *I materiali votivi della grotta del Colle di Rapino.* CstipiVot 15. Rome.

Gustafsson, Gabriella 2000. *Evocatio Deorum: Historical and Mythical Interpretations of Ritualised Conquests in the Expansion of Ancient Rome.* Acta universitatis Upsaliensis, Historia Religionum 16. Uppsala.

Haack, Marie-Laurence 2003. *Les haruspices dans le monde romain.* Bordeaux.

Habinek, Thomas, and Schiesaro, Alessandro (eds.) 1997. *The Roman Cultural Revolution.* Princeton, NJ.

Haensch, Rudolf 1997. *Capita provinciarum.* Mainz.

Haensch, Rudolf 2006. "'Religion' und Kulte im juristischen Schrifttum der Hohen Kaiserzeit," in: Elm et al. (2006: 233–48).

Hajjar, Youssef 1977. *La triade d'Héliopolis-Baalbek: Son culte et sa diffusion à travers les texts littéraires et les documents iconographiques et épigraphiques.* 2 vols. Leyden.

Hajjar, Youssef 1985. *La triade d'Héliopolis-Baalbek: Iconographie, théologie, culte et sanctuaires.* Montreal.

Halkin, Léon 1953. *La supplication d'action de grâces chez les Romains.* Paris.

Hänlein-Schäfer, Heidi 1985. *Veneratio Augusti: Eine Studie zu den Tempeln des ersten römischen Kaisers.* Rome.

Hänlein-Schäfer, Heidi 1996. "Die Ikonographie des Genius Augusti im Kompital- und Hauskult der frühen Kaiserzeit," in: Alastair Small (ed.), *Subject and Ruler: The Cult of the Ruling Power in Classical Antiquity.* Ann Arbor, 73–9.

Hanson, John A. 1959. *Roman Theater-Temples.* Princeton, NJ.

Hardie, P. 1986. *Virgil's Aeneid: Cosmos and Imperium.* Oxford.

Harland, Philip 2003. *Associations, Synagogues and Congregations: Claiming a Place in Ancient Mediterranean Society.* Minneapolis.

Harmon, Daniel E. 1978. "The public festivals of Rome," *ANRW II.16, 2.* 1440–68.

Harrison, Thomas J. 2000. *Divinity and History: The Religion of Herodotus.* Oxford.

Hartmann, M. 2005. *Die frühlateinischen Inschriften und ihre Datierung: Eine linguistisch-archäologisch-paläographische Untersuchung.* Münchener Forschungen zur historischen Sprachwissenschaft 3. Bremen.

Hatzfeld, J. 1919. *Les trafiquants italiens dans l'orient hellénique.* Paris.

Hauken, T. 1998. *Petition and Response: An Epigraphic Study of Petitions to Roman Emperors.* Bergen, 181–249.

Heck, Eberhard 1987. *Me Theomachein: Die Bestrafung des Gottesverächters. Untersuchungen zu Bekämpfung und Aneignung römischer religio bei Tertullian, Cyprian und Laktanz*. Frankfurt.

Heimerl, A. 2001. *Die römischen Lampen aus Pergamon vom Beginn der Kaiserzeit bis zum Ende des 4. Jhs. n. Chr*. Pergamenische Forschungen 13. Berlin.

Heine, Ronald E. 2004. "The beginnings of Latin Christian literature," in: Frances Young, Lewis Ayres, and Andrew Louth (eds.), *The Cambridge History of Early Christian Literature*. Cambridge, 131–41.

Heinzelmann, M., Ortalli, J., Fasold, P., and Witteyer, M. (eds.) 2001. *Römischer Bestattungsbrauch und Beigabensitten: in Rom, Norditalien und den Nordwestprovinzen von der späten Republik bis in die Kaiserzeit* (= *Culto dei morti e costumi funerari romani: Roma, Italia settentrionale e province nord-occidentali dalla tarda Repubblica all' età imperiale*). Wiesbaden.

Henig, Martin 1984. *Religion in Roman Britain*. London.

Henrichs, Albert 1985. " 'Der Glaube der Hellen': Religionsgeschichte als Glaubensbekenntnis und Kulturkritik," in: William M. Calder, Hellmut Flashar, and Theodor Lindken (eds.), *Wilamowitz nach 50 Jahren*. Darmstadt, 263–305.

Herz, Peter 1975. *Untersuchungen zum Festkalender der römischen Kaiserzeit nach datierten Weih- und Ehreninschriften*. Mainz.

Herz, Peter 1978. "Kaiserfeste der Prinzipatszeit," *ANRW II.16, 2*. 1135–1200.

Herz, Peter 1997. "Herrscherverehrung und lokale Festkultur im Osten des römischen Reiches (Kaiser/Agone)," in: Cancik and Rüpke (1997: 239–64).

Herz, Peter 2000. "Endzeitstimmung und Zukunftserwartung in augusteischer Zeit," in: U. G. Leinsle and J. Mecke (eds.), *Zeit – Zeitenwechsel – Endzeit: Zeit im Wandel der Zeiten, Kulturen, Techniken und Disziplinen*. Schriftenreihe der Universität Regensburg 26. Regensburg, 157–69.

Hesberg, Henner von 1985. "Zur Plangestaltung der Coloniae Maritimae," *Römische Mitteilungen 92*. 127–50.

Hesberg, Henner von 1992. *Römische Grabbauten*. Darmstadt.

Heurgon, J. 1957. *Trois études sur le "Ver sacrum."* Brussels.

Hickson, Frances V. 1993. *Roman Prayer Language: Livy and the Aeneid of Vergil*. Stuttgart.

Hickson Hahn, Frances 2004. "The politics of thanksgiving" in: Christoph F. Konrad (ed.), *Augusto Augurio: Rerum humanarum et divinarum commentationes in honorem Jerzy Linderski*. Stuttgart, 31–51.

Hinard, François (ed.) 2000. *Histoire romaine. I: Des origines à Auguste*. Paris.

Hinard, François, and Dumont, Jean Christian (eds.) 2003. *Libitina: Pompes funèbres et supplices en Campanie à l'époque d'Auguste*. Paris.

Hofter, M. and Heilmeyer, W.-D. (eds.) 1988. *Kaiser Augustus und die verlorene Republik*. Exhibition catalogue. Berlin.

Hölkeskamp, Karl-Joachim 1987. *Die Entstehung der Nobilität: Studien zur sozialen und politischen Geschichte der Römischen Republik im 4. Jhdt. v. Chr*. Stuttgart.

Hölkeskamp, Karl-Joachim 2004. *Rekonstruktionen einer Republik: Die politische Kultur des antiken Rom und die Forschung der letzten Jahrzehnte*. Munich.

Holland, Louise Adams 1961. *Janus and the Bridge*. Rome.

Hölscher, Tonio 1967. *Victoria Romana: Archäologische Untersuchungen zur Geschichte und Wesensart der römischen Siegesgöttin von den Anfängen bis zum Ende des 3. Jhd. n. Chr*. Mainz.

Hölscher, Tonio 1980. "Die Geschichtsauffassung in der römischen Repräsentationskunst," *JdI 95*. 265–321.

Hölscher, Tonio 1984. *Staatsdenkmal und Publikum: Vom Untergang der Republik bis zur Festigung des Kaisertums in Rom.* Xenia – Konstanzer althistorische Vorträge und Forschungen 9. Constance.

Hölscher, Tonio 1988. "Historische Reliefs," in: Hofter and Heilmeyer (1988: 351–400).

Hölscher, Tonio 1993. "Mythen als Exempel der Geschichte," in: Fritz Graf (ed.), *Mythen in mythenloser Gesellschaft: Das Paradigma Roms.* Stuttgart, 67–87.

Hölscher, Tonio 1998. *Öffentliche Räume in frühen griechischen Städten.* Heidelberg.

Hopkins, Keith 1965. "Elite mobility in the Roman Empire," *P&P 32.* 12–29.

Horbury, W. 1998. "The cult of Christ and the cult of the saints," *New Testament Studies 44.* 444–69.

Hörig, Monika, and Schwertheim, Elmar 1987. *Corpus Cultus Iovis Dolicheni (CCID).* Leyden.

Horstmanshoff, H. F. J., and Stol, M. (eds.) 2004. *Magic and Rationality in Ancient Near Eastern and Graeco-Roman Medicine.* Studies in Ancient Medicine 27. Leyden.

Howgego, C. J. 1995. *Ancient History from Coins.* London.

Howgego, C. J., Heuchert, V., and Burnett, A. M. 2005. *Coinage and Identity in the Roman Provinces.* Oxford.

Hubaux, Jean 1958. *Rome et Véies: Recherches sur la chronologie légendaire du Moyen Âge romain.* Paris.

Humbert, Michel 1978. *Municipium et civitas sine suffragio: L'Organisation de la conquête jusqu'à la guerre sociale.* Rome.

Humm, Michel 1996. "Les origines du pythagorisme romain: problèmes historiques et philosophiques," *Les Études classiques 64.* 339–53.

Hummel, Pascale 2000. *Histoire de l'histoire de la philologie.* Geneva.

Humphrey, John H. 1986. *Roman Circuses: Arenas for Chariot Racing.* London.

Hunink, Vincent 1997. *Apuleius of Madauros, Pro se de magia (Apologia).* Amsterdam.

Inglebert, H. 1996. *Les romains chrétiens face à l'histoire de Rome.* Paris.

Jameson, Michael H. 1988. "Sacrifice and animal husbandry in classical Greece," in: C. R. Whittaker (ed.), *Pastoral Economies in Classical Antiquity.* Cambridge, 87–119.

Jameson, S. 1966. "Two Lycian families," *Anatolian Studies 16.* 125–37.

Jannot, Jean-René 1998. *Devins, dieux et démons: Regards sur la religion de l'Étrurie antique.* Paris.

Jocelyn, H. D. 1972. "The poems of Quintus Ennius," *ANRW I.2.* 987–1026.

Johns, C. M. 1996. *The Jewellery of Roman Britain: Celtic and Classical Traditions.* London.

Johnson, Mark J. 1997. "Pagan-Christian burial practices of the fourth century: shared tombs?" *Journal of Early Christian Studies 5.1.* 37–59.

Johnston, Sarah Iles 1990. *Hekate Soteira.* Atlanta, GA.

Johnston, Sarah Iles 2005. *Religions of the Ancient World: A Guide.* Cambridge, MA.

Jones, Arnold H. M. 1940. *The Greek City from Alexander to Justinian.* Oxford.

Jones, Christopher 1978. *The Roman World of Dio Chrysostom.* Cambridge, MA.

Jones, Christopher 1999. *Kinship and Diplomacy in the Ancient World.* Cambridge, MA.

Jones, Siân 1997. *The Archaeology of Ethnicity: Constructing Identities in the Past and the Present.* London.

Jordan, David R. 1985. "A survey of Greek *defixiones* not included in the special corpora," *Greek, Roman and Byzantine Studies 26.* 151–97.

Jordan, David R. 1991. "A new reading of a phylactery from Beirut," *ZPE 88.* 61–9.

Jordan, David R. 2001. "New Greek curse tablets (1985–2000)," *Greek, Roman and Byzantine Studies 41.* 5–46.

Jordan, David R., Montgomery, Hugo, and Thomassen, Einar (eds.) 1999. *The World of Ancient Magic*. Bergen.

Jost, M. F. P. 2000. *Die Patrozinien der Kirchen der Stadt Rom vom Anfang bis in das 10. Jahrhundert*. 2 vols. Neuried.

Jouin, Martine, and Méniel, Patrice 2001. "Les dépôts animaux et le fanum gallo-romain de Vertault (Côte-d'Or)," *Revue Archéologique de l'Est 50*. 119–216.

Jürgens, H. 1972. *Pompa diaboli: Die lateinischen Kirchenväter und das antike Theater*. Tübinger Beiträge zur Altertumswissenschaft, 46. Stuttgart.

Kähler, Heinz 1966. *Seethiasos und Census: Die Reliefs aus dem Palazzo Santa Croce in Rom*. Monumenta artis Romanae 6. Berlin.

Kähler, Heinz 1970. *Der römische Tempel*. Berlin.

Kaizer, Ted 2002. *The Religious Life of Palmyra: A Study of the Social Patterns of Worship in the Roman Period*. Stuttgart.

Kaizer, Ted 2004. "Religious mentality in Palmyrene documents," *Klio 86*. 165–84.

Kaizer, Ted 2005. "Leucothea as Mater Matuta at Colonia Berytus," *Syria 82*. 199–206.

Kajanto, I. 1957. *God and Fate in Livy*. Turku.

Kajava, Mika 1998. "Visceratio," *Arctos 32*. 109–31.

Kaufmann-Heinimann, Annemarie 1998. *Götter und Lararien aus Augusta Raurica: Herstellung, Fundzusammenhänge und sakrale Funktion figürlicher Bronzen in einer römischen Stadt*. Forschungen in Augst 26. Augst.

Kienast, Dietmar 1999. *Augustus: Prinzeps und Monarch*. 3rd edn. Darmstadt.

Kiley, Mark (ed.) 1997. *Prayer from Alexander to Constantine: A Critical Anthology*. New York.

Kippenberg, Hans G. 1995. "Lokale Religionsgeschichte von Schriftreligionen: Beispiele für ein nützliches Konzept," in: Hans G. Kippenberg and Brigitte Luchesi (eds.), *Lokale Religionsgeschichte*. Marburg, 9–11.

Kippenberg, Hans G. 1997. "Magic in Roman civic discourse : why rituals could be illegal," in Peter Schäfer and Hans G. Kippenberg (eds.), *Envisioning Magic:A Princeton Seminar and Symposium*. Studies in the History of Religions 75. Leyden, 37–63.

Kippenberg, Hans G. 2002. *Discovering Religious History in the Modern Age*, trans. Barbara Harshaw. Princeton, NJ.

Klein, Richard 1968. *Tertullian und das römische Reich*. Heidelberg.

Kleiner, Diana E. E. 1992. *Roman Sculpture*. New Haven, CT.

Kloppenborg, John S., and Wilson, Stephen G. (eds.) 1996. *Voluntary Associations in the Graeco-Roman World*. London.

Klose, D. O. A. 2005. "Festivals and games in the cities of the East during the Roman Empire," in: Howgego et al. (2005: 125–33).

Klumbach, H. 1961. *Lampenbilder und Terra Sigillata*. Jahrbuch des Römisch-Germanischen Zentralmuseums 8. Mainz, 190–4.

Knoch, O. B. 1991. "Gab es eine Petrusschule in Rom?" *Studien zum Neuen Testament und seiner Umwelt 16*. 105–26.

Koch, Carl 1932. "Mola salsa," *RE 15.2*. 2016–17.

Koch, Carl 1960. "Die altrömische Staatskult im Spiegel augusteischer und spätrepublikanischer Apologetik," in: C. Koch, *Religio: Studien zu Kult und Glauben der Römer*. Nuremberg, 176–204 (translated as "Roman state cult in the mirror of Augustan and late Republican apologetics" in: Ando 2003: 296–329).

Koch, Guntram 1993. *Sarkophage der römischen Kaiserzeit*. Darmstadt.

Kokkinia, C. 2000. *Die Opramoas-Inschrift von Rhodiapolis: Euergetismus und soziale Elite in Lykien*. Bonn.

Kolb, Frank 2004. "*Praesens deus*: Kaiser und Gott unter der Tetrarchie," in: Alexander Demandt, Andreas Goltz, and Heinrich Schlange-Schöningen (eds.), *Diokletian und die Tetrarchie*. Millennium Studies 1. Berlin and New York, 27–37.

Körner, Christian 2002. *Philippus Arabs: Ein Soldatenkaiser in der Tradition des antoninisch-severischen Prinzipats*. Untersuchungen zur antiken Literatur und Geschichte 61. Berlin.

Kotansky, R. 1991. "Magic in the court of the Governor of Arabia," *ZPE 88*. 41–60.

Kotansky, R. 1994. *Greek Magical Amulets 1*. Opladen.

Kraabel, A. Thomas 1978. "Paganism and Judaism: the Sardis evidence," in: *Paganisme, Judaisme, Chretienisme*. Melanges Marcel Simon. Paris, 13–33 (= Overman and MacLennan 1992: 237–56).

Kraabel, A. Thomas 1979. "The Diaspora synagogue: archaeological and epigraphic evidence since Sukeni," in: *ANRW II.19, 1*. 477–510.

Kraabel, A. Thomas 1981. "The social systems of six Diaspora synagogues," in: Joseph Gutmann (ed.), *Ancient Synagogues: The State of Research*. Brown Judaic Studies. Chico, CA, 79–91 (= Overman and MacLennan 1992: 258–67).

Kraabel, A. Thomas 1982. "The Roman Diaspora: six questionable assumptions," *JRS 33*. 445–64 (= Overman and MacLennan 1992: 1–20).

Kraabel, A. Thomas 1987. "Unity and viversity among Diaspora synagogues," in: Lee I. Levine (ed.), *The Synagogue in Late Antiquity*. Philadelphia, 49–59 (= Overman and MacLennan 1992: 21–34).

Kraus, Christina S. 1994. " 'No second Troy': topoi and refoundation in Livy, Book V," *TAPhA 124*. 267–89.

Krause, Carl 1931. "Hostia," *RE*, Suppl. *5*. 236–82.

Krauss, Franklin B. 1930. *An Interpretation of the Omens, Portents, and Prodigies Recorded by Livy, Tacitus, and Suetonius*. Philadelphia.

Kugel, James L. 2003. *The God of Old: Inside the Lost World of the Bible*. New York.

Kühlborn, J.-S. 1988. "Germanien und Rom," in: Hofter et al. (1988: 530–41, 580–605).

Kunz, Heike 2006. *Sicilia: Religionsgeschichte des römischen Sizilen*. Religion der römischen Provinzen 4. Tübingen.

Künzl, Ernst 1979. "Le argenterie," in: F. Zevi (ed.), *Pompei 79*. Naples, 211–28.

Künzl, Ernst 1988. *Der römische Triumph: Siegesfeiern im antiken Rom*. Munich.

Kuttner, A. L. 1995. *Dynasty and Empire in the Age of Augustus: The Case of the Boscorelae Cups*. Berkeley.

La Regina, A. 1966. "Le iscrizioni osche di Pietrabbondante e la questione di *Bovianum vetus*," *Rheinisches Museum 109*. 260–86.

La Rocca, E. 2002. "Le basiliche cristiane 'a deambulatorio' e la sopravvivenza del culto eroico," in: F. Guidobaldi and A. Guiglia Guidobaldi (eds.), *Ecclesiae Urbis 2*. Vatican City, 1109–40.

Lafferty, M. K. 2003. "Translating faith from Greek to Latin: Romanitas and Christianitas in late fourth-century Rome and Milan," *Journal of Early Christianity 11*. 21–62.

Lamberton, R. 1986. *Homer the Theologian*. Berkeley.

Lampe, P. 1989. *Die stadtrömischen Christen in den ersten beiden Jahrhunderten*. 2nd edn. Tübingen, 301–7.

Lane Fox, Robin 1986 [1997]. *Pagans and Christians in the Mediterranean World from the Second Century AD to the Conversion of Constantine*. London (French edn. 1997).

Lang-Auinger, C. (ed.) 2003. *Hanghaus 1 in Ephesos: Funde und Ausstattung*. Forschungen in Ephesos VIII/4. Vienna.

Lapidge, Michael (ed.) 1996. *Wallace Martin Lindsay: Studies in Early Medieval Latin Glossaries*. Aldershot.

Latte, Kurt 1914. "Immolatio," *RE 9/1*. 1112–33.

Latte, Kurt 1960. *Römische Religionsgeschichte*. Munich.

Laurence, R., and Wallace-Hadrill, A. (eds.) 1997. "Domestic space in the Roman world: Pompeii and beyond," *JRA* (Portsmouth), Suppl. *22*.

Le Bonniec, Henri 1958. *Le culte de Cérès à Rome: Des origines à la fin de la république*. Paris.

Le Gall, J. 1976. "Evocatio," in: *Mélanges offerts à Jacques Heurgon 1*. Collection de l'École française de Rome 27. Rome, 519–24.

Le Roux, Patrick 1995. *Romains d'Espagne: Cités et politique dans les provinces*. Paris.

Le Roux, Patrick 1998. *Le Haut-Empire romain en Occident d'Auguste aux Sévères*. Paris.

Lefèvre, Eckard 1989. *Das Bild-Programm des Apollo-Tempels auf dem Palatin*. Constance.

Legouilloux, Martine 2000. "L'hécatombe de l'ekklesiaterion de Posidonia-Paestum: le témoignage de la faune," in: Stéphane Verger (ed.), *Rites et espaces en pays celte et méditer-ranéen? Etude comparée à partir du sanctuaire d'Acy-Romance (Ardennes, France)*. Rome, 341–51.

Lehmann, Yves 1986. "Religion et politique autour des 'Antiquités divines' de Varron," *REL 64*. 92–103.

Lehmann, Yves 1997. *Varron théologien et philosophe romain*. Collection Latomus 237. Brussels.

Leibundgut, A. 1977. *Die römischen Lampen in der Schweiz: Eine kultur- und handels-geschichtliche Studie*. Bern.

Lejeune, M. 1990. *Méfitis d'après les dédicaces lucaniennes de Rossano di Vaglio*. Louvain-la-Neuve.

Lendon, J. E. 1997. *Empire of Honor: The Art of Government in the Roman World*. Oxford.

Leon, H. J. 1960. *The Jews of Ancient Rome*. Philadelphia.

Leppin, Hartmut 2004. "Zum Wandel des spätantiken Heidentums," *Millennium 1*. 59–82.

Letta, C. 1992. "I santuari rurali nell'Italia centro-appenninica: valori religiosi e funzione aggreg-ativa," *MEFRA 104*. 109–24.

Leumann, Manu 1937. "Review of Ernout et Meillet, *Dictionnaire étymologique de la langue Latine*," *Gnomon 13*. 27–36.

Levene, D. S. 1993. *Religion in Livy*. Leyden.

Levick, Barbara 1967. *Roman Colonies in Southern Asia Minor*. Oxford.

Levine, Lee I. 1996. "Diaspora Judaism in late antiquity and its relationship to Palestine: evidence from the ancient synagogue," in: B. Isaac and A. Oppenheimer (eds.), *Studies on the Jewish Diaspora in the Hellenistic and Roman Periods 12*. Tel Aviv, 139–58.

Levine, Lee I. 1998a. "Synagogue leadership: the case of the archisynagogue," in: Martin Goodman (ed.), *Jews in a Graeco-Roman World*. Oxford, 181–94.

Levine, Lee I. 1998b. *Judaism and Hellenism in Antiquity: Conflict or Confluence?* Seattle.

Levine, Lee I. 1999. "The patriarch and the ancient synagogue," in: Steven Fine (ed.), *Christians and Polytheists in the Ancient Synagogue: Cultural Interaction during the Greco-Roman Period*. London, 87–100.

Levine, Lee I. 2000. *The Ancient Synagogue: The First Thousand Years*. New Haven, CT.

Levison, Wilhelm 1946. *England and the Continent in the Eighth Century*. Oxford.

Lewy, H. 1978. *Chaldean Oracles and Theurgy*. 2nd edn. Paris.

Lichtenberger, Achim 2003. *Kulte und Kultur der Dekapolis: Untersuchungen zu numisma-tischen, archäologischen und epigraphischen Zeugnissen*. Wiesbaden.

Lieberg, Godo 1973. "Die 'theologia tripartita' in Forschung und Bezeugung," *ANRW I.4*. 63–115.

Liebeschuetz, J. H. W. G. 1979. *Continuity and Change in Roman Religion*. Oxford (repr. 1989).

Liebeschuetz, J. H. W. G. 1999. "The significance of the speech of Praetextatus," in: Polymnia Athanassiadi and Martin Frede (eds.), *Pagan Monotheism in Late Antiquity.* Oxford, 185–206.

Lieu, Judith, North, John, and Rajak, Tessa (eds.) 1992. *The Jews among Pagans and Christians in the Roman Empire.* London.

Lieu, Samuel N. C. 1994. *Manichaeism in Mesopotamia and the Roman East.* RG-RW 118. Leyden.

Lightfoot, Jane L. 2003. *Lucian, On the Syrian Goddess: Edited with Introduction, Translation and Commentary.* Oxford.

Lightstone, Jack N. 1984. *The Commerce of the Sacred: Mediation of the Divine Among Jews in the Greco-Roman Diaspora.* Chico, CA.

Lightstone, Jack N. 1988. *Society, the Sacred and Scripture in Ancient Judaism.* Waterloo, ON.

Lightstone, Jack N. 2002. "The Rabbis' Bible: the canon of the Hebrew Bible and the early Rabbinic guild," in: Lee Martin McDonald and James A. Sanders (eds.), *The Canon Debate.* Peabody, MA, 163–84.

Lightstone, Jack N. 2005. "Urbanization in the Roman Levant and the inter-religious struggle for success," in: Richard Ascough (ed.), *Religious Rivalries and the Struggle for Success in Sardis and Smyrna.* Waterloo, ON, 211–45.

Lindenberger, James M. 1994. *Ancient Aramaic and Hebrew Letters,* ed. Harold Richards Kent. Atlanta, GA.

Linder, Amnon 1987. *The Jews in Roman Imperial Legislation.* Detroit and Jerusalem.

Linderski, Jerzy 1982. "Cicero and Roman divination," *La Parola del Passato 37.* 12–38.

Linderski, Jerzy 1985. "The *Libri Reconditi,*" *HSCPh 89.* 207–34.

Linderski, Jerzy 1986. "The augural law," *ANRW II.16, 3.* 2146–312.

Linderski, Jerzy 1993. "Roman religion in Livy," in: Wolfgang Schuller (ed.), *Livius: Aspekte seines Werkes.* Xenia 31. Constance, 53–70.

Linderski, Jerzy 1995. *Roman Questions: Selected Papers.* HABES 20. Stuttgart.

Lindsay, Wallace M., and Thomson, H. S. 1921. *Ancient Lore in Medieval Latin Glossaries.* Oxford.

Ling, R. 1991. *Roman Painting.* Cambridge.

Littleton, C. Scott 1982. *The New Comparative Mythology: An Anthropological Assessment of the Theories of Georges Dumézil.* 3rd edn. Berkeley.

Long, Charlotte R. 1987. *The Twelve Gods of Greece and Rome.* Leyden.

Lott, J. Bert 2004. *The Neighborhoods of Augustan Rome.* Cambridge.

Lozano, F. 2002. *La religiòn del poder: el culto imperial en Athenas en época de Augusto y los emperadores Julio-Claudios.* BAR 1087. Oxford.

Lücke, S. *Syngeneia: Epigraphish-historische Studien zu einem Phänomen der antiken griechischen Diplomatie.* Frankfurt.

Lüderitz, G. 1983. *Corpus jüdischer Zeugnisse aus der Cyrenaika.* Beihefte zum Tübinger Atlas des vorderen Orients B, 53. Wiesbaden.

Luoghi 1996. *I luoghi degli dei.* Chieti.

Luterbacher, Franz 1904. *Der Prodigienglaube und Prodigienstil der Römer.* Burgdorf (repr. Darmstadt 1967).

Maas, Michael 1992. *John Lydus and the Roman Past.* London.

MacBain, Bruce 1982. *Prodigy and Expiation: A Study in Religion and Politics in Republican Rome.* Brussels.

MacMullen, Ramsay 1981. *Paganism in the Roman Empire.* New Haven, CT (French edn. 1987).

MacMullen, Ramsay 1984. "Notes on Romanization," *Bulletin of the American Society of Papyrologists 21.* 161–74.

MacMullen, Ramsay 1987. *Constantine*. 2nd edn. London.

Maier, Jean Louis 1987. *Le dossier du Donatisme 1: des origines à la mort de Constance II (303-361)*. Texte und Untersuchungen 134. Berlin.

Manuwald, Gesine 2001. *Fabulae praetextae: Spuren einer literarischen Gattung der Römer*. Munich.

Margolioth, Mordechai 1966. *Sepher Ha-Razim*. Jerusalem.

Markus, Robert 1990. *The End of Ancient Christianity*. Cambridge.

Marrou, Henri I. 1978. "Survivances païennes dans les rites funéraires des donatistes," in: *Hommage à Joseph Bidez et à Franz Cumont*. Collection Latomus 2. Brussels, 193–203.

Martens, M. 2004a. "The mithraeum in Tienen (Belgium): small finds and what they can tell us," in Martens and De Boe (2004: 25–48).

Martens, M. 2004b. "Re-thinking sacred 'rubbish': the ritual deposits of the temple of Mithras at Tienen," *JRA 17*. 333–53.

Martens, Marleen, and De Boe, Guy (eds.) 2004. *Roman Mithraism: The Evidence of the Small Finds*. Tienen.

Martin, Hanz G. 1987. *Römische Tempelkultbilder: Eine archäologische Untersuchung zur späten Republik*. Studi e materiali del Museo della civiltà Romana 12. Rome.

Martin, J.-P. 1982. *Providentia deorum: recherches sur certains aspects religieux du pouvoir impérial romain*. Rome.

Mastandrea, P. 1979. *Un neoplatonico latino: Cornelio Labeone*. EPRO 77. Leyden.

Mastrocinque, Attilio 1988. *Lucio Giunio Bruto: ricerche di storia, religione e diritto sulle origini della repubblica romana*. Trento.

Mastrocinque, Attilio 2005a. *From Jewish Magic to Gnosticism*. Tübingen.

Mastrocinque, Attilio 2005b. "Cosmologie e impero in Giuliano l'Apostata," *Klio 87*. 154–76.

Mattern, Torsten 2001. "*Dignis digna*: Innenräume stadtrömischer Tempel," *Antike Welt 32*. 57–63.

Mattiocco, M. (ed.) 1989. *Dalla villa di Ovidio al santuario di Ercole*. Sulmo.

Mayer, Marc (ed.) 1992. *Religio deorum: actas del coloquio internacional de epigrafía "Culto y sociedad en Occidente."* Barcelona.

Mazza, M. 1963. "Studi Arnobiani, I: la dottrina dei 'viri novi' nel secondo libro dell' 'Adversus nationes' di Arnobio," *Helikon 3*. 111–69.

McBrearty, Madeleine 1986. "The Leiden Papyrus: introduction and translation." MA thesis. Concordia University, Montreal (microfiche: Ottawa, ON, National Library of Canada, 1987).

McClelland, Charles 1980. *State, Society, and University in Germany 1700–1914*. Cambridge.

McCormick, M. 1986. *Eternal Victory: Triumphal Rulership in Late Antiquity, Byzantium, and the Early Medieval West*. Cambridge.

McCutcheon, Russell T. 1995. "The category 'religion' in recent publications: a critical survey," *Numen 42*. 284–309.

Meadows, A. M., and Williams, J. H. C. 2001. "*Moneta* and the monuments: coinage and politics in Republican Rome," *JRS 91*. 27–49.

Meeks, Wayne A., and Wilken, Robert L. 1978. *Jews and Christians in Antioch in the First Four Centuries of the Common Era*. Missoula, MT.

Merkelbach, Reinhold 1978. "Der Rangstreit der Städte Asiens und die Rede des Aelius Aristides über die Eintracht," *ZPE 32*. 287–96.

Merkelbach, Reinhold 1984. *Mithras*. Königstein.

Merkelbach, Reinhold, and Stauber, Josef 2002. *Steinepigramme aus dem griechischen Osten*. Band 4. Leipzig.

Meyer, Marvin W., and Smith, Richard (eds.) 1999. *Ancient Christian Magic: Coptic Texts of Ritual Power*. Princeton, NJ.

Meyers, Eric M. 1999. "The Torah shrine in the ancient synagogue: another look at the evidence," in: Steven Fine (ed.), *Jews, Christians and Polytheists in the Ancient Synagogue: Cultural Interaction during the Greco-Roman Period*. London, 201–23.

Meyer-Zwiffelhoffer, Eckhard (1999). Πολιτικως ἀρχεον: *Zum Regierung der senatorischen Statthalter in der kaiserzeitlichen griechischen Provinzen*. Stuttgart.

Michels, Agnes K. 1954/5. "Early Roman religion, 1945–1952," *CW 48*. 25–35, 41–5.

Michels, Agnes Kirsopp 1967. *The Calendar of the Roman Republic*. Princeton, NJ.

Michels, Agnes Kirsopp 1976. "The versatility of *religio*," in: *The Mediterranean World: Papers Presented in Honor of Gilbert Bagnani*. Peterborough, ON, 36–77.

Mikalson, Jon D. 2003. *Herodotus and Religion in the Persian Wars*. Chapel Hill, NC.

Millar, Fergus 1990. "The Roman *coloniae* of the Near East: a study of cultural relations," in: H. Solin and M. Kajava (eds.), *Roman Eastern Policy and Other Studies in Roman History*. Helsinki, 7–58.

Millar, Fergus 1992. *The Emperor in the Roman World*. 2nd edn. London.

Millar, Fergus 1993a. *The Roman Near East, 31 BC–AD 337*. Cambridge, MA.

Millar, Fergus 1993b. "The Greek city in the Roman period," in: Mogens Herman Hansen (ed.), *The Ancient Greek City-State*. Copenhagen, 232–60.

Mirecki, Paul, and Meyer, Marvin W. (eds.) 2002. *Magic and Ritual in the Ancient World*. Leyden and Boston.

Mirkovic, Miroslava 1994. "*Beneficiarii consularis* in Sirmium," *Chiron 24*. 345–404.

Mitchell, Stephen 1993. *Anatolia: Land, Men and Gods in Asia Minor*. 2 vols. Oxford.

Mitchell, Stephen 1999. "The cult of *Theos Hypsistos* between pagans, Jews, and Christians," in: Polymnia Athanassiadi and Michael Frede (eds.), *Pagan Monotheism in Late Antiquity*. Oxford, 81–148.

Modrzejewski, J. M. 1991. *Les juifs d'Egypte de Ramses II à Hadrien*. Paris.

Moede, Katja 2004. "Ritual und Bild: Die Darstellung religiöser Rituale im römischen Relief." Dissertation. Greifswald.

Moles, John 1993. "Livy's Preface," *PCPS 39*. 141–68.

Momigliano, Arnaldo 1955–92. *Contributi alla storia degli studi classici e del mondo antico*. 9 vols. Rome.

Momigliano, Arnaldo 1984. "The theological efforts of the Roman upper classes in the first century BC," *Classical Philology 79*. 199–211 (= Ando 2003: 147–63).

Momigliano, Arnaldo 1986. "The disadvantages of monotheism for a universal state," *Classical Philology 81*. 285–297 (= Momigliano 1987: 142–58).

Momigliano, Arnaldo 1987. *On Pagans, Jews, and Christians*. Middletown, CT.

Mommsen, Theodor 1859. "Die Ludi Magni und Romani," *Rheinisches Museum* N.F. *14*. 79–87.

Montanari, Enrico 1988. *Identità culturale e conflitti religiosi nella Roma repubblicana*. Rome.

Moralee, J. 2004. *"For Salvation's Sake": Provincial Loyalty, Personal Religion and Epigraphic Production in the Roman and Late Antique Near East*. New York.

Morel, Jean-Paul 1992. "Ex-voto par transformation, ex-voto par destination: à propos du dépôt votif de Fondo Ruozzo à Teano," in: *Mélanges P. Lévêque* 6. Besançon, 221–32.

Moussy, Claude 1966. *Gratia et sa famille*. Publications de la Faculté des lettres et sciences humaines de l'Université de Clermont-Ferrand 2.25. Paris.

Mouterde, René 1930. *Le glaive de Dardanos: objets et inscriptions magiques de Syrie*. Mélanges de l'Université Saint-Joseph 15, 3. Beyrouth.

Mratschek, S. 2001. "*Vota et frequentationes*: Heiligenkult und gesellschaftliche Kontakte des Paulinus von Nola auf dem Apostelfest in Rom," XXIX Incontro di studiosi dell'antichità cristiana: Pietro e Paolo e il loro rapporto con Roma nelle testimonianze antiche. *Studia Ephemeridis Augustinianum 74.* 261–75.

Muth, Susanne 1998. *Erleben von Raum – Leben im Raum: Zur Funktion mythologischer Mosaikbilder in der römisch-kaiserzeitlichen Wohnarchitektur.* Archäologie und Geschichte 10. Heidelberg.

Naumann, G. 1933. *Griechische Weihinschriften.* Halle.

Nelis-Clément, Jocelyne 2000. *Les beneficiarii: militaires et adminstrateurs au service de l'empire(Ier s. a.C–VIe s. p.C.).* Bordeaux.

Néraudau, Jean-Pierre 1979. *La jeunesse dans la littérature et les institutions de la Rome républicaine.* Paris.

Neudecker, Richard 1988. *Die Skulpturenausstattung römischer Villen in Italien.* Beiträge zur Erschliessung hellenistischer und kaiserzeitlicher Skulptur und Architektur 9. Mainz.

Neudecker, Richard 1998. "The Roman villa as a locus of art collections," in: A. Frazer (1998: 77–91).

Neusner, Jacob 1993. *Judaic Law from Jesus to the Mishnah: A Systematic Reply to Professor E.P. Sanders.* Atlanta, GA.

Neusner, Jacob 1995. *Judaism in Modern Times.* Oxford.

Niebuhr, Barthold G. 1828–32. *Römische Geschichte.* Berlin.

Nilsson, Martin Person 1988. *Geschichte der griechischen Religion 2: Die hellenistische und römische Zeit.* 4th edn. Handbuch der Altertumswissenschaft 5, 2, 2. Munich.

Nock, Arthur Darby 1972. *Essays on Religion and the Ancient World.* Oxford.

Norden, Eduard 1939. *Aus Altroemischen Priesterbuechern.* Leipzig (2nd edn. 1995).

Noreña, C. F. 2001. "The communication of the emperor's virtues," *JRS 91.* 146–68.

North, John 1976. "Conservatism and change in Roman religion," *Papers of the British School at Rome 44.* 1–12.

North, John 1979. "Religious toleration in Republican Rome," *PCPS 25.* 85–103 (= Ando 2003: 199–219).

North, John 1990. "Diviners and divination at Rome," in: John North and Mary Beard (eds.), *Pagan Priests: Religion and Power in the Ancient World.* Ithaca, NY, 51–71.

North, John 1993. "Roman reactions to empire," *Scripta Classica Israelica 12.* 127–38.

North, John 1995. "Religion and rusticity," in: Timothy J. Cornell and Kathryn Lomas (eds.), *Urban Society in Roman Italy.* London, 135–50.

North, John 1998. "The books of the *pontifices*," in: *La mémoire perdue: Recherches sur l'administration romaine.* Rome, 45–63.

North, John 2000. *Roman Religion.* New Surveys in the Classics 30. Oxford.

Nouilhan, Michèle 1989. "Les lectisternes républicains," in: Annie-France Laurens (ed.), *Entre hommes et dieux: Le convive, le héros, le prophète.* Paris, 27–40.

Noy, David 1993–5. *Jewish Inscriptions of Western Europe. 1: Italy (excluding the City of Rome), Spain and Gaul. 2: The City of Rome.* Cambridge.

Noy, David 1998. "Where were the Jews of the Diaspora buried?" in: Martin Goodman (ed.), *Jews in a Graeco-Roman World.* Oxford, 75–92.

Noy, David 2000. *Foreigners at Rome: Citizens and Strangers.* London.

Noy, David, and Bloedhorn, Hanswulf 2004. *Syria and Cyprus: Inscriptiones Judaicae Orientis. Vol. 3.* Texts and Studies in Ancient Judaism 102. Tübingen.

Noy, David, and Horbury, W. (eds.) 1992. *Jewish Inscriptions of Greco-Roman Egypt.* Cambridge.

Noy, David, Panayotov, Alexander, and Bloedhorn, Hanswulf (eds.) 2004. *Inscriptiones Judaicae Orientalis. Vol. 1: Eastern Europe.* Tübingen.

Ogden, Daniel 2002. *Magic, Witchcraft, and Ghosts in the Greek and Roman Worlds: A Sourcebook.* Oxford.

Ogilvie, R. M. 1969. *The Romans and their Gods in the Age of Augustus*. London.

Opelt, Ilona 1980. *Die Polemik in der christlichen lateinischen Literatur von Tertullian bis Augustin*. Heidelberg.

Orlin, Eric 1997. *Temples, Religion and Politics in the Roman Republic*. Leyden.

Orr, D. G. 1978. "Roman domestic religion: the evidence of the household shrines," *ANRW II.16, 2*, 1557–91.

Ortalli, Jacopo 2001. "Il culto funerario della Cispadana romana," in: Heinzelmann et al. (2001: 215–42).

Ostrow, Stephen E. 1990. "The *Augustales* in the Augustan scheme," in: Raaflaub and Toher (1990: 364–79).

Overman, J. Andrew, and MacLennan, Robert S. (eds.) 1992. *Diaspora Jews and Judaism: Essays in Honor of and in Dialogue with A. Thomas Kraabel*. University of South Florida Studies in the History of Judaism 41. Atlanta, GA.

Pagden, Anthony 1995. *Lords of All the World: Ideologies of Empire in Spain, Britain and France, c. 1500–c. 1800*. New Haven, CT.

Pailin, David 1984. *Attitudes to Other Religions*. Manchester.

Pailler, Jean-Marie 1988. *Bacchanalia: La répression de 186 av. J.-C. á Rome et en Italie*. Rome.

Painter, K. S. 1977. *The Mildenhall Treasure: Roman Silver from East Anglia*. London.

Painter, K. S. 2001. *The Insula of the Menander at Pompeii 4: The Silver Treasure*. Oxford.

Palmer, Robert E. A. 1970. *The Archaic Community of the Romans*. Cambridge.

Palmer, Robert E. A. 1974. *Roman Religion and Roman Empire: Five Essays*. Philadelphia.

Panciera, S. 1990. "Le iscrizioni votive latine," *Scienze dell'antichità 3–4*. 905–14.

Pani Ermini, L. 1989. "Santuario e città fra tarda antichità e altomedioevo," *Settimane di Studio del Centro Italiano di Studi sull'Alto Medioevo 36/2*. 837–77.

Péché, Valerie, and Vendries, Christophe 2001. *Musique et spectacles à Rome et dans l'occident romain sous la République et le Haut Empire*. Paris.

Pergola, P., and Barbini, P. M. 1999. *Le catacombe romane: Storia e topografia*. 2nd edn. Rome.

Petzl, Georg 1994. *Die Beichtinschriften Westkleinasiens*. Bonn.

Petzl, Georg 1998. *Die Beichtinschriften im römischen Kleinasien und der Fromme und Gerechte Gott*. Opladen.

Phillips, C. Robert 1986. "The sociology of religious knowledge in the Roman Empire to A.D. 284," *ANRW II.16, 3*, 2677–773.

Phillips, C. Robert 1988. "The *Compitalia* and the *Carmen Contra Paganos*," *Historia 37*. 383–4.

Phillips, C. Robert 1991a. "Misconceptualizing classical mythology." Repr. in: Richard Buxton (ed.), *Oxford Readings in Greek Religion*. Oxford 2000, 344–58.

Phillips, C. Robert 1991b. "*Nullum crimen sine lege*: socioreligious sanctions on magic," in Christopher Faraone and Dirk Obink (eds.), *Magika Hiera: Ancient Greek Magic and Religion*. New York, 260–76.

Phillips, C. Robert 1996. "Rev. Jan Bremmer, *Greek Religion*," *CP 91*. 281–6.

Phillips, C. Robert 2000a. "Walter Burkert *In Partibus Romanorum*," *Religion 30*. 245–58.

Phillips, C. Robert 2000b. "Ancient Roman religion in the late 1990s," *Religious Studies Review 26*. 140–5.

Phillips, C. Robert 2001. "Sondergötter," *NP 11*. 713–14.

Phillips, C. Robert 2004. "Weinstock, Stefan (1901–71)," in: Robert B. Todd (ed.), *The Dictionary of British Classicists 3*. Bristol, 1043–6.

Piétri, Charles 1976. *Roma christiana*. 2 vols. Rome.

Piétri, Charles 1997. *Christiana respublica: éléments d'une enquête sur le christianisme antique*. Collection de l'École Française de Rome 234, 1–3. 3 vols. Rome.

Piétri, Charles 2004. *Naissance d'une chrétienté (250–430)*. Histoire du christianisme des origines à nos jours 2. Paris.

Piranomonte, Marina (ed.) 2002. *Il Santuario della Musica e il Bosco Sacro di Anna Perenna*. Rome.

Piso, Ioan 2003. *Das Heiligtum des Jupiter Optimus Maximus auf dem Pfaffenberg/Carnuntum: Die Inschriften*. Vienna.

Pleket, Harry W. 1981. "Religious history as the history of mentality: the 'believer' as servant of the deity in the Greek world," in: Versnel (1981a: 152–92).

Poccetti, P. 1979. *Nuovi documenti italici a completamento del manuale di E. Vetter*. Pisa.

Poccetti, P., [and Nava, M. L.] 2001. "Il santuario lucano di Rossano di Vaglio: una nuova dedica ad Ercole," *MEFRA 113*. 95–122.

Pollini, John 1990. "Man or god: divine assimilation and imitation in the Late Republic and Early Principate," in: Raaflaub and Toher (1990: 334–63).

Porten Palange, F. P. 2004. *Katalog der Punzenmotive in der arretinischen Reliefkeramik*. Römisch-Germanisches Zentralmuseum. Kataloge vor- und frühgeschichtlicher Altertümer 38. Mainz.

Porton, Gary 2001. "Who was a Jew," in: Jacob Neusner and Allan J. Avery-Peck (eds.), *Judaism in Late Antiquity 2.3.2*. Leyden, 197–218.

Potter, David S. 2004. *The Roman Empire at Bay AD 180–395*. London.

Poultney, J. W. 1959. *The Bronze Tables of Iguvium*. Baltimore, MD.

Preisendanz, K., and Henrichs, A. (eds.) 1973–4. *Papyri Graecae Magicae*. Stuttgart.

Preller, Ludwig 1883. *Römische Mythologie*. 3rd edn. Berlin.

Prescendi, Francesca forthcoming. *Décrire et comprendre le sacrifice: Les réflexions des Romains sur leur propre religion à partir de la littérature antiquaire*. Potsdamer Altertumswissenschaftliche Beiträge. Stuttgart.

Price, Simon 1984. *Rituals and Power: The Roman Imperial Cult in Asia Minor*. Cambridge.

Price, Simon 1999. "Latin Christian apologetics: Minucius Felix, Tertullian, and Cyprian," in: Mark Edwards, Martin Goodman, and Simon Price (eds.), *Apologetics in the Roman Empire: Pagans, Jews and Christians*. Oxford, 105–29.

Prosdoscimi, A. 1984. *Le tavole iguvine 1*. Florence.

Prosdoscimi, A. 1985. "Rite et sacrifice dans les tables d'Iguvium," in *Sodalitas: Scritti in onore di Antonio Guarino*. Naples, 3317–40.

Prosdoscimi, A. 1989. "Le religioni degli Italici," in: *Italia omnium terrarum parens*. Milan, 477–545.

Purcell, Nicolas 1983. "The *apparitores*: a study in social mobility," *Papers of the British School at Rome 51*. 125–73.

Purcell, Nicholas 2005. "Romans in the Roman world," in: Galinsky (2005: 85–105).

Putnam, Michael C. J. 2001. *Horace's Carmen Saeculare*. London.

Quass, F. 1982. "Zur politischen Tätigkeit der munizipalen Aristokratie der griechischen Ostens in der Kaiserzeit," *Historia 31*. 188–213.

Quass, F. 1993. *Die Honoratiorenschicht in der Städten der griechischen Ostens*. Stuttgart.

Raaflaub, Kurt (ed.) 1986. *Social Struggles in Archaic Rome: New Perspectives on the Conflict of the Orders*. Berkeley.

Raaflaub, Kurt, and Toher, Mark (eds.) 1990. *Between Republic and Empire: Interpretations of Augustus and His Principate*. Berkeley.

Radke, Gerhard [1965] 1979. *Die Götter Altitaliens*. Fontes et Commentationes 3. 2nd edn. Münster.

Radke, Gerhard 1987. *Zur Entwicklung der Gottesvorstellung und der Gottesverehrung in Rom*. Darmstadt.

Raepsaet-Charlier, Marie-Thérèse 1993. *Diis deabusque sacrum.* Paris.

Rajak, Tessa 1996. "Jews as benefactors," in: B. Isaac and A. Oppenheimer (eds.), *Studies on the Jewish Diaspora in the Hellenistic and Roman Periods 12.* Tel Aviv, 17–36.

Rajak, Tessa 1998. "The gifts of god at Sardis," in: Martin Goodman (ed.), *Jews in a Graeco-Roman World.* Oxford, 229–40.

Rajak, Tessa 1999. "The synagogue within the Greco-Roman city," in: Steven Fine (ed.), *Jews, Christians and Polytheists in the Ancient Synagogue: Cultural Interaction during the Greco-Roman Period.* London, 161–73.

Rajak, Tessa, and Noy, David 1993. "*Archisynagogoi*: office, title and social status in the Greco-Roman synagogue," *JRS 83.* 75–93.

Rajak, Tessa, and Noy, David 2002. "Synagogue and community in the Graeco-Roman Diaspora," in: John R. Bartlett (ed.), *Jews in the Hellenistic and Roman Cities.* London, 22–38.

Ramsey, J. T., and Licht, A. L. 1997. *The Comet of 44 B.C. and Caesar's Funeral Games.* Atlanta, GA.

Rapp, Claudia 2005. *Holy Bishops in Late Antiquity.* Berkeley.

Rasmussen, Susanne W. 2003. *Public Portents in Republican Rome.* Rome.

Rawson, Elizabeth 1974. "Religion and politics in the late second century B.C. at Rome," *Phoenix 28.* 193–212.

Rawson, Elizabeth 1985. *Intellectual Life in the Late Roman Republic.* Baltimore, MD.

Rebillard, Éric 2003a. *Religion et sépulture: L'église, les vivants et les morts dans l'Antiquité tardive.* Paris.

Rebillard, Éric 2003b. "The cult of the dead in Late Antiquity: towards a new definition of the relation between the living and the dead," in: J. Rasmus Brandt, S. Sande, O. Steen, and L. Hodne (eds.), *Rome AD 300–800: Power and Symbol, Image and Reality.* Rome, 47–55.

Reeder Williams, E. 1984. *The Archaeological Collection of the Johns Hopkins University.* Baltimore, MD, and London.

Renoirte, T. 1951. *Les "conseils politiques" de Plutarque: Une lettre ouverte aux Grecs à l'époque de Trajan.* Louvain.

Reverdin, Olivier, and Rudhardt, Jean (eds.) 1980. *Le sacrifice dans l'Antiquité.* Entretiens sur l'Antiquité classique 27. Geneva.

Reynolds, Joyce 1982. *Aphrodisias and Rome.* JRS Monographs 1. London.

Reynolds, Joyce, and Tannenbaum, R. 1987. *Jews and Godfearers at Aphrodisias: Greek Inscriptions with Commentary.* Cambridge Philological Society Supplements 12. Cambridge.

Reynolds, L. D., and Wilson, N. G. 1991. *Scribes and Scholars.* 3rd edn. Oxford.

Ribichini, S. (ed.) forthcoming. *Saturnia Tellus.*

Richardson Jr., Lawrence 1988. *Pompeii: An Architectural History.* Baltimore, MD.

Richardson Jr., Lawrence 1992. *A New Topographical Dictionary of Ancient Rome.* Baltimore, MD.

Richardson, Peter 1996. "Early synagogues as *collegia* in the Diaspora and Palestine," in: Kloppenborg and Wilson (1996: 90–110).

Rieger, Anna-Katharina 2004. *Heiligtümer in Ostia: Studien zur antiken Stadt.* Studien zur antiken Stadt 8. Munich.

Rives, James B. 1995. *Religion and Authority in Roman Carthage from Augustus to Constantine.* Oxford.

Rives, James B. 1999. "The decree of Decius and the religion of the Empire," *JRS 89.* 135–54.

Rives, James B. 2001. "Civic and religious life," in: John Bodel (ed.), *Epigraphic Evidence.* London, 118–36.

Rives, James B. 2002. "Magic in the XII Tables Revisited," *CQ 52.* 270–90.

Rix, Helmut 2000. "Oskisch brateis bratom, lateinisch grates," in: A. Hintze and E. Tichy (eds.), *Anusantatyai: Festschrift für Johanna Narten zum 70. Geburtstag.* Dettelbach, 207–29.

Rix, Helmut 2002. *Sabellische Texte: Die Texte des Oskischen, Umbrischen und Südpkenischen.* Heidelberg.

Robert, Louis 1977. "La titulaire de Nicée et de Nicomédie: la gloire et la haine," *HSCPh 81.* 39ff. (= *Opera minora selecta 6* (1989) 211–49).

Robinson, D. M. 1924. "Some Roman terra-cotta savings-banks," *American Journal of Archaeology 28.* 239–50.

Robinson, M. 2002. "Domestic burnt offerings and sacrifices at Roman and pre-Roman Pompeii, Italy," *Vegetation History and Archaebotany 11.* 93–9.

Rogers, Guy M. 1991. *The Sacred Identity of Ephesos: Foundation Myths of a Roman City.* London.

Rohde, Erwin 1898. *Psyche.* 2nd edn. 2 vols. Leipzig.

Rohde, Georg 1936. *Die Kultsatzungen der römischen Pontifices.* Berlin.

Ronke, Jutta 1987. *Magistratische Repräsentation im römischen Relief: Studien zu standes- und statusbezeichnenden Szenen.* 3 vols. Oxford.

Rose, Herbert Jennings 1913. "Italian 'Sondergötter,'" *JRS 3.* 233–41.

Rose, Herbert Jennings 1934. "Altheim: revolutionary or reactionary?" *HTR 27.* 33–51.

Rose, Herbert Jennings 1935. "*Numen inest*: 'animism' in Greek and Roman religion," *HTR 28.* 237–57.

Rose, Herbert Jennings 1943. "Robert Ranulph Marett, 1866–1943," *Proceedings of the British Academy 29.* 357–70.

Rose, Herbert Jennings 1960. "Roman religion 1910–1960," *JRS 50.* 161–72.

Rosenberger, Veit 1998. *Gezähmte Götter: Das Prodigienwesen der römischen Republik.* HABES 27. Stuttgart.

Rossum-Steenbeek, Monique van 1998. *Greek Readers' Digests? Studies on a Selection of Subliterary Papyri.* Leyden.

Rostad, Aslak 2002. "Confession or reconciliation? The narrative structure of the Lydian and Phrygian 'confession inscriptions,'" *Symbolae Osloenses 77.* 145–64.

Rothblatt, Sheldon 1968. *The Revolution of the Dons: Cambridge and Society in Victorian England.* London.

Roth-Rubi, K. 1997. "Silber und Terra Sigillata im Vergleich: Zur Herkunft einiger glattwandiger Gefässe aus dem Hildesheimer Silberfund," in: M. Boetzkes and H. Stein (eds.), *Der Hildesheimer Silberfund: Original und Nachbildung. Vom Römerschatz zum Bürgerstolz.* Exhibition Catalogue. Hildesheim.

Rougier, L. 1959. *La religion astrale des Pythagoriciens.* Paris.

Rüpke, Jörg 1995a. *Kalender und Öffentlichkeit: Die Geschichte der Repräsentation und religiösen Qualifikation von Zeit in Rom.* RGVV 40. Berlin.

Rüpke, Jörg 1995b. "*Fasti*: Quellen oder Produkte römischer Geschichtsschreibung?" *Klio 77.* 184–202.

Rüpke, Jörg 1997. "Römische Religion und Reichsreligion: Begriffsgeschichtliche und methodische Bemerkungen," in: Hubert Cancik and Jörg Rüpke (eds.), *Römische Reichsreligion und Provinzialreligion.* Tübingen, 3–23.

Rüpke, Jörg 2001 [2007]. *Die Religion der Römer: Eine Einführung.* Munich (2nd edn. 2006; Italian edn. 2004; English edn. 2007; Czech edn. 2007).

Rüpke, Jörg 2003. "*Libri sacerdotum*: Wissenschaftsgeschichtliche und universitätsgeschichtliche Beobachtungen zum Ort von Georg Wissowas Religion und Kultus," in: Philippe Borgeaud and Francesca Prescendi (eds.), *Georg Wissowa (1857–1931): Cent ans de religion romaine. Archiv Für Religionsgeschichte 5.* Munich, 16–39.

Rüpke, Jörg 2004a. "Religion und Gruppe: Ein religionssoziologischer Versuch zur römischen Antike," in: Brigitte Luchesi and Kocku von Stuckrad (eds.), *Religion im kulturellen Diskurs: Festschrift Kippenberg*. Berlin, 235–57.

Rüpke, Jörg 2004b. "Roman religion," in: Harriet I. Flower (ed.), *The Cambridge Companion to the Roman Republic*. Cambridge, 177–94.

Rüpke, Jörg 2005a. *Fasti sacerdotum: Die Mitglieder der Priesterschaften und das sakrale Funktionspersonal römischer, griechischer, orientalischer und jüdisch-christlicher Kulte in der Stadt Rom von 300 v.Chr. bis 499 n.Chr.* 3 vols. Potsdamer Altertumswissenschaftliche Beiträge 12/1–3. Stuttgart (English edn. 2008).

Rüpke, Jörg 2005b. "Varro's *tria genera theologiae*: religious thinking in the late Republic," *Ordia prima 4*. 107–29.

Rüpke, Jörg 2006a. "Literarische Darstellungen römischer Religion bei lateinischen Apologeten des Christentums: Universal- und Lokalreligion bei Tertullian und Minucius Felix," in: Elm et al. (2006: 209–23).

Rüpke, Jörg 2006b. "Religion in the *Lex Ursonensis*," in Ando and Rüpke (2006: 34–46).

Rüpke, Jörg 2006c. *Zeit und Fest: Kulturgeschichte des Kalenders*. Munich.

Rutgers, Leonard Victor 1995. *The Jews in Late Ancient Rome: Evidence of Cultural Interaction in the Roman Diaspora*. RG-RW 126. Leyden.

Rutgers, Leonard Victor 1998. *The Hidden Heritage of Diaspora Judaism*. 2nd edn. Leuven.

Rutgers, Leonard Victor 2001. "Death and afterlife: the inscriptional evidence," in: Jacob Neusner, Allan J. Avery-Peck, and Bruce Chilton (eds.), *Judaism in Late Antiquity 3, 4*. Leyden, 293–310.

Rutter, K. (ed.) 2001. *Historia nummorum: Italy*. London.

Ryberg, Inez Scott 1955. *Rites of the State Religion in Roman Art*. Memoirs of the American Academy in Rome 22. Rome.

Saller, R. P. 1991. *Personal Patronage under the Early Empire*. Cambridge.

Salmeri, G. 2000. "Dio, Rome, and the civic life of Asia Minor," in: S. Swain (ed.), *Dio Chrysostom: Politics, Letters, and Philosophy*. Oxford, 53–92.

Salzman, Michele R. 1987. "Superstitio in the Codex Theodosianus and the persecution of pagans," *Vigiliae Christianae 41*. 172–88.

Salzman, Michele R. 1990. *On Roman Time: The Codex-Calender of 354 and the Rhythms of Urban Life in Late Antiquity*. Berkeley.

Samter, Ernst 1901. *Familienfeste der Griechen und Römer*. Berlin.

Samuel, Alan E. 1972. *Greek and Roman Chronology: Calendars and Years in Classical Antiquity*. Munich.

Sanders, Edward P. 1992. *Judaism, Practice and Belief: 63 BCE–66 CE*. London.

Sanders, Edward P. 1999. "Common Judaism and the synagogue in the first century," in: Steven Fine (ed.), *Jews, Christians and Polytheists in the Ancient Synagogue: Cultural Interaction during the Greco-Roman Period*. London, 1–17.

Santini, Claudio 1988. "Il lessico della spartizione nel sacrificio romano," in: Grottanelli and Parise (1998: 293–302).

Sanzi di Mino, M. R., and Staffa, A. R. 2000. "Il santuario italico-romano della dea Feronia in località Poggio Ragone di Loreto Aprutino (PE)," *RPAA 69* (1996–7), 155–86.

Sapouna, P. 1998. *Die Bildlampen römischer Zeit aus der Idäischen Zeusgrotte auf Kreta*. BAR International Series 696. Oxford.

Sartre, Maurice 1997. *Le Haut-Empire romain: Les provinces de Méditerranée orientale d'Auguste aux Sévères*. Paris.

Sartre, Maurice 2005. *The Middle East under Rome*. Cambridge, MA.

Sauer, Eberhard 2003. *The Archaeology of Religious Hatred in the Roman and Early Medieval World*. Stroud.

Sauer, Eberhard 2005. *Coins, Cult, and Cultural Identity: Augustan Coins, Hot Springs and the Roman Baths at Bourbonne-les-Bains*. Leicester.

Sauron, Gilles 1994. *Quis deum? L'expression plastique des idéologies politiques et religieuses à Rome à la fin de la République et au début du principat*. Rome.

Saxer, V. 1989. "L'utilisation par la liturgie de l'espace urbain et suburbain: l'exemple de Rome dans l'antiquité et le haut moyen âge," in: *Actes du XIe Congrès International d'Archéologie Chrétienne 2*. Vatican City, 917–1032.

Schäfer, Thomas 1980. "Zur Ikonographie der Salier," *Jahrbuch des Deutschen Archäologischen Instituts 95*. 342–73, figs. 20–3.

Schäfer, Thomas 1989. *Imperii insignia. Sella curulis und fasces: Zur Repräsentation römischer Magistrate*. Mainz.

Schallmayer, Egon, Eibl, Cordula, Ott, Joachim, Preuss, Gerhard, and Wittkopf, Esther 1990. *Der römische Weihebezirk von Osterburken I*. Corpus der griechischen und lateinischen Beneficiarier–Inschriften des Römischen Reiches. Stuttgart.

Schattner, Thomas G., and Suárez Otero, José 2004. "Monte de Facho (Spanien)," *Archäologischer Anzeiger 2004, 2*. 328–32.

Schefold, Karl 1962. *Vergessenes Pompeji: Unveröffentlichte Bilder römischer Wanddekorationen in geschichtlicher Folge herausgegeben*. Bern.

Schefold, Karl 1998. *Der religiöse Gehalt der antiken Kunst und die Offenbarung*. Kulturgeschichte der antiken Welt 78. Mainz.

Scheid, John 1985a. "Numa et Jupiter ou les dieux citoyens de Rome," *Archives de Sciences Sociales des Religions 59*. 41–53.

Scheid, John 1985b. *Religion et piété à Rome*. Paris (2nd edn 2001).

Scheid, John 1987. "Polytheism impossible; or, the empty gods: reasons behind a void in the history of Roman religion," in: Francis Schmidt (ed.), *The Inconceivable Polytheism*. Paris, 303–25.

Scheid, John 1990. *Romulus et ses frères: Le collège des Frères Arvales, modèle du culte public dans la Rome des empereurs*. BEFAR 275. Paris.

Scheid, John 1991. "Sanctuaires et territoire dans la colonia Augusta Treverorum," in: J.-L. Brunaux (ed.), *Les sanctuaires celtiques. Actes du colloque de Saint-Riquier, 1990*. Paris, 42–57.

Scheid, John 1993. "Cultes, mythes et politique au début de l'empire," in: Fritz Graf (ed.), *Mythen in mythenloser Gesellschaft: Das Paradigma Roms*. Stuttgart, 109–27.

Scheid, John 1995. "Les espaces culturels et leur interprétation," *Klio 77*. 424–32.

Scheid, John 1996. "*Graeco ritu*: a typically Roman way of honoring the gods," *HSCPh 97*. 15–31.

Scheid, J. 1997. "Pline le Jeune et les sanctuaires d'Italie," in: A. Chastagnol, S. Demougin, and C. Lepelley (eds.), *Splendidissima ciuitas: Etudes d'histoire romaine en hommage à François Jacques*. Paris [1996], 241–58.

Scheid, John 1998a. "Les livres Sibyllins et les archives des quindécimvirs," in: Claude Moatti (ed.), *La mémoire perdue: Recherches sur l'administration romaine*. Rome, 11–26.

Scheid, John 1998b. *Commentarii fratrum Arvalium qui supersunt: les copies épigraphiques des protocoles annuels de la confrérie arvale (21 av.–304 ap. J.-C.)*. Collection Roma antica 4. Rome.

Scheid, John 1998c. "Les incertitudes de la *uoti sponsio*: observations en marge du *uer sacrum* de 217 av. J.-C.," in: Michel Humbert and Yves Thomas (eds.), *Mélanges de droit romain et d'histoire ancienne: Hommage à la mémoire d'André Magdelain*. Paris, 417–25.

Scheid, John 1998d. "La piété des procurateurs des Gaules et des Germanies," *Cahiers du Centre Gustave Glotz 9*. 265–75.

Scheid, John 1998e. "Déchiffrer des monnaies: réflexions sur la représentation figurée des jeux séculaires," in: Claire Auvray-Assayas (ed.), *Images romaines*. Études de littérature ancienne 9. Paris, 13–35.

Scheid, J. 1999a. "Hiérarchie et structure dans le polythéisme romain: façons romaines de penser l'action," *Archiv für Religionsgeschichte 1*. 184–203 (= Scheid 2005c: 58–83).

Scheid, John 1999b. "Aspects religieux de la municipalisation: quelques réflexions générales," in: M. Dondin-Payre and M.-T. Raepsaet-Charlier (eds.), *Cités, municipes, colonies: Les processus de municipalisation en Gaule et en Germanie sous le Haut Empire romain*. Paris, 381–423.

Scheid, John 2003. *An Introduction to Roman Religion.*, trans. Janet Lloyd. Edinburgh (French edn. 1998).

Scheid, John 2004. "Interdits et exclusions dans les banquets sacrificiels romains," in: Grottanelli and Milano (2004: 123–39).

Scheid, John 2005a. "Augustus and Roman religion: continuity, conservatism, and innovation," in: Galinsky (2005: 175–93).

Scheid, John 2005b. "Epigraphie ou identité religieuse ou l'art de la traduction," in: Janine Desmulliez and Christine Hoet-van Cauwenberghe (eds.), *Le monde Romain à travers l'épigraphie: Méthodes et pratiques*. Lille, 217–29.

Scheid, John 2005c. *Quand faire c'est croire: Les rites sacrificiels des Romains*. Paris.

Scheid, John 2005d. "Arvales," *ThesCRA 5*. 92–3.

Scheid, John 2006. "Rome et les grands lieux de culte d'Italie," in: Annie Vigourt, Xavier Loriot, Agnès Bérenger-Badel, and Bernard Klein (eds.), *Pouvoir et religion dans le monde romain, en hommage à Jean-Pierre Martin*. Paris, 75–86.

Scheid, John forthcoming, a. "Körperbestattung und Verbrennungssitte aus der Sicht der schriftlichen Quellen," in: Fasold et al. (forthcoming).

Scheid, John forthcoming, b. "Les activités religieuses des magistrats romains," in: Rudolf Haensch and Johannes Heinrichs (eds.), *Der Alltag der Römischen Administration* (forthcoming).

Schilling, Robert 1954. *La religion romaine de Vénus*. Paris.

Schlesier, Renate 1994. *Kulte, Mythen und Gelehrte: Anthropologie der Antike seit 1800*. Frankfurt.

Schmidt, Manfred G. 2004. *Einführung in die lateinische Epigraphik*. Darmstadt.

Schnegg-Köhler, Bärbel 2002. *Die augusteischen Säkularspiele*. Archiv für Religionsgeschichte 4. Munich.

Schneider, Rolf Michael 1990. "Augustus und der frühe römische Triumph," *Jahrbuch des Deutschen Archäologischen Instituts 105*. 167–205.

Schnurbein, S. von 1974. "Bemerkenswerte Funde aus einer Töpferei des Hauptlagers von Haltern," *Germania 52*. 77–80.

Schöllgen, Georg 1984. *Ecclesia sordida? Zur Fragen der sozialen Schichten frühchristlicher Gemeinden am Beispiel Karthagos zur Zeit Tertullians*. Münster.

Scholz, Udo W. 1973. "Suovetaurilia und Solitaurila," *Philologus 117*. 3–28.

Schörner, Günther 2003. *Votive im römischen Griechenland: Untersuchungen zur späthellenistischen und Kaiserzeitlichen Kunst- und Religionsgeschichte*. Altertumswissenschaftliches Kolloquium 7. Stuttgart.

Schraudolph, Ellen 1993. *Römische Götterweihungen mit Reliefschmuck aus Italien: Altäre, Basen und Reliefs*. Heidelberg.

Schubert, Werner 1984. *Jupiter in den Epen der Flavierzeit*. Frankfurt.

Schütte-Maischatz, Anke, and Winter, Engelbert 2004. *Doliche – Eine kommagenische Stadt und ihre Götter: Mithras und Iupiter Dolichenus.* Asia Minor Studien 52. Bonn.

Schwab, Raymond 1984. *The Oriental Renaissance: Europe's Rediscovery of India and the East, 1680–1880,* trans. Gene Patterson-Black and Victor Reinking. New York (German edn. 1950).

Schwarte, Karl-Heinz 1994. "Diokletians Christengesetz," in: Rosemarie Günther and Stefan Rebenich (eds.), *E fontibus haurire: Beiträge zur römischen Geschichte und zu ihren Hilfswissenschaften. Heinrich Chantraine zum 65. Geburtstag.* Studien zur Geschichte und Kultur des Altertums N. F. 1, 8. Paderborn, 203–40.

Schwartz, Seth 1998. "The Hellenization of Jerusalem and Shechem," in: Martin Goodman (ed.), *Jews in a Graeco-Roman World.* Oxford, 37–46.

Scott, A. Brian 1969. *Hildeberti Cenomannensis Episcopi: Carmina Minora.* Leipzig.

Scott, S. 1997. "The power of images in the late-Roman house," in: Laurence and Wallace-Hadrill (1997: 53–67).

Scullard, Howard H. 1981. *Festivals and Ceremonies of the Roman Republic.* London.

Segal, Robert 1998. *The Myth and Ritual Theory.* Oxford.

Seiler, F. 1992. *Casa degli Amorini dorati (VI 16,7.38).* Häuser in Pompeji 5. Munich.

Selinger, Reinhard 2004. *The Mid-Third Century Persecutions of Decius and Valerian.* 2nd rev. edn. Frankfurt.

Settis, S., La Regina, A., and Agosti, G. 1988. *La Colonna Traiana.* Turin.

Sfameni Gasparro, Giulia 1982. *Gnostica et Hermetica.* Rome.

Sfameni Gasparro, Giulia 2002. "Magie et magiciens: le débat entre chrétiens et païens aux premiers siècles de notre ère," *Res Orientales* (*Charmes et sortilèges: Magie et magiciens*) 14. 239–65.

Sgubini Moretti, A. M. 1982/4. "Statue e ritratti onorari del Lucus Feroniae," *RPAA 55–6.* 71–109.

Shapiro, H. Alan, Giannotta, Kristina, and Hoff, Rolf von den 2004. "Dance," *ThesCRA 2.* 299–343.

Sharpe, Eric J. 1975. *Comparative Religion: A History.* New York.

Sheppard, A. R. R. 1984/6. "Homonoia in the Greek cities of the Roman Empire," *Ancient Society 15–17.* 229–52.

Sherk, Robert K. 1988. *The Roman Empire: Augustus to Hadrian.* Translated Documents of Greece & Rome 6. Cambridge.

Sherwin-White, A. N. 1973. *The Roman Citizenship.* Oxford.

Sider, Robert Dick 1978. "Tertullian *On the Shows:* an analysis," *Journal of Theological Studies* ns *29.* 339–65.

Siebert, Anna Viola 1999. *Instrumenta Sacra: Untersuchungen zu römischen Opfer-, Kult und Priestergeräten.* RGVV 44. Berlin.

Simon, Erika 1986. *Augustus: Kunst und Leben in Rome um die Zeitenwende.* Munich.

Sisani, S. 2001. *Tuta Ikuvina: Sviluppo e ideologia della forma urbana a Gubbio.* Rome.

Skutsch, Otto 1985. *The Annals of Quintus Ennius.* Oxford.

Smadja, Elisabeth 1986. "La Victoire et la religion impériale dans les cités d'Afrique du nord sous l'empire romain," in: *Les grandes figures religieuses: Fonctionnement pratique et symbolique dans l'Antiquité.* Besançon, 503–19.

Smallwood, Mary 2001. *The Jews Under Roman Rule from Pompey to Diocletian: A Study in Political Relations.* 2nd edn. Boston.

Smith, Christopher J. 1996a. *Early Rome and Latium: Economy and Society c. 1000 to 500 BC.* Oxford.

Smith, Christopher J. 1996b. "Dead dogs and rattles: time, space and ritual sacrifice in Iron Age Latium," in: John Wilkins (ed.), *Approaches to the Study of Ritual*. Accordia Specialist Studies on the Mediterranean 2. London, 73–90.

Smith, Christopher J. 1999. "Reviewing archaic Latium: settlement, burials, and religion at Satricum," *JRA 12*. 453–75.

Smith, Christopher J. 2005. "The beginnings of urbanization in Rome," in: Barry Cunliffe and Robin Osborne (eds.), *Mediterranean Urbanization 800–600 BC*. Proceedings of the British Academy 126. Oxford, 91–111.

Smith, Christopher J. 2006. *The Roman Clan: The Gens from Ancient Ideology to Modern Anthropology*. Cambridge.

Smith, Jonathan Z. 1978. *Map is not Territory: Studies in the History of Religion*. Studies in Judaism in Late Antiquity 23. Leyden.

Smith, Jonathan Z. 1990. *Drudgery Divine: On the Comparison of Early Christianities and the Religions of Late Antiquity*. Chicago.

Smith, Jonathan Z. 1995. "Trading places," in: Marvin Meyer and Paul Mirecki (eds.), *Ancient Magic and Ritual Power*. RG-RW 129. Leyden, 13–27.

Smith, Jonathan Z. 1998. "Religion, religions, religious," in: Mark C. Taylor (ed.), *Critical Terms for Religious Studies*. Chicago, 269–84.

Smith, Morton 1971. *Palestinian Parties and Politics that Shaped the Old Testament*. New York.

Souris, G. 1984. "Studies in provincial diplomacy under the Principate." DPhil, Cambridge.

Spaeth, Barbette S. 1996. *The Roman Goddess Ceres*. Austin, TX.

Spawforth, A. J., and Walker, S. 1985. "The world of the Panhellenion I: Athens and Eleusis," *JRS 75*. 78–104.

Spawforth, A. J., and Walker, S. 1986. "The world of the Panhellenion II: Three Dorian cities," *JRS 76*. 88–105.

Spera, L. 1998. "*Ad limina apostolorum*: santuari e pellegrini a Roma tra la tarda antichità e l'alto medioevo," in: C. Cerreti (ed.), *La geografia della città di Roma e lo spazio del sacro*. Rome, 1–104.

Spera, L. 2003. "Il territorio della Via Appia: forme trasformative del paesaggio nei secoli della tarda antichità," in: Philippe Pergola, Ricardo Santangeli Valenzani, and Rita Volpe (eds.), *Suburbium: Il suburbio di Roma dalla crisi del sistema delle ville a Gregorio Magno*. Rome, 267–330.

Spickermann, Wolfgang (ed.) 2001. *Religion in den germanischen Provinzen Roms*. Tübingen.

Spickermann, Wolfgang 2003. *Germania superior: Religionsgeschichte des römischen Germanien I*. Religion der römischen Provinzen 2/1. Tübingen.

Spickermann, Wolfgang 2007. *Germania inferior: Religionsgeschichte des römischen Germanien II*. Religion der römischen Provinzen 2/2. Tübingen.

Stambaugh, J. E. 1978. "The functions of Roman temples," *ANRW II.16, 1*. 554–608.

Stamper, John W. 2005. *The Architecture of Roman Temples: The Republic to the Middle Empire*. Cambridge.

Stanfield, J.-A., and Simpson, G. 1990. *Les potiers de la Gaule centrale: Recherches sur les ateliers de potiers de la Gaule centrale 5*. Revue archéologique sites, hors-série 37. Gonfaron.

Steidl, Bernd 2005. "Die Station der beneficiarii consularis in Obernburg am Main," *Germania 83*. 67–94.

Steinby, Eva M. (ed.) 1993–2000. *Lexicon topographicum urbis Romae*. Rome.

Steiner, Heinrich 1989. *Das Verhältnis Tertullians zur antiken Paideia*. St. Ottilien.

Stemmer, K. 1992. *Casa dell'Ara massima (VI 16,15–17)*. Häuser in Pompeji 6. Munich.

Stern, Menahem 1974–84. *Greek and Latin Authors on Jews and Judaism*. Jerusalem.

Stern, Sacha 2002. "Jewish calendar reckoning in the Graeco-Roman cities," in: John R. Bartlett (ed.), *Jews in the Hellenistic and Roman Cities*. London and New York, 107–16.

Sterz, St. A. 1994. "Aelius Aristides' political ideas," *ANRW II.34, 2*. 1248–70.

Steuernagel, Dirk 1999. "'Corporate identity': Über Vereins-, Stadt- und Staatskulte im kaiserzeitlichen Puteoli," *Mitteilungen des Deutschen Archäologischen Instituts Rom106*. 149–87.

Steuernagel, Dirk 2004. *Kult und Alltag in römischen Hafenstädten: Soziale Prozesse in archäologischer Perspektive*. PawB 11. Stuttgart.

Stewart, Peter 2003. *Statues in Roman Society: Representation and Response*. Oxford.

Stewart, Zeph (ed.) 1972. *Arthur Darby Nock: Essays on Religion and the Ancient World*. 2 vols. Oxford.

Stilp, Florian 2001. *Mariage et suovetaurilia: Etude sur le soi-disant "Autel de Domitius Ahenobarbus."* Revue d'Antiquité Suppl. 26. Rome.

Stirling, L. M. 2005. *The Learned Collector: Mythological Statuettes and Classical Taste in Late Antique Gaul*. Ann Arbor.

Stocking, George 1987. *Victorian Anthropology*. New York.

Stocking, George 1996a. *After Tylor: British Social Anthropology 1888–1951*. London.

Stocking, George 1996b. *Volksgeist as Method and Ethic*. Madison.

Stoll, Oliver 2001. *Zwischen Integration und Abgrenzung: Die Religion des Römischen Heeres im Nahen Osten*. St. Katharinen.

Strange, James F. 2001. "The synagogue as metaphor" in: Jacob Neusner and Allan J. Avery-Peck (eds.), *Judaism in Late Antiquity 2, 3, 4*. Leyden, 93–120.

Stray, Christopher 1998. *Classics Transformed: Schools, Universities, and Society in England, 1830–1960*. Oxford.

Strobel, Karl 1993. *Das Imperium Romanum im "3. Jahrhundert": Modell einer historischen Krise? Zur Frage mentaler Strukturen breiterer Bevölkerungsschichten in der Zeit von Marc Aurel bis zum Ausgang des 3. Jh. n. Chr.* Historia Einzelschriften 75. Stuttgart.

Strubbe, Johannes H. M. 1991. "Cursed be he that moves my bones," in: C. A. Faraone and D. Obbink (eds.), *Magika Hiera: Ancient Greek Magic and Religion*. New York, 33–59.

Strubbe, Johannes H. M. 1997. *ARAI EPITUMBIOI: Imprecations against Desecrators of the Grave in the Greek Epitaphs of Asia Minor. A Catalogue*. Bonn.

Strubbe, Johannes H. M. 2003. "Cultic honors for benefactors in the cities of Asia Minor," in: Lukas de Blois, Paul Erdkamp, Olivier Hekster, Gerda De Klein, and Stephan Mols (eds.), *The Representation and Perception of Roman Imperial Power: Proceedings of the Third Workshop of the International Network Impact of Empire (Roman Empire c. 200 B.C.–A.D. 476), Netherlands Institut in Rome, March 2023*. Amsterdam.

Stylow, Armin U. 2005. "Fuentes epigráficas para la historia de la Hispania Ulterior en época republicana," in: Enrique Melchor Gil, Joaquin Mellado Rodríquez, and Juan Francisco Rodríquez Neila (eds.), *Julio César y Corduba: Tempo y espacio en la campaña de Munda (49–45 A.C.)*. Cordova, 247–62.

Süßenbach, U. 1977. *Christuskult und kaiserliche Baupolitik bei Konstantin*. Bonn.

Swain, Simon 1996. *Hellenism and Empire: Language, Classicism, and Power in the Greek World, AD 50–250*. Oxford.

Swain, Simon, and Edwards, Mark (eds.) 2004. *Approaching Late Antiquity: The Transformation from Early to Late Empire*. Oxford.

Syme, Ronald 1939. *The Roman Revolution*. Oxford.

Syme, Ronald 1958. *Tacitus*. Oxford.

Symonds, Richard 1986. *Oxford and Empire*. London.

Szemler, George J. 1971. "*Religio*, priesthoods and magistracies in the Roman republic," *Numen 18*. 103–31.

Szemler, George J. 1972. *The Priests of the Roman Republic: A Study of Interactions between Priesthoods and Magistracies.* Brussels.

Tagliamonte, G. 1996. *I Sanniti*, Rome.

Tambiah, Stanley J. 1968. "The magical power of words," *Man 3/2.* 175–208.

Tambiah, Stanley J. 1981. "A performative approach to ritual," *Proceedings of the British Academy 65, 1979.* 116–42.

Taylor, Lily R. 1931. *The Divinity of the Roman Emperor.* Middletown, CT.

Tcherikover, Victor, and Fuks, Alexander 1957–64. *Corpus Papyrorum Judaicarum.* 2 vols. Cambridge, MA.

Teixidor, Javier 1977. *The Pagan God: Popular Religion in the Greco-Roman Near East.* Princeton, NJ.

Thee, F. C. R. 1984. *Julius Africanus and the Early Christian View of Magic.* Hermeneutische Untersuchungen zur Theologie 19. Tübingen.

Thomas, Y. 1990. "L'institution de l'origine: *sacra principiorum populi romani*," in: Marcel Detienne (ed.), *Tracés de fondation.* Louvain, 143–70.

Thornton, Agatha 1976. *The Living Universe: Gods and Men in Virgil's Aeneid.* Leyden.

Thuillier, Jean-Paul 1985. *Les jeux athlétiques dans la civilisation étrusque.* Rome.

Thulin, C. O. 1912. "*Haruspex*," *RE 7/2.* 2431–68.

Thür, H. 2005. *Hanghaus 2 in Ephesos: Die Wohneinheit 4. Baubefund, Ausstattung, Funde.* Forschungen in Ephesos VIII/6. Vienna.

Tobin, J. 1997. *Herodes Attikos and the City of Athens: Patronage and Conflict under the Antonines.* Amsterdam.

Tolotti, F. 1982. "Le basiliche cimiteriali con deambulatorio del suburbio romano," *Mitteilungen des Deutschen Archäologischen Instituts Rom 89.* 153–211.

Tomlin, Roger S. 2002. "Writing to the gods in Britain," in: Alison E. Cooley (ed.), *Becoming Roman, Writing Latin?* Portsmouth, 165–79.

Torelli, Mario 1982. *Typology and Structure of Roman Historical Reliefs.* Ann Arbor.

Torelli, Mario 1984. *Lavinio e Roma: Riti iniziatici e matrimonio tra archeologia e storia.* Rome.

Torelli, Mario 2002. "Le basiliche circiformi," in: F. Guidobaldi and A. Guiglia Guidobaldi (eds.), *Ecclesiae Urbis 2.* Vatican City, 1097–108.

Toutain, Jules 1907–20. *Les cultes païens dans l'Empire romain 1: les provinces latines.* 3 vols. Paris.

Toynbee, A. J. 1965. *Hannibal's Legacy.* London.

Toynbee, J. M. 1971. *Death and Burial in the Roman World.* Ithaca, NY.

Tranoy, Alain 1981. *La Galice romaine: Recherches sur le nord-ouest de la péninsule ibérique dans l'Antiquité.* Paris.

Trebilico, P. R. 1991. *Jewish Communities in Asia Minor.* Cambridge.

Turcan, Marie 1986. *Les Spectacles: Introduction, texte critique, traduction et commentaire.* Sources Crétiennes 332. Paris.

Turcan, Robert 1980. "Le sacrifice mithriaque: innovations de sens et de modalité," in: Reverdin and Rudhardt (1980: 343–58).

Turcan, Robert 1988. *Religion romaine.* Iconography of Religions 17.1–2. Leyden.

Turcan, Robert 1989. *Les cultes romains dans le monde romain.* Paris.

Turcan, Robert 1996. *The Cults of the Roman Empire.* Oxford.

Turlan, J. 1955. "L'obligation *ex voto*," *Revue historique du droit français et étranger 33.* 502–36.

Vaage, Leif (ed.) 2006. *Religious Rivalries and Relations among Pagans, Jews, and Christians.* Waterloo, ON.

Vaahtera, Jyri 2001. *Roman Augural Lore in Greek Historiography: A Study of the Theory and Terminology*. Historia Einzelschriften 156. Stuttgart.

Valantasis, Richard 2000. *Religions of Late Antiquity in Practice*. Princeton, NJ.

Van Andringa, William (ed.) 2000. *Archéologie des sanctuaires en Gaule romaine*. Saint-Etienne.

Van Andringa, William 2002. *La religion en Gaule romaine: Piété et politique (Ier–IIIe siècle ap. J.-C.)*. Paris.

Van Andringa, William 2003. "Cités et communautés d'expatriés sous l'Empire: le cas des *Cives Romani consistentes*," in: Nicole Belayche and S. Mimouni (eds.), *Les Communautés religieuses dans le monde gréco-romain: Essais de définition*. Turnhout, 49–60.

Van Andringa, William, and Lepetz, Sébastien 2003. "Le ossa animali nei santuari: per un'archeologia del sacrificio," in: Olivier de Cazanove and John Scheid (eds.), *Sanctuaires et sources dans l'Antiquité*. Naples, 85–96.

van der Horst, Pieter W. 1999. "Was the synagogue a place of Sabbath worship before 70 CE?" in: Steven Fine (ed.), *Jews, Christians and Polytheists in the Ancient Synagogue: Cultural Interaction during the Greco-Roman Period*. London, 18–43.

van Straten, Folker T. 1974. "Did the Greeks kneel before their gods?" *Babesch 49*. 159–89.

van Straten, Folker T. 1976. "Daikrates' dream: a votive relief from Kos, and some other *kat' onar* dedications," *Babesch 51*. 1–27.

van Straten, Folker T. 1981. "Gifts for the gods" in: Versnel (1981a: 65–151).

Vanggaard, Jens. H. 1988. *The Flamen: A Study in the History and Sociology of Roman Religion*. Copenhagen.

Vasunia, Phiroze 2005. "Greek, Latin and the Indian Civil Service," *PCPS 51*. 35–71.

Vendries, Christophe, and Péché, Valerie 2004. "Music romaine," *ThesCRA 2*. 397–415.

Vermaseren, Maarten J. 1956–60. *Corpus inscriptionum et monumentorum religionis Mithriacae*. The Hague.

Vermaseren, Maarten J. 1971. *Mithriaca 1: The Mithraeum at S. Maria Capua Vetere*. Leyden.

Vermaseren, Maarten J. 1977. *Cybele and Attis: The Myth and the Cult*. London.

Vermaseren, Maarten J. 1981. "Mithras in der Römerzeit," in: Maarten J. Vermaseren (ed.), *Die orientalischen Religionen im Römerreich*. EPRO 93. Leyden, 96–120.

Vermaseren, Maarten, J., and van Essen, C. C. 1965. *The Excavations in the Mithraeum of the Church of Santa Prisca in Rome*. Leyden.

Versnel, Henrik S. 1970. *Triumphus*. Leyden.

Versnel, Henrik S. (ed.) 1981a. *Faith, Hope and Worship: Aspects of Religious Mentality in the Ancient World*. Leyden.

Versnel, Henrik S. 1981b. "Religious mentality in ancient prayer," in: Versnel (1981a: 1–64).

Versnel, Henrik S. 1991. "Beyond cursing: the appeal to justice in judicial prayers," in: C. A. Faraone and D. Obbink (eds.), *Magika Hiera: Ancient Greek Magic and Religion*. New York. 60–95.

Versnel, Henrik S. 2002. "The poetics of the magical charm" in: Mirecki and Meyer (2002: 105–58).

Veyne, Paul 1959. "Le monument des suovétauriles de Beaujeu (Rhône)," *Gallia 17*. 79–100; figs. 3–5.

Veyne, Paul 1986. "Une évolution du paganisme gréco-romain: injustice ou piété des dieux, leurs ordres et 'oracles,'" in: Paul Veyne, *La société romaine*. Repr. Paris, 1991, 281–310.

Veyne, Paul 1989. "S'assoeir auprès des dieux, fréquenter les temples: la nouvelle piété sous l'Empire," *Revue de Philologie 63*. 175–94.

Veyne, Paul 1990. *Bread and Circuses: Historical Sociology and Political Pluralism*. Harmondsworth.

Veyne, Paul 1999. "Prodiges, divination et peur des dieux chez Plutarque," *Revue d'Histoire des Religions 216.* 387–442.

Veyne, Paul 2000. "Inviter les dieux, sacrifier, banqueter: quelques nuances de la religiosité gréco-romaine," *Annales (Histoire, Sciences Sociales) 55.* 3–42.

Veyne, Paul 2005. *L'Empire gréco-romain.* Paris.

Wagenvoort, Hendrik 1947. *Roman Dynamism.* Oxford.

Wallace, Anthony F. C. 1966. *Religion: An Anthropological View.* Chicago.

Wallace-Hadrill, Andrew 1994. *Houses and Society in Pompeii and Herculaneum.* Princeton, NJ.

Wallace-Hadrill, Andrew 2005. "*Mutatas formas:* the Augustan transformation of Roman knowledge," in: Galinsky (2005: 55–84).

Wallraff, Martin 2001. *Christus Sol Invictus.* Münster.

Waltzing, Jean-Pierre 1931. *Tertullien, Apologétique: Commentaire analytique, grammatical et historique.* Paris.

Wardman, Alan 1982. *Religion and Statecraft among the Romans.* London.

Watson, Alan 1993. *International Law in Archaic Rome: War and Religion.* London.

Watson, Alaric 1999. *Aurelian and the Third Century.* London.

Watts, Edward J. 2006. *City and School in Late Antique Athens and Alexandria.* Berkeley.

Weinfeld, Morton 2002. *Like Everyone Else, But Different: The Paradoxical Success of Canadian Jews.* Toronto.

Weinreich, Otto 1912. "THEOI EPÊKOOI," *Athener Mitteilungen 37.* 1–68 (= *Ausgewählte Schriften 1*, Amsterdam (1969), 131–95).

Weinstock, Stefan 1946. "Martianus Capella and the cosmic system of the Etruscans," *JRS 36.* 101–29.

Weinstock, Stefan 1949. "Rev. H. J. Rose, *Ancient Roman Religion*," *JRS 39.* 166–7.

Weinstock, Stefan 1960. "Two archaic inscriptions from Latium," *JRS 50.* 112–18.

Weinstock, Stefan 1961. "Rev. Kurt Latte, *Römische Religionsgeschichte*," *JRS 51.* 206–15.

Weinstock, Stefan 1971. *Divus Julius.* Oxford.

Welles, C. Bradford 1969. "The gods of Dura-Europos," in: R. Stiehl and H. E. Stier (eds.), *Beiträge zur alten Geschichte und deren Nachleben: Festschrift F. Altheim 2.* Berlin, 50–65.

Welles, C. Bradford, Fink, Robert O., and Gilliam, J. Frank 1959. *The Parchments and Papyri: The Excavations at Dura-Europos. Final Report 5.1.* New Haven, CT.

Wellmann, M. 1928. *Die PHYSIKA des Bolos und der Magier Anaxilaos aus Larissa 1.* Abhandlungen der Preussischen Akademie der Wissenschaften. Berlin.

Wide, Sam 1912. "Griechische und römische Religion," in: Alfred Gercke and Eduard Norden (eds.), *Einleitung in die Altertumswissenschaft 2.* 2nd edn. Leipzig, 167–272.

Wiebe, Donald 2004. "Implications of the 'modes of religiosity theory' for the scientific study of religion," *Method and Theory in the Study of Religion 16.* 234–40.

Wiegels, Rainer 1988. "Mithras und Haruspex im römischen Speyer," *Mitteilungen des Historischen Vereins der Pfalz 86.* 5–34.

Wilamowitz-Moellendorff, Ulrich von 1921. *Geschichte der Philologie.* 3rd edn. Leipzig.

Wilamowitz-Moellendorff, Ulrich von 1931–2. *Die Glaube der Hellenen.* 2 vols. Berlin.

Wille, Günther 1967. *Musica Romana: Die Bedeutung der Musik im Leben der Römer.* Amsterdam.

Willems, H. and Clarysse, W. (eds.) 2000. *Les Empereurs du Nil.* Exhibition Catalogue. Paris.

Williams, J. H. C. 2005. "The newer rite is here? Vinous symbolism on British Iron Age coins," in: C. C. Haselgrove and D. Wigg-Wolf (eds.), *Iron Age Coinage and Ritual Practices.* Mainz, 25–39.

Williams, Margaret 1998. "The structure of the Jewish community in Rome," in: Martin Goodman (ed.), *Jews in a Graeco-Roman World*. Oxford, 215–28.

Wiseman, Timothy P. 1994. "*Conspicui postes tectaque digna deo*: the public image of aristocratic and imperial houses in the late Republic and early Empire," in: Timothy P. Wiseman, *Historiography and Imagination: Eight Essays on Roman Culture*. Exeter, 98–115; 154–61.

Wiseman, Timothy P. 1995a. *Remus: A Roman Myth*. Cambridge.

Wiseman, Timothy P. 1995b. "The god of the Lupercal," *JRS 85*. 1–22.

Wiseman, Timothy P. 1998. *Roman Drama and Roman History*. Exeter.

Wiseman, Timothy P. 2001. "Reading Carandini," *JRS 91*. 182–93.

Wiseman, Timothy P. 2004. *The Myths of Rome*. Exeter.

Wissowa, Georg 1904. "Echte und falsche 'Sondergötter' in der römischen Religion," in: Georg Wissowa, *Gesammelte Abhandlungen zur römischen Religions- und Stadtgeschichte*. Munich, 304–26.

Wissowa, Georg 1912. *Religion und Kultus der Römer*. Handbuch der Altertumswissenschaft 5, 4. Munich (repr. 1971).

Witschel, Christian 1999. *Krise – Rezession – Stagnation? Der Westen des römischen Reiches im 3. Jahrhundert n. Chr.* Frankfurt.

Woodman, A. J. 2004. *Tacitus: The Annals*. Indianapolis.

Woolf, Greg 1998. *Becoming Roman: The Origins of Provincial Civilization in Gaul*. Cambridge.

Wörrle, Michael 1988. *Stadt und Fest im kaiserzeitlichen Kleinasien: Studien zu einer agonistischen Stiftung aus Oinoanda*. Munich.

Wörrle, Michael forthcoming. "Limyra in der frühen Kaiserzeit," in: Christof Schuler (ed.), *Griechische Epigraphik in Lykien*.

Wülker, Ludwig 1903. *Die geschichtliche Entwicklung des Prodigienwesens bei den Römern: Studien zur Geschichte und Überlieferung der Staatsprodigien*. Leipzig.

Young, Frances, Ayres, Lewis, and Louth, Andrew (eds.) 2004. *The Cambridge History of Early Christian Literature*. Cambridge.

Zanker, Paul 1983. "Der Apollontempel auf dem Palatin: Ausstattung und politische Sinnbezüge nach der Schlacht von Actium," *Città e Architettura nella Roma Imperiale*, Analecta Romana, supplementa *10*. 21–40.

Zanker, Paul 1987 [1988]. *Augustus und die Macht der Bilder*. Munich (English edn. 1988).

Zanker, Paul 1998. *Pompeii: Public and Private Life*, trans. D. L. Schneider. Cambridge, MA.

Zanker, Paul 1999. "Mythenbilder im Haus," in: R. F. Docter and E. M. Moormann (eds.), *Proceedings of the XVth International Congress of Classical Archaeology, Amsterdam, July 12–17, 1998*. Allard Pierson Series 12. Amsterdam, 40–8.

Zanker, Paul 2000. "Bild-Räume und Betrachter im kaiserzeitlichen Rom," in: Adolf H. Borbein, Tonio Hölscher, and Paul Zanker (eds.), *Klassische Archäologie: Eine Einführung*. Berlin, 205–26.

Zanker, Paul, and Ewald, Björn Christian 2004. *Mit Mythen leben: Die Bilderwelt römischer Sarkophage*. Munich.

Zavaroni, A. 2004. "Note sull'iscrizione italica di Rapino," *ZPE 149*. 227–31.

Ziegler, R. 1985. *Städtisches Prestige und kaiserzeitliche Politik: Studien zum Festwesen in Ostkilikia im 2. und 3. Jahrhundert n. Chr.* Düsseldorf.

Ziethen, G. 1994. *Gesandte vor Kaiser und Senat: Studien zur römischen Gessandschaftswesen zwischen 30 v. Chr. und 117 n. Chr.* St. Katharinen.

Zilling, Henrike Maria, 2004. *Tertullian: Untertan Gottes und des Kaisers*. Paderborn.

Ziolkowski, Adam 1992. *The Temples of Mid-Republican Rome and their Historical and Topographical Context*. Saggi di Storia antica 4. Rome.

General Index

Academy 97, 378
accensi 334–5
accession of emperors 77, 118, 121, 220, 430
acclamation 96, 414
acerra 257
acta see *commentarii*
actors 227, 237, 245, 276, 278, 280, 284, 351–2
adoption 73, 80, 252, 313
adventus 256, 412
adynaton 295
adytum 209
aedes Mariana 66–7
aedes sacra 205–6
aediculae 197, 199
aediles 224, 226, 230, 335
aeditumus 332
aedituus 209
aeneatores 249, 252
Aeneid 55, 133–5, 212
aes signatum 143
Agape 407
ager peregrinus 298
agones 231, 421–2, 424
agon Solis 102
Agonium 179
aition 214
alchemy 380

alio die 299
almsgiving 116
altars
    Belvedere 80
    of Angera 265
    of Hercules 56, 268
    of the *Vicomagistri* 260
    of Victory 120, 122
    see also arae
amphitheater 192, 222, 350, 360–1, 376, 404, 414, 422–3, 434, 468–9, 470
amulet 158, 199, 279, 289, 340, 361–2, 370–1, 387–8
ancestors 69, 85, 134, 145–6, 151, 308, 315, 320, 348, 359, 369–70, 380, 408, 441, 454, 462
androgyny 244, 382; *see also* hermaphrodites
angels 113, 161, 361, 369–70, 389
aniconic worship 62, 206, 383
anima mundi 383
animal sacrifice 7, 87, 98, 111–12, 116, 119–22, 150, 165, 167–8, 229, 258, 263–4, 268, 271, 275, 332, 333–4, 388, 390
animism 10, 20, 23–6, 41
annales 130
    maximi 13, 294
anthropology 11–12, 19–26, 41, 276

anthropomorphic depiction 2–3, 37, 41, 114, 206
apices 144, 152
Apis bull 85
Apocrypha 351, 356, 379–80, 384, 386
Apollonian triad 218
apologists 256, 392, 457–71
apostle 107, 148, 410, 412–13, 415, 420–3
apotheosis 80, 212, 214, 315
apparatus ludorum publicorum 230
apparitores 34, 334–7, 341
arae 183–5, 206
    Borghese 165
    Consi 223
    Domitius Ahenobarbus 165, 170
    Pacis augustae 134, 171–2, 255
    see also altars
arches 94, 219–20, 250–1, 260, 413–15
    of Constantine 251, 257, 415, 417
    of Titus 256
archierosyna 112
archisynagogus 374–5
archives 15, 209, 372
    Archive Wall 323
archon 373
arenas 411, 416, 422, 468–70
Areopagus 328
Arians 105, 119
aristocracy 35, 59, 63, 65–7, 72–4, 87, 124, 179, 189, 232, 292, 317, 319, 321–2, 328–9, 374–5, 381, 416, 419
Aristotelianism 379, 381
Armilustrium 179
Arval Brethren *see fratres Arvales*
ascetism 97, 354, 386, 468
assemblies 292, 299, 326
    provincial 112
associations 39, 93, 276, 279, 371, 373, 375, 398, 468
astrology 141, 292, 339–41, 379, 380, 382, 384, 388–9, 394, 399
astronomy 363, 390
asylum 61, 311
atheism 360, 368, 390
athletes 319, 360, 416, 419, 421–4

augurium salutis 299
augury 36, 40, 42, 60, 70, 75, 132, 147, 151–2, 206, 292–3, 298–9, 303, 332, 334, 338–9, 435, 447
Augustales 79, 82
Augustan
    cult 217, 279
    marriage laws 105
    religion 73, 77
Augustus (title) 83, 117–18, 158, 160
auspicia 40, 42, 48, 50, 132, 139, 147, 167, 178, 206, 292–3, 299–300, 339, 442–3, 452
    oblativa 293
authority
    Christian 112, 120–1
    moral 100
    religious 58–60, 66, 177, 299, 304, 351, 364, 369, 385, 443
    spiritual 122
avodah 358
axes 152, 155, 168, 332, 334, 449, 464

Bacchanalia 14, 64, 70, 284, 437
banquets 5, 64, 80, 116, 121–2, 132, 184, 193, 208, 210, 212, 214, 230, 267–71, 329, 409, 412, 452
baptisterium 455
Bar Kochba rebellion 346, 368
barbarians 94, 96, 168, 255–6, 260, 392, 414
basilicas 123, 354, 372, 412, 414–24, 434
    Aemilia 67
    Apostolica 412, 415–16, 419
    Constantini 414
baths 209, 218, 388
    Baths of Caracalla 396
belief 1, 6, 13, 24, 26, 41, 58–9, 80, 101, 107, 109–10, 113–14, 121, 138, 141, 181–2, 187, 247, 285–6, 289, 309, 311, 339, 352, 360, 378–9, 383–4, 386–8, 390, 392, 400, 402, 406, 409, 459, 461–2, 467, 470
biga 224
birds 36, 132, 171, 206, 264, 278, 299, 452

birth 80, 92, 102, 116, 138, 141, 237–8, 247, 281–2, 293, 295, 303, 314, 318, 329, 358, 362, 375, 398, 416, 464
birthdays 73, 91, 93, 120, 178, 237, 307, 363, 409, 435, 448, 469
bishops 98–9, 101, 105, 110, 112, 115, 118, 120–5, 407, 409–10, 419, 426
boars 170, 171
bodies 23, 32, 114, 116, 270–1, 284, 315, 383, 404, 409–11, 414
bos mas 173
boundary stones 45, 141, 301
Brahmins 392
brateis datas 47–8
bread 115, 211, 164, 267–8
brides 279, 393
Buddhism 100
bulls 46, 150, 165–71, 173, 239, 240, 260, 393, 395, 398, 401–2, 403, 433, 449, 455
bulla 279
burials 6, 33–5, 113–16, 186–7, 238, 269, 295, 315, 409–10, 413, 415, 419, 424
  ground 114–16, 206, 263
  practice 2, 115, 187

caduceus 143, 150, 154–5, 254
Caesareum 448
cakes 35, 115, 267, 278, 281, 332–3
calendar 2, 8, 15, 26, 38–42, 66, 70, 72–3, 82, 87, 89, 91, 111–13, 115, 117, 121, 124, 177–9, 211–12, 222–3, 226, 230, 232, 234, 261, 276, 281–2, 288, 307, 316, 339, 351, 359, 363–4, 392, 397, 417–18, 423, 435, 439–40, 448
  lunar 364
  reform 178–9
camilli 332–4
candles 120
canonization 356
canopy 420
capite velato 165, 167, 171, 257, 258
Capitoline festival 224
Capitoline triad 89, 268, 434, 440, 447
capricorns 197
Cara Cognatio 115

Caristia 115–16, 124
Carmen Saeculare 77, 244, 245–6
carmina 129, 236, 245, 255, 259, 278, 287–8
  malum 14
  sacrum 401–2
Carmentalia 179
Castra peregrinorum 399
catacombs 115, 412, 417–18, 426
  Catacomb of Callixtus 408–9
  Catacomb of Priscilla 409
catechism 390, 469
Catholic Christianity 1, 18, 105, 120, 459
cattle 47, 264, 266, 348
celebration 76, 111, 121, 124, 224, 275, 364, 390, 410, 417, 419, 424–5, 435
celibacy 105
cellae 55, 87, 206–7, 209, 215, 220, 396
cemeteries 101, 115, 237, 279, 408–13, 417–19, 424
Cerberus 379
Cerialia 179, 226
Chaldeans 338, 340, 379–87
  oracle 387, 391
chariots 159, 171, 232, 399
  races 121, 222–4, 229, 232, 269, 289, 361
children 47, 90, 190, 213, 228, 237–8, 270, 279, 286–7, 293, 306, 308, 313–14, 374
chi-rho 104, 159–61
Christianization 108, 159, 161, 365, 418, 447
Christmas 417
Chronograph of 354 CE 111, 124, 417–18, 426
churches 36, 52–3, 58, 98–101, 103–5, 107, 110, 114–16, 119–20, 122, 125, 159, 185, 276, 331, 351, 354, 361, 370, 391, 408–9, 412–26, 455
  S. Clemente 408
  S. Crisogono 408
  S. Croce in Gerusalemme 412
  S. Felicità 53
  S. Prisca 399, 401–3
  S. Sebastiano 412
  Ss. Giovanni e Paolo 408

churches (*cont'd*)
  Ss. Marcellinus and Petrus 412
  St. Laurentius 412
  St. Paul 412
  St. Peter 412
  St. Sebastian 412, 419
cinctus Gabinius 264
circitor 400
circumcision 362–3
circuses 5, 111–12, 117, 121–2, 124, 222,
    229, 269, 339, 415, 417, 419, 421–3,
    468–70
  Circus Flaminius 75, 226
  Circus Maximus 112, 121, 222–3, 269,
    406, 416–17, 423–4
citharas 215, 228
clergy 101, 103, 105, 111–16, 119, 407,
    417
Clitumnus fons 213, 283
clubhouses 206, 221
clupeus virtutis 151
codification 346, 434
coin sacrifice 213
collegia 6, 79–80, 167–8, 178, 220, 232,
    252–3, 263, 268, 275, 293, 299, 310,
    334, 355, 437, 443
  Arvalis 76, 240, 281; *see also fratres
    Arvales*
  augural 72, 146–7, 298–9, 334
  compitalicia 199
  pontifical 61, 72, 447
  priestly 60–1, 63, 65–6, 80, 102, 132,
    150–1, 217, 267, 277, 292, 298, 334,
    435
  quindecemviral 90
  religious 6–7, 60–1
  of the *vicomagistri* 165
columbaria 187
comet 80, 293, 315
commemoration 131, 409–10, 422
commentarii of priests 8, 13–14, 177, 282,
    293–4, 336
Commodeia 319
compita 78, 165–6, 207
Compitalia 79, 82, 167, 199, 279, 332
confession 446
confessor 99, 101, 411, 421–2

coniectrix 338
consecratio 206
consensus deorum hominum 304
Constitutio Antoniniana 92, 431
Constitutio Apostolica 115
Consualia 179, 223–4, 469
conversion 96, 111, 114, 362–3, 400,
    413–14, 460
Corax (Mithraic grade) 398
cornicines 249, 332
Cornucopia 150, 154, 157, 197, 314
corona civica 151, 167
corpse 443
corpus Christi 276
cosmology 388–9
cosmos 361, 380–1, 383, 388–9
cows 43, 138, 173, 264, 334, 433
cremation 114, 187
crossroad 17, 322
crown 153, 280, 399
crucifixion 105
cult
  adoption of 62, 89, 96, 368, 442, 463,
    467
  association 165
  of the dead 276
  domestic 34, 38, 59, 141, 180, 188–9,
    191–3, 197, 201, 217, 219–20,
    238–40, 245, 277–9, 407
  foreign 62–4, 70
  image 5, 7, 197, 205–11, 217, 220,
    393, 396–402
  local 62, 207, 210, 437
  music 261
  musicians 252
  personnel 211, 258
  private 38, 113–14, 123
  provincial 81
  public 4, 38, 69, 73, 84, 87, 107,
    109–13, 116–18, 120, 122, 124, 156,
    252–3, 275, 375, 435, 444
  relief 400–1
  statue 55, 87, 144, 149, 152, 218–19,
    283, 393, 441
  symbol 357
  urban 84, 212
  see also imperial cult

culter 334
cultus deorum 227
cura ludorum publicorum 224–6, 230–1, 328
curses 213, 286–9
    self- 242
    tablet 185
cymbals 249
Cynics 78

damnatio memoriae 415
dance 198, 214, 228–9, 237, 244, 249–59, 261, 278, 332
Day of Atonement 358, 365, 370
deacons 407, 411
death 34, 77, 80, 96–7, 101–2, 104, 116–17, 123, 187, 237, 287, 291, 302–3, 314, 325, 336, 338, 382, 392, 395, 396, 397, 398–9, 410, 421, 423, 432, 447, 462
decemviri sacris faciundis 226
Decennalia 254
dedicatory formula 180
defixio(nes) 263, 269, 286, 289
deification 23, 62, 69, 75, 77, 81, 87, 90–1, 95, 210
demigods 305, 315
demons 16, 113, 186, 289, 339–40, 361, 379, 389, 399, 424, 459, 470
dendrophoroi 398
depositio episcoporum 417–18
depositio martyrum 412, 418, 423
deus praesens 400
devotio 44, 68, 239, 281, 287–8, 312
di immortales 5, 56
diadem, royal 85, 312
dies depositionis 409
dies fasti/nefasti 179
dies natalis 409, 418
Divalia 179
divi 54, 80, 447
divi filius 80
divination 6, 106, 235, 263, 292, 301–2, 336–7, 341, 379, 383–4, 388, 391
doctrine 97, 99
dogs 37, 51, 89, 264, 398

domus
    divina 54, 94, 102
    ecclesiae 408
    publica 40
Donatist 99, 105, 123
dorsulae 264
dreams 137, 285, 292–3, 302, 338, 340–1, 369, 391

eagles 143, 315
earthquakes 148, 220, 294, 304, 323, 340
Easter 106, 120–1, 124, 158, 365, 408, 413, 417, 424
ecclesiastical history 430
eclipse 293
ecstasis 269
ecumenical synod 105
Ecurria see Equirria
Edict of Milan 104, 413
ekpyrosis 383
elections 65–6, 77–8, 144, 238, 245, 261, 267, 298–9, 301, 304, 310, 316, 321, 463
elephants 295
Eleusinian mysteries 102
endogamy 355, 359, 362, 369
entrails 171, 300, 336, 338–9
ephebe 361
epiclesis 55, 181, 280, 284, 402
Epicureanism 379, 386
episcopacy 123–4, 408
episcopalis audientia 105
epithets of gods 50, 69, 87, 102, 131, 180, 186, 232, 240, 280, 409, 411, 449–50
epula publica 407, 412
Epulones 63, 133, 333
epulum Iovis 268–9
Equirria 179, 223, 234, 469
equus October 137
Etrusca disciplina 15–16, 336, 384, 388
eucharist 407, 409–13, 422
euergetism 148, 305, 307, 318–19, 326–30, 451
Euhemerism 132
eusebeia 279
evocatio 37, 62, 69–70, 75, 83, 239, 441–2
exauguratio 442

execution 404
exegesis 48, 131, 137
exhumation 14
exorcist 384
expiation 60, 77, 138–9, 141, 244, 247,
   264, 270, 278, 289, 293–303, 366
extispicy 266, 283, 300, 334
ex-voto 54, 92, 281, 284

fabula praetexta 228
faith 421, 469
fas 278
fasces 155, 165, 260, 334, 432
Fasti 72–3
  Antiates maiores 178–9
  Praenestini 178
  Vaticani 212
fathers 75, 77, 80, 88, 91, 102, 104, 111,
   114, 120, 213, 263, 276, 307, 311,
   313, 318, 327, 329, 332, 373–5,
   382, 386, 388–9, 459; *see also pater*
   familias
fauissae 17, 284
feasts 86, 115, 178, 211, 238, 258, 318
  of Booths 364–5
  of Esther (Purim) 363–5
Feldherrensarkophage 168
Feralia 115–16, 179, 287–8
fercula 171, 260, 333
feriae 37–8, 179, 222, 283, 296; *see also*
  holidays
Feriale Duranum 435, 448
Fetiales 242, 248
fictores 332
fidicines 249, 256, 332
fish 264
flamines 39–42, 69, 87, 112, 401
  Dialis 39, 48, 76, 78, 332
  Martialis 48
  Quirinalis 48
flaminica 332
Floralia 52
flutes 235, 237, 249, 258, 261, 264, 332,
  335
Fontinalia 179
food 35, 116, 206, 220, 268, 270–1, 296,
  330, 341, 363, 397

forums 40, 54, 69, 86, 89, 148, 205,
   218–20, 230, 237, 339, 372, 395,
   397, 432, 434
  Forum Augustum 74, 134
  Forum Boarium 37, 42, 268, 297
  Forum Romanum 74–5, 80, 302–3
fountains 94, 188, 206, 208, 470
fratres Arvales 76, 176, 177, 208, 212,
   214, 237, 243, 253, 267, 277, 281,
   332; *see also collegium Arvalis*
  Acta 8, 14, 212, 240, 247, 281–2
fulgurales libri 336
funerals 4, 35–6, 115, 129, 222, 252,
   257, 261, 270–1, 292, 409, 469–70;
   see also burials
  association 406
  curses 286
  games 329
  inscription 338, 347, 379
  meals 116
  prayer 409
  rites 85, 120, 125, 221, 238, 264, 270
Furrinalia 179

Galli 63
games 4, 42, 100, 102, 109–11, 117–18,
   121–4, 131, 153, 217, 222–34, 269,
   296, 301, 318–19, 323, 327, 329,
   360, 410, 417, 419, 421, 423–4, 439,
   468–70; *see also ludi*
  plebeian 63
gardens 52, 68, 188–9, 192, 197, 208
  temple 208
garland 280
gerousia 323, 326, 328, 374
gerousiarch 373
gesta martyrum 424
ghetto 406
gladiators 105, 111, 121, 196, 222, 327,
   404, 468
gnosticism 100, 380, 384, 386–9, 391
goats 264
goetes 288, 339
gospel 410
Graeco ritu 62–4, 102, 218, 225–6, 237,
   264, 266, 271, 277
graffiti 56, 177, 399, 401, 412

grain 37
grammateus 113, 373–4
grove 14, 45, 50–5, 205–6, 208, 210, 212–14, 221, 238, 253, 279, 286
guttus 333
gymnasia 189, 192, 318, 326, 360, 372, 434
gymnosophist 380

Hannukah 363
harioli 6, 338
haruspicy 106, 266, 293–302, 335–8, 382, 391, 401
hazzan 374
healing 130, 133, 182, 370
hearths 237, 264, 277
Hebrew 347, 356, 365, 369, 455, 459
hecatomb 269
Heliocentrism 391
Heliodromus (Mithraic grade) 399
Hellenization 3, 225, 319–20, 347, 349, 367, 371, 450
heralds 143, 254, 277, 432; *see also praecones*
Hercolei 394
heresies 17, 98, 106, 119–20, 123, 346, 365, 384, 388, 460
Hermaistai 394
hermaphrodites 295, 297–8
Hermeticism 385–7, 389
herms 192
heroes 189, 191, 331, 369, 393, 414, 419–20, 422, 465
heroa 52, 329, 415
hiereis 373, 375
hieros agon 319
hieros logos 401
high priests 217, 328, 358–9
hippopotamus 199
holidays 4, 66, 79, 111–12, 115, 117, 120–1, 124, 179, 222, 365, 370, 435, 469; *see also feriae*
holocaust 267, 271
holy men 97–8, 362, 370–2, 384
Holy Trinity 118, 120
homonoia 324, 326
homooúsios 105

honey 399, 404
horses 89, 143, 223–4, 264, 289, 311
    races 63, 223
house
    of Augustus 215–16
    of the Ara Massima 188
    of the Colored Capitals 190–1
    of the Ephebe 190
    of the Golden Cupids 192
    of M. Lucretius Fronto 190
    of the Menander 193
    of a Priest 199
    of the Red Walls 199–200
    of the Tragic Poet 201
    of the Vettii 198–9
human sacrifice 269
hut of Romulus 215
hymns 1, 77, 80, 236–7, 244–5, 247, 277, 297, 395, 401–2, 413
    Arval 237, 244
    Salian 236
hypogea 409

iconography 147, 153, 162, 168–70, 254, 271, 393, 402, 449
identity 31, 88, 90, 163, 210, 296, 298, 355, 359–60, 367, 371–2, 382, 397–400, 448, 453
Ides (*Eidus*) 179, 339
idolatry 6, 18, 111, 206, 468–9
Iguvine Tables 2, 48, 50
illness 92
images (*imagines*) 4–5, 7, 85, 87, 117, 158, 162, 165, 206–7, 209, 211, 214, 218, 229, 233, 250, 254–5, 259, 382, 385, 396, 401, 416, 442, 448–9, 452
immolation 168, 173, 264, 334
imperial cult 2, 8, 68–9, 79–86, 91, 106, 111–12, 116, 135, 140, 150, 162, 184, 199, 221, 252–3, 310–11, 314–16, 323–34, 346, 360, 371, 379, 386, 431, 444–8, 467
imperialism 430, 442
imperium 225, 440, 442
    cum auspiciis 304
impiety 327, 390
inauguration 170–1, 237, 245, 299, 364

incantation 371
incense 115, 120, 165, 167, 183, 254,
    258, 263–4, 268–70, 275, 280, 310,
    333–4, 361, 390, 397, 402, 452
indulgentia 309
inhumation 114, 286
initiation 102, 386–8, 390, 392–4,
    398–404
instaurare 266
interpretatio Graeca 181
interpretatio Romana 87, 181, 436
invocation 94, 240–1, 276, 279
ira de(or)um 227
Iseum 206
Islam 17, 364, 377

Judaism 2, 5–6, 11, 18, 97, 110, 123,
    149, 180, 284, 305, 315, 325, 331,
    345–77, 384–93, 406, 410, 449, 467
jugs 152, 165, 333, 264

kalathos 449
kalatores 332
Kalendae 179
Keddushah 366

labarum 159, 160–1, 418, 422
lamella 387–8
lamps 20, 188, 195–7, 213, 364, 393
lapsi (Christians) 99, 107
lararia 180, 188, 193, 198–200
Latinization 347, 425, 459
laurel 79, 151, 167, 197, 232, 260, 264,
    269, 296
law
  augural 442
  of Moses 356, 361
  pontifical 443
  priestly 437
  sacred 89; *see also lex sacra*
  see also lex
lead tablets 93, 280, 287–8
lectisternia 266, 268, 296, 452
lectors 45, 46, 165, 167, 335
Lemuria 179
Leo (Mithraic grade) 398
Lernetalia 179

Levites 331, 359, 362, 369
lex 434; *see also* law
  Aemilia 13
  coloniae Iuliae Genetivae 435
  Cornelia 339
  de flamino Narbonensis 178
  Flavia municipalis 438
  Irnitana 335
  Lucerina 14
  Ogulnia 72
  sacra 178, 435–6, 445
libationes 79–80, 153–4, 165–8, 171,
    173, 213, 258, 263–5, 269–71, 276,
    279–80, 334, 452
libelli 100
Liberalia 41, 179, 212, 469
library 14–16, 189, 209, 211, 215–17
lictors 35, 334, 432
lightning 60, 106, 293–9, 302, 304, 336
litatio 266, 285
literacy 15, 185, 401
literature 17, 41, 52, 98, 119, 129, 132–3,
    141–2, 189, 209, 215, 218, 261, 351,
    354–6, 359–60, 364, 366, 377, 386,
    400, 425, 430, 441–2, 457–8
liticines 249, 332
liturgy 226–7, 232, 269, 318, 346, 365–6,
    374–5, 409–10, 418, 422–5; *see also*
    cult
litui 146–7, 152, 163, 206, 332
loot 5, 61, 139, 215, 221, 224, 256, 260,
    297
lot 218, 287, 292
Lucaria 179
lucus 277
lucus Feroniae 45, 54
ludi 63, 70, 111–12, 121–2, 224, 228,
    231, 269, 277, 296, 468–70; *see also*
    games
  annui 222
  Apollinares 226, 230
  Ceriales 226, 230
  circenses 63, 111–12, 121, 223–4,
    231–2, 406, 423
  Florales 226, 230
  funebres 222
  magni 224–5, 469

maximi 224–5
Megalenses 68, 226, 230, 268
plebei 63, 226, 230, 269, 423, 469
publici 222–33
Romani 224–6, 230, 423, 469
saeculares 8, 75–6, 78, 82, 217, 225–6, 246, 271, 277, 302
scaenici 26, 63, 75–6, 82, 223, 225, 229, 231, 233, 269, 470
Tarentini 225
Victoriae 231
Victoriae Caesaris 231–2
votivi 224, 230
ludiones (lydiones) 253–4
Lupercalia 121, 124–5, 179, 264
lustratio 170, 295, 269
  agri 278
  exercitus 171
lustra 77, 117
Lusus Troiae 253
lyres 215, 218, 249, 252, 264, 280, 332

Maccabees 350, 370
magi 280, 287, 338–41, 379–84, 387–9, 401
magic 14, 23, 25, 97, 185, 213, 236, 263, 267, 275–6, 280–1, 286–91, 338–40, 361, 387–8, 391
magistri 165–6, 199, 214, 217, 263, 277
Manicheism 100, 102–3, 108
mantele 334
marriage 4, 314, 351, 362, 464
Martenses 394
martyrdom 8, 98, 101–3, 116, 123, 222, 370, 409–26, 440, 458, 460, 468
mastigophoroi 254
Matralia 179
matron 176, 270, 277, 297
mausoleum 210, 413, 419
meals 100, 172, 207, 211, 279, 397–8, 407, 412
meat 20, 211, 267–8, 271, 283, 293, 348, 363, 397, 439
Meditrinalia 179
Melitians 99–100
memoria 14, 201, 210, 411

mensae 165, 206, 267
Mercuriales 394
mercy 96
Messiah 304–5, 314
metempsychosis 381
Miles (Mithraic grade) 398
military 3, 7, 15, 58, 67–8, 80–1, 91, 94, 105, 156, 162, 168, 171, 196, 225, 227–9, 233, 238, 242, 252–3, 260, 279, 297–8, 304, 310, 395–6, 400, 403, 413, 435–6, 451, 455
ministri 220, 332
minority 99, 176, 311, 345, 347, 350, 352, 354–5, 357, 372, 377
minyan shtarot 364
miracles 97, 136, 384, 386, 398, 462
Mishna 363
Mithraea 90, 206, 268, 387, 390, 394–402, 403, 455
Mithraism 2, 6, 384, 387, 389–90, 392–5, 397–8, 401–5
Mithra-Yašt 399
mola salsa 264–6
monks 110, 122, 289
monogamy 362
monotheism 96–7, 102, 108, 113, 312, 315, 359–61
  Jewish 382
  solar 114, 119
monstra 336
Montanists 106, 468
moon 382, 398
morality 59
mos 55
mos maiorum 14
mothers 67, 91, 141, 217, 279, 307, 332, 373–4, 382
mourning 271, 409
mules 223, 295
municipalia sacra 55, 438
municipia 54–5, 86, 89–90, 95, 264, 334–5, 431–2, 436–9, 444, 471
music 16, 133, 189, 229, 237, 249–54, 257–62, 332, 382, 432
mutitationes 268
myrtle 383
mystagogues 403

mysteria 37, 63, 151, 181, 209, 284, 381, 386, 390–4, 401, 430
mythology 3–5, 11, 17–20, 25, 27, 31–8, 42, 47, 61, 131, 133–4, 142–3, 153, 176, 188–98, 212–14, 217, 228, 233, 300, 315, 384–5, 388–90, 398–400, 406, 416–18, 440, 451, 453, 458

Na(ha)r 45
natales of Constantinople 120
natales of Rome 100, 120
nature 45, 52, 88, 113, 283, 288, 295, 325, 380, 383, 389, 458, 463
 sanctuaries 208
Navigium Isidis 124, 281
Nazareth Decree 14
necromancy 369
necropoleis 33, 210, 221, 270, 419
neokoroi 150, 153, 319, 324–6, 448
Neoplatonism 8, 97–8, 113, 119, 384–6, 388–9, 394
Neo-Pythagoreanism 6, 381–2
Neptunalia 179
New Testament 8, 98, 351, 455
New Year 120, 178, 194, 197, 213, 223, 307, 365, 370
night 77, 117, 263, 277, 283, 287, 308, 339
Nonae 179, 339
Novatians 106
novendiale sacrum 115, 296, 297
Novensides 14
numerology 381, 386, 389
numina 20, 23, 81, 83, 84, 94, 113, 227, 233
nuncupatio votorum 312
nymphs 38, 190, 212–14, 280, 398
Nymphus (Mithraic grade) 393

oaken wreath 79
oaths 50, 80, 90, 144–5, 237, 239, 241–2, 247, 286, 308, 311–12, 315, 431, 434, 440
obnuntatio 66, 435
October equus 264
offerings 35, 67, 101, 115, 120, 123, 153, 164–5, 184, 189, 235, 237, 242,
263–4, 266–70, 275–6, 279, 281, 283–4, 340, 366
oinochoe 87
Old Testament 98, 347, 351, 356, 455
olives 383
Olympieion 85
omens 36, 43–4, 66, 70, 80, 138, 140, 248, 266, 299–303, 336
 mortis 301
One (*Hen*) 97, 113, 389–90
Opalia 179
Opiconsivia 179
oracles 103, 130, 217–18, 287, 292, 304, 350, 384–5, 398, 446
oracula Chaldaica 388
orations 104, 116, 311, 318, 320–1, 330
ordines 39, 42, 280, 323, 329, 337
 equestris 459
Orphism 382, 384–6
orthodoxy 23, 70, 105, 110, 119–20, 123, 384, 387
orthopraxy 58, 150
oscilla 192
ostenta 293, 336
ostiarius 332
otium 189, 192
owls 143, 295, 340
oxen 46, 48, 87, 173, 240, 281–2, 285, 334

paganism 6, 17–18, 23, 92, 96–9, 102–24, 163, 275, 315, 331, 346–7, 350–5, 358, 360, 362–3, 366, 369, 385–6, 390–1, 399, 406–9, 413, 456, 459–62, 471
pagus 87, 89, 91
paideia 317, 329
palaestra 189
pallium 408
Panathenaia 228
panem et circensis 233
Panhellenion 320, 321
pantheon 4–5, 37, 54, 62, 69, 80, 84–8, 109, 112, 177, 181, 231, 283, 288, 361, 391, 439, 447, 463
Parentalia 4, 32, 115
Parilia 4, 179, 277–8, 285

Passover 364–6
pastophori 398
Pater (Mithraic grade) 280, 393, 399, 402–3
pater patratus 241–2
paterae 87, 152, 165–6, 333–4
patres familias 6, 180, 198, 237, 245, 277
patriarchs 364, 366, 370, 373, 375
patricians 35, 39, 42, 224, 283
patronage 46, 75, 79, 83–6, 89, 92–3, 119, 145, 156, 193, 239, 321, 346, 349, 354–5, 373, 376, 402–3, 419, 426, 454
pax 182
   Augusta 75, 80, 305
   de(or)um 60, 227, 278, 293
   Romana 84, 95
penetrale 209
Pentecost 364
perjury 242
Perses (Mithraic grade) 398–9
persecution 96, 99, 101–5, 108–9, 222, 408–9, 411, 415, 422
philosophy 6, 8, 96–8, 113–14, 132–3, 138, 189, 300, 318, 350, 378–87, 389–91, 408, 453, 458–66, 470
philotimia 318
piacula 286
pietas 227, 265, 279, 286, 408
piety 7, 62, 67, 74, 90–5, 100, 129, 132, 137, 146, 148, 154, 188, 276, 390, 400, 402, 410, 437; *see also pietas*
pigs 48, 87, 144, 165, 167–8, 239–41, 266, 333, 397
pilgrimage 364, 366, 370, 413, 424, 453
Pistis 285
Platonism 113, 381, 383–4, 389, 391, 392
plebeians 42, 72, 146, 224, 226, 246, 283, 299
podiums 55, 206, 209, 215, 220–1, 277, 401, 403
poetry 4, 25, 33, 39, 76, 130–8, 142, 193, 215, 227, 236, 244–5, 248, 261, 288, 304–6, 314–15, 318, 320, 339, 366–7, 378–9, 382, 385–6, 390, 395, 398, 426, 444, 461–4, 470

polygamy 362
polymorphism 389
polytheism 6–7, 14, 16–17, 85, 90, 114, 278, 389, 456
pomerium 433–4, 443
pompae 223, 228–9, 234, 407
   circenses 111–12, 232, 253–4
   deorum 229
   funebris 409
   minor 173
   triumphalis 254, 260
pontifices 13–15, 39, 42, 55, 60–1, 66, 74, 115, 120, 132, 151, 223, 244, 279, 333–4, 435, 438, 443, 447, 494–7
   maximus 39–40, 64, 66, 73–4, 77–8, 106, 120, 152, 217, 333, 412, 443, 447
popes 77, 118, 124, 409, 424
poplar 383
Poplifugium 179
porta Carmentalis 297
porta Collina 231, 295
portenta 60, 136, 140, 293
porticos 51, 87, 159, 183, 189, 206, 208, 211, 215–19, 412
   Porticus Octaviae 150
   porticus Tulliana 220
portraits 143–4, 328
Portunalia 179
Poseidoniastai 394
poultry 194, 229–30, 264, 332, 396–7
praecantrix 338
praecones 277, 335–7; *see also* heralds
praefationes 87, 169, 264, 280, 334
praesens deus 80
praesides omnium ludorum publicorum 224–5, 232
prayers 5, 44–5, 50, 87, 91, 103, 115, 122, 159, 160, 175, 186, 204, 235–48, 259, 265–6, 278, 281, 285, 287, 302, 312, 335, 340, 356–9, 365–8, 370–5, 388–9, 409, 417, 423, 434, 467
presbyters 118, 365, 373, 375, 407, 418, 421
priestesses 63, 208, 217, 331

priesthood 1–6, 13–14, 42, 60, 69, 76–7, 102, 109, 150–1, 164, 171–3, 181, 209–10, 214, 236, 246, 252–3, 255, 294–5, 317, 327–9, 331, 335, 432, 434, 437, 439, 447, 453–4, 470
principes 75, 167, 207, 217, 222
privileges 76, 267, 319, 323, 329, 346–8, 361, 363, 374–5, 467
probatio victimae 173
prodigies 60–1, 69, 136–40, 206, 209, 292–303, 336, 462
profanum 305
Progonoi 454
prophecy 67, 131–6, 218, 226, 293, 300, 302, 304, 338–9, 356–7, 365–9, 380–5, 388, 392
proseuche 356, 372
prostitution, ritual 50, 106, 117
providentia deorum 102, 313, 379
psalms 359, 365, 413
Pseudepigrapha 351, 356, 385
pueri et puellae patrimi matrimique 332
pullarii 332
pulvinar 232, 267
purification 41, 77, 101, 124, 334, 357–8, 366
purity 116, 280, 359, 368–9, 399
  laws 351, 357
Pyrrhiche 228
Pythagoreanism 132, 379–84, 388–9, 391

quadrigae 215, 260
Quindecemviri sacris faciundis 217, 277, 302, 443
Quinquatrus 179
Quirinalia 179

rabbinic
  Judaism 377
  literature 351, 363–4
  movement 346, 355, 357
rabbis 351, 364, 377
rams 170–1, 194
raven (Mithraic grade) 398
reburial 14
refrigerium 115
Regia 40, 295

Regifugium 41, 179
Reichsreligion 430, 437
religio 227, 279, 339, 341
  licita 467
  neglecta 227
  Romana 459
Renaissance 17–18, 27, 31, 430
res religiosa 114
res sacrae 5
resurrection 409
revelation 59, 385, 388
revenge 74, 287
rex sacrorum 39–40, 332–3
rhomboi 386
rider-gods 446
rites 14, 38, 40, 43–4, 47–8, 84–5, 87, 109, 115–16, 120, 134, 165–6, 223–4, 227–8, 265, 268, 276, 281, 289, 336; *see also* cult
  private 39, 115, 123; *see also* cult, domestic
ritual fast 296, 370
ritualism 18, 291
Robigalia 41, 179
Romanitas 17, 64, 152
Romanization 3, 55, 81, 89, 93, 150, 329, 347, 371, 418, 425, 445, 459

Sabbath 348, 356, 359, 364–5
sacerdotes provinciae 112
sacra 305, 438
sacra gentilica 238
sacred writings 132, 293, 336, 356–7
sacrificial animals 170–3, 258, 260–1, 280, 285, 300
sacrilege 54, 110, 129, 158, 302
sacrosanctity 80
saecula 76, 277
sage 365
Salii 237, 253, 255–6
salvation 74, 80, 284, 381, 386, 390, 392, 404, 412
Sanctorale 418
sanctus 366
sarcophagi 8, 168, 186, 383, 418, 422
Saturnalia 4, 114, 121, 130, 179
schism 99–100, 123

schools 98, 114, 121, 378, 447
scorpions 398, 403
scribae 334–5, 373
sculptures 188, 191–2, 197, 200–1, 235, 247, 448
Sebasteion 448
Second Sophistic 323, 453, 455
Second Temple 356
sects 119, 353, 375, 386, 388, 456, 468
sellisternia 226, 266
Septimontium 46
Septuagint 347
Serapeum 15, 206
sermons 112, 122, 259, 356, 362, 365, 370, 423–4
servi publici 332
seven-branched candelabra 357
sheep 87, 168, 239–41, 264, 266, 333
shrines 40, 61, 74, 78, 109, 165, 180, 186, 191, 196–200, 206–8, 217–18, 220, 237–8, 413, 424, 442, 447, 455
Sibylline Books 47, 60, 62, 132, 217–18, 225, 245, 293, 384
signs (*signa*) 60, 104, 137, 140–1, 160, 206, 210, 336–7, 415
sikinnis 229
simpulum 152
simulacra 206
sin 99, 110–11, 113, 124, 358, 399, 404, 446
sistra 249, 386
sitella 218
Skepticism 11, 40, 59, 68, 138, 141, 300
slaves 45, 72–3, 78–9, 180–3, 199, 208, 211, 220, 244–5, 263, 289, 304, 311, 332, 334–5, 347, 363, 396, 400, 408, 410
snakes 141, 159, 198, 386, 398
sodales 63, 268, 333
    Augustales 334
sodalicium 382
solar (heliocentric) theology 391
solitaurilia 170
Solomonic wisdom 384, 387
solstice 397
sons 104, 118, 120
Sondergötter 14

soothsayers 132, 141, 218, 300, 302, 340–1
sophists 288, 320, 325, 391
sorcery 339, 362; *see also* magic
sôter (tou kosmou) 80, 93, 283, 305
souls 80, 97, 285, 315, 381, 383, 385–6, 389–90, 399
sows 48, 270
spells 186, 236, 289, 338–9, 382, 387, 389
spes publica 159
sphinx 18
springs 36, 46–7, 158, 206, 213, 238, 384
    sanctuary 208
stadia 318, 326, 360, 419, 422
stars 379, 380–1, 383–5, 388, 463
statues 4, 7, 47, 54, 68–9, 80, 85, 89, 93–4, 131, 146, 173, 177, 180, 182, 189, 192, 197, 207, 210, 215, 217–18, 220, 229, 232, 238, 252, 266–7, 286, 296, 302, 305, 311, 318, 328, 387, 414, 441, 448; *see also* images; statuettes
statuettes 1, 4, 35, 54, 94, 167, 191–3, 197–201, 207, 238; *see also* statues
stelae 92, 183, 186, 210, 285, 398, 422, 446
Stoicism 283, 378–9, 381–4, 389–90, 392, 404
sub-deacon 407
suffimenta 277
suicide 416
sun 308, 383–4, 392, 398–9, 417
Sunday 105, 120–1, 407, 418, 424, 426
suovetaurilia 170–1, 173–4
superstitio 5, 97, 112, 115, 121, 199, 275–6, 287, 338–41, 459, 468
supplicationes 100, 238, 247–8, 270, 281, 294, 296–7
swine 264
symbols 3, 7, 36, 106, 143, 146–55, 159–60, 163–4, 167, 172, 174–5, 213, 215, 231, 285, 292, 334, 404, 419
symposia 193, 195, 214, 267

synagogues 206, 211, 346–50, 354,
    356–7, 360–8, 370–7, 455
syncretism 384
syngeneia 320
synods 98, 105

tabellae defixionum 185
tabula dealbata 294, 296
taurobolia 90, 281, 283
tauroctonies 394, 398, 401
taurus 173
tegula Capuana 2
teletai of Mithras 395, 399
temenos 51, 284
templa 61, 205–6, 299, 394
    temple of the Sun 102
temple doors 207, 209, 217, 220, 238
temple guardians 209, 448
tensa 232
Terminalia 179
text, cultic 6, 32, 86, 177, 239
thaumaturgist 384
theaters 43, 53, 68, 76, 94, 111, 122, 148,
    208–10, 225, 227–9, 231, 234, 252,
    254, 257, 269, 311, 325–7, 350,
    360–1, 468–9
theoí sýnnaoi 185
theologia naturalis 378, 381
theology 6, 16, 98–9, 107, 113, 118–19,
    248, 280, 285, 311, 315, 360, 378,
    380, 382–91, 429, 463–5
theophany 398
theos 81
    epiphanes 309, 310
theoxenia 226, 452
theurgy 98, 361–2, 385–91
thiasos 192, 254
thrones 86, 100, 104, 340, 403, 414
tibia 261
tibicines 165, 167, 228, 249, 256–8, 332,
    335
togas 41, 64, 86, 165, 255–6, 263, 277,
    333, 363, 433
    praetexta 165, 167
    virilis 279, 363
tombs 114–16, 125, 173, 177, 185–7,
    207, 210, 257, 271, 286, 349,

369–70, 374, 410–14, 418–20, 423;
    see also funerals
Torah 356–7, 359–60, 364–8, 377
traditor 99
trapezomata 452
tria genera theologiae 462
tripods 143, 150, 165, 168, 217–18, 257,
    388
tripudium 168, 253, 255–6, 261, 299–300
triumphs 96, 129, 131, 159, 170–1, 223,
    232, 238, 244–6, 250–1, 254–6,
    259–60, 292, 302, 404, 409, 414
Trojan origin 137
tropaia 410, 414, 418, 422
trumpets 252
*tubicines sacrorum publicorum populi
    Romani* 249, 252, 260–1, 280
Tubilustrium 179, 252
tunicae 256, 333, 393, 449
Twelve Tables 13, 14, 288
tympana 249

Underworld 52, 77, 135, 266, 267, 269,
    271, 288, 339

vates 218
venationes 230
ver sacrum 285
Vestal Virgins 4, 39–40, 76, 120, 264,
    295, 334
Vestalia 179, 264
veterans 181, 432, 447
viatores 334–5
vicennalia 109, 169
vici 89, 90, 94, 165–6, 199, 310, 332,
    397
vicomagistri 73, 166–7, 310, 332
vicoministri 79, 332
victimarii 165, 168, 332–4
victoria Caesaris 233
victoriae populi Romani 231, 233
victories 53, 69, 75–6, 93–5, 102, 104–5,
    108, 129, 131, 139, 156, 159, 168,
    213, 215, 218, 224, 231–3, 239,
    245–6, 260, 269, 280–1, 289, 302,
    312, 411–18, 421–3
Villa dei Misteri 393

Vinalia 179
vintage 120, 439
Virgo Vestalis parentat 115
virtus 63, 192
vitio creatum 298–9
Volkanalia 179
votive items 2, 5, 35–6, 41–2, 45–7, 52,
    62, 69, 87, 91–3, 121, 124, 169–73,
    180–3, 192, 206–7, 213, 223–6,
    230–1, 235–41, 245–8, 259, 267,
    270–1, 275–6, 279–87, 291, 296,
    312–13, 331, 361, 366, 370, 446
Vulgata 425
vultures 147

weddings 279, 340
widows 123

wine 87, 115, 167, 197, 214, 258,
    264–70, 275, 280, 334, 341, 397,
    398
witches 369
wolves 43, 46, 295, 297, 301–3
women 7, 90, 101, 114, 124, 141, 196,
    199, 212, 237–8, 257, 268, 276, 279,
    281, 338–9, 341, 358, 393, 396, 404,
    422, 435
worship 62–4, 205, 207, 222–6, 237, 263,
    386, 410, 435–6, 440–9, 452, 456,
    464

xenia 192

Ziborium 420
Zoroastrian tradition 100

Index of Personal Names

1 GODS

Abaddir 435
Acerronius 55
Adolenda 14
Adonis 94, 455
Aeacus 379
Aequitas 156
Aesculapius 64, 88, 185, 264, 284
  Augustus 86
Africa Caelestis 83
Aglibol 446, 450
Allat 450
Alma 92
Amor 192
Ancharia 463
Angitia 53
Anna Perenna 205, 210, 212–14, 280
Annona 407
Anubis 94
Aphlad 94, 455
Aphrodite 67, 85, 117, 361
Apollo 37, 39, 63, 74–7, 80, 86, 88,
    103–4, 130, 133, 143, 150, 190,
    199–200, 205, 207, 210–11, 215–18,
    226, 234, 285, 288, 297, 305, 381,
    384, 395, 446, 453–4, 469
  Actius 153–4, 156, 215
  Palatinus 207, 214, 217–18

Philia 85
Phoebus 86, 245, 311
  Sosianus 171, 251, 257, 260
Ares 13
Arethusa 143
Artahe 90
Artemis 85, 94, 143, 149, 284, 381, 446,
    448–9, 455
  Laphria 85
Astarte 91
Atargatis 452, 463
Atepomarus 182
Athena 37, 85, 143, 217, 381, 446,
    449
Attis 390, 392
Augusta Emerita 83
Azzanathkona 94, 446, 455

Baal-Shamin 450
Bacax 93, 181
Bacchus 64, 76, 188, 192–3, 199, 437
Bandua Boleccus 86
Bel 446, 450
Belenus 463
Bes 85, 94
Bindus 181
Bonus Eventus 86

Caelestis 463
Castor and Pollux 37
Cautes 398
Cautopates 398
Celle 52
Ceres 42, 51–2, 56, 63, 87, 171, 226,
    234, 264, 270–1, 278, 296, 407, 469
Cerfian 51
Cerfius Martius 45
Cernunnos 88
Charon 379
Christ 1, 14, 99, 107, 118, 122, 124,
    159–60, 162, 339, 365, 388, 406,
    410, 413, 415, 418, 420–3, 430, 459
Circe 443
Clementia 156
Cohvetena 86
Coinquenda 14
Concordia 75, 154, 283
  Augusta 75
Consentius 16
Consiva 40
Consus 223, 469
Conventina 91
Cretus 94
Cronus 131
Cupid 195, 199
Cybele 196, 249, 390, 392, 398, 442

Daphne 190
Dea Dia 208, 212, 253, 277
Dea Nehalennia 181
Dea Roma 2, 81, 93, 144, 323
Dea Syria 452
dei patrii 181
dei Penates 15, 38, 201, 268, 270, 275,
    279, 440–1
Delventinus 463
Deus Lar Berobreus 183
Deus Turmsgada 181
Di Manes 115, 186–7, 239, 271, 287
Diana 36, 43–4, 86, 148, 182, 215, 245,
    281
  Maxima 86
  Planciana 67
Dii Magifae 181
dii propitii 197

Dionysus 76, 85, 307
Dioscuri 144
Dis (Pater) 77, 225
Disciplina 91
diva Augusta 315
divus Augustus 315
diva Claudia virgo 315
divus Constantinus 159
divus Iulius 80–1, 135
Dusares 446, 463

Eilithyai 77
Elpis Sebaste 157
Epona 91
Er 388
Erinye 196
Eros 188

Fatum 77
fauns 38
Felicitas 156
Feronia 45, 54–5
Fides 286
Fisus Sacus 49
Fisus Sancius 60
Flora 63, 234, 469
Fons perennis 398
Fortuna 36–7, 197, 199, 207, 220, 454
  Augusta 90, 205, 207, 218–20, 307
  Equestris 443
Frugifer 83, 92
Furiae 135, 193

Genius 2, 6, 79–80, 87, 94, 154, 161,
    167, 188, 198–201, 207, 264, 275,
    279, 310–11, 440
  Augusti 166, 268
  loci 182, 184, 414
  municipi 86
  populi Romani 169
  Senatus 2, 169
Grabovius gods 49–50

Hades 379, 381
Harpocrates 85, 392
Hecate 385–8
Helios 143, 309, 361, 390

Hera 130, 133
  Licinia 56
Hercules 37, 45–7, 51, 85–6, 91, 143–4,
    184, 192, 199, 200–1, 217, 286, 307,
    315, 383, 406, 419
  Curinus 56
  Epitrapezios 193
  Invictus 68
  Musarum 62, 131
  Pompeianus 67
Hermes 130, 361, 385–6, 388
  Trismegistus 385
Hilaritas 156
Homonoia 85
Hondus Cerfius 60
Honos 66, 302
Horus 94
Hosios kai Dikaios 446
Hunte 51

Ianus 72, 144, 264
Iaô 384
Idaea 196
Idiatte 90
Isis 8, 85–6, 97, 119, 124, 189, 221, 249,
    257, 261, 269, 283, 291, 392, 398,
    453
  Pelagia 86
Iuno 37, 50, 55, 130, 133, 217, 238, 434,
    447
  Curitis 52
  Regina 77, 83, 239, 244, 281, 297
  Sospita 37, 45
Iuno (of a female) 279, 310
Iuppiter 37, 39, 44, 47–51, 76, 88, 102,
    130–5, 149, 155–6, 168–9, 182, 199,
    223–4, 234, 239, 241, 246, 260, 264,
    269, 276, 280–1, 286, 297, 301, 311,
    315, 366, 382, 412, 434, 440, 442,
    447, 450, 469
  Anxur 55
  Capitolinus 67, 90, 92, 171, 217, 286,
    308
  Capitolinus Optimus Maximus 35,
    156
  Conservator 156
  Custos 156
  Dolichenus 91, 392, 455

Grabovius 49
Heliopolitanus 93
Hunte 51
Latiaris 469
Liber 55
Municipalis 90
Optimus Beelseddes 450
Optimus Maximus 77, 86, 90–1, 130,
    133, 141, 223–6, 238, 240, 280,
    449–50
Optimus Maximus Balmarcod 450
Optimus Maximus Dolichenus 449
Optimus Maximus Heliopolitanus 449
paganicus 183
Sabazios 392
Statius 142
Stator 297
Tarpeianus 109
Victor 156
Iustitia 381
Iuventas 302–3

Lahus Paraliomegus 86
Larentia 467
Lares 32, 38, 78–9, 84, 115, 121, 165,
    167, 180, 188, 197–201, 207, 243–4,
    266, 268, 275, 279, 281, 310, 332
  Augusti 86, 197
  Callaeciae 83
  Compitales 86
  Viales 86
Latona 217
Lenus Mars 87
Liber (Pater) 42, 76, 89, 469
Libera 42
Liberalitas 156
Libertas 301
  Augusta 86
Luna 93, 188, 383

Marduk 62
Mars 13, 39, 43–4, 46–51, 74–5, 86, 91,
    137, 143, 170, 182, 188, 190, 223,
    236–7, 239–40, 243–4, 253, 264,
    295, 469
  Augustus 86, 182
  Grabovius 49
  Hodius 60

Lenus 87
Mullo 87
Pater 280
Ultor 156, 279, 285, 448
Victor 280
Mater Magna (Deorum Idaea) 62–4, 68,
  70, 84, 90, 218, 226, 234, 249, 268,
  283, 390, 442–3, 469
Mater Matuta 36, 435, 436
Matronae 183
Medusa 190–1
Mefitis 47, 51–2, 55
  Utiana 55
Melqart 37
Men 446
Mercurius 92, 130, 181–2, 190, 194–5,
  198–200, 391
  Augustus 86
  Canetonnensis 193
Minerva 37, 47, 55, 156, 190, 192,
  195–6, 199, 238, 382, 434, 447
  Medica 284
  Sulis Minerva 186
Mithras 7, 90, 97, 268, 270, 386–7,
  392–3, 394–5, 398–403, 404, 455
  D(eus) S(ol) I(nvictus) M(ithras) 115,
  401
  Invictus 401
  Invictus Nabarze 401
Moira 77
Mullo 87, 182
Muses 13, 131
Mutunus 467

Nebu 450
Nemesis 85, 285, 286
Nemi 281
Neptunus 182, 264, 383, 469
Nike 143
Nodens 287
Nortia 463
Numiternus 463
nymphs 38, 190, 212–14, 280, 398

Obodas 463
Olympian gods 75, 229, 234, 296, 392
Onuava 90–1
Osiris 85, 453

Pales 278
Persephone 56
Pertunda 279
Philologia 391
Pietas 86, 154, 156–7
  Augusta 86
Pluto (Dis) 77
Poemana 86
Praestota 45, 50
  Cerfia 45
Proserpina 77, 137, 225
Providentia 307
  Augusta 314

Quirinus 39, 49–50

Rea 86
Rego 86
Reshef 450
Robigo 37, 264

Sacra Moneta 158
Salus 154, 156, 161–2
Sandan 145
Saturnus 60, 64, 74, 131, 144, 464
satyrs 229, 253
Securitas 156
Selene 385
Semo Sancus Dius Fidius 60
Semones 243, 244
Sequana 92
Serapis 85, 89, 97, 111, 464
Shadrafa 450
Silvanus 7, 182, 287
Sol 93, 104, 108, 114, 161, 215, 383,
  398, 403
  Elagabal 156
  Invictus 102, 401, 417
  Invictus Mithras 392; *see also* Mithras
Spes 156
  Augusta 157
Sterculus 465, 467
Sulis Minerva 186
Summanus 14
Sunuxal 88

Tanit 133
Tefer Jovius 49–50

Tellus 239, 264, 281
Terminus 442
Terra Mater 77, 91
Teutates 181
Theos Hypsistos 114
Torsa 50–1
Trebus Iovius 49–50
Turmasgada 182
Tursa Cerfia 45

Uni 37, 133

Varsutina 463
Vediovis 36
Venus 7, 17, 51, 62, 67–8, 70, 85–6,
　　131–2, 188, 190, 192–3, 197, 315,
　　382, 470
　Erycina 62, 68
　Genetrix 69, 232
　Pompeiana 199
　Victrix 68–9, 83, 231
Veroca (Verora) 86
Vesta 74, 148, 154, 208, 217–18, 264,
　　440, 448

Victoria 52, 75, 91, 93, 143, 160–2, 169,
　　197, 199, 231, 234, 302, 311
　Augusta 75, 86
　Sullana 231
Viradecthis 91
Virtus 66, 302, 454
Visidianus 463
Vofionus 49
　Grabovius 49
Vulcanus 60, 264

Yarhibol 446, 450
YHWH 284, 315, 357, 359–60, 365–72,
　　375, 384

Zeus 85, 94, 130–1, 143, 196, 307, 309,
　　315, 446, 449, 454
　Alsenos 92
　Ammon 307
　Ampeleites 446
　Betylos 449
　Olympios 454
　Patarenos 92
　Polieus 85
　Thallos 92, 446

2 HUMANS

Aaron 360
Abraham 276, 357, 359
Acheloos 213
Achilles 137
Actaeon 406
Aelius Heracleides 320
Aelius Verus 313
Aemilius Paullus 261
Aeneas 33–4, 36, 38, 61, 67–8, 85,
　　131–4, 137–8, 214, 217, 440–1
Agathocles 47
Agnes 419
Agrippa 325
Alaric 423
Alaric II 351
Alcimus 395

Alcmaeon the Pythagorean 381
Alexander of Abonouteichos 384
Alexander, bishop of Alexandria 99, 105–6
Alexander the Great 3, 81, 99, 105–6,
　　143, 159, 305, 307, 366, 394, 450,
　　454
Alexander Polyhistor 381
Alexander Severus 96
Alexandra 289
Ambrose 115–16, 120, 122–3
Ammianus Marcellinus 16, 109, 119, 138,
　　142
St. Anastasia 424
Anaxilaos of Larissa 380, 388
Anchises 132
Andromeda 190–1

Andronikos 130
T. Annius Luscus 433–4
P. Anteios Antiochus 320
Antinoos 319
Antiochus III 226
Antiochus IX Cyzicenus 395
Antonia Tryphaina 326
Antoninus Pius 149, 170, 254, 313, 321, 394
C. Antonius 151
M. Antonius (triumvir) 69, 74, 76, 80–1, 151, 215, 299, 444, 449
M. Antonius Polemon 318, 320
Apion 360
Apollonius of Tyana 340, 384
Sex. Apudius 313
L. Apuleius 8, 261, 288, 291, 338, 387
M. Apuleius Eurycles 328
Aquilas 347
Arcadius 121
Ariadne 188
Aristeides 8, 323, 330
Aristophanes 228
Aristotle 31
Arius 99–100, 105–6, 118
Arnobius 15–16, 389, 457–8
Arrius Antoninus 322
Artemidoros of Chalcis 285, 340
Ascanius 137
Asclepigenia 386
Ascyltos 190, 197
Ateius Capito 77
Athanasius 106, 118
Atia 305
Attalos Paterklianos 196
Atticus 319, 327
Attius Navius 300
Augustine 8, 14–16, 37, 16, 113, 115, 122–4, 279, 382, 423–4, 457, 458
Augustus 23, 33, 56, 58, 64, 68, 71–86, 93–4, 133–4, 148, 151–6, 164–7, 178, 197, 199, 201, 207, 212, 215, 217, 225, 233, 244, 246, 252–3, 279, 281, 285, 299, 302–3, 305, 307–10, 313, 315–17, 323, 338, 340, 380, 430, 432, 434, 436, 439–40, 447, 449; *see also* Octavian

Aurelian 99, 102, 416
M. Aurelius, *see* Marcus Aurelius
Ausonius 16, 391

Barbatio 288
Barea Soranus 341
Basil of Caesarea 423
Bibulus 66
Bolus Mendesius 379–80
Brutus 75, 151

Caecilian 99, 105
Caedicius 399
C. Iulius Caesar 33, 58, 65–70, 72–3, 74, 77, 80, 85, 87, 133–5, 151, 155, 178–9, 215, 231–3, 246, 281, 298, 302, 304–5, 307, 315, 337, 382–3, 433, 435
Calepodius 409
Caligula 153, 154, 219, 308–9, 313, 326, 350
Calpurnia 302
Calpurnius Piso 288
Camena 13
Camillus 239, 277, 283, 444
Caracalla 15, 92, 431
Cassandra 193
Cassius 75
Cassius Hemina 464
Catilina 302
Cato the Elder 13, 134–6, 238–41, 264, 276, 282, 285, 288, 300, 338, 433
Catullus 398
Celsus 338, 379, 399
Censorinus 15, 16
Charax 320
Charisius 16
M. Tullius Cicero 13, 18, 33, 59, 61, 66, 88, 188–9, 192, 223, 270, 276–9, 291, 294, 299–304, 338–9, 341, 345, 350, 366, 378–9, 382–3, 391, 432–3, 452, 458, 468
L. Cincius 13, 16–17
Claudia Severa 373, 376
Claudius 152–3, 337, 346, 439–40
Tib. Claudius Andragathos Attalos 320–1
Claudius Charax 318

Tib. Claudius Livianus 395
M. Claudius Marcellus 298–9, 336
C. Claudius Nero 297
Claudius Piso Tertullinus 321
P. Claudius Pulcher 300
Cleanthes the Stoic 382–3
Clement of Alexandria 98
Clement of Rome 421
P. Clodius Pulcher 277, 301–2
Commodus 157, 313, 319–20, 400
Conrutus 383
Constans 117
Constantine 96, 104–25, 155, 158–62,
　　346, 374–5, 397, 408, 410, 412–25
Constantine II 159
Constantius 103–4, 109–10, 117–18, 120,
　　159, 288
Cornelius Labeo 15–16, 384
Cornelius Nepos 464
P. Cornelius Lentulus Sura 302
P. Cornelius Scipio Africanus 301
Q. Cornificius 151
Croesus 394
Cyprian 98–9, 101, 424, 457, 458
Cyrus 394

Damascius 386
Damasippus 380
Damasus 120, 123, 413, 425
Decentius 160
Decius 96, 98, 100–1, 103, 109, 408,
　　431, 434
P. Decius Mus 239, 312, 336
Democritus 379–80, 384
Denys of Alexandria 101
Dexippus 15
Diadumenianus 325
Dido 212
Dio 85, 93, 318, 324, 326–7, 330
Diocles 402
Diocles of Peparethus 137
Diocletian 15, 96, 99–100, 102–3, 105,
　　108–9, 158
Diodorus Siculus 464
Dionysius of Halicarnassus 8, 14–15, 229,
　　253, 255, 336, 383
Domitian 156–7, 240, 326, 439–40

Domitilla 409
Cn. Domitius Calvinus 151
Domitius Corbulo 311
Q. Domitius Tutus 193
Donatus 99, 105

Egeria 55
Elagabalus 150, 153, 156, 391
Encolpius 190, 197
Endymion 188
Q. Ennius 130–4
Epameinondas 329
Epicharmus 132
Epicurus 378–9
Ethpeni 400–1
Eudocia 161
Eunapius 386, 388, 391
Eurycles 319
Eusebius of Caesarea 103, 106, 111, 116,
　　159, 416, 422
Eusebius of Myndos 387
Eusebius of Nicomedia 99, 106
Ezra 366, 369

Fabius Maximus 336
Fabius Pictor 33, 137, 229, 382
Fausta 162
Faustina II 313–14
Festus 8, 16, 299, 438–9
Filocalus 426
Firmicus Maternus 387, 392
Firmidius Severinus 400
Firmus Catus 340
Flavia Nicolais Saddane 436
Flavius Arrianus 318
Fronto 14, 322
Q. Fulvius Flaccus 56
M. Fulvius Nobilior 62

Galba 141, 439
Galerius 103–4
Gallienus 102
Ganymede 315
Gellius 13, 16, 431–2, 436, 438
Germanicus 281, 288, 383
Geryon 46
Gordian III 93

Granius Licinianus 382
Gratian 120, 123, 391
Gregory of Nazianz 423
Gregory of Nyssa 423

Hadrian 85–7, 93, 169, 311, 313, 321, 326, 328, 431–2, 447
Haman 365
Hanna 370
Hannibal 45, 130, 137, 139, 297, 301, 336
Hanno 242–3
Hasdrubal 297
Helen of Troy 384–5
Helena 105
Hephaestus 38
Heraclitus 378
Herculius 102
Herodes Atticus 318–19, 327
Herodes the Great 370
Herodotus 136, 139, 142, 394, 452–3
Hieronymus 425–6, 460
Hippolytus 98, 388
Homer 4, 13, 130–3, 136, 385, 446
Honorius 121, 347
Horace 74, 76–7, 244–5, 261, 304, 339, 350
Hypatia 391

Iamblichus 98, 386, 388–90
Ignatius of Antioch 410
Iosephus 325, 346, 348, 350, 355, 360, 363, 370
Iovian 119
Iovius 102
Irenaeus 388
Isaiah 366
Isidore of Seville 15, 332
Iulia, daughter of Augustus 313
Iulia Domna 83
Iulian the Theurgist 387
Iulianus Apostata 8, 114, 118, 125, 385, 386–7, 390–1
Iulius Africanus 384
C. Iulius Eurycles Herclanus L. Vibullius Pius 319
Iulius Obsequens 293, 296

Iulus 36, 68, 133
Iustina 123
Iustinian 347
Iustinian II 162
Iustinus 407–8
Iuvenal 350

Jacob 369
John Chrysostom 122, 362, 365, 370–1, 423
John Lydus 15–17, 27
Joseph, son of Jacob 369, 464
Joshua 356
Josiah 369
Jugurtha 302

Kotys 308

Labienus 66
Lactantius 103, 256, 457–8
Laevius 382
Laurentia 465
Lentulus Spinther 151
Leo 423
Lepidus 77, 78, 151
Leucippus 380
Leucothea 436
Libanios 117, 287–8, 322
Liberius 118
L. Licinius Lucullus 338
C. Licinius Mucianus 340
Licinius 104, 106, 159, 161, 413
Livia 216, 302, 315, 447
Livius Andronicus 13, 130, 227, 244
M. Livius Salinator 297
Livy 8, 16, 33, 44, 64, 136–42, 229, 236, 239, 241–2, 248, 285, 293–4, 296–7, 336, 437, 441–2, 458
Longinianus 113
Lucan 134–5, 142
Lucian of Antioch 98
Lucian of Samosata 8, 320, 379, 393, 452
C. Lucretius Menander 403
M. Lucretius Fronto 190, 379
Lucullus 215, 339
Luscus 434
Lysippus 193

Macrinus 325
Macrobius 15–17, 114, 391, 441
Maecenas 338
Magnentius 109, 160
Maioran 99
Mani 100, 399
Manius Aquilius 69
C. Manlius 170
T. Manlius Torquatus 336
Marcellina the Carpocritian 384
Marcellus 313
Marcinia 56
Marcion 408
Marcus Aurelius 89, 250–1, 313–14, 323, 328
Marcus the Valentinian 380, 384, 387–8
C. Marius 52, 65–7, 302, 337, 382
Marius Victorinus 16
St. Mark 410
Martial 193, 350
Martianus Capella 16, 391
Ma[rt]inus 396
Ma[tern]inus 396
Maxentius 104–5, 412–18, 422
Maximianus 102
Maximinus Daia 103, 278
Maximus of Ephesus 387, 390, 422
Maximus of Madaura 113
Maximus of Tyre 113
Medea 193
L. Memmius Rufus 326
Metrodoros of Scepsis 380
Michelangelo 74
Miltiades 417
M. Minucius 146
P. Minucius 146
C. Minucius Augurinus 145
M. Minucius Faesus 146–7
Minucius Felix 8, 457–8
Mithridates VI Eupator 305, 380
Modestinus 339
Monica 115
Moses 351, 357, 359–61, 369
Mucius Scaevola 69
Munatius Plancus 74
Myron 215

Cn. Naevius 130–4, 137, 142, 228
Narcissus 188
Nehemiah 366, 369
Neptunalios 380
Nero 134, 141, 148, 152, 253, 288, 292, 309, 311–15, 341, 383, 406, 421
Nerva 89, 152, 156, 281, 313, 325
Nestorius 214, 386
Nicolaus of Damascus 325
Nigidius Figulus 13, 15–16, 382–3, 388
Niobe 217
Sex. Nonius Sufenas 231
Noumenios 389
Novatian 99, 409
Novius Vindex 193, 200, 261
Numa Pompilius 18, 39, 132, 153, 252–3, 378, 383, 390
Nymphus 393

Octavian 69, 73–6, 80, 147, 151, 258, 302, 305, 381–2, 444, 449; *see also* Augustus
Odysseus 137
Opramoas 319
Orestes 196
Origen 98, 399
Orpheus 382, 385, 388
Ostanes 380, 384
Otho 141
Ovia Pacia 47
Ovid 8, 17, 23, 25, 39, 52, 80, 212–14, 315, 350, 442

Sex. Pacuvius 313
Pamphylos 380
Paul of Samosata 99
Paul of Tarsus 148, 284, 362–3, 365, 406, 408, 410–15, 418, 421
Paulus Diaconus 17
Pausanias 320, 453
Pelagius 289
Periplectomenus 338
Perseus 190–1, 320
Pescennius Niger 324
Peter the Apostle 120, 124, 363, 410–15, 417–18, 421

Petronius 193, 197
Philip the Arab 98, 100, 108
Philo of Alexandria 346, 350, 354–5, 360,
    366–7, 370, 374
Philostratus 8, 319, 340, 391
Pisistratos 37
Cn. Plancus 67
Plato 97, 291, 378, 381, 383, 385,
    388–400
Plautus 242–3, 245, 284, 338
Pleminius 139
Pliny the Elder 21, 52, 86, 188–9, 235,
    247, 258, 287, 338, 387, 458, 464
Pliny the Younger 14, 56, 87, 282, 350,
    443
Plotinus 97, 102, 385, 388–9
Plutarch 8, 52, 137, 255, 261, 318, 321,
    326, 330, 395, 453–4
Plutarch the Thaumaturgist 386
Polemon 308, 325
Polybius 59, 73, 192
Sex. Pompeius 215
Cn. Pompeius Magnus 65, 67–9, 134–5,
    148, 151, 215, 231–3, 302, 321,
    382–3, 454
L. Pompeius Paulinianus 90
Pomponius Atticus 192
L. Pomponius Molo 153
Q. Popilius Pytho 325
Porphyry 98, 384–5, 388–91, 392, 394,
    399–400
Poseidonius 381, 395
Praetextatus 114, 117, 409
Proclus 289, 386, 388
Propertius 25, 215, 261
Proteus 385
Publius Valerius 36
Pyrrhus 131, 139
Pythagoras 378, 380–2, 387

Quintilian 236

Rachel 370
Remus 32, 34, 75, 132, 137, 304,
    415
Rhoemetalkes 308

Romulus 32, 34, 39, 43, 61, 75, 132, 137,
    147, 214, 304, 415, 432

Sallustius 119, 136
Salustius 390–1
Salutaris 448
Salvina 289
Saoteros of Nicomedia 319
Saturninus 83, 84
Sceva 362
Scipio Africanus 67
Scribonia 340
N. Scribonius Libo Drusus 340–1
Seianus 314
Seleucus Nicator 454
C. Sempronius Gracchus 301, 337
Tib. Sempronius Gracchus 65, 301, 336
Seneca 238, 283, 291, 339, 458, 468
Senecianus 287
Septimius Severus 149, 324
M. Servilius Nonianus 340
Servius 15–17, 36–7, 332, 444
Severus 422
Sibyl of Cuma 214
Sibyl of Tibur 90
Sicinus 123
Silvester 417
Simon Magus 380, 384
Sixtus II 101, 411
Socrates 394
Solomon 356
Soter 407
Spartacus 304, 404
T. Statilius Lambrias 327
Statius 135, 395
Stephanus Byzantius 397
Strabo 52, 54, 437
Suetonius 16, 76, 85, 157, 350, 382, 458,
    468–9
Sulla (Felix) 35, 65, 67–8, 151, 231–3,
    288, 293, 298, 302, 321, 337, 381
Symmachus 16–17, 109, 122
Syrianus 381

Tacitus 8, 76, 87, 136, 138, 140–2, 311,
    340, 350, 447, 458, 464

Tarquinius Priscus 38
Tarquinius Superbus 34, 37–8
Tertullian 8, 16, 111, 399, 459–64,
　　466–71
Thales 278
Themistocles 329
Theodosius I 110, 120–1, 123, 201, 350
Theodosius II 125, 161, 346–7
Theophanes of Mytilene 321
Theophrastus 379
Theopompus 33
Tiberius 55, 73, 141, 157, 162, 168, 178,
　　252, 288, 292, 313–14, 325, 340–1,
　　383, 434, 439, 447
Timaeus of Tauromenium 137
Tiridates 311–12
M. Tittius 373, 376
Titus 85, 439–40
Titus Flaminius 69
Totila 121
Trajan 56, 84–5, 89, 148, 171, 256, 281,
　　311–13, 326–7, 329, 333, 443
Trajan Decius 85
Trimalchio 190, 193, 197
M. Tullius 219–21
Tullus Hostilius 294

Ulpian 434
Ursinus 123

Valens 119, 388
Valentinian I 117, 119, 123
Valentinian II 120, 347, 350, 408

Valentinus 380, 387
Valerian 96, 98, 101–2, 408, 411
Valerius 139
Valerius Antias 294
D. Valerius Dionysius 376
Valerius Iustus 90
Valerius Maximus 235
Valerius Soranus 382
M. Terentius Varro 8, 13–16, 27, 33, 37,
　　41–2, 189, 253, 378, 382–5, 433,
　　438, 442, 458, 462–9, 471
Vatinius 339
C. Velleius 379
Verica 152
Verres 66, 192, 337
Verrius Flaccus 8, 13, 16, 39, 350, 366, 438
L. Verus 328, 401
Vespasian 141, 148, 240, 310, 438–40
Vetranio 160–1
Victor 408
Vipsanius Agrippa 313
Virgil 33, 42, 52, 55, 76, 133–5, 212,
　　305, 385, 426, 444, 458
Vitellius 156, 256
Vitruvius 75, 209, 434
Volusii Saturnini 54

Xenophon 394
Xerxes 380, 393

Zachalias of Babylon 380
Zephyrinus 408
Zoroaster 380–1, 384, 386, 392–3

Index of Places

Abdera 380

Abella 45, 57

Achaea 319

Acropolis 75

Actium 156, 215, 317

Aegeis 319–20, 330

Aelia Capitolina 447

Aezani 449

Africa 5–6, 61, 83, 86, 89, 92–4, 99, 102, 105, 112, 123–4, 183, 188, 191, 347–9, 365, 371, 396, 412, 423, 449, 457–63

Agnone 51–2, 57

Aizanoi 328

Akraiphia 309

Alba Longa 34, 36, 241–2, 441

Alburnus Maior 93

Alexandria 15, 88, 99, 118, 120, 141, 157, 215, 310, 361, 374, 391, 422, 444

Alexandria Troas 319

Allia 339

Alps 82, 432

Altbachtal 90

Ambracia 131

Anagnia 14

Anath 455

Anatolia 3, 286, 381, 394–5, 399, 442, 446

Antia 463

Antioch 88, 99, 119, 152, 287, 365, 370, 450–1, 455

Antium 39, 73, 443

Aosta 400

Apamea 388, 399

Apennines 437

Aphrodisias 85, 323, 328

Apollonopolis Heptokomia 86

Apulia 294

Apulum (Alba Iulia) 185, 285

aquae Cutiliae 52

Aquilonia 44

Aquincum 184–5, 401

Aquitaine 90

Arabia 3, 289, 446, 463

Arcadia 449

Arezzo 195

Argos 320

Aricia 36

Ariminum 123

Armenia 3

Arricia 257, 433

Arsinoe 93

Asculum 463

Asia 6, 178, 307, 328, 350, 362, 366, 373, 442, 449

Asia Minor 61–2, 85–6, 88, 143–4, 254, 302, 307–8, 316, 319, 325, 328, 330, 346–50, 364, 371, 382, 433, 446, 448, 450, 456

Assos 308

Assyria 453
Astigi 86
Atella 297
Athens 33, 37, 62, 75, 85, 117, 143, 187,
    228, 302, 319–21, 327–8, 328, 446,
    453
Attica 386
Augsburg 396
Augusta Emerita 83
Augusta Treverorum (Trier) 90, 106, 185,
    397
Aventine 223, 226, 297, 399

Babylon 62, 122, 380, 450
Baetica 86, 89, 178
Bath (Aquae Sulis) 186
Bay of Naples 77, 393
Beaujeu 170
Belginum-Wederath 94
Beneventum 173, 394
Beroea 325–6
Berthouville 193
Berytus (Beirut) 289–90, 435, 447,
    450
Bethel 369
Bethlehem 370
Biesheim 396
Bithynia 321, 324
Bithynia et Pontus 312, 443
Black Sea 3, 91
Bonn 88, 396
Bordeaux 90
Boscoreale 193
Bosra 289
Bovillae 36
Braga 84
Britannia 86–7, 91, 93, 152, 177, 186,
    396
Bulla Regia 122
Byzantium 27, 375, 423–4

Caere 170
Calydon 85
Campania 33, 38, 45, 52–4, 130, 189,
    193, 418, 432
Campus Martius 68, 137, 210, 226, 238,
    245, 253

Capena 45, 55
Capitol 6, 13, 35–6, 48, 61–2, 77, 89,
    91, 93, 111, 141, 155, 223, 238, 252,
    259–60, 268, 277, 279, 286, 295, 301,
    412, 434–5, 449
Cappadocia 390
Capracotta 52
Capua 57, 182, 297, 393, 403–4, 432–4
Caria 85, 323
Carnuntum 91, 94, 404
Carpathia 3
Carthage 2, 13, 77, 83–4, 89–90, 99, 101,
    105, 122, 130–1, 133, 226, 289, 297,
    300, 409, 424, 435, 441, 459–60,
    468–9, 471
Carthago Nova 152
Casinum 463
Castel S. Elia 257
Chaironeia 318
Chaourse 194
Chave (Aqua Flavia) 90
Cibyra 320
Cilicia 320, 395
Circeii 443
Città Castellana 165
Civita Danzica 50
Civita di Tricarico 54
Claros 446
Clitumne 56
Cologne 81, 88
colonia Iulia Felix Lucoferonensium 54
Colosseum 148, 252, 414
columna Minucia 67, 145–6
Commagene 395
Como 56
Constantinople 17, 105–6, 120, 122–4,
    159, 161, 416
Convenae 88, 90, 93
Corinth 85, 192
Cortijo del Tajo 86
Costa Dorada 396
Crimae 181
Crotona 56
Cuicul (Djemila) 89
Cyprus 141, 307, 387, 409
Cyrenaica 360–1, 373, 376
Cyzikus 326

Dacia 91, 93, 285, 414, 449
Dalmatia 90
Danube 86, 91, 396–7, 400
Daphne 88
Decapolis 450, 456
Delos 394
Delphi 130, 217, 226, 288, 388, 446,
    453
Didyma 446
Dolichenus (Dülük) 395, 449
Drepanum 300
Dura-Europos 91, 94, 282, 363, 393, 397,
    399, 400–1, 446, 448–9, 454–6

Egypt 3, 85–6, 92, 94, 100, 157, 177,
    189, 289, 311, 331, 338–40, 346, 356,
    360, 364–5, 367, 370–2, 379–80,
    384–8, 392–3, 396, 422, 444, 464
Elaea 323
Elbe 81
Eleusis 63
Elis 302
Els Munts 396
Emesa 91
Ephesus 81, 85, 143, 148–50, 153,
    201, 284, 325, 328, 446, 448–51,
    455
Epidaurus 64, 327
Esquiline 284
Etruria 2, 32–8, 42–5, 49, 51, 57, 75,
    144–5, 223–5, 234, 252, 298, 300, 337,
    389, 433
Euphrates 395, 448, 454–5
Europe 5–6, 32, 346, 430

Falisca 45, 52
Ferentinum 298
Firmum Picenum 177
Florence 169, 283
Forum Claudii Vellensium (Martigny) 396,
    401
Forum Clodii 81
Forum Iulium 232
Fregellae 437–8
Frusino 297
Fucino (lake) 53
Furfo 55

Gabii 208, 442
Galicia 83, 88
Galilee 459
Gallia Belgica 87, 397
Gallia Lugdunensis 87
Gaul 34, 43–4, 87, 89, 92, 94, 102, 112,
    192–3, 269, 302, 338, 387, 396, 397,
    422
Gaza 289
Gellep 396
Geneva 400
Geneva (lake) 396
Gerasa 94
Germania 3, 94, 186, 196, 400, 401
Germania Superior 177, 183, 395–6
Gravisca 37
Greece 2–4, 19, 35–8, 61–2, 69, 75, 77,
    85–6, 130, 133, 136–7, 139, 302, 309,
    328–9, 347–9, 364, 371, 380, 446, 450,
    453
Grotta del Colle 50
Güglingen 396
Gytheion 447

Hadrian's Wall 91
Haltern 197
Hawarte 390
Hawran 181
Hebron 370
Heidelberg 396
Heilbronn 396
Heliopolis (Baalbek) 149, 449
Hellespont 340
Herculaneum 379
Hernicia 46
Hierapolis 452–3
Hirpinia 46, 52
Hispellum 56, 106, 112
Histria 91
Huarti (Hawarti) 399

Iberia 313
Iguvium (Gubbio) 45–6, 49–51
Illyricum 160, 297
India 2, 19, 27, 380
Inn 396
Interamna 314

Iran 399
Irni 335
Isola Sacra (Ostia) 221
Israel 2, 6, 276, 345–8, 356–61, 363–4,
  366–70, 373, 375

Jerusalem 149, 331, 346, 355, 357–9,
  364–71, 413, 447, 449
Judaea 141, 345, 371, 395, 400
Judah 6, 356

Krefeld 396
Kornelimünster 88
Kyzikos 308

Lanuvium 45
Laodicea 320
Larissa 338
Lateran 408, 412, 414, 418, 420–1
Latium 32–7, 42, 44, 51–2
Lavinium 36–8, 42, 51, 137, 214, 440–1
Lebanon 149, 449
Leontopolis 367
Lesbos 81
Levant 86, 345–9, 364, 371, 374, 450,
  456
Liris 52, 437
Locri 56, 139
Lucania 51, 54
Lugdunum (Lyon) 81, 90, 170, 187, 195,
  400, 422
Lugo (Léon) 83–4, 86
Lusitania 83
Lycia 319, 329, 395
Lydia 284–5, 395, 446

Mabog 452
Macedonia 325, 347–9, 364, 371
Magna Graecia 54, 56, 136, 225
Mainz 403
Mamertine 47
Mamre 106, 275
Mantinea 319
Martigny 401
Maryport 91, 184
Mauretania 463
Megara 192

Mesopotamia 3, 384–5, 435, 446
Messana 47
Messapia 130
Messene 386
Metaurus 297
Middle East 346, 362, 364
Milan 104, 115, 118, 122–3
Mildenhall 188
Milvian Bridge 111, 160, 412–13
Minturnae 297
Moesia Inferior 395
Mogontiacum (Mainz) 184, 393, 399,
  403
Mola 45
Montcournet 194
Monte de Facho 183, 185
Morken-Harff 183, 185
Mount Eryx 62
Mount Olympus 395
Mount Pfaffenberg 94
Mündelsheim 396
municipium Asisinatuum 183
Mytilene 81

Nabataea 446
Nag Hammadi 386
Naples 191, 310, 403
Narbo 81, 89
Narbonensis 178
Narnia 463
Naulochos 215
Nescania 86
Nicaea 81, 85, 93, 105, 319, 324–5
Nicomedia 81, 103, 319, 324–5, 443
Nisibis 399
Nola 114
Noricum 395, 396, 463
Nuits-Saint-Georges 90
Numidia 114, 337

Obernburg 183
Oinoanda 254
Olympia 131
Onias 367
Oreto Aprutino 55
Orontes 449
Osterburken 183

Osteria dell'Osa 33, 42
Ostia 21, 119, 293, 396–400, 402
Osuna 435
Oxford 20, 22–3

Padan-Aram 369
Paelignia 46–7, 55–6
Paestum 54, 269
Palatine 62, 74–5, 77, 205, 207, 210–11,
    215–16, 218, 223, 226, 252, 277, 397
Palestine 2–3, 105, 275, 289, 345, 351,
    364–6, 368, 393, 446, 448, 450–6
Palmyra 91, 99, 102, 182, 447
Pamphylia 395
Parincris 50
Parino 50
Paris 88, 171
Patras 85
Peloponnese 447
Pergamum 81, 88, 150, 196, 215, 302,
    323, 327, 388
Persia 2, 7, 100–1, 104–5, 119, 143, 369,
    384, 387, 392–3, 394–5
Pesch 183, 185
Pessinus 206
Pfaffenburg 91
Pharsalus 68–9, 135, 231, 302
Philippi 75, 156, 285
Phoenicia 2, 35, 37–8, 289–90, 450
Phrygia 63, 92, 282, 391, 392, 446
Picenum 44–6
Pietrabbondante 53, 57
Pisaurum 45
Platea 320
Plautus 291
Po 432
Pola (Pula) 185
Pompeii 188–93, 195, 200–1, 205, 207,
    218–19, 264, 393; *see also* house *in*
    general index
Pons Aeni 396
Ponza 393
Potenza 55
Praeneste 35, 39, 73
Prusa 318, 321, 326–7
Puteoli 279
Pyrgi 37

Quintana (Künzing) 396–7

Raetia 395, 396–7
Rappino 50
Reate 46, 295
Regillus (lake) 37
Remuria 32
Rennes 87
Rhine 86
Rhineland 183
Rhodes 143
Rhodiapolis 319
Riegel 397
Romania 449
Rome *see individual areas here and*
    buildings in the general index
Rosia Montana 93
Rossano di Vaglio (Lucania) 47, 51, 55,
    57

Sabine territory 46, 52
Sabratha 89
Saguntum 86
Saint-Pé-d'Ardet 90
Salona 89–90
Salzburg 396
Samnium 44, 46, 51–4, 298, 336
Samosata 452
Samothrace 284
Sardis 361
Satricum 36, 42
Scalae Caci 215
Schwarzwald 397
Seben 182
Sechtem 396
Seine 92, 284
Sentinum 43–4
Serapeum of Alexandria 88
Serra di Vaglio 55
Serra Lustrante d'Armento 54
Shekem 369
Sicily 61–2, 137, 178, 213, 227
Side 325
Singili Barba 86
Sirmium 183
Smyrna 150, 320, 323, 325, 327
Sora 382

Soracte 55
Sorrento 218
Spain 61, 81, 86–91, 139, 152, 183, 186, 191, 335, 396, 406, 433, 435, 438, 440
Sparta 319–20
Speyer 401
St. Bernhard 177
Strasburg 248
suburbium 423–4
Sulmona 56
Synnada 30–1
Syracuse 143, 192
Syria 3, 7, 91, 93, 102, 152, 226, 269, 287, 289–90, 370, 390, 393, 399, 402, 446–53, 455–6, 463

Tadinum (Gualdo Tadino) 45
Taranto 54
Tarentum 130
Tarragona 396
Tarsus 145, 320
Tauromenium 137, 178
Tegea 449
Thebaid 422
Thebes 135
Thibilis 93
Thignica 183, 185
Thracia 308
Thugga 89
Tiber 61, 212, 284
Tibur 208
Tibus 91
Tienen 397
Tigris 340
Timnin el-Tahta 450
Tours 116
Tralles 302
Trasimene 47, 296
Tria Fata 412
Troy 3, 34, 38, 61, 130–4, 226, 228, 393, 440

Tucci 86
Turda 91
Turkey 312, 448–9, 456
Tuscany 53, 192
Tusculum 185, 189
Tyre 278

Uganda 22
Uley 186
Umbria 2, 43–5, 49, 56, 112, 314
United States of America 22, 81
Urso 89, 335, 337, 433, 435, 439–40, 445

Vaise 195
Vatican 80, 391, 406, 411–12
Veii 34, 37, 185, 239, 285, 441, 444
Verona 185
Vesuvius 188, 193, 198–200, 220
Via Appia 115, 297, 412, 415, 417
Via Ardeatina 419
Via Flaminia 148, 212
Via Labicana 412
Via Lationa 297
Via Nomentana 419
Via Ostiense 411–12
Via Praenestina 412, 419
Via S. Gregorio 164
Via Sacra 36
Via Tiburtina 412
Via Triumphalis 415
Vibia 115
Vienna 422
Virunum 396
Volcanal 38
Vulsinii 463

Wiesloch 396
Würzburg 424

Zama 301